ISBN 978-1-331-32393-8
PIBN 10174338

1 MONTH OF
FREE
READING

at
www.ForgottenBooks.com

By purchasing this book you are eligible for one month membership to ForgottenBooks.com, giving you unlimited access to our entire collection of over 1,000,000 titles via our web site and mobile apps.

To claim your free month visit:
www.forgottenbooks.com/free174338

THE
LIFE AND OPINIONS OF
JOHN BUNCLE
ESQUIRE

BY

THOMAS AMORY

With an Introduction by

ERNEST A. BAKER, M.A.

LONDON:

GEORGE ROUTLEDGE AND SONS, LIMITED

NEW YORK: E. P. DUTTON & Co.

1904

INTRODUCTION

THE *History of John Buncle* has never been a popular book. It is hardly possible to imagine a period whose standard of taste and culture would render it popular. Yet it is safe to predict that it will always, as in the past, be an object of interest to the connoisseur, the explorer of curious by-paths of literature, and to all who have a liking for the eccentricities of human nature, when conjoined with strength and shrewdness, and with candour of expression. Thrice during the last century was the book disinterred from the obscurity that covered it, and on each occasion by a critic distinguished by this taste for originality. Charles Lamb, in *The Two Races of Men*, hits off the book with delightful humour when he says, "In yonder nook, John Buncle, a widower-volume, with ' eyes closed,' mourns his ravished mate." Hazlitt's enthusiasm led him, ill advisedly, to compare the author with a genius of a far superior order :—

"The soul of Francis Rabelais passed into John (*sic*) Amory, the author of *The Life and Adventures of John Buncle*. Both were physicians, and enemies of too much gravity. Their business was to enjoy life. Rabelais indulges his spirit of sensuality in wine, in dried neats'-tongues, in Bologna sausages, in botargos. John Buncle shows the same symptoms of inordinate satisfaction in tea and bread-and-butter. While Rabelais roared with Friar John and the monks, John Buncle gossiped with the ladies, and with equal and uncontrolled gaiety. These two authors possessed all the insolence of health, so that their works give a fillip to the constitution ; but they carried off the exuberance of their natural spirits in different ways. The title of one of Rabelais' chapters (and the contents answer to the title) is, ' How they chirped over their cups.' The title of a corresponding chapter in *John Buncle* would run thus : ' The author is invited to spend the evening with the divine Miss Hawkins, and goes accordingly ; with the delightful conversation that ensued.'"

The essay is so well known and so sententious that it has probably led many a man to take its judgments on trust, and not trouble to peruse the book for himself. Leigh Hunt, on the contrary, in that charming literary *vade mecum* of his, *A Book for a Corner*, entices one to get the book and read it, or rather to roam about in its leisurely and discursive pages. But whoever has been so tempted hitherto must have met with an initial difficulty, the extreme scarcity of the work. Amory published the first volume in 1756, along with a complete edition in four volumes, 12mo. Another edition appeared in three volumes in 1825, since which date the chances of coming across the book in any form have steadily grown more remote.

What is the peculiar attraction of *John Buncle* ? That a book is merely a literary curiosity, or that it contains excellent passages interspersed amid a huge extent of tedious prosing, is certainly not the thing to secure the interest of Lamb, Hazlitt, Leigh Hunt. What fascinates in the book is the vigour and the frankness with which a most exceptional, yet, in a way, a most representative kind of man reveals the whole of his character. For John Buncle is an eccentric only in the sense that he carries very common traits of character to a strange excess. In his love of good living, his sensuality combined with a pharisaic animus against vice, in that blind egotism and portentous arrogance, one might perceive the exaggeration of certain national qualities, with which the author, who was in the first case anonymous, shows his sympathy by exalting them to the degree of absurdity. John Bull, at least one side of him, was caricatured, unintentionally, in *John Buncle*. And the sectarian spirit that is so deeply ingrained in the national character is faithfully portrayed in *John Buncle* the unitarian, with his dogmatism and utter intolerance, and his delight in wordy argument untempered by the slightest capacity for understanding his adversary's point of view.

▼

It is, in fact, such a paradox of a book that it tempts everyone to fly into paradoxes. Buncle himself is so hot in denouncing immorality and yet so immoral ; condemns sensuality with so much eloquence yet is so shamelessly sensual ; is so sincere and yet such a hypocrite ; so fervent in his religious zeal, yet degrades religion so unblushingly to consecrate his unholy appetites. " It is impossible," said Leigh Hunt, " to be serious with John Buncle, Esq., jolly dog, Unitarian, and Bluebeard ; otherwise, if we were to take him at his word, we should pronounce him, besides being a jolly dog, to be one of a very selfish description, with too good a constitution to correct him, a prodigious vanity, no feeling whatever, and a provoking contempt for everything unfortunate, or opposed to his whims. He quarrels with bigotry, and is a bigot ; with abuse, and riots in it. He hates the cruel opinions held by Athanasius, and sends people to the devil as an Arian. He kills off seven wives out of pure incontinence and love of change, yet cannot abide a rake or even the poorest victim of the rake, unless both happen to be his acquaintances. The way in which he tramples on the miserable wretches in the streets is the very rage and triumph of hard-heartedness, furious at seeing its own vices reflected on it, unredeemed by the privileges of law, divinity, and success. But the truth is, John is no more responsible for his opinions than health itself, or a high-mettled racer. He only ' thinks he's thinking.' He does, in reality, nothing at all but eat, drink, talk, and enjoy himself. Amory, Buncle's creator, was in all probability an honest man, or he would hardly have been innocent enough to put such extravagances on paper."

Leigh Hunt also says in the same place : " John's life is not a classic : it contains no passage which is a general favourite : no extract could be made from it of any length to which readers of good taste would not find objections. Yet there is so curious an interest in all its absurdities ; its jumble of the gayest and gravest considerations is so founded in the actual state of things ; it draws now and then such excellent portraits from life ; and, above all, its animal spirits are at once so excessive and so real, that we defy the best readers not to be entertained with it, and having had one or two specimens, not to desire more. Buncle would say, that there is ' cut and come again ' in him like one of his luncheons of cold beef and a foaming tankard."

The Life of John Buncle has many of the same merits as the life of Samuel Pepys, not the least of which is the unconscious humour of the book. Buncle himself is utterly devoid of a sense of humour ; his heavy seriousness is something unconscionable. But I doubt if there be a more egregious example in literature of the unintentionally comic. The entire plan, or no-plan, of the book, with its aimless narrative and irrelevant digressions (the story seems to exist for the sake of the digressions) is so absurd ; and the idea is so comic of the man going out to try his fortune in the world, " not like the Chevalier La Mancha, in hopes of conquering a kingdom, or marrying some great Princess ; but to see if I could find another good country girl for a wife, and get a little more money ; as they were the only two things united, that could secure me from melancholy, and confer real happiness."

He puts the case with inimitable gravity : " In the next place, as I had forfeited my father's favour and estate, for the sake of christian-deism, and had nothing but my own honest industry to secure me daily bread, it was necessary for me to lay hold of every opportunity to improve my fortune, and of consequence do my best to gain the heart of the first rich young woman who came in my way, after I had buried a wife. It was not fit for me to sit snivelling for months, because my wife died before me, which was, at least, as probable, as that she should be the survivor ; but instead of solemn affliction, and the inconsolable part, for an event I foresaw, it was incumbent on me, after a little decent mourning, to consecrate myself to virtue and good fortune united in the form of a woman."

Most diverting of all are the scenes of love-making, a kind of love-making which is, surely, quite unique in literature or in life. What coy maiden was ever wooed after the manner employed to win the " illustrious Statia " ? Indelicacy almost ceases to be indelicate when it becomes so elephantine.

" Ponder, illustrious Statia, on the important point. Consider what it is to die a maid, when you may, in a regular way, produce heirs to that inestimable blessing of life and favour, which the munificence of the Most High was pleased freely to bestow, and which the great Christian mediator, agent, and nego· ciator, republished, confirmed, and sealed with his blood. Marry then in regard to the gospel, and let it be the fine employment of your life, to open gradually the treasures of revelation to the understandings of the little Christians you produce. What do you say, illustrious Statia ? Shall it be a succession, as you are an upright Christian ? And may I hope to have the honour of sharing in the mutual satisfaction that must attend the discharge of so mo· mentous a duty ? "

Needless to say, the lady is not proof against such eloquence ; and the nuptials are concluded with a dispatch befitting the urgency of the obligation. The disquisitions on fluxions, geometry, algebra (with diagrammatic illus· trations), on the Hebraic covenant, the rite of circumcision, and similarly erudite topics, that take the place of amorous small talk, are equally enter· taining in a way that their author never intended. The young ladies are charming in spite of their prodigious learning ; but more charming is the force which their personal attractions add to their reasoning. " But is there no other way," asks John Buncle of an accomplished female who has been demonstrating a curious mathematical theorem, " of paying £100 in guineas and pistoles, besides the six ways you have mentioned ? " ' There is no other way,' *the fine girl answered.*" There is something most refreshing to hear Buncle, the epicure, the amorous, and the successful, delivering himself gravely on the subject of resignation to the decrees of providence :—

" This is a summary of my past life ; what is before me heaven only knows. My fortune I trust with the Preserver of men, and the Father of spirits. One thing I am certain of by observation, few as the days of the years of my pil· grimage have been, that the emptiness, and unsatisfying nature of this world's enjoyments, are enough to prevent my having any fondness to stay in this region of darkness and sorrow. I shall never leap over the bars of life, let what will happen ; but the sooner I have leave to depart, I shall think it the better for me."

" 'Tis a very interesting," as Charles Lamb says, " and an extraordinary compound of all manner of subjects, from the depth of the ludicrous to the heights of sublime religious truth. There is much abstruse science in it above my cut, and an infinite fund of pleasantry. John Buncle is a famous fine man, formed in Nature's most eccentric hour." And with all its defects and its offences against good taste, Lamb said emphatically to some one who objected to the epithet so applied, *The Life of John Buncle* is " a healthy book." It is perhaps a tribute to the originality of the book, and no detri· ment to its real merits, that a Saturday Reviewer called it " a book which nowadays would have been dated from Colney Hatch, or, more likely, sup· pressed by the care of relatives." And that the *Biographie Universelle* should run it down is, perhaps, testimony as emphatic to its truly English qualities.

John Buncle is virtually a sequel to an earlier book of Amory's published in 1755, entitled, *Memoirs containing the Lives of several Ladies of Great Britain* : " A History of Antiquities, Productions of Nature, and Monuments of Art ; Observations on the Christian Religion as professed by the Established Church and Dissenters of every Denomination ; Remarks on the Writings of the Greatest English Divines : with a Variety of Disquisitions and Opinions relative to Criticism and Manners ; and many Extraordinary Actions." This is another Unitarian romance, as eccentric, rambling and bizarre in style as *John Buncle*, which it resembles in every respect save that it is, perhaps, even less like any other sort of book on record, and has less of the personal element in it. But such episodes as the casual meeting of the author with the beautiful Miss Bruce, in a little mansion set amidst " the finest flowering greens," in a sequestered spot among " the vast hills of Northumberland," a meeting that is, of course, the prelude to a lengthy discourse on Philosophic

Deism ; such characters as Miss West, Julia Desborough and Charles Benlow, paragons of virtue, wisdom and orthodox Unitarianism ; with their adventures in the wilds of northern England, the Hebrides, and a sort of Deistic Utopia in the Cape Verde Islands, might have been taken from the pages of *John Buncle.* A reader of the latter volume might easily fancy himself familiar with such incidents as the two following, taken from the *Memoirs* :—

"They were riding to Crawford Dyke, near Dunglass, the place I intended for, and by a wrong turn in the road came to Mrs. Benlow's house instead of going to Robin's Toad, where they designed to bait.' It was between eight and nine at night when they got to her door ; and as they appeared, by the richness of their riding-dress, their servants, and the beautiful horses they rid, to be women of distinction, Mrs. Benlow invited them in, and requested they would lie at her house that night, as the inn they were looking for was very bad. Nothing could be more grateful to the ladies than this proposal. They were on the ground in a moment ; and all sat down soon after, with the greatest cheerfulness, to a fine dish of trouts, roasted chickens, tarts, and sparragrass. The strangers were quite charmed with everything they saw. The sweet rural room they were in, and the wild beauties of the garden in view, they could not enough admire ; and they were so struck with Mrs. Benlow's goodness, and the lively, happy manner she has of showing it, that they conceived immediately the greatest affection for her. Felicity could not rise higher than it did at this table. For a couple of hours we laughed most immoderately."

"As I travelled once in the month of September, over a wild part of Yorkshire, and fancied in the afternoon that I was near the place I intended to rest at, it appeared, from a great water we came to, that we had for half a day been going wrong, and were many a mile from any village. This was vexatious ; but what was worse, the winds began to blow outrageously, the clouds gathered, and, as the evening advanced, the rain came down like waterspouts from the heavens. All the good that offered was the ruins of a nunnery, within a few yards of the water, and among the walls, once sacred to devotion, a part of an arch that was enough to shelter us and our beasts from the floods and tempest. Into this we entered, the horses, and Moses, and his master, and for some hours were right glad to be so lodged. But, at last, the storm and rain were quite over, we saw the fair rising moon hang up her ready lamp, and with mild lustre drive back the hovering shades. Out then I came from the cavern, and as I walked for a while on the banks of the fine lake, I saw a handsome little boat, with two oars, in a creek, and concluded very justly, that there must be some habitation not far from one side or other of the water. Into the boat therefore we went, having secured our horses, and began to row round, the better to discover. Two hours we were at it as hard as we could labour, and then came to the bottom of a garden, which had a flight of stairs leading up to it. These I ascended. I walked on, and, at the farther end of the fine improved spot, came to a mansion. I immediately knocked at the door, sent in my story to the lady of the house, as there was no master, and in a few minutes was shown into a parlour. I continued alone for a quarter of an hour, and then entered a lady, who struck me into amazement. She was a beauty, of whom I had been passionately fond when she was fourteen and I sixteen years of age. I saw her first in a French family of distinction, where my father had lodged me for the same reason as her parents had placed her there ; that is, for the sake of the purity of the French tongue ; and as she had a rational generosity of heart, and an understanding that was surprisingly luminous for her years ; could construe an Ode of Horace in a manner the most delightful, and read a chapter in the Greek Testament with great ease every morning ; she soon became my heart's fond idol ; she appeared in my eyes as something more than mortal. I thought her a divinity. Books furnished us with an occasion of being often together, and we fancied the time was happily spent. But all at once she disappeared. As she had a vast fortune, and as there was a suspicion of an amour, she was snatched away in a moment, and for twenty years from the afternoon she vanished, I could not see her or hear of her : whether living or dead, I knew not till the night I am speaking of, that I saw come into the room, the lovely Julia Desborough transformed into Mrs. Mort. Our mutual surprise was vastly great. We could not speak for some time. We knew each other as well as if it had been but an hour ago we parted, so strong was the impression made. She was still divinely fair ; but I wondered she could remember me so well, as time and many shaking rubs had altered me very greatly for the worse. See how strangely things are brought about ! Miss Desborough was removed all the way to Italy, kept many years abroad that she might never see me more, and in the character of Mrs. Mort, by accident, I found her in solitude in the same country I lived in, and still my friend. This lady told me, she had buried an admirable husband a few years ago, and, as she never had any liking to the world, she devoted her time to books, her old favourites, the education of her daughter, and the salvation of her soul. Miss Mort and she lived like two friends. They read and spun some hours of their time every day away.

"They had a few agreeable neighbours, and from the lake and cultivation of their gardens derived a variety of successive pleasures. They had no relish for the tumultuous pleasures of the town ; but in the charms of letters and religion, the philosophy of flowers, the converse of their neighbours, a linen manufactory, and their rural situation, were as happy as their wishes could rise to in this hemisphere. All this to me was like a vision. I wondered, I admired. Is this Miss Desborough with whom I was wont to pass so many hours in reading Milton to her, or Telemaque, or L'Avare de Moliere ? What a fleeting scene is life ! But a little while and we go on to another world. Fortunate are they who are fit for the remove, who have a clear conception of the precariousness and vanity of all human things, and by virtue and piety so strive to act what is fairest and most laudable, and so pass becomingly through this life, that they may in the next obtain the blessed and immortal abodes prepared for those who can give up their account with joy."

Though his admiration for the female sex was always enthusiastic, it i· not until he gets to the sequel that our author begins to show the sincerity (f his appreciation by marrying them. When he does begin, his perseverance is limited only by his profound respect for human and divine legislation. John Buncle is a Mormon born out of due time. Had he lived in the day of Joe Smith, he would, beyond all manner of doubt, have proved his belief in a religion so consistent with the dictates of reason and the constitution of man by becoming one of the most distinguished of the Latter-Day Saints. Buncle represents the man who, in Meredith's phrase, has neither rounded Seraglio Point nor doubled Cape Turk ; yet his constitutional respect for law, rather the letter than the spirit, is such that he finds a pleasure in restraining his polygamous instincts—and denouncing those of other people. Buncle's conscience was, in truth, a curious faculty. So long as he kept to the strict article of a definite, but somewhat shaky, code of morals, he was never tired of pluming himself upon his virtue, and complimenting those people who agreed with him. When once he begins to argue with himself or his detractors upon ethical questions, then his unconscious humour becomes most delectable. His apology to such as objected to the brevity of his periods of mourning for his deceased wives and his haste in securing another partner, has been quoted often enough, but I will venture to quote it again :—

"I reply, that I think it unreasonable and impious to grieve immoderately for the dead. A decent and proper tribute of tears and sorrow, humanity requires ; but when that duty has been paid, we must remember, that to lament a dead woman is not to lament a wife. A wife must be a living woman. The wife we lose by death is no more than a sad and empty object, formed by the imagination, and to be still devoted to her, is to be in love with an idea. It is a mere chimerical passion, as the deceased has no more to do with this world, than if she had existed before the flood. As we cannot restore what nature has destroyed, it is foolish to be faithful to affliction. Nor is this all, if the woman we marry has the seven qualifications which every man would wish to find in a wife, beauty, discretion, sweetness of temper, a sprightly wit, fertility, wealth, and noble extraction, yet death's snatching so amiable a wife from our arms can be no reason for accusing fate of cruelty, that is, providence of injustice ; nor can it authorise us to sink into insensibility, and neglect the duty and business of life. This wife was born to die, and we receive her under the condition of mortality. She is lent but for a term, the limits of which we are not made acquainted with ; and when this term is expired, there can be no injustice in taking her back ; nor are we to indulge the transports of grief to distraction, but should look out for another with the seven qualifications, as it is not good for man to be alone, and as he is by the Abrahamic covenant bound to carry on the succession in a regular way if it be in his power. Nor is this all, if the woman adorned with every natural and acquired excellence is translated from this gloomy planet to some better world, to be a sharer of the divine favour, in that peaceful and happy state which God hath prepared for the virtuous and faithful, must it not be senseless for me to indulge melancholy and continue a mourner on her account, while she is breathing the balmy air of paradise, enjoying pure and radiant vision, and beyond description happy ? "

His other motives for desiring to get married as often as he decently could, and the workings of his very peculiar conscience, are revealed with wonted frankness in the following statement of his mental deliberations when confronted with the responsibility of a choice of brides :—

" Against staying longer than two or three days, I had many good reasons that made it necessary for me to depart : beside the unreasonableness of my being an expense to Mr. Turner in his absence, or confining his sister to the country ; there was Orton-Lodge, to which I could not avoid going again : and there was Miss Melmoth, on whom I had promised to wait, and did intend to ask her if she would give me her hand, as I liked her and her circumstances, and fancied she would live with me in any retreat I pleased to name ; which was a thing that would be most pleasing to my mind. It is true, if Charles Turner had come home, while I stayed at his house, it was possible I might have got his sister, who was a very great fortune : but this was an uncertainty however, and in his absence, I could not in honour make my addresses to her : if it should be against his mind, it would be acting a false part. while I was eating his bread. Miss Turner to be sure had fifty thousand pounds at her own disposal, and so far as I could judge of her mind, during the three days that I stayed with her at Skelsmore-Vale, I had some reason to imagine her heart might be gained : but for a man worth nothing to do this, in her brother's house without his leave, was a part I could not act, though by missing her I had been brought to beg my bread."

The moral, religious, and speculative digressions that take up by far the greater space in the book are of singularly little interest to us. They contain no original thought, and merely display the extent of their author's erudition. The utmost praise one can give is that now and then he puts a commonplace well, as for instance :—

" How shall we account for such things ? By saying, that the world that now is, and the world that is to come, are in the hands of God, and every transaction in them is quite right, though the reason of the procedure may be beyond our view. We cannot judge certainly of the ends and purposes of Providence, and therefore to pass judgment on the ways of God, is not only impious, but ridiculous to the last degree."

Beyond that his science is absurd, his speculations are vain, and his reasoning, in spite of its pompous phrasing, very shallow.

Amory's exaggerated descriptions of scenery, in the *Memoirs*, and the earlier part of *John Buncle*, have drawn upon his head a great deal of ridicule. Perhaps he has been laughed at rather unfairly, and more allowance ought to have been made for the ideas of the time when he wrote. With hardly any exception, the eighteenth century writers who have tried to delineate savage scenery have been afflicted by emotions of nervousness and stupefaction that seem rather absurd nowadays. This is how Pennant describes the scenery of Derwentwater : " Here all the possible variety of Alpine scenery is exhibited, with all the horror of precipice, overhanging rock, or insulated pyramidal hills, contrasted with others whose smooth and verdant sides, swelling into immense aerial heights, at once please and surprise the eye. The two extremities of the lake afford most discordant prospects : the southern is a composition of all that is horrible, an immense chasm opens," and so on. Dr. Brown, in his famous letter, finds that " the full perfection of Keswick consists of three circumstances, *beauty*, *horror*, and *immensity* united." " On the opposite shore," says he, " you will find rocks and cliffs of stupendous height, hanging broken over the lake in horrible grandeur, some of them a thousand feet high, the woods climbing up their steep and shaggy sides, where mortal foot never yet approached. On these dreadful heights the eagles build their nests ; a variety of waterfalls are seen pouring from their summits, and tumbling in vast sheets from rock to rock in rude and terrible magnificence," etc. At Malham Cove, in Craven, one of the spots, probably, where Buncle encountered an impassable range of unscalable " mountains," the poet Gray found it " safer to shelter yourself close to its bottom " (lest any of the rocks at the summit should give way and overwhelm the spectator), " and trust to the mercy of that enormous mass, which nothing but an earthquake can stir." " I stayed there," he continues, " not without shuddering, a quarter of an hour, and thought my trouble richly paid, for the impression will last for life." West, of Ulverston, the author of the earliest guide to the Lakes, who fell foul of Gray for his hyperbolic descriptions, speaks of " an arrangement of vast mountains, entirely new, both in form and colouring of rock ; large hollow craters scooped in their bosoms, once the seeming seats of raging liquid fire, though at present overflowing with the purest water, that foams down the craggy brows." Here we can almost picture the tarns on the hill-tops described by Buncle, their depths communicating with the " abyss." And again we can realize some of his difficulties in travelling when we read of another writer who found the lake of Wastwater " of access most laborious from the nature of its surrounding soil, which is utterly devoid of tenacity." West goes on, " The lower parts are pastured with a motley herd ; the middle tract is assumed by the flocks, the upper regions (to man inaccessible) are abandoned to the birds of Jove." Mr. W. P. Haskett Smith quotes Mrs. Radcliffe touching the ascent of Saddleback : " The views from the summit are exceedingly extensive, but those immediately under the eye on the mountain itself so tremendous and appalling that few persons have sufficient resolution to experience the emotions which those awful scenes inspire." " When we had ascended about a mile," says another writer, " one of the party, on looking round, was so astonished with the different appearance of objects in the valley so far beneath us that he declined proceeding. We had not gone much further till the other companion was suddenly taken ill and wished to loose blood and return."

Buncle's romantic pen, sketching freely from memory, and biassed by his constitutional megalomania, went very little farther, after all, when he turned these awe-inspiring fells into ranges of impassable mountains. The lakes, the tarns, the bogs, and the waterfalls are still there, and may have similar effects on people who are prepared by a suitable education to be appalled. Stainmore Forest has always been one of the wildest districts in Britain, and in Amory's day still retained an evil reputation for murders and highway robberies. The burning river may have had its origin in a reminiscence of bog-fires, more plentiful then than now. The adjoining district of Craven possesses genuine marvels enough in the way of caves, pot-holes and underground water-channels, wet and dry, to furnish a Jules Verne with ample materials for romance. Buncle has simply multiplied the existing caverns and magnified their proportions. If we make proper allowance for the attitude of the time as regards natural sublimity, I think Amory is not a much more flagrant offender against truth and probability than the author of *Lorna Doone*.

John Buncle is a personage of definite lineaments whom, once known, we can never forget or confuse with any other personage, real or fictitious : his author, Thomas Amory, is a very vague and unsubstantial being indeed. Yet there is much to be said, if only on internal evidence, for the view that in the creation we may recognize the authentic features of the author himself. There is a certain class of books that convince their reader, although it might be impossible to prove the case by actual reason, that they are autobiographical, in the sense that they express, more or less consciously, the character of their writers.   One feels it in reading them, the perception is intuitive and irresistible.   Whether it be the accent given to unimportant traits, or the emergence of more intimate peculiarities, or something altogether un-definable and intangible, we feel it, quite independently of external evidence, in reading *David Copperfield, Pendennis,* or *Jane Eyre,* and even minor works like *The Fool of Quality.*   We feel it, never more strongly, whilst perusing *The Life of John Buncle,* so strongly that it would require cogent proofs of the contrary to unsettle our convictions.   The reader must judge from the following summary of what can be ascertained about Thomas Amory, from the statements of himself, his son, and other persons, whether the validity of the intuitive view is confirmed in the present instance.

A letter appeared in the *St. James's Chronicle* on October 25, 1788, inquiring as to the authorship of *John Buncle,* and it was replied to in a letter, which can be referred to in the *Gentleman's Magazine* (vol. lviii. p. 1062), stating that the unknown author was Thomas Amory, a native of Ireland, who had been bred to some branch of the profession of physic, and was now living as a recluse on a small fortune in Orchard Street, Westminster, with a country house to which he occasionally retired at Bellfont, near Hounslow.   The corres-pondent went on to describe Amory as " A man of a very peculiar Look and Aspect, though at the same time, he bore quite the Appearance of a Gentleman. He read much ; and scarce ever stirred, but like a Bat, in the Dark of the Evening ; and then he would take his usual Walk ; but seemed to be always ruminating on speculative Subjects, even while passing along the most crowded Streets."   This elicited a reply from the son of the mysterious author, Robert Amory, M.D., who controverted certain erroneous statements, and gave a genealogy of the Amorys, whose lineage he traced to Amory de Montford, who married the sister of Henry II., and was created Earl of Leicester. Amory "was not a native of Ireland.   His Father, Councillor Amory, attended King William to Ireland, and was appointed Secretary for the for-feited Estates in that Kingdom, and was possessed of very extensive Property in the County of Clare.   He was the youngest Brother of Amory or Damer, the Miser, whom Pope calls ' the Wealthy and the Wise ' ; from whom comes Lord Milton, etc., etc.   My Grandfather married the Daughter of Fitzmaurice, Earl of Kerry ; Sir William Petty another Daughter ; and the Grandfather of the Duke of Leinster another."   He goes on to state that Thomas Amory lived on Mill Bank, Westminster, and for a few years rented a house at Bedfont.   He never had but one wife, and Robert Amory was himself the only surviving child.   At that date, 1788, his father was still living, though now ninety-seven years old.   When young he was a very handsome man. He had published many religious and political tracts, poems and songs.   He now lived in complete seclusion, not seeing anybody.

This letter was replied to by Louis Renas, who threw doubt and contumely on the alleged genealogy, which he characterized as "an idle tale, void of foundation or probability."   The insult drew out a further letter from Dr. Amory, who in an irritated manner reasserted his original statements, and wound up by insinuating that his correspondent's real name was "Mr. Louis the Ass," whence he said it would be easy for the Heralds Office to find out his family connections.   This pretty controversy came to an end with a letter from L. Renas, dated April 20, 1790, in which he apologized for a slight error in his previous communications, and admitted that Thomas Amory was indeed the grandson of a lord—Baron Kerry—but reiterated his other contentions. There can be little doubt that Robert Amory, M.D., had inherited some of the eccentricities and a good deal of the temper of his father, who was as fond of a dispute as his hero, John Buncle.

Amory, if not a native of Ireland, seems to have lived in Dublin at some period, and to have been acquainted with Swift. In 1751, on the publication of Lord Orrery's remarks on the life and writings of Dr. Swift, the following advertisement appeared in the *Whitehall Evening Post*, but there is no record that the pamphlet was ever printed : " Soon will be published a Letter to Lord Orrery in answer to what his Lordship says in his late remarks in praise of Swift's Sermon on the Trinity ; being an attempt to vindicate the divinity of God the Father Almighty, and to convince his Lordship, if he has a mind open to conviction, that the tritheistic discourse preached by the Dean of St. Patrick's is so far from being that masterpiece my Lord Orrery calls it that it is in reality the most senseless and despicable performance ever produced by orthodoxy to corrupt the divine religion of Jesus Christ. By Thomas Amory, Esq." One would like greatly to read this fulmination by a man who, to judge by the disposition of his fictitious counterpart, was quick to wrath, a good hater, and outdid even that other eccentric of genius, George Borrow, in the violence of his enmity for Roman Catholics, and most other people who disagreed with him. In 1776 appeared an anonymous work entitled *John Buncle, junr., Gentleman*, 12 mo, Dublin, the author of which was a certain Dr. Cogan. An anonymous pamphlet that appeared in the same year as the *Memoirs*, entitled, " A Letter to the Reviewers occasioned by their account of a book called *Memoirs*, etc." was presumably written by Amory. In *Notes and Queries* for January 27, 1855, is quoted a letter from " Amouri," (Thomas Amory) to an unnamed lady, enclosing a copy of verses composed by ten gentlemen, including the writer, in praise of a certain Molly Rowe. The following stanza is signed " T. Amory " :—

" In the dance, through the couples ascudding,
How graceful and light does she go !
No Englishman ever lov'd pudding
As I love my sweet Molly Rowe."

The pudding simile is certainly in the vein of John Buncle. The letter is dated from Newton in Yorkshire, July th' 8, 1773. Amory died on November 25, 1788, at the age of ninety-seven.

It is regrettable that the *Dictionary of National Biography* and the latest edition of Chambers's *Cyclopædia of English Literature* should still persist in the statement that the author of *John Buncle* must have been disordered in his intellect, in spite of the indignation with which this charge, advanced in the *General Biographical Dictionary*, in 1798, was repudiated by an able writer in the *Retrospective Review* (vol. vi., 1822). Although it is insinuated that anybody who admires the book must likewise be in want of medical treatment, we can afford to bear the reflection with equanimity in the distinguished company of Lamb, Hazlitt, Leigh Hunt, and other able men who have confessed a liking for this strange book.

E.A.B.

DRAMATIS PERSONÆ

John Buncle, the supposed autobiographer.
Mr. John Bruce, his private tutor.
Harriot Noel, his first love, cut off by small-pox on the eve of their marriage.
Mr. Noel, her father, owner of Eden Park.
Soto Finn, or O'Fin, Buncle's servant.
Dr. Whaley, Dean of Derry, his fellow-passenger in crossing from Dublin to Whitehaven.
Pierce Gavan, a fellow-commoner of Buncle's at Trinity College, Dublin; has a marvellous escape from drowning.
Charles Henley, a young merchant, drowned in crossing the Irish Sea.
Whitwell, the mate of the packet.
Miss Melmoth, Buncle's first wife, dies of fever at the end of two years.
Charles Turner, an old university friend, living in the wilds of Westmoreland and Yorkshire.
John Price, a farmer near Stainmore Forest, an old schoolfriend from Dublin.
Martha, his wife, learned in divinity.
Mrs. Burcot (Azora), Superior of the female republic living at Burcot Lodge.
Mrs. Fletcher (Antonia), her friend and confidant among the hundred young women forming the community.
The twenty philosophic recluses of Ulubrae.
Miss Harcourt, a learned young lady, foundress of a house of Protestant recluses in Richmondshire.
Mr. Harcourt, her father.
Mr. Berrisfort, a learned gentleman.
Miss Berrisfort, his sister, a daring horsewoman.
Miss Fox, their cousin.
The three Flemings, devout Roman Catholics, farmers in Stainmore, one of whom Buncle converts.
Mr. Henley, the philosophic proprietor of the Groves of Basil.
Statia, his daughter, Buncle's second wife, who dies in two years of small-pox.
Ten Ivonist friars and their ten wives in a Protestant monastery near Harrogate.
Miss Antonia Cranmer, a young lady of large fortune, who becomes Buncle's third wife, and dies of small-pox at the end of two years.
Agnes Vane, her cousin.
Dorick Watson, a converted Roman Catholic, turned recluse.
Mr. Gollogher
Mr. Gallaspy
Mr. Dunkley
Mr. Makins   Six Irish gentlemen whom Buncle meets with at Harrogate, his contemporaries at Trinity College, Dublin.
Mr. Monaghan
Mr. O'Keefe
Charles Hunt, owner of a small estate in Kildare in Buncle's boyhood.
Elizabeth, his daughter, ruined and deserted by Mr. R.
Miss Spence, of Westmoreland, Buncle's fourth wife, dies in six months of a malignant fever.
Miss Fox (Imoinda), an old flame of Buncle's.
Oliver Wincup, Esq., of Woodcester, an agreeable acquaintance.
Miss Veyssiere, a dashing young beauty, sacrificed to a rich old man.
Miss Turner, sister of Buncle's friend, Charles Turner, his fifth wife, killed in six weeks by a carriage accident.
Martha Jacquelot, her friend.
Miss Hinxworth, a gentleman's daughter, carried off by O'Regan.
O'Regan, an Irish dancing master.
Tom Clancy, landlord of the *Cat and Bagpipe*, near Knaresborough.
Miss Martha Tilston   Two beautiful young heiresses, wards of their tyrannical uncle
Miss Althea Llandsoy   Old Cock.
Old Cock, a villainous lawyer.
Ribble, a little old man, skilled in chemistry.
Richmond, his cousin, an invalid through debauchery.
Avery Moncton, a deluded husband, who turns hermit.
Edmund Curll, the famous bookseller, satirized by Pope in the *Dunciad*.
Carola Bennet, a courtesan who is married and reformed by a young clergyman.
Dunk the miser.
Miss Dunk, his daughter, afterwards Mrs. Stainville, and then the sixth Mrs. Buncle: dies in two years of small-pox.
Dr. Stainville, who exhumes and marries Miss Dunk.
Dr. Fitzgibbons, an Irish gentleman.
Julia, his daughter, Buncle's seventh wife, drowned shortly after their union.

The Life of John Buncle, Esq.

Nec Vixit Male, qui Natus Moriensque fefellit.

THAT the transactions of my life, and the observations and reflections I have made on men and things, by sea and land, in
various parts of the world, might not be buried in oblivion, and
by length of time be blotted out of the memory of men, it has
been my wont, from the days of my youth to this time, to write
down memorandums of every thing I thought worth noticing,
as men and matters, books and circumstances, came in my way ;
and in hopes they may be of some service to my fellow-mortals
I publish them. Some pleasing and some surprising things the
reader will find in them. He will meet with miscellany thoughts
upon several subjects. He will read, if he pleases, some tender
stories. But all the relations, the thoughts, the observations,
are designed for the advancement of valuable learning, and to
promote whatsoever things are true, whatsoever things are honest,
whatsoever things are just, whatsoever things are pure, whatsoever things are lovely, whatsoever things are of good report.

About fifty years ago the midwife wheeled me in, and much
sooner than half a century hence, in all human probability, death
will wheel me out. When Heaven pleases, I am satisfied. Life
and death are equally welcome, because equally parts of my
way to eternity. My lot has been a swarthy one in this first
state, and I am in hopes I shall exchange worlds to advantage.
As God, without all peradventure, brought his moral creatures
into being, in order to increase their virtue, and provide suitable
happiness for the worthy, the most unfortunate here may expect
immutable felicity at last, if they have endeavoured, in proportion to what power they had, to render themselves useful
and valuable, by a sincerity and benevolence of temper, a dis-
interestedness, a communicativeness, and the practice of those
duties, to which we are obliged by the frame of our nature,
and by the relations we bear to God, and to the subjects of his
government.

For my part, I confess that, many have been the failings of my
life, and great the defects of my obedience. But in the midst
of all my failings and imperfections, my soul hath always sym-
pathised with the afflicted, and my heart hath ever ached for the
miseries of others. My hand has often relieved when I wanted

1   B

the shilling to comfort myself, and when it hath not been in my power to relieve, I have grieved for the scanty accommodations of others. Many troublesome and expensive offices I have undertaken to do good to men, and ever social and free have I been in my demeanour, easy and smooth in my address ; and therefore I trust that, whenever I am removed from this horizon, it will be from a dark and cloudy state, to that of joy, light, and full revelation. This felicitates my every day, let what happen from without. This supports me under every affliction, and enables me to maintain a habit of satisfaction and joy in the general course of my life.

The things of my childhood are not worth setting down, and therefore I commence my life from the first month of the seventeenth year of my age, when I was sent to the university, in 1720, and entered a pensioner, though I had a larger yearly allowance than any fellow-commoner of my college. I was resolved to read there, and determined to improve my natural faculties to the utmost of my power. Nature, I was sensible, had bestowed no genius on me. This, and understanding, are only the privilege of extraordinary persons, who receive from Heaven the happy conjunction of qualities, that they may execute great and noble designs, and acquire the highest pitch of excellence in the profession they turn to, if they will take the pains to perfect the united qualities by art, and carefully avoid running into caprice and paradox ; the rocks on which many a genius has split. But then I had a tolerable share of natural understanding, and from my infancy was teachable, and always attentive to the directions of good sense. This I knew might rise with some labour, to a half merit, though it could never gain immortality upon any account : and this was enough for me. I wanted only to acquire such degrees of perfections as lay within the small sphere nature had chalked out for me.

To this purpose I devoted my college life to books, and for five years that I resided in the university, conversed so much with the dead that I had very little intercourse with the living. So totally had letters engaged my mind, that I was but little affected towards most other things. Walking and music were my favourite recreations, and almost the only ones I delighted in. I had hardly a thought at that time of the foolish choices and pursuits of men, those fatal choices and pursuits which are owing to false judgments, and to a habit of acting precipitantly, without examining the fancies and appetites ; and therefore very rarely went into the pleasures and diversions which men of fortune in a university too commonly indulge in. My relaxation after study was my german-flute and the conversation of some ingenious, sober friend, generally my private tutor, Mr. JOHN BRUCE, who was a bright and excellent man, and of whom you will find a large account in the first volume of my *Memoirs of several Ladies of Great Britain*, 1755, 8vo, p. 7. If the weather permitted, I walked out into the country several miles. At this exercise I had often one or other with me ; but for the most part was obliged to go alone. My dog and my gun however were diversion enough on the way, and they frequently led me into scenes of entertainment, which lasted longer than the day. Some of them you will find in this *Journal*. The history of the beautiful HARRIET NOEL you shall have by and by.

At present, my scheme requires me to set down the method I pursued in my readings, and let my reader know the issue of my studies. My time I devoted to philosophy, cosmography, mathematics, and the languages, for four years, and the fifth I gave to history.

The first book I took into my hand, after receiving my note of admission, was the *Essay* of that fine genius, Mr. LOCKE, and I was so pleased with this clear and accurate writer, that I looked into nothing else, till, by reading it three times over, I had made a thorough acquaintance with my own understanding. He taught me to examine my abilities, and enabled me to see what objects my mind was fitted to deal with. He led me into the sanctuary of vanity and ignorance, and showed me how greatly true knowledge depended on a right meaning of words, and a just significancy of expression. In sum, from the *Essay* my understanding received very great benefits, and to it I owe what improvement I have made in the reason given me. If I could, I would persuade all young gentlemen to read it over and over with great attention, and I am sure. they would find themselves very richly rewarded for their pains in reading it. They would acquire that justness and truth of understanding, which is the great perfection of rational beings.

When I had done, for a time, with this admirable *Essay*, I then began to study the first principles of things, the structure of the universe, the contexture of human bodies, the properties of beasts, the virtues of plants, and the qualities of metals, and was quite charmed with the contemplation of the beautiful order and wise final causes of nature in all her laws and productions. The study had a delightful influence on the temper of my mind, and inspired into it a love of order in my heart, and in my outward manners. It likewise led me to the great first cause, and in repeated views of harmony, wisdom, and goodness, in all the works of nature, riveted upon my mind a fixed conviction, that all is under the administration of a general mind, as far remote from all malice as from all weakness, whether in respect of understanding, or of power. This gave me a due affection towards the infinitely perfect Parent of Nature ; and as I contemplated his glorious works, I was obliged in transports to confess, that he deserved our love and admiration. This did also satisfy me, that whatever the order of the world produces, is in the main both just and good, and of consequence that we ought in the best manner to support whatever hardships are to be endured for virtue's sake : that acquiescence and complacency with respect to ill accidents, ill men and injuries, ought to be our part under a perfect administration ; and with benignity and constancy we must ever act, if there be a settled persuasion that all things are framed and governed by an universal mind. Such was the effect the study of natural philosophy had upon my soul. It set beyond all doubt before me the moral perfection of the Creator and Governor of the universe. And if this Almighty God, I said, is perfect wisdom and virtue, does it not follow that he must approve and love those who are at due pains to improve in wisdom ; and what he loves and delights in, must he not make happy ? This is an evident truth. It renders the cause of virtue quite triumphant.

But upon ethics or moral philosophy I dwelt the longest. This is the proper food of the soul, and what perfects it in all the virtues and qualifications of a gentleman. This science I col- lected in the first place from the antient sages and philosophers, and studied all the moral writers of Greece and Rome. With great pleasure I saw that these immortal authors had delineated, as far as human reason can go, that course of life which is most according to the intention of nature, and most happy ; had shown that this universe, and human nature in particular, was formed by the wisdom and counsel of a Deity, and that from the constitution of our nature various duties arose : that since God is the original independent being, complete in all possible per- fection, of boundless power, wisdom, and goodness ; the Creator, Contriver, and Governor of this world, to whom mankind are indebted for innumerable benefits most gratuitously bestowed ; we ought to manifest the most ardent love and veneration toward the Deity, and worship him with affections of soul suited to the pre-eminence and infinite grandeur of the original cause of all ; ought to obey him, as far as human weakness can go, and humbly submit and resign ourselves and all our interests to his will ; continually confide in his goodness, and constantly imitate him, as far as our weak nature is capable. This is due to that original most gracious power who formed us, and with a liberal hand supplies us with all things conducive to such pleasure and happiness as our nature can receive. That in respect of mankind, our natural sense of right and wrong, points out to us the duties to be performed towards others, and the kind affections implanted by nature, excites us to the discharge of them : that by the law of our constitution and nature, justice and benevolence are prescribed ; and aids and an intercourse of mutual offices required, not only to secure our pleasure and happiness, but to preserve ourselves in safety and in life ; that the law of nature, or natural right, forbids every instance of injustice, a violation of life, liberty, health, property ; and the exercise of our honourable, kind powers, are not only a spring of vigorous efforts to do good to others, and thereby secure the common happiness ; but they really procure us a joy and peace, an inward applause and external advantages ; while injustice and malice, anger, hatred, envy, and revenge, are often matter of shame and remorse, and contain nothing joyful, nothing glorious : in the greatest affluence, the savage men are miserable ; that as to ourselves, the voice of reason declares, that we ought to employ our abilities and opportunities in improving our minds to an extensive knowledge of nature in the sciences ; and by diligent meditation and observation, acquire that prudence, justice, temperance, and fortitude, which should constantly govern our lives. That solid prudence, which abhors rashness, inconsiderateness, a foolish self-confidence and craft, and under a high sense of moral excellence, considers and does what is really advantageous in life. That justice, which constantly regards the common interest, and in subserviency to it, gives to each one whatever is due to him upon any natural claim. That temperance, which restrains and regulates the lower appetites, and displays the grace and beauty of manners. And that fortitude, which represses all vain and excessive fears, gives us a superiority to all the external accidents of our mortal state, and strengthens the soul against all toils or dangers we may be exposed to in discharge of our duty ; as an early and painful death with virtue and honour is highly preferable to the longest ignominious life, and no advantages can be compared, in point of happiness, with the approbation of God, and of our own hearts.

That if in this manner we live prepared for any honourable services to God, our fellows, and ourselves, and practise piety toward God, good-will toward men, and immediately aim at our own perfection, then we may expect, notwithstanding our being involved in manifold weaknesses and disorders of soul, that the divine goodness and clemency will have mercy on such as sincerely love him, and desire to serve him with duty and gratitude ; will be propitious and placable to the penitents, and all who exert their utmost endeavours in the pursuit of virtue : and since the perfection of virtue must constitute the supreme felicity of man, our efforts to attain it must be effectual in obtaining complete felicity, or at least some lower degree of it.

This beautiful, moral philosophy, I found scattered in the writings of the old theist philosophers, and with great pains reduced the various lessons to a system of active and virtuous offices : but this I knew was what the majority of mankind were incapable of doing ; and if they could do it, I saw it was far

inferior to revelation. *E*very Sunday I appropriated to the
study of revealed religion, and perceived as I read the sacred
records, that the works of Plato, and Cicero, and *E*pictetus, and
all the uninspired sages of antiquity, were but weak rules in
respect of the divine oracles. It is the mercy and power of God
in the triumphs of grace, that restores mankind from the bondage
and ignorance of idolatry. To this the sinner owes the conversion
of his soul. It is the statutes of the Lord that rejoice the heart
and enlighten the eyes. What are all the reasonings of the philosophers to the melody of that heavenly voice which cries continually "Come unto me all ye that travail and are heavy laden,
and I will refresh you." And what could their lessons avail
without those express promises of grace and spiritual assistance,
which the blood of the new covenant confirms to mankind ?
The philosophy of Greece and Rome was admirable for the times
and men : but it admits of no comparison with the divine lessons
of our holy religion, and the charter of God's pardon granted to
us by his blessed Son. Beside, the philosophers were in some
degree dark and doubtful in respect of death and futurity ; and
in relation to this world, there is not a power in their discourses,
to preserve us from being undone by allurements, in the midst
of plenty, and to secure our peace against the casualties of fortune,
and the torments of disappointments ; to save us from the cares
and solicitudes which attend upon large possessions, and give
us a mind capable of relishing the good things before us ; to make
us easy and satisfied as to the present, and render us secure and
void of fear as to the future. These things we learn from revelation, and are informed by the sacred records only, that if we are
placed here in the midst of many fears and sorrows, and are often
perplexed with evils in this world ; they are so many warnings
not to set up our rest here, but to keep a steadfast eye upon the
things which God has prepared for those who love him. It is
the gospel informs us, there is another scene prepared for the
moral world, and that justice only waits to see the full proof of
the righteousness, or unrighteousness of men : that that scene
will open with the judgment seat of Christ, and we shall either
receive glory and immortality, if we have obeyed the calls of
grace to virtue and holiness ; or, be doomed to the most dreadful
miseries, if we reject the counsel of God, and live quite thoughtless
of the great concerns of eternity. These considerations made
me prefer revealed religion, in the beginning of my rational life.
The morality of the antient philosophers I admired. With
delight I studied their writings, and received, I gratefully confess,
much improvement from them. But the religion of our blessed
Lord I declared for, and look on the promised Messiah as the
most consummate blessing God could bestow, or man receive.
God having raised up his son Jesus, sent him to bless you, in

turning every one of you from your iniquities. And would men but hear and obey this life-giving Redeemer, his gospel would restore reason and religion to their rightful authority over mankind ; and make all virtue, and true goodness, flourish in the earth.

But I must observe that, by the religion of the *New Testament*, I do not mean any of those modern schemes of religion, which discover the evident marks and signatures of superstition and enthusiasm, or of knavery and imposture ; those systems which even miracles cannot prove to be true, because the pieties are absurd, inconsistent, and contradictory. The notions that are not characterized by the reason of things, and the moral fitness of actions, I considered as repugnant to the veracity, wisdom and goodness of the Almighty, and concluded, that that only could be Christian religion, which bore the visible marks and signatures of benevolence, social happiness, and moral fitness, and was brought down from heaven to instruct mankind in the worship of one eternal mind, and bring them to repentance, and amendment of life. This was the religion I found in my Bible. I saw with pleasure, as I thoughtfully went through the divine pages, that natural religion is the foundation and support of revelation : supplies the defects of nature, but never attempts to overthrow the established principles of it, and casts new light upon the dictates of reason, but never overthrows them. Pure theism, and Christ the appointed Mediator, Advocate, and Judge, by a commission from God the Father, to me appeared to be the gospel ; and the directions of the Holy Spirit, to believe in one supreme independent first cause, and worship in spirit and truth this one God and Father of all, in the name of Christ Jesus ; as the disciples of the Messiah ; to copy after the life of our blessed Saviour, and to the utmost of our abilities, obey all his commands. This was the religion I found in the writings of the apostles, and I then determined to regard only this gospel doctrine.

The manner of my studying cosmography and mathematics is not worth setting down, as there was nothing uncommon in it. In the one I only learned to distinguish climates, latitudes, and the four divisions of the world ; the provinces, nations, kingdoms and republics comprised therein, and to be able to discourse upon them. And in the other, I went no farther than to make myself a master of vulgar and decimal arithmetic, the doctrine of infinite series, and the application of algebra, to the higher geometry of curves. Algebra I was charmed with, and found so much pleasure in resolving its questions, that I have often sat till morning at the engaging work, without a notion of its being day till I opened the shutters of my closet. I recommend this study in particular to young gentlemen, and am satisfied, if they would but take some pains at first to understand it, they would have so great a relish for its operations, as to prefer them many an evening to clamorous pleasures ; or, at least, not be uneasy for being alone now and then, since their algebra was with them.

In reading history, my last year's principal employment, during my residence in college, I began with the best writers of antient history and ended with modern times, epochs, centuries, ages ; the extent of empires, kingdoms, commonwealths ; their progress, revolutions, changes and declensions ; the number, order, and qualities of the princes that have reigned over those states and kingdoms, their actions military and civil ; the characters and actions of the great men that flourished under them ; and the laws, the arts, learning and manners, I carefully marked down, and observed not only how the first governments were formed, but what the progress was of industry and property, which may be called the generative principle of empire.

When I had done with antient history, I sat down to the best modern stories I could get, and read of distant nations before I began to study my country's constitution, history and laws. When I had finished the histories of France, Spain, Italy, and Germany, and many more, then I turned to Great Britain, and in the first place took a view of the English constitution and government, in the antient books of the common law, and some more modern writers, who out of them have given an account of this government. From thence I proceeded to our history, and with it joined in every king's reign the laws then made. This gave me an insight into the reason of our statutes, and showed me the true ground upon which they came to be made, and what weight they ought to have. By this means I read the history of my country with intelligence, and was able to examine into the excellence or defects of its government, and to judge of the fitness or unfitness of its orders and laws. By this method I likewise knew enough of the law for an English gentleman, though quite ignorant of the chicane, or wrangling and captious part, and was well acquainted with the true measure of right and wrong. The arts how to avoid doing right, and to secure one's-self in doing wrong, I never looked into.

Thus did I read history, and many noble lessons I learned from it—just notions of true worth, true greatness, and solid happiness. It taught me to place merit where it only lies, not in birth, not in beauty, not in riches, not in external show and magnificence, not in voluptuousness ; but, in a firm adherence to truth and rectitude ; in an untainted heart, that would not pollute or prostitute its integrity in any degree, to gain the highest worldly honours, or to ward off the greatest worldly misery. This is true magnanimity : and he alone can be truly happy, as well as truly great, who can look down with generous contempt upon everything that would tempt him to recede in the smallest degree from the paths of rigid honesty, candour and veracity.

Es modicus voti, presso lare, dulcis amicis;
Jam nunc astringas ; jam nunc granaria laxes;
Inque luto fixum possis transcendere nummum
Nec glutto sorbere salivam Mercurialem ?
Hæc mea sunt, teneo, cum vere dixeris : Esto
Liberque ac sapiens, prætoribus ac Jove dextro.
Sin tu, cum fueris nostræ pauló ante farinæ,
Pelliculam veterem retines, et fronte politus
Astutam vapido servas sub pectore vulpem ;
Quæ dederam suprà, repeto, funemque reduco.
Nil tibi concessit ratio : digitum exere peccas,
Et quid tam parvum est ? Sed nullo thure litabis,
Hæreat in stultis brevis ut semuncia recti
Hæc miscere Nefas :—

Are you moderate in your desires, frugal, and obliging to your friends ? Do you know when to spare, and when to be liberal, as occasion requires ? And can you give a check to your avarice, in spite of all temptations which are laid in your way? Can you refrain from being too greedy in your pursuit after riches ? When you can sincerely affirm that you are master of yourself, and of all these good qualities, then you are free indeed, and wise, by the propitious power of Jove and the Prætor.

But if you retain the old habits of a slave, and harbour ill qualities, under the hypocritical appearance of virtue, you are as much a slave as ever, while thus enslaved to your vices. Philosophy gives no indulgence to vice, makes no allowance for any crime. If in wagging your finger, you acted against reason, you transgress, though the thing be of so trifling a nature. All the sacrifices you can offer will never pass for a drachm of rectitude, while your conduct is faulty. Wisdom is incompatible with folly.

When to be bountiful, and when to spare,
And never craving, or oppress'd with care ;
The baits of gifts, and money to despise,
And look on wealth with undesiring eyes ;
When thou can'st truly call these virtues thine,
Be wise and free by Heav'n's consent and mine.
But thou, who lately of the common strain,
Wert one of us, if still thou dost retain
The same ill habits, the same follies too,
Gloss'd over only with a saint-like show,
Then I resume the freedom which I gave,
Still thou art bound to vice, and still a slave.
Thou canst not wag thy finger, or begin
The least slight motion, but it tends to sin.
How's this ? Not wag my finger, he replies ?
No, friend ; not fuming gums, nor sacrifice,
Can ever make a madman free, or wise.
Virtue and vice are never in one soul :
A man is wholly wise, or wholly is a fool.

This is the great lesson, that virtue alone is true honour, true freedom, and solid, durable happiness. It is indeed its own reward. There are no satisfactions equal to, or comparable with virtuous, rational exercises ; nor can virtuous dispositions, and well improved moral powers be rewarded, or receive happiness suited to their nature, but from their exercises and employments about proper objects. And as virtue gives pleasure here in proportion to the improvements it makes, far beyond all that mere sense can yield, in the most advantageous circumstances of outward enjoyment ; so in a state to come, it shall be so placed as its improvements require, that is, be placed in circumstances that shall afford it business or employment proportioned to its capacity, and by means thereof the highest satisfaction. Such a basis for building moral instructions upon we find in history. We are warned in some pages to avoid the miseries and wretchedness which many have fallen into by departing from reason or virtue : and in others, we meet with such virtuous characters and actions, as set forth the charms of integrity in their full lustre, and prove that virtue is the supreme beauty, the supreme charm : that in keeping the precepts of moral rectitude, we secure a present felicity and reward ; and have a presage of those higher rewards which await a steady course of right conduct in another world. —Glorious, natural virtue ! Would mankind but hearken to its voice, and obey its dictates, there would be no such beings as invaders, delinquents, and traitors, in this lower world. The social inclinations and dispositions would for ever prevail over the selfish appetites and passions. The law of benevolence would be the rule of life. The advancement of the common good would be the work of every man.

The case however is, that the generality of mankind are too corrupt to be governed by the great universal law of social nature, and to gratify ambition, avarice, and the like, employ a cunning or power, to seize the natural rights and properties of others : and therefore, to natural virtue, grounded on the reason and fitness of things, in themselves, the first and principal mean of securing the peace and happiness of society, it was necessary to add two other grand principles, civil government and religion, and so have three conducible means to social happiness. These three are necessary to the being of a public, and of them, religion, as I take it, is of the first consequence ; for the choice few only mind a natural virtue, or benevolence flowing from the reason, nature, and fitness of things : and civil government cannot always secure the happiness of mankind in particular cases : but religion, rightly understood, and fixed upon its true and proper foundation, might do the work, in conjunction with the other two principles, and secure the happiness of society. If mankind were brought to the belief and worship of one only true God, and to a sincere obedience to his will, as we have it discovered in revelation, I think, appetite and passion would cease to invade by violence or fraud, or set up for private interest in opposition to the public

stock or common good.   But, alas ! Religion is so far from being
rightly understood, that it is rendered by some explainers the
most doubtful and disputable thing in the world.   They have
given it more phases than the moon, and made it everything and
nothing, while they are screaming or forcing the people into their
several factions.   This destroys the moment of religion, and the
multitude are thereby wandering into endless mazes and perplexities, and rendered a hairing, staring, wrathful rabble ; instead of · being transformed into such Christians as filled the
first church at Jerusalem ; Christians who acknowledged and worshipped God the Father Almighty, in the name of Christ, that
is, under a belief of that authority and power which the Father of
the universe has, for the good of mankind, conferred upon him ;
and in humility and meekness, in mortification and self-denial,
in a renunciation of the spirit, wisdom, and honours of this world,
in a love of God, and desire of doing God's will, and seeking only
his honour, were, by the gospel, made like unto Christ.   Golden
religion !   Golden age !   The doctrine of Christianity was then
a restoration of true religion : the practice of Christianity, a
restoration of human nature.   But now, alas ! too many explainers are employed in darkening and making doubtful the
revealed will of God, and by paraphrases, expositions, commentaries, notes, and glosses, have almost rendered revelation useless.
What do we see in the vast territories of popery, but a perfect
diabolism in the place of the religion of our Lord ? doctrines the
most impious and absurd, the most inconsistent and contradictory in themselves, the most hurtful and mischievous in their
consequences ; the whole supported by persecution, by the sophistry of learned knaves, and the tricks of juggling priests.   And
if we turn our eyes from these regions of imposture and cruelty,
to the realms of protestants, do we not find some learned Christian
critics and expositors reducing the inspired writings to a dark
science ? without regard to the nature and intrinsic character of
their doctrines, do they not advance notions as true and divine,
which have not one appearance of divine authority ? but on the
contrary, militate with the reason of things, and the moral fitness
of actions ; and are so far from being plain and clear, free from all
doubtfulness, or ambiguity, and suited to the understandings
and capacity of men, that the darkness of them renders such pretended revelations of little service ; and impeaches the veracity,
wisdom, and goodness of God !   Alas ! too many explainers are
clamorous, under the infallible strength of their own persuasions,
and exert every power to unman us into believers.   How the
Apostles argued for the great excellency and dignity of Christianity is not with them the question ; so far as I am able to judge
from their learned writings ; but the fathers, and our spiritual
superiors have put upon the sacred writings the proper expli-

cations ; and we must receive the truth as they dispense it to us. This is not right, in my conception.   I own it does not seem to answer the end of the Messiah's coming, which was to restore Reason and Religion to their rightful authority over mankind ; and to make all virtue, and true goodness, flourish in the earth ; the most perfect blessing to be sure that God could bestow on man, or man receive from God.   This blessing we must miss, if human authority is to pin us down to what it pleases to call sense of scripture, and will set up the judgment of fallible men as the test of Christianity.   The Christian laity are miserable indeed, if they be put under an obligation to find that to be truth which is taught by these leaders.   In truth, we should be un- happy men, with a revelation in our churches and our closets, if the leaders had a right to make their own faith pass for the faith of the Apostles ; or, if we refused it, might lance the weapons of this world at their people.   What must we do then as true Christians ?   I think for myself, that we ought to form our judgment, in matters of faith, upon a strict, serious and impartial examination of the holy scriptures, without any regard to the judgment of others, or human authority whatever : that we ought to open the sacred records, without minding any systems, and from the revealed word of God learn that Christianity does not consist in a jingle of unintelligible sounds, and new fundamentals, hewn out by craft, enthusiasm, or bigotry, and maintained with an outrage of uncharitable zeal, which delivers Christians to the flames of an eternal hell : but, that the heavenly religion of our Lord consists in looking on the promised Messiah, as the most consummate blessing God could bestow, or man receive ; and that Jesus is that Messiah ; in acting according to the rules of the gospel, and in studying to imitate God, who is the most per- fect understanding nature, in all his moral perfections ; in be- coming the children of God by being, according to our capacity, perfect as he is perfect, and holy as he is holy, and merciful as he is merciful ; and in our whole moral behaviour as like to him as possible.

In a word, to flee injustice, oppression, intemperance, impurity, pride, unmercifulness and revenge : to practise justice, piety, temperance, chastity, humility, beneficence, and placability : to turn from our iniquities to the practice of all virtue : and through the alone mediation of the only-begotten Son of God, believe in and worship the eternal mind, the one supreme spirit, in hope of a glorious immortality, through the sanctification of the Holy Ghost.   These are the things the Lord came down to teach man- kind.   For the *New Testament* itself then we must declare, and look upon it as the only guide, or rule of faith.   It is now the only deliverer of the declarations of our Lord : and the rule in our inquiry is, that every thing necessary to be believed by a Christian, is in those books not left to be gathered by consequences, or implications ; but the things necessary to obtain the favour of God promised to Christians are expressly declared.   If this was not the case—if things absolutely necessary were not expressly proclaimed to be so, the gospel revelation would be no rule at all.*

But it is time to tell my reader the story of the beautiful HARRIET NOEL, which I promised in a preceding page (p. 3, ante). On the glorious first of August, before the beasts were roused from their lodges, or the birds had soared upwards, to pour forth their morning harmony ; while the mountains and the groves were overshadowed by a dun obscurity, and the dawn still dappled the drowsy east with spots of grey ; in short, before the sun was up, or, with his auspicious presence, began to animate inferior nature, I left my chamber, and with my gun and dog, went out to wander over a pleasant country.   The different aspects and the various points of view were charming, as the light in fleecy rings increased ; and when the whole flood of day descended, the embellished early scene was a fine entertainment.   Delighted with the beau-

---

* To the plain and satisfactory method of seeking for the faith in the sacred books, there are many adversaries and many objections raised.   There are, says a great man, a very numerous body of Christians who know no other guides but the living guides of the present church ; and acknowledge no other faith, for the faith once delivered to the saints, but that which is now delivered to them by their present rulers, as such.

To establish this point, the greater part of these lay down the infallibility of the present church, and of every man of the past ages, through whose mouth, or by whose hands, the present traditions of faith have descended to them.   And this, indeed, would be a very good method, if that single proof of infallibility could be proved.   But this is a point so gross and so utterly void of all proof, that a great body of the Christian world have broke lose from the power of this monster, and declared for the *New Testament* itself, as the only guide or rule of faith ; the only deliverer of the faith to us of later ages.

When this comes however to be put in practice, too many of the same persons who set the scriptures up as the only guide, turn round on a sudden, and let us know, that they m ean by it, not these sacred original writings themselves, but the interpretations, or sense, put upon them by our spiritual superiors, to which we are bound to submit, and put under an obligation to find that to be the truth which is taught by these leaders.

But to this we reply with reason, that though we ought to pay a regard of serious attention to those whose business it is to find out and dispense the truth, and show the respect of a due examination of what they affirm ; yet we must not yield the submission due only to infallibility.   It is our glory not to submit to the voice of any man.   We must reserve that regard, for God, and for Christ, in matters of faith once delivered to the saints.

Others, again, of the reformed, tell us, that the surer way of knowing what was delivered above eighteen hundred years ago, is to take the original faith from the Councils and Fathers, grave and good men, who met and wrote for the settling of the faith.   And to this we answer, that these wise and good men cannot give so good an account of the faith contained in the original books as the books themselves which contain it.

To give an example to the purpose.   If we would know the doctrine of the Church of England at the Reformation, it is not the writings of particular divines, many years after that period, that we must consult ; or any assembly of them ; but the authentic acts and declarations, and sermons, made and recorded at the time ; for many of the doctrines thought essential at the Reformation, have been since changed by gradual alterations ; by explainers using their own style and manner of expression, and introducing their own scheme of philosophy, and judgment in commenting, into the scheme of doctrine to be explained.   This produces great variation from what was once settled.   What was once esteemed fundamental is thereby altered.   Let this be applied to the first Christian writers, after the Apostles were departed, and as their language and philosophy were various, and they differed from one another, great variations must creep into the doctrines delivered by them.   It follows then, that nothing but what is recorded in the first original books themselves can be firm and stable to us in points of faith.   In the original books only we can find the faith, without that confusion and darkness, which human explications and additions have brought in by way of light.

ties of this morning, I climbed up the mountains, and traversed through many a valley. The game was plenty, and for full five hours, I journeyed onward, without knowing where I was going, or thinking of a return to college.

About nine o'clock however I began to grow very hungry, and was looking round to see if I could discover any proper habitation to my purpose, when I observed in a valley, at some distance, something that looked like a mansion. That way therefore I moved, and with no little difficulty, as I had a precipice to descend, or must go a mile round, to arrive at the place I wanted : down therefore I marched, got a fall by the way that had like to have destroyed me, and after all, found it to be a shed for cattle. The bottom however was very beautiful, and the sides of the hills sweetly copsed with little woods. The valley is so divided, that the rising sun gilds it on the right hand, and when declining, warms it on the left.

> —— Veniens dextrum latus aspiciat Sol,
> Lævum discedens curru fugiente vaporet.

A pretty brook here likewise babbles along, and even Hebrus strays not round Thrace with a purer and cooler stream.

> Fons etiam rivo dare nomen idoneus, ut nec
> Frigidior Thracam nec purior ambiat Hebrus.

In this sweet and delicious solitude, I crept on for some time by the side of the murmuring stream, and followed as it winded through the vale, till I came to a little harmonic building, that had every charm and proportion architecture could give it. It was situated on a rising ground in a broad part of the fruitful valley, and surrounded with a garden, that invited a pensive wanderer to roam in its delightful retreats, and walks amazingly beautiful. Every side of this fine spot was planted thick with underwood, and kept so low, as not to prevent a prospect to every pleasing remote object.

Finding one of the garden doors left open, I entered immediately, and to screen myself from the scorching beams of the sun, got into an embowered way, that led me to a large fountain, in a ring or circular opening, and from thence, by a gradual, easy, shady ascent, to a semicircular amphitheatre of evergreens, that was quite charming. In this were several seats for ease, repast, or retirement ; and at either end of it a rotunda or temple of the Ionic order. One of them was converted into a grotto or shell-house, in which a politeness of fancy had produced and blended the greatest beauties of nature and decoration. The other was a library, filled with the finest books, and a vast variety of mathematical instruments. Here I saw Miss NOEL sitting, and so intent at writing, that she did not take any notice of me, as I stood at the window, in astonishment, looking at the things before me, and especially at the amazing beauties of her face, and the splendour of her eyes ; as she raised them now and then from the paper she was writing on, to look into a Hebrew Bible, that lay open upon a small desk before her. The whole scene was so very uncommon, and so vastly amazing, that I thought myself for a while on some spot of magic ground, and almost doubted the reality of what my eyes beheld ; till Miss NOEL, by accident, looked full at me, and then came forward to the open window, to know who I wanted.

Before I could answer, I found a venerable old gentleman standing by my side, and he seemed much more surprised at the sight of me than his daughter was ; for, as this young lady told me afterward, she guessed at once the whole affair ; seeing me with my gun and dog, in a shooting dress ; and knew it was a natural curiosity brought me into the garden, and stopped me at the window, when I saw her in such an attitude, and in such a place. This I assured them was the truth of my case, with this small addition, however, that I was ready to perish for want of something to eat ; having been from four in the morning at hard exercise, and had not yet broke my fast. If this be the case, says the good old man, you are welcome, sir, to *Eden Park*, and you shall soon have the best breakfast our house affords.

Upon this Mr. NOEL brought me into his house, and the lovely HARRIET made tea for me, and had such plenty of fine cream, and extraordinary bread and butter set before me, that I breakfasted with uncommon pleasure. The honour and happiness of her company rendered the repast quite delightful. There was a civility so very great in her manner, and a social goodness so charming in her talk and temper, that it was unspeakable delight to sit at table with her. She asked me a number of questions relating to things and books and people, and there was so much good sense in every inquiry, so much good humour in her reflections and replications, that I was entirely charmed with her mind ; and lost in admiration, when I contemplated the wonders of her face, and the beauties of her person.

When breakfast was over, it was time for me to depart, and I made half a dozen attempts to rise from my chair ; but without her laying a rosy finger on me, this illustrious maid had so totally subdued my soul, and deprived me of all motive power, that I sat like the renowned Prince of the Massagetes, who was stiffened by enchantment in the apartment of the Princess Phedima, as we read in *Amadis de Gaul*. This Miss NOEL saw very plain, and in compassion to my misfortune generously threw in a hint now and then, for a little farther conversation to colour my unreasonable delay. But this could not have been of service much longer, as the clock had struck twelve, if the old

gentleman, her father, had not returned to us, and told me, he
insisted on my staying to dine with him ; for he loved to take a
glass after dinner with a facetious companion, and would be
obliged to me for my company. "At present," continued he,
"you will excuse me, sir, as business engages me till we dine ;
but my daughter will chat the hours away with you, and show
you the curiosities of her library and grot. HARRIET will supply
my place."

This was a delightful invitation indeed, and after returning
my hearty thanks to the old gentleman for the favour he did me,
I addressed myself to Miss NOEL, when her father was gone,
and we were walking back to the library in the garden, and told
her ingenuously, that though I could not be positive as to the
situation of my soul, whether I was in love with her or not, as I
never had experienced the passion before, nor knew what it was to
admire a woman, having lived till that morning in a state of
indifference to her sex, yet I found very strange emotions within
me, and I was sure I could not leave her without the most lively
and afflicting inquietude. "You will pardon, I hope, madam, this
effusion of my heart, and suffer me to demonstrate by a thousand
and a thousand actions, that I honour you in a manner unutterable,
and, from this time, can imagine no happiness but with you."

"Sir," this inimitable maid replied, "you are an entire stranger
to me, and to declare a passion on a few hours' acquaintance,
must be either to try my weakness, or because you think a young
woman is incapable of relishing any thing but such stuff, when
alone in conversation with a gentleman. I beg then I may hear
no more of this ; and as I am sure you can talk upon many more
rational subjects, request your favour to give me your opinion
on some articles in this Hebrew Bible you see lying open on the
table in this room. My father, sir, among other things, has taken
great pains to instruct me, for several years that I have lived
with him in a kind of solitary state, since the death of my mother,
whom I lost when I was very young, and has taught me to read
and understand this inspired Hebrew book ; and says we must
ascribe primævity and sacred prerogatives to this language.
For my part, I have some doubts as to this matter, which I
dare not mention to my father. Tell me, if you please, what you
think of the thing ?"

"Miss NOEL," I answered, "since it is your command that
I should be silent as to that flame your glorious eyes and understanding have lighted up in my soul, like some superior nature,
before whom I am nothing, silent I will be, and tell you what I
fancy on a subject I am certain you understand much better than
I do. My knowledge of the Hebrew is but small, though I have
learned to read and understand the *Old Testament* in the ante-
Babel language.

"My opinion on your question is, that the Biblical Hebrew was the language of Paradise, and continued to be spoken by all men down to, and at the time of Moses writing the *Pentateuch*, and long after. Abraham, though bred in Chaldea, could converse freely with the Egyptians, the Sodomites, and the King of Gerar ; nor do we find that any variety of speech interrupted the commerce of his son Isaac with the several nations around, or that it ever stopped Jacob in his travels. Nay, the Israelites, in their journeys through the deserts of Arabia, after they had been some hundred years in Egypt, though joined by a mixed multitude, and meeting with divers kinds of people, had not corrupted their language, and were easily understood, because it was then the universal one. The simplicity and distinctness of the Hebrew tongue preserved its purity so long and so universally. It could not well be degenerate till the knowledge of nature was lost, as its words consist but of two or three letters, and are perfectly well suited to convey sensible and strong ideas. It was at the captivity,† in the space of seventy years, that the Jews by temporising with the ignorant victors, so far neglected the usage of their own tongue, that none but the scribes or learned men could understand Moses's books."

"This, I confess," said Miss NOEL, "is a plausible account of the primævity and pre-eminence of the sacred Hebrew, but I think it is not necessary the account should be allowed as fact. As to its being the language in Paradise, this is not very probable, as a compass of eighteen hundred years must have changed the first language very greatly by an increase of words and new inflections, applications, and constructions of them. The first few inhabitants of the earth were occupied in few things, and wanted not a variety of words ; but when their descendants invented arts and improved sciences, they were obliged to coin new words and technical terms, and by extending and transferring their words to new subjects, and using them figuratively, were forced to multiply the senses of those already in use. The language was thus gradually cultivated, and every age improved it. All living languages are liable to such change. I therefore conclude, that the language which served the first pair would not do for succeeding generations. It became vastly more copious and extensive, when the numbers of mankind were great, and their language must serve conversation and the ends of life, and answer all the purposes of intelligence and correspondence. New words and new terms of speech, from time to time, were necessary, to give true ideas of the things, actions, offices, places,

† The captivity here spoken of began at Nebuzaradan's taking and burning the city and temple of Jerusalem, and sending Zedekiah, the last king, in chains, to Nebuchadnezzar, who ordered his children to be butchered before his face, his eyes to be put out, and then thrown into a dungeon, where he died. This happened before our Lord, 588 years ; after the flood, 1766 ; of the world, 3416.

and times peculiar to the Hebrews. *E*ven Hutchinson allows
there was some coinage, some new words framed. We find in
the latter prophets words not to be met with in the *Pentateuch :*
and from thence we may suppose, that Moses used words unknown to Nimrod and Heber : and that the men at Shinaar *
had words which the people before the flood were strangers to.
*E*ven in the seventeenth century, there must have been a great
alteration in the language of Adam ; and when the venerable
Patriarch and his family came into a new world, that was in a
different state from the earth before the deluge, and saw a vast
variety of things without precedent in the old world, the alterations in nature and diet, must introduce a multitude of new terms
in things of common experience and usage ; as, after that
amazing revolution in the natural world, not only the clouds
and meteors were different, and the souls that were saved had
a new and astonishing view of the ruin and repair of the system ;
but Noah did then begin to be an husbandman ; he planted a
vineyard ; he invented wine ; and to him the first grant was
given of eating flesh. All these things required as it were a new
language, and the terms with mankind increased. The Noahical
language must be quite another thing after the great events of
the flood. Had Methuselah, who conversed many years with
Adam ; who received from his mouth the history of the creation
and fall, and who lived six hundred years with Noah, to communicate to him all the knowledge he got from Adam ; had this
ante-diluvian wise man been raised from the dead to converse
with the post-diluvian fathers, or even with Noah, the year he
died, that is three hundred and fifty years after the flood ; is
it not credible from what I have said, that he would have
heard a language very different from that tongue he used in
his conversations with Adam even in the nine hundred and
thirtieth year of the first man ? † I imagine, Methuselah would

* Shinaar comprehends the plain of Chaldea or Babylonia in Asia ; and the " men of
Shinaar " were the first colony that Noah sent out from Ararat, the mountains of Armenia,
where the Ark rested after the flood, to settle in the grand plains of Babylonia, twelve hundred
miles from Ararat. This was in the days of Peleg, two hundred and forty years after the
flood, when the eight had increased to sixty thousand ; which made a remove of part of them
necessary.

† The extraordinary longevity of the ante-diluvians is accounted utterly incredible by
many moderns ; but it did not appear so unnatural to the early ages of Paganism. Let
no one, says Josephus, upon comparing the lives of the antients with our lives, and with
the few years which we now live, think that what we have said of them is false. I have
for witness to what I have said, all those who have written antiquities, both among the Greeks
and Barbarians. For even Manetho, who wrote the Egyptian History ; and Berosus, who
collected the Chaldean Monuments ; and Mochus and Hostiæus ; and besides these, Hierony-
mus the Egyptian, and those who composed the *Phœnician history,* agree to what I here
say. Hesiod also, and Hecutæus, and Hallanicus, and Acusilaus ; and besides these, Ephorus
and Nicolaus of Damascus, relate that the ancients lived a thousand years.

The antient Latin authors likewise confirm the sacred history in this branch : and Varro
in particular, made an.enquiry, What the reason was that the antients lived a thousand
years ?

[The author had here promised " a continuation of this note in the *Appendix,*" but it
may be proper to notice, that the first volume of this work was printed in 1756, and the second

not have been able to have talked with Noah, at the time I have mentioned, of the circumstances that then made the case of mankind, and of the things of common experience and usage. He must have been unable to converse at his first appearance ? "

" What you say, madam," I replied, " is not only very probable, but affords a satisfaction unexpected in a subject on which we are obliged, for want of data, to use conjectures. I yield to your superior-sense the notion, that the *Scriptures* were written in the language of Paradise. Most certain it is, that even in respect of our own language, for example, the subjects of Henry I would find it as much out of their power to understand the English of George the First's reign, were they brought up again, as the ordinary people of our time are at a loss to make anything of the English written in the first Henry's reign. But when I have granted this, you will be pleased to inform me, how Abraham and his sons conversed and commerced with the nations, if the Hebrew was not the universal language in their time ? If the miracle at Babel was a confusion of tongues, as is generally supposed, how did the holy family talk and act with such distant kings and people ? Illuminate me, thou glorious girl, in this dark article, and be my teacher in Hebrew learning, as I flatter myself you will be the guide and dirigent of all my notions and my days. Yes, charming HARRIET, my fate is in your hands. Dispose of it as you will, and make me what you please."

" You force me to smile," the illustrious Miss NOEL replied, " and oblige me to call you an odd compound of a man. Pray, sir, let me have no more of those romantic flights, and I will answer your question as well as I can ; but it must be at some other time. There is more to be said on the miracle at Babel, and its effects, than I could dispatch between this and our hour of dining, and therefore, the remainder of our leisure till dinner, we will pass in a visit to my grotto, and in walking round the garden to the parlour we came from." To the grotto then we went, and to the best of my power I will give my reader a description of this splendid room.

In one of the fine rotundas I have mentioned, at one end of the green amphitheatre very lately described, the shining apartment was formed. Miss NOEL's hand had covered the floor with the most beautiful mosaic my eyes have ever beheld, and filled the arched roof with the richest fossil gems. The mosaic painting on the ground was wrought with small coloured stones or pebbles, and sharp pointed bits of glass, measured and proportioned

to which the *Appendix* was to have been added, did not make its appearance till 1766, and then without the promised addition. What the Appendix was intended to comprise will be found more fully noticed in the introductory portion to this volume. The *material* connected with the dispersion at Babel, was derived by the author, from Blomberg's *Life of Edmund Dickinson, M.D.*, 1739, 8vo, of which subsequent notice will be made. ED.]

together, so as to imitate in their assemblage the strokes and colour of the objects, which they were intended to represent, and they represented by this lady's art, the Temple of Tranquillity, described by Volusenus in his dream.

At some distance the fine temple looks like a beautiful painted picture, as do the birds, the beasts, the trees in the fields about and the river which murmurs at the bottom of the rising ground ; '' *Amnis lucidus et vadosus in quo cernere erat verii generis pisces colludere.*'' So wonderfully did this genius perform the piece, that fishes of many kinds seem to take their pastime in the bright stream. But above all, is the image of the philosopher, at the entrance of the temple, vastly fine. With pebbles and scraps of glass, all the beauties and graces are expressed, which the pencil of an able artist could bestow on the picture of Democritus. You see him as Diogenes Laertius has drawn him, with a philosophical joy in his countenance, that shews him superior to all events. *Summum bonorum finem statuit esse lætitiam, non eam quae sit eadem voluptati, sed eam per quam animus degit perturbationis expers ;* and with a finger, he points to the following golden inscription on the portico of the temple :

Flagrans sit studium bene merendi de seipso,
Et seipsum perficiendi.

That is, " by a rectitude of mind and life, secure true happiness and the applause of your own heart, and let it be the labour of your every day, to come as near perfection as it is possible for human nature to get." This mosaic piece of painting is indeed an admirable thing. It has a fine effect in this grotto and is a noble monument of the masterly hand of Miss NOEL.

Nor was her fine genius less visible in the striking appearance of the extremely beautiful shells and valuable curiosities, all round the apartment. Her father spared no cost to procure her the finest things of the ocean and rivers from all parts of the world, and pebbles, stones, and ores of the greatest curiosity and worth. These were all disposed in such a manner as not only shed a glorious lustre in the room, but shewed the understanding of this young lady in natural knowledge.

In one part of the grot were collected and arranged the stony coverings of all the shell-fish in the sea, from the striated patella and its several species, to the pholades in all their species ; and of those that live in the fresh streams, from the suboval limpet or umbonated patella and its species, to the triangular and deeply striated cardia. Even all the land shells were in this collection, from the pomatia to the round-mouthed turbo. The most beautiful genera of the sea-shells, intermixed with fossil corals of all the kinds ; with animal substances become fossil ; and with copper-ores, agates, pebbles, pieces of the finest marmora and alabastritæ, and the most elegant and beautiful marcasites, and crystals, and spars. These filled the greatest part of the walls, and in classes, here and there, were scattered, as foils to raise the lustre of the others, the inferior shells.

Among the simple sea-shells, that is, those of one shell, without a hinge, I saw several rare ones, that were neither in Mrs. O'HARA's nor in Mrs. CRAFTON's grottos in Fingal, as I observed to those ladies.* The shells I mean are the following ones.

The SEA-TRUMPET, which is in its perfect state, nine inches long, an inch and half diameter at its mouth or irregular lip, and the opening at the small end about half an inch. The surface is a beautiful brown, prettily spotted with white, and the pipe has fourteen annular ridges that are a little elevated, and of a fine purple colour.

The ADMIRAL is vastly beautiful, a voluta two inches and a half long, and an inch in diameter at the head, from whence it decreases to a cone with an obtuse point. The ground colour is the brightest, elegant yellow, fiuer than that of Sienna marble, and this ground so variegated with the brightest colours, that a little more than a third part of the ground is seen. Broad fasciæ, the most charmingly varied, surround it, and the clavicle is the most elegant of objects in colours, brightness, and irregularities. There is a punctuated line of variations that runs in the centre of the yellow fascia, and is wonderfully pretty. This beautiful East-Indian sells at a great price.

The CROWN IMPERIAL is likewise extremely beautiful. This voluta is four inches long, two in diameter at the top, and its head adorned with a charming series of fine tubercles, pointed at the extremities. The ground is a clear pale, and near the head and extremity of the shell, two very beautiful zones run round. They are of the brightest yellow, and in a manner the most elegant, are variegated with black and white purple. It is also an East-Indian.

---

* I had once a sweet little country house in the neighbourhood of those ladies, and used to be often at their gardens and grottos. Mrs. CRAFTON had the finest shells, but her grot was dull and regular, and had no appearance of nature in the formation. She was a pious plain, refined lady, but had not a fancy equal to the operation required in a shell-house.

The excellent, the polite, the well-bred, the good and unfortunate Mrs. O'HARA had a glorious fancy. She was a genius, and had an imagination that formed a grotto wild and charming as Calypso's. Her fancy did likewise form the garden, in which the grotto stood near the margin of a flood, into a paradise of delights. Many a pleasing, solitary hour, have I passed in this charming place ; and at last saw all in ruins ; the garden in disorder, and every fine shell torn from the grotto. Such are the changes and chances of this first state ; changes wisely designed by Providence as warnings not to set up our rest here : that we may turn our hearts from this world and with all our might labour for that life which shall never perish.

What ruined Mrs. O'HARA's grotto deprived me of my little green and shady retreat. CHARLES O'HARA, this lady's husband, a strange man, from whom I rented my pretty farm, and to whom I had paid a fine to lower the rent, had mortgaged it, unknown to me, to the famous DAMER, and that powerful man swallowed all. All I had there was seized for arrears of interest due of Mr. O'HARA, and as I was ever liable to distrainment, I took my leave of Fingal.

The HEBREW LETTER, another voluta, is a fine curiosity. It is two inches in length, and an inch and a quarter in diameter at the top. It is a regular conic figure, and its exerted clavicle has several volutions. The ground is like the white of a fine pearl, and the body all over variegated with irregular marks of black, which have a near resemblance of the Hebrew characters. This elegant shell is an East-Indian.

The WHITE VOLUTA, with brown and blue and purple spots. This very elegant shell, whose ground is a charming white, is found on the coast of Guinea, from five to six inches in length, and its diameter at the head often three inches. It tapers gradually, and at the extremity is a large obtuse. Its variegations in its spots are very beautiful, and its spots are principally disposed in many circles round the shell.

The BUTTERFLY is a voluta the most elegant of this beautiful genus. Its length is five inches in its perfection, and two and a half broad at the head. The body is an obtuse cone : the clavicle is pointed, and in several volutions. The ground is the finest yellow, and beautified all over with small brown spots, in regular and round series. These variegations are exceeding pretty, and as this rare East-Indian shell has beside these beauties three charming bands round the body, which are formed of large spots of a deep brown, a pale brown, and white, and resemble the spots on the wings of butterflies, it is a beautiful species indeed. The animal that inhabits this shell is a limax.

The TULIP CYLINDER is a very scarce and beautiful native of the East-Indies, and in its state of perfection and brightness of colour, of great value. Its form is cylindric, its length four inches, and its diameter two and a half, at its greatest increase. Its clavicle has many volutions, and terminates in an obtuse point. The ground colour is white, and its variegations blue and brown. They are thrown into irregular clouds in the most beautiful manner, and into some larger and smaller spots. The limax inhabits this fine shell.

I likewise saw in this grotto the finest species of the purpura, the dolia, and the porcellana. There was of the first genus the thorny woodcock : of the second the harp shell : and of the third, the argus shell.

The THORNY WOODCOCK is ventricose, and approaches to an oval figure. Its length, full grown, is five inches ; the clavicle short, but in volutions distinct ; and its rostrum from the mouth twice the length of the rest of the shell. This snout and the body have four series of spines, generally an inch and a half long, pointed at the ends, and somewhat crooked. The spines lie in regular, longitudinal series. The mouth is almost round, but the opening is continued in the form of a slit up the rostrum. The colour of this American, and extremely elegant shell, is a tawny yellow, with a fine mixture of a lively brown, and by bleaching on the coasts, it gets many spots of white.

The BEAUTIFUL HARP is a Chinese ; three inches and a half long, and two and a half in diameter. The shell is tumid and inflated, and at the head largest. It has an oblong clavicle in several volutions, pointed at the extremity, and the other extreme is a short rostrum. The whole surface is ornamented with elevated ribs, that are about twice as thick as a straw, and as distant from each other as the thickness of four straws. The colour is a fine deep brown, variegated with white and a paler brown, in a manner surprisingly beautiful.

The extremely elegant ARGUS is from the coast of Africa, and is sometimes found in the East-Indies. Its length, in a state of perfection, is four inches and a half ; its diameter three. It is oblong and gibbous, has a wide mouth, and lips so continued beyond the verge, as to form at each extremity a broad and short beak. The colour is a fine pale yellow, and over the body are three brown fasciæ : but the whole surface, and those fasciæ are ornamented with multitudes of the most beautiful round spots, which resemble eyes in the wings of the finest butterflies. The limax inhabits this charming shell. This creature is the sea-snail.

The CONCHA OF VENUS was the next shell in this young lady's collection that engaged my attention. One of them was three inches long, and two and a half in diameter. The valves were convex, and in longitudinal direction deeply striated. The hinge at the prominent end was large and beautifully wrought, and the opening of the shell was covered with the most elegant wrinkled lips, of the most beautiful red colour, finely intermixed with white ; these lips do not unite in the middle, but have slender and beautiful spines round about the truncated ends of the shell. This shell of Venus is an American, and valued by the collectors at a high rate.

But of all the curious shells in this wonderful collection, the HAMMER OYSTER was what I wondered at most ; it is the most extraordinary shell in the world. It resembles a pick-ax, with a very short handle and a long head. The body of the shell is in the place of the handle of the instrument, and is four inches and a half long, and one inch and a half in diameter. What answered to the head of the pick-ax was seven inches long, and three quarters of an inch in diameter. This head terminates at each end in a narrow obtuse point, is uneven at the edges, irregular in its make, and lies crosswise to the body : yet the valves shut in the closest and most elegant manner. The edges are deeply furrowed and plaited, and the lines run in irregular directions. The colour without is a fine mixture of brown and purple ; and within a pearly white, with a tinge of purple. This rare shell is an

*E*ast-Indian, and whenever it appears at an auction is rated
very high. I have known ten guineas given for a perfect one.
  With a large quantity of these most beautiful shells, which are
rarely seen in any collections, and with all the family of the
pectens, the cardiæ, the solens, the cylinderi, the murexes, the
turbines, the buccina, and every specis of the finest genera of
shells, Miss NOEL formed a grotto that exceeded every thing of
the kind I believe in the world ; all I am sure that I have seen,
except the late Mrs. HARCOURT's in Richmondshire ; which I
shall give my reader a description of, when I travel him up those
*E*nglish Alpes. It was not only, that Miss NOEL's happy fancy
had blended all these things in the wildest and most beautiful
disposition over the walls of the rotunda ; but her fine genius
had produced a variety of grots within her grotto, and falling
waters, and points of view.   In one place was the famous
Atalanta, and her delightful cave : and in another part, the
Goddess and Ulysses' son appeared at the entrance of that grot,
which under the appearance of a rural plainness had every thing
that could charm the eye : the roof was ornamented with shell-
work ; the tapestry was a tender vine, and, limpid fountains
sweetly purled round.
  But what above all the finely fancied works in Miss NOEL's
grotto pleased me, was, a figure of the philosopher *E*pictetus, in
the centre of the grot.   He sat at the door of a cave, by the side
of a falling water, and held a book of his philosophy in his hand,
that was written in the manner of the antients, that is, on parchment rolled up close together.   He appeared in deep meditation,
and as part of the book had been unfolded and gradually extended,
from his knee on the ground, one could read very plain, in large
Greek characters, about fifty lines.   The *E*nglish of the lesson
was this—

" THE MASTER SCIENCE

  " All things have their nature, their make and form, by which
they act, and by which they suffer.   The vegetable proceeds
with a perfect insensibility.   The brute possesses a sense of what
is pleasurable and painful, but stops at mere sensation.   The
rational, like the brute, has all the powers of mere sensation, but
enjoys a farther transcendent faculty.   To him is imparted the
master-science of what he is, where he is, and the end to which
he is destined.   He is directed by the canon of reason to reverence
the dignity of his own superior character, and never wretchedly
degrade himself into a nature to him subordinate.   The master-
science, he is told, consists in having just ideas of pleasures and
pains, true notions of the moments and consequences of different
actions and pursuits, whereby he may be able to measure, direct

or controul his desires or aversions, and never merge into miseries. Remember this Arrianus. Then only, you are qualified for life, when you are able to oppose your appetites, and bravely dare to call your opinions to account ; when you have established judgment or reason as the ruler in your mind, and by a patience of thinking, and a power of resisting, before you choose, can bring your fancy to the test of truth. By this means, furnished with the knowledge of the effects and consequences of actions, you will know how you ought to behave in every case. You will steer wisely through the various rocks and shelves of life. In short, Arrianus, the deliberate habit is the proper business of man ; and his duty, to exert upon the first proper call, the virtues natural to his mind ; that piety, that love, that justice, that veracity, that gratitude, and that benevolence, which are the glory of human kind. Whatever is fated in that order of incontroulable events, by which the divine power preserves and adorns the whole, meet the incidents with magnanimity, and co-operate with chearfulness in whatever the supreme mind ordains. Let a fortitude be always exerted in enduring ; a justice in distribution ; a prudence in moral offices ; and a temperance in your natural appetites and pursuits. This is the most perfect humanity. This do, and you will be a fit actor in the general drama ; and the only end of your existence is the due performance of the part allotted you."

Such was Miss NOEL's grotto, and with her, if it had been in my power to choose, I had rather have passed in it the day in talking of the various fine subjects it contained, than go in to dinner ; which a servant informed us was serving up, just as I had done reading the above recited philosophical lesson. Back then we returned to the parlour, and there found the old gentleman. We sat down immediately to two very good dishes, and when that was over, Mr. NOEL and I drank a bottle of old Alicant. Though this gentleman was upwards of eighty, yet years had not deprived him of reason and spirits. He was lively and sensible, and still a most agreeable companion. He talked of Greece and Rome, as if he had lived there before the æra of Christianity. The Court of Augustus he was so far from being a stranger to, that he described the principal persons in it ; their actions, their pleasures, and their caprices, as if he had been their contemporary. We talked of these great characters. We went into the gallery of Verres. We looked over the antient theatres. Several of the most beautiful passages in the Roman poets this excellent old man repeated, and made very pleasant, but moral remarks upon them.

" The cry," said he, "still is as it was in the days of Horace :—

O cives, cives, quaerenda pecunia primum est ;
Virtus post nummos.—

Unde habeas nemo quaerit, sed oportet habere.
Quorum animis, a prima lanugine, non insedit illud ?

" And what Catullus told his Lesbia, is it not approved to this day by the largest part of the great female world ?

> Vivamus, mea Lesbia, atque amemus,
> Rumoresque Senum severiorum,
> Omnes unius aestimemus assis.
> Soles occidere et redire possunt,
> Nobis, cum semel occidit brevis lux,
> Nox est perpetua una dormiendo.
> Hæc discunt omnes ante Alpha et Beta puellæ.

The girls all learn this lesson before their A B C ; and as to the opinion of the poet, it shews how sadly the Augustan age, with all its learning, and polite advantages, was corrupted : and as Virgil makes a jest of his own fine description of a paradise of the *Elysian* fields ; as is evident from his dismissing his hero out of the ivory gate ; which shews he was of the school of Epicurus ; it is from these things manifest, that we can never be thankful enough for the principles and dictates of revealed religion : we can never sufficiently adore the goodness of the most glorious *Eternal* for the gospel of Jesus Christ ; which open the unbounded regions of eternal day to the virtuous and charitable, and promises them a rest from labour, and ever blooming joys ; while it condemns the wicked to the regions of horror and solid darkness ; that dreadful region, from whence the cries of misery for ever ascend, but can never reach the throne of mercy. O heavenly religion ! designed to make men good, and for ever happy ; that preserves the dignity of human nature, guards and increases virtue, and brings us to the realms of perfect reason and excellent glory.

" But," continued this fine old gentleman, " Tibullus has ever pleased me in the description of his mistress :—

> Illam quicquid agit, quoquo vestigia flectit,
> Componit furtim subsequiturque decor ;
> Seu solvit crines, fusis decet esse capillis ;
> Seu compsit comptis est veneranda comis.
> Urit seu Tyria voluit procedere puella ;
> Urit seu nivea candida veste venit.
> Talis in æterno felix Vertumnus Olympo
> Mille habet ornatus, mille decenter habet.

" These elegant lines contain an inimitably beautiful description of outward grace, and its charming effects upon all who see it. Such a grace, without thinking of it, every one should strive to have, whatever they are doing. They should make it habitual to them. Quintilian seems to have had these fine lines in view, in his description of outward behaviour : 'Neque enim gestum componi ad similitudinem saltationis volo, sed subesse aliquid, in hac exercitatione puerili, unde nos non id agentes, furtim decor ille discentibus traditus subsequatur.' *Cap.* 10. I am not for having the mein of a gentleman the same with that of a dancing-master ; but that a boy while young should enter upon this exercise, that it may communicate a secret gracefulness to his manner ever after."

In this manner did the old gentleman and I pass the time, till the clock struck five, when Miss NOEL came into the parlour again, and her father said he must retire, to take his evening nap, and would see me at supper ; for with him I must stay that night. "HARRIET, make tea for the gentleman. I am your servant, sir," and he withdrew. To HARRIET, then, my life, and my bliss, I turned ; and, over a pot of tea, was as happy, I am sure, as ever with his Statira sat the Conqueror of the World. I began to relate once more the story of a passion, that was to form one day, I hoped, my sole felicity in this world ; and with vows and protestations affirmed that I loved from my soul. "Charming angel," I said, "the beauties of your mind have inspired me with a passion that must increase every time I behold the harmony of your face ; and by the powers divine, I swear to love you as long as Heaven shall permit me to breathe the vital air. Bid me then either live or die, and while I do live, be assured that my life will be devoted to you only." But in vain was all this warmth. Miss NOEL sat as unmoved as Erycina on a monument, and only answered, with a smile, "Since your days, sir, are in my disposal, I desire you will change to some other subject, and some article that is rational and useful ; otherwise I must leave the room."

"To leave me," I replied, "would be insupportable ; and, therefore, at once I have done. If you please then, madam, we will consider the miracle at Babel, and enquire into the language of the world at that time. Allowing, as you have proved in our late conversation, that the language after the flood was quite another thing from that used in Paradise, and of consequence, that Moses did not write in that tongue which Adam and Eve conversed in ; nor is Hebrew of that primævity which some great men affirm ; yet, if there was a confusion of tongues at Babel, and many languages were spoken in the earth in the days of Abraham, how did he and his sons converse so easily with the various nations they passed through, and had occasional connexions with ? For my part, I think with Hutchinson, that the divine interposition at Babel was for quite another end, to wit, to confound their confession, and cast out of their minds the name or object of it, that a man might not listen to the lip or confession of his neighbour. They were made to lose their own lip, and to differ about the words of their atheistical confession."

" As to a confusion of confessions," replied Miss NOEL, " it appears to me to be a notion without any foundation to rest on. The argument of Hutchinson that the word ' shepah,' the name for a lip, when used for the voice or speech, is never once in the Bible used in any other sense than for confession, is not good ; because, though ' *shephah* ' is often generally used for religious discourse or confession, yet the phrases, ' other lips ' and ' other tongues,' are also used for ' other languages, utterances, pronunciations, dialects ' St. Paul, i *Corinthians*, ch. 14, v. 21, 22 ; applies *shephah* to language or dialect, in his quotation from the prophet *Isaiah*, ch. 28, v. 11, 12. He says, in the law it is written, ' With *men of* * other tongues and other lips will I speak unto this people, and yet for all that they will not hear me.' And the words of the prophet are, speaking of Christ promised ; ' with stammering lips, and another tongue will he speak to this people.' It is evident from this, that the Hebrew word *shephah* here signifies tongues or languages, and not confessions or discourse. So the apostle applies it, and explains the prophet : and by ' stammering lips,' *Isaiah* means the ' uncouth pronunciations of barbarous dialects,' or languages of the nations, which must produce in strangers to them ridiculous lips or mouths ; and in this he refers undoubtedly to the stammering and strange sounds at the Babel confusion, when God, by a miracle and visible exhibition, distorted their organs of speech, and gave them a trembling, hesitation and precipitancy, as to vocal and other powers. In short, the miraculous gift of tongues would in some measure affect the saints, in respect of pronunciation, as the Miracle of Babel did the people of that place.† Nor is this the

* The words *men of* are not in the Greek.

† To this stammering or uncouth pronunciation of barbarous dialects the prophet *Ezekiel* refers, chap. 36, v. 3, " Ye are made to come upon the lip of the tongues " : that is, ye are become a bye-word even in the heathen gabble, among the babbling nations where ye are in captivity. Holloway, the author of *Letter and Spirit*, says, the word barbarous, used in so many languages, (with only their respective different determinations) for persons of strange or foreign tongues, is a monument of the great confusion at Babel ; this word being a corruption of the reduplicate Chaldee word *Balbel*, by changing the *l* in each place into *r*. Some say, the word in the other languages is derived from the Arabic *Barbar*, to " murmur like some beast." Scaliger defines it, Pronunciatio vitiosa et insuavis, literasque male exprimens, blæsorum balborumque more : which was hitting upon the truth as to part of the original manner of the confusion. Indeed *Blæsus* and *Balbus*, in Latin, are both derived in like manner from *Bal* and Balbel. The Welsh have preserved a noble word for this barbarism of confused language in their compounded term *Baldwraidd :* which is a plain compound of the Hebrew *Bal*, and *Dabar*, without any other deflection from the original Hebrew, than that of changing the *b* in the latter member of the word *Dabar* into the Welsh *w*, a letter of the same organ. Moreover, from their said *Baldwraidd*, and *Das*, we again derive our *Balderdash :* which therefore signifies strictly, a heap of confused or barbarous words, like those of the gabble of dialects, orginally gendered at Babel. See *Letter and Spirit*. ch. 11. It is very remarkable, that this learned gentleman says he had been long of Hutchinson's mind, as to a confusion of confessions, and not of tongues ; but on weighing the matter, is now of another opinion. *Ibid.* p. 115. Therefore, Hutchinson not infallible, but out for once, and as Dr. Sharp well observes, this may be an earnest of deserting Hutchinson in other points of his new hypothesis. See Dr. Sharp's *Two Discourses on the Hebrew Tongue and Character* against Holloway. His *Two Discourses on Elohim, and Defence*. And his *Three Discourses on* cherubim. The Hutchinsonians lay the stress of their hypothesis on the Biblical Hebrew, being the language of Adam in Paradise ; and if this be taken from them, they are left in a poor way indeed.

only place in Scripture where *shephah*, lip, signifies language, pronunciations, and dialects ; and where there is reference to the confusion of tongues at Babel, *Isaiah*, speaking of the privileges of the godly, says, ' Thou shalt not see a fierce people, of a deeper speech than thou canst perceive, (of a deeper lip than thou canst hear, *Heb.*) of a stammering or ridiculous tongue, that thou canst not understand. This is enough in answer to Hutchinson and his fautors, in respect of what they say on the confusion at Babel. This proves that the word *shephah*, lip signifies language, utterance, dialect, as well as confession or discourse ; and therefore, Moses, in his account of the Miracle at Babel, might have mean'd a confusion of languages. That he did mean this, is plain, not only from a tradition gone out into all the earth, which is a matter of greater regard than Hutchinson's fancy ; but because the sacred oracles allude to this event. Beside St. Paul aforementioned, the royal prophet in *Psalm* lv. ver. 9, refers to the means of the division of tongues, and denounces a curse in terms taken from that inflicted at Babel. ' Swallow up, O Lord, and divide their tongues.' This seems to describe the manner of that confusion ; that the substance of the one language was sunk or swallowed up in the vast chaos of universal babble ; and that out of that jargon it was again, by another act, divided or broken into many particular dissonant dialects, or tongues."

" All this," I said, " is very just, and gives me delight and satisfaction. I am now convinced, not only that Hebrew was not the language of Paradise, or that Adam did not speak the tongue the old world used immediately before the confusion at Babel ; but likewise, that the division there, was a division and confusion of the one language then spoken ; and not a confusion of confessions, as Hutchinson affirms. Inform me, however, if you please, what you mean by that tradition you mentioned which declared the Miracle of Babel to be a confusion of languages."

" The Jews' tradition," replied Miss NOEL, " is preserved in their *Targum*, and tells us, that the whole earth, after the flood, was of one speech, or sort of words, and when at their first remove from Ararat, they came to Shinar, they consulted to build them a city, and a tower for a house of adoration, whose head might reach to, or be towards, the heavens, and to place an image of the host of heaven for an object of worship on the top of it ; and to put a sword in his hand, that he might make war for them against the divine armies, to prevent their dispersion over the whole earth. Whereupon the word of the Lord was revealed from Heaven, to execute vengeance upon them, and the Lord corrupted their tongue, broke their speech into seventy languages, and scattered them over the face of the whole earth. No one knew what his fellow said ; and they slew one another, and ceased from building the city. Therefore he called the name of it

Babel ; because there the Lord mingled together the tongues of
all the inhabitants of the other.   This you read in the *Targum*
that was written before the days of Jesus Christ, as the Jews
affirm ; or, if not so early, yet it is a very antient book, and the
doctor who composed it must certainly know the meaning of the
word *shephah* better than Hutchinson.   It appears, upon the
whole, that the argument of this famous modern is without
foundation.''   '

   " It is, indeed," I answered, " but then I am not able to conceive
how Abraham and his sons conversed with so many nations, or
how the Hebrew that Moses wrote in was preserved.   Illuminate
me in these things, illustrious HARRIET, and from your fine understanding, let me have the honour and happiness of receiving
true Hebrew lessons.   Proceed, I beseech you, and stop not
till you have expounded to my understanding the true nature
of Cherubim ?   What do you think of Hutchinson's Rub and
Rubbin, and of his notions of *Ezekiel's* cherubic form."

   " To talk of Cherubim and *Elohim*," resumed Miss NOEL,
" and say all that ought to be said, to speak to any purpose ;
of the three heads and four visages, the bull, the man, the lion,
and the eagle, mentioned in the prophet, requires more knowledge in Hebrew learning than I· pretend to be mistress of, and
must take up more time than there is now to spare.   I may
hereafter, however, if you should chance to come again to our
house, let you know my fancies upon these grand subjects, and
why I cannot accord with Hutchinson and my father, in their
notion of the Cherubim's signifying the unity of the essence,
the distinction of the persons, and man's being taken into the
essence by his personal union with the second person, whose
constant emblem was the lion.   This, I confess, appears to my
plain understanding very miserable stuff.   I can see no text
either in the *Old Testament*, or in the *New*, for a plurality of beings,
co-ordinate and independent.   The sacred pages declare there is
one original perfect mind.   'The Lord shall be king over all the
earth.   In that day there shall be ONE LORD, and his name
ONE,' says the prophet *Zachariah*, speaking of the prodigious
revolution in the Gentile world, whence in process of time, by
the gospel of Jesus Christ, the worship of one true God shall
prevail all over the earth, as universally as Polytheism had done
before.   This I dare not observe to my father, as he is an admirer
of Hutchinson, and will not bear any contradiction ; but my
private judgment is, that Hutchinson on the Cherubim and
Elohim or Eloim, is a mad commentator, as I may show you,
if we ever happen to meet again.

   " At present, all I can do more on the Hebrew subject, is to
observe that, in respect of the preservation of the Hebrew tongue,
I imagine the one prevailing language before the Miracle of Babel,

which one language was afterwards called Hebrew, though divided and swallowed as it were at the tower, was kept without change in the line of Shem, and continued their tongue. This cannot be disputed, I believe. I likewise imagine, it must be allowed that this Hebrew continued the vernacular tongue of the old Canaanites. It is otherwise unaccountable how the Hebrew was found to be the language of the Canaanites, when the family of Abraham came among them again, after an absence of more than two hundred years. If they had had another tongue at the confusion, was it possible for Abraham, during his temporary sojournments among them, and in the necessities of his peregrination, to persuade so many tribes to quit their dialect, and learn his language ; or, if his influence had been so amazing, can it be supposed, they would not return again to their old language, after he had left them, and his family was away from them more than two hundred years ? No, sir ; we cannot justly suppose such a thing. The language of the old Canaanites could not be a different one from the Hebrew. If you will look into Bochart,* you will find this was his opinion. That great man says, the anté-Babel language escaped the confusion two ways, viz., by the Canaanites, through God's providence preserving it in their colonies for the future use of the Hebrews, who were to possess the land ; and by the patriarch Heber, as a sacred depositum for the use of his posterity, and of Abraham in particular.

"This being the case: the Phœnician or Canaanitish tongue, being the same language that the line of Heber spoke, with this only difference, that by the latter it was retained in greater purity, being in the mouths of a few, and transmitted by instruction ; it follows, that Abraham and his sons could talk with all these tribes and communities ; and as to the other nations he had communication with, he might easily converse with them, as he was a Syrian by birth, and to be sure could talk the Aramitish dialect as well as Laban his brother. The Aramitish was the customary language of the line of Shem. It was their vulgar tongue. The language of the old world, that was spoken immediately before the confusion, was called Hebrew from Heber, which they reserved for sacred uses."

---

† The great Samuel Bochart, born at Rouen, in 1599, was the minister of the reformed church in the town of Caen, in Normandy. His principal works are his *Phaleg* and *Canaan ;* works that show an amazing erudition, and ought to be well read by every gentleman ; you should likewise have his *Hierozoicon, or History of Animals mentioned in the Sacred Books.* It is a good supplement to his *Scripture Geography.* His sermons and dissertations are also very valuable. Bochart died suddenly in the Academy at Caen, on Monday, 16th May, 1667, in the sixty-eighth year of his age. Brieux wrote the following fine epitaph on him :—
    Scilicet hæc cuique est data sors æquissima, talis
    Ut sit mors, qualis vita peracta fuit.
    Musarum in gremio teneris qui vixit ab annis.
    Musarum in gremio debuit ille mori.

Here Miss NOEL ended, and my amazement was so great, and my passion had risen so high for such uncommon female intelligence, that I could not help snatching this beauty to my arms, and without thinking of what I did, impressed on her balmy lips half a dozen kisses. This was wrong, and gave very great offence, but she was too good to be implacable, and on my begging her pardon, and protesting it was not a wilful rudeness, but the magic of her glorious eyes, and the bright powers of her mind, that had transported me beside myself, she was reconciled, and asked me, if I would play a game at cards ? " With delight," I replied, and immediately a pack was brought in. We sat down to cribbage, and had played a few games, when by accident Miss NOEL saw the head of my german flute, which I always brought out with me in my walks, and carried in a long pocket within-side my coat. " You play, sir, I suppose, on that instrument," this lady said, " and as of all sorts of music this pleases me most, I request you will oblige me with anything you please." " In a moment, I answered, and taking from my pocket book the following lines, I reached them to her, and told her I had the day before set them to one of Lully's airs, and instantly began to breathe the softest harmony I could make—

A SONG

ALMIGHTY love's resistless rage,
No force can quell, no art assuage :
While wit and beauty both conspire,
To kindle in my breast the fire :
The matchless shape, the charming grace,
The easy air, and blooming face,
Each charm that does in Flavia shine,
To keep my captive heart combine.

I feel, I feel the raging fire !
And my soul burns with fierce desire !
Thy freedom, Reason, I disown,
And beauty's pleasing chains put on ;
No art can set the captive free,
Who scorns his offer'd liberty ;
Nor is confinement any pain,
To him who hugs his pleasing chain.

Bright Venus ! Offspring of the sea !
Thy sovereign dictates I obey ;
Submissive own thy mighty reign,
And feel thy power in every vein :
I feel thy influence all-confest,
I feel thee triumph in my breast !
'Tis there is fix'd thy sacred court,
'Tis there thy Cupids gaily sport.

Come, my Boy, the altar place,
Add the blooming garland's grace ;

Gently pour the sacred wine,
Hear me, Venus ! Power divine !
Grant the only boon I crave,
Hear me, Venus ! Hear thy slave !
Bless my fond soul with beauty's charms,
And give me Flavia to my arms.*

Just as I was finishing this piece of music, old Mr. Noel came into the parlour, in his wonted good humour, and seemed very greatly pleased with me and my instrument. He told me, I was the young man he wanted to be acquainted with, and that if it was no detriment to me, I should not leave him this month to come. " Come sir," continued this fine old gentleman, " let me hear another piece of your music—vocal or instrumental as you will, for I suppose you sing as well as you play." " Both you shall have, Sir," I replied, " to the best of my abilities, and by way of change, I will give you first a song, called

THE SOLITUDE.

YE lofty mountains, whose eternal snows
　Like Atlas seem to prop the distant skies ;
While shelter'd by your high and ample brows
　All nature's beauties feast my ravish'd eyes :
And far beneath me o'er the distant plain
The thunders break, and rattling tempests reign.

* As this song is a short imitation of the nineteenth *Ode* of the first book of Horace, it is worth your while, Reader, to see how the Rev. P. Francis has done the whole. I will here set down a few lines :

　　" Urit me Glyceræ nitor
　　　Splendentis pario marmore purius :
　　Urit grata protervitas,
　　　Et vultus nimium lubricus aspici."
Which lines are imitated in the first verse of the above song, and a part of the second ; and the ingenious Mr. Francis renders them in the following manner—
　　" Again for Glycera I burn,
　　And all my long forgotten flames return.
　　As Parian marble pure and bright,
　　　The shining maid my bosom warms ;
　　Her face too dazzling for the sight,
　　　Her sweet coqueting—how it charms ! "
The following :
　　" In me tota ruens Venus
　　　Cyprum deseruit—"
of which the third verse of the song is an imitation, Mr. Francis translates thus :
　　" Whole Venus rushing through my veins,
　　No longer in her favourite Cyprus reigns."
And the lines :
　　" Hic vivum mihi cespitem, hic
　　　Verbenas, pueri, ponite thuraque
　　Bimi cum patera meri :
　　　Mactata veniet lænior hostia : "
Which are imitated in the fourth verse of the song, Mr. Francis translates as follows,
　　" Here let the living altar rise,
　　　Adorn'd with every herb and flower ;
　　Here flame the incense to the skies,
　　　And purest wines libation pour ;
　　Due honours to the Goddess paid,
　　　Soft sinks to willing love the yielding maid."

C

Here, when Aurora with her cheerful beam
 And rosy blushes marks approaching day ;
Oft do I walk along the purling strea'n,
 And see the bleating flocks around me stray :
The woods, the rocks, each charm that strikes my sight,
Fills my whole breast with innocent delight.

Here gaily dancing on the flow'ry ground
 The cheerful shepherds join their flute and voice ;
While thro' the groves the woodland songs resound,
 And fill th' untroubled mind with peaceful joys.
Music and love inspire the vocal plain,
Alone the turtle tunes her plaintive strain.

Here the green turf invites my wearied head
 On nature's lap to undisturb'd repose ;
Here gently laid to rest, each care is fled ;
 Peace and content my happy eye-lids close.
Ye golden flattering dreams of state adieu !
As bright my slumbers are, more soft than you.

Here free from all the tempests of the great,
 Craft and ambition can deceive no more !
Beneath these shades I find a blest retreat,
 From Envy's rage secure, and Fortune's power :
Here call the actions of past ages o'er,
Or truth's immortal source alone explore.

Here far from all the busy world's alarms,
 I prove in peace the Muse's sacred leisure :
No cares within, no distant sound of arms,
 Break my repose, or interrupt my pleasure.
Fortune and Fame ! Deceitful forms ! Adieu !
The world's a trifle far beneath my view.

This song delighted the old gentleman exceedingly. He told me, he was charmed with it, not only for the fine music I made of it, but the morality of it, and liked me so much, that I was most heartily welcome to make his solitary retreat my home, as often and as long as I pleased.   And indeed I did so, and continued to behave in such a manner, that in two months time, I gained so entirely his affections, and so totally the heart of his admirable daughter, that I might have her in wedlock when I pleased, after the expiration of that current year, which was the young lady's request, and be secured of his estate at his death ; beside a large fortune to be immediately paid down ; and this, though my father should refuse to settle anything on me, or Miss NOEL, my wife. This was generous and charming as my heart could desire. I thought myself the happiest of men. *Every* week I went to *E*den Park, one time or other, to see my dear Miss NOEL, and pay my respects to her worthy father. We were while I stayed a most happly family, and enjoyed such satisfactions as few I believe have experienced in this tempestuous hemisphere. Mr.

NOEL was passionately fond of his daughter, and he could not regard me more if I had been his own son, I loved my Harriet' with a fondness beyond description, and that glorious girl had all the esteem I could wish she had for me. Our mutual felicity could rise no higher till we gave our hands, as we had already plighted our hearts.

This world is a series of visionary scenes, and contains so little solid, lasting felicity, as I have found it, that I cannot call life more than a deception ; and, as Swift says it, " He is the happiest man, who is best deceived." When I thought myself within a fortnight of being married to Miss NOEL, and thereby made as completely happy in every respect as it was possible for a mortal man to be, the small pox stepped in, and in seven days time, reduced the finest human frame in the universe to the most hideous and offensive block. The most amiable of human creatures mortified all over, and became a spectacle the most hideous and appalling. This broke her father's heart in a month's time, and the paradise I had in view, sunk into everlasting night.

My heart, upon this sad accident, bled and mourned to an extreme degree. All the tender passions were up in my soul, and with great difficulty could I keep my ruffled spirits in tolerable decorum. I lost what I valued more than my life ; more than repeated millions of worlds, if it had been possible to get them in exchange. This engaged, beloved partner, was an honour to her sex, and an ornament to human kind. She was one of the wisest and most agreeable of women ; and her life quite glorious for piety to God, compassion to the necessitous and miserable, benevolence and good will to all, with every other grace and virtue. These shone with a bright lustre in her whole deportment, and rendered her beloved, and the delight of all that knew her. Sense and genius were in her united, and by study, reflection, and application, she improved the talents, in the happiest manner. She had acquired a superiority in thinking, speaking, writing, and acting ; and in manners, her behaviour, her language, her design and her understanding was inexpressibly charming. Miss NOEL died in the 24th year of her age, the 29th of December, in the year 1724.

This dismal occurrence preyed powerfully on my spirits for some time, and for near two months, I scarcely spoke a word to any one. I was silent, but not sullen. As my tears and lamentations could not save her, so I knew they could not fetch her back. Death and the grave have neither eyes nor ears. The thing to be done upon so melancholy an occasion, is to adore the Lord of infinite wisdom, as he has a right to strike our comforts dead ; and so improve the awful event, by labouring to render our whole temper and deportment Christian and divine, that we may be able to live, while we do live, superior to the strokes of fortune and the calamities of human life ; and when God bids us die, in whatever manner, and at whatever time it may be, have nothing to do but to die, and so to enter into our master's joy.   This is wisdom.   This good we may extract from such doleful things. This was the effect my dear Miss NOEL's death had on me, and when I saw myself deprived of so invaluable a thing in this world, I determined to double my diligence in so acting my part in it, that whenever I was to pass through the last extremity of nature, I might be dismissed with a blessing to another world, and by virtue of the sublime excellencies of our holy religion, proceed to the abodes of immortality and immutable felicity.

I wish I could persuade you, reader, to resolve in the same manner.   If you are young, and have not yet experienced life, believe me, all is vanity, disappointment, weariness, and dissatisfaction, and in the midst of troubles and uncertainties, we are hastening to an unknown world, from whence we shall never again return.   Whether our dissolution be near, we know not ; but this is certain, that Death, that universal conqueror, is making after us apace, to seize us as his captives ; and therefore, though a man live many years, and rejoice in them all, which is the case of very few, yet let him remember the days of darkness.

And when death does come, our lot may be the most racking pains and distempers, to fasten us down to our sick-beds, till we resign our spirits to some strange region, our breath to the common air, and our bodies to the dust from whence they were taken.   Dismal situation l   If in the days of our health, we did not make our happiness and moral worth correspond,did not labour, in the time of our strength, to escape from wrong opinion and bad habit, and to render our minds sincere and incorrupt ; if we did not worship and love the supreme mind, and adore his divine administration, and all the secrets of his providence.   If this was not our case, before corruption begins to lay hold of us, deplorable must we be, when torments come upon us, and we have only hopeless wishes that we had been wiser, as we descend in agonies to our solitary retreat : to proceed from thence to judgment.   Language cannot paint the horrors of such a condition.   The anguish of mind, and the torture of body, are a scene of misery beyond description.

Or, if without torment, we lie down in silence, and sink into the land of forgetfulness, yet, since the Lord Jesus is to raise us from the regions of darkness, and bring us to the sessions of righteousness, where all our actions are to be strictly tried and examined, and every one shall be judged according to the deeds done in the body, whether they have been good or evil ; what can screen us from the wrath of that mighty power, which is to break off the strong fetters of death, and to throw open the iron gates of the grave, if injustice, cruelty, and oppression, have been our practice in this world ; or if, in the neglect of the distressed and hungry, we have given up ourselves to chambering and wantonness, to gluttony and voluptuousness ? It is virtue and obedience, acts of goodness and mercy, that only can deliver us. If we worship in spirit and in truth the most glorious of immortal beings, that God who is omnipotent in wisdom and action, and perform all the offices of love and friendship to every man, then will our Lord pronounce us the blessed of his Father. If we do evil, we shall come forth into the resurrection of damnation. This merits your attention, reader, and I hope you will immediately begin to ponder, what it is to have a place assigned in inconceivable happiness or misery for ever.

Having thus lost Miss NOEL, and my good old friend, her worthy father, I left the university, and went down to the country, after five years and three months absence, to see how things were posited at home, and pay my respects to my father ; but I found them very little to my liking, and in a short time, returned to Dublin again. He had lately married in his old age a young wife, who was one of the most artful, false, and insolent of women, and to gratify her to the utmost of his power, had not only brought her nephew into his house, but was ridiculously fond of him, and lavishly gratified all his desires. Whatever this little brute, the son of a drunken beggar, who had been a journeyman glover, was pleased, in wantonness, to call for, and that his years, then sixteen, could require, my father's fortune in an instant produced ; while scarcely one of my rational demands could be answered. Money, clothes, servants, horses, dogs, and all things he could fancy, were given in abundance ; and to please the basest of women, and the most cruel step-mother that ever the devil inspired to make the son of another woman miserable, I was denied almost everything. The liberal allowance I had at the university was taken from me. Even a horse to ride out to the neighbouring gentlemen, was refused me, though my father had three stables of extraordinary cattle ; and till I purchased one, was forced to walk it, wherever I had a mind to visit. What is still more incredible, if anything of severity can be so, when a mother-in-law is sovereign, I was not allowed to keep my horse even at grass on the land, though five hundred acres of freehold estate surrounded the mansion, but obliged to graze it at a neighbouring farmer's. Nor was this all the hard treatment I received. I was ordered by my father to become the young man's preceptor ; to spend my precious time in teaching this youngster, and in labouring to make the little despicable dunce a scholar. All this was more than I could bear. My life became insupportable, and I resolved to range even the wilds of Africa, if nothing better offered, rather than live a miserable slave under the cruel tyranny of those unrelenting oppressors.

My father, however, by the way, was as fine a gentleman as
ever lived, a man of extraordinary understanding, and a scholar ;
likewise remarkably just and good to all the world, except myself,
after I left the university : and to do him all the justice in my
power, and vindicate him so far as I am able, I must not conceal,
that great as the ascendancy was, which my mother-in-law had
over him, and as much as he was henpecked by that low-bred
woman, who had been his servant maid, yet it was not to her
only that my sufferings were owing.   Religion had a hand in
my misery.   False religion was the spring of that paternal
resentment I suffered under.

It was my father's being wont to have prayers read every
night and morning in his family, and the office was the litany of
the common prayer-book.   This work, on my coming home,
was transferred from my sister to me, and for about one week I
performed to the old gentleman's satisfaction, as my voice was
good, and my reading distinct and clear ; but this office was far
from being grateful to me, as I was become a strict Unitarian,
by the lessons I had received from my private tutor in college,
and my own examinations of the vulgar faith.   It went against
my conscience to use the tritheistic form of prayer, and became
at last so uneasy to me, that I altered the prayers the first Sunday
morning, and made them more agreeable to Scripture as I conceived.   My father at this was very highly enraged, and his
passion arose to so great a height, upon my defending my con-
fesion, and refusing to read the established form, that he called
me the most impious and execrable of wretches, and with violence
drove me from his presence.   Soon after, however, he sent me
Lord Nottingham's *Letter to Mr. Whiston*, and desired I would
come over to him when I had carefully read it over.   I did so,
and he asked me what I thought of the book.   I answered, that
I thought it a weak piece, and if he would hear me with patience,
in relation to that in particular, and to the case in general, perhaps
he might think my religion a little better than at present he
supposed it to be.   " I will hear you," he said, " proceed."   I
then immediately began, and for a full hour repeated an apology
I had prepared.*   He did not interrupt me once, and when I
had done, all he replied was, " I see you are to be placed among
the incurables.   Begone," he said, with stern disdain ; and I

* The reader will find this apology in the *Appendix* to this life, [see note, p. 41, ante].
By scripture and argument, without any regard to the notions of the fathers, I there endeavour
to prove, that God the Father, the beginning and cause of all things, is One Being, infinite in
such a manner, that his infinity is an infinity of fulness as well as immensity ; and must be
not only without limits, but also without diversity, defect or interruption : and of consequence his Unity so true and real, that it will admit of no diversity or distinction of persons :—
that as to the Lord Jesus Christ, he was the servant chosen of this tremendous God, to redeem
mankind ; but his holy soul so far in perfection above Adam or any of his posterity, and possessed so   much a greater share of the indwelling of the divine life and nature than any other
creature, that he might, compared to us, with a just figure of speech, be called God.

resolved to obey. Indeed it was impossible for me to stay, for my father took no farther notice of me, and my mother-in-law and the boy, did all they could invent to render my life miserable.

On the first day of May, 1725 ; early in the morning, as the clock struck one, I mounted my excellent mare, and with my boy O'FIN, began to journey as I had projected, on seeing how things went. I did not communicate my design to a soul, nor took my leave of any one, but in the true spirit of adventure, abandoned my father's dwelling, and set out to try what fortune would produce in my favour. I had the world before me, and Providence my guide. As to my substance it consisted of a purse of gold, that contained fifty Spanish pistoles, and half a score moidores ; and I had one bank note for five hundred pounds, which my dear Miss NOEL left me by her will, the morning she sickened ; it was all she had of her own to leave to any one. With this I set forward, and in five days time arrived from the Western extremity of Ireland at a village called Ring's-end, that lies on the Bay of Dublin. Three days I rested there, and at the Conniving House,* and then got my horses on board a ship that was ready to sail, and bound for the land I was born in, I mean Old England.

The wind, in the afternoon, seemed good and fair, and we were in hopes of getting to Chester the next day ; but at midnight a tempest arose, which held in all the horrors of hurricane, thunder and lightning, for two nights and a day, and left us no hope of escape. It was a dreadful scene indeed, and looked as if the last fatal assault was making on the globe. As we had many passengers, their cries were terrific, and affected me more than the flashing fires and the winds. For my part, I was well reconciled to the great change, but I confess that nature shrunk at the frightful manner of my going off, which on the second night, I expected every moment. At last, however, we got into Whitehaven. It pleased the great King of all the earth to bid the storm *Have done.*

Four remarkable things I noticed while the tempest lasted. One was that the Dean of Derry, DR. WHALEY, whom we had on board, who had nineteen hundred a year from the church, for

---

* The Conniving-House, as the gentlemen of Trinity call'd it in my time, and long after was a little public house, kept by Jack M'Lean, about a quarter of a mile beyond Rings-end, on the top of the beach, within a few yards of the sea. Here we used to have the finest fish at all times, and in the season, green peas and all the most excellent vegetables. The ale here was always extraordinary, and every thing the best ; which, with its delightful situation rendered it a charming place of a summer's evening. Many a happy evening have I passed in this pretty thatched house with the famous LARREY GROGAN, who played on the bag-pipes extremely well ; dear JACK LATTIN, matchless on the fiddle, and the most agreeable of companions ; that ever charming young fellow, JACK WALL, the son of counsellor Maurice Wall the most worthy, the most ingenious, the most engaging of men ; and many other delightful fellows, who went in the days of their youth to the shades of eternity. When I think of them and their evening songs "We will go to Johnny M'Lean's to try if his ale be good or not etc." and that years and infirmities begin to oppress me—What is life !

teaching the people to be Christians, was vastly more afraid than one young lady of the company, who appeared quite serene. The Dean, though a fine orator at land, was ridiculous in his fears at sea. He screamed as loud as any of the people : but this young lady behaved, like an angel in a storm. She was calm and resigned, and sat with the mate and me during the second night discoursing of the divine power, and the laws of nature in such uproars. By the way, neither mate, nor master, nor hand could keep the deck. The ship was left to the mercy of the winds and waves.

The second remarkable thing was that as this young lady went naked into bed in her cabin, the first night before the tempest began to stir, it was not many hours till a sea struck us upon the quarter, and drove in one of our quarter, and one of our stern dead lights, where we shipped great quantities of water, that put us under great apprehensions of foundering, and filled so suddenly the close wooden bed in which Miss MELMOTH lay, that had I not chanced to be leaning against the partition, and snatched her out, the moment I felt myself all over wet, and half covered with the breaking sea, she must inevitably have perished. I ran up on deck with her in my arms, and laid her almost senseless and naked there, and as there was no staying many minutes in that place, I threw my great coat over her, and then brought her down to my own berth, which I gave her, and got her dry clothes from her trunk, and made her drink a large glass of brandy, which saved her life. She got no cold, which I thought very strange, but was hurt a little in the remove. When all was over she protested she would never go naked into bed, on board ship, again.

The third particular was, that there were some officers on board, most monstrously wicked men, and when we were given over by the captain, and no hope he thought of being saved, these warriors lamented like young children, and were the most dismal disturbing howlers on board : yet, when we got on land, they had done with O Lord, O Lord, and began again their obscene talk, and to damn themselves at every word to the centre of hell.

The fourth thing was this. There was on board with us a young gentleman of my acquaintance, one PIERCE GAVAN, who had been a fellow-commoner in my time of Trinity, Dublin. The first day of the storm, he was carried over-board by a rolling sea, and fairly lodged in the ocean, at above twenty yards distance from the ship ; but the next tumbling billow brought him back again. He was laid on the deck without any hurt. On the contrary, one CHARLES HENLEY, a young merchant, was beat over, and we never saw him more.

HENLEY was not only a man of sense and prudence, who had an honest mind, and a cultivated understanding, but by search and enquiries into the doctrines, institutions and motives of revealed religion, had the highest regard for the truths of genuine Christianity, and chose the best means in his power to make himself acceptable to God.

GAVAN, on the contrary, had no sense of religion, nor did he ever think of the power and goodness of God. He was a most profane swearer, drank excessively, and had the heart to debauch every pretty woman he saw, if it had been possible for him to do so much mischief. Yet this man, who never reformed that I heard, and whose impieties have even shocked young fellows who were no saints, was astonishingly preserved ; and HENLEY, who had the most just natural notions, and listened to Revelation, perished miserably ! How shall we account for such things ? By saying, that the world that now is, and the world that is to come, are in the hands of God, and every transaction in them is quite right, though the reason of the procedure may be beyond our view. We cannot judge certainly of the ends and purposes of Providence, and therefore to pass judgment on the ways of God, is not only impious, but ridiculous to the last degree. This we know for certain, that whenever, or however, a good man falls, he falls into the hand of God, and since we must all die, the difference as to time and manner, signifies very little, when there is an infinite wisdom to distinguish every case, and an infinite goodness to compensate all our miseries. This is enough for a Christian. Happy is the man, and for ever safe, let what will happen, who acts a rational part, and has the fear and love of God in his thoughts. With pleasure he looks into all the scenes of futurity. When storms and earthquakes threaten calamity, distress, and death, he maintains an inward peace.

May 10th.—When we had obtained the wished for shore, the passengers all divided. The Dean and his lady, and some other ladies, went one way, to an inn recommended to them by a gentleman on board ; the warriors and Gavan marched to another house ; and the young lady, whose life was by me preserved, and I, went to the Talbot, which the mate informed me had the best things and lodgings, though the smallest inn of the town. This mate, one WHITWELL, deserves to be particularly mentioned, as he was remarkable for polite breeding, good sense, and a considerable share of learning, though a sailor ; as remarkable this way, as the captain of the ship was the other, that is for being the roughest and most brutal old tar that ever commanded a vessel.

WHITWELL the mate, about thirty-six years of age at this time, told me, he was the son of a man who once had a great fortune, and gave him a university education, but left an estate so encumbered with debts, and ruined with mortgages, that its income was almost nothing, and therefore the son sold the remains of it

and went to sea with an East India captain, in the twenty-second
year of his age, and was so fortunate abroad, that he not only
acquired riches, in the four years time that he trafficked about,
between Batavia and the Gulph of Persia, but married a young
Indian lady, the daughter of a Rajah, or petty Prince in the Mogul
Empire ; who was rich, wise and beautiful, and made his life so
very happy, for the three years she lived, that his state was a
Paradise, and he seemed a little sovereign.   But this fleeting
scene was soon over, and on his return to England with all his
wealth, their ship was taken by the pirates of Madagascar, who
robbed him of all he had, and made him a miserable slave for
more than two years, when he escaped from them to the tawny
generation of Arabs, who lived on the mountains, the other side
of this African island, who used him with great humanity ; their
chief being very fond of him, and entertaining him in his mud-
wall palace : he married there a pretty little yellow creature,
niece to the poor ruler, and for twelve months was very far from
being miserable with this partner, as they had a handsome
cottage and some cattle, and this wife was good-humour itself,
very sensible, and a religious woman ; her religion being half
Mahometanism and half Judaism.   But she died at the year's
end, and her uncle the chief, not living a month after her, WHIT-
WELL came down from the mountains to the next sea coast under
the conduct of one of the Arabians, his friend, and meeting with
a European ship there, got at last to London.   A little money he
had left behind him in England, by way of reserve, in case of
accidents, if he should ever return to his own country, he regained,
and with this dressed himself, got into business, and came at
last to be mate of the ship called the Skinner and Jenkins.   His
destiny, he added, was untoward, but as he had thought, and
read, and seen enough in his wide travels, to be convinced, the
world, and every being, and every atom of it were directed and
governed by unerring wisdom, he derived hopes and comforts
from a due acknowledgment of God.   There are more born to
misery than to happiness, in this life ; but all may die to be for
ever glorious and blessed, if they please.   This conclusion was
just and beautiful, and a life and sentiments so uncommon I
thought deserved a memorial.

Miss MELMOTH and I continued at the Talbot for three weeks.
and during that time, breakfasted, dined, and supped together.
Except the hours of sleep we were rarely from each other.   We
walked out together every day, for hours conversed, sometimes
went to cards, and often she sung, delightfully sung, while on
my flute I played.   With the greatest civility, and the most exact
good manners, we were as intimate as if we had been acquainted
for ages, and we found a satisfaction in each other's company,
as great as lovers generally experience ; yet not so much as one

syllable of the passion was mentioned : not the least hint of love on either side was given, while we stayed at Whitehaven : and I believe neither of us had a thought of it. It was a friendship the most pure and exalted, that commenced at my saving her life, in the manner I have related, and by some strange kind of magic, our notions and inclinations, tempers and sentiments, had acquired such a sameness in a few days, that we seemed as two spiritual *socias*, or duplicates of each other's mind. Body was quite out of the case, though this lady had an extravagance of beauty. My sole delight was that fine percipient, which shed a lustre on her outward charms. How long this state would have lasted, had we continued more time together, and had the image of the late Miss NOEL been more effaced, or worn out of the sensory of my head, I cannot say ; but while it did last, there could be nothing more strange. To see two young people of different sexes, in the highest spirits and most confirmed health live together, for twenty-one days, perfectly pleased with each other, entirely at their own disposal, and as to fortune, having abundautly enough between them both for a comfortable life ; and yet never utter one word, nor give a look, that could be construed a declaration of the passion, or a tendency towards a more intimate union ; to complete that connexion which nature and providence requires of beings circumstanced as we were : was very odd. We sat up till the clock struck twelve every night, and talked of a vast variety of things, from the Bible down to the *Clouds* of Aristophanes, and from the comedies and tragedies of Greece and Rome to the *Minerva* of Sanctius, and Hickes's *Northern Thesaurus*. Instead of Venus or any of her court, our conversation would often be on the *Morals* of Cicero, his *Academics*, and *De Finibus ;* on the English or the Roman History ; Shakespeare's scenes of nature, or maps of life ; whether the *Œdipus* or the *Electra* of Sophocles was the best tragedy ; and the scenes in which Plautus and Terence most excelled. Like two critics, or two grammarians, antiquarians, historians, or philosophers, would we pass the evening with the greatest cheerfulness and delight.

Miss MELMOTH had an astonishing memory, and talked on every subject extremely well. She remembered all she had read. Her judgment was strong, and her reflections always good. She told me her mother was another Mrs. Dacier, and as her father was killed in a duel, when she was very young, the widow MELMOTH, instead of going into the world, continued to live at her country seat, and diverted herself with teaching her daughter the languages of Greece and Rome, and in educating her heart and mind. This made this young lady a master of the Latin tongue and Greek, and enabled her to acquire a knowledge so various and fine, that it was surprising to hear her expatiate and explain. She talked with so much ease and good humour, and had a manner so cheerful and polite, that her discourse was always entertaining, even though the subject happened to be, as it was one evening, the paulo post future of a Greek verb. These things, however, were not the only admirable ones in this character. So happily had her good mother formed and instructed her mind, that it appeared full of all the principles of rational honour, and devoted to that truly God-like religion, which exalts the soul to an affection rather than dread of the supreme Lord of things, and to a conviction that his laws lead us both to happiness here and hereafter. She thoroughly understood the use and excellence of Revelation, and had extracted from the inspired volumes everlasting comfort and security under the apprehensions of the divine power and majesty : but she told me she could not think rites and outward performances were essential to real religion. She considered what was just and beautiful in these things as useful and assisting only to the devout mind. In a word, this young lady was wise and good, humble and charitable. I have seen but one of her sex superior to her in the powers of mind and the beauties of body, and that was Miss NOEL. Very few have I known that were equal.

The second day of June, Miss MELMOTH and I left Whitehaven, and proceeded from thence to Westmoreland. We travelled for five days together, till we came to Brugh under Stainmore, where we stayed a night at Lamb's, a house I recommend to the reader, if ever he goes that way ; and the next morning we parted. Miss MELMOTH and her servants went right onwards to Yorkshire, and I turned to the left to look for one CHARLES TURNER, who had been my near friend in the university, and who lived in some part of the north east extremity of Westmoreland, or Yorkshire. But before we separated on the edge of Stainmore, we stopped at the Bell to Breakfast, which is a little lone house on a descent to a vast romantic glen, and all the public house there is in this wild silent road, till you come to JACK RAILTON, the quaker's house at Bows. We had a pot of coffee and toast and butter for breakfast, and, as usual, we were very cheerful over it ; but when we had done, and it was time to depart, a melancholy, like a black and dismal cloud, began to overspread the charming face of CHARLOTTE, and after some silence, the tears burst from her eyes. "What is the matter, Miss MELMOTH," I said : "what makes this amazing change ? " "I will tell you, sir," this beauty replied. "To you I owe my life, and for three weeks past have lived with you in so very happy a way, that the end of such a scene, and the probability of my never seeing you more, is too much for me." "Miss MELMOTH," I answered, "you do me more honour than I deserve in shedding tears for me, and since you can think me worth seeing again, I promise you upon my sacred word, that as soon as I have found a beloved friend of mine I am going up the hills to look for, and have paid my respects to him for a while, if he is to be found in this desolate part of the world, I will travel with my face in the next place, if it be possible, towards the east-riding of Yorkshire, and be at Mrs. AsGIL's door, where you say you are to be found." This restored the glories to CHARLOTTE's face again, and for the first time I gave Miss MELMOTH a kiss, and bade her adieu.

June 8th.—Having thus lost my charming companion, I travelled into a vast valley, enclosed by mountains whose tops were above the clouds, and soon came into a country that is wilder than the campagna of Rome, or the uncultivated vales of the Alps and Appenines. Warm with a classical enthusiasm, I journeyed on, and with fancy's eye beheld the rural divinities, in those sacred woods and groves, which shade the sides of many of the vast surrounding fells, and the shores and promontories of many lovely lakes and bright running streams. For several hours I travelled over mountains tremendous to behold, and through vales the most enchanting in the world. Not a man or house could I see in eight hours time, but towards five in the afternoon, there appeared at the foot of a hill a sweetly situated cottage, that was half covered with trees, and stood by the side of a large falling stream : a vale extended to the south from the door, that was terminated with rocks, and precipices on precipices, in an amazing point of view, and through the flowery ground, the water was beautifully seen, as it winded to a deeper flood at the bottom of the vale. Half a dozen cows were grazing in view : and a few flocks of feeding sheep added to the beauties of the scene.

To this house I sent my boy, to inquire who lived there, and to know, if for the night I could be entertained, as I knew not where else to go. O'FIN very quickly returned, and informed me, that one farmer PRICE was the owner of the place, but had gone in the morning to the next town, and that his wife said I was welcome to what her house afforded. In then I went, and was most civilly received by an exceedingly pretty woman, who told me her husband would soon be at home, and be glad, she was sure, to see me at their lonely place ; for he was no stranger to gentlemen and the world, though at present he rarely conversed with any one. She told me, their own supper would be ready in an hour hence, and in the meantime would have me take a can of fine ale and a bit of bread. She brought me a cup of extraordinary malt-drink and a crust, and while I was eating my bread, in came Mr. PRICE.

The man seemed very greatly astonished at entering the room, and after he had looked with great earnestness at me for a little while, he cried out, " Good heaven ! What do I see l FALSTAFF,

my class-fellow, and my second self. My dear friend you are
welcome, thrice welcome to this part of the world." All this
surprised me not a little, for I could not recollect at once a face
that had been greatly altered by the small-pox : and it was not till
I reflected on the name PRICE, that I knew I was then in the house
of one of my school-fellows, with whom I had been most intimate,
and had played the part of Plump Jack in *Henry the Fourth*,
when he did Prince Henry. This was an unexpected meeting
indeed : and considering the place, and all the circumstances
belonging to the scene, a thing more strange and affecting never
came in my way. Our pleasure at this meeting was very great,
and when the most affectionate salutations were over, my friend
PRICE proceeded in the following manner.

" Often have I remember'd you since we parted, and exclusive
of the Greek and English plays we have acted together at Sheridan's school,* in which you acquired no small applause, I have
frequently thought of our frolicsome rambles in vacation time,
and the merry dancings we had at Mother Red-Cap's in Back-
Lane ; the hurling matches we have play'd at Dolphin's-barn,
and the cakes and ale we used to have at the Organ-house on
Arbor-Hill, These things have often occurred to my mind : but
little did I think we should ever meet again on Stainmore-hills.
What strange things does time produce l It has taken me from a
town life to live on the most solitary part of the globe :—and it
has brought you to journey where never man I believe even
thought of travelling before." " So it is," I replied, " and strange
things, dear JACK, may happen yet before our eyes are closed :
why I journey this untravelled way, I will inform you by and by ;
when you have told me by what strange means you came to dwell
in this remote and silent vale." " That you shall know," said he,
" very soon, as soon as we have eaten a morsel of something or
other which my dear MARTHA has prepared against my return.
Here it comes, a fowl, bacon and greens, and as fine I will answer
as London market could yield. Let us sit down, my friend and
God bless us and our meat."

Down then we sat immediately to our dish, and most excellent
every thing was. The social goodness of this fond couple added
greatly to the pleasure of the meal, and with mirth and friendship
we eat up our capon, our bacon, and our greens. When we had
done, PRICE brought in pipes and tobacco, and a fresh tankard of
his admirable ale. " Listen now, said he, " to my story, and then
I will hearken to yours.

" When I left you at Sheridan's school, my remove was from

---

* The School-house of the famous Dr. Sheridan, in Capel Street, Dublin, where many of
the younger branches of the most distinguished families in Ireland, at that period received
the first rudiments of their education ; was formerly King James II.'s Mint-house. The
only view of it extant, is a vignette in Samuel Whyte's *Poems*, printed by Subscription at
Dublin, in 1793. 8vo. p. 44. ED.

Ireland to Barbadoes, to become a rich uncle's heir, and I got by
my Indian airing a hundred thousand pounds. There I left the
bones of my ·mother's brother, after I had lived two years in that
burning place, and from thence proceeded to London, to spend
what an honest, laborious man had long toiled to save. But I had
not been above three months in the capital of England, when it
came into my head to pass some time in France, and with a girl I
kept made haste to the French metropolis. There I lived at a
grand rate, and took from the French Opera-house another whore.
The Gaul and the Briton were both extreme fine girls, and agreed
so well together, that I kept them both in one house. I thought
myself superlatively happy in having such a brace of females, and
spared no cost in procuring them all the finery and pleasures that
Paris and London could yield. I had a furnished house in both
these cities, and with an expensive equipage went backwards and
forwards. In four years time I spent a great deal of money, and
as I had lost large sums at play, and these two whores agreed in
the end to rob me, and retire with the money, where I should never
discover them, I found myself in very middling circumstances,
and had not six hundred pounds left in the fourth year from my
uncle's death. How to dispose of this and myself was now the
question. What I should do, was my deliberation, to secure bread
and quiet ? Many a thoughtful hour this gave me, and at length
I determined to purchase a little annuity. But before this could
be effected, I went down to Westmoreland, on an information I
had received, that my two ladies were at Appleby with other
names, and on my money appeared as women of fortune. But
this journey was to no purpose, and I was preparing to return to
London, when my wife you saw at the head of the table a while
ago, came by chance in my way, and pleased me so well with her
good understanding, face and person, that I resolved to marry
her, if she would have me, and give her the management of my five
hundred pounds on a farm, as she was a farmer's daughter, and
could manage one to good advantage. Her father was lately
dead, and this little mountain farm she continued to occupy :
therefore nothing could be more to my purpose, if I could prevail
on her to make me her husband, and with some difficulty she did,
to my unspeakable felicity. She had no money worth mentioning : but her house was pretty and comfortable, and her land had
grain and cattle ; and as I threw into her lap my five hundred
pounds, a little before we were married, to be by her disposed of
and managed, according to her pleasure she soon made some good
improvements and additions, and by her fine understanding, sweet
temper, and every christian virtue, continues to render my life so
completely happy ; so joyous and delightful ; that I would not
change my partner and condition, for one of the first quality and
greatest fortune. In her I have every thing I could wish for in a

wife and a woman, and she makes it the sole study and pleasure of her life to crown my every day with the highest satisfactions and comforts. Two years have I lived with her on these wild mountains, and in that time I have not had one dull or painful minute, but in thinking that I may lose her, and be the wretched survivor. That thought does sometimes wound me. In sum, my friend, we are the happiest oɩ wedded mortals, and on this small remote farm, live in a state of bliss to be envied. This proves that happiness does not flow from riches only : but, that where pure, and perfect love, strict virtue, and unceasing industry, are united in the conjugal state, they can make the Stainmore mountains a Paradise to mortals in peace and little.

" But it is not only happiness in this world that I have acquired by this admirable woman, but life eternal. You remember, my friend, what a wild and wicked one I was when a school-boy, and as Barbadoes of all parts of the globe is no place to improve a man's morals in, I returned from thence to Europe as debauched a scelerate as ever offended Heaven by blasphemy and illiberal gratifications. Even my losses and approaching poverty were not capable of making any great change in me. When I was courting my wife, she soon discerned my impiety, and perceived that I had very little notion of hell and heaven, death and judgment. This she made a principal objection against being concerned with me, and told me she could not venture into a married connexion with a man, who had no regard to the divine laws, and therefore, if she could not make me a Christian, in the true sense of the word, she would never be Mrs. PRICE.

" This from a plain country girl, surprised me not a little, and my astonishment rose very high, when I heard her talk of religion, and the great end of both, a blessed life after this. She soon convinced me that religion was the only means by which we can arrive at true happiness, by which we can attain to the last perfection and dignity, of our nature, and that the authority and word of God is the surest foundation of religion. The substance of what she said is as follows. I shall never forget the lesson.

" The plain declarations of our Master in the Gospel restore the dictates of uncorrupted reason to their force and authority, and give us just notions of God and ourselves. They instruct us in the nature of the Deity, discover to us his unity, holiness, and purity, and afford certain means of obtaining eternal life. Revelation commands us to worship one Supreme God, the Supreme Father of all things ; and to do his will, by imitating his perfections, and practising everything recommended by that law of reason, which he sent the Messiah to revive and enforce : that by repentance, and righteousness, and acts of devotion, we may obtain the divine favour, and share in the glories of futurity ;

for, the Supreme Director, whose goodness gives counsel to his powers, commanded us into existence to conduct us to everlasting happiness, and therefore teaches us by his Son to pray, to praise, and to repent, that we may be entitled to a nobler inheritance than this world knows, and obtain life and immortality, and all the joys and blessings of the heavenly Canaan. This was the godlike design of our Creator. That superior agent, who acts not by arbitrary will, but by the maxims of unclouded reason, when he made us and stationed us in this part of his creation, had no glory of his own in view, but what was perfectly consistent with a just regard to the felicity of his rational subjects.

"It was this made the apostle show Felix the unalterable obligations to justice and equity ; to temperance, or a command over the appetites ; and then, by displaying the great and awful judgment to come, urge him to the practice of these, and all the other branches of morality ; that by using the means prescribed by God, and acting up to the conditions of salvation, he might escape that dreadful punishment, which in the reason and nature of things, is connected with vice, and which the good govern· ment of the rational world requires should be inflicted on the wicked ; and might on the contrary by that mercy offered to the world through Jesus Christ, secure those immense rewards, which are promised to innocence and the testimony of an upright heart. This faith in Christ, St. Paul placed before the Roman governor in the best light. He described the complexion and genius of the Christian faith. He represented it as revealing the wrath of God against all immorality ; and as joining with reason and uncorrupted nature, enforcing the practice of every moral and social duty.

"What effect this discourse had on Felix," continued MARTHA, "in producing faith, that is, morality in an intelligent agent, we are told by the apostle. He trembled : but iniquity and the world had taken such a hold of him, that he dismissed the subject and turned from a present uneasiness to profit and the enjoyment of sin. He had done with St. Paul, and sacrificed the hopes of eternity to the world and its delights.

"But this," concluded MARTHA, " will not I hope be your case. As a judgment to come is an awful subject, you will ponder in time, and look into your own mind. As a man, a reasonable and social creature, designed for duty to a God above you, and to a world of fellow creatures around you, you will consider the rules of virtue and morality, and be no longer numbered with those miserable mortals, who are doomed to condemnation upon their disobedience. Those rules lie open in a perfect gospel, and the wicked can have nothing to plead for their behaviour. They want no light to direct them. They want no assistance to support them in doing their duty. They have a gospel to bring them to life and salvation, if they will but take notice of it ; and if they will not walk in the light of God's law, this gospel must be their judgment and condemnation.''

'' Say then, Sir,'' MARTHA proceeded, '' can you be prevailed on to think of religion in its native purity and simplicity, and by the power of the gospel, to act with regard to virtue and piety, that when Christ shall come not only in the power, but in the wisdom and the justice of God, to judge the world, you may be secured from that misery and distress, which is prepared for iniquity ; and enjoy that eternal life, which is to be the portion of the righteous ? ''

'' In this extraordinary manner did MARTHA HARRINGTON discourse me, and the effect of it was that I began a thorough reform from that hour. My rational life from that happy day commenced, and I entered seriously into my own breast, to think in earnest of that solemn judgment to come. What MARTHA said was so clear and strong, that I had not a thought of replying, but truth at once entirely subdued my heart, and I flew to the Son of God, to request his intercession with the Father of the Universe for the pardon of all my crimes. The dignity and end of my being has since been the subject of my meditations, and I live convinced, that everything is contemptible, that is inconsistent with duty and morality. This renders even my pleasures more agreeable. This gives eternal peace to my mind.''

Here PRICE ended his remarkable story, and according to our agreement, I began to relate what happened to me from the time we parted at school, and concluded with informing him, that I was going in search of CHARLES TURNER, my near friend, when fortune brought me to his house : that this gentleman lived somewhere towards the confines of Cumberland and the North Riding of Yorkshire, but where the spot was I could not tell, nor did I know well how to go on, as the country before me seemed impassable, on account of its mountains, precipices, and floods. '' I must try, however, what can be done ; not only in regard to this gentleman ; but, because I have reason to think it may be very much to my advantage, as he is very rich, and the most generous of men. If he is to be found, I know I shall be welcome to share in his happiness as long as I please, nor will it be any weight to him.'' PRICE to this replied, that I was most heartily welcome to him as long as I pleased to stay, and that though he was far from being a rich man, yet he had every day enough for himself and one more ; and his MARTHA he was sure would be as well pleased with my company, as if I had been his own brother, since she knew I was his esteemed friend. In respect of the way, he said, he would enable me to find Mr TURNER, if he could, but the country was difficult to travel, and he doubted very much if one could go to the extremity of Cumberland or Yorkshire over the hills ; but we would try, however, and if it was possible, find out Mr. TURNER's house. Yet solely with him I must not stay, if he could be seen. I must live between both, till I got some northern girl, and had a wife and habitation of my own : " and there is," continued Price, " not many miles from me, a sweet pretty lass, the daughter of a gentleman farmer, who is a very good man, and would, I believe, upon my recommendation, give you his girl and a sum of money, to sit down on those hills." " This is vastly kind, Jack," said I, " and what I shall gratefully remember so long as I live. I may ride many a mile I am sure, and be an adventurer many a long day, before I meet with such offers again. Your sweetly situated house and good things, with a fine northern girl and money down, are benefits not to be met with every day. But at present the object I must pursue is my university friend, CHARLES TURNER, and if you please to do me the great favour of guiding me so far as you can over this wild, uninhabited land, after I have stayed with you for the first time, two or three days, and promise to abide many more hereafter if it be in my power, we will set out in quest of what I want." " As you will," my friend PRICE replied, " and for the present let us be gay. Here comes my beloved with a little bowl of punch, and as she sings extremely well, and you have not forgot I fancy our old song, we will have it over our nectar. You shall represent Janus and Momus, and I will be Chronos and Mars, and my wife Diana and Venus. Let us take a glass first—' THE LIBERTIES OF THE WORLD,' and then do you begin." We drank, and in the following manner I went on.

SONG.

JANUS.
Chronos, Chronos, mend thy pace,
A hundred times the rolling sun, .
Around the radiant belt has run,
    In his revolving race.
Behold, behold, the goal in sight,
Spread thy fans, and wing thy flight.

CHRONOS.
Weary, weary of my weight,
Let me, let me drop my freight,
And leave the world behind.
        I could not bear
        Another year
The load of human kind.

MOMUS.
Ha ! ha ! ha ! ha ! ha ! ha ! well hast thou done,
    To lay down thy pack,
    And lighten thy back.
The world was a fool, e'er since it begun.

And since neither Janus, nor Chronos, nor I,
  Can hinder the crimes,
  Or mend the bad times,
'Tis better to laugh than to cry.

CHORUS.

'Tis better to laugh than to cry.

JANUS.

Since Momus comes to laugh below,
  Old Time begin the show!
That he may see, in every scene,
What changes in this age have been;

CHRONOS.

Then goddess of the silver bow begin!

DIANA.

With horns and with hounds I waken the day,
And hye to my woodland walks away;
I tuck up my robe, and am buskin'd soon,
And tye to my forehead a waxing moon;
I course the fleet stag, unkennel the fox,
And chase the wild goats o'er summits of rocks,
With shouting and hooting we pierce through the sky:
And echo turns hunter, and doubles the cry.

CHORUS.

With shouting and hooting we pierce through the sky,
And echo turns hunter, and doubles the cry.

JANUS.

Then our age was in its prime,

CHRONOS.

Free from rage,

DIANA.

——————— And free from crime.

MOMUS.

A very merry, dancing, drinking,
Laughing, quaffing, and unthinking time.

CHORUS.

Then our age was in its prime,
Free from rage, and free from crime.
A very merry, dancing, drinking,
Laughing, quaffing, and unthinking time.

MARS.

Inspire the vocal brass, inspire;
The world is past its infant age
    Arms and honour,
    Arms and honour,
Set the martial mind on fire,
And kindle manly rage.
Mars has look'd the sky to red;
And peace, the lazy good, is fled.
Plenty, peace, and pleasure fly;

The sprightly green
In Woodland walks, no more is seen ;
The sprightly green has drank the Tyrian dye.

CHORUS.

Plenty, peace, and pleasure fly ;
    The sprightly green
In Woodland walks, no more is seen ;
The sprightly green has drank the Tyrian dye.

MARS.

Sound the trumpet, beat the drum,
Through all the world around :
Sound a reveille, sound, sound,
    The warrior God is come.

CHORUS.

Sound the trumpet, beat the drum,
Through all the world around ;
Sound a reveille, sound, sound,
    The warrior God is come.

MOMUS.

Thy sword within the scabbard keep,
    And let mankind agree ;
Better the world were fast asleep,
    Than kept awake by thee.
The fools are only thinner,
    With all our cost and care ;
But neither side a winner,
    For things are as they were.

CHORUS.

The fools are only thinner,
    With all our cost and care ;
But neither side a winner,
    For things are as they were.

VENUS.

Calms appear, when storms are past,
Love will have its hour at last :
Nature is my kindly care ;
Mars destroys, and I repair :
Take me, take me, while you may,
Venus comes not ev'ry day.

CHORUS.

Take her, take her, while you may,
Venus comes not ev'ry day.

CHRONOS.

The world was then so light,
I scarcely felt the weight ;
Joy rul'd the day, and love the night.
But since the queen of pleasure left the ground,
    I faint, I lag,
    And feebly drag
The pond'rous orb around.

MOMUS, *pointing to Diana.*

All, all, of a piece throughout ;
The chace had a beast in view ;

DIANA, *to Mars.*
Thy wars brought nothing about ;

MARS, *to Venus.*

Thy lovers were all untrue.

VENUS, *to Janus.*
'Tis well an old age is out,
And time to begin a new.

CHORUS.

All, all, of a piece throughout ;
Thy chace had a beast in view ;
Thy wars brought nothing about ;
Thy lovers were all untrue :
'Tis well an old age is out,
And time to begin a new.

In this happy manner did we pass the night in this wild and frightful part of the world, and for three succeeding evenings and days, enjoyed as much true satisfaction as it was possible for mortals to feel. PRICE was an ingenious, cheerful, entertaining man, and his wife had not only sense more than ordinary, but was one of the best of women. I was prodigiously pleased with her conversation. Though she was no woman of letters, nor had any books in her house except the *Bible,* Barrow's and Whichcot's *Sermons,* Howell's *History of the World,* and the *History of England* yet from these few, a great memory, and an extraordinary conception of things, had collected a valuable knowledge, and she talked with an ease and perspicuity that was wonderful. On religious subjects she astonished me.

As Sunday was one of the daies I staid there, and PRICE was obliged in the afternoon to be from home, I passed it in conversation with his wife. The day introduced religion, and among other things I asked her, which she thought the best evidences of Christianity ? The prophecies or the miracles ?

" Neither," Mrs. PRICE replied. " The prophecies of the Messiah recorded in the Old Testament, are a good proof of the Christian religion, as it is plain from many instances in the New Testament, that the Jewish converts of that generation understood them to relate to our Lord ; which is a sufficient reason for our believing them. Since they knew the true intent and meaning of them, and on account of their knowing it, were converted ; the prophecies for this reason should by us be regarded as divine testimony in favour of Christ Jesus. Then as to miracles, they are to be sure a means of proving and spreading the Christian religion, as they shew the divine mission of the Messiah, and rouse

the mind to attend to the power by which these mighty works
were wrought. Thus miracle and prophecy shew the teacher came
from God. They contribute to the establishment of his kingdom,
and have a tendency to produce that faith which purifies the heart,
and brings forth the new birth.

" But the greater evidence for the truth of our holy religion,
appears to me to be that which converted the primitive Christians,
to wit, the powerful influence which the gospel has on the minds
of those who study it with sincerity, and the inward discoveries
Christ makes to the understanding of the faithful by his light
and good spirit. This exceeds the other evidences, if the heart
be honest. The gospel is irresistible, when the spirit of God
moves upon the minds of Christians. When the divine power,
dispensed through Christ, assists and strengthens us to do good,
and to eschew evil, then Christianity appears a religion worthy
of God, and in itself the most reasonable. The complete salvation deserves our ready acceptation. That religion must charm
a reasonable world, which not only restores the worship of the
one true God, and exhibits, in a perfect plan, those rules of
moral rectitude, whereby the conduct of men should be governed,
and their future happiness secured ; but, by its blessed spirit,
informs our judgments, influences our wills, rectifies and subdues
our passions, turns the bias of our minds from the objects and
pleasures of sense, and fixes them upon the supreme good. Most
glorious surely is such a gospel."

" But does not this operation of the spirit," said I, " which
you make the principal evidence for Christianity, debase human
nature, and make man too weak, too helpless and depending
a being ? If voluntary good agency depends on supernatural
influence and enlivening aid, does not this make us mere patients,
and if we are not moral agents, that is, have not a power of
choosing or refusing, of doing or avoiding, either good or evil, can
there be any human virtue ? Can we in such case approve
or disapprove ourselves to God. To me it seems that man was
created to perform things natural, rational, and spiritual, and
has an ability to act within the reach of his agency, as his duty
requires. I think the moral fitness of things is a rule of action
to conduct our actions by, and that the great advantage of revelation consists in its heavenly moral lessons, and the certainty
of that future judgment and retribution, which has a powerful
influence upon a rational mind, and strongly inclines a reasonable
being to save his soul, by so acting in this world as to avoid
everlasting misery, and ensure the favor of God, and eternal
happiness in another world. This appears to me more consistent with the nature and the truth of things. It is more to
the honour of human nature, if I mistake not, and gives more
glory to God."

To this Mrs. PRICE answered, that " as she was sensible of the shortness of her own understanding, and believed the faculties of the human mind in general were weak and deficient, she could not see any thing unreasonable in supposing the thing formed depended on, and was subject to the Creator that made it. It cannot be absurd, surely, to say, that so weak and helpless a being as man, depends entirely on God. Where in the nature of things can we fix a standard of certainty in understanding, and stability in practice, but in the fountain of truth, and all perfection ?

" But to our better comprehending this matter, let us take a view of primitive Christian religion. Christianity is a divine institution, by which God declares himself reconciled to mankind for the sake of his beloved son, the Lord Jesus Christ, on condition of repentance, amendment of life, and perseverance in a state of holiness ; and that we might be able to perform the things required of us, he offers the assistance of his good spirit. This last offer in a proper sense, is salvation ; ' for according to his mercy, he saved us, by the washing of regeneration, and the renewing of the Holy Ghost. By grace are ye saved through faith, and that not of yourselves ; it is the gift of God.' We find, then, that there are two parts in the Christian religion : one, external and historical ; the other, internal and experimental. The first comprehends what is no more to be repeated, though the effects are lasting and permanent, to wit, the life and good works of Jesus, his miracles, death, and resurrection ; which declare him spotless virtue, perfect obedience, and the Son of God with power. And in the second part, we have that standing experience of a divine help, which converts and supports a spiritual life. It is true, both the parts have a near relation, and in conjunction produce the good ends of religion. The second is the effect of the first. Redemption from the power of sin, sanctification, and justification, are blessings wrought in us by the good spirit of him, who without us did many glorious things, that he might redeem us from all iniquity, and purify unto himself a peculiar people zealous of good works ; and that they who live should not henceforth live into themselves, but unto him that died for them, and rose again. But it is in the second part that the excellence of our holy religion consists. We have no ability of ourselves to take off our minds from the things that are evil, and engage them in the work of religion and godliness. This is the gift of God. It is a continued miracle that cleanses that polluted fountain, the heart, and therefore I call this experience the principal evidence of the Christian religion. It is the glory of Christianity, and renders it the perfection of all religions."

"That Christianity," I replied, " is the perfection of all religions, is granted ; but that we have no ability to save our souls without a supernatural operation on them, this is what I have still some doubt of. A careful examination of the subject, produces some hard objections, and therefore, madam, I will lay my difficulties before you, that your fine natural understanding may remove them, if it be possible. I will be short on the article, for many words would only darken it.

" In the first place, then, as to man's inability to live a religious life, and practice the precepts of the gospel, it must be the effect of the human composition, or the effect of the agency of the serpent. If the former, it is chargeable upon the author of the composition ; if the latter, upon the agent which acts upon it. Man could not be culpable, I think, for a bad life, in either case. If my nature be weakness itself, or the serpent is superior to me, what good can be required of me ? Can the supreme reason call for brick, where there are no materials to make it with ? will you say yes, because he gives supernatural ability to perform ? But then, can this be called man's action ? It is the action of the author by his miserable creature, man ; and in such case, may we not say, that though commands are given to man to obey revealed laws, yet the obedience is performed by God ?

" In the next place, as man in his natural capacity, and all his natural powers, are the work of God, and as truly derived from him as any supernatural powers can be, it follows, I imagine, that a voluntary agent's making a right use of the powers of his nature, is as valuable as his being compelled to act well and wisely by a supernatural power. To assert, then, such experiences or operations, to me seems to misrepresent the nature of a being excellently constituted to answer the good purposes he was created for. I am likewise, at present, of opinion, that depreciating our natural abilities, does not give so much glory to God as you imagine."

To this Mrs. PRICE replied, "that by the operation of the spirit, she did not mean that man was purely passive, and had no part in the working out his salvation, but that God co-operates with man, and without destroying the faculty of reason, improves it by convincing and enlightening the understanding, and by moving and inclining the will towards such objects as are acceptable to himself, and from those that are contrary to his gospel. The mind in this manner enlightened and affected, begins to act, and as the spirit moves upon the soul, the quickened man, under the divine direction, does all the good the scripture commands him to do, and eschews the evils he is ordered to avoid. By God through Christ, he practices the excellent virtues recommended in the holy books, and for this reason, the righteousness which Christians bring forth, is called in scripture the righteousness of Christ, the righteousness of God, and the right-

eousness of faith.   Christ is the efficient.   We, through him, are
made able to act.   Notwithstanding the weakness and in-
capacity of our nature, yet through faith in the power of God,
which is given to all who believe in him, we are enabled to flee
immorality and vice, and by a life of virtue and piety, to enjoy
the pleasure of a sweet reflection, and the praises of unpolluted
reason.

" That this is the case of man, the sacred writings declare in
a thousand places, and set forth the exceeding greatness of
God's power in this respect.   The ministry of the gospel appears
to have been ordained for this end, and the perfection of the
Christian religion to rest on this particular thing.   ' The Lord
died for our sins, and rose again for our justification, that we,
through the power of his resurrection, might be made righteous.'
And the apostle adds, ' I am not ashamed of the gospel of Christ.
for it is the power of God unto salvation, to every one that believeth, to the Jew first, and also to the Greek, for therein is the
righteousness of God revealed from faith to faith.'   And that
the promise of the Holy Ghost had reference not only to the
great effusion of the spirit at Pentecost, which was a solemn
confirmation of the new and spiritual dispensation of the gospel ;
but also to that instruction which Christians of every age were
to receive from it continually, if they attended to it, is evident
from the promise of Christ, I will pray the Father, and he shall
give you another comforter, (the spirit of truth) that he may
abide with you for ever.'   This spirit was to supply the place
of his personal presence.   It was to become a teacher and comforter to his disciples and followers to the end of time, to enlighten and incline their minds to piety and virtue, to enable
them to do all things appertaining to life and to godliness, and to
have a faith in God's power and all-sufficiency.   This is the
glorious specific difference of Christianity from all other religions.
We have an inward instructor and supporter always abiding with
us.   And what can be a higher honor to mankind, or an act of
greater love in God, than for him to interpose continually, and
by his holy spirit restore the teachable aud attentive to that
purity and uprightness in which he at first created man ?
Glorious dispensation !   Here is a complete reparation of the
loss sustained by transgression.   We are created anew in Christ
Jesus, and are made partakers of the divine nature.   Surely
this is the utmost that can be expected from religion.   In short,
continued Mrs. Price, " it is to me a most amazing thing, to see
men of sense disclaim this help, argue for self-sufficiency and
independency, and receive only the outward appearance of the
son of God, in a literal, historical, aod formal proiession of Christianity !   This will never do the work.   The outward appearance
of the Son of God only puts us in the capacity of salvation ; it is

the inward appearance by the power and virtue of the spirit
that must save us. The end of the gospel is repentance, forgiveness of sins, and amendment of manners ; and the means
of obtaining that end, is Christianity in the life, spirit, and
power of it."

"You talk extremely well, madam," said I, "upon this subject, and have almost made me a convert to the notion of an
inward appearance of the Son of God ; but I must beg leave to
observe to you, that as to what you have added, by way of explication and vindication of the operation of the spirit, to wit,
that man has agency, and God co-operates with it, by which
means the man is enabled to apply his agency to the performance
of good ; this does not seem to me to make the matter quite plain.
The virtue or goodness of an agent must certainly arise from a
right exercise of his own power, and how then can God's co-
operating with him make a better man ? Can such co-operation
add any thing to my virtue, if my goodness is to be rated in
proportion to the exertion of my own will and agency ? If I am
not able to save a man from drowning, though I pity him, and
do my best to preserve his life ; but God gives me strength, or
co-operates with me, and so the man is saved ; can this add
any thing to my virtue or goodness ? It would be indeed an
instance of God's goodness to the man ; but as to myself, I did
no more with the divine co-operation than I did without it.
I made all the use I could of what power I had. This seems to
me a strong objection against the inward appearance : nor is it
all there is to object. If I see a man in a deep wet ditch, in a
dangerous and miserable way, and am prompted by a natural
affection, and the fitness of relieving, to exert a sufficient strength
I have, to take the man out of his distress, and put him in a
comfortable way, which is a thing I really did once, and thereby
saved a useful life ; in this case there was good done by an agent,
without any supernatural co-operation at all. Many more
instances might be produced ; but from what has been said, is it
not plain that much good may be done without any interposition ;
and, with it, that no good can be added to the character of the
agent ?

"But you will say, perhaps, that the good disposition of the
agent in such cases, is supernatural operation, and without such
operation, he could not make a right use of his ability. To this
we reply, that if by disposition is meant a given power to distinguish betwixt motive and motive, and so to judge of moral
fitness and unfitness ; or, a power to act from right motives,
when such are present to the mind ; these cannot be given,
because they are the powers which constitute a man a moral agent,
and render him accountable for his actions. Without them he
could not be a subject of moral government.

" And if you mean by the term disposition, God's presenting such motives to the mind, as are necessary to excite to right action ; the answer is, that though God may kindly interpose, and in many instances, by supernatural operation, present such motives to the mind, yet such operation cannot be always necessary, in order to our doing good.   In many cases we see at once what good ought to be done, and we do it instantly of ourselves unless the natural faculties be prevented by false principles. If our fellow-creature falls into the fire, or has a fit, while we are near him, the fitness of relieving him, and the natural compassion essential to our constitution, will make us fly to his assistance, without a supernatural operation.   We want no divine impulse to make us interpose.   Without being reminded, we will do our best to recover the man, if superstition or passion hath not misled the natural powers of the mind.   In a great variety of things, the case is the same, and when at a glance we see the fitness of action, there is an immediate production of good.

" It is not just, then, to assert that the heart cannot be the spring of good actions, without the actings of God.   It is the seat and source of both evil and good.   Man is capable of giving glory to God, and of doing the contrary.   He is constituted to answer all the purposes of social felicity, and to act a part suitable to, and becoming that reason and understanding, which God hath given him to guide his steps ; and he may, on the contrary, by abusing his liberty act an unsocial part in the creation, and do great dishonour to his Maker, by the evil imaginations of his heart, and the violence his hand commits.   This hath been the state of human nature from the fall to the flood, and from the flood to our time.   The human race have a natural ability for good or evil, and are at liberty for the choice of either of these. ' If thou doest well, Cain, who has power, and is at liberty to do evil, thou shalt be accepted ; and if thou doest not well, who hast power, and is at liberty to do good, sin lieth at the door.' If this had not been the case of Cain, and of others since his days, it seems to me, at present, that God would act an unequal part with his creatures.   Can happiness or misery be called reward or punishment, unless the creature can voluntarily choose or avoid the thing which renders him the object of infliction or glory ? I think not.   ' For we must all appear before the judgment seat of Christ, that every one may receive the things done in his body according to that he hath done, whether it be good or bad.'   The agency of a serpent will be no plea then, for a Cain, I suppose : nor will Abel's title to an inheritance depend only on the good brought forth in him by the Lord.   And as to a self-sufficiency or independency in all this, as often charged, I can see none, for the reason already given, to wit, that my natural powers are as much the gift of God to me as supernatural powers can be, and render me as dependent a being. They are derived from him. It is his given powers I use, and if I make a right use of them, to answer the great and wise purpose I was created for, the good application must be as valuable as if I had applied supernatural powers to the same purpose."

" What you say, sir," answered Mrs. PRICE, " has reason in it, to be sure : but it seems inconsistent with the language of the *Bible*, and takes away the grace of God entirely, and the principal evidence of the Christian religion : As to the necessary guilt of mankind, Moses says, ' and God saw, that the wickednesses of man was great in the earth ; and that every imagination of the thoughts of his heart, was only evil continually : and it re- pented the Lord, that he had made man on the earth, &c.' And again ; ' The earth also was corrupt before God, and the earth was filled with violence : and God looked upon the earth, and behold it was corrupt, for all flesh had corrupted his way on the earth. And God said unto Noah, the end of all flesh is come before me, for the earth is filled with violence through them and behold, I will destroy them with the earth. But Noah found grace in the eyes of the Lord.' The prophet *Jeremiah* does likewise affirm, ' The heart is deceitful above all things and desperately wicked.' And St. Paul declared from *Psalm* 14 and 53, ' There is none righteous, no, not one ; there is none that understandeth, there is none that seeketh after God. They are all gone out of the way, they are altogether become unprofit- able ; there is none that doth good, no not one. Their throat is an open sepulchre ; with their tongues have they used deceit ; the poison of asps is under their lips : whose mouth is full of cursing and bitterness. Their feet are swift to shed blood. Destruction and misery are in their ways. And the way peace have they not known.'

" Then as to grace, or the operation of the Spirit, to cure this miserable condition of mankind, Peter said unto them, ' Repent, and be baptized every one of you, in the name of Jesus Christ, for the remission of sins, and ye shall receive the gift of the Holy Ghost, for the promise is unto you and your children, and to all that are afar off.' This is a very extensive declaration both as to time and place. After Peter had told the people, ' the God of our fathers raised up Jesus whom ye slew, and hanged on a tree, him hath God exalted with his right hand, to be a prince and a saviour, for to give repentance unto Israel, and forgiveness of sins, and we are his witnesses of these things, and so also is the Holy Ghost, whom God hath given to them that obey him,' the apostle adds, then they (the Gentiles) were filled with the Holy Ghost.' All who obeyed, without distinction, had the Holy Ghost given them, and it was a witness to them of the truth of Christ's divine mission, and the good effects of it, according to the promise of the Lord, to wit, ' he shall testify of me.'

"St. Paul likewise tells us, ' if any man have not the spirit of Christ, he is none of his. And if Christ be in you, the body is dead because of sin, but the spirit is life, because of righteousness ; but if the spirit of him that raised up Jesus from the dead, dwell in you, he that raised up Christ from the dead, shall also quicken your mortal bodies by his spirit that dwelleth in you. Therefore brethren, we are debtors, not to the flesh to live after the flesh, for if ye live after the flesh ye shall die ; but if ye through the spirit do mortify the deeds of the body, ye shall live. For as many as are led by the spirit of God, they are the sons of God. For ye have not received the spirit of bondage again to fear, but ye have received the spirit of adoption, whereby we cry Abba Father, the spirit itself beareth witness with our spirit, that we are the children of God.' Here we see the necessity of having the spirit of Christ, and that those who have it not, do not belong to him. They are none of his. We may likewise observe, that it mortifies the deeds of the body, and quickens the soul to a life of holiness ; the passage likewise shews, that the spirit bears witness with our spirits, and by an evidence peculiar to itself, gives us a certain sense, or understanding of it.

" In short, sir, a great number of texts might be produced to show not only the work and effect of the divine spirit upon our minds ; but that, it is an evidence, the principal evidence and ground of certainty to believers, respecting the truth of Christianity. I will mention however only two or three more, and then shall be glad to hear what you say to those things.

" ' What man knoweth the spirit of man, save the spirit of man which is in him ? even so the things of God knoweth no man, but the spirit of God. Now we have received not the spirit of the world, but the spirit which is of God, that we might know the things which are freely given to us of God. Ye have an unction from the Holy one, and ye know all things. These things I have written to you, concerning them that seduce you ; but the anointing which ye have received of him, abideth in you, and ye need not that any teach you, but as the same anointing teacheth you of all things, and is truth, and is no lie, and even as it hath taught you, ye shall abide in it. Hereby we know that he abideth in us by his spirit, which he hath given us. Hereby we know that we dwell in him, and he in us, because he hath given us of his spirit."

" What do you say to all this ? do not the sacred passages I have repeated seem to declare in the plainest manner the necessary iniquity of man ; that this is to be cured only, and his nature rectified by the operation of the divine spirit ; and that the effusion of the spirit, both as to instruction and evidence, was not peculiar to the infancy of Christianity ? This appears to my understanding. The very essence of the Christian religion I think from these scriptures consists in the power and efficacy of the spiritual principle.''

"What you have said, madam," I replied, "seems strong indeed in defence of the weakness of man, and the operation of the spirit, and I should be of your way of thinking as to the manifestation of it, but that I imagine the thing may be explained in a different manner. Let us review our religion, if you please, and perhaps we may find, that another account may be given of sanctification, and the renewing the mind into a state of holiness.

"When God called this world into being, his purpose was existence. This I think was the case. True religion was to form and fix every good principle in the human mind, produce all righteousness in the conversation, and thereby render mankind the blessed of the universal Father. They were to worship the one true God ; the possessor of all being, and the fountain of all good ; to believe on him, and have their trust and dependence always on him ; to be pure and peaceable, gentle and full of mercy, without partiality, without hypocrisy, and so devoted to holiness and obedience, to every virtue and every good work which the law of reason can require from men ; that after a long life spent in acting a part the most honourable to God, and the most advantageous to mankind, in obeying the dictates of reason, and thereby imitating the example of God ; they might be translated to the regions of immortality, where the first and great Original displays as it were face to face the perfections of the Deity, and from an all-perfect and holy being receive the vast rewards he has prepared for those, who, in this first state, have been to all the purposes of life and religion, perfect as he is perfect. For these reasons did the supreme director, the greatest and the best Being in the universe, command the human race into existence. He gave them faculties to conduct them here through various scenes of happiness to the realms of immortality and immutable felicity. It was a Godlike design l

" But it was not very long before this human race became corrupt, and not only did evil in the sight of the Lord, but ceased to apprehend the first cause as one most perfect mind. The natural notions of moral perfection which reason and the light of nature supply, they no longer minded, nor thought of what is fit and reasonable to be done in every case. The passions began to influence and direct their lives : just and pure ideas of the Deity were lost, false ones took place, and the mischief and its fatal consequences became very great. It was a melancholy scene l The exalted notions of one glorious God, and of that true religion which subsists in the expectation of a future state, were no longer known, nor did the race ever think of approving themselves in the eye of an all perfect and holy being, Superstition and iniquity prevailed, and the spread of evil was wide.

" God saw that the wickedness of man was great in the earth," the thoughts of his heart evil continually, &c. as you have before quoted from the book of Genesis and because the wickedness of the tenth generation was so great, and men no longer endeavoured after those perfections, which are natural and proper to rational minds ; no longer thought of conforming themselves to the divine nature, or strove to imitate the excellencies of it, though constituted to give glory to their Maker, and endued with a reason and understanding sufficient to teach them the rule of duty, and guide their steps in the ways of true religion ; but against the light of their own minds, acted the most impious and unsociable part : therefore God repented that he had made them, that is, he did what is the product of repentance in men, when they undo, as far as it is in their power what they repent of, and destroyed his own work by that desolating judgment, the flood. This seems to be the truth of the case. The words of Moses do not mean the state of human nature on account of the fall. They express only the wickedness of the tenth generation as a reason for the deluge at that time. There is not the least ground for asserting from this passage in the sacred historian, that man was unable to do good by his natural powers, and that his crimes arose from resisting the actings of God upon his mind. The impiety of this generation was a mere abuse of free will, and acting against the plain dictates of their own minds ; therefore, when wilful oppression and sensuality filled the earth, God destroyed the world by an inundation. Noah only, who was a just man, and perfect in his generation, with his family escaped.

" This terrible execution of an awful vengeance on the guilty race, demonstrated to the survivors, and to all ages to come, the great malignity of sin, and the uncontrollable supremacy of the divine government. As the venerable patriarch and his family sailed over the bosom of the boundless ocean of waters, and above the wrecks and ruins of this terrestrial world, they adored with grateful hearts, the Almighty Father of virtue and goodness, who had so wonderfully preserved them, and were convinced by the amazing, striking evidence, that sin is the greatest infamy and degradation of our reason and nature ; that it has an insuperable repugnancy and irreversible contrariety, to our true happiness, and is infamous, pernicious, and ruinous, by the sentence of the Almighty. The dreadful event unanswerably evinced his constant actual cognizance of enormous faith and manners, and his unchangeable displeasure with them. This truth, which was learn'd at first, by the expulsion from Paradise, and the sad inheritance

of mortality, they saw again republished in the most awful manner·
This gave undoubtedly a very religious turn to their minds, and
they determined to adhere to those excellent principles and practices, which had been, through God's goodness, their security in
the general desolation, and to flee the contrary malignant ones
which had procured that desolation on the rest. In a degree
suitable to their nature and ability, they resolved to imitate the
perfections of God, and to employ the powers and faculties of
reason in endeavouring to be just, and righteous, and merciful.
And as the amazing operation of God in the deluge called for their
wonder and praise, we must think their hearts glowed with the
sense of his goodness to them, and that they extolled his mercy
and power in the salvation they had received. So we are told
by an inspired writer. Noah restored the antient rites of divine
service, and built an altar to the Lord, ' And the Lord smelled
a sweet savour, and said, never any more will I curse the ground
for man's sake, though the imagination of man's heart is evil
from his youth ; ' because he will not hearken to the voice of
reason, and with the greatest ardour and contention of mind,
labour to attain a conformity to the divine nature in the moral
perfections of it which is the true dignity of man, and the utmost
excellence of human souls. ' Neither will I again smite any more
every living creature as I have done. While the earth remaineth,
seed time and harvest, and cold and heat, and summer and winter,
and day and night shall not cease.'

" Thus did God enter into a covenant with Noah, and his sons,
and their seed ; and as the late amazing occurrences must incline
the spectators of the flood to piety and goodness ; and the fathers
of the post-diluvian world were careful to instruct their children
in the several parts of the stupendous fact, and from the whole
inculcate the being and perfections of God, his universal dominion
and actual providence and government over all things, his love
of virtue and goodness and infinite detestation of all sin ; to which
we may add, that the imitation of God is not a new principle
introduced into religion by revelation, but has its foundation in
the reason and nature of things ; we may from hence conclude
that the rising generation were persons of conspicuous devotion,
and followed after the moral virtues, the holiness, justice and
mercy which the light of nature discovers. They were, I believe,
most excellent mortals for some time. They obeyed to be sure
every dictate of reason, and adored and praised the invisible
Deity ; the supreme immutable mind.

" But this beautiful scene had an end, and man once more forgot his Maker and himself. He prostituted the honour of both,
by robbing God of the obedience due to him, and by submitting
himself a slave to the elements of the world. When he looked up
to the heavens, and saw the glory of the sun and stars, instead of

praising the Lord of all, he foolishly said, these are thy gods, O Man ! An universal apostacy from the primitive religion prevailed. They began with the heavenly bodies, or sydereal gods, and proceeded to heroes, brutes, and images, till the world was overflowed with an inundation of idolatory, and superstition : even such superstition, as nourished under the notion of religion, and pleasing the gods, the most bestial impurities, the most inhuman and unnatural cruelties, and the most unmanly and contemptible follies. Moral virtue and goodness were totally extinguished. When men had lost the sense of the supreme Being, the Creator, Governor, and Judge of the world, they not only ceased to be righteous and holy, but became necessarily vicious and corrupt in practice ; for iniquity flows from corrupt religion, as the waters from the spring. The principles and ceremonies of the established idolatries gave additional strength to men's natural inclinations, to intemperance, lust, fraud, violence, and every kind of unrighteousness and debauchery. Long before the days of Moses this was the general case. Idolatry had violated all the duties of true religion, and the most abominable practices by constitution were authorized. The Phalli* and the Mylli,† rites that modesty forbids to explain, were esteemed principal parts of their ritual ; virgins before marriage were to sacrifice their chastity to the honour of Venus ;‡ men were offered upon the altars for sacrifices ; and children were burned alive to Moloch and Adramalech. In a word, the most abominable immoralities

* " Ex ea re tum privatim tum publice lignea virilia thyrsis alligates per eam solennitatem gestabant : fuit enim *Phallus* vocatum membrum virile." Schædius *de Diis Germanis*, edidit Keyslero, 1728, 8vo. p. 130.

† " Heraclides Syracusius libro de vetustis et sancitis moribus scribit apud Syracusios in perfectis thermophoriis, ex sesamo et melle fingi pudenda muliebria, quæ per ludos et spectacula circumferebantur, et vocabantur *Mylli*."—Athenæi *Deipnos*, l. 14. p. 647.

‡ This is taken notice of by the prophet Jeremiah. " The women also with cords about them, sitting in the ways, burn bran for perfume ; but if any of them, drawn by some that passeth by, lie with her, she reproacheth her fellow, that she was not thought as worthy as herself, nor her cord broken."—*Baruch*, ch. 6. v. 43.

Herodotus, who lived almost two centuries after, in explanation of this passage of the prophet *Baruch*, tells us, " Every woman at Babylon, was obliged, once in her life, to sit down openly in the temple of Venus, in order to prostitute herself to some stranger : They enter into the temple, and sit down crowded with garlands, some continually going out, and others coming in : The galleries where they sit are built in a straight line, and open on every side, that all strangers may have a free passage to choose such woman as they like best. Those women who excel in beauty and shape are soon dismissed : but the deformed are sometimes necessitated to wait three or four years, before they can satisfy the law. The men declared their choice by throwing money into the lap of the woman they most admired, which she was by no means to refuse, but instantly retire with the man that accosted her, and fulfil the law. Women of rank, for none were dispensed with, might sit in covered chariots for the purpose whilst their servants waited at a distance till they had done." See *Herodotus, translated by Isaac Littlebury*, 1709, 8vo. vol. 1. p. 125.

Strabo also furnishes an account to the same purpose, lib. 16. p. 745 ; and Justin observes, the reason for this custom, was ne sola impudria videretur, *i.e.* lest Venus alone should appear lascivious.—Lib. 18. cap. 5.

As to the breaking of the woman's cord, Dr. Hyde says, their lower garments were tied with small and weak cords made of rushes, " qui ad congrediendum erant frangendi." Purchas confirms this notion ; having seen the thing practised in his travels in the east, *Pilgr.* book 1. ch. 12. p. 65. But Grotius on *Baruch* says, the meaning was, the women had cords given them, as a token that they were under the vow of prostitution, which when they had performed, the cord was properly said to be broken ; for every vow may be called universally prevailed; with the encouragements of religion, men were led into intemperance, uncleanness, murders, and many vices, inconsistent with the prosperity and peace of society, as well as with the happiness of private persons ; and that such iniquities might have a perpetual source, the most shameful idolatries were preserved in opposition to the knowledge and worship of the one true God. So general was this corruption and idolatry, that the infection seized the descendants of Shem, the pious race. Even Terah, the father of Abram, we find charged with it. And Abram himself was culpable I think in this respect, as the word *Asebes* imports. It is rendered in our *Bible* ungodly, but it signifies more properly idolatry, and that is what St. Paul in the 4th chapter to the *Romans* hints. The apostle speaking of Abraham, says, but to him that worketh not, but believeth in him that justifieth the ungodly, that is, an ungodly idolator, who has no manner of claim to the blessings of God, he must be justified upon the foot, not of his own prior obedience, but of God's mercy.

" In such a calamitous state, a revelation to restore the law of nature, and make it more fully and clearly known, to enforce its observance, to afford helps and motives to the better performance of what it enjoins, and relieve the guilty mind against all its doubts, would certainly be a merciful vouchsafement from God to mankind, and be much for their advantage and happiness ; and therefore, in the 428th year from the flood, to provide for the restoration of the true religion, and preserve the knowledge and worship of the one true God on earth, in opposition to the prevailing idolatry, and the gross immoralities that were the effects of idolatrous principles and practices, Jehovah commanded Abraham to leave his country, his kindred, and his father's house, and proceed with his family to the land of Canaan. Here God entered into covenants with Abraham and his posterity,* to be

vinculum, or a cord. As I take it, the case was both as Hyde and Grotius relate it. I was in company with a physician, who had spent many years of his life in the East, and he assured me, he had seen both circumstances practised in the kingdom of Cranganor.

As to the woman's burning incense or bran for a perfume, it was the custom before coition by way of charm and incentive. When a Babylonian and his wife had a mind to correspond, they always first lit up the fuming pan, imagining it improved the passion. So in the *Pharmaceutria* of Theocritus, p. 33. we see Simætha is using her incantation, " nunc furfures sacrificabo," Πιτυρον, the word made use of in Jeremiah's *Epistle.* And as if all this had not been lust enough in their religion, it was farther declared in their ritual, that those were best qualified for the sacerdotal function, who were born of mothers who conceived them of their own sons.

In respect of human sacrifices, if you would have a full account of them, consult the following authors, and you will find that the Canaanites were far from being the only Pagans who were guilty of this unnatural barbarity. Selden *de Diis Syris.* Segort. 1. c. 6. and all the authors he quotes. Grotius on *Deut.* 18. Isaac Vossius *de Orig. Idol.* 1. 2. c. 5. Dion Vossius on Maimon. *de Idol.* c. 6· Lud. Vives *Notes on St. Aug. de Civit. Dei.* l. 7. c. 19. Ouzelius et Elmenhorstius *Notes on Min. Fœlix.* Spenceri *de Legibus Hebræorum.* 1. 2. c. 13· And Fabricius *Bibliographia.* c. 9.

* Bishop Sherlock well observes, that " two covenants were given to Abraham, one a temporal covenant, to take place in the land of Canaan—the other, a covenant of better hope , to be performed in a better country."—*Discourse on Prophecy.* p. 134.

instruments in the hands of Providence for bringing about great designs in the world, that he and his posterity were to be the church of God, and depositaries of a hope, that the covenant limited to Abraham and his chosen seed, was to grow in the fulness of time into a blessing upon all the nations of the earth.   Abraham was at this time seventy-five years old, and God added to the patriarchal worship the visible mark of circumcision, as a seal of a covenant between himself and Abraham.

" Yet how fit soever such a visible mark might be, to keep in remembrance the covenant between God and the family of Abraham, it was found in experience, insufficient to preserve them from the idolatrous customs of their neighbours.   Some new laws, some further constitutions of worship were to be added, or, as the family of Abraham were situated in the midst of idolators and unrighteous ones, it was foreseen they would soon fall from the essentials of religion ; and instead of preserving a right knowledge of God, of his being, perfections and government, a just sense of the reverence all men owe to him, from a firm belief of his being, power, dominion, justice, and goodness, and an hearty concern to obey the known will of God in all things ; doing what is pleasing in his sight, seeking, and hoping their perfection and happiness, in the likeness, and in the image of God ; they would, on the contrary, serve other Gods, and make their idolatry, not a matter of harmless speculation, but a fountain of the most dangerous immoralities ; and therefore, as it was highly fit in itself, and well becoming the wisdom of God, he gave Moses a christianity in hieroglyphics, that is, a tabernacle, a shechinah, a priesthood, an altar, sacrifices, laws moral, and ceremonial, with every constituent part of the Hebrew ritual ; being figures of a better shechinah, temple, priest, altar, sacrifice, revelation, and blessings— figurative representations of the more perfect constitutions in the days of Messiah the King.   This was in the year 875 after the flood, and in 1491 before Christ.   By a ritual so becoming the wisdom of God, given for a preservative against idolatrous principles, and as a dispensation preparatory to that future heavenly religion, the Hebrew nation were guarded against the surrounding corruptions of the world, and raised up the defenders of true religion, to preserve the knowledge and worship of the one true God.

" But as mankind would not follow the light of nature, which is sufficient, when attended to for a constant universal practice of piety and morality ; so neither would they be engaged by various revealed laws, from time to time given, and by the calls and lessons of many prophets, to the practice of true religion and righteousness ; but as the heart is the seat and source of wickedness in man, according to the prophet *Jeremiah*, so even the hearts of the Jews became deceitful above all things, and desperately wicked. And the prophet goes on to shew, not the necessary inability of man without experiences, or an operating spirit within, as you suppose, madam; but that, though men thus wickedly deceive one another, yet they cannot possibly by such a wilful desperate piece of wickedness deceive their Maker, because to him the most secret recesses of their hearts lie open ; and, cousequently, in the issue, they deceive themselves, seeing God, who knows the deceit which is lodged in their hearts, will render unto them according to their works, and according to the fruit of their doings : so that their hope and expectation will be disappointed, even as a partridge is disappointed that sitteth on eggs, and hatcheth them not.

"And as St. Paul says from the fourteenth and fifty-third *Psalm*, there was none righteous, no not one ; there is none that understandeth, there is none that seeketh after God ; and so on, as you, madam, have quoted the verses, in which the apostle did not intend to shew the necessary pollution of man without the help of grace ; but the groundlessness of that opinion which the Jews had gone into, that they were the only people which pleased God ; for they were as guilty as the Gentiles were in transgressing the law of nature. Neither of them had any legal title to justification. They were all very great transgressors. The throat of Jew and Gentile an open sepulchre : their tongues, deceit : the poison of asps under their lips : their mouths, full of cursing and bitterness : their feet swift to shed blood. Destruction and misery in their ways : and the way of peace have they not known : Therefore the justification of the Jew as well as the Gentile must be of grace, and not of debt.

"In this was manifested the inestimable love of God in the redemption of the world by Jesus Christ. Though Jew and Gentile were qualified to discern and do both good and evil, and the Jew had a written law as a further assistance, but nevertheless they violated the plain dictates of natural reason, and the divine precepts of the law, and by unrighteousness and impurity, rendered themselves objects of judgment and condemnation ; yet the Father of the universe, in compassion to mankind, sent a divine teacher from heaven, Christ, the true prophet that was to come into the world, and by his divinely revealed testimony and authority, attempts to abolish the superstition of men, reclaim their wickedness, and bring them back to the true sp ritual worship of God, and to that holiness of life and manners which is agreeable to the uncorrupted light and dictates of nature. This was love. The blessed God, in compassion to human ignorance and wickedness, contracted by men's own fault, gives them an express revelation of his will, and re-establishes the rule of pure uncorrupt religion and morality. He declares those terms of sinful man's reconcilement to him which he was pleased to accept,

Grace is manifested in the gospel to turn men from their vanities, or idol service, unto the living God, who made heaven and earth, and by the doctrine and sacrifice of Jesus Christ, to redeem us from all iniquity, and purify to himself a peculiar people, zealous of good works :—That denying all ungodliness and worldly lusts, we should live soberly, righteously, and godly in this present world, looking for that blessed hope, and the glorious appearance of the great God ; who will judge the world by that divine person, and great temporary minister, whom he sent before to destroy sin, and the kingdom of Satan ; and to bring mankind into a perfect obedience to the will of the supreme Being.   This renders Christianity a heavenly thing.   Revelation thus explained is beautiful and useful to an extreme degree.   It does not contradict but strengthens the obligations of natural religion."

"Your account, Sir," said Mrs. PRICE, "of man and religion is different indeed from mine, and I must allow your explications have reason in them : but still they do not satisfy me, nor can I part with my own opinion.   Two things in particular to me appear very strange in your scheme.   It seems to take away the necessity of the Christian revelation, if natural religion, duly attended to, was perfect, and sufficient for virtue and holiness, and thereby to gain the favour of God.   If reason alone can do the work, if men please, then what need of the gospel ?   If men will consider, and without consideration, no scheme can be of service ; they may as well turn their thoughts to the law of nature as to the law of grace, if there is no difference betwixt the rule of nature and the law of Christ, with regard to the knowledge of God, the maker of heaven and earth, and the worship due to him on that account, and the practice of virtue and morality.

"In the next place, if I understand you right, the grace of God is of no use at all in religion, as you account for salvation.   What is out of order within us, in the mind and its faculties, the will and its affections, and wants to be set right in good thought and works, our own reason, in your notion of religion, is sufficient to regulate, and unassisted by the illumination of the holy spirit of God, we may live in an uncorrupted state of piety and morality, and so save our souls, if we please.   This is what I cannot believe. The grace of God in the gospel is the glory and comfort of the Christian religion.   A divine operation that renews and sanctifies the mind is an invaluable blessing, and in a manner inexpressibly charming, satisfies me beyond hesitation, that the Christian religion is true, while it puts me in the actual possession of the good effects of it.   The spirit of God discovers to me the state of my own mind, in all the circumstances of a Christian life, sets my follies, my neglects, and my failings, in order before me, which is the first right step in order to the overcoming them ; and then observing the discoveries I was not able to make myself, and ι aving a strong faith in the divine power and sufficiency, I am enabled to gain victories my insufficient reason could never obtain. May this divine monitor then abide in my breast. It is by the heavenly assistance of the holy spirit only, as vouchsafed in the Christian dispensation, that I can secure for myself eternal life. The wise and prudent of this world may think as they please of this matter, and produce reasonings against it beyond my power to answer ; but for my part, I must consider it as the principle of my salvation, and I think I cannot be thankful enough for the inestimable blessings. It is to me a glorious instance of the great wisdom and goodness of God."

"Madam," I replied, "in relation to your first objection, that I make no difference between revealed and natural religion, for nature is as sufficient as grace, in my account, I assure you that I think the revelation of the gospel excels the best scheme of natural religion that could be proposed ; in declaring the terms of reconcilement, in demonstrating the divine wrath against sin, in the method of shewing mercy by the death of God's beloved son, and the promise of free pardon on the condition of repentance and newness of life. This manner gives unspeakable comfort to repenting sinners. It gives the greatest encouragement to engage them to the love of God, and the practice of all his commandments an encouragement that reason could not discover. To Christianity, therefore, the true preference is due. Though philosophy or the doctrine of reason may reform men, yet the Christian religion is a clearer and more powerful guide. It improves the light of reason by the supernatural evidence and declaration of God's will, and the means of man's redemption is a more efficacious motive and obligation to universal obedience than nature could ever with certainty propose. A revelation that has the clearest and strongest evidence of being the divine will, must be the most easy and effectual method of instruction, and be more noticed than the best human teaching ; and this will of God being truly and faithfully committed to writing, and preserved uncorrupt, must always be the best and surest rule of faith and manners. It is a rule absolutely free from all those errors and superstitions, both of belief and practice, which no human composure was ever before free from, or, probably would have been free from, without the assistance of such a revelation. Nor is this all. This is not the only superior excellence of our holy religion.

" A Mediator and crucified Redeemer brought into the Christian revelation, has a noble effect on a considering mind, and shews the reasonableness of the gospel-dispensation. The wisest and most rational heathens ever were for sacrifices and mediators, as the greatness of God was thereby declared, and that not only sin deserved punishment, but men's lives to be forfeited by their breach of the divine laws ; and when a divine person, made man, like unto us, appears instead of all other mediators, by whom, as the instrument of the means of salvaton, we are to offer up our prayers to the only true God ; and his voluntary dying in testimony of the truth of his mission and doctrine, is apponted to be instead of all other sacrifices, and to remain a memorial that God requires no atonement of us, but repentance and newness of life ; and the spotless virtues and obedience of this divine Redeemer, are to be a most perfect and moving example for us to imitate ; this renders Christianity worthy of God, and makes it the perfecion of religion. Great then are the advantages which the revelation of Christ Jesus has above mere reason, darkened by the clouds of error and a general corruption It is the most perfect rule of life. It is the most powerful means to promote a constant uniform practice of virtue and piety It advances human nature to its highest perfection, fills it with all the fruits of righteousness, and grants us privileges and blessings far superior to what we could attain any other way.

" With regard to the second objection, that I take away the grace of God, to preserve the dignity of human nature, this is far from my intention. I do indeed think, that as the gospel was given for the noblest purpose ; to wit, to call in an extraordinary manner upon mankind, to forsake that vice and idolatry, the corrupt creed of polytheism, the guilt of superstition, their great iniquities, violent passions, and worldly affections, which are all contrary to reason, and disgrace human nature ; and to practise that whole system of morality, which they must know to be most useful to them ; that they might turn to a religion which had but one object, the Great Invisible Being, all-knowing, and all-sufficent, to whom all the intelligent world are to make their devout applications ; because he is an infinite, independent, sovereign mind, who has created all things, and absolutely rules and governs all ; possesses all natural perfections, exists in all duration, fills all space with his presence, and is the omniscient witness of all their difficulties and wants ; and that since they were bound by all the ties of moral duty to obey this one God, and observe the rational institutions of religion, therefore they should make it the labour of their whole lives to excel in holiness and righteousness, and by virtue and piety unite themselves to God, and entitle themselves to glory at the great day. That as this is the nature, end, and design of the Christian revelation, so I do think the gospel of our salvation the word of truth, as an apostle calls it, is sufficient for the purpose, without immediate impulses. As we have a reasonable,intellectual nature, there is no want of mechanical powers. The words of Christ, which are the words of God, are, our life, and will, if attended to, powerfully enable us to practise good works, and to excel, and persevere therein. I can do all these things, through Christ, who strengtheneth me, that is, through the written directions of Christ, and through the arguments and motives of the Christian doctrine   To say otherwise of the gospel is, in my opinion, injurious to it.

" God may, to be sure, give special aids to men, whenever he thinks fit. He may, by an extraordinary agency, render our faculties more capable of apprehension, where divine things are concerned, may awaken a dormant idea, which lay neglected in the memory, with unusual energy ; may secretly attract the more attentive regard of the mind, and give it an inclination and an ability of tracing its various relations, with an unusual attention, so that a lustre before quite unknown shall be, as it were, poured upon it ; the spirit of God may render the mind more susceptible and more tenacious of divine knowledge ; I believe he often does by interposition, if in the spirit of Christ's doctrine we ask it of the great Father of Lights, the author of all the understanding divided among the various ranks of created beings ; who, as he first formed the minds of angels and men, continues the exercise of their intellectual faculties, and one way or another communicates to them all the knowledge of every kind which they possess ; in which view all our knowledge of every kind may be called a revelation from God, and be ascribed, as it is by Elihu in Job, to the inspiration of the Almighty. This the holy Spirit may do, and dissipate a prejudice that opposes truth. But this is not always necessary, nor always to be expected. It is evident from the gospel, that our Lord rather speaks of his word and doctrine, as the aids to save men's souls, than of himself, or spirit, personally considered. Abiding in him, and he in them, as necessary to their bearing fruit, signifies a strict and steady regard to his word, and the influence of that upon our minds. ' If ye abide in me, and my words abide in you ; ye shall ask what ye will, and it shall be done unto you : ' that is, ' If you continue to believe in me, and to pay a steady regard to my doctrine, you will be highly acceptable to God.'

" In short, ' as no man can come unto me,' says our Lord, ' except the Father which hath sent me draw him ; ' that is no man will receive my pure, sublime and spiritual doctrine, unless he have first gained some just apprehensions concerning the general principles of religion ; but if he has a good notion of God and his perfections, and desires to advance in virtue, he will come unto me, and hearken to that revelation, which contains the best directions for the performance of all the duties, and the greatest incitement to virtue, piety and devotion, so, no man can come to the Father but by the Son, that is, by obeying the written word and proceeding in that way in which the Son has declared it to be the will of the Father, that men should come to him, namely by keeping God's commandments, and by repentance and amendment of life ; there being no other name, or way given among men, but this way given or declared by Jesus Christ, by which they may be saved. In all this, there is not a word of supernatural light or operation ; though such operation, as before observed, there may be. There is not a hint of man's natural inability.

" To the glorious gospel then, the gospel of our salvation, the word of truth, the word of life, let us come, and with diligence and impartiality study it. Let us follow the truth we there find in every page, and it will enable us to triumph over the temptation of allurement and of terror. We shall become the children of God by the spirit of adoption. We shall be easy and happy in this life, and glorious and ever blessed in that which is to come. If we obey the gospel of the Son of God, and hearken to his word, he will take us under his guardian care. He descended from heaven, to deliver us from everlasting ruin, he purchased us with the price of his own blood, and if we live up to the word of truth, he will conduct us safely through life and death, into the abode of holy and happy spirits, and at length raise our bodies from the dust, and fix our complete persons in a state of immortal glory and felicity. This is my sense of religion. Where I am wrong I shall ever be glad to be set right."

Mrs. PRICE made no reply, and so ended this remarkable conversation. On whose side the truth is, the reader is to judge. What she advances for supernatural operation is strong and pious ; and considering Mrs. PRICE had no learning, and was almost without any reading, I thought it very wonderful to hear her on this, and many other subjects. She was such another genius as Chubb, but on the other side of the question ; if she had been able to write as sensibly and correctly as she talked on several articles of religion, she would have made a good author. So much goodness and good sense I have not very often found in her kind. They merit a memorial in a journal of the curious things that have occurred to me in my life-time.

The thirteenth of June, 1725, I took my leave of my friend, JOHN PRICE, and his admirable wife, promising to visit them again as soon as it was in my power, and proceeded on my journey in quest of Mr. Turner. I would not let PRICE go with me, on second thoughts, as many sad accidents might happen in this rough and desolate part of the world, and no relief in such case to be found. If I fell, there was no one belonging to me to shed a tear for me ; but if a mischief should befal JACK PRICE, his wife would be miserable indeed, and I the maker of a breach in the sweetest system of felicity that love and good sense had ever formed. This made me refuse his repeated offers to accompany me. All I would have was a boy and horse of his, to carry some provisions wet and dry, as there was no public-house to be found in ascending those tremendous hills, or in the deep vales through which I must go ; nor any house that he knew of beyond his own.

With the rising sun then I set out, and was charmed for several hours with the air and views. The mountains, the rocky precipices the woods and the waters, appeared in various striking situations every mile I travelled on, and formed the most astonishing points of view. Sometimes I was above the clouds, and then crept to enchanting vallies below. Here glens were seen that looked as if the mountains had been rent asunder to form the amazing scenes, and there, forests and falling streams covered the sides of the hlls. Rivers in many places, in the most beautiful cascades, were tumbling along ; and cataracts from the tops of mountains came roaring down. The whole was grand, wonderful, and fine. On the top of one of the mountains I passed over at noon, the air was piercing cold, on account of its great height, and so subtle, that we breathed with difficulty, and were a little sick. From hence I saw several black subjacent clouds big with thunder, and the lightning within them rolled backwards and forwards, like shining bodies of the brightest lustre. One of them went off in the grandest horrors through the vale below, and had no more to do with the pike I was on than if it had been a summit in another planet. The scene was prodigiously fine. Sub pedibus ventos et rauca tonitrua calcat.

Till the evening, I rid and walked it, and in numberless windings round impassable hills, and by the sides of rivers it was impossible to cross, journeyed a great many miles, but no human creature, or any kind of house, did I meet with in all the long way, and as I arrived at last at a beautiful lake, whose banks the hand of nature had adorned with vast old trees, I sat down by this water in the shade to dine, on a neat's tongue I had got from good Mrs. PRICE ; and was so delighted with the striking beauties and stillness of the place, that I determined to pass the night in this sweet retreat. Nor was it one night only, if I had my will, that I would have rested there. Often did I wish for a convenient little lodge by this sweet water-side, and that with the numerous swans, and other fowl that lived there, I might have spent my time in peace below, till I was removed to the established seat of happiness above.

Had this been possible, I should have avoided many an affliction, and had known but few of those expectations and disappointments, which render life a scene of emptiness, and bitterness itself. My years would have rolled on in peace and wisdom, in this sequestered, delightful scene, and my silent meditations had been productive of that good temper and good action, which the resurrection of the dead, the dissolution of the world, the judgement day, and the eternal state of men, requires us to have. Free from the various perplexities, and troubles I have experienced by land and sea, in different parts of the world, I should have lived, in this paradise of a place, in the enjoyment of that fine happiness, which easy country business and a studious life afford ; and might have made a better preparation for that hour which is to disunite me, and let my invisible spirit depart to the shades of eternity. Happy they, who in some such rural retirement, can employ some useful hours every day in the management of a little comfortable farm, and devote the greater portion of their time to sacred knowledge, heavenly piety, and angelic goodness ; which cannot be dissolved when the thinker goes, nor be confined to the box of obscurity, under the clods of the earth ; but will exist in our souls for ever, and enable us to depart in peace to the happy regions. This has ever made me prefer a retired country life, when it was in my power to enjoy it. But be it town or country, the main business, my good readers, should be to secure an inheritance in that eternal world, where the sanctified live with God and his Christ. Getting, keeping, multiplying money ; dress, pleasure, entry ; are not only little things for such beings as we are : they are indeed sad principal work for creatures that are passing away to an everlasting state : there to lament their lost day, and talents misapplied, in dreadful agonies, in the habitations of darkness ; or to remain for ever in the habitations of light, peace, and joy ; if you have laboured to obtain, and improve in the graces and virtuous qualities which the gospel recommends. These are the treasure and possession worth a Christian's acquiring. These only are portable into the eternal world ; when the body that was clothed in purple and fine linen, and fared sumptuously every day, is laid in a cold and narrow cave. Take my advice then, reader. Be ready. Let us so think and act in this first state, that in the next, we may meet in the regions of purity and righteousness, serenity and joy.

The lake I have mentioned was the largest I had seen in this wild part, being above a mile in length, and more than half a mile broad ; and the water that filled it burst with the greatest impetuosity from the inside of a rocky mountain, that is very wonderful to behold. It is a vast craggy precipice, that ascends till it is almost out of sight, and by its gloomy and tremendous air, strikes the mind with a horror that has something pleasing in it. This amazing cliff stands perpendicular at one end of the lake, at the distance of a few yards, and has an opening at the bottom, that is wide enough for two coaches to enter at once, if the place was dry. In the middle of it there is a deep channel, down which the water rushes with a mighty swiftness and force, and on either side, the stone rises a yard above the impetuous stream. The ascent is easy and flat. How far it goes, I know not, being afraid to ascend more than forty yards; not only on account of the terrors common to the place, from the fall of so much water with a strange kind of roar, and the height of the arch which covers the torrent all the way : but because as I went up, there was of a sudden, an increase of noise so very terrible, that my heart failed me, and a trembling almost disabled me. The rock moved under me, as the frightful sounds encreased, and as quick as it was possible for me, I came into day again. It was well I did ; for I had not been many minutes out, before the water overflowed its channel, and filled the whole opening in rushing to the lake. The increase of the water and the violence of the discharge were an astonishing sight. I had a fortunate escape.

As the rocky mountain I have mentioned, is higher than either Snowden in North-Wales, or Kedar-Idris in Merionethshire, which have been thought the highest mountains in this island ; that is, it is full a mile and a half high from the basis, as I found by ascending it with great toil on the side that was from the water, and the top was a flat dry rock, that had not the least spring, or piece of water on it, how shall we account for the rapid flood that proceeded from its inside ? Where did this great water come from ? I answer, might it not flow from the great abyss, and the great encrease of it, and the fearful noise, and the motion of the rock, be owing to some violent commotion in the abyss, occasioned by some natural or supernatural cause ?

That there is such an abyss, no one can doubt that believes revelation, and from reason and history it is credible, that there are violent concussions on this vast collection of water, by the divine appointment : and therefore, I imagine it is from thence the water of this mountain proceeds, and the great overflowing and terrifying sound at certain times. To this motion of the abyss, by the divine power exerted on it, I ascribe the earthquakes ; and not to vapour, or electricity. As to electricity, which Dr. Stukely makes the cause of the deplorable downfall of Lisbon, in his book on *The Philosophy of Earthquakes ;* there are many things to be objected against its being the origin of such calamities ; one objection is, and it is an insuperable one, that electrical shocks are ever momentary, by every experiment, but earthquakes are felt for several minutes. Another is, that many towns have been swallowed up in earthquakes, though Lisbon was only overthrown. Such was the case of the city of Callao, within two leagues of Lima. Though Lima was only tumbled into ruins, October 28, 1746 ; yet Callao sunk downright with all its inhabitants, and an unfathomable sea now covers the finest port in Peru, as I have seen on the spot. In the earthquake at Jamaica, June 7, 1692, in which several thousands perished, it is certain, that not only many houses, and a great number of people, were entirely swallowed up ; but that, at many of the gapings or openings of the earth, torrents of water that formed great rivers, issued forth. This I had from a man of veracity then on the spot, who was an eye-witness of these things, and expected himself every minute to descend to the bowels of the earth, which heaved

and swelled like a rolling sea.   Now to me the electrical stroke
does not appear sufficient to produce these things.   The power
of electricity, to be sure is vast and amazing.   It may cause great
tremors and undulations of the earth, and bring down all the
buildings of a great city ; but as to splitting the earth to great
depths, and forcing up torrents of water, where there was no
sign of the fluid element before, I question much if the vehemence
of the elemental electric fire does this.   Beside, when mountains
and cities sink into the earth, and the deepest lakes are now seen
to fill all the place where they once stood, as has been the case in
many countries, where could these mighty waters come, but from
the abyss ?   The great lake Oroquantur in Pegu, was once a vast
city.   In Jamaica, there is a large deep lake where once a mountain stood.   In an earthquake in China, in the province of Sanci,
deluges of water burst out of the earth, Feb. 7, 1556, and inundated the country for 180 miles.   Many more instances of this
kind I might produce, exclusive of Sodom, the ground of which
was inundated by an irruption of waters from beneath, which
now forms the Dead Sea ; after the city was destroyed by fire
from above ; that the land which had been defiled with the unnatural lusts of the inhabitants might be no more inhabited, but
remain a lasting monument of the divine vengeance on such
crimes, to the end of the world ; and the use I would make of those
I have mentioned, is to show that these mighty waters were from
the furious concussion of the abyss that caused the earthquakes.
Electricity, I think, can never make seas and vast lakes to be
where there were none before.   Locherne, in the county of Ferma-
nagh, in the province of Ulster in Ireland, is thirty three miles
long, and fourteen broad, and as the old Irish *Chronicle* informs us, was once a place where large and populous towns
appeared, till for the great iniquity of the inhabitants, the
people and their fair habitations were destroyed in an earthquake,
and mighty waters from the earth covered the place, and formed
this lake.   Could the electrical stroke produce this sea that was
not to be found there before the destruction ?   Is it not more
reasonable to suppose, that such vast waters have been forced
by a supernatural commotion from the great abyss, in the earthquake that destroyed the towns which once stood in this place ?

   To this then, till I am better informed, I must ascribe such
earthquakes as produce great rivers and lakes ; and where no
waters appear, I believe the earthquakes are caused by the immediate finger of God ; either operating on the abyss, though not so
as to make the water break out on the earth or by directing the
electrical violence or stroke ; or otherwise acting on the ruined
cities and shattered places.

   For my part, I think it is a grievous mistake in our philosophical
enquiries, to assign so much to second causes as the learned do.

The government of the universe is given to matter and motion, and under pretence of extolling original contrivance, the execution of all is left to dead substance. It is just and reasonable, in which even Newton and M'Laurin agree, to suppose that the whole chain of causes, or the several series of them, should centre in him, as their source and fountain ; and the whole system appear depending upon him, the only independent cause. Now to me this supposition does not appear either just or reasonable. I think the noble phænomena of nature ought to be ascribed to the immediate operation of the Deity. Without looking for a subtile elastic medium, to produce gravity ; which medium Sir Isaac confesses he had no proof of ; nor is there in reality such a thing in the universe ; I imagine the divine Newton would have done better, if, after establishing the true system by nature, by demonstrating the law of gravity, he had said this gravity was the constant and undeniable evidence of the immediate influence of the Deity in the material universe. A series of material causes betwixt Deity and effect, is, in truth, concealing him from the knowledge of mortals for ever. In the moral government of the world, second causes do, because free-agents act a part ; but, in the material universe to apply them, to me seems improper, as matter and motion only, that is, mechanism, come in competition with the Deity. Most certainly he constantly interposes. The divine power is perpetually put forth throughout all nature. Every particle of matter, must necessarily, by its nature, for ever go wrong, without the continued act of Deity. His everlasting interposition only can cause a body moving in a circle to change the direction of its motion in every point. Nor is it possible for subtile matter, the supposed cause of gravity, to know to impel bodies to a centre, with quadruple force at half the distance.

And as in gravity, and in the cohesion of the parts of matter, the Deity is, and acts in the motion of the celestial bodies, and in the resistance the least particles make to any force that would separate them ; so is his immediate power, I think for myself, exerted not only in earthquakes and tides, but in the circulations of the blood, lymph, and chyle, in muscular motion, and in various other phaenomena that might be named. Books I know have been written, and ingenious books they are, to show the causes of these things, and trace the ways they are performed by the materials themselves ; but these explications never satisfied me. I had as many questions to ask, after reading these books, as I had before I looked into them, and could find no operator but infinite power, conducted by infinite wisdom.

As to the force of the moon, in raising tides, and, that spring tides are produced by the sum of the actions of the two luminaries, when the moon is in *Syzygy*, there is much fine mathematical reasoning to prove it, which the reader may find in Dr. Halley's abstract of Sir Isaac Newton's *Theory of the Tides ;* and in Dr. Rutherforth's *System of Natural Philosophy ;* but nevertheless, the concomitance of water and luminary, or the revolutions of ocean and moon answering one another so exactly that the flow always happens when the moon hangs over the ocean, and the spring tides when it is nearer the earth, which is supposed to be in the new and full moon ; this does not prove to me, that the periodical flux and reflux of the sea is derived from mechanism. As we have two ebbs and two flows in twenty-four hours, and the moon comes but once in that time to our meridian, how can the second ebb and flow be ascribed to it ? and when, beneath the horizon, in the opposite hemisphere, the moon crosses the meridian again, is it credible, that from the eastern and southern ocean, round Good Hope and Cape Horn, it should as soon overflow our coasts, as when it is vertical to the shores of Guinea ?

If the moon, in conjunction with the sun, by pression and attraction, was the princpal cause of flux and reflux, why is there no established tide on the Mediterranean sea, though of a vast breadth, and two thousand miles in length from the Streights of Gibraltar to the coasts of Syria and Palestine ; but only some irregular and unaccountable swellings and falls in a few places of this sea, to wit, at Tunis, Messina, Venice, and Negropont ; and these swellings, as I have seen, flowing sometimes four, five, six or seven, and eight times in twenty-four hours ; in the most irregular manner ; against the fixed laws of pression and attraction, ascribed to the moon and sun, on a supposition of their causing the tides ?   If pression, and the strong attractive power of the moon, and the weaker influence of the sun, forces the immense ocean twice a day from its natural quietus, and rolls it in tides, why has the Caspian sea no tide ; no swelling or flow, regular or irregular, excepting that sometimes, in the space of sixteen years, and never sooner, it rises many fathoms, and drowns the adjacent country ; to the almost ruin, sometimes of Astracan in Asiatic Russia ; as happened when I was there to embark for Persia ? If it be said, that this is properly a lake, having no communication with the ocean ; yet, I answer, that it is in every quality of saltness, &c. as much a sea as any other sea ; and large enough for the luminaries attraction and pression ; being five hundred miles from north to south, and near four hundred miles in bredth from east to west : I say, large enough to avoid continuing necessarily in equilibrium, as Dr. Rutherforth says must be the case, on account of the small extent of this sea.   Five hundred by four hundred miles of sea does not require that such a sea should press equally, or that the gravity of its water should be equally diminished in every part of it, and so out of the powers, addititious and ablatitious, of the luminary ; that is, the force, with which the moon encreases the waters gravity, and the force,

with which the moon diminishes the waters gravity. If the
moon in zenith or nadir did the work, the equilibrium of the
Caspian might be destroyed, as well as any other equilibrium
of water, by force, addititious or ablatitious, or by the sum of
these forces ; therefore, there might, by this theory, be tides in
the Caspian sea, though not great ones. There are small as well
as great tides. The tides of the Atlantic ocean are inferior in
every respect to those of the larger Pacific ocean. A quarter of a
great circle of the earth, that is, an extent of ocean from east to
west 90°, is only required, that the tides may have their full motion. A tide of less motion may be in such an extent of sea as
the Caspian.

In the last place, how does *the Theory of Tides* account for the
regular peculiarity of the flux and reflux of the Atlantic, different
from all other tides ; while at Bathsha in the kingdom of Tun-
quin there never is more than one tide in twenty-four hours ;
and some day no tide ? For my part, I resolve the whole in
the immediate power of the Deity. This power is gravity,
attraction, repulse. The inactivity of matter requires the constancy and universality of divine power to support the material
universe, and move it as occasion requires ; that is, as infinite
wisdom sees most conducive to the benefit of his creation.

Men of fine imagination may make a wonderful display of
mathematical learning in accounts of gravity, &c. combined with
principles of mechanism ; and electricity, which is called the
immediate officer of God Almighty ; but the truth is a constant repetition of divine acts in regular and irregular motions
of the earth and the seas. The finger of God moves the land
and the waters.

In the case of earthquakes, as electricity, or aerial power, is
insufficient to produce them in my opinion, for two reasons,
before given ; to wit, that the electrical stroke is ever single and
momentary, but the vibrations of the earth, in a quake, are often
three and four minutes, and have held to seven minutes, and that
besides the swelling and trembling of the earth, it has so opened
at those times, as to swallow not only houses and people, but
even mountains, and to send forth great rivers and vast waters.
And, as subterranean fire and vapour, I think, can never do such
work, for many reasons that may be offered, we must, I think,
ascribe the earthquakes to the immediate impression of divine
power ; by which a city is tumbled into ruins in three or four
minutes, in the sad manner Lisbon was destroyed the first of
November, 1755, or, the water of the great abyss is with such
violence moved, |that it shakes the arches of the earth, and
where infinite wisdom directs, is enabled by Almighty Power to
open the globe with tremendous noises, and pour forth vast
torrents of water, to cover a land where once a flourishing

city has stood. The electric stroke cannot be more dreadful
than such exertion of omnipotence. The immediate action
of the Deity, to destroy, must be as efficacious surely
as any subordinate agent or cause : and it must be more
terrible to the mind, as there can be no supposition of accident
in ruin this way : but we see as it were the almighty arm, exerting
an irresistible force, that could in the same few moments that a
large town and its inhabitants are destroyed, shake the whole
world into one dreadful ruin, or separate it into nothing. To
my apprehension, the aerial power of electricity is not so fearfully striking, as the Creator's appearing, on the spot, to shake
terribly the earth : and if we consider, that it is on account of
sin, that God resigns his omnipotence to his wrath, and commands his whole displeasure to arise, must not this account of an
earthquake have the greatest tendency to reform the manners
of surviving people ?

As to the muscular motion, if it be rightly considered, it appears very plainly to proceed from a living force, impressed ab
extra ; that mechanism does not act as cause in this affair ; but
the divine power acts in the case, as it does in many different
places of the human body at once, and with inexpressible
variety.

Various are the accounts that learned men have given of
muscular motion, and ingenious are their reasonings on the subject : but they are not satisfactory, nor do they at all explain
the thing, and account for it. What is a muscle ?

It is to be sure a bundle of small blood vessels, consisting of
arteries and their returning veins, laid one upon another in their
parallel plates, running through the whole length of the muscle ;
and at small intervals, these blood vessels, or longitudinal red
and fleshy fibres, are contorted and bound about with small
transverse, and spiral ramifications and twinings of the nerves.
This is a muscle : it has two ends, or tendons, fastened to two
bones, one of which is fixed, and the other moveable ; and by the
contraction of the muscle, the moveable bone is drawn upon its
fulcrum towards a fixed point. This is indisputable ; and it is
likewise certain, that the muscles are to be distinguished into
those of voluntary, and those of natural or necessary motion :
that the voluntary muscles have antagonists, which act alter-
nately in a contrary direction, that is are contracted by the
command of the will, while the others are stretched, and again
are extended, while the others contracted : but the necessary
muscles have contracting and extending powers within themselves,
and need no antagonists.

This being the true state of the muscles, the question is, what
causes that elasticity, spring, or power of contraction and restoration, which their nervous coats and fibres have, to recover them

selves against a given weight or force that stretches them ? The reply is, that many unanswerable reasons can be given to prove, that this contractive restitutive force does not depend on the mixture effervescence, or rarefaction of any fluids, humours, or liquors within the body ; and there is one convincing experiment that shews it.

Lay open the thorax of a dog, as I have often done ; and take a distinct view of that famous muscle, the heart, in its curious and wonderful motion, while the animal is still alive. In diastole, the muscle is very red and florid, soft and yielding to the touch, and through it the vital fluid glows and shines ; it appears in this state fully replenished and distended with blood ; but in systole, as soon as it begins to contract, and the blood rushes out by the compression of the contracting fibres, the heart loses its florid colour, and becomes pale and livid, compact and solid, and evinces that, during this state of it, the muscle contracts inwardly into its own dense substance, and takes up less space than before, till it returns to its diastole ; then the blood which flowed from it with velocity, during systole through the coronary veins into the auricles, rushes back into it through the coronary arteries, restores the glowing florid colour, and inflates the muscle, in order to strain the nerve for the next contraction. It is plain from hence, that the heart has less blood and fluid in time of contraction, and that the contraction is not caused by the addition of another fluid from the nerves, as the learned have asserted.

And as to what they say of the longitudinal fibres being divided into innumerable little cells or bladders, which have communications with the blood vessels and nerves, and that in these vesicles, the blood and nervous fluid mix, ferment, and by rarefaction and expansion, swell and blow up the cells, and thereby inflate and distend the muscle, and increase its thickness, while its length is shortened ; this is so perplexed and unreasonable an hypothesis, that I am astonished how men of sense ever came to think of such a doctrine. There is no such nervous fluid to be found, to cause this fermentation, rarefaction, &c. ; and if there was, expansive force must lengthen as well as thicken, and the muscle could not be shortened in length, and swelled in thickness. The natural action of the fluids upon the solids is, to increase dimensions proportionably every way, that is, in the direction of the axis and conjugate diameter equally. Beside, if there was expansion, circulation must stop. The distention of the vesicles, and the rapid exit of the rarefying fluid could not be at once.

The plain account of the matter is then, that muscular motion is performed by the elasticity of the nervous fibrillæ, contracting and restoring themselves against the stretching force of the

circulating blood.   The contraction of the muscles straitens and
compresses the blood-vessels, and forces the blood with impetuosity through the heart ; and this squeezing or propelling force
gives the fluid an impetus, that makes it return with violence
upon the muscles, in the course of its circulation ; then by force
and impulse, it stretches the transverse and spiral nervous fibres,
and so extends the contracted muscle, that drove it by contraction from itself.   Upon this the blood-vessels having obtained
their due extent and capacity, the distending force of the blood
of consequences ceases : but the moment it does, the contractive
power of the nerves begins to act again, and restores them to a
contracted dense state, by a force exactly equal to that which
extended them ; till the returning propelled blood re-enters the
muscle, and stretches it again, as before described.   Such are
the two wonderful counter-forces that produce the natural involuntary motion of the heart, and carry on the circulation of
the blood.   You see with your eyes, in the opened live dog this
alternate contraction and extension ; and as the stretching
power is but a consequence of the contracting power, contraction
is the spring of this wonderful action, in which our will or free
agency has no concern.   And to what shall we ascribe this astonishing operation, this amazing contractive power, so exactly as to
time, and so constantly continued on the muscles of natural or
necessary motion ; till the æquilibrium by some means or other
be broken and the motion is preternaturally interrupted and
suspended ? Will the great mechanical reasoners say, that
matter does this wonder—matter, that is blind and impotent ?
Stuff : we must ascribe to a cause wise and powerful, not only the
original contrivance of the thing, but the execution of this extraordinary scene.   While you gaze upon this noblest muscle
of the dog, you see the Deity at work.

And if we turn our eyes from the muscles of mere natural
involuntary motion, which performs by a contracting power
acting within them ; to those muscles which move the bones
and members of our bodies, by the command of the will, how
adorable is the wisdom and goodness of the Almighty Author
of nature, not only in providing the animal machine with antag-
onistical muscles, one of which is contracted, while the other is
extended ; but for stimulating, contracting, and compressing the
nervous elastic cords and blood-vessels, as our minds command
or determine ! there is no possibility of accounting for the directions at pleasure of the antagonistic muscles, but by resolving
them into the continual presence and action of the first cause.
He enforces and executes.   It is the active principle gives energy
and motion both to voluntary and necessary muscles.   This, I
think, is the truth of philosophy.   To suppose every thing to be
effect without cause, is to reduce religion and philosophy to the

same desperate state. It destroys all the principles of reason, as well as of virtue and moral conduct.

To say all that can be said, in as few words as possible, upon this article, it is not only the muscular motion, necessary and spontaneous,* that is caused by the action of the Deity ; but the constant motions in the stomach, lungs, intestines, and other parts of the body, are caused by an acting Divine Power. It can be demonstrated, that in the action of soft bodies upon soft bodies, the motion is always diminished ; and of consequence it must be greatly lessened in the yielding softness of the flesh and fluids of animal bodies. We see how soon water settles, after motion imprest, by the bare attrition of its parts on one another ; although it has no obstacles to encounter, or narrow passages to move through. What then can we think of motion in such narrow twining meanders, as veins, arteries, intestines, and lacteal vessels, through which the fluids of animal bodies are conveyed to parts innumerable ? while the blood, lymph, and chyle creep through such narrow winding vessels, the whole motion of those fluids must be consumed every instant by the attrition of their parts, and the force of consequence be renewed every instant. Here is a perpetual miracle. The Divine Power urges on these fluids ten thousand ways at once. Reason must confess a miraculous power indesinently and variously put forth in our bodies ; while ignorance and vanity in vain attempts to account mechanically for the circulation of those fluids. We are not only fearfully and wonderfully formed in the womb, but fearfully and wonderfully preserved every minute ! creating power never ceases.†

The conclusion of the matter is, that the plain argument for the

---

* That even spontaneous motion is performed by the divine power, is proved in the first part of a most excellent book, entitled, *An Enquiry into the Nature of the Human Soul*, [by John Baxter, the third and best edition was printed in two volumes, 8vo, in 1745 ; a third followed in 1750]. I shall only observe here that motion is spontaneous, as it is begun and ended by the living being itself, without physical necessity : but it is above the power and knowledge of the spontaneous being, as it is performed mechanically : the motive power is immediately impressed by the Creator, who is the only mover, as well as the first mover. How adorable is this condescension ! the Creator exerts his power in consequence of the spontaneity of his living creatures ! But is not this low work for the supreme Lord of heaven and earth, says the mechanical reasoner ? No. Lowness of work is not applicable to the Creator of all things. He is as much the Creator of the meanest insect, as of the highest intelligence. It is his perpetual power, exerted in cohesion, that keeps all the parts of matter in the bodies of living creatures together. Philosophy cannot be hurt by admitting his power His omnipotence is displayed to our senses in the most despicable weed of the field as well as in the bright rolling orbs of heaven. In calling such things low work, we forget what infinite power implies, and what infinite goodness prompts.

† Should it be asked, why was such an intricate structure of such materials employed, or such a laborious method contrived, by the organization of dead matter, if it no way serves to produce motion, but rather consumes the force impressed ? the answer is, that this consuming mechanism is no inconvenience in nature, if we consider who renews the motive power. We are forced to be frugal of our little power : but this is not applicable to the Deity. The governing power of the Deity is creating power. Beings made up of matter and spirit require such a supplying power, and in the various work God instructs his rational beings, and displays his omnipotence in wisdom and action.

existence of a Deity, obvious to all, and carrying irresistible conviction with it, is from the evident contrivance and fitness of
things to one another, which we meet with through all the parts
of the universe.   There is no need of nice and subtile reasoning
in this matter ; a manifest contrivance immediately suggests a
contriver.   It strikes like a sensation and artful reasonings
against it may puzzle us, but it is without shaking our belief.   No
person, for example, who knows the principles of optics, and the
structure of the eye, can believe that it is formed without skill in
that science ; or that the ear was formed without the knowledge
of sounds.   This is a just argument, and forces our assent.   But
the great M'Laurin should not have stop'd here.   The plain
argument for the existence of a Deity grows stronger, when we
add to it what is evident as divine contrivance, to wit, the constant
interposition of God, to support and move his creatures.   Original
contrivance in the works of the creation is adorable.   We are
certain, demonstratively certain, that the heavens, the land, and
the waters, and all the creatures in them contained, are the works
of the living God ; but it is the present performance that strikes
us like a sensation.   With inexpressible pleasure we see creating
power with our eyes.   Which ever way we turn them, we behold
Almighty Power employed, and continually acting under the
direction of infinite knowledge.

Since things are so, and all the works of nature, in the common
voice of reason, declare the power and wisdom of the Creator, and
speak his goodness in the innumerable mighty things he continually performs for our preservation and happiness, the contemplation of them should warm our hearts with the glory of the
Almighty, and make us continually praise and adore that Almighty
providence, which formed and sustains not only the human race
and this terrestrial globe, but numberless other worlds and their
inhabitants, that hang in infinite space.   These mighty things
displayed, ought surely to produce the most devout prayers, and
songs of praises in no common strain ; and especially, if we add
to those works of nature, that second creation, the still greater
work of grace.   Such omnipotence in wisdom and action, and such
amazing goodness as we see in the christian gospel, should,
I think, engage us to love and adore so great and good a
Being as our Creator, and induce us to devote our lives to
him.

For my part, when I consider the mighty scene and prospect
of nature, and turn my thoughts from thence to God's word, that
heavenly law, which directs our will and informs our reason and
teaches us in all things how to pursue our own happiness, I am so
struck with a sense of infinite wisdom, goodness, and action, that
I cannot help extolling the king of the universe for the greatness
of his power and mercy, and am necessarily engaged in a scene

of praise and devotion. Indeed the heart must be as hard and cold as marble, that does not glow, nor is inflamed with adoration to the great author of all things ; after viewing with attention even one particular only in the works of nature, that material sun, which now shines out with light and beauty to animate and refresh the world ; and in the creation of grace, that sun of righteousness, who sheds forth the choicest blessings of Heaven upon the inhabitants of the earth. Can we be silent, who behold and enjoy those things ! alas l too many can. Neither the heavens, which declare the glory of God, nor the days of the gospel, nor the righteousness of the new law are regarded by them. But the wise will ever join with all their hearts, in the most exalted prayer and praise, and adore the giver of those good and perfect gifts ; for all his blessings vouchsafed us ; and especially, for the charter of his pardon granted by his blessed Son, and the promises of everlasting happiness and glory in a life to come, reason must declare it just to offer up religious praise, and make the greatest mental and moral improvement we can in this first state.

Another extraordinary thing I saw in the place I have mentioned, was a water on the top of a hill, which stood at the other end of the lake, and was full as high as the mountain, from the side of which the water poured into the lake. This loch measured three quarters of a mile in length, and half a mile over. The water appeared as black as ink, but in a glass it was clear as other water, and bright in running down. It tasted sweet and good. At one end, it runs over its rocky bank, and in several noisy cascades, falls down the face of the mountain to a deep bottom, where a river is formed, that is seen for a considerable way, as it wanders along. The whole is a striking scene. The swarthy loch, the noisy descending streams, clumps of aged trees on the mountain's side, and the various shores and vallies below, afford an uncommon view. It was a fine change of ground, to ascend from the beautiful lake, encompassed with mountains, and adorned with trees, into which was poured from a gaping precipice, a torrent of streams ; and see from the reverse of an opposite hill, an impetuous flood descending from the top to the finest points of view in the wildest glens below.

What line I had with me, for experiments on waters and holes, I applied to this loch, to discover the depth, but with three hundred yards of whipcord my lead could reach no ground, and from thence, and the blackness of the water, and the great issuing stream, I concluded, justly I think, that it went down to the great abyss, the vast treasury of waters within the earth. Many such unfathomable lochs as this have I seen on the summits of mountains in various parts of the world, and from them, I suppose, the greatest part of that deluge of waters came that drowned the old world. This leads me to say something of the flood.

Many books have been written in relation to this affair, and while some contend for the overflowing of the whole earth to a very great height of waters, and some for a partial deluge only, others will not allow there was any at all. The divine authority of Moses they disregard. For my part I believe the flood was universal, and that all the high hills and mountains under the whole heaven, were covered. The cause was forty days heavy rain, and such an agitation of the abyss, by the finger of God, as not only broke up the great deep, to pour out water at many places, but forced it out of such bottomless lochs as this I am speaking of on the mountain's top, and from various swallows in many places. This removes every objection from the case of the deluge, and gives water enough in the space of one hundred and fifty days, or five months of thirty days each, to over-top the highest mountains by fifteen cubits, the height designed. The abyss in strong commotion, or violent uproar, by a power divine, could shake the incumbent globe to pieces in a few minutes, and bury the whole ruins in the deep. To me, then, all the reasoning against the deluge, or for a partial flood appear sad stuff. Were this one loch in Stanemore to pour out torrents of water, down every side, for five months, by a divine force on part of the abyss, as it might very easily, by such means do, the inundation would cover a great part of this land ; and if from every loch of the kind on the summits of mountains, the waters in like manner, with the greatest violence, flowed from every side out of the abyss, and that exclusive of the heavy rains, an earthquake should open some parts of the ground to let more water out of the great collection, and the seas and oceans surpass their natural bounds, by the winds forcing them over the earth, then would a universal flood very soon prevail. There is water enough for the purpose, and as to the supernatural ascent of them, natural and supernatural are nothing at all different with respect to God. They are distinctions merely in our conceptions of things. Regularly to move the sun or earth ; and to stop its motion for a day ; to make the waters that covered the whole earth at the creation, descend into the several receptacles prepared for them ; and at the deluge to make them ascend again to cover the whole earth, are the effect of one and the same almighty Power ; though we call one natural, and the other supernatural. The one is the effect of no greater power than the other. With respect to God, one is not more or less natural or supernatural than the other.

But how the waters of the deluge were drawn off at the end of the five months, is another question among the learned. The ingenious Keill, who wrote against the two ingenious theorists says the thing is not at all accountable in any natural way ; the draining off, and drying of the earth, of such a huge column of waters could only be effected by the power of God : natural causes both in decrease and the increase of the waters must have been vastly disproportionate to the effects ; and to miracles they must be ascribed. This, I think, is as far from the truth, as the theorists ascribing both increase and decrease to natural causes. God was the performer to be sure in the flood and the going off, but he made use of natural causes in both, that is, of the things he had in the beginning created. The natural causes he is the author of were at hand, and with them he could do the work. The sun evaporated ; the winds dried ; and the waters no longer forced upwards from the abyss, subsided into the many swallows or swallow-holes, that are still to be seen in many places, on mountains and in vallies ; those on the mountains being necessary to absorb that vast column of waters which rose fifteen cubits above the highest hills.

A swallow is such another opening in the ground as Eldine Hole in Derbyshire,* and in travelling from the Peak to the northern extremity of Northumberland, I have seen many such holes in the earth, both on the hills and in the vales. I have likewise met with them in other countries. By these swallows, a vast quantity of the waters to be sure went down to the great receptacle ; all that was not exhaled, or licked up by the winds ; or, except what might be left to increase the former seas of the antediluvian world into those vast oceans which now encompass the globe, and partly to form those vast lakes that are in several parts of the world. These things easily account for the removal of that vast mass of waters which covered the earth, and was in a mighty column above the highest hills. Every difficulty disappears before evaporation, the drying winds, the swallows, and perhaps the turning seas into oceans ; but the three first things now named were sufficient, and the gentlemen who have reasoned so ingeniously against one another about the removal of the waters, might have saved themselves a deal of trouble, if they had reduced the operation to three simple things, under the direction of the first cause. The swallows especially must do great work in the case, if we take into their number not only very many open gulphs or chasms, the depth of which no line or sound can reach ; but likewise the communications of very many parts of the sea, and of many great unfathomable lochs, with the abyss. These absorbers could easily receive what had before come out of them. The sun

* *Eldine-Hole* in *Derbyshire* is a mile south of *Mamtorr*, and four miles east of *Buxton*. It is a perpendicular gulph or chasm, which I tried to fathom more than once, and sound it by my line, and by the measure of sound at the rate of sixteen feet one twelfth in one second, the measure Dr. *Halley* allows near the earth for the descent of heavy bodies ; to be one thousand two hundred and sixty-six feet, or four hundred and twenty-two yards down to the water ; but how deep the water is cannot be known. I suppose it reaches to the abyss. This chasm is forty yards long above ground, and ten over at its broadest part : but from the day there is a sloping descent of forty yards to the mouth of the horrible pit, and this is only four yards long and one and a half broad. Two villains who were executed at *Derby* not long ago, confessed at the gallows, that they threw a poor traveller into this dreadful gulph, after they had robbed him.

by evaporation, with the wind, might take away what was raised. There is nothing hard then in conceiving how the waters of the deluge were brought away.

But as to the lake I have mentioned, into which a rapid flood poured from the bowels of the mountain, what became of this water the reader may enquire.   To be sure, as it did not run off in any streams, nor make the lake rise in the least degree, there must have been a communication in some parts of its bottom, between the water of it and the abyss.   As the loch on the top of the mountain I have described had no feeders, yet emitted streams, and therefore must be supported by the abyss ; so this lake, with so powerful a feeder, not running over, or emitting water any way, must discharge itself in the abyss below.   The case of it must be the same as that of the Caspian Sea.   In to this sea many rivers pour, and one in particular, the Volga I mean, that is more than sufficient, in the quantity of water it turns out in a year, to drown the whole world.   Yet the Caspian remains in one state, and does not overflow its banks, excepting, as before observed, sometimes in the space of sixteen years.   It must by passages communicate with the great deep.   It refunds the rivers into the great abyss.   The case of the Mediterranean sea is the same ; for, though a strong current from the Atlantic continually sets through the Strait of Gibraltar, yet these waters do not make it overflow the country round it, and, of consequence, they must be carried off by a subterranean passage, or passages, to the abyss.

From the lake I proceeded the next morning, June 14, 1725, toward the north-east end of Westmoreland, having passed the night in a sound sleep under the trees by the water-side, but was forced by the precipices to shape my course from four in the morning till eight, to the north-west, and then the road turned east-north-east, till I came to a great glen, where a river made a rumbling noise over rocks and inequalities of many kinds, and formed a very wild, wonderful scene.   The river was broad and deep, and on an easy descent to it, was an assemblage of stones, that ran in length about a hundred feet, in breadth thirty feet, and somewhat resembling the Giant's Causeway, in the county of Antrim, and province of Ulster, in Ireland ; nine miles north-east from the pretty town of Colerain.   The Giant's Causeway, reader, is a prodigious pile of rocks, eighty feet broad, twenty feet above the rest of the strand, and that run from the bottom of a high hill above two hundred yards into the ocean.

The assemblage of stones I am speaking of are columns with several corners, that rise three yards above the ground and are joined as if done by art ; the points being convex and concave, and thereby lying one in another.   These columns have five and six sides, a few of them seven ; and a number of them nicely and exactly placed together make one large pillar from one foot to two in diameter. They are so nicely joined, that although they have five and six sides, as I before said, yet their contexture is so adapted, as to leave no vacuity between them ; the prominent angles of one pillar fitting, and falling exactly into the hollows left them between two others, and the plain sides exactly answer to one another ; so that those hexagons and pentagons of columnar marble appear as if finished by the hands of the most masterly workmen. All the pillars stood exactly perpendicular to the plane of the horizon.

Doctor Foley, in No. 212, of the *Philosophical Transactions*, speaking of the Giant's Causeway, seems to think these wonderful pillars are composed of the common sort of craggy rock by the sea side ; and the authors of the *Complete System of Geography* are of opinion, they resemble the lapis basaltes ; but some think they are a sort of marble. Now the truth is, the basaltes of the antients is a very elegant and beautiful marble of a fine deep glossy black, like high polished steel, and is always found erect in the form of regular angular columns, composed of a number of joints, fitted together, and making pillars ; so that where such pillars are seen, they are undoubtedly the columnar marble, or touch-stone of the antients. Dr. John Hill, in his *History of Fossils*, gives a good account of the nature of this body, and mentions several places it is to be found in ; but seems not to have heard there was any of it among the northern mountains of our country.

This marble is one of the noblest productions of nature, and of all the fossil kingdom, the most astonishing body. If art is requisite for the formation of many things we see daily done with elegance and beauty ; then certainly, mind itself, even the supreme mind, must have caused such effects as these astonishing marble pillars ; which lie in vast compound perpendicular columns at great depths in the earth, none being in beds of strata, like the other marbles ; and rise in such beautiful joints and angles, well fitted together, more than six and thirty feet above ground in some places. No other way could those wonderful productions have come into being, but by that intelligent, active power, who speaks intelligibly to every nation by his works. To talk as some people do, that necessity, which destroys the very idea of intelligent and designing activity, or chance—which is an utter absurdity—or the sea, according to Telliamed, generated and formed this genus of marble, and so wonderfully distinguished it from all the other marmora ; by making it into pentagon, hexagon and septagon columns, and rendering the points of the columns convex and concave, and so amazingly joining them together, that the prominent angles of one pillar fall exactly into the hollow left between two others, and the plain sides exactly answer to one another, as before observed, while all of them stand up perpendicular, contrary to the quality of all other marbles, and some lie in beds of strata. To talk I say of the sea, a chance, a necessity, doing this, or any thing of so wonderful a kind is to produce schemes founded in ignorance, and eversive of true knowledge, instead of giving a rational, intelligible account of the formation of the world, its order and appearances. In this wonderful production, a due attention perceives infinite art and power. Did we want that variety of things which employ the consideration of rational men, and force the tongues of thinking men to acknowledge creating power, this marble alone would be sufficient to demonstrate equal power directed by infinite wisdom.

Another extraordinary thing I saw in a valley not far from that where the basaltes stands, is a boisterous burning spring. It rises with great noise and vibration, and gushes out with a force sufficient to turn many mills. The water is clear and cold, but to the taste unpleasant, being something like a bad egg. I judged from the nature of its motion that the water would take fire, and having lit my torch, soon put it in a flame. The fire was fierce, and the water ran down the vale in a blaze. It was a river of fire for a considerable way, till it sunk under ground among some rocks, and thereby disappeared. After it had burned some time, I took some boughs from a tree, and tying them together, beat the surface of the well for a few minutes, and the burning ceased. The water was not hot, as one might expect, but cold as the coldest spring could be. There are a great number of such springs in the world, but this is the largest I have read of, or seen. It differs from that of Broseley in Shropshire, within six miles of Bridge-north, in this respect, that Broseley-well will not continue to burn for any time, unless the air be kept from it ; to which purpose they have enclosed it in an iron cistern with a cover to it ; and to experiment the boiling a piece of meat by the fire of this spring, they clap the pot close down when the cover is taken up, and then it burns as long as they will ; making the largest joint of meat fit to eat in half the time the strongest culinary fire could do the work. As to the medicinal virtues of the spring, in the mountains, I can only say, that as it has a copious sulphur, and from thence flames like a spirit of wine, it is probable it might be as effectual in communicating sanity in various cases, as the famous burning spring is in the palatinate of Cracow of the lesser Poland mentioned in the *Leipsic Acts*, for 1684, p. 326. And as to the extinguishing this fire by beating it with twigs, it must be for the reason given by Mr. Denis, that as the inflammability of such springs is to be ascribed to sulphur, and to its exhalations bursting out of the water ; so this floating flame, which is too subtle to heat the water, is stifled, by involving these spirits in the aqueous particles, by brushing the surface with brooms.

Conradus tells us, concerning the Polish spring, that at one time, when it was kindled by lightning, the people neglected to put it out and the stream proceeded on fire for almost three years, and reduced all the neighbouring wood to ashes. It is really a wonderful sight to see such a river of fire, and adorable must be that power, who has caused such things. To say that matter and motion circumscribe and regulate such powers, is idle to the last degree. It is an inversion of reason. The very existence of the water and sulphur of this spring, must be by the power of the Creator constantly put forth upon it, which causes the parts to be what we call such things ; and the motion of both must be an impression ; for motion is not essential to matter. Nothing else could produce them, and a cause there must be equal to the various and wonderful effects of both, a cause that is infinity, wise and powerful. The Deity is every where present, and every where active. His power is indesinently working, gives existence to the various creatures and produces the most noble phænomena in nature. All we see, all we feel, fire and water, the universal variety of inanimate and animate creatures, are only the effects of his creating power constantly repeated. The existence of the whole world is a continual new creation ; and therefore it becomes the bounden duty of all rational creatures, to worship this Almighty Power, as well for his works of creation, as for the ways of his providence. Great and wonderful are thy works, O Lord God Almighty ! and just and righteous are thy ways, O King of saints : who would not fear thee, O Lord, and glorify thy name, because thou art holy.

From the burning fountain we proceeded for half an hour in the same valley right onwards, and then turned to the left in a course to the west, for about a mile, which brought us to the bottom of a steep mountain, we must ascend, or go no farther. It was hard to get the horses over this, and no less difficult to descend with them to a deep bottom on the other side of the hill : but with great hazard to ourselves and the beasts, we came down in safety. On the top of this mountain I saw another large loch that was black as ink in appearance, though bright when taken up in a glass ; which as before observed, must be owing I suppose to its top communicating with the abyss below ; and in the bottom we descend to, there was a swallow larger than the one I saw before. I could make no discovery as to its depth, either by line or sound ; nor did my lead touch any water. On the sloping way from the first chasm in day to the gulph, were several lateral chambers, that descended one yard in six ; but though the bottom was hard, the horrors of the places hindered me from going far. I went to the end of the first, which was sixty seven yards, and having looked into the second, to which a narrow short pass leads enquirer, I made what haste I could back ; for the opening discovers a space so vast, dismal, and frightful, that it strike one to the heart. The bottom, as far as my light could enable me to distinguish, was a continuance of stone ; but neither top nor sides were to be seen. It is a horrible place.

Leaving this bottom, we mounted another very high and dangerous hill, and from the top of it descended into twenty acres of as rich and beautiful ground as my eyes had ever seen. It was covered with flowers and aromatic herbs ; and had, in the centre of it, a little grove of beautiful trees ; among which were fruits of several kinds. A flowing spring of the purest water was in the middle of this sweet little wood, and ran in pretty windings over the ground. It refreshed and adorned the field, and it was beautiful to see the deer from the hills, and the goats come down from the cliffs, to drink at these streams. The whole was surrounded with precipices that ascended above the clouds, and through one of these rocky mountains there was an opening that had a stupendous appearance.

It was a vast amazing arch, that had some resemblance of the Gothic aisle of a large cathedral church, and terminated in a view of rocks hanging over rocks in a manner frightful to behold. It measured an hundred yards in length, forty in breadth, and I judged it to be fifty yards high. The pending rocks in view inclosed a space of four acres, as it appeared to me, and the bottom was so very deep that it looked like night below. What line I had could not reach it, nor could I make any thing of the depth by sound. It seemed to me to be a vast swallow that went down to the abyss. The whole was a scene that harrowed the soul with horror.

By the spring in the little grove I have mentioned, I sat down at eight in the morning, to breakfast on something that one of my squires produced from his store, while the other was looking for a passage or way onwards, between those vast precipices that surrounded us. Two hours he wasted in an enquiry, and then returned, to let me know there was no passage that he could find : the enclosed rocks were one continued chain of impassable mountains. Here then I thought was my *ne plus ultra*. As the man affirmed there was no getting beyond the vast inclosing cliffs that walled in this charming spot of earth, I imagined for some time, that I must of necessity return, and give over all thoughts of getting to the borders of Cumberland or Bishopric that way. It seemed impossible to proceed, and that was no small trouble to my mind. It was a great journey round, and if I did ride it, I knew not where to turn in on the confines of the country my friend lived on ; for I had lost his directions, and had only a small remembrance of his dwelling somewhere on the north edge of Westmoreland or Yorkshire, or on the adjoining borders of Cumberland, or the county of Durham. What to do I could not for some time tell : going back I did not at all like, and therefore, to avoid it if possible, resolved to pass the day in trying if I could find my way out, without climbing the mountain again that I had lately come down. Round then I walked, once, and to no manner of purpose, for I did not see any kind of pass ; but the second time, as I marched on observing the hill, I took notice of a large clump of great trees in an angle or deep corner, that seemed to stand very oddly, and in the mountain above them there appeared as I thought a distance or space that looked like an opening. I soon found it was so, and that at the back of this little wood, there lay a very narrow way, only broad enough for two horses a-breast : that it extended due west for more than a mile, and then west north west for a quarter of a mile, till it terminated in a plain that was several miles in circumference, and intirely surrounded with hills. This I discovered in walking the pass by myself, and then returned to bring the horses and men, through this amazing way. It was quite dark, mere night all along ; and the bottom very bad. It was likewise very dangerous. It was evident from the ground that stones had fallen from the tops of the hills ; and should any descend from so vast a height on us, though even small ones, they would without all peradventure be immediate death.

The plain we came into from the defile, was above a mile over to the opposite hills, and across it was a walk of aged oaks, that seemed, in such a place, as the avenue that leads to the fairy castle of wishes. If there are such things, as Dr. Fowler, bishop of Gloucester, bath in one of his books affirmed, then here, I said, in this fine romantic region, where all the charms of the field, the forest, the water, and the mountains, are united, may be their favourite mansion, and perhaps they will admit me into their fairy castle, then commences their friendship, and when they have all breathed on me, it is but wishing for the future, and the completion of every desire is granted the moment it is formed. Would not this be complete happiness ? what do you say, Reflection ?

" No ! " answered Reflection, as we rode up this avenue " Imagination may form fine pictures of felicity from an indulgence in every wish ; but, so blind are mankind to their own real happiness, that it is oftener to the gratification than to the disappointment of their wishes that all their misery is owing. We often choose what is not consonant to the welfare of our nature, and strive to avoid these incidents which are fated in the order of incontrollable events for our good. Frequently do we labour to secure the things that debase us into slaves, and overwhelm us with calamity ; but seldom do we desire, rarely do we strive to obtain those objects, and acquire that station, which are most likely to render humanity as perfect as it can be in this world, rational and godlike, and thereby crown our lives with true happiness. Many a man has pursued a Venus, an estate, an honour with much toil and wonderful activity, and when possessed of the fancied blessing, have been made very miserable mortals. The wished-for beauty has often made even the husband wretched. An aching scar is often covered with the laurel : and in respect of envied great fortunes, gaudy is the thing without, and within very often is mere bitterness. The wisdom is as to this world, not to get from the fairies a power of enjoying all that fancy may desire, if that was possible ; but, to act well and wisely, in the most reasonable, lovely, and fair manner, and propose nothing of ourselves, but with a reserve that supreme wisdom permits it ; welcoming every event with cheerfulness and magnanimity, as best upon the whole, because ordained of infinite reason ; and acquiescing in every obstruction, as ultimately reservable to divine providence. This," continued Reflection, " in respect of this life, were there no other, is preferable to the castle of wishes, if we could find it at the end of this avenue*."

But if another life is taken into the question, the argument grows stronger against a power of enjoying all we could wish for, as we are accountable creatures, and are pouring fast out of time into eternity, religion undoubtedly ought to be the main business of mortals ; that religion which is a living principle, spring or root of actions in the soul ; wrought there by the hand of him that made us ; and which requireth us to honour and fear God, as the supreme Lord, to esteem him as the chief good ; and to exercise and express that honour, that fear, and that esteem, by all the means, and in all the ways which reason and revelation appoint for such exercise and expression ; that we may gain the love of the Almighty, and obtain the established seat of happiness above : but such force hath the objects of sense upon the mind, that it is more than probable they would outweigh the distant hopes of religion, if wishing could bring in even a tenth part of of what the vanity of man, and his senses would call for. It would be so far from being an advantage to mankind, if they could wish and have vast fortunes, all the pleasures and pomps and honours of the world, that they would thereby be deprived of the rational joys of life, and be influenced to think no more of the excellency and beauty of religion, and the good consequences of serving God truly. They would not even divide themselves between this world and the other. The idol gods of this state would have all their service. The wish then should be for daily

* In the second volume of *Familiar Letters between the Characters in David Simple,* the reader will find an excellent story in relation to *wishing,* which the ingenious female writer calls ' a Fragment of a Fairy Tale,' in the conclusion of which there is the following sensible observation : " The good *Fairy* came often to visit me, and confirmed me in my resolution, never again to be so unreasonable, as to desire to have all my wishes completed ; for she convinced me, that the short-sighted eyes of mortals were not formed to see, whether the event of any of their own wishes would produce most happiness or misery : and that our greatest felicity, often arises from the very disappointment of those desires, the gratification of which, at the first view, seems to be necessary to our welfare."—*Familiar Letters, ut supra* 1747, 8vo. vol. ii. p. 225. 272.

bread and of the kingdom of God may come, his will be done in our souls. In these are comprised the greatest and most valuable blessing, and we are sure we can obtain them, if we will add to asking an industry and prudence in acquiring, and take care by culture, to bring up the seeds of virtue and holiness. This is enough to make us as happy here as reason can desire. We have a sufficiency to go through this world to that other where we are to be stationed for ever, and against the accidents of the way, we have the supports which innocence and virtue to the good administer. Peace and tranquillity of mind here, and hopes full of comfort with respect to hereafter, are the ingredients of our happiness ; a happiness the greatest ! and we are certain that he upon whose mercy and goodness we confess we exist, will, in regard to our confidence and trust, our faith and religion, when this fleeting scene is over, make us glorious and ever blessed in the kingdom he has prepared for those that rely on the Divine Goodness, and do their best to advance the state of true virtue in the world. Let us not regret, then, the want of a Castle of Wishes. Let us not have a desire of that wealth, dominion, and splendour, which lives in contempt of the prophets, and riots in the heinous pleasures of irreligion.

Let our great Master's Will be made the rule of all our actions, and let his interest be regarded, as our interest. Let us consult his honour, as our own honour ; and having food and raiment, be content, as we are hastening away with a never ceasing pace, to the realms of eternity and unmixed bliss. This is reason and light. This only deserves our care. There is nothing worth wishing for, but the happiness of God's presence in our hearts ; and the more immediate communications of his love and favour in the regions of day.

Thus did Reflection entertain me, as I rode up this grand shady walk, which looked like the avenue I had read of in the *Tales of the Fairies*, and brought me to a natural grotto, more beautiful than Ælian's description of Atalanta's, or that in Homer, where Calypso lived. It was a large cavern at the bottom of a marble mountain, and without, was covered round with ivy, that clung about some aged oaks, on either side of the entrance, that seemed coeval with the earth on which they grew. Abundance of large laurel trees, in clumps, adorned an extensive area before the door ; and saffron, and hyacinths, and flowers of many colours, covered in confused spots the green carpet. The beautiful ground refreshed the sight, and purified the air ; and to enhance the beauties of the spot, a clear and cold stream gushed from a neighbouring rock ; which watered the trees and plants, and seemed to combat with the earth, whether of them most contributed to their growth and preservation. It was a sweet rural scene. For charms and solitude the place was equally to be admired.

E

The inside of this grotto was a beautiful green marble, extremely bright, and even approaching to the appearance of the emerald. It was thick set with shells, and those not small ones, but some of the largest and finest kinds : many of them seemed as it were, squeezed together by the marble, so as to show the edges only but more were to be seen at large, and filled with the purest spar. The whole had a fine effect, and as the cave had been divided by art into six fine apartments, and had doors and chimneys most ingeniously contrived, both the mansion and its situation charmed me in a high degree. On either side of it were many cottages, pretty and clean, and as sheep were feeding on the field, some cows grazing, and various kinds of tame fowl before the doors, I concluded it was an inhabited place, before I saw any one.

44. The first human being I beheld, was an old woman, who appeared at the grotto door, and I requested her to inform me, who lived in this delightful place ; and which was my best way to Cumberland or Bishopric ? Sir, replied the good old woman, you are welcome to Burcot Lodge. Women only are the inhabitants of this spot : and over the hills before you, you must go, to get to the countries you mention. We are a hundred souls in all that live here, and our mistress, superior and head, is a young woman. Her name is Azora. Yonder she comes, goodness itself, and as it is now seven in the evening, too late to proceed any farther in this part of the world, you had better walk up to her, and pay her your respects. Great was my surprise at what I heard. A little female republic among those hills was news indeed and when I came near Azora, my astonishment increased.

She was attended by ten young women, straight, clean, handsome girls, and surpassed them in tallness. Her countenance was masculine, but not austere : her fine blue eyes discovered an excellence of temper, while they showed the penetration of her mind. Her hair was brown, bright and charming ; and nature had stamped upon her cheek a colour, that exceeded the most beautiful red of the finest flower. It was continually as the maiden blush of a modest innocence. She was dressed in a fine woollen stuff, made in the manner shepherdesses are painted, and on her head had a band or fillet like what the ladies now wear, with a bunch of artificial flowers in her hair. She had a very small straw hat on. In her hand, she held a long and pretty crook ; and as her coats were short, her feet were seen, in black silk shoes, and the finest white stockings, and appeared vastly pretty. She struck me greatly. She was a charming, and uncommon figure. When I came up to Azora, I could hardly forbear addressing her, as the son of Ulysses did the supernal ; " O vous qui que vous soiez, mortelle ou deesse, quoiqu'a vous voir on ne puisse vous prendre que pour une divinité, seriez-vous insensible au malheur d'un fils, etc." Whoever you are, a mortal or a goddess, though sure your aspect speaks you all divine, can you, unmoved, behold a hapless son, by fate expelled, and urged by unrelenting rage, to wander through the world, exposed to winds and seas, and all the strokes of adverse fortune, till he arrived in this land of felicity and peace ? But on better thoughts I only said, I am your most humble servant, madam, and told her I believed I had lost my way, and knew not where to go. To which she replied, " you are welcome, sir, to our hamlet, and to the best entertainment it affords, only tell me," she added with a smile, " what could induce you to travel this unbeaten road, and how did you pass the precipices and rivers you must have met with in the way ? " " Curiosity, madam," I answered, " was one cause ; that I might see a country no traveller had been in ; and my next inducement, to find a valuable friend ; who lives somewhere upon the northern border of this county, or Yorkshire, or on the adjoining limits of Cumberland or Durham ; but on which I do not know ; and as I come from Brugh under Stancmore, I judged it the shortest way by a great many miles, and the likeliest to succeed in my inquiry after my friend, then as to hills and waters, many dangerous ones I have gone over, and with great toil and fatigue have got thus far." " This," AZORA said, " is a rational account of your journey, and as there are many difficulties still before you, you are welcome to rest with us till you are refreshed, and able to proceed.

By this time we reached the grotto door, and upon entering the first apartment, I saw another lady, dressed in the same manner, and seemed to be of the same age, that is, about six and twenty, as I was told. This was AZORA'S companion and friend. She was a very pretty woman, though inferior to AZORA in charms ; but her mind was equally luminous and good. Neither she nor AZORA were learned women, this is, they understood no other language than the English tongue, and in that they had but a small collection of the best books ; but those few they had read well, and they had capacities to think. In reason, philosophy, and mathematics, they were excellent, and in the most agreeable manner, discovered in conversation the finest conceptions of the most excellent things. AZORA, of the two, was by much the best speaker. Her voice was delightful, and her pronunciation just, strong, clear, and various. With unspeakable pleasure did I listen to her, during three days that I happily passed with her and her companion, and received from both many valuable informations. I thought I understood algebra very well, but I was their inferior, and they instructed me ; and on the fundamental points of religion, they not only out-talked me, but out-reasoned me. It is very strange, I confess. It is very true, however.

AZORA, in particular, had an amazing collection of the most rational philosophical ideas, and she delivered them in the most pleasing dress, with as much ease as she breathed. She asked me, after I had feasted on an excellent supper, how religion went on in the world ; and what was the condition of that which came from supernatural communication, as she phrased it ? and when I told her, that our excellent divines did all that was possible for men to do, to turn the world from superstition of every kind, to that express revelation which restores the dictates of uncorrupted reason to their force and authority ; which teaches the knowledge of one supreme Spirit or God, and the nature of that worship which is due to a Being not confined to, or dependent upon particular places, or circumstances ; but always and everywhere present with us : she answered, that such clergymen are glorious, and cannot be enough admired ; and great is the unreasonableness of the men who opposed them, and forced them into the field of disputation, from their holy labour of instructing the people in penetential piety and sanctification ; I mean the infidels and the bigots.

"What can be more unjust and impious," AZORA continued, "than for men to declaim against a revelation which displays the paternal regard of God for his creatures, by doing more than was strictly necessary for their happiness, as they had his original law of reason before he gave them the gospel ; and which enables us to extend our knowledge even as to those things which we are by nature capable of knowing ; which awakens us to duty, and advises us how to walk in the ways of prudence and safety. To reject such an extraordinary method of saving us, is senseless and culpable indeed. Surely, when superstition and enthusiasm has led mankind into errors, we ought to adore the divine goodness for re-communicating a knowledge of true religion ; of duty in this life, and of what we are to expect in that which is to come. We can never be thankful enough for a revelation, that has a tendency to promote the happiness of mankind both here and hereafter. The opposition, in my opinion, is without excuse ; as the external evidence of history, miracles, and prophecy for the gospel, is incontestably strong, when fairly examined ; must appear with force to a modest, candid, impartial inquirer ; and as the internal evidence for the sacred letters, their usefulness and excellence, must be obvious to every attentive capacity, that delights in the pursuit of religion and virtue. Truth and candour, then, those infidels are strangers to. They are not fair reasoners. They are haughty, over-bearing declaimers.

"Nor can I think much better," said AZORA, "of those great and reverend men, who preach and write to prove the weakness of human reason, and that the prime law of our creation, the law of nature, is imperfect, insufficient, and obscure ; and there•

fore, supernatural communication was absolutely necessary ; who add to this, things inconceivable and contradictory, and insist upon our believing articles too hard for rational beings. This is misrepresenting rationals, if we believe the Scriptures, and is so far from being of service to the cause of Christianity, as in Charity we must suppose those great men by such writing and preaching do intend ; that it does, on the contrary, very greatly hurt revealed religion. It is to such wrong defences of revelation that antichristian deism owes its chief strength. Our holy religion wants not any real evidence that can be desired by the modest, candid, and impartial ; but if great and learned men will deny the perfection of the primary law of God and substitute in the place of recommunicated nature, an invented gospel, that swells with useless mysteries, and hard doctrines ; great damage must fall upon the true gospel. An unintelligible religion is no religion. It can be of no concern, with regard to rational creatures ; and strong minds will laugh at its pieties."

" But exclusive of invented mysteries," I said, " which are to be sure sad stuff in the works of those great men, and deplorably corrupt the simplicity of the gospel, to me it is not so plain, that mankind could by reason acquire just and adequate ideas of the existence and nature of the supreme Being, or know that they had immortal souls, and would expose themselves to eternal unavoidable misery in a future state, in proportion to the demerit of their thoughts and actions in this world ; but might secure everlasting felicity by worshipping one supreme, universal, omnipotent, eternal, omnipresent, and intelligent spirit, and doing all the good we have an opportunity and power to do in this life. I question if reason can make us clear and certain on these articles. The reason of the bulk of mankind cannot do it, I think. Therefore, the gospel was absolutely necessary for the salvation of men."

AZORA to this replied, that " faith in Christ, and all his own institutions, were of high value indeed ; and beautiful his religion appears, when it is fairly represented, as an institution that has no other end than morality, the most noble end, and the most worthy of God ; and that declares the practice of all the moral offices to be superior to any inward accomplishment, or outward Christian institution : but she could not allow, that Christianity was absolutely necessary : for the common reason of men, without launching out into the unfathomable ocean of metaphysical subtilties, appears upon trial to be able to discover the fundamental points of religion ; and from the things that are made, from our moral capacities and powers, and from our relations to one another, to know the Supreme Being, his attributes and perfections, and that we are accountable to our great Creator."

" If men will think, they must perceive without the reason of a Newton or Clarke, the existence of a spiritual influence in all the parts of inanimated matter, and the existence of their own spirits or souls. To which ever part of matter we look, we see a spirit employed. An influencing being, endued with the faculties of perception, activity, and volition, is plain. The accidental qualities of matter, called attraction, repulsion, and communication of motion, evince that material and vegetable nature, and all the parts of inanimated matter, are actuated by one supreme and universal Spirit : I say One Spirit, because it is evident from a sameness of volition, that is, from one and the same faculty of volition, manifest throughout all nature, that there are not several distinct, independent spirits. In attraction, repulsion and communication of motion ; there appears no different faculty of volition, but a different exercise of the same faculty of volition, which, for wise reasons, makes some parts of matter cohere strongly, as stone and metal,—some weakly, as earth, etc. ; some repel, while others attract ; some elastic, and others non-elastic. In all these cases, one spirit only is the actor : that Being who holds all perfection in himself, and by an absolute command over all parts of matter, forms and manages it as his wisdom sees best ; just as his adorable providence governs us, and disposes of us, by such laws as reason, consulting the good of the whole society, declares it to be best for us to obey : best, most surely, as it is the glory of the Almighty to be constantly and without any deviation governed by the eternal and immutable laws of good and right, just and equal. All is the operation of one and the same universal spirit. Identity is visible. The various kinds of attraction, repulsion, etc., only show the un-limited power of the Deity, in actuating matter as his established rules require. Were several arbitrary supreme spirits to act over matter, the consequence would be a breach of regularity, uniformity, and constancy, in the laws of nature, and that con-fusion would appear instead of beauty and order.

" Thus common reason confesses that there is one infinite universal, supreme spirit, who actuates and governs the universe ; and from the heavens, the earth, and ourselves, we are as certain that there is a Creator and Lord of all the Worlds, who directs every atom of it, and animates every material form, as we are of anything demonstrated to us. And as he is not only the Creator but the Manager and Preserver of every being, there can be no power equal to him. He must be omnipotent. He must likewise be eternal and omnipresent ; for there was no superior power to receive existence from, nor is there a superior power to confine it. As to his infinite intelligence, his being the Author and Preserver of all things demonstrates it.

" In respect of the human soul," AZORA continued, " it is impossible for perception to proceed from the body, or from any motion or modification of parts of the body ; and therefore, there must be a mind in which our ideas must be produced and exist. If the ideas of sensation may be supposed to be occasioned by the different motions of the constituent parts of the brain, yet they cannot be those motions. The motions can only enable a spiritual percipient to note them and remember them, and as to reflection, the other part of the perceptive faculty, attention, and contemplation, it is not possible they can proceed from the different motions into which the parts of the brain are put ; because they are employed solely about perceptions which were only in the mind. The case is the same as to many other qualities or faculties ; in the designing quality, the inventing quality, the judging quality, the reasoning quality, the compounding quality, the abstracting quality, the discerning quality, the recollective quality, the retentive quality, the freedom of will, the faculty of volition, and especially the foreseeing faculty : these cannot be the faculties of matter. Such qualities must exist ultimately and solely in mind. Can foresight, for example, be the work of matter, when it is employed about things and actions which have not yet happened, and for that reason cannot be the objects of the senses ? No surely. It must be the spiritual part of the compound that acts upon the occasion : in all the intelligent faculties which we comprehend under the complex idea of understanding, spirit only can be the performer.

" There is a soul or mind then in man, and that it is immortal and accountable, is as evident as that the retentive faculty, that is, retaining ideas received by reflection, does not pertain to body, but it is a natural quality of the soul only, and does not proceed from its union with the body : for, as perception and retention prove the human mind to be a distinct being, and that it has qualities which cannot proceed from the body, therefore it must still continue a spirit unless annihilated by its Creator, and must, after its separation, be endued with the qualities which are the faculties of soul only. The reason is plain. These qualities cannot be destroyed without a cause, but separation is no cause, as the quality or qualities did not proceed from, or depend on union, therefore the soul is immortal, unless we suppose what cannot be supposed, that its Creator puts an end to its being. We must know, after death, that we exist. We must remember a past existence, and call to mind every idea we had formed in this life by reflection.

" As to our being accountable hereafter for the deeds we have done in this first state of existence, this can admit of no speculation ; for as we have received from our Creator the eternal law of reason, which enables us to distinguish right and wrong, and to govern the inferior powers and passions, appetites and senses, if we please ; as we are endued with an understanding which can acquire large moral dominion, and may, if we oppose not, sit as queen upon the throne over the whole corporeal system ; since the noble faculty of reason was given to rectify the soul and purify it from earthly affections ; to elevate it above the objects of sense, to purge it from pride and vanity, selfishness and hypocrisy, and render it just, pious, and good ; of consequence, God has a right to call us to account for our conduct in this first state, and will reward or punish, in a most extraordinary manner ; as the principles and actions of man have been righteous ; or, his life and character stained by unjust dispositions and filthy deeds.   This is plain to common reason.   Every understanding must see this, how wrong soever they wilfully act.   As God by his nature must abhor iniquity, and love what is honest, pure, and good ; he must reward the piety and worthy behaviour of those, who act according to reason in this life, and with views beyond the bounds of time, endeavour to proceed each day to more exalted ideas of virtue : but, the mortals who deviate from rectitude and goodness, and wilfully live workers of iniquity, must expect that God, the Father of Spirits, the Lover of truth, and the patron of righteousness and virtue, will proportion future punishments to present vices, and banish them to the regions of eternal darkness.   From the natural lights of our understanding we have the highest reason to conclude this will be the case. The truths are as evident to a reflection, as that this world, and we who inhabit it, could not have had eternal existence, nor be first formed by any natural cause ; but must have been originally produced, as we are now constantly preserved, by the supreme and universal spirit.   This is the excellent law of reason or nature.   There is a light sufficient in every human breast, to conduct the soul to perfect day, if men will follow it right onwards, and not turn into the paths that lead to the dark night of hell.''

AZORA'S religions notions amazed me, and the more, as they were uttered with a fluency and ease beyond anything I had ever heard before.   In the softest, sweetest voice, she expressed herself, and without the least appearance of labour, her ideas seemed to flow from a vast fountain.   She was a master indeed in the doctrine of ideas.   Her notion of them and their formation was just as possible ; and in a few minutes she settled everything relating to them.   Her ideas of activity and passivity afforded me much instruction, as did her notions of space, matter, and spirit : and what is still more extraordinary, she had a fine conception of an electrical fluid, which is thought to be a discovery made very lately, and made use of it to prove, not that it is the ultimate cause of effects, but that everything is caused and directed by an immaterial spirit.   An immaterial spirit was her favourite article, and it was to me a fine entertainment to hear her on that subject ; from the one supreme spirit down to the spirit of brute animals. But to conclude our conversation on religion ; I observed to AZORA, that "if things were so, and the law or reason was so perfect and sufficient, then I could not see that there was any want at all of the religion of favour, since that of nature was enough to confirm us in rectitude and holiness, if we would obey its directions ; and to show us the way to the mansions of angels. Why the law of grace at so great an expense, if the rule of reason can make us good here, and for ever happy hereafter ? "

AZORA replied, that she had before answered this question by observing, that "excellent as the primary law of the creation was, yet revelation was of the greatest use, as it enables us to extend our knowledge even as to the things which we are by nature capable of knowing ; and as it restored to the world the law of reason, that is, true religion, when superstition and enthusiasm had established false religion. This renders Christianity glorious were there nothing more to be said for it. But this is not all we can say.

"The best of mortals are weak, and the most of them are so fully employed about things temporal, that it is impossible so much good should proceed from mere human reason as from a plain easy gospel, that delineates duty in the most intelligible manner, and contains the absolute command of the great God, to renounce vicious habits, impure desires, worldly tempers, and frame ourselves to purity, sincerity, and devotion ; as the only means that can secure his felicitating presence and gain us admission to the delightful seats of separate souls made perfect. In this the gospel is far preferable to reason.

"Beside, as wilful disobedience strikes at the being and government of God, and devotedness to the Lord of all the worlds, in trust and resignation, is the perfection of religion, the example of the Son of God in his humiliation, his cross, his death, make an instance of resignation so consummate and instructive, that we not only learn from it what reason cannot half so well instruct us in ; I mean the amiableness of virtue, the excellency of holiness, and the merit of absolute and unreserved obedience ; but, we are roused to an imitation of this grand character ; both on account of its beauty, and the promise of our sitting down with Christ in his throne, if, according to our measure, we work all righteousnes, and overcome our present temptations and trials, even as he also overcame, and is set down with his Father in his throne. Reason is nothing compared to this. The gospel dispensation by this means is fitted to render us virtuous, holy, and thoroughly good, in a method the law of nature could never do."

"And more than this, when the God of heaven saw his creatures and children every where going wrong, without any help amongst themselves, and therefore sent his son to set them right ; to set before them the unchangeable rule of everlasting righteousness in its original purity and perfection, and not only explain and enforce it by the most powerful considerations, but apply the commands of supreme reason to the government of the thoughts and passions of the heart ; that duty and virtue in the principle, and habit of universal rectitude towards both God and man, might be the practice of all the earth, and mankind become a people holy to the Lord ; He, the Universal Father, the better to effect this blessed purpose, added two things to religion, which have a power that reason wants to make us conform to God, and the eternal laws of righteousness, in principle, temper, and life. One is, Christ's appearing to put away sin by the sacrifice of himself, by his becoming a sin-offering. The other is the assistance of the Spirit of God. The oblation of the son, and the grace of the Father, have effects in religion, in changing and sanctifying, that reason is an utter stranger to.

" The sum of the whole is, the gospel, that word of truth and power, enters the hearts, and breaks the power of sin in the soul. The holy life of Christ sets us an example, that we should walk in his steps, and obey the will of the infinitely wise Creator ; that, like him, we should accord by obedience with the harmony of God's moral government, and rather die than break or obstruct it by any wilful sin. And by his being a sin-offering, he not only put an end to all sin-offerings, which both Jews and Gentiles were wont to offer ; * but, by his being the most precious one in the universe, showed God's great displeasure against sin, and in his obedience to the Father, even unto death, that we ought to cease from evil, and by a righteous obedience render ourselves worthy of God the Father's love. That we may do so we have the promise of the Spirit to enable us to turn from sin and Satan to the living God, that by the acting principle of sanctification, wrought within us by the hand of him that made us, without the least force on our will, we may perfect our souls in purity and holiness, exercise acts of love and benevolence, and worship the one true God in and through the one true Mediator. Reason alone, excellent as it is, cannot produce anything like this.

" The religion of favour in these respects surpasses the law of nature. By the first law of the creation, reason, we may acquire that righteousness, which is an habitual rectitude of soul, and right actions flowing from it : but sanctification, that influencing principle, which adds holiness to righteousness, belongs, as I

---

* When a plague afflicted the Massilienses, they fed a poor man deliciously, and adorned him with sacred vestments ; then led him through the city, and sacrificed him, by throwing him headlong down from a steep rock, after the people had poured their execrations upon him, and prayed that all the calamities of the city might fall upon him. Such practice shews that Christ being offered for the sins of the whole world, was in conformity to the ideas of mankind. The *Jews* had their devoted animal, and the *Gentiles* had their sacrificed poor man, and other ways.

take it, to the law of grace.   It is given to those who ask it, not for
the sake of but through Christ."

"All this," I answered, "is just and fine, and I have only to
request, for my farther instruction, that you will be pleased,
madam, to explain yourself a little more on the articles of a sin-
offering, and grace ; for I have always thought there was a darkness sat upon these parts of revealed religion, and have often
wished for what I have not yet found, a head capable of giving me
entire satisfaction on these points : but from what I have heard
you say, I must now suppose that all my doubts, relative to the
two subjects, you have the power to remove."   "My power,"
replied AZORA, "is no more than a plain understanding, that in
this still and peaceful region, has been at liberty, to think without
being corrupted by sophistry, school-nonsense, or authority ; and,
as to giving satisfaction on the heads you mention, or any other,
it is not what I pretend to : but my opinion you shall have since
you ask ; " and in the following manner AZORA proceeded.

"As to our Lord's becoming a sin-offering, I conceive, in the
first place, that God ordained it, because he saw it needful, and
necessary to answer many and great ends.   It must be right, and
what in the reason and nature of things ought to be, though we
were not able to comprehend the reasons that made it needful.
It must have been the properest way to make up the breach between heaven and earth, since infinite wisdom appointed it.

"In the next place, as the death of this great person not only
gave the highest attestation to the truth of his doctrine, and confirmed every word he had preached ; to the encouragement of
sinners to repent, and the great consolation of saints ; but has
afforded us such a noble pattern of obedience, as must have an influence on intelligent beings, and excite them to practice obedience
to all the commands of God, and perfect resignation to his will
in every case ; which are some excellent reasons for Christ's dying ; so did Almighty God make this farther use of it, that he
appointed the blood of Christ, which was shed to produce the
essence of sanctification in the soul, to wit, devotedness, trust,
and resignation to the Almighty Father of the universe, to be the
blood of a new covenant, shed for many for the remission of sins.
This seems to me to take in the whole case.   Christ by obedience
to the death, which happened in the natural course of things, is
held out to the world a pattern of self-sacrifice in the cause of truth
and virtue, a sample of that perfect religion, not my will, but thine
be done ; the glorious gospel is thereby confirmed ; and our redemption is effected by the blood of the Son of God.   As Moses,
the mediator between God and Israel, repeated to the people the
laws and judgments of God, and received their consent to the divine commands ; entered this covenant in his book, offered
sacrifices of praise and friendship, and then confirmed the covenant

in the most solemn manner, by dividing the blood of the sacrifices into parts ; one part of which he sprinkled on the altar, to ratify God's part of the covenant ; and with the other part sprinkled the people, that is, the twelve princes, the heads, or the twelve pillars, which represented the twelve tribes, and then awfully cried out with a strong voice, ' Behold the blood of the covenant Jehovah has made with you : ' so did the Lord Jesus Christ, the mediator between God and all mankind, teach the people by his gospel to rectify their notions, to regulate their affections, to direct their worship ; with the judgments that were to be the consequence of disobedience, the rewards prepared for those who obey ; and then declared, in relation to his death, ' This is my blood of the new covenant. The blood I must shed on the cross will seal, ratify, and confirm a pardoning covenant, and by virtue thereof, upon repentance and conversion, the world is washed clean through the blood of the Lamb.' This, I think for myself, renders the thing very plain and easy. The death of the Son of God was taken into the plan of redemption, not to pacify God's anger ; for God could be no otherwise pleased or delighted with the blood of his Son, than as his shedding it was an act of the highest obedience and a noble pattern to all the rational creation ; but his blood was made the seal of a pardoning and justifying covenant ; and by the death of Christ, the most powerful means to prevent sin, and to draw sinners to obey the commands of heaven, God demonstrated his love and mercy to mankind. I fancy I am clear. In this view of the matter, I can see no difficulty in being justified freely by the grace of God, through the redemption which is in Christ Jesus. God is the sole original and fountain of redemption The Son, and his gospel are the great instruments. Lo ! I come to do thy will, O my God, the Son declares : and the blood be shed, the better to bring the human race to wisdom, rectitude and happiness, is appointed by our merciful, good, and gracious Father, to be the seal and ratification of a new covenant. Moloch might want cruel and bloody sacrifice to pacify him ; but the Father of the universe sent his Christ to deliver his commands, and made the death which he foresaw would happen by his Son's delivering such commands to impious men, to be a covenant between Jehovah and the people, that Jesus should be considered as a propitiation for our sins, and his death be an eternal memorial of the Almighty's love, and abhorrence of iniquity. There can no objection lie against this. To me this appears the most rational and beautiful scheme that infinite wisdom could contrive. Most glorious and good is our God. Most happy may mortals be, if they please. The virtuous obedience of our Lord hath obtained from God a right and power to abolish death. His blood hath confirmed the covenant of grace, and his gospel hath brought life immortal into light.

"As to the influence of the spirit," AZORA continued, "that there is such a living principle in the human soul, cannot, I think, be denied, if revelation is to be believed ; but the mode of influencing is not perhaps to be explained otherwise than by saying, that our gracious and good Father makes now and then some friendly impressions upon our minds, and by representing in several lights the terrors and promises of the gospel, excites our hopes and fears, As I apprehend, we can go very little further. It is easy, I think. to prove from the scriptures, that as the extraordinary assistance of the Holy Ghost was necessary for planting Christianity at first ; so is a supernatural assistance of the Holy Ghost, though not in so illustrious a manner, still necessary to enable us to perform the conditions of the gospel. Though God has recalled the more visible signs of his presence, yet to be sure he continues to influence some way or other. I cannot suppose the Holy Ghost has wholly withdrawn himself from the church. ' The renewing of the Holy Ghost,' St. Peter says, ' was a promise made to them and to their children, and to those that were afar off, even as many as God should call ; ' and as human nature has the same weakness and passions, and extravagancies of former ages, there is as much need of a divine assistance now as in the time of the apostles : nay, more need, I think, at present, as miracles are ceased. There must be a weight of supernatural power to press within, as there are now no flashings from the sky, or extraordinary appearances without, to prove the certainty of our religion, and make us consider its promises, threatenings, and rules : but the way this supernatural principle acts, as before observed, is hard to determine, any more than what I have said, and instead of wasting our time in enquiries how the thing is done, our business is to render ourselves capable of so great a blessing, by not grieving this holy spirit, lest he depart from us ; and resolving with the psalmist, to walk with a perfect heart, and to set no wicked thing before our eyes. We must strive to improve religious thoughts : we must labour hard to obey the written rules ; God will then give us the grace sufficient for us. To our considerable talent of natural power to do good, our Father will add the advantages of his spirit. If we desire to be good, he will make us good in conjunction with our own application and pains ; by a gradual process, and human methods. If nature gives her utmost actings, the author of nature will move, and direct and assist her where she is weak. Both the grace and the providence of God may be likened to a little spring concèaled within a great machine : to the known given powers of the machine, the operations of it are ascribed, and all its events imputed ; yet it is the small secreted spring that directs, draws, checks, and gives movement to every weight and wheel. The case cannot be exactly alike, as a compound of matter and spirit is different from a machine : but it may suggest I imagine some imperfect idea of the affair : a very imperfect one, I confess, for if we were thinking ever so long of the matter, grace after all would be what the apostle calls it, an unspeakable gift. A gift surmounting our apprehensions as well as it does our merit. The theory of it may be perhaps too excellent for us, and our part is, not to determine how, but with honest hearts to pray, that a ray from heaven may open, and shine upon our understanding, clear it from prejudices and impostures, and render it teachable, considerative and firm ; may inspire good thoughts, excite good purposes, and suggest wholesome counsels and expedients. This the divine power may easily do, without depriving us of free will, or lessening our own moral agency. That power may extinguish an imagination we strive to get rid of : may remove an impediment we labour to be freed from : may foil a temptation we do our best to resist. If we do all we can, and implore the divine aid, there is no doubt but the Almighty may give his free creatures such power and dispositions, as will carry them innocently and safely through the trials of this first state. On such conditions, God, the Father of spirits, the friend of men, the patron of righteousness and all virtue, will, without all peradventure, distribute his grace to every mortal in proportion to the measures of necessary duty."

Here Azora ended, and I sat for some minutes after in great admiration. Her fancy furnished ideas so very fast, and speaking was so very easy to her, without one pang in the delivery, or the least hesitation for hours, as she could, if she pleased, so long discourse ; her judgment was so strong, and her words so proper and well placed, that she appeared to me a prodigy in speaking, and I could have listened to her with delight and amazement the whole night. But exactly at ten o'clock, the old woman I mentioned before, who first bid me welcome to Burcot-Lodge, came into the chamber with candles, and Azora told me, that if I would follow Gladuse, she would light me to bed ; this I did immediately, after wishing the ladies good night, and my guide brought me to her own cottage, which was next door to the grotto. She showed me into a small clean room, neatly and prettily furnished, and there I found a good bed. Down I lay as soon as I could, being much fatigued, and as the sun was rising, got up again, to write what I could remember to have heard Azora say. My memory from my childhood has been very extraordinary. I believe there are few living exceed me in this respect. The greatest part of what I read and hear, remains with me, as if the book was still before me, or the speaker going on. This enables me to write down, with much exactness, what I care to note, and I can do it for the most part in the relater's or talker's own words, if I minute it in my short hand within twenty-four hours after reading or discoursing. Upon this account, I can say, that I lost very little of all that Azora was

pleased to let me hear ; or, of the discourses I had with her ingenious companion, ANTONIA FLETCHER.

June 15th.—When I had done writing, I went out to wait upon
the ladies, and found them in their fine gardens, busily employed
in the useful and innocent diversion which the cultivation of some
of the greatest beauties of the creation affords. They had every
kind of fruit-tree in their ground, every plant and flower that
grows, and such a variety of exotic rarities from the hotter climate
as engaged my admiration, and finely entertained me for many an
hour, during my stay in this place. They both understood gardening to perfection, and continually lent their helping hands to
the propagation of every thing. The digging and laborious work
was performed by many young women, who did it with great
activity and understanding, and the nicer parts these ladies executed. I was astonished and delighted with their operations of
various kinds. It was beautiful to see with what exquisite skill
they used the knife, managed graffs, and cyons, directed the
branches and twigs in posture on espaliers, and raised flowers.
They had everything in perfection in their kitchen garden and
physic garden. Their fruits, roots, and herbs for the table, were
most excellent ; their collection of herbs for medicine the most
valuable : and as the whole contrivance of the gardens approached
nature, and beautiful in grass, gravel, and variety of evergreens,
I was led with delight through the whole, till I came into the green-
house. There I saw AZORA and ANTONIA at work, and paid them
the compliments they deserved.

Immediately after my arrival, breakfast was brought in, choco-
late and toast, and the ladies were extremely pleasant over it.
They asked me a great many questions about the world, and were
so facetious in their remarks, and pleased with my odd account of
things, that they laughed as heartily as I did, and that was at no
small rate. This being done, we walked over every part of the
gardens, and AZORA did me the honour not only to shew me all the
curiosities, and improvements she had made, in the management
of seeds, flowers, plants, and trees ; but, lectured on various fine
objects that appeared in our way, with a volubility of tongue, and
a knowledge of the subjects, that was amazing indeed. Were I to
set down what she said even on sallads, cucumbers, cauliflowers,
melons, asparagus, early cabbages, strawberries, rasberries, cur-
rants, goosberries, apples, pears, plums, cherries, apricots, &c,. and
especially her propagation of mushrooms, champignons, and but-
tons ; this, exclusive of exotics, and flowers, would make I believe
an octavo ; and in relation to exotics and flowers, I am sure she
talked twice as much, and of every thing extremely well. I never
did hear any thing like her. The discourse cost her no more than
the breath of her nostrils.

But at last we came to a fish-pond, that was an acre of water, and I assure you, reader, in half an hour's time the illustrious AZORA not only talked more of fish and ponds than the ingenious and honourable Roger North, of Rougham in Norfolk, hath written on these subjects in his excellent *Discourse*, printed in 1713, in 8vo. ; but, mentioned many useful things relative to them, which Mr. North was a stranger to. She told me, among other matters, that there was only pike and perch in her pond, and the reason of it was because she loved pike above all fish, and as the jacks were fish of prey, no fish but the perch could live with them : the perch on account of the thorny fins on its back, escapes the pike's voracious appetite. She farther informed me, that the jacks in her pond were the finest in the world, as I would see at dinner, and the reason of it was owing to the high feeding she took care they had every day ; beside the entrails of what fowl and sheep her people killed for her table and themselves, the pike had blood and bran mixed in plenty, and all the frogs she could get from a neighbouring fen ; for of them the jacks are most fond. This made the fish extraordinary ; and as the water was current through the pond, and the bottom of various depths from one to six feet, that the spawn may have shallow water to lie in, and the fry shallow water to swim in, as they both required, this was the reason, that one acre of water in such a manner, produced double the quantity of fish to what a pond of still water and a bottom all of one depth, could have. See, continued AZORA, what multitudes there are. They know me, as I feed them myself every day, and tamely come up, cruel tyrants as they are, to get their meat. Here she called ' jack, jack,' and throwing in a basket of unfortunate frogs, it was wonderful to see how those devouring monsters appeared, and voraciously swallowed the poor things.

AZORA was going to proceed to another pond of carp and tench, which she had at the other end of her gardens, and let me know how that was ordered, so as to produce the largest and finest fish : but a bell rung for morning prayers, at ten o'clock, and she immediately turned towards a chapel. She asked me if I would attend divine service, and upon my answering, with pleasure, desired me to come on. In the church I saw every soul of the community assembled, and while I chose to sit on one of the benches among the people, at some distance, that I might the better observe every thing done, the ladies ascended by a few steps into a reading desk, and AZORA began with great devotion, to pray in the following manner :

" O Christ, our blessed mediator, pray for us that our faith fail not, and through thy merits and intercession, Lord Jesus, let our prayer be set forth in the sight of Almighty God as incense, and the lifting up of our hands as a morning sacrifice.

" Almighty and everlasting God, thou pure and infinite Spirit, who art the great cause and author of nature, and hast established the world by thy wisdom, and stretched out the heavens by thy discretion ; upon whom depends the existence of all things, and by whose providence we have been preserved to this moment, and enjoyed many blessings and undeserved advantages ; graciously accept, we beseech thee, our grateful sense and acknowledgements of all thy beneficence towards us ; accept, O Lord, our most hearty and unfeigned thanks for all the instances of thy favour which we have experienced ; that we have the use of our reason and understanding, in which many fail, and have had refreshing sleep and quiet the past night ; for delivering us from evil, and giving us our daily bread ; for all the necessaries, conveniencies, and comforts, which thy liberal hand hast provided for us, to sweeten human life, and render it more agreeable than otherwise it could be in this day of our exercise, probation and trial. While we live, we will praise and magnify thy awful name, and join in ascribing, with the glorious and innumerable heavenly host, honour, power, and thanksgiving to the eternal God, who sits on the throne of supremacy unrivalled in majesty and power.

" But especially, O great and blessed God, adored be thy goodness for so loving the world, as to give thy only begotten Son, to the end, that all who believe in him, should not perish, but have everlasting life ; for his humbling himself even to the death upon the cross, and shedding his blood for the remission of our sins. Great and marvellous are thy works of mercy, O Lord God, Almighty ! who can utter all thy praise ? Praise our God, all ye his servants, and ye that fear him, small and great. Amen ; allelujah. Blessing and honour, and glory, and power be unto him that sitteth upon the throne, and to the Lamb for ever and ever.

" O God and Father of our Lord Jesus Christ, have mercy on us dust and sin, weakness and imperfection, and enter not into strict judgment with us, thine unrighteous and unworthy servants. We confess, with shame and grief, that we have violated thine holy laws, and abused thy tender mercies : that we have followed too much the devices and desires of our own hearts, and in numberless instances have offended against a most righteous governor, a most tender and compassionate Father, and a most kind and bounteous benefactor. In thought, word, and deed, many have been our offences ; and many are still our imperfections. We have sinned against Heaven, and before thee, and have thereby deserved thy just displeasure. But our hope and confidence is in thine infinite mercy, O God, and that according to thy promises declared unto mankind in Christ Jesus, our Lord, thou wilt spare them who confess their faults, and restore them that are penitent. We do earnestly repent, and are heartily sorry for all our misdoings. Through faith we offer up the Lamb that was slain to the eternal God for the redemption of our souls ; believing the worthiness of our Lord Jesus Christ to be a full, perfect, and sufficient sacrifice, oblation and atonement for the sins of a repenting world, and therefore resolving, with all our strength, to imitate his spotless virtue, and perfect obedience. Pardon us, then, we beseech thee, and blot out our iniquities. Deliver us, we pray, in the name of the Lord Jesus, from the evil consequences of all our transgressions and follies, and give us such powers and dispositions as will carry us innocently and safely through all future trials.

"Create in us, O God, pure hearts, and renew right spirits within us. Cast thy bright beams of light upon our souls, and irradiate our understandings with the rays of that wisdom which sitteth on the right hand of thy throne. Let thy holy spirit enable us to act up to the dignity of our reasonable nature, and suitably to the high character, and glorious hopes of Christians ; that we may subordinate the affairs and transactions of time to serve the interests of our souls in eternity ; that we may shake off this vain world, and breathe after immortality and glory ; that we may live in perfect reconciliation with the law of everlasting righteousness, truth, and goodness ; and so comply with thy nature, mind, and will, O eternal and sovereign spirit, thou God most wonderful in all perfections, that we may fully answer the relation we stand in to thee. Relieve and ease our consciences O blessed Lord, by the blood of sprinkling, according to our several conditions of body and mind ; and supply us with suitable grace and strength.

"We beseech thee, in the next place, Almighty Lord, to take us into thy protection this day, and suffer no being to injure us, no misfortune to befal us, nor us to hurt ourselves by any error or misconduct of our own. Give us, O God, a clear conception of things, and in all dangers and distresses, stretch forth the right hand of thy majesty to help and defend us. From sickness and pain, and from all evil and mischief, good Lord deliver us this day, and be propitious unto us, we beseech thee.

"And while we remain in this world, O Father, Lord of heaven and earth, secure us from everything that is terrible and hurtful, and keep us in peace and safety. From all sad accidents and calamitous events, from all tormenting pains and grievous diseases, good Lord deliver us ; and bless us with so much health and prosperity, as will enable us to pass our time here in contentment and tranquility.

"And when the time of our dissolution shall come, by the appointment of thy adorable wisdom, O Father of mercies and the God of all comforts, grant us a decent and happy exit ; without distraction of mind or torments of body : let thy servants depart in peace, and suddenly die in the Lord.

"We pray, likewise, for the happiness of all mankind : that they may all know, and obey, and worship thee, O Father, in spirit and in truth, and that all who name the name of Christ, may depart from iniquity, and live as becomes his holy gospel. We beseech thee to help and comfort all who are in danger, necessity, sickness, and tribulation : that it may please thee to sanctify their afflictions, and in thy good time to deliver them out of all their distresses. If we have any enemies, O Lord forgive them, and turn their hearts. •

"Our father, etc."

When this extraordinary prayer was done, which was prayed with a very uncommon devotion, such as I never had seen before ; they all stood up, and AZORA said, " Let us sing the nineteenth psalm to the praise and glory of the most high God," and immediately raised it. Then all the people joined, and a psalm was sung to perfection indeed. AZORA and ANTONIA had delightful voices, and as they understood music very well, they had taught this congregation so much church harmony, as enabled them to perform beyond anything I have ever heard in any assembly of people. The whole scene was a strange and pleasing thing. They met again at four in the afternoon ; and this is the work of their every day. At ten and four they go to prayers, and after it sing a psalm ; concluding always in the following way. " May the grace of our Lord Jesus Christ procure us the love of God, that the Almighty Father of the universe may bless us with the heavenly assistance of the Holy Ghost."

As to the evening-office of devotion at this place, it was, exclusive of the first address, and the concluding Lord's Prayer, quite different from that of the morning ; and because some readers may be pleased with a sight of another of AZORA's religious compositions, I here set it down.

"O Christ, our blessed mediator, pray for us, that our faith fail not, and through thy merits and intercession, Lord Jesus, let our prayer be set forth in the sight of Almighty God as incense, and the lifting up of our hands as an evening-sacrifice.

"O God, who art the Father and Lord of all beings, and the eternal and inexhaustible fountain of mercy, we beseech thee to be merciful unto us, and to blot out all our transgressions for we truly repent of our wilful imperfections, our failings and neglects, in every instance of thy law, and our duty : and through faith we offer up to thee the lamb that was slain for the redemption of our souls : believing the worthiness of our Lord Jesus to be a full, perfect, and sufficient sacrifice, oblation and atonement for the sins of a repenting world, and therefore resolving, with all our strength, to imitate his spotless virtue and perfect obedience.

"Remember not, then, O Lord, our iniquities, neither take thou vengeance for our sins ; but as we sincerely believe thy holy gospel, and are truly penitent, as we entirely and willingly forgive all, who have, in any instance or in any degree, offended, or injured us, and are truly disposed and ready to make all possible reparation, if we have injured any one, have mercy upon us miserable sinners, and as thou hast promised by thy Son, pardon and forgive us all our sins, and restore us again to thy favour. Hear in heaven, thy dwelling place, and when thou hearest, accept us to thy mercy. O spare us whom thou hast redeemed by thy Son's most precious blood, and make us partakers of that salvation which thou hast appointed in Christ Jesus our Lord, and our souls shall bless thee to eternity.

" And that we may no more offend thee, or transgress the rule of virtue or true religion, but may hereafter truly please thee both in will and deed, and faithfully observe the right statutes, and all thy precepts, endue us, O Lord with the grace of thy holy spirit, that we may amend our lives according to thy holy word. Vouchsafe we beseech thee, to direct, sanctify and govern both our hearts and bodies in the ways of thy laws, and in the works of thy commandments ; and so teach us to number our days that we may apply our hearts unto wisdom, and mind those things which are in conjunction with our everlasting welfare. O let us be always under thy communication and influence, and give that light to our minds, that life to our souls that will raise us to a nearer resemblance of thee, and enable us to ascend still higher, towards the perfection of our nature. Let us be transformed by the working of thy grace and spirit into the image of thy Son. Conform us to his likeness, O blessed God, and make us, body and soul, an habitation for thyself ; that in our hearts we may continually offer up to thee, holy, sublime, and spiritual sacrifices.

" From all evil and mischief, good God deliver us, and defend us we beseech thee, from everything terrible and hurtful. Take us under thy protection the remaining part of this day, and grant us a night of peace, through Jesus Christ our Lord.

" And forasmuch as our earthly house of this tabernacle shall be dissolved, and that in a few years at farthest, it may be in a few minutes, we must descend to the bed of darkness, and acknowledge corruption to be our father, and the worms our sister and mother, grant, O everlasting God, that we may depart in peace, and by an improved principle of divine life, under the influence of the gospel be translated to that eternal world, where God dwells, where Christ lives, and sanctified souls enjoy endless life and the purest pleasures, for evermore.

" That it may please thee, most gracious and good God, to have mercy on the whole race of mankind, and to bless them with all things pertaining to life and godliness : let the light of thy glorious gospel shine upon the nations darkened by superstition, that they may worship thee who art God from everlasting to everlasting, and cultivate and establish in their minds the most pure, benevolent, and godlike dispositions. We beseech thee for all Christian churches ; that their behaviour may, by the influence of thy blessed spirit, be suitable to their holy profession, and their conversation upright and unblamable. Where any have departed from the purity and simplicity of the gospel, lead them, O God, to the right practice and knowledge of their holy religion ; and grant that they may feel the comfortable and sanctifying effects of it ; and in their lives show forth its praise to others. We farther pray, most merciful Father, for all that are destitute or afflicted, either in body, mind, or estate ; that from Heaven, the habitation of thy glory and goodness, thou would send them relief, and, if it be possible, put an end to their present calamities and troubles. O thou Father of mercies, and God of all consolation, bind up the broken in heart, and comfort those that mourn. We have a real sense of the miseries of the distressed part of mankind, and offer up for them our prayers to thee, through Jesus Christ our Lord."

A THANKSGIVING.

" O God, the author of all good, and the fountain of all happiness, we offer up our thanksgivings and praises unto thee, for thy great goodness to us, and to all mankind. We praise and magnify thy holy name for all thy mercies ; for our existence, and the use of our reasoning powers and faculties ; for the health and strength we enjoy, and for all the comforts and conveniences of life : for these thy gifts we adore thee, O munificent parent of good, and pray that a deep and efficacious sense of thy goodness may remain upon our hearts, and be a principle of constant and cheerful obedience to thy holy laws.

" But especially we offer up the acknowledgments of our hearts and mouths for all that thy Son Jesus Christ did, and taught, and suffered, in this world, to save us from our sins, and to conduct us to true and everlasting happiness. We bless thee for the glorious gospel, and for bringing us more effectually, by revelation, to the knowledge of thee, and the practice of our duty. For this merciful appointment, and for all thy mercies, which respect another and a better life than the present ; for every instance of thy tender regard to us, and for the manifold experiences which we have had of thy loving kindness ; we offer up the tribute of unfeigned thanks. Our souls do magnify thee, O Lord God most excellent and good, and all the powers within us praise thy holy name. To thee be glory in the church by Christ Jesus, throughout all ages, world without end. To thee, O thou God of love, be rendered by all beings endued with reason, all honour and obedience, both now, and for ever.

" Almighty and everlasting God, who has promised to hear

the petitions of them that pray unto thee in thy Son's name, we beseech thee of thy great mercy, to accept the sacrifice of prayer and praise, which we have this evening offered up to thy divine Majesty ; and for the relief of our wants, and the manifestation of thy power and glory, grant us those things which we have requested, if thou seest it consistent with our chief and eternal good.   In the name of thy Son Jesus Christ, and his disciples, we pray, and in his words conclude the services of this day.

"Our Father, who art in heaven, hallowed be thy name, etc."

After this, they all stood up, and as in the morning, AZORA said, " let us sing to the praise and glory of God the 148th psalm." She sung the first verse alone, and at the second, they all joined, and went through the whole in a fine and heavenly manner. Then the service concluded with this benediction.

THE BENEDICTION.

" May the God of grace and peace be with us and bless us, May his holy spirit keep us from falling, and preserve us blameless, unto the coming of our Lord Jesus Christ."

Thus ended the evening and morning offices of worship at Burcot Lodge, and as I cannot sufficiently praise, so I could not enough admire the religion and piety of this congregation.   The purity of their worship was charming : and in the ladies and their people a devotion was manifest, that looked more like that of heavenly spirits, than of beings in an animal frame ; who are warped with the customs of the world, and perplexed with difficulties which arise from sensible objects.   They appeared in high admiration of God, endeared to his righteous government, devoted to his holy laws, and powerfully drawn to imitate him in all his imitable perfections.   Not one idle word, or careless look, did I hear or see during the whole time of divine service ; but, like creatures fixed unchangeably in the interest of religion and virtue, and delighted with the joys of piety, their hearts melted in every part of their devotions, and their breasts were filled with the most grateful transporting adorations and affec-tions.   So much beautiful religion I had not often seen in any assembly.   They had a true sense indeed of the love and goodness of God, and of the Grace and charity of Jesus Christ.   They had all been carefully instructed by a wise and excellent man, who was not long since removed from them by death ; and his daughter the admirable AZORA, in conjunction with his niece, the amiable ANTONIA, took all possible pains, since the decease of Mr. Burcot, to maintain the power of religion in their community, and keep the people hearty and steady in the principles and practice of it.   This brings me again to the history of AZORA.

AZORA BURCOT was the daughter of a gentleman who was once possessed of a very great fortune, and by a fatal passion for the grand operation, and an opinion of the possibility of finding the philosopher's stone, he wasted immense sums in operations to discover that preparation, which forces the fæces of infused metals to retire immediately on its approach, and so turns the rest of the mass into pure gold ; communicating the malleability and great ductility of that metal, and giving it true specific gravity, that is, to water, as eighteen and one half is to one. His love of that fine, ancient art, called chymistry, brought him into this misfortune. For improvement and pleasure, he had been long engaged in various experiments, and at last, an adept came to his house, who was a man of great skill in the labours and operations of spagyrists, and persuaded him it was possible to find the stone ; for he, the adept, had seen it with a brother, who had been so fortunate as to discover it, after much labour and operation. The colour of it was a pale brimstone and transparent, and the size of that of a small walnut. He affirmed that he had seen a little of this scraped into powder, cast into some melted lead, and turn it into the best and finest gold. This had the effect the adept desired, and from chymistry brought Mr. Burcot to alchymy. Heaps of money he wasted in operations of the most noble elixir by mineral and salt ; but the stone after all he could not find : and then, by the adept's advice, he proceeded in a second method, by maturation, to subtilize, purify, and digest quicksilver, and thereby convert it into gold.* This likewise came to nothing, and instead of the gold he expected, he had only heaps of mercury fixed with verdegrease, which gives

* There is a third way to make gold, to wit, by separation, for every metal contains some quantity of gold ; but the quantity is so small that it bears no porportion to the expense of getting it out : this last way the Spagyrists never attempt ; and as for the two other methods, maturation, and transmuting by the grand elixir, the happy hour will never come, though so many ingenious men have often thought it drawing nigh. To console them for the loss of their fortunes they have had some comfortable moments of reflection, that they have been within some minutes of success, when crack I all is gone and vanished on a sudden, and they have nothing before them but cinders and broken crucibles. It is very strange then that a man of Dr. Dickenson's great veracity and skill in chymistry, should affirm the thing was actually done in his presence by an adept ; and the more so, as his friend, the Honourable Robert Boyle, told him the thing was an impossibility. Dickenson's words are, " Nec potui sane quantacunque mihi fuerit opinio de ista re, quin aliquoties animi penderem donec illustris ea demonstratio quam vestra excellentia, biennio jam elapso, coram exhibuit, omnem ansam dubitandi mihi præcidisset." And again " Plaucit dominationi vestræ claro experimento ante oculos facto animum meum ad opus accendere atque ; etiam quæstionum mearum solutiones, quantum licerat, promittere." *Vide Epistola dd Theod. Mundanum Philosophum Adeptum, de Quintessentia Philosophorum, de Vera Physiologia, &c. Oxon.* 1686. This is very surprising ; and the more so, as the greatest watchings and closest application, in searching after the stone, are all in vain, unless the stars shed a propitious influence on the labours of the Spagyrist : the work must be begun and advance in proper planetary hours, and depends as much on judicial astrology, as on fire, camphire, salt, labour and patience : but judicial astrology is no science. It is a mere farce. I must conclude then, that the hands of Mundanus the adept, were too quick for the doctor's eyes, and he deceived him by legerdemain: that all the books on the subject are fraudulent descriptions to deceive the credulous ; and what Mundanus told Dickenson of Sir George Ripley, canon of Bridlington, in Yorkshire in the reign of Edward the Fourth, and of Raymund Lully, was mere invention. He affirmed that Ripley sent the knights of Rhodes an hundred thousand pounds to support them in their wars against the Turks : and that Lully assisted Edward I. king of England, with six millions of gold, towards carrying on the Crusade. This piece of secret history he assures us he found in an ancient manuscript of indisputable authority, *quod inculpatæ fidei registris innotescit ;*

it a yellow tinge, and more deeply coloured with turmeric. Gold
it seemed, but, on trial in the coppel, it flew away in fumes and
the adept made off. Too late this good and learned man saw
he had been imposed on, and that the Spagyrists are in reality
what Dr. Dickenson calls them, *Enigmatistinubivagi.* *

Chymistry, reader, is a fine and ancient art. The analysing
of sensible bodies by fire, to discover their real powers and virtues,
is highly praiseworthy, and the surprising experiments we make,
fill the mind of an inquirer after truth with the greatest veneration
for the wonderful author of nature ; but more than this, is a sad
romance that ends in empty pockets. Never think then of *The
Hermetical Banquet,* Glauber's *Golden Ass,* or the *Philosopher's
Magical Gold.*† By the law of honest industry, endeavour to be
rich if you can, for this sole reason, that it is more blessed to give
than to receive ; and if that lies not within your capacity, or
means, be content with peace and little. There is more true
happiness in daily bread, and the possession of the divine and
social virtues, than in tons of gold without holiness and a strong
attachment to virtue.

When Mr. Burcot found he had almost ruined himself, and
that he was no longer able to live as he had done, he laid his
melancholy case before his daughter AZORA, and asked her advice,
what he should do ? Her counsel was, to retire immediately to
this part of Stanemore, which was an unvalued part of his estate,
and bring as many of his tenants as he could persuade to inhabit

a manuscript that no one ever saw except Mundanus himself ; *penes me* indeed, it was to be
found only in his own head.

Ripley is in great repute among the adepts to this day, and his famous unintelligible and
mysterious book is called *A Compound of Alchymie conteyning Twelve Gates.* He inscribed
the manuscript to Edward IV. but the editor dedicated it to Queen Elizabeth, affirming
that it contained the right method of making the philosopher's stone and *aurum potabile.*
Lully was a very learned man for the latter end of the thirteenth century, and wrote several
books in Latin ; *Generales Artium Libri. Libri Logicales, Philosophici et Metaphisici :
Variarum Artium Libri : Libri Spirituales Prædicabiles,* and the *Vade Mecum Lulli :* which
treats more particularly on the Philosopher's Stone.

* *Life of Edmund Dickenson, M.D. Physician in Ordinary to Charles II., and James II.* by
William Nicolas Blomberg, 1739, 8vo. p. 135. From this work, the whole that has here
been advanced respecting Alchymy, is extracted, pp. 87–139.

† As to the aurum potabile mentioned by Ripley, which was then and long after esteemed
a panacea, or universal medicine, it is now a question if there can be a tincture of gold ; for
if it be only a division of the lests, or minims of gold, by the spicula of aqua regia, and these
minims thrown into oil of rosemary where they swim, it is no radical tincture of gold, and
the sole virtue lies in the oil of rosemary. The oil may be evaporated ; the gold dust remains ;
and that by melting is reduced to a lump of gold again. This I have experimented. But
the alchymists say, gold may be reduced into a gum of substance like honey, without any
corrosive, and that gum steeped in spirit of wine acquires a ruby colour. An ounce of this
is to be mixed with sixteen ounces of another liquor, and we have aurum polabile ; sovereign
in all distempers. This seems to me to be a second part of the romance. The making of
this golden gum is a secret we can no more come at than the philosopher's stone. The adepts
however assert it, and assure us, that Moses could make aurum potabile, as is evident from
his pulverising the golden calf, and giving it to the children of Israel to drink. This great
man, who wrote 540 years before Homer : 200 before Sanchoniatho ; and 350 before the
Trojan war, was, as they inform us, an adept.

[The story of "pulverising the golden calf," a rabbinical impertinence, which Calmet in
his *Commentaire Literal sur l'Exode,* ch. xxxii. ver. 20. owns himself ashamed to mention,
as well as the probability, that Moses was an adept, has met with a full investigation in the
Life of Edmund Dickenson, noticed ut supra, pp. 162–171. ED.]

this fine tract of land ; to sell what remained of his fortune, and with the money procure as many of the necessaries or comforts of living as could be had, to get in particular some young trades-men and their wives by offered rewards in this place ; to build cottages for the people ; and render the fine caverns in the rock as habitable and pleasing for themselves as art could render them. "Here," said AZORA, "we shall live more happy than we could do, if still possessed of a fortune to make an appearance in the world. We shall enjoy by industry and prudence every good thing that rational life can require, and live secured from the strokes of fortune, and the world's contempt. Strangers to vanity and the pleasures of high life, in this delightful retreat, we shall pass our happy days as in a region of goodness, know-ledge, and joy ; and the predominant bent of our hearts will be to wisdom, and virtue, and to ascend into the realms of perfect day." "Happy advice," the father of AZORA said, and the thing was immediately done. A colony was quickly established here, and everything was settled and ordered in the most advantageous manner. Cattle, instruments, and grain to sow the land were sent in ; clothes and every material the little republic could want were provided, and every hand was as useful as we could wish. "For four years," AZORA continued to inform me, "we lived in peace and tranquillity, and never once regretted the loss of our fortunes. We were happier far than when we had thousands. Industry, knowledge, and religion, were our employment. The night to come of pain and death gave us no uneasiness. We lived as the Christians of the first two centuries, and rather longed for than feared that event, which is to remove us to growing brightness for ever and ever. But a fever came in among us and swept away my father, and every man of our little republic, several women likewise, perished ; but a hundred souls remained. Ninety-eight women, besides ANTONIA and AZORA. These loved me too well," she continued, "to abandon me ; and as they were happily situated, and many of them had learned their husbands trades, they agreed and swore to spend their lives with me here and be as serviceable as possible, without admitting any men to live among us. They are so in the highest degree : they are all useful and pious as I could wish them, and under the heavens there is not a happier society of mortals. We have the best of everything : all we want, and in reason could wish for."

Here AZORA ended her relation, and I wondered greatly at what I heard ; nor did my admiration lessen when I saw how she governed this community, and they employed their time. Her great understanding enlightened and directed them, in the execution of everything serviceable and ingenious ; and she lived before their eyes an example of the greatest industry, and the most exalted piety. They, on the other hand, were as useful

and religious as possible, and so heartily and faithfully discharged
social duties, in every instance, that they seemed as one great
capacity and power at work, to promote every convenience and
good.   Some of them, as I have said, were at work in the gardens :
others in the fields : various trades and occupations were going
on within doors and without, and all were employed in ways that
best subserved the general welfare.   In their behaviour, there
was nothing wild, insolent, or arch, to be seen : no swellings of
vanity and pride : no passion to disoblige : no intention to offend :
but, every one, discreet and calm ; good-humoured, and very
civil ; worthily sustaining their various relations, and each attentive to her own incumbent duty.   Their labours were but a
diversion to them, and they lived in tranquillity and plenty.
Their clothing was coarse, but very good, clean, and handsome.
There was not one ragged or dirty person among them ; nor any
with bad shoes and stockings.   In all respects they seemed a
most happy community.   AZORA studied, to the utmost degree,
the advantage and happiness of these people : and they, in return,
made their duty a vigorous and cheerful service.   Most of the
conveniences and comforts of life they had within their own little
territory ; flesh and fish, mutton, kid, and venison ; corn for
bread, every vegetable ; malt-drink, meath, and cyder ; all in
great plenty, and most excellent ; wool and flax for clothing ;
good candles ; and wood enough for firing.   What things they
wanted two of them rode for to the nearest town, and not only
purchased such goods with the money they got by sale of several
commodities, especially knit thread stockings and gloves ; but
always at such times brought in some cash to their mistress,
and she gave part of it among the people, to buy them little
things they fancied.

As to the ten young women I mentioned, who walked after
Azora when first I saw her, they were the daughters of some
widows in this little republic, and by her chosen, not only to be
her attendants and upper servants, and to look after her dairy,
her bees, her poultry, and her aviary ; which was the finest I have
ever seen, for the variety of birds, and as it was turfed, to avoid
the appearance of foulness on the floor, and so large as to give the
birds some freedom of flight ; but, on account of their good
understanding, in which they far excelled their fellows.   These
girls were carefully instructed by AZORA and ANTONIA, and beside
being taught the fine works of the needle, learned music, and the
elements of the mathematics from the ladies.   The eldest of
these girls was but twenty, and the youngest eighteen, and they
all surprised me very greatly with their quickness in answering
very hard arithmetical questions.   They could not only add,
subtract, multiply, divide, find a fourth proportional, and extract
roots of every kind with exactness and readiness, and apply

them upon all common occasions ; but were perfect in fractions vulgar and decimal. They had even gone as far in algebra as the resolution of simple equations.

Finding them one morning at figures, I asked the youngest of them, what was the number, that $\frac{2}{3}$ of it with 4 over, amounted to the same as $\frac{7}{12}$ of it with 9 over ? She immediately translated the question from common language into algebra $\frac{2x}{3} + 4 = \frac{7+}{12}$ +9 : and quickly discovered the unknown quantity x to be $x = 60$: Then she took it in synthetically, $\frac{2}{3}$ of $60 = 40 + 4 = 44 : \frac{7}{12}$ of $60 = 35 + 9 = 44$.—(Synthetically is tracing property from number : —Analytically is tracing number from property). This made me wonder very greatly. I asked another of them, if she bought 20 loaves for 16 pence, all of them twopenny, penny, and farthing ones—how many would she have of each ? She answered 5 twopenny loaves, 3 penny ones, and 12 farthing loaves ; for the equations were $x + y + z = 20$ and $8x + 4y = z = 64$. From whence by subtraction, $7x + 3y = 44$, and of consequence, $y = \frac{44 - 7 +}{3}$ $= 14 - 2x + \frac{2 - x}{3}$.

I asked a third, how many ways she could pay 20*l.* in pistoles, guineas, and moidores, at 17*s.*, 21*s.* and 27*s.* the pistole, the guinea, and the moidore ?. She replied in a very little time, 9 ways, to wit, 11 pistoles, 5 guineas, and 4 moidores—8 pistoles, 1 guinea, 9 moidores—8 pistoles, 10 guineas, 2 moidores—17 pistoles, 4 guineas, 1 moidore—2 pistoles, 2 guineas, 12 moidores —2 pistoles, 11 guineas, 5 moidores—5 pistoles, 6 guineas, 7 moidores—5, 15, 0—and 14 pistoles, 0 guineas, 6 moidores. This was a hard operation.

I asked another of these young women, if her lady gave her 297 guineas and 339 pistoles, to pay 6 men a hundred pounds apiece in guineas and pistoles only, as was agreed, how could she contrive to pay them, and dispatch the thing ? I will tell you, sir, she answered, very soon. x represents my guineas, and y my pistoles, and $21x + 17y = 2,000$, of consequence, $x = \frac{2000 - 17y}{21}$ $= 95 + \frac{5 - 17y}{21}$, etc. and quickly discovered, that the first man should have 92 guineas and 4 pistoles:—the second man, 75 guineas and 25 pistoles :—the third, 58 guineas, 45 pistoles :—the fourth, 41 guineas and 67 pistoles :—the fifth, 24 guineas and 88 pistoles : —and the sixth man, 7 guineas and 109 pistoles. This was admirable. But is there no other way, I said, of paying 100*l* in

guineas and pistoles, besides the six ways you have mentioned ?
There is no other way, the fine girl answered.   If a seventh man
was to be paid 100*l*. in these two kinds of money, he must be
paid in one of these six methods.   This was true.   I was charmed
with what I heard.

While I was thus engaged with the maids, AZORA and ANTONIA
came into the room, and fiuding how I had been employed, they
began to talk of problems, theorems, and equations, and soon
convinced me, that I was not superior to them in this kind of
knowledge ; though I had studied it for a much longer time, and
had taken more pains than ever they did.   Their fine understandings saw at once the things that made me sweat many an
hour, and in less time than I required for an operation, they could
answer the most difficult questions, and do anything in simple
quadratic equations, and in the composition and resolution of
ratios.   This I thought very wonderful ; especially as they had
been taught no longer than one year by Mr. Burcot ; and that
they had acquired the most abtruse part of their knowledge by
their own application.   I note the thing down as one of the
strangest and most extraordinary cases that ever came in my
way : perhaps, that ever was heard.   It is such a specimen of
female understanding, as must for ever knock up the positive
assertions of some learned men, who will not allow that women
have as strong reasoning heads as the men.

By the way, I observe, exclusive of these two ladies that I have
seen many of the sex who were distinguished for accuracy and
comprehensiveness, not only in the science, where known and
required quantities are denoted by letters, but in other fine parts
of learning   I have little right to pretend to anything extraordinary in   understanding, as my genius is slow, and such is
common in the lower classes of men of letters ; yet, my application
has been very great : my whole life has been spent in reading
and thinking : and, nevertheless, I have met with many women,
in my time, who, with very little reading have been too hard for
me on several subjects.   In justice, I declare this ; and am very
certain from what I have heard numbers of them say, and seen
some of them write, that if they had the laboured education the
men have, and applied to books with all possible attention for
as many years as we do ; there would be found among them as
great   divines   as   Episcopius,   Limborch,   Whichcote,   Barrow,
Tillotson, and Clarke ; and as great mathematicians, as M'Laurin,
Saunderson, and Simpson.   The critics may laugh at this assertion, I know they will : and, if they please, they may doubt my
veracity as to what I relate of the two ladies, and the ten young
women, in Burcot-Hamlet ; but what I say is true notwithstanding.   Facts are things too stubborn to be destroyed by
laughing and doubting.

As to the ladies I have mentioned, they both did wonders in specious arithmetic ; but AZORA was the brightest of the two, and in pure algebra, had gone much farther than ANTONIA. With wonder I beheld her, while she answered the most difficult questions as fast as fingers could move ; and in the solution of cubics, and the resolution of equations, both according to Des Cartes, laborious method, and the better universal way, by converging series, work with a celerity and truth beyond what I have ever seen any man do. Nor was it only algebra independent of geometry that she understood. She could apply its reasoning to geometrical figures, and describe the loci of any equations by the mechanical motion of angles and lines. She was in this respect the greatest prodigy I ever saw.

But it was not on account of this excellence that I so much admired AZORA, and honour her memory so greatly as I do ; nor because she talked so excellently on various subjects, as I have related ; but, for her knowledge of the truths of Christianity, and the habits of goodness she had wrought into her soul ; for the care she took of the people under her government, by communicating every felicity in her power, to their bodies and minds ; and the pure religion of Christ Jesus, which she publicly maintained, in all the beauty of holiness and, in a just fervour of practice. She was herself, in her manners and piety, a fine copy of those blessed women who conversed with our Lord and his apostles : and her society, in innocence and goodness, in usefulness and devotion, seemed an epitome of the first Christian church at Jerusalem. Under a just impression of the most heavenly principles they all lived, and strictly regarded their several offices. As the gospel directs, they worshipped a first cause, the Deity, as the disciples of the Christ of God, our holy mediator ; and the authority of a being of infinite wisdom, and unchangeable rectitude of nature, had made such an impression upon their minds, that they laboured continually to acquire that consecration and sanctity of heart and manners, which our divine religion requires. Excellent community ! happy would Europe be, if all her states were like this people. A false religion would not then prevail ; nor would superstition be the idol to which the world bows down. The evils, which now dishonour human nature, and infest society, would not be seen among us ; nor those excesses of passion be known, which are the parent of discord and calamity, and render this lower world one scene of sin and sorrow : but, as revelation inculcates, as reason suggests, mankind would worship the Almighty Principle, the One God, the Only True God, with a worship suitable to the nature of a Being, who is not confined to, or dependent upon, particular places and circumstances, who is always, and everywhere present with us ; and like the ministers attending on the glorious throne of the Monarch of the world, they would, according to our measure, be pure, benevolent mortals, and as perfect in goodness, as men can be within the degree and limit of their nature. In a word, the supreme Father of all things would then be the God of all Christians ; and in doing his will, in imitating his perfections, and in practising everything recommended by the great and universal law of reason, that law which God sent our Lord to revive and enforce ; they would find the greatest pleasure. Such were the people of Burcot-Hamlet. AZORA and ANTONIA were indeed most glorious women.*

* AZORA BURCOT died in 1732, six years after I left them, but ANTONIA FLETCHER was [1756] living in the same happy situation ; and by advising the young women to marry some young men of those mountains, has made an alteration in the community for the better, and encreased the number of her people. The settlement is now like to continue, and they find many advantages from having men among them. The rising generation thereby acquired, now proves a blessing to the first colony, whom years have rendered much weaker and dependent than when I first saw them. AZORA, a little before she died, did intend to get in a recruit of female children for the support of the society : but ANTONIA judged it was much better to let the young girls of the community get honest youths for their spouses ; for, by this means, they can never want young people to assist and comfort them, and to encrease and perpetuate their happy republic. For these reasons, she sent for some young men to several neighbouring villages in Richmondshire, to make several things wanting and to dig, and work in the gardens, for so much by the year certain ; and as they were smitten with the clean, civil girls of Burcot-Hamlet, several marriages soon ensued, and infants were produced before the twelve months had expired. More than half of the twenty women that married, had twins the first year, and all of them had strong healthy children. The ten extraordinary girls I mentioned, got very good husbands, and as ANTONIA was particularly kind to them on their marrying, and gave to all the wedded folks great encouragement in profitable gardens and houses, grain and cattle, they and their spouses became rather more dutiful and useful to their mistress and ruler than otherwise, and in gratitude, and for the sake of their children, did their best to please Mrs. FLETCHER, and encrease the common felicity. In this condition I found them on my second arrival at Burcot-Hamlet. They were a flourishing village, and a most happy people. My second visit was in 1739, fourteen years after the first ; and I saw them a third time in 1752. They were then all well, and enjoyed every comfort of life that can proceed from good and useful manners. Mrs. FLETCHER, though now in years, has no sign of age in her constitution, and still leads a most active and pious life. She is a subaltern providence to them, and with the tenderest care, makes it the labour of her every day to secure and advance the temporal and eternal interest of the people : but their souls are her main care. She performs to them divine service twice every day, as good AZORA was wont to do. She reads the best sermons to the aged, and constantly catechises the young ones. She is a blessed woman.

By the way, reader, I must observe to you, that in travelling over that part of Richmondshire, which is called Stanemore, I found several small villages, that are not mentioned in Camden, or the *Britannia Antiqua et Nova,* or in *England's Gazetteer :* and though not so pretty and happy as Burcot in the northern end of the fells of Westmoreland ; yet in tolerable condition, and remarkable on account of several things and people ; though they live entirely on what their spot affords, and have little communication with their countrymen beyond the mountains that separate the inhabitants of Stanemore from the rest of England. I took notice, in particular, that although those poor remote people had not faculties adapted to large measures of knowledge, nor have ministers to teach them, or churches to pray in ; yet they were not alienated from the taste and feelings of humanity, nor strangers to the momentous principles of true Christianity. They had the Bible, and could read it. They instructed their children in virtue and religion, and lived themselves as the intelligent subjects of an Almighty Governor ; in a firm belief that God will distinguish the virtue and the offence of mankind hereafter, by suitable tokens of his favour, or displeasure. All this I saw in several villages of Stanemore-mountains. I lived for some time among the poor people : and I mention their case here, that you may have the less reason to imagine there is anything incredible in my account of the extraordinary state of Burcot-Hamlet.

As to the Stanemore-part of Richmondshire, Camden, and the authors of the other *Britannia,* and the tourmen, &c. never so much as saw this country at a distance, I am very sure. The very little they say of it is false and ridiculous. Camden places Bows before Gretabridge. He says, in this desolate and solitary, this mountainous and vast tract called Stanemore, there is but one inn in the middle of it for the entertainment of travellers, whereas, in truth, there is no inn at all in what is properly called Stanemore : the inn Camden speaks of

The 18th of June, 1725, I took my leave of Mrs. BURCOT and Mrs. FLETCHER, for so they would be called, as they informed me, after I had once used the word Miss ; and from this fine place, proceeded on my journey, by a paper of written directions I had received from them : as there was a pretty good, though a long and tedious way out of the mountains, if a traveller knew the passes and turnings ; but otherwise, it was either impossible to go on ; or a man must journey at the hazard of his life a thousand times a day, in crossing waters and precipices.

Our first labour was to ascend a very narrow steep way in the side of a mountain, which went up due north for a full mile, and brought us to another large, standing, black and unfathomable

is the Bell I mentioned before, where I breakfasted with Miss MELMOTH ; and lies on the left side of a fine turnpike road from Bows to Brugh, in Westmorland, the high-way to Carlisle ; but though this road is a part of Stanemore, running in a direct line from Gretabridge through Bows to Brugh, eighteen miles of delightful ground, both on account of the excellence of the way, and the fine views of mountains and vales on either hand, for twelve miles, from a beautiful ruin of a Roman castle at the end of the town,* yet this is but the southern beginning of Stanemore. That vast tract of mountains, glens, and valleys, forest, rock, and water, the most wonderful land in the world, for forty miles to the end of the country, if it was possible to go straight on, lies on the right hand of this road, as you ride to Brugh under Stanemore ; or, on your left, as you come from Westmoreland to Catarracton or Catarrick.

Here, by the way, let me tell you, Reader, lives RALPH HAWKWELL, who keeps an excellent house, where you may get choice things, after a ride of twenty two miles, if you come from Boroughbridge to go to the north ; or of fifteen miles, if from Greta-bridge, for the south ; provided you have the *rem* ; and if you have not, though you were an apostle of a man RALPH would have very little regard for you. Indeed, every where in the north, where the best of things are to be had, I have always found travelling there as expensive as near London. Many I know give a different account, but the reason is, either they never were there ; or they travel in a pilgrim-like manner. You must take care, then, to have money enough, if ever you undertake the northern expedition I have frequently gone upon : and as it is not safe carrying much cash with you, for there are rogues in that part of the world, as well as in this ; they rob even on Stanemore road ; and in riding over the great moor that lies between Brugh and Appleby, there is a little ale-house to be seen at a good distance, on the right hand, at the entrance of a wood, at the bottom of a range of vast fells, where highwaymen sometimes resort ; I was pursued by two of them, not long ago, and to the excellence of my horse, owed the saving of my purse, and perhaps my life · they were well mounted, but I kept an hundred yards ahead of them for several miles, while, as fast as they could stretch away, they chased me till near the town of Brugh. I was all alone, my fellow having received a mischief, and being obliged to stay a day behind ; and the rogues did swear and hoot most horribly, and fired three shots at me ; but my horse was as good as ever spanked it along, and I cut him up, and pricked him over the turf, like the wind away. I say, then, as it is not safe travelling with all the money necessary for such a long journey, the best way is, when cash runs low, to lie by to rest for a week, and put your notes in order, in some town and by one of the dealers, or manufacturers of the place, draw on your friend, or goldsmith in London, for what you want, and by the return of the post, you will be paid the money where you are. In this manner I did, when I was last at Richmond, in the north-riding of Yorkshire. Being in want of money, I asked a gentleman with whom I chanced to dine

* By the way, I suspect from Bishop Horsley's account of the Roman castle or station that he never was on the spot, but had his relation from the surveyor he sent out to find the length of this Roman wall, and take other dimensions and notes for his *Britannia Romana* I mean Mr. Cay, who published the late map of Northumberland, which Bishop Horsley employed him to make. He does not describe the fort and situation, and the adjacent country, as if he had been there himself : nor can I think he ever rode from this castle to Brugh or Burgh under Stanemore, or from Brugh, the Roman Veteræ, to Brovocum, now Brougham-Castle, a great and curious Roman ruin. The finest things relating to them, he has omitted, and many antiquities that are to be found in off-sets by the way. I question, likewise, if ever he saw with his own eyes, the eastern and western terminations of the Roman wall. If he was at Newcastle, and really did ride over Lonsdale marsh to Tunnocelum, a marsh where I had like to have lost my life ; it is surprising that a man of his understanding and taste for antiquities, should give no better account of these places. For my part, I could not see what he saw : nor did he see what I saw at the end of the town of Boulness.

water, on the top of this high hill.   There was no appearance of any feeders to supply this frightful lake, and therefore, and on account of its blackness, the surface must communicate with the abyss.   From this water we rode due east for half an hour, and then descended to a sandy valley, where flames were rising from the ground.   The fire came up without noise, smoke, or smell, and appeared to me very wonderful ; but such things are common in many parts of the world.   In the side of one of the Apennines, I have seen a large blazing vale.   The learned tell us, this is owing to rich veins of bitumen, which crops in such places, and the heat of the air between the hills, in shallow valleys, causes it to burn.   This crop of bitumen, and accension by the agitation

how I could supply myself with £20 by draft on one in the capital ; and he directed me to his neighbour, who let me have what I had occasion for at moderate exchange, as soon as he heard from his friend in London.   I might have had any money I named in this way ; and so, in other places of trade.

I hope, reader, you will excuse this little digression, because it is meant well ; and for the same reason, I imagine you will pardon me for advising you, in the next place, should the fates ever bring you to Cataractonium, in order to proceed to the northern extremity of our country ; to go four miles out of your way to see Richmond town, before you set out for Gretabridge, to JOSEPH MARSHALL'S ; the best house of the two inns there.   The delightful romantic situation of Richmond, and the fine curiosities about the town, will afford you an agreeable entertainment for a couple of days ; and if you like going at night to a club of very worthy, sensible men of this town, who are very civil to strangers, you may pass the evening in a very pleasing way ; or if you have a taste for dancing, and prefer the conversation of a fine girl to a pipe and more serious discourse, there is a small polite assembly of as pretty women as ever gladdened the heart of man.   My method, while there, was to smoke one night with the club ; and the next I devoted to the ladies.   We made up ten couple, and had the hemp-dressers one night, which is, you know, if you are a dancing reader, the most difficult, and laborious of all the country dances ; and no where have I seen the ground more actively beat, or, in juster measure.   Life and truth and charms were in perfection in those Richmond girls.   I was there in 1729, 1737, and again in 1752, and the sensible club, and bright assembly, were still in being ; but no more than three did I see, of men or women, in 37, that were there in 29 ; and in 52, they were all strangers to me.   Some were married away ; some had removed ; and others were translated to the shades of eternity.   This was to me a moral lesson.   When I looked round the assembly room the last time I was there, and found every glorious girl of my acquaintance was gone, and that years had rendered me almost unfit to join with the ladies then present, in the dancings of the night, a philosophical sadness came powerfully upon my mind, and I could not help sighing in the midst of harmony, and a blaze of charms.   This life, I saw was a fleeting scene indeed.

And now, reader, as to the Stanemore-country, if it should ever come into your head, to wander over this wild and romantic part of our world, at the hazard of your neck, and the danger of being starved, your route is, when you have passed the turnpike on Stanemore, in your way to Brugh, to turn off to the right, beyond the public-house, and ascend a fine rising valley you will see between two mountains, till you come to the top of the first hills : then proceed, if you can, in the course I have described, and wherever it is in your power, tend to the north-east, for that is the way out.   This is one way into the heart of Stanemore in Richmondshire, and will bring you, by the way, among the dreadful northern fells of Westmoreland ; a frightful country, and a fatiguing march.

Another way to the Stanemore Alps, is behind JACK RAILTON'S, the quaker's house at Bows.   Hire a guide from him, and his man will bring you as he did me once through a very surprising way of deep bottoms to a public house at Eggleston, on the border of Richmond-Stanemore.   There rest that night, and early the next morning, proceed due north, when you can, with another guide, and you will come to mountains upon mountains, rapid rivers and headlong torrents, that form amazing and tremendous scenes.   Or, as this way is neither comfortable, nor very safe, it is a better road to the confines, or beginning of Stanemore, to ride from Gretabridge to Bernard Castle, and from Bernard Castle to Eggleston, about sixteen miles, as I judge, for it is not measured, and then set out for the mountains from Eggleston, as before directed.   I have been told there is another way into Stanemore, through Bishoprick ; but as I am a stranger to it, I can only say what I have heard, that it is worse than the bottoms I went through from the quaker's house.   This is enough, reader, to shew you how to get into Stanemore, if you have the curiosity and heart to visit that very wild and wonderful land.

of hot air, is well fancied, I own : but it does not give me full satisfaction. I think of this, and many other natural things, as Moyle does of the aurora borealis : that these uncommon appearances should be looked on with wonder and admiration, and raise in us a due reverence of their great Author, who has shown his Almighty power and wisdom in forming such an infinite variety of productions in all parts of the universe. Philosophy undertakes to account for everything. I am sure it is in many cases mistaken.

Having passed the burning valley, we rode through a river, that was up to the horses bellies, very rapid, and a bad bottom, and then proceeded along a steep hill side, the course N.W. till we came to a rich low land, that was covered with flowers and aromatic shrubs, and adorned with several clumps of oak, chestnut, and white walnut trees. This plain is about twenty five acres, surrounded with stony mountains, some of which are very high and steep, and from the top of one of the lowest of them, a cataract descends, like the fall of the river Niagara in Canada, or New France, in North America. Swifter than an arrow from a bow the rapid river comes headlong down in a fall of an hundred and forty feet, which is three feet more than the descent of Niagara. The river here, to be sure, is not half so large as that which comes from the vast lakes of Canada, but it is a great and prodigious cadence of water, and tumbles perpendicularly in as surprising a manner, from as horrible a precipice ; and in this very nearly resembles the Niagara Fall ; that as you stand below, as near the fall as it is safe to go, you see the river come down a sloping mountain for a great way, as if it descended from the clouds It is a grand and amazing scene. The water issues from a great lake on the top of a mountain that I found very hard to ascend, and the lake has many visible feeders from hills upon hills above it, which it is impossible to climb.

18 June.— It was twelve o'clock by the time we arrived at this water fall, and therefore I sat down by the side of it to dine, before I attempted to get up to the top of the precipice, and see from whence this water came. While my eyes were entertained with the descending scene, I feasted on a piece of venison pasty, and some fine ale, which, among other provisions, Mrs. Burcot had ordered her servants to put up for me : but as I was thus happily engaged, my lad, O'Fin, had climbed up to the top of the waterfall, and was going to land from a tree that grew out of the rocky mountain near the summit of the hill, when his foot slipped, and he came tumbling down in a miserable way. I expected him in pieces on the ground, as I had him full in my view. There seemed no possibility of an escape, and yet he received no harm. In the middle of the descent, he stuck in another projecting thick tree, and from it came safely down. This was a deliverance.

F

Providence often saves us in a wonderful manner, till the work appointed to be finished is done, or the limited time of our trial over. In relation to such escapes, I could give myself as an instance many a time, and will here mention one extraordinary case.

As I travelled once in the county of Kerry in Ireland, with the White Knight, and the Knight of the Glen,* we called at Terelah O Crohane's, an old Irish gentleman, our common friend, who kept up the hospitality of his ancestors, and showed how they lived, when Cormac MacCuillenan, the Generous, from whose house he descended ; was king of Munster and archbishop of Cashel in the year 913.† There was no end of eating and

* Such knights were honourable creations made by the Irish kings. We have an account of them in the *Psalter of Tarah*, before the reigns of Conaire the Great, A.M. 3970, ante Christum 34 ; Cormac Ulfadda, A.D. 230 ; and the glorious Brien Boiroimhe, A.D. 1027 : the three greatest monarchs that ever Ireland had. Fitzgerald, the first knight of Glen, was so made by the immortal Brien Boiroimhe, who fell in the bloody fight between him and Maolmorda king of Leinster, who had joined with the Danes, A.D. 1239. The king of Ireland and the king of Leinster slew each other ; and with Brien Boiroimhe set the glory of Ireland. The states from this time began to decay ; and Roderic O'Connor, who came to the crown, A.D. 1168, was the last king of Ireland. Our Henry II., got the king-dom A.D. 1172, by two means ; one of which was a grant the Pope made of it to him ; who was allowed by the natives to be supreme Lord of the island in temporals, and the nobility had by commission resigned it to him, after the death of Brien Boiroimhe. The other mean, and what effectually did the work, was the king of Leinster's joining with Strangwell, who was at the head of the English forces, and had married that king's daughter. An old chronicle says she was the most beautiful woman upon earth of her time, and very learned ; but inferior nevertheless in beauty and learning to the six princesses we read of in the *Psalter of Tarah*, who were fair beyond all mortals that ever lived, and wonderful in the extent of their know-ledge ; to wit—

The princess Mac Diarmuid.
The princess Mac Reagien.
The princess Mac Faolian.
The princess Mac Kennedy.
The princess O'Heyn.
The princess O'Flaherty.

These six were Druidesses, says the *Psalter of Tarah*.

By the way, reader, let me tell you, that from this same *Psalter of Tarah*, I wrote out one of the finest and most improving love stories that ever I read. It is called ' the Adventure of Terlagh Mac Shain and the beautiful Gara O'Mulduin ; which happened in the reign of Cormac Ulfada, king of Ireland, in the year of salvation 213, that Faon Maccumhail, com-monly called Fian Maccul, the mighty champion, beat the Picts, and brought off among other prisoners, the beautiful Ciarnuit, daughter to the king of the Picts, whom Cormac Ulfada took for his concubine." This story is likewise more shortly told in *The Red Book of Mac Eogane*, a very valuable old Irish manuscript : and from both those books I will give my reader the best part of this adventure as soon as I can see a proper place to bring it in.

† This Cormac Cuillenan wrote the famous *Psalter of Cashel*, a very extraordinary and valu-able book, which he composed from antient poems of the bards, who thus wrote their history, and from venerable records, as this king and prelate declares in his will. The clause is this " My psalter, which preserves the ancient records and monuments of my native country, which are transcribed with great fidelity, I leave to Ronal Cashel, to be preserved to after-times and ages yet to come." There is another remarkable clause in this great man's will, to wit, " My soul for mercy I commit to heaven ; my body leave to dust and rottenness." There is not a word of any saint in it ; and of consequence, there was no saint-worship then in Ireland.

Cormac wrote his will the day before he fought the bloody battle of Maghailbe with the king of Leinster, and therein fell. It begins in this manner :

" Summon'd away by death, which I perceive
Approaches ; for by prophetic skill,
I find that short will be my life and reign :
I solemnly appoint that my affairs
Shall thus be settled after I am dead ;

drinking and the famous DOWNE FALVEY played on the harp. For a day and a night we sat to it by candle-light, without shirts or clothes on ; naked excepting that we had our breeches and shoes and stockings on ; and I drank so much Burgundy in that time, that the sweat ran of a red colour down my body ; and my senses were so disordered, that when we agreed to ride out for a couple of hours to take a little air, I leaped my horse into a dreadful quarry, and in the descent was thrown into a large deep water that was in a part of the frightful bottom, and by that means saved my life. When I came above water I swam very easily out of the pit, and walked up the low side of the quarry as sober as if I had not drank a glass. This is a fact, whatever the critics may say of the thing. All I can say to it is my hour was not come.

Having dined, and shot a bustard that weighed forty pounds, I went on again, the course northwest for half a mile, and then to my astonishment, it trended to the south for more than an hour ; which was going back again : but at last it turned about, and for half an hour, we went to the north-west again, and then due east for a long time, till we came to hills upon hills that were very difficult to pass. We were obliged to alight at many of them, and walk up and down them, which was a delay of many

> And thus I constitute my latest will :
> My royal robe embroider'd o'er with gold,
> And sparkling with the rays of costly jewels ;
> Well suited to a state of majesty,
> I do bequeath &c.———
> My coat of mail of bright and polish'd steel
> Will well become the martial king of Ulster,
> To whom I give it ; and my golden chain
> Shall the most pious Muchuda enjoy
> As a reward, &c.———
> My golden vestment for most sacred use,
> And my royal wardrobe I hereby give
> To &c.———"

Now from this antique piece verbally translated, I think it is evident, that the kings of the four provinces of Ireland were not such poor and ignorant chiefs as ¦ they are generally imagined to be ; and of consequence, that one of the four to whom the other three did homage, and who was therefore called the king of Ireland, was always a potent prince, and could do great matters, when they were all united. This consideration, I fancy, and the address let me add of Anselm, archbishop of Canterbury, and of Lanfranc, archbishop of the same see, " to Mortogh O'Brien king of Ireland, and Terlagh O'Brien king of Ireland, Moriardacho Glorioso and Terdeluacho Magnifico. To the most magnificent Terlagh O'Brien, king of Ireland, our benediction," &c. as you may read them at large in Usher's *Primordia* * ought to give some credit to O'Flaherty's *Ogygia*, Keating's *History*, and Mac Curtins' *Annals* ; which those writers really took from very ancient records, and principally from the very valuable manuscripts, called the *Psalters of Cashel* and *Tarah.*

What the *Psalter of Cashel* was I have told you, reader ; and as to the Psalter *of Tarah* the history of it is this.—On a tract of land called Tarah, that was taken from the province of Leinster, and added to the county of Meath, stood the largest of the four vast palaces of the kings of Ireland, and at that grand fabric there was a triennial meeting of the states of the kingdom, called the royal assembly of Tarah. There they enacted laws, examined the ancient chronicles and records, and purged them from all false and spurious relations, settled genealogies, and considered noble exploits. All the things that received the assembly's approbation were registered, and transcribed into the royal records, and they called this journal the *Psalter of Tarah.*

---

* These letters were written by the English archbishops to the Irish kings, Turlogh and Murtogh, in the years 1098 and 1110.

hours : but we did it at last, and came into a large sandy opening, that had a number of rapid streams breaking over it, that fell from the mountains, and with the forest on the surrounding hills, formed a wild and pleasing scene.   Over this we went for half a mile, and then came to a long glen, so very deep and narrow that it was quite night when we got to the bottom of it, though the sun was not yet down ; and it brought to my remembrance Anchises' son, the wandering prince of Troy, when he descended to the shades below.   It had the appearance indeed of some such place, and was a frightful way, as hills, like Caucasus and Atlas, were close on either hand of us, and a river roared through the bottom of the steep descent ; which we were obliged to walk down on foot.   This could not be the right road I was certain. Azora and Antonia could never pass this deep and rapid flood It was too much for any man to venture into, without knowing where the torrent went, or how the channel of the river was formed.

Up then I came again to the day, and resolved to pass the night at the foot of one of the woody hills, on the margin of the streams that sounded sweetly over the shores : but how to proceed the next morning I knew not.   As my paper of directions did not mention the dark steep descent we had been down, but a little valley that lay due east, through which we were to go : no such vale could we see, and of consequence, in some turning of the road, we had gone wrong.

When I came among the trees, on the side of one of the mountains, I began to look for some convenient resting-place, while my two boys were picking the bustard, and preparing a fire to roast it for supper, and wandered a good way till I saw a pretty hermitage in an open plain like a ring, and going up to it, found the skeleton of a man.   He lay on a couch in an inward room without any covering, and the bones were as clean and white as if they had come from the surgeon's hands.   The pismires to be sure had eaten off the flesh.   Who the man was, a paper lying on the table in a strong box informed me.   It was called

THE CASE OF JOHN ORTON.

" I was twenty years old when Charles II. was restored, in 1660 ; and being master of large fortunes, and educated in an aversion to puritans and republican principles, went into all the licentiousness and impieties, which overspread and corrupted this nation, when that profligate prince ascended the throne.   I drank up to the excess of the times : I debauched every woman I could get within my power, by gold, treachery, or force ; maid, wife, and widow : I murdered several men in duels ; and blasphemed the God of heaven continually.   The devil was my first and last toast ; and, in a club I belonged to, I proceeded to such scarce credible

wickedness, as to perform the part of the priest in our infernal
sodality, and after using the words of consecration over the
elements, gave the prophane bread and wine in the most horrible
manner. I was the most abominable of mortals; Contrary
to all the dictates and principles of wisdom, virtue, and honour
I acted ; bound myself in bondage to Satan ; and lived the most
execrable slave to the vilest inclinations, and most heinous habits.
Scratch was the name I had for the evil one, and upon all occasions
I invoked him. The last words I said every night, after lying
down, were ' Scratch, tuck me in.'

"In this diabolical manner did I pass my life away till I was forty,
and in twenty years time committed every evil that can dishonour
human manners, and infest society. I was a disgrace to my
species, and unworthy of the name of man.

"But as I went on in this manner, and gloried only in outdoing
the greatest scelerates in impiety and debauchery, in being the
chief instrument of Satan, and striving to bring every soul I
got acquainted with, in subjection to the flesh and the devil ;
maliciously committing all manner of sin ; and with greediness
executing the suggestions of a defiled imagination, and the
purposes of the most corrupt heart ; I was struck one night
with the most excruciating torment of body ; and had, at the
same time, such unspeakable horrors upon my mind, that I
believe my condition resembled the state of the damned. The
tortures all over my frame, were beyond the pains any rack
could cause ; but were less afflicting than the panic fear that harrowed my soul under a lively sense of eternal vengeance, for
the crying enormities and impurities of my life. All my crimson
crimes were held as in a mirror before me ; the most diabolical
impieties against heaven, and the most shocking cruelties to
men ; the numbers I had drank to death, and secured in the
service of hell ; the men I had sent to the other world by combat
at pistol and sword ; and the women I had ruined, not only in
this life, but perhaps, for evermore ; the miseries I had brought
upon families, and the manifold afflictions I had been the author
of for years after years, by night and by day ; all these offences
I saw like the hand-writing on the wall, and in a horror and con-
sternation of mind, that words cannot describe, lay a miserable
spectacle for two nights and two days. Tormented, perplexed,
and confounded, I rolled from side to side, and condemned
myself and my folly in the most doleful complaints ; but dared
not look up to a just judge and offended God. No slumber
for this time did approach my eyes ; but in agonies I shook
with a frightful violence, and thought every moment, that the
demons my fancy had in view, were going to force my miserable
soul away to everlasting inflictions, in the most dismal cavern
of hell. Spent, however, at last, I fell into a short sleep. I had

half an hour's rest, and in that slumber imagined, I heard a small voice say, ' As I live, saith the Lord, I have no pleasure in the death of the wicked ; but that the wicked turn from his way, and live : Turn ye, turn ye from your evil ways ; for why will ye die, O house of Israel. Rend your heart, and not your garments, and turn unto the Lord your God : for he is gracious and merciful, slow to anger, and of great kindness, and repenteth him of the evil.'

" Upon this I awaked, and found my pains were gone. To heaven I lifted my eyes, and as the tears poured down my face, cried out to God for mercy. " O God be merciful to me a sinner. Have mercy on me dust and sin, the vilest of all sinful creatures. To me belongs nothing but shame and confusion of face eternally. My portion should in justice be the lake of everlasting fire and brimstone. But O Lord God most mighty, O holy and most merciful Father, to thee belongeth infinite goodness and forgiveness. O remember not my sins and transgressions, my great and numberless provocations, and my trespasses that are grown up even unto heaven. Have mercy upon me, O God, after thy great goodness, and according to the multitude of thy mercies, do away mine offences. I have a hearty sense and detestation of all my abominations, and with a true contrition of heart, I repent of all my iniquities. Wash me, then, I beseech thee, O Father of mercies ; wash my polluted soul in the blood of the holy Jesus, and forgive me all my sins, as I offer up a troubled spirit, and a broken and contrite heart, which thou hast promised not to despise. And grant, O Lord God, my Father, that I may from this hour, by the guidance and direction of thy sanctifying spirit, bid a final adieu to all ungodliness and iniquity ; and consecrate myself entirely to thee, to serve thee with humility, love and devotion, and for the remainder of my life, give thee the sacrifices of righteousness, through Jesus Christ our Lord.'

" When I had thus implored the mercy of the Almighty, in a torrent of tears, with strong cryings, I found my heart quite easy, and my mind so filled with delights and comforts, that I cannot describe the strange happiness of my condition : but how to secure this felicity was the question. I was afraid of the world, and trembled when I thought of its temptations : beside, the great wickedness of my past life made it necessary that I should live in an extraordinary state of penitence, and by great mortification and piety, make what amends I could for sinning against heaven in the most atrocious manner ; and wilfully for a long series of years, breaking every law of the just and holy governor of the world. A change of mind, and common piety, were not enough for such a wretch as I had been. I was unworthy of the innocent comforts of life. I ought to breathe in sighs, and speak in groans. I resolved then to be a reform indeed, and in this part of Stanemore mountains, which I was well acquainted with, spend the remainder of my days, in the labours of a penitential piety.

"As I had no relations living, I sold what estates I had left, and gave almost the whole money among the poor. With the little I kept, I bought what necessary things I should want in my solitude; and with tools and seeds, some clothes and linen, a few books, and other little matters, retired to this spot in the year 1681. I had some working men from the next village, to build me the little hut I live in; to sow my garden with every vegetable, and put some fruit-trees in the ground; to cut me a pile of firing from the woody hills; and make my place as convenient as my intended life could require. All this was soon done, and then I was left alone; in the possession of everything I had a wish for in this world. It is now twenty years since my arrival here, and in all the time, I have not had one sick or dismal hour. My garden and my cottage employ me in agreeable labours, to furnish my table with roots and fruits; which is what I mostly live on; having nothing more but goat's milk, and now and then a sea-biscuit; my drink being water, and sometimes a cup of meath of my own making.

"When I am weary of working, I sit down to study my *B ible*, and in that most perfect treasure of saving knowledge, I find such joy and satisfaction as make my life a scene of heavenly happiness, and charm me into raptures the nearer I approach to the hour of my dissolution. That will be a blessed hour. By the amazing mercy of God, vouchsafed through the Lord Jesus, my crimson sins are pardoned; and when the voice of the Son of God, the thunder of the dreadful trumpet will awake all the dead, I shall have my part in the first resurrection, and ascend with the blessed to the eternal mansions of the sky. Adored be thy goodness, most glorious *E*ternal. Inestimable is thy love in the redemption of sinners by the gospel, and the sacrifice of the holy Jesus !

"Fellow mortal, whoever thou art, into whose hands this paper cometh, take my advice, and remember thy latter end. If, like me, thou hast been betrayed by the demons into great impieties and presumptuous sins, and hast been persuaded to abdicate heaven, and its eternal hopes, in exchange for illicit gratifications of every kind, and the pleasures of this world then, like me, repent, and in tears and mortification, implore the mercy of heaven. Turn to the everlasting Father of mercies, and the God of all comforts, after his own manner, with humility, sorrow, and resolutions of amendment, and in the name of Lord Jesus Christ, implore his compassion and forgiveness, and he will repent and turn unto thee. He will wash you in the blood of Jesus, and make you whiter than snow. When he sees the sinner a great way off in tears, fasting, and prayer, he will run unto him, and fall upon his neck and kiss him. You will become the beloved of the Father, and be reinstated in the favour of the greatest and most glorious of immortal beings. He will bless you here with that peace that passeth all understanding. He will bless you for ever hereafter with glory and honour in the kingdom he has prepared for the benevolent, the pure, and the honest. But if you continue to offend your Creator, and violate the laws of the God of heaven, then will you live exposed to judgments in this world, and most certainly will depart in confusion and misery. The demons you obeyed will gather round the pale, the guilty, the affrighted ghost of you, eager to involve your wretched spirit in their own horrors, and will drag it to their dismal regions. And when all the monuments of human power, wealth and pride, shall be overthrown ; the earth itself be in a blaze, and the sea turned into vapours, at the descent of the Son of God, to judge the vast congregation of the sons of men, the amazing assembly of mortals, unheard of generations raised from the grave to have all their actions tried ; every condition ever-lastingly determined ; then will you be placed in that division which will call upon the rocks to hide them, and the hills to cover them from the face of the Judge ; but in vain attempt to secret themselves from an infinite eye, and an Almighty power. Then will the terrors of the gospel stand in full force against thee, and in the dreadful sentence pronounced against the guilty you must share—Depart from me, ye cursed, into everlasting fire. O dreadful doom ! what a tremendous day to sinners ! and to see the righteous acquitted, and before your eyes ascend in triumph and splendour into the mansions of glory, to live the happy favourities of God and Christ for never-ending ages ; while you are driven forward to the infernal prison, and shut up in the habitations of eternal darkness and torments, the very thought of it, if you will think seriously of it, is enough to curdle the blood, and wither in a moment every unlawful joy that sin can produce in bloom and glory. The despair, the sighs, the groans, the doleful shrieks, when the wicked are driven off to the regions of blackness and darkness for ever, are inexpressible. Think then. Think in time, my fellow mortal and profit by the blood of a Saviour. Study his gospel. Hear his ministers. Regard the alarms of conscience, and submit to the influence of the holy Spirit.

And if you are not that monster of iniquity I once was, before I obtained the divine mercy, by a timely and severe repentance, yet, as in heaven so in hell, there are many mansions, and if you do not work out your salvation according to the terms of the gospel, and make every law of Christ the rules of your behaviour ; if you do not act continually as related to God, to each other, and to another world, and seek first the kingdom of God, and the righteousness thereof, you will utterly disqualify yourself for the rewards and happiness of heaven, though your conduct may be far from meriting the most dreadful inflictions in another world. The gains of unrighteousness, or meddling with any forbidden fruit, is a violation of the laws of God that must ruin you for ever ; though the punishment for so doing cannot be equal to the torments prepared for the tyrant and oppressor, the murderer, the adulterer, the drunkard, and offenders in the highest crimes, We must cease to do evil, and learn to do well, in order to be saved. Not according to promises and prayers at last, not according to legacies to be paid to the poor when we are dead, shall we be judged ; but, as we have rectified the judgment and the will, made virtue the governor of the heart, and in all things sought God's glory, not our own. This do, and you will live.

" JOHN ORTON."

May 1, 1701.

This extraordinary paper surprised me very greatly, and when from reading it, I turned my eyes to the bones of JOHN ORTON, I could not help breaking out in the following reflection. And is this the once lively, gallant, drinking JACK ORTON, who thought for forty years that he was made for no higher end than to gratify every appetite, and pass away time in a continual circle of vanity and pleasure! Poor skeleton, what a miserable spectacle art thou! Not the least remain of activity and joy, of that sprightliness and levity of mind, that jocund humour and frolic, which rendered thee the delight of the wild societies of thy youthful time : grim, stiff, and horrid, is the appearance now ; vain mirth and luxury, licentious plays and sports, can have no connection with these dry bones.

O Death, what a change dost thou make l The bulk of mankind are averse to serious thought, and hearken to the passions more than to the dictates of reason and religion : to kill time, and banish reflection, they indulge in a round of dissipations, and revel in the freedom of vicious excesses : their attention is engrossed by spectacle and entertainments, and fixed to follies and trifles ; giddy and unthinking, loose and voluptuous, they spend their precious hours in the gay scenes of diversions, pomp and luxury ; and as if the grave and a judgment to come, were a romance of former times, or things from which they are secured, never think of these important and momentous subjects ; with minds bewitched by exorbitant pleasure, and faculties enervated and broken by idle mirth and vanity, they pass their every day away without any of that consideration which becomes reasonable beings, and creatures designed for a state of immortality : but at last, you appear, and in a moment turn delight and admiration, into aversion and horror : strength, wealth, and charms, you instantly reduce to weakness, poverty, and deformity, in the first place ; and then, to a skeleton like the bones before me.

Nor is this the worst of the great revolution. When death approaches, the amusements of sense immediately fail, and past transactions in every circumstance of aggravation, crowd into the mind : conscience reproaches loudly, the heart condemns, and the sick tremble at the apprehensions of a vengeance they laughed at in the days of diversion, and the midnight hours of the ball : as they come near the black valley, they see the realities of a future state ; and agonies convulse their souls : terrors till then unknown enter their breasts ; and, in anxieties that are incapable of being uttered, and expectations the most torturing, on a review of life, they pass from the plains of time into the ocean of eternity. Here lies the frame, like the dry bones before me ; but, the soul is gone to the sessions of righteousness ; and perhaps, the dreadful sentence of the divine justice is pronounced on it. This is a tremendous affair, that calls for timely and serious consideration. *E*ternity l *E*ternal misery l They that have done evil, to come forth unto the resurrection of damnation.

I will take thy advice then, thou glorious penitent, JOHN ORTON ; and since it is in my power to come forth unto the resurrection of life, and obtain immortality, honour, and glory, with the righteous, in the kingdom of their father, I will open the reforming gospel night and morning, and by its heavenly directions regulate my conduct. I am determined to make a wise and serious preparation for death and judgment. To the best of my power, I will provide for that day, when the prayers and charities of the righteous will be brought forth as their memorials before the tribunal of Jesus Christ.

This is the thing to be minded. The brightest scenes of wordly prosperity, and grandeur, are contemptible, when they do not accord with virtue and piety. Death, in a few years, blends the prince and the meanest subject, the conqueror and the slave, the statesman, the warrior and the most insignificant in one promiscuous ruin ; and the schemes, the competitions, and the interests, which have engaged the chief attention of the world, are brought to nothing, and appear, too often, ridiculous : but righteousness is unchangeably glorious, and in the universal ruin, receives no detriment : when all human power and policy will be extinct : concealed piety and persecuted virtue, will again appear, and be owned as his by the Lord of Hosts, in that day when he maketh up his jewels.

I will love thee therefore, O Lord my strength ; yea, I will love thee : and it shall ever be my heart's desire, that my soul may behold by faith in itself, as in a glass, the glory of the Lord, able and ready to change it into the same image from glory to glory, reflected upon, and conveyed to it by the Spirit of the Lord. May my portion here be this blessed transforming union, that I may be made partaker of the divine nature, by impressions from it.* I shall then have all I wish, and all I want. With a settled indifference I shall then look upon the highest advantages of this world. I shall have nothing to hope or to fear. The will of God will be to me unmixed felicity.

Such was the soliloquy I spoke, as I gazed on the skeleton of JOHN ORTON ; and just as I had ended, the boys brought in the wild turkey, which they had very ingeniously roasted, and with

---

* The expression, " partaker of the divine nature by impressions from it," may, perhaps, be thought by some readers, to approach to vision ; and to contradict my own opinion before delivered, in relation to this subject : let me observe then, that by impression, I here mean no more, than bright beams of light cast upon the soul by the present Deity ; as he sits all power, all knowledge, in the heart, and dispenses such rays of wisdom to the pious petitioner, as are sufficient to procure a lasting sense of spiritual heavenly things. God is not only in heaven. He dwelleth indeed in the heaven of heavens after the most glorious manner, as the High and Lofty One, and by some splendid appearance, manifests a presence to the senses of the blessed spirits * ; but as he is an infinite Spirit, diffused through all things filling as well as containing them, seeing and knowing all, even the most secret things ; for, His eyes, to speak after a popular manner, are ten thousand times brighter than the sun, beholding all the ways of men and considering the most secret paths ; knowing all things ere ever they were created, and looking upon all things after they were perfected : it follows, that since nothing can exclude the presence of this infinite Spirit ; then, in Him we live, move, and have our being : He is not far from any of us ; but although he is above all, yet he is through all, and in us all ; within us, as well as without us ; and therefore, in the hearts of the faithful, he must be considered, as an immense, intellectual, pure light, ready to enlighten and enliven them, and to shed forth the bright beams of his love upon them. I imagine this illustrates the thing. To me it seems reason.

---

* As to the expression just now used, to wit, that this infinite Spirit manifests himself to the senses of his blessed subjects—it may be asked how this can be—can the eye behold what is infinite and invisible ?

The answer is this, that although God's essence be invisible, yet there is a glory, the train and attendance of his essence, which exhibits a bodily and sensible vision of God. He decketh himself with light as with a garment. This is the dwelling of his essence. He dwelleth in light that is unapproachable.

We must distinguish then between the essential and the majestatic presence of God. The majestatic presence is the discovery of his essential presence in a determinate place by a magnificent luminous appearance ; and this the apostle calls the excellent glory, *megalo-prepous doxīs*. This glory appeared on Mount Sinai six days together. It rested and dwelt in the sanctuary. It filled the house. Moses saw its back parts, that is, a small measure and scantling of it, in proportion to the weakness of his mortal eyes : but, in the other world, when mortals shall have put on immortality, and our bodies shall be invested with the new powers of spirituality and incorruption, then face to face, we shall be able to see the whole lustre of divine Majesty, as familiarly as one man beholdeth the face of another.*

There are two ways then, as an excellent man observes, of seeing God, to wit, by intelligence, and, in some manner, by sense : but we must not imagine that these two make up the beatific vision. There is a cause of more importance to beatitude. The sight and contemplation of the divine glories is our act ; but the act of God is the communication of them. This makes the saints perfectly blessed. By the communication of the divine glories, we come to be, not bare spectators, but, θειας κοινονοι φυσεος, partakers of the divine nature.

As we are more obliged, says the writer I have mentioned to the sun, who is the cheer and vigour of nature, and the very life of all animal and vegetable beings : for his influences than for his sight, so are the heavenly inhabitants much more obliged to God for their recep-tions from him as the fountain of life and wisdom, than for the sight and contemplation of him as the subject of perfection. This illustrates the matter, and we may say, there is a third way of seeing God, to wit, in the enjoyment of him ; the beamings of his favour, and the effusions of his love, passing through the whole man, and producing an intimate sensation of him both in body and soul, and filling both with an unconceivable and endless delectation. This is seeing God as he is.

---

* As grateful objects of sense make up a great part of human delectation ; may we not suppose, that this glory of God, accommodated to our senses, will produce a more ravishing and transcendent delight, than all the objects in nature are capable of producing.

some of Mrs. BURCOT'S fine ale and bread, I had an excellent
supper. The bones of the penitent ORTON I removed to a hole
I had ordered my lad to dig for them ; the skull excepted, which
I kept, and still keep on my table, for a memento mori ; and that
I may never forget the good lesson, which the percipient who once
resided in it, had given. It is often the subject of my meditation.
When I am alone of an evening, in my closet, which is often my
case, I have the skull of JOHN ORTON before me, and as I smoke a
philosophic pipe, with my eyes fastened on it, I learn more from
the solemn object, than I could from the most philosophical
and laboured speculations. What a wild and hot head once
how cold and still now ; poor skull, I say : and what was the
end of all thy daring frolics and gambols—thy licentiousness
and impiety ?—A severe and bitter repentance. In piety and
goodness JOHN ORTON found at last that happiness the world
could not give him. There is no real felicity for man, but in
reforming all his errors and vices, and entering upon a strict
and constant course of virtue. This only makes life comfortable ;
renders death serene and peaceful ; and secures eternal joy and
blessedness hereafter. Such are the lessons I extract from the
skull of JOHN ORTON.

When I had supped, I went about, to see what things ORTON
had left behind him in his little cottage, and I found a field bed-
stead large enough for two, with a mattrass, silk blankets, quilt,
and cotton curtains ; two oak stools, and a strong square table
of the same wood. An oak settee, on which his bones lay ;
a silver lamp to burn oil in ; a tinder-box and matches ; a case
of razors, six handsome knives and forks in a case ; half a dozen
china plates, two china dishes ; and two pint mugs of the same
ware ; half a dozen drinking-glasses, a large copper kettle, a
brass skillet, two silver spoons, and a silver ladle ; in a chest
were clothes and linen, shoes and stockings, and various useful
matters; There were pens, ink, and paper in a writing-desk,
and half a score guineas ; and on a shelf over it, a dozen good
books ; three of which were, a large *English* Bible, *Thomas à
Kempis* and Sir Walter Raleigh's *History of the World :* under
the shelf hung a plain gold watch, and a large ring sun-dial. In
a dark closet, I found a box of sea-biscuits, many flasks of oil
for eating, and jars of it for the lamp ; honey, salt and vinegar ;
four dozen of quart bottles of meath, and two stone bottles,
that held three gallons each, full of brandy : this I suppose was
against the days of weakness or sickness. He had not used a pint
of this liquor.

Having found these things within doors, I proceeded from
the house to the garden, which lay at a small distance from the
little thatched mansion, and contained about four acres ; it had
been very beautifully laid out, and filled with the best fruit-trees,

and all the vegetables : but it was run to ruin and high weeds, and shewed that its owner had been long dead. I suppose he died soon after the date of his paper ; for, I observed, that many prior dates had been struck out ; and had he lived after the year 1701, he would, in all probability, have razed that likewise, and set down 1702. Some sudden sickness must have seized him ; and perhaps, when he found himself sinking, he laid himself out naked on the wooden couch where I found his skeleton. I can no otherwise account for his having no kind of covering over him. As to his bones being so clean, that to be sure was performed by the ants. I took notice of many nests here of the larger ants, in holes under the roots of great trees.

That the pismires are the best preparers of a skeleton is not only certain from the account the missionaries give of the coming on of the ants in Pegu ; when in one night's time, the vast swarms of them that approach, reduce every human creature they can fasten on to clean bones ; which makes the people set fire to their habitations, when they have notice given them by a kind of small monkey they keep for the purpose of the motion of this terrible enemy ; but it is plain from what I have often experimented.

When I want to make a skeleton of any small animal, I put the dead creature in a box with holes in it among the ants, in their habitations, or nests, or in such parts of the house as a whole tribe will often march to, through several rooms, in one track or certain road, to eat sugar or sweetmeats they have discovered, and then in two or three days, they will perform, what the finest knife cannot execute. The big ants which are larger than a common house fly, and are seldom less than six thousand in a nest, will clear the bones of a rat in half a night's time.

There was a pretty little wooden summer-house in the centre of the garden, and in it had been in pots some curious plants and flowers. Here were various tools, and many instruments of gardening. It appeared from them, and the great variety of things in the ground, that ORTON must have used himself to hard labour, and found great pleasure in his improvements and productions. There was a deal of art and ingenuity to be traced in the wild wilderness the garden was grown into. It was plain from a book, called *The Carthusian Gardener*, which lay on a table in the summer-house, that he had made that business his study. Round this summer-house were the remains of many hives on benches, but the bees were all gone, and the stock ruined.

All these things, and the place, set me a thinking, and soon suggested to my fancy, that in my condition, I could not do better than succeed ORTON on the premises : but, without turning hermit. Here is, I said, a pretty small thatched mansion, that might easily be enlarged, if more rooms were wanting ; and a garden, which labour would soon restore to its usefulness and beauty, and make it produce the best vegetables in plenty. Here is fish in the waters, fowl of every kind, and deer on the mountains. Here are goats in great herds, for milk, for kids, and when cut, for excellent venison. Here is the finest water, and by getting bees, as ORTON had, meath may be made that will be equal to the best foreign wine. As to the situation, it is most delightful. Nothing can be more charming than these shores and breaking waters, the rocky precipices and the woody hills, which surround this little region. What then should hinder but that I here sit down, and put an end to my adventures ; as the few things that are wanting may be had at the next town, and a stock for years be in a few days secured ? The man I am looking for may never be found ; and if I should meet with him, his circumstances and temper may be changed : then, as to the world, I know not how to deal in any kind of business ; and to live on the small fortune in my possession, must reduce me to poverty very soon. Here then it is good for me to reside, and make myself as happy as I can, if it be not in my power to be as happy as I would. I have two lads with me, who are active, useful young men, willing to work, and pleased to stay wherever I am ; and if I can commence a matrimonial relation with some sensible, good-humoured, dear delightful girl of the mountains, and persuade her to be the cheerful partner of my still life, nature and reason will create the highest scenes of felicity, and we shall live as it were in the suburbs of heaven. My lads too may pick up among the hills, upon scripture principles, two bouncing females : and a state will in a little time be formed. This is fine. For once in my life I am fortunate. And suppose this partner I want in my solitude could be MISS MELMOTH, one of the wisest and most discreet of women ; a thinking bloom, and good-humour itself in a human figure ; then, indeed I must be happy in this silent, romantic station. This spot of earth would then have all the felicities. Resolved. ' Conclusum est contra Manicheos,' said the great St Austin, and with a thump of his fist, he cracked the table.

Thus was my head employed, while I smoked a pipe after supper, and I determined to return to ORTON'S mansion, after I had found a way out of Stanemore ; but the previous question was, how I should get out of the place I was in, without going back, as there appeared no passage onwards. I tried every angle the next morning, to no purpose, and in vain attempted some hills that were too steep for the horses. Down then I went again to the bottom of the black and narrow glen afore-mentioned, and with light observed the rumbling deep river. It appeared more frightful than the first time I saw it and there was no venturing into it. This troubled me not a little, as the water was not above eight yards broad, and there was an ascending glen on the other side of it, that appeared to rise into a fine woody country. It was not half the length of that we had descended, nor near so steep ; it began to widen at the distance of a hundred yards from the water, so as to show, at the summit, a fine plain encompassed with a sweep of forest. We could see the sun shining there. The view in contrast was quite charming.

For some time I stood in this perplexed condition by the water side, and could not tell what to do, when one of the lads came running to me, to let me know, that as he carefully examined the sides of the glen we came down, he discovered to the left, about fourscore yards above the river, a pass wide enough for one horse to go through, and he believed it was a way out. This was reviving news, and upon going into it, I found that it went straight on among the mountains, like a rent, or open crack, for three hundred yards, and then turned to the left for about fifty more, when it winded a little, and began to extend wider and wider every yard, till it brought us by several turnings to the beginning of a fine valley, where we again found the river we had seen in the bottom of the deep glen, and perceived that it ended in a great water, and went off in some subterranean way. The mountains were almost close to this fine water, on either hand, for near half a mile, and made a delightful rural scene. We could see the river, as we looked up it, come tumbling on for a great way between the steep rocky precipices ; and the broad bright lake it formed between vast frowning mountains, with wood and lawns in it, at the end of the vale, were altogether a view most charming. This made me more highly value Orton Lodge.

There is a cave there likewise, that adds great beauty to the place, and in charms and wonders, exceeds the grot of Tunis, a few miles east of Carthage, directly under Cape Bonn, formerly called the promontory of Mercury, where Æneas sheltered after the storm ; * and St. Donat's Cave † in Glamorganshire, which

---

* Dr. Shaw, in his *Travels*, shews that the cave near Cape Bonn was the grot which Virgil describes in the following manner :

    " Defessi Æneadæ, quæ proxima litora, cursu
    Contendunt petere, et Lybiæ vertuntur ad oras.
    Est in secessu longo locus : insula portum
    Efficit objectu laterum, quibus omnis ab alto
    Frangitur inque sinus scindit sese unda reductos.

---

† St. Donat's Cave, by the vulgar called Reynard's Church, in Glamorganshire is on hundred and sixty feet in length, the breadth forty-three, and the height thirty-four. Every spring tide fills it with water, and has smoothed it to perfection. At the upper end of it, there is a grand seat, arched into the stone, and near it a falling-spring of fresh water drops into a cistern it has made. The rushing tides have made good seats in the sides of the rock, and from them you have a view of the channel, which is seven leagues. Every ship that sails to and from Bristol, is seen, and the mountains of Somersetshire bound the prospect that way. The cliff over the cave is almost double the height of the grot, and to the very edge of the precipice, the cattle come to graze, to avoid the insects, who will not approach the sea-breezes. The whole is a charming scene.

is much more beautiful than the African grot described in the first *Æneid*.

> Hinc atque hinc vastæ rupes, geminique minantur
> In cœlum scopuli. Quorum sub vertice late
> Æquora tuta silent. Tum sylvis scena coruscis
> Desuper horrentique atrum nemus imminet umbra;
> Fronte sub adversa scopulis pendentibus antrum,
> Intus aquæ dulces, vivoque sedilia saxo,
> Nympharum domus."

The weary Trojans ply their shatter'd oars
To nearest land, and make the Lybian shores.   **D**

The Trojans, weary'd with the storms, explore
The nearest land, and reach the Lybian shore.   **P**

Within a long recess there lies a bay,
An island shades it from the rolling sea,
And forms a port secure for ships to ride,
Broke by the jutting land on either side:
In double streams the briny waters glide.   **D**

Far in a deep recess, her jutting sides
An isle projects, to break the rolling tides
And forms a port, where, curling from the sea
The waves steal back, and wind into a bay.   **P**

Betwixt two rows of rocks, a sylvan scene
Appears above, and groves for ever green.   **D**

On either side, sublime in air, arise
Two tow'ring rocks, whose summits brave the skies;
Low at their feet the sleeping ocean lies:
Crown'd with a gloomy shade of waving woods,
Their awful brows hang nodding o'er the floods.   **P**
A grot is form'd beneath, with mossy seats
To rest the Nereids, and exclude the heats:
Down through the crannies of the living walls
The crystal streams descend in murm'ring falls.   **D**

Oppos'd to these, a secret grotto stands,
The haunt of Nereids, fram'd by nature's hands;
Where polish'd seats appear of living stone,
And limpid rills, that tinkle as they run.   **P**

There lies a harbour far within the land,
Commodious form'd by an opposing isle:
Which breaking as a mound the furious waves,
They run divided, calmer then unite.
On each side rocks, and two with steepy height
Aspiring touch the clouds, safe at whose feet
The waters far and near pacific sleep.
Distant from these a sylvan scene, beyond,
To bound the prospects, woods with horrent shade.
Op'ning to view, beneath the hanging rocks
A cave; within, a fountain pure; and seats
Form'd from the living stone; the cool recess
Of nymphs.   **S**

This grot within a mountain over-shaded with trees, and lying open to the sea, with a cliff on each side and not far from Carthage, answers so well to the Nympharum domus of Virgil,[*] that I think we need not doubt of its being the cave into which the gallant Æneas led the gracious queen: but that it ever was a quarry, and that pillars were made by the workmen to support the roof, as Dr. Shaw says, does not seem to be the case. The whole grot, which goes in thirty-six fathoms under the hill, its arches, and pillars were undoubtedly by the hand of nature; like many others I have seen. So it appeared to me. I could not see the least sign of a labouring hand in this cave.

---

[*] The kingdom of Tunis in the west of Barbary in Afric, was once the celebrated republic of Carthage. The city of Carthage was about four miles from the spot the city of Tunis now

The cave in Stanemore is in the bottom of a perpendicular mountain of a vast height, the east side of the lake and four yards from the shore. The entrance is a grand sweep, high and broad as the grot, that is, in breadth fifty two feet, in height fifty nine. It is an hundred and forty seven feet long. The stone of it is extremely beautiful ; of a yellow and reddish colour, bright and glittering, and beautifully variegated with arched and undulated veins of various tinges. I broke off a piece of it, and found it a congeries of plates of spar, stained with a fine mixture of colours. It is a species of the alabaster, called *Marmor Onychites*, on account of its tabulated zones, resembling those of the onyx, and is very little inferior to the Ægyptian alabaster. This Stanemore stone is far beyond the Cornish and Derbyshire alabaster. The caverns there are but encrusted with a sparry substance, as I have found upon various examinations ; and, as is evident to every eye that sees the workman making the elegant vases and chimney-columns we have of the alabaster of those counties ; whereas in Stanemore this alabaster consists of strata of sparry substance, though somewhat coarser than this kind of Ægyptian stone.

The top of the cave is a bold arch, finished beyond all that art could do, and the floor as smooth as it is possible to make the stone. At the far end of the grot, there are a dozen rows of seats like benches, that rise one above another. The uppermost will. hold but two people, on each of the others a dozen may sit with ease ; they make the place look as if it was the assembly room, or council chamber of the water-nymphs. There was no water dropping from the roof of this cave ; but in a thousand places, where moss had agreeably covered the walls, it crept through the sides, and formed streams that ran softly over the ground, and had worn it smooth. It brought to my remembrance some very poetical lines in *Lucretius :*—

> " Noctivagi sylvestria templa tenebant
> Nympharum, quibus exibant humore fluente
> Lubrica, proluvie larga lavere humida saxa,
> Humida Saxa super viridi stillantia musco
>   Et partim plano scatere atque erumpere campo."

> "And then by night they took their rest in caves,
> Where little streams roll on with silent waves ;
> They bubble through the stones, and softly creep,
> As fearful to disturb the nymphs that sleep.
> The moss spread o'er the marbles, seems to weep."

This was exactly the case of the water in this fine cave. In

stands on. Many ruins of it are still remaining. This glorious city, was twenty-three miles round, and built near an hundred years before Rome, was taken and utterly rased by young Africanus, that is, Scipio Æmilianus, before Christ 146 years. It had disputed with Rome for the empire of the world, for the space of 118 years. The most beautiful village in the world, called Marsa, now stands in the western point of ancient Carthage, and from thence it is a fine walk to Dido's Cave under Cape-Bonn.

the lowest harmony, it gently fell over the slanting floor, and as Oldham has it—

> "Away the streams did with such softness creep,
> As 'twere by their own murmurs lull'd asleep."

Such was the delightful spot I at last discovered, when I thought I was come to the *ne plus ultra*, that is, had gone on till I could go no further ; and now seeing how my way lay, I departed from Orton Lodge betimes the next morning, June 19th, leaving my lad O'Fin to keep possession of the place till I returned, and with the other boy went through the lawns in the wood I have mentioned at the end of the vale. This brought me to a range of mountains most frightful to behold, and to the top of them, with great toil, we made a shift to climb, and from thence descended through many perils to a bottom between the hills we had come down, and some mountains that stood at a small distance from them. This low ground trended north and north-west for an hour, and then turned north-east for three hours more, a very bad way ; stony and wet, and some stiff pieces of road : but the bottoms brought us at last into a large and spacious plain, that was surrounded with hills, whose tops and sides were covered with antient trees and lofty groves, and some mountains whose heads were above the clouds. Flowers and clover, and other herbs, adorned the ground, and it was watered with many never-drying streams. The plain seemed a vast amphitheatre, by nature formed ; and variety and disposition refreshed the eyes whatever way they turned.

In the very centre of this ground, I found a house and gardens that charmed me very much. The mansion had a rusticity and wildness in its aspect, beyond anything I had seen, and looked like a mass of materials jumbled together without order or design. There was no appearance of rule in any part, and where a kind of proportion was to be seen, it seemed as a start into truth, by the inadvertent head of blind chance. It was the most Gothic whimsical, four-fronted thing, without, that ever my eyes beheld ; and within, the most convenient, comfortable dwelling I have seen.

This edifice, which looks more like a small Gothic cathedral, than a house, stands in the middle of large gardens, which are not only very fine, but uncommon, and different from all the gardens I have been in. There is no more rule observed in them, than in the house ; but the plantations of trees, and plots of flowers, the raised hills, the artificial valleys, the streams that water these vales, and the large pieces of water, and lakes, they have brought in and formed, are inexpressibly charming and fine. Wild and natural they seem, and are a beautiful imitation of the most beautiful scenes of nature. The wilderness, the openings, the parterres, the gardens, the streams, the lakes, the cascades, the valleys, and the rising grounds, in the most various disposition, and as if art had little, or no hand in the designs, have an admirable effect upon the eye.

The passages from valley to valley, between the hills they have made, are not by formal straight walks, but by windings in various ways, which are decorated with little grotto's, and diversified in the manner of laying out the ground : the streams and canals sometimes serpent, and sometimes spread away. Rocks are artfully placed, seem to push the waters off, and on the banks are seeming wild productions of flowers. As the hills and risings are sprinkled with flowery trees, so are these banks with all the sweets that grow. Small boats are on the running streams, and over them in many places, are winding bridges of wood, most ingeniously and finely made. These streams which they have from the mountains, supply the larger pieces of water ; and in the largest of those lakes they had raised a rock, in the most natural manner. On this is a summer-house of great beauty. It is the reverse of the mansion, and has every charm that pure architecture could give it. It is large enough for a small family.

When I came up to this seat, which the owners of it call Ulubræ, some gentlemen, who were in the gardens, saw me, and saved me the trouble of asking admission, by inviting me in with the greatest civility ; but they seemed under a vast surprise at my arrival ; and much more so, when I gave them an account of the way I had travelled. It appeared almost incredible. They had not a notion of such a journey. They told me I was in Yorkshire now, and had been so when I ascended the high mountains that are some miles behind the hills that surround their house ; but they did not imagine there was any travelling over those mountains, and the alps upon alps beyond them, to Brugh under Stanemore. The way, they said, was very bad from their house to Eggleston, or Bowes, on account of bills, waters, and wet bottoms ; it was worse to travel northward to Bishoprick ; and scarce passable to the north-east to Cumberland. What then must it be to journey as I had done over the northern fells of Westmoreland, and the bad part of Yorkshire-Stanemore I had passed.

"It was a terrible way," I replied, "and what I often despaired of coming through, even at the hazard of my life. Frequently we were locked in by chains of precipices, and thought we should never find a pass : some of the mountains were so steep, that it was with the greatest difficulty we could lead the horses up and down them : and many rivers were so rapid and rocky at bottom, that we were often in danger of being lost ; beside, if fortune had not conducted us to the habitations of people we little expected to find, we might have perished for want of food, as my servant could not bring from Brugh provisions sufficient for so long and uncertain a way. All these difficulties I saw very soon ; in less than a day's ride to the north from the Bell Inn on the southern edge of Stanemore ; a little lone public-house, that lies half-way the turn-pike road, on the left hand, as the traveller goes from Bowes to Brugh, Penrith, and Carlisle ; but friendship and curiosity were too many for all the obstacles in the way, and in hopes of finding a beloved friend, who lives somewhere towards the northern edge of Yorkshire or Westmoreland, or on the neighbouring confines of Bishoprick, or Cumberland ; and that I might see a part of England, which even the borderers on it are strangers to, and of which Camden had not an idea " ; * I went on, "and have had success thus far. The journey has been worth my pains. I have beheld the most delightful scenes, and met with very extraordinary things : and should I find my friend at last, my labours will be highly rewarded indeed."

The gentlemen I was talking to, seemed to wonder very much at me and my discourse ; and as the rest of the society by this time came into the parlour, they introduced me to them, and then related what I had said. They all allowed it was very extraordinary, and requested I would oblige them with some particulars that occurred. I did so immediately, and told them, among other things, of my reception at Burcot Lodge, and of the skeleton of JOHN ORTON which I found in the cottage on the side of the woody hill. I let them know the goods and conveniences I saw there, and that I was so pleased with the beauties of the place, the little mansion, the once fine gardens, and the useful things on the premises, that I intended to return to it, and make it my summer retreat ; that I had left a man there to that purpose, who was at work in the garden, and expected to be back in a month's time, with such things as were wanting to make it an agreeable and comfortable little country house.

The philosophers wondered not a little at what they heard. If they were surprised at seeing me as a traveller in such a place, they were much more astonished at my relation. They could not enough admire Mrs BURCOT and Mrs FLETCHER. The history of the penitent ORTON, they thought very strange. They told me they were glad I had a thought of making Orton Lodge a summer retreat, and hoped it would occasion my calling upon them many times ; that I should always be heartily welcome to

---

* I have already observed [p. 126], that Camden, and every other describer of England, had not the least notion of Stanemore, that is, the north fells of Westmoreland and the northern mountains of Richmondshire : and as to the people who live on the borders of Stanemore, I could not find so much as one man in Richmond, Greta-bridge, Bowes, and Brugh, that had been any length of way up the mountains. When I asked RAILTON, the quaker, a very knowing man, who keeps the George at Bowes, what sort of a country Stanemore was ? He answered, "It is, after a few miles riding more wild and mountainy than the highlands of Scotland, and impassable "; nay, my landlord at Eggleston, some miles within Stanemore, knew nothing of the mountains upon mountains that are far beyond his house.

their house, and might with less difficulty go backwards and
forwards, as their lodge was at my service, whenever I was pleased
to do them the favour to call. This was civil, and I returned
them the thanks they deserved.

Here dinner was brought in, and with these gentleman I sat
down to several excellent dishes. There was the best of every
kind of meat and drink, and it was served up in the most elegant
manner : their wine in particular was old and generous, and they
gave it freely. We took a cheerful glass after dinner, and laughed
a couple of hours away in a delightful manner. They were quite
polite, friendly and obliging ; and I soon found in conversing
with them, that they were men of great reading, and greater
abilities. Philosophy had not saddened their tempers.
They were as lively, companions, as they were wise and learned
men.

These gentlemen are twenty in number, men of fortune, who
had agreed to live together, on the plan of a college described
by *Evelyn* in his letter to the Hon. Robert Boyle ; but, with this
difference, that they have no chaplain, may rise when they please,
go and come as they think fit, and every one is not obliged to
cultivate his garden. *Every* member lays down a hundred
pounds on the first day of the year, and out of that fund they
live, pay their servants, keep their horses, and purchase everything
the society requires. What is wanting at home, this stock
produces, and is to be expended only at Ulubræ, for everything
necessary and comfortable, except raiment and horses. When
they are abroad, it is at a plus-expence.

I call these gentlemen philosophers, because exclusive of their
good morals, they devote the principal part of their time to
natural philosophy and mathematics, and had, when I first saw
them, made a great number of fine experiments and observations
in the works of nature, though they had not been a society for
more than four years. They make records of everything extraordinary which comes within their cognizance, and register every
experiment and observation. I saw several fine things in their
transactions, and among them a most ingenious and new method
of determining expeditiously the tangents of curve lines ; which
you know, mathematical reader, is a very prolix calculus, in the
common way : and as the determination of the tangents of
curves is of the greatest use, because such determinations exhibit
the quadratures of curvilinear spaces, an easy method in doing
the thing, is a promotion of geometry in the best manner. The
rule is this.

Suppose B D E the curve, B C the *abscissa* $= x$, C D the
ordinate $= y$, A B the tangent line $= t$, and the nature of the
curve be such, that the greatest power of y ordinate be on one
side of the equation ; then $y^3 = -x^3 - x x y + x y y - a^3 + a a y$

—$a\,a\,x + a\,x\,x - a\,y\,y$: but if the greatest power of y be wanting, the terms must be put $= O$

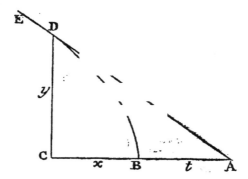

Then make a fraction and numerator ; the numerator, by taking all the terms, wherein the known quantity is, with all their signs ; and if the known quantity be of one dimension, to prefix unity, and of two, 2, if of three, 3, and you will have—$3\,a^3 + 2\,a\,a\,y - 2\,a\,a\,x + a\,x\,x - ay\,y$:

The fraction, by assuming the terms wherein the abscissa x occurs, and retaining the signs, and if the quantity x be of one dimension, to prefix unity, as above, etc., etc. ; and then it will be—$3\,x^3 - 2\,x\,x\,y + x\,y\,y - a\,a\,x + 2\,a\,x\,x$: then diminish each of these by x, and the denominator will be—$3\,x\,x - 2\,x\,y + y\,y - a\,a + 2\,a\,x$.

This fraction is equal to A B, and therefore t is $=$

$$\frac{-3\,a^3 + 2\,a\,a\,y - 2\,a\,a\,x + a\,x\,x - a\,y\,y}{-3\,x\,x - 2\,x\,y + y\,y - a\,a + 2\,a\,x}$$

In this easy way may the tangents of all geometrical curves be exhibited ; and I add, by the same method, if you are skilful, may the tangents of infinite mechanical curves be determined. Many other fine things, in the mathematical way, I looked over in the journal of these gentlemen. I likewise saw them perform several extraordinary experiments.

They make all the mathematical instruments they use, and have brought the microscope in particular, to greater perfection than I have elsewhere seen it. They have them of all kinds, of one and more hemispherules, and from the invented spherule of Cardinal de Medicis, not exceeding the smallest pearl placed in a tube, to the largest that can be used. They had improved the double reflecting microscope, much farther than Marshal's is by Culpeper and Scarlet, and made several good alterations in the solar or camera obscura microscope ; and in the catoptric microscope, which is made on the model of the Newtonian telescope.

In one of their best double reflecting optical instruments, I had a better view of the variety and true mixture of colours than ever I saw before. The origins and mixtures were finely visible. In a common green ribbon, the yellow, the light red and a blue, appeared distinct and very plain ; the lively green was a yellow and blue : in a sea green, more blue than yellow : the yellow was a light red and a pellucid white. All the phœnomena of colours were here to be found out.

In this instrument, the finest point of a needle appeared more blunt and unequal, and more like a broken nail, than I had before seen it. The finest edge of a razor was like the back of a dog, with the hair up. The finest paper, was great hairs, cavities, and unevenness, and the smoothest plate of glass, was very rough, full of cracks, fissures and inequalities. Very different, indeed, are the things finished by human art from the things finished by the hand of nature. The points, the edges, the polish, the angles, everything that nature produces, appear in the instrument in a perfection that astonishes the beholder.

In the views I here took of the vegetable world, with my eye thus armed, I saw many extraordinary things I had never observed before. I took notice, in particular, that a sage leaf is covered with a kind of cobweb, in which swarms of little active creatures, with terrible horns and piercing eyes are busily employed : a mulbery leaf was an amazing flexus or network : we can see but nine ribs on the sigillum Solomonis ; whereas my armed eye perceived here seventy-four : in a nettle I observed its whole surface covered over with needles of the most perfect polish, every one of which had three points, points very different from our finest points, not flat, but to perfection sharp ; and that these needles rested on a base, which was a bag of a flexible substance, in form of a wild cucumber, and filled with a sharp, poisonous liquor : this is discharged at the extremity of every point of the needles that cover the surface of the nettle : from a hole visible in every point the poison is thrown out, and excites a sense of pain ; and a heat arises as the blood flows more copiously to the wounded part. By pressing with my finger the extremity of the prickles, the bag of poison fell ; and on taking off my finger, it swelled again. What a piece of workmanship is here in a nettle ! Wonderful are thy works, O Lord God Almighty !

A leaf of sorrel in this microscope exhibited to my eye oblong, rough and straight atoms, sharp as needles, and from thence the tongue is twinged. In a bud cut away with a fine needle from a steeped seed of a French-bean, I saw the entire plant ; and in an almond so cut away, the perfect tree. Many other wonderful things I observed of the vegetable kingdom, in the microscopes of these gentlemen.

As to the animal kingdom, my observations on it, in the optical instruments at Ulubræ, were so many, that I could fill a volume with the things I saw : but, as I have little room or time to spare, I shall only mention two or three. In the double reflecting telescope, a louse and a flea were put ; which are creatures that hate each other as much as spiders do, and fight to death when they meet. The flea appeared first in the box, and as he was magnified very greatly, he looked like a locust without wings ; with a roundish body, that is obtuse at the end, and the breast covered with an armature of a triangular figure ; the head small in proportion to its body, but the eyes large, red, and very fierce ; his six legs were long, robust and made for leaping ; the *antennæ* short, but firm and sharp ; its tail was scaly, and full of stings, and its mouth pointed into active pincers : his colour was a deep purple.

The louse in white was next brought on, and had a well shaped, oblong indented body : his six legs were short, made for walking and running, and each of them armed at the extremity with two terrible claws : the head was large, and the eyes very small and black : its horns were short and jointed, and could be thrust forward with a spring. Its snout was pointed, and opened, contracted, and penetrated in a wonderful manner.

The first that was brought on the stage was the flea, and to show us what an active one he was, he sprung and bounced at a strange rate : the velocity of his motions in leaping were astonishing ; and sometimes, he would tumble over and over in a wanton way : but the moment the louse appeared, he stood stock still, gathered himself up, and fixed his flashing eyes on his foe. The gallant louse did with a frown for some time behold him, and then crouching down, began very softly to move towards him, when the flea gave a leap on his enemy, and with his dangerous tail and pinching mouth began to battle with great fury ; but the louse soon made him quit his hold, by hurting him with his claws and wounding him with his sharp snout. This made the flea skip to the other side of the box, and they both kept at a distance for near a minute looking with great indignation at each other, and offering several times to advance. The louse did it at last in a race, and then the flea flew at him, which produced a battle as terrible as ever was fought by two wild beasts. Every part of their bodies was in a most violent motion, and sometimes the flea was uppermost, but more frequently the louse. They did bite, and thrust, and claw one another most furiously, and the consequence of the dreadful engagement was, that the flea expired, and the louse remained victor in the box : but he was so much wounded, that he could scarce walk. This battle was to me a very surprising thing, as each of them was magnified to the size of two feet : but considering what specs or atoms of animated matter they were, it was astonishing to reflection to behold the amazing mechanism of these two minute things, which appeared in their exertions during the fray. It was still more strange to see the aversion these small creatures had to each other, the passions that worked in their little breasts, and the judgment they showed in their endeavours to destroy one another. It is indeed a wonderful affair : nor was it the least part of admiration to see through the extraordinary transparencies of the louse, the violent circulation of the blood in its heart. This was as plain to my eye, as red liquor forced by a pump in several experiments through circulating glass pipes. As to the dead flea it was opened, and by the camera obscura or solar microscope, which magnifies the picture of such a body as a flea, to eight feet ; * we saw the intestines distinguished and arranged in a manner that cannot be enough admired. It was full of eggs, and in every egg were many half-formed young ones.

The water Aranea, or great water spider, was next put in, and made a wonderful appearance in his greatly magnified state. It is the largest of the spider kind, except the native of Apulia, called the Tarantula, and is furnished at the head with a hard black forceps which resembles that of the Apulian araneus : the colour of its oval body is a bluish black, and has a transverse line and two spots hollowed in it ; its eight legs are very long, the joints large, and the little bones of the feet have different articulations : it was armed with bristles like a boar, and had claws very black, not unlike an eagle : it had eight eyes and six of them were disposed in form of a half moon on the forehead ; the other two were on the crown of the forehead : one to the left, the other to the right. This disposition affords light to the whole body, and as these eyes are well furnished with crystalline humours, they are sharp sighted beyond all creatures, and so nimbly hunt down flies : the mouth was full of teeth, and they looked like short thick hairs.

---

* Though the image of a flea may be magnified to eight feet, by removing farther off the white paper screen, on which the picture of the object is thrown very beautifully from the object posited in a single pocket microscope that is fastened to a tube to the solar microscope, yet the image or picture is more distinct and exact, when not enlarged to more than three feet, on the opposite side of the darkened room. By the way, reader, the solar microscope is the most entertaining of all the microscopes, and by it without any skill in drawing you may easily make an exact picture of any animal or object you can put into the fastened pocket microscope. The object is so intensely illuminated by the sun beams collected by a convex lens, that are thrown on it by a looking-glass, that its picture is most perfect and plainly represented on the white screen. You may have a mite, or one of the imperceptible animals of rotten wood, so truly and greatly magnified, as easily to sketch out the exact image of it in all its wonderful parts, with a pencil or pin : and in this amusing work, and in transferring the objects from the solar to the double reflecting microscope, the catoptric microscope, and the microscope for opaque objects, how usefully and delightfully might a young man of fortune employ many hours that are miserably sauntered away or consumed in senseless and illicit delights ?

In opposition to this amphibious creature, which walks on the mud at the bottom of standing waters, as well as on the banks, the silvery-green bodied spider was put into the box, which is one of the class that lives in the woods, where it squats down on the branches of trees, and throws four of its legs forward, and four backward, extending them straight along the bow ; but the great water aranea, with his terrible weapon, the black forceps, in a minute destroyed it, and we took the dead body out, to put in its place the red and yellow spider, which is a larger and stronger kind ; this made a battle for two minutes, and hurt his foe ; but he could not stand it longer and he expired at the victor's feet.

These things were a fine entertainment to me, as I had not before seen a solar, catoptric, or improved double-reflecting microscope. I had now a nearer view of the skilful works of the supreme Artificer. With admiration I beheld the magnified objects, the wonderful arrangement of the intestines of the flea, the motion and ebullition of the blood of a louse, the various spiders, their forms, so astonishingly framed, the gnat, that elephant in so small a miniature, the amazing form of the ant, the astonishing claws and beautiful wings of a fly ; the bones, nerves, arteries, veins, and moving blood in this very minute animal ; the wonderful bee, its claws, its colours, and distinct rows of teeth, with which it sips the flowers, and carries the honey home in its stomach, but brings the wax externally on its thighs, and a thousand other things which manifest a Creator. In every object I viewed in the optical instruments, my eyes beheld one wise being and supreme cause of all things. Every insect, herb, and spire of grass, declare eternal power and godhead. Not only the speech and language of the heavens, but of all the works and parts of nature is gone out into all the earth and to the ends of the world ; loudly proclaiming, that thou, O God, art Lord alone : Thou hast made heaven, the heaven of heavens, and all their hosts ; the earth, and all things that are therein ; therefore be thou our Lord God for ever and ever.

The library belonging to these gentlemen is a very fine one, and contains many thousand volumes ; but is much more valuable for the intrinsic merit, than the number of the books : and as to ancient manuscripts, there is a large store of great value : they had likewise many other curious monuments of antiquity ; statues, paintings, medals, and coins, silver, gold, and brass; To describe those fine things would require a volume. Among the books, I saw the editions of the old authors, by the famous printers of the fifteenth and sixteenth centuries ; editions greatly prized and sought after by most of the learned ; but these gentlemen did not value them so much as the editions of the classics, that have been published within this last century ; especially the quarto editions done in Holland. They showed me many errors in the Greek authors by the Stephens' ; and as to Plantin, exclusive of his negligence, in several places, his Italic character they thought far inferior to the Roman in respect of beauty. All this was true, and it is most certain that the best corrected book are the best editions of the classics. They are the best helps for our understanding them. There is no reason then for laying out so much money for the old editions, when in reality the modern ones are better.

One of the books in this library, which I chanced to take into my hand was the famous *Vindiciæ contra Tyrannos*, which came out in Latin and French in 1579, under the name of Stephanus Junius Brutus, and is " A Defence of Liberty against Tyrants." This treatise proves, in the first place, that subjects are not bound to obey princes, if they command that which is against the law of God ; as the worship of a consecrated wafer, and the theology of St. Athanasius, marianolatry, the demonolatry, and all the diabolism of popery. Secondly, That it is lawful to resist a prince, who like James II. endeavours to ruin the true church, and makes the superstition of Rome the religion of the land. Thirdly, That it is lawful to resist a prince, when he oppresses and strives to ruin a state ; like Charles I. who would have exercised a power contrary to the interest of his people, contrary likewise to that of the protestant religion ; * and when James II.

* Many instances can be produced of Charles the First's exerting a power contrary to the interest of the protestant religion ; and a capital one is, this king's express and strict orders, signed with his own hand, to captain John Pennington, to deliver, which he did, in obedience thereto, a squadron of the naval forces of England, consisting of eight men of war, into the hands and absolute power of the French king ; and Charles directed, " that in case of disobedience in the English captains to that order, Pennington was to sink them." These naval forces enabled the Gaulish king to break and suppress the power of the Rochelle protestants : this was an unjustifiable step indeed in Charles' reign : and if to this we add thousand acts of this said sovereign Lord, which were the cause of all the disagreements differences and contentions between his majesty and his people, that happened in his reign, and the sources of public calamity, it is certainly most amazing, to see the memory of this prince treated equally, if not superior to the most celebrated martyrs ! torrents of tears have I seen pour from the eyes of our mourning theologers on the 30th of January. I remember one time, when Dr. Warren preached the *commemoration sermon* at St. Margaret's Westminster, that he wept and sobbed so bitterly and calamitously, that he could hardly get out the following concluding words of his fine discourse, the Roy—Royal Ma—Martyr—the —holy Martyr—the—the—blessed Martyr.

Nor can I forget [Dr. Delany] the learned author of *The Life of David*. This gentleman preached before the late Duke of Devonshire in Christ-Church, on Monday, January 30 1737, from these words, ‘ Take away the dross from the silver, and there shall come forth a vessel for the finer.—Take away the wicked from before the king, and his throne shall be established in righteousness." *Prov.* ch. 25.

In this fine sermon, the Dr. gave us the picture of a Man as like Charles I. as Phalaris was to the apostle St. John : he then deprecated the murder which are his own words, and in the most piteous manner, with tears informed us, that God gave us this prince in his mercy and took him away in his indignation : " A prince." said the doctor, " who was a true lover of his people, compassionate of their errors and misfortunes and religiously tender of their well-being. He equally understood and practised religion in its purity ; and he died defending it. King Charles the First of blessed memory ! " Here the preacher wept, and then proceeded to abuse the opposers of this royal contender for absolute prerogatives ; as absolute as those the eastern or civil law potentates claim ; and then, to make and apply observations and inferences to the persons and characters of the present times, he told the

began his tyranny, by dispensing with the penal statute of
25 *Car.* II. in the case of Sir *Edward* Hales notwithstanding the
true religion, the honour of Almighty God, the safety of the
government, and the public good and peace of the nation depend
upon this act of 25 *Car.* II., and Fourthly, That neighbour princes
or states, may be or are bound by law, to give succours to the
subjects of other princes, afflicted for the cause of true religion,
or oppressed by manifest tyranny. These truths are finely
proved in this extraordinary book. The excellent author
evinces, that justice requires, that tyrants and destroyers of
the commonwealth be compelled to reason. Charity challenges
the right of relieving and restoring the oppressed. Those that
make no account of these things, do as much as in them lies to

Lord Lieutenant, and the House of Lords, among other admirable things, that " they should
remember how the lay lords had consented to deprive the bishops of their seats in parliament,
and rob the spiritual lords of their rights and privileges ; which drew down a just judgement
upon themselves ; for they, the said lay lords, were soon after voted useless : have a care
then, lay lords, how you act for the future against the spiritual lords. Maintain, for the time
to come, a strict and inviolable regard to the rights, privileges, and properties of the spiritual
lords."

This advice, by the way, appeared to me very singular, and I think, on the contrary, that
it would be well for our church, if our bishops were obliged to leave the court, the parliament
and their politics, and then spend their lives in labouring in the vineyard of Christ, in their
several dioceses. What have priests to do with baronies and acts of state ; men that ought
above all other men to be content with food and raiment, and to withdraw themselves from
the world, that by their continued conversation with God, and attention only to the sacred
prescriptions of the gospel, they might appear replenished with that divine power and virtue
which by prayer, and all the exercises of piety and penitence, they had implored ; and by
their examples and instructions, brighten and inflame the people with the love of God, and
improve the good in goodness, and correct and reform the wicked. This would be acting
like bishops indeed. The holiness of our prelates lives, and their fervour in teaching mankind the truths of Jesus Christ would soon advance the cause of their master. They would
bring the people to conform to the will of the Lord, and cause the learned to purify the de-
filements of genius : that pride and vanity, that curiosity and self-love which are incompatible with an accomplished purity of heart. But as to " Charles the First, of blessed
memory," certain I am, that whatever Dean Delany may think of him, this prince did really
contend for the cardinal maxims of the civil law, and died, not for true religion, as this doctor
says, but to advance the civil laws above the constitution and laws of Britain, and thereby
acquire an absolute dominion. *Quod principi placuit legis habet vigorem.* It appears from
matters of fact, that his pleasure was to be the law. In him was to reside the sole power
of imposing taxes on the people. This power, and other powers contrary to the fundamental
form of this government ; this king of blessed memory assumed and challenged as rights
under the name of his undoubted prerogatives, and grasped the pretence so hard, as never
to part with it, till he wanted strength to hold it. THIS IS THE MARTYR ! ! ! His reign was
a provoking violation of parliamentary rights, and a cruel oppression of his subjects.

Instead then of the fine laboured reasons offered by Dr. Delany to the Lord Lieutenant of
Ireland, to account for the way of Providence in the tragical death of this king, he might
have said, That whereas this prince had departed from the known laws of the land to an
arbitrary power, and not only the pressures and sufferings of the people, under this method
of governing, were innumerable ; but the fundamental form and original constitution of
Britain, on which the protestant religion and the liberty of Europe depend ; was in danger
of being subverted, and for ever destroyed, therefore did Providence deliver up this king into
the hands of wicked men, who had usurped the administration of affairs ; that the mortification in the constitution might be cured by the death of this destroying prince ; and the
violence of his exit remain a monument *in terrorem* to all future kings of England ; to have
a care how they offer to make any alteration or change in the original form of government ;
for violations of the constitution had brought Charles the First to the block. This had been
a reasonable account of that sad affair. It is supported by matters of fact.

N.B. The contentions between his Majesty and the house of commons began about the
following essential points.

1. The power the king assumed, and challenged as a right, to impose taxes, levy monies,
and impose duties on merchandizes, without a previous grant thereof in parliament.

drive piety, justice, and charity out of this world that they may
never more be heard of.

I asked one of these gentlemen, if he knew who was the author
of this book ; for it was ascribed to various men.   He told me,
that the learned Hubert Languet was the reputed author, as we
find in De la Mare's eulogium upon him ; but De la Mare was
misinformed by Legoux.   The great Du Plessis * was the author.

2. That the commons were obliged to observe and obey the king's messages, in giving
precedency to the matter of supplies, preferable to the redress of grievances, and to depend
on royal promises for time and opportunity to dispatch other business.
3. That the commons had no right and power of enquiring into the demeanour of the
king's ministers and nearest servants, and impeaching them for misdemeanours.
4. That the king could in his courts below, take cognizance of, and censure the debates of
the commons,
5. That the king could, by warrants signed with his own hand, arrest and imprison his
subjects ; and especially the members of parliament, for what they said and did in parliament.
These illegal and destructive acts of power King Charles I. claimed as his prerogatives,
and exercised them as long as he was able, with great rigour, and extraordinary circumstances ; and how such a general oppression, and rendering the two estates of lords and
commons of no signification, can make the memory of this prince blessed ; or, how his
suffering in the manner he did, in defence of such absolute, law-giving power, that was inconsistent with the constitution, and with the reasons upon which it is founded, can render
him a holy and blessed martyr, is past my comprehension.   I should rather choose to say,
that since that monarch would not act for the protection, happiness, and safety of his people,
but by a continued exertion of sovereign power, endeavoured to oppress and ruin them, and
change the form of government, his arbitrary principles brought him to a dismal extremity.
This, as before observed, is the truth of the case.   May his death be a warning to future
English kings ; that they may govern with parliaments, and exert their powers for the protection, safety, and happiness of the people.
* The great Du Plessis de Mornay was born on the 5th of November, 1549.   He wrote
several excellent books, and one that is invaluable, *on the Eucharist*, against the papists,
which was published in 1598.   This book produced the famous conference between Du Plessis
Mornay and Cardinal Perron, at Fontainbleau in the year 1600.   The victory at this conference is by the papists ascribed to Perron ; but the protestants, with more justice affirm,
that Du Plessis was victor at Fontainbleau.   Jacques Davy du Perron, bishop of Evreux, published at the time, a book on this conference, in which he gives a pretended true account of it,
and illustrates and defends his cause : but to this the great Mornay replied, and made a poor
devil of Perron.   See those pieces, reader, and you will be finely entertained ; for, Perron,
though a papist, was a great man.   Du Plessis died at his barony La Foret in Poictou, Nov.
13, 1623, aged 74 ; having retired to his country seat after Louis XIII. had taken from him
the government of Saumur.
Cardinal Du Perron, born Nov. 25, 1556, was trained up in the reformed religion with great
care ; but went off to popery on the preferments offered him by Henry III.   As, on the contrary, Du Plessis Mornay had been educated a papist, but became a protestant, to the loss
of the greatest preferments.—It was Du Perron that converted to popery the famous Henry
Sponde, bishop of Pamiers, and abridger of the *Annals* of Baronius, dedicated to Perron ;
and, in conjuction with Cardinal D'Ossat, he made a papist of Henry the Fourth of France.
It was owing to the management of this Cardinal de St. Agnes, in the conclave, and to
D'Ossat, that wicked fellow, Paul V.* was created pope and Cardinal Baronius lost
the popedom.   Bellarmine however who was likewise one of the fifty-nine cardinals in that
conclave, might have had it, but he refused it.   Those things we find in the *Lettres de Guy
Patin*, Vol. I. in Godeau *Melanges*, critiques apud Antillion, and in the *Histoire des Con-
claves*.   Cardinal Du Perron, died at Paris, in 1618, aged 63.
Leo XI. who reigned but twenty-five days, died in the fifty-third year of his age, in 1605 ;
was succeeded by Paul Borghese alias Paul V., who died 28th of Jan, 1621 ; aged 68 ; having
for his successor Ludovisio, called Gregory XV.
D'Ossat was born Aug. 23, 1536.   His five volumes of *Letters* are a master piece, in politics,
and next to Father Paul's *History of the Council of Trent*, are the best books you can look
into, reader, for an exact and full description of the artifices of the Court of Rome.   Remarkable was the saying of this Cardinal, when Henry IV. of France was stabbed : " If there was

* So Marbais, a doctor of divinity, who knew this pope well, assures us, vid. *Requeste a
Empereur, Leyde,* 1613, p. 223.

D'Aubigné,* whose word is sterling, affirms it.   See here, said
Mr. Seymour, the second volume of D'Aubigne's *History*, book ii.
ch. ii. p. 108, " il paroissoit un autre livre qui s'appelloit Junius,

the least pretext for such assassinations, they ought to be contrived and executed by the
heretics, whom the king separated from and abandoned, and thereby gave them reason
to be afraid of him ; but they never made the least attempt of this kind, neither against him,
nor the five kings his predecessors, though their majesties made the most cruel butcheries
of the Huguenots." D'Ossat died at Rome : March 13, 1604, in the sixty-seventh year of
his age.

Baronius was born Oct. 30, 1538.   His *Ecclesiastical Annals* in twelve volumes, folio,
containing the history of the church for twelve centuries, ending at the year 1198, have been
well called the twelve labours of the Roman Hercules.   It is a prodigious work.   The reading,
the erudition, the judgment, the order, and method of the author, are amazing ; but an unhappy prejudice for papal rights, and Romish pieties, attaches him continually to the Roman
cause, without the least regard to truth, and makes it plain, that he was not as he affirms,
assisted from above in this work.   The most judicious of the Roman Catholic writers say
" Il seroit a souhaiter qu'il eut été exempt des preventions que son education et son païs lui
avoient inspirées."   Isaac Casaubon, in his fine *Exercitations*, says with much justice of this
great man ; " qui denique merita sua in ecclesiam, si immoderato partium studio non cor-
rupisset, dignus erat sine controversia, cui omnes et veteres et recentiores, qui illam eruditionis
partem attigerunt, assurgerent, et fasces submitterent.   Sed vir eruditissimus quando a
scriptionem se accingebat, de approbanda fide sua ex æquo omnibus, sicuti par erat fidelem
historicum, adeo nihil cogitavit ; ut contra, id summo studio videaturegisse ne,qui in negotio
religionis alia sequebantur castra ullum usquam æquitatis vestigium in suis scriptis reperirent
Adeo in defensione illarum partium quas probabat, totus est ubique historiam professus,
non solum theologum, sed etiam persæpe disputatorem è schola agit, locos communes ad
narratione historica digrediens, sæpissime contexit ; Protestantes passim nullo discrimine,
convitiis, maledictis et infandis calumniis incessit.   Jura principum, quæ a paucis seculis
obtentu religionis imminui ceperunt, ita cupide, quoties datur occasio, contrahit, arrodit,
everitit, ut natum in regno noscere nequeas ; educatum, altum et auctum Romæ facile agnos-
cas.   Denique ita se gessit Baronius totis 12 suorum annalium tomis, ut qui dubitari nollet,
præcipium sibi scopum fussie, papalem monarchiam stabilire, amplificare, et ad cœlum usque
evehere."   This is a just character of the *Annals* of Baronius.   The best edition of this work,
is the English translation of it by Hall a doctor of the Sorbonne.   It is not only preferable
to the French, Italian, and every other translation, but far better than the original Latin, on
account of Hall's corrections, and most learned notes and dissertations.

Baronius in writing his *Annals* ascribes the guidance and success of his pen, to the favour
of the most holy Mary, the mother of God.   " To her whom I acknowledge the whole
to be received, I offer these *Annals*, &c.   To her by whom the whole of this gift comes to us
from God, to the most holy Virgin, the most safe ark in which our labours may be kept, and
in safe custody protected, we offer these *Annals*, that she may sanctify them with her blessing.
For the entireness of his net, after his having cast it so often, and the continuance of his
strength fresh and green in his old age ; all was from the grace of Abisag, their shunamite
cherishing his aged bones ; the most holy and pure virgin favouring the work begun, and
taking care of, and happily promoting all his affairs."   What must a true Christian say to
this ?

Many are the abridgements of the *Annals* ; but the best is that of Henry Sponde, the
apostate, aforementioned.   Baronius died Jan. 30, 1607, aged 68.

After all, the *Centuries of Magdebourg*, which were published in 1559 and 1560, are the
most valuable body of ecclesiastical history.   Baronius, who pretended to answer them by
his *Annals*, is undoubtedly the finest writer ; but the ministers, Matthias Flaccius, Jean
Vigand, Matthew le Judin, Basil Faber, Nicholas Gallus, and Andrew Corvin, are the learned

---

* Theodore Agrippa D'Aubigné, the favourite of Henry IV., was born in the year 1550,
and died 1631, aged 80.   He wrote several curious things ; but his great and principal work
is his *Universal History*, containing the transactions from 1550 to 1601, in three folio volumes.
This is a very extraordinary history, and contains many curious relations that are nowhere
else to be found.   He was obliged to leave France on account of this history and died
at Geneva.   His two satires, called *La Confession de Sancy* and *Les Aventures du Baron de
Fœneste*, are fine things.   Du Chat's edition of the latter, which is really a very curious
thing, is well worth reading.   The best edition is that printed at Cologne in 1729, in two
small volumes 12mo.

[The life of this extraordinary man, was written with much elegance and perspicuity, by
Mrs. Sarah Scott, and printed in 1772, in one volume, 8vo. Ed.]

ou Défense contre les Tyrans, fait par M. Du Plessis, renommé pour plusieurs excellens livres." And again D'Aubigné says that "M. Du Plessis lui a avoué qu'il en estoit l'auteur," *ib.* book ii. ch. 15, p. 91.

Another extraordinary book I saw in this library, was the famous piece *de Libertate Ecclesiastica*, written against the papal usurpations, at the time his holiness Camille Borghese, commonly called Paul V., had the memorable contest with the Venetians ; and upon enquiring, who was the author of this scarce and valuable book ; which is even superior to Father Paul's book upon the same subject in defence of the liberties of mankind ; Mr. Trenchard the president of the society, showed me Cappel's

men to whom we are indebted for the noblest collection of historical truths in ecclesiastical affairs, that ever appeared in the world. They are honest writers indeed. Every page of their work discovers a zeal for truth, and the glory of Christ ; while Baronius sadly labours for a pontifex maximus, and the cheats of Rome. The work of the centuriators extends to the thirteenth century, and every century contains sixteen chapters : the first is a summary of the things to be recited ; then the second treats of the place and extent of the church ; the third, of persecution and peace ; the fourth, of doctrine ; the fifth of heresies ; the sixth, of ceremonies and rites ; the seventh, of policy and government ; the eighth, of schism ; the ninth, of synods ; the tenth, of bishops ; the eleventh, of heretics ; the twelfth, of martyrs ; the thirteenth, of miracles ; the fourteenth, of the Jews ; the fifteenth, of religions separated from the church ; and the sixteenth, of broils and political changes. In this clear and distinct manner are the things of every age treated.

Bellarmine, born the 4th of October, 1542, was a man of great learning in the works of the fathers, councils, canon-law, and church history ; and wrote several laboured things ; but his chief performance is his body of Controversy, in four volumes folio ; which the catholics think very fine : They shew, indeed, great reading ; but, ignorance of the sense of scripture, and are quite void of argument. There is not one article of popery tolerably well defended in the four volumes. Every exposition and vindication is senseless and ridiculous. He died Sept. 17th 1621, aged 79.

Isaac Casaubon, who wrote the *Exercitations* on Baronius ; was born Feb. 18, 1559, died in 1614, in the 55th year of his age and was interred in Westminster Abbey.

Besides his *Exercitations*, he published several learned works and animadversions commentaries on Persius, Polybius, Athenæus, Strabo, Suetonius, and Diogenes Laertius. It was he, having purchased the MS. at a great price, first published in Greek, Polyænus' *Stratagems of the Antients in War*, in the year 1589 ; but the Latin version added to it, was done by Justus Vulteus ; and we have since had a more correct edition of Polyænus, by Pancratius, in the year 1690. The *Epistolæ Casauboni* are likewise valuable things ; but of most merit are his *Exercitations*, and his Persius. His *Commentary on Persius* is admirable, not only for a just explication of his incomparable author, but for much fine classical learning which he has scattered through it ; and for his *Exercitations* against Baronius, the friend of truth must be for ever charmed with them. It is to be lamented that we have but sixteen of them. They go no farther than to the thirty-fourth year of Jesus Christ, and relate principally to Baronius's bad explication of scripture.

Two Jesuits, Boullenger and Jean L'Heureux, wrote against the *Exercitations* ; but the defence of Baronius by Endemen Jean, the name L'Heureux went by, is very weak, as you will soon see, reader, on turning him over. And as to Julius Cæsar Boullenger, the other monk, when you have read his *Dissertation* against Casaubon, and Bishop Montague's *Animadversions* on that dissertation, you will perceive he was a poor creature.

It is remarkable, that Isaac Casaubon's two sons Henry and Meric, both went off to popery, and died in France, apostate priests in the Romish church ; though their father had fled from that country for the sake of the protestant religion, and was one of the best defenders of the reformed faith. He was one of the judges at the famous conference between Du Plessis and Perron : and, by the way, I think it equally remarkable, that the grandson of the great primate Usher, and the only remaining person of the archbishop's family, should be the most violent papist I ever saw. I knew the man in Dublin, and never heard so outrageous a catholic as he was. He said, to my astonishment, that " his grandfather was a great light but burn'd with his head downwards in this world, till he drop'd into hell in the next."

As to the conference between Du Plessis and Perron, about the Eucharist and other matters, besides the two pieces I have mentioned, to wit, Perron's account of it, and Mornay's answer

Assertion of the True Faith against Rosweius the Jesuit. And in
the following passage. "In ecclesiastica, antiquitate quam non
esset Tyro Casaubonus, docuit A.D. 1607. libro singulari de
libertate ecclesiastica, cujus jam paginæ 264. typis erant editæ,
cum rex Henricus IV. Compositis jam Venetorum cum pontifice
Romano controversiis, vetuit ultra progredi, et hoc ipsum quod
fuerat inchoatum supprimi voluit, ut ejus pauca nunc extent
exemplaria," p. 17. And in the same book, I saw some manuscript references to Casaubon's *Lettres*, p. 628, 632, and 647, and
to one place in Scaliger's *Letters*, edit, 1627, p. 345. Several places
I turned to, and saw that Casaubon hinted to his friends, that
he was the author of the book *de Ecclesiastica Antiquitate.*
Scaliger * affirms it. The words "Vetuit ultra progredi, et hoc

---

to the account, you will find a good relation of it in the *Histoire de l'Edit de Nantes*, tom i.
p. 343, et suivante ; and see further on this article Sully's *Memoirs.*
    The ingenious and excellent Miss Mornay, of Shelford Park, is descended from the great
Phillip Mornay Du Plessis, and the last of the house of Du Plessis now [1756] living. Her
grandfather, Jacques de Mornay, was great grandson to Du Plessis Mornay, and came over
to England on the revocation of the edict of Nantes, in the year 1685, when Lewis XIV, with
the same hand that signed the revocation of the edict of Nantes, granted to the reformed
religion, by Henry IV., in 1598, in the ninth year of his reign ; likewise signed an order
for eighty thousand merciless dragoons and other troops, to march against his protestant
subjects and force them by plundering and torturing, to turn papists.
    I say with the same hand, because the twelfth article of the edict signed by this cruel
and perfidious prince in the forty-third year of his reign, is as follows : "And furthermore
Those of the said pretended reformed religion, till such time as it shall please God to illuminate
them may abide in the towns, and places of our kingdom, countries and lands of our dominion
and continue their traffic, and enjoy their goods, without being molested or hindered on
account of the said pretended reformed religion, provided they do not assemble to exercise
it, &c." This was a monstrous cheat and highly perfidious to deceive and ensnare his poor
subjects. Something might be said for the edict of revocation, if Lewis had declared, that
to quell the agitations of his conscience he must revoke the edict of Nantes, though he had
sworn to the observation of it ; and that he allowed a certain time to his protestants subjects,
after which they must either turn catholics, or quit the kingdom, with their families and
effects, or else they should be exposed to such and such treatment. This had been plain
and honest dealing, though an arbitrary proceeding : but to give it under his hand to his
subjects, that they "might stay and continue their traffic, enjoy their goods without being
molested or hindered on account of their religion," and at the same time leave them to the
mercy of the dragoons ; Was not this an heinous act ? "Had he been guilty of this single
one only,' says Laval, in the sixth volume of his excellent *History of the Reformation in
France,* "it would have imprinted such a spot on his reputation, that all the waters of the
Seine were not sufficient to wash it away."
    * Joseph Scaliger, born Aug. 4, 1544, died in the 65th year of his age, at Leyden, Jan, 21,
1609. His father, Julius Cæsar Scaliger, died in the 75th year of his age, October 21, 1558.
    The father was a papist, the son a protestant ; were both great men in the republic of letters
and both wrote many books, but the son was by far the greatest man.
    What I like best of the father's works, are his *Poetics.* His *Account of the Latin Tongue*,
and his *Exercitations against Cardan.* These are fine pieces. His *Problems on Aulus Gellius*
are also excellent.
    The works of Joseph the son, are as follows,—*Commentarii in Appendicem Virgilii. Notae
in librum Varroni de Re Rustica. Conjecturæ in Varronem de Lingua Latina. Castigationes
in Valerium Flaccum. Notæ in Tertullianum de Pallio, cum Tractatus de Equinoctiis. Loci
cujusdam Galeni Difficillimi Explicatio. Elenchus Tribæresii Nicolai Serarii. Confutatio
ejusdem Serarii Animadversorum in Scaligerum. Castigationes et Notæ in Eusebii Chronica.
Thesaurus Temporum. Elenchus utriusque Orationis Chronologicæ Davidis Paræi. Con-
jectanea de Nonni Dionystaticis. Notæ in Opera Ausonii. Emendatio Temporum. Veterum
Græcorum Fragmenta. Cyclometrica Elementa duo. Appendix ad Cyclometriam suam.
Ausoniarum Lectionum libri duo. Emendationes ad Theocriti, &c. Idyllia. Notæ in Hip-
pocratem. Notæ et Castigationes, in Tibullum, Catullum, Propertium. Epistolarum Volumen.
Commentarii in Manilium. Animadversiones in Melchioris Guillandini Commentarium in
Tria Plinii de Papyro Capita. Epistola adversus Barbarum et Indoctum Poema Patroni
Clientis Lucani. Diatriba de Decimis in Lege Dei. Notitia Galliæ. Diatriba de Europæorum*

ipsum quod fuerat inchoatum supprimi voluit," accounts for its being published imperfect ; which all that see it wonder at.

Many other extraordinary books and manuscripts I saw in this library, and a great number of fine curiosities ; but I can only mention one particular more. *Engraven* on a beautiful cornelian I saw the Roman god of bounds, with these words, " Concedo Nulli," and one of the gentlemen asked me, what I supposed the meaning of this design ? The emblem, I answered, was a very just one, and in my opinion meant, that truth must never be given up. That, it was replied, was not the meaning of it, though my thought was not unjust. The design is to put one in mind of death, of which *terminus* is the most just emblem ; and he says, " Concedo Nulli," I favour none, I suffer none to pass the limit. " There is," continued the gentleman, "a little curious history depends on this. Here is a gold medallion, on one side of which you see the image of the great *Erasmus*, and on the other this fancy ; which he always wore in a ring, and from thence I had the medallion struck. *Erasmus* asked the famous Carvajal the Spanish cordelier, just as I did you, what the meaning of this ring was. Carvajal, who had had some contests with *Erasmus* and hated him greatly, said ' it owed its being without all peradventure, to the pride of *Erasmus*, and meant, that he would never yield, right or wrong, to any one in the republic of letters.' *Erasmus* answered, that ' his explication was quite wrong, and that on the contrary, he used the device, to kill his pride, and put him in mind of death, which suffers not the greatest men to pass the short limit of time allotted them.' This pleased me much, and I resolved to get the fancy on a cornelian for a seal."

Linguis, &c. Judicium de quadam Thesi Chronologica. Expositio Numismatis Argenti Constantini Imperatoris. Orphei Poetæ Hymni Sacri Versibus Antiquis Latine Expressi Martials Select Epigram. Versiones Græce. Sophoclis Ajax Characteri Vetere Conversus. In Æschyli Prometheum Prologus. Animadversiones in Epigrammata, &c. Cornelii Galli. Animadversiones in Cyclopem Euripidis. Dionysius Cato cum Notis. De Equinoctiorum Anticipatione Diatriba. Varia Poemata Latina. Poemata Græca versa ex Latino. &c. Notæ in Panegyricum ad Pisones. Castigatio Kalendarii Gregoriani. Interpretatio Proverbioru-Arabicorum cum Scholiis. De Arte Critica Diatriba. Notæ in Novum Testamentum. Hyppoliti Canon Paschalis, cum Commentariis. De Re Nummaria Dissertatio. Discours de la Jonction des Mers, &c. Discours sur Milice Romaine. Lettres touchant l'Explication à quelques Medailles. Prætio in Origines Linguæ Latinæ. Scaligerana. Epistola in Fabrium Paulinum. Animadversiones in Locos Controversos Roberti Titii. Vita Julii Cesaris Scaligeri cum Epistola de Vetustate et Splendore Gentis Scaligera.

These are the works of Joseph Scaliger, and in them one meets with so various and fine an erudition, and so much valuable criticism, that if the reader of fortune will take my advice he will get them all into his closet as soon as possible ; and at the same time, the four excellent pieces I have mentioned of Julius Cæsar Scaliger, the father of Joseph.

The great Louis Cappel author of the *Assertion of the True Faith,* was a protestant minister at Saumur. He was born October 14, 1583, and died at Saumur, the 16th of June, 1658, aged 75. He was likewise the author of that excellent book called, *Arcanum Punctuationis Revelatum* ; and of another very valuable work, intitled *Critica Sacra.* His son, Jean Cappel, turned papist, and died a despicable apostate in the Romish church.

There were two other Cappels, protestant ministers ; both Jacques, one who died in 1585 the other in 1624, who were both authors of several controversial pieces against popery. They were however weak writers, when compared with the learned Louis Cappel.

Another extraordinary thing these gentlemen showed me was a hole leading to some wonderful caverns in the side of a mountain, about a mile to the north of their house. It resembles at the entrance, Penpark-hole, in Gloucestershire,* within three miles of Bristol ; but with this difference, that Penpark-hole was once a lead ore pit, and one is let down by ropes through two tunnels to the chamber ; whereas the entrance of the place I am speaking of is the work of nature, a steep and narrow descent of twenty-three yards, which I went down by having a rope under my arm and setting my hands and feet against the sides of the passage, till I came to a flat rough rock, which opened two yards and a half one way, and four yards the other way. This little cavern was two yards high. We went from it into a more easy sloping way, which brought us downward for thirteen yards, till we came to another cavern, that was six yards long, and four and a half broad. Here we found a perpendicular tunnel, two yards wide, and sixty-seven yards deep ; but where it went to, and what

* In Penpark-hole you are let down by ropes fixed at the top of the pit, four fathom perpendicular, and then descend three fathoms more, in an oblique way, between two rocks, which brings you in a perpendicular tunnel, thirty-nine yards down, into which you descend by ropes, and land in a spacious chamber, that is seventy-five yards in length, forty-one in breadth, and nineteen yards high, from the margin of a great water, at the north end of it, to the roof.   This water is twenty-seven yards in length, twelve in breadth, and generally sixteen deep.   It is sweet, bright, and good drink.   It rises sometimes several feet, and at other times sinks two feet below its usual depth.   The torches always burn clear in this chamber, nor is the air in the least offensive, though fifty-nine yards from the surface of the earth, and separated from the day by such deep tunnels, and an oblique descent between them.   The great tunnel is about three yards wide, and in the south side of it thirty yards down, nine yards before you come to the opening of the chamber, or cavity below, is a passage thirty-two yards in length, three and a half high, and three yards broad.   It is the habitation of bats, and towards the end of it, a sloping hole goes to some other place.   This passage, and the tunnels, and the chamber below, are all irregular work.

Penpark-hole has long been an object of curiosity, and induced many to leave " the roddie lemes of daie," to explore its terrific and gloomy subterranean caverns. The descent of Captain Sturmy in 1669, and of Captain Collins in September 1682, are on record ; but few later visitors of such scenes, so dismal and dreary as are rarely to be paralleled and, of which the most fervid imagination can form at best an inefficient and faint idea, have published any descriptive account. Mr. George Symes Catcott, who more than once gratified his curiosity in attempting further discoveries in those ' regions of horror and doleful shades ' : on a visit to this place on Easter Monday, April 17, though the year is not mentioned, describes the chamber noticed in the preceding note as about ninety feet long, and fifty-two broad, with a hard rocky vaulted roof, about thirty feet above the water ; but when the water is at the lowest, it is supposed to be at least about ninety feet, so that even with the assistance of torches the summit cannot be distinctly seen. The roof appears to be of nearly an equal height in every part ; and very much resembles the ceiling of a Gothic cathedral. This place is rendered awful by the great reverberation which attends the voice when speaking loud, and still more so by the pendent rocks which sometimes break in very large pieces from overhead and the sides, riveting forcibly on the mind the most horrific tremor and dreadful apprehensions of personal danger. The water, agreeably to the preceding description, is stated by Mr. Catcott, to be in many places seven or eight fathoms deep, but " in August 1762, it was found not more than one fathom." In conclusion of the notice of this dreadful chasm, the melancholy circumstance of the poor traveller being thrown headlong by the villains who had robbed him, into Eldine-hole, near Derby may recur to the reader, when he is told that on the 17th of March, 1775, the Rev. Mr. Newnam, fell by accident into this tremendous cavern, and was no more seen. Public curiosity was excited, and for some weeks a vast concourse of persons were brought together daily, to visit this ill-boding and gloomy spot. Some few persons summoned sufficient fortitude to descend into and explore the yawning gulph, and the result of these inquiries were communicated by Mr. Catcott, to an excellent, but long since discontinued work, the *Literary Magazine*, March 1793, pp. 206–9. ED.

caused the noise below, the gentlemen who came thus far with me, could not tell ; for they had never ventured into it, nor could they persuade any of their people to be let down to the bottom though they had found by the lead that there was hard ground below. " I will then," I said, " explore this subterranean realm, if you will let me and my lad down, with proper conveniences for an enquiry of the kind, and I dare say I will give you a good account of the region below." " This," they answered, " was not safe for me to do. I might perish many ways. The damps and vapours might kill me at once ; or my lights by them might be put out, or kindle the vapour of the place below." " But to this, I said that I was sure the noise we heard at the bottom was some running water, and wherever that was in the caverns of the earth, the air must be pure and good. So Mr. Boyle says in his *General History of the Air*, and so I have often found it in my descents to the deepest mines." " As you please then," the gentlemen replied," you shall have everything you can desire, and be let down very safely, however you may fare when you get to the ground : and when you want to come up, pull the packthread you have in your hand, that will be tied to a bell at the top of the tunnel, and you shall be immediately drawn up again." These things being agreed they let me down in a proper basket the next morning at eight o'clock, with a lighted torch in my hand, and soon after, my man Ralph followed with everything I had required. I was more than half an hour going down, for the rope was given like a jack line from the engine it came from. I saw several dismal lateral holes by the way ; but no mischief or inconvenience did I meet with in my passage to the ground.

When I came to the bottom, I found I was in a chamber of a great extent, and though a hundred and three yards from the day, breathed as free as if I had been above ground. A little river made a noise in its fall from a high rock, within four yards of the spot I landed on, and ran with impetuosity in a rough channel I knew not where. The water was not deep, as we found with our poles, and but three yards broad, and therefore we crossed it, at a hundred yards from the fall, to get into a cavern that had an arched entrance, on the other side, within two yards of the stream. Our course to the crossing was due west, and then we went to the north, on passing the water, and walking up the second cave.

In it we ascended for seventy-nine yards, an easy rising way, and then came to a swallow, into which a river that ran towards us fell. Our course to this place was due north, but as the flood came from the west, we turned next to that point, and by the side of this water marched fifty yards. The cavern was so wide we could not see the walls, and the roof was of a vast height.

At the end of fifty yards, the river appeared due north again, and by its side we went for ten more, till we came to another vast cavern, that was a steep ascending opening, down which the river very musically came.   This place was so like Pool's Hole, that I might think myself in the Peak.   It was just such another grand opening, up the inside of a mountain, and had not only the descending flood, but as many beautiful stalactical concretions on the rising way ; which formed the most beautiful pillars, walls, and figures of the finest carved work ; but in this it differed from Pool's Hole * that the ascending opening in Richmondshire is much wider ; the rough, open steep, much higher to the roof ; and this steep reaches to the summit of the vast hills, and ends in an opening in day.   We came out this way on the top of an exceeding high mountain, after we had climbed from the bottom to the upper end four hundred and seventy nine yards ; add to this two hundred and twenty nine yards, the way we had come from the bottom of the tunnel to the beginning of the watery steep, and our march through the mountain, from the time we parted with the gentlemen, to our getting out at the top of it, was seven hundred and eight yards.

This was a laborious route, and at the hazard of our lives many times, performed.   Once, in particular, my lad RALPH fell into the river with his torch in the great ascent, and in striving to save his life I lost the other light I carried in my hand.   This reduced us to a state of the blackest darkness, and in that con- dition, we could not stir.   It was a horrible scene.   It chilled my blood, and curdled it in my veins, but I had a tinder-box, matches and wax candle, in my pocket, and soon recovered the desirable light ; at which we lighted other torches, and proceeded to ascend the rough and rocky steep, till we came to the fountain that made the descending flood.   The opening upwards from that became very narrow, and the slant so great, that it was extremely difficult to go on ; but as I could see the day at the end of it, I resolved to strive hard, and mount, if possible, these

* Pool's-hole, about a mile west of Buxton-wells in Derbyshire, is in the whole length from the entrance to the farthest ascent, but two hundred and thirty yards.   The account of this in Camden's *Britannia* is very imperfect, and next to nothing : and what the authors of the *Tour through Great-Britain* say of it, even in their fifth edition, in the year 1753, only shows to one who has been there, and carefully examined it, that neither Daniel Defoe, nor those since concerned in improving and correcting the four volumes of the Tour, ever were in the inside of Pool's-hole.   Their description of this, like a thousand other places in those volumes, is mere imagination, with some things from Cotton's false account ; and the fancy not only wrong, but very bad.   I would describe it here, but that the reader will find me in Derbyshire before I take my leave of him, if death does not prevent, and I shall then give a full and true history of this high and rough country ; its waters, curiosities, and anti- quities.   At present, I shall only observe, to abate the wonder of my passing from the bottom of the inside of one of the Richmond mountains to the plain on the top of it, that the hill in which is Pool's-hole is open within side, in the ascent, so far, that five yards more of aper- ture would bring one to the outside of the top : and I believe it is very possible for art to make an entrance that way, as nature has done at the bottom.

remaining sixty yards. In short, we did the work. As before related we came out this way, and from the dismal caverns of night ascended to a delightful plain ; from which we again beheld the glorious sun, and had the finest points of view. It was by this time noon, and under the shade of some aged trees, that grew on the banks of a great lake, on the summit of this vast hill, I sat down to some bread and wine I had brought with me for relief. Never was repast more sweet. I was not only fatigued very much : but, had been in fear as to my ever climbing up, and knew not how to get down, when I had mounted two thirds of the way. The descent was a thousand times more dangerous than the going towards the top.

When I had done, I walked about to see if there was any way down the mountain's sides, to go to Ulubræ, from whence I came ; but for miles it was a frightful perpendicular rock, next that place and impossible for a goat to descend ; and on the side that faced Bishoprick, a fine country house and gardens, about a quarter of a mile off, in a delightful valley, that extended with all the beauties of wood and lawn, meadow and water, from the foot of the mountain I was on, the precipice here was a terrible way for a man to venture down ; but it was possible to do it with a long pole, at the hazard of his life, as the rocks projected in many places, and the side went sloping off ; and therefore I resolved to descend. I could not think of going back the way I came ; since I had got safe into day again, I thought it better to risk my limbs in the face of the sun, than perish as I might do in the black and dismal inside of those tremendous hills. Besides, the house in my view might be perhaps the one I wanted. It was possibly my friend TURNER might live there.

With art and caution then I began to descend, and so happily took every offered advantage of jutting rock and path in my way, that without any accident I got in safety down ; though the perils were so great, that often I could not reach from rock to rock with my pole. In this case, I aimed the point of my pole at the spot I intended to light on, and clapped my feet close to it, when I went off in the air from the rock : the pole coming first to the place broke the fall, and then sliding gently down by it, I pitched on the spot I designed to go to, though six, seven, or eight fathoms off, and the part of the rock below not more than a yard broad. It is a frightful piece of activity to a bystander, but the youths on the mountains of Ireland make nothing of it, they are as expert at this work as the Teneriffe men, from them I learned it ; and made RALPH so perfect in the action, while he travelled with me, that he could go from rock to rock like a bird.

When we came to the ground, I sent my man before me to the house, with my humble service to the master of it, Mr. HARCOURT, and to let him know, that I had travelled through the inside of one of the high mountains that surrounded his house, and on coming out on the top of it, had made the precipice next him my road to the valley he lived in ; that I knew not which way to turn next, in order to go to Cumberland, and begged leave to dine with him, and receive his information. This strange message, delivered by RALPH with much comic gravity, that gentleman could not tell what to make of ; as I had ordered my young man not to explain himself, but still say that we had travelled the inside of the mountain, and came down the precipice. This was so urprising a thing to Mr. HARCOURT and his daughter, that they walked out with some impatience to see this extraordinary traveller, and expressed no little amazement when they came near me. After a salute, Mr. HARCOURT told me he did not understand what my servant had said to him ; nor could he comprehend how I arrived in this valley, as there was but one passage into it at the front of his house ; and my being on foot too, increased the wonder of my appearing in the place : but whatever way I came, I was welcome to his house, and he would show me the way in.

"My arrival here, Sir," I replied, "is to be sure very strange, and would be almost incredible to hear told by another person, of one that journeyed two hundred and twenty nine yards deep, to the foundation of this Alp, on the other side of it, then ascended a hollow way, till he got out at the top, and came down a high and frightful precipice to the vale below : but here I am a proof of the fact. I will explain how it was done ; " and I began to relate every particular at large.

"But tell me, Sir," Miss HARCOURT said, "if you please, why did you not return the way you came ; since the other side of the mountain is impossible to descend, as you inform us on account of its being a perpendicular steep ; and that you must have hazarded your life a thousand times, in coming down the way you did with the pole ? I tremble as I look at the place, and only with fancy's eye, see you on the descent. Beside, the gentlemen you left on the other side of the hill will conclude you lost, and be very greatly troubled on the account."

"My reason, Madam," I answered, "for coming down this very dangerous way, was, because I thought it, with all its perils, much safer than the inside road I had come. My activity I had reason to think, was superior to the difficulties of the outward way, and if I should fall, it would be in the light of heaven, with a human habitation in view, that might afford me some relief, if I only broke my bones ; but, if in descending the very steep and horrible caverns of the hill, which with the greatest difficulty I climbed up, I should happen to get a fall, as in all human probability I would, and break a limb in these most dismal cavities of eternal night, I must have perished in the most miserable manner, without a possibility of obtaining any relief. Nor is this all, madam, the thing that brought me here among the mountains of Richmondshire, was to find a gentleman of my acquaintance, and when I saw your house from the top of the mountain, I did not know but it might be his. I fancied it was, as the situation answered my friend's description of the spot he lived on.

" And if it had been his, madam, it would have put an end to all my toils ; for I am a wanderer upon the face of the earth, through the cruelty of a mother-in-law, and the unreasonableness of a rich father, who has forsaken me because I will not submit to the declarations and decisions of weak and fallible men, in matters of pure revelation and divine faith, and own the infallibility of the orthodox system. Because the ascent of my mind could not go beyond the perception of my understanding, and I would not allow that the popular confession is the faith once delivered to the saints, therefore I was thrown off, and obliged to become the pilgrim you see before you."

This history of a forlorn, seemed stranger to the young lady and her father than even the account of my journey through the inside of a mountain, and down a precipice that a goat would scarce venture. They were both very greatly amazed at my relation, and Mr. HARCOURT was about to ask me some questions, when one of his servants came to let him know that dinner was serving up, and this put an end to our conversation. The master of the house brought me into a fine room, and I saw on the table an elegant dinner, there was likewise a grand sideboard, and several men servants attending. Miss HARCOURT sat at the head of the table, and at her right hand two young ladies vastly handsome, whom I shall have occasion to mention hereafter in this journal ; two ladies more were on the other side of her, pretty women, but no beauties ; and next them sat three gentlemen ; sensible, well-behaved men ; one of them a master of music, the other a master of languages, and the third a great painter ; who were kept in the house on large salaries, to teach the young lady these things. Mr. HARCOURT placed me by himself, and was not only extremely civil, but manifested a kind of fondness as if he was well pleased with my arrival. He and his daughter took great care of me, and treated me as if I had been a man of distinction rather than the poor pilgrim they saw me, with my staff in my hand. The young lady talked to me in a very pleasant manner, and as I saw the whole company were inclined to be very cheerful I club'd as much as I could to promote good-humour, and encrease the festivity of the table. We laughed the afternoon away in a charming manner, and when we had done, we all went to walk in the gardens. Here the company soon separated, as the various beauties of the place inclined various minds to different

things and parts.   Some pensively roamed in shady walks, some
sat by playing fountains, and others went to gather fruits and
flowers.   I had the honour to walk with Miss HARCOURT to a
canal at some distance, and as we went, this young lady told me,
she did not well understand me as to what I had said of religion
being concerned in my becoming a traveller, and desired me to
be a little more particular.   " That I will," and immediately proceeded in the following manner.

" My father, Madam, is a man of great learning, virtue and
knowledge, but orthodox to the last degree, and sent me to the
university on purpose to make me a theologer, that I might be an
able defender of the *Creed of St. Athanasius,* and convince the
poor people of the country he lived in, and in good time, he fondly
hoped, the inhabitants of many other countries : that notwithstanding the symbol I have mentioned is what no human apprehension can comprehend, and the judgment hath nothing to act
on in consideration of it ; that there is nothing to be understood
in that symbol, nor can a man form any determination of the
matter therein contained ; yet they must believe this great and
awful mystery : that three persons and Gods are only one person
and God ; and, on peril of eternal misery, they must confess that,
Father, Son, and Holy Ghost, though three Beings, as distinct
as any three things in the universe, yet are only one Being.   This
mystery I was to preach up in his church, a church in a field, near
his house, to which he had the right of presenting, and enflame
the people against reason; that traitor to God and religion, which
our adversaries, the Christian deists, would make Lord and King
in opposition to faith.   I was to tell my beloved, that reason is
a carnal sensual devil, and that instead of hearkening to this
tempter, they must assent to those heavenly propositions, which
give wisdom without ideas, and certainty without knowledge.
You must believe, my beloved, that none is before or after the
other.   None is greater or less than another.   The infidels call
this an unintelligible piece of nonsense : but it is, my beloved, a
very transcendent mystery.   It does, we must own, stagger and
astonish us, being a thing beyond our reach to comprehend ; but,
it must be believed, on peril of eternal misery as I before observed :
and it is easy to be believed, for this plain reason, given by a very
learned and pious bishop of our church ; to wit, that it is too high
to be by us comprehended.   This was the opinion of that great
prelate.   Bishop Beveridge, in his *Private Thoughts,* p. 52, to
which book I refer you, my beloved, for more of his admirable
reasoning on this capital article, and further observe to you, that
not only this most pious bishop, and many other most excellent
prelates were of this way of thinking ; but all the most admirable
divines have declared in their sermons and other matchless writings, that the more incredible the Athanasian creed is, and the

fuller of contradictions, the more honour we do to our God in believing it. It is the glory of orthodox Christians, that their faith is not only contrary to the carnal mind, but even to the most exalted reason. In matter of faith, we must renounce our reason, even though it be only the thing that distinguishes us from the beasts, and makes us capable of any religion at all. No human arguments are to interfere in this victorious principle : the catholic faith is the reverse of rational religion, and except a man believe it faithfully, he must go into everlasting fire and brimstone.*

" In this manner, Madam, like a mad bigot, a flaming zealot, and a sublime believer, was I to preach to the people of Ireland, and be an apostle for that faith which is an obedience to unreasonable commands : but unfortunately for my father's design : and fortunately for my soul ; I was, on entering the university, put into the hands of a gentleman, who abhorred modern orthodoxy, and made the essential constitutive happiness and perfection of every intelligent being consist in the conformity of our mind to the moral rectitude of the Divine Nature. This excellent man convinced my understanding, that even faith in Christ is of an inferior nature to this, and that it is only the means to obtain it. Such a conformity and obedience of the heart and conscience to the will of God ought to be my religion, as it was the religion of our Saviour himself.

" Thus, Madam, was I instructed by a master of arts, my private tutor, and when to his lessons I added my own careful examinations of the vulgar faith, and the mind of our Lord, as I found it in the books, I was thoroughly satisfied, that an act of faith is an act of reason, and an act of reason an act of faith, in religious matters ; that our Lord was not the great God ; nor a part of that compound, called the Triune-God ; the miserable invention of divines ; but, a more extraordinary messenger than the prophets under the law chosen by the divine wisdom, to publish the will of God to mankind, and sent under the character of his son, and spiritual heir of his inheritance the church, to new-form the ages, and fix such good principles in the minds of men, as would be productive of all righteousness in the conversation :

* Little did I think when I talked in such a manner to Miss HARCOURT against the famous symbol, that I should ever find in the book of a most learned man and excellent divine, the same kind of arguments seriously produced in favour of the Creed of St. Athanasius; yet this strange thing has time brought on, and thereby convinced the world, that the greatest learning and the most exalted piety, employed in the cause of mystery, can become so extravagant and erring as to maintain that a thing incomprehensible to human reason can be revealed, and that the more incomprehensible it is to human reason, and the more senseless it appears to human understanding, the more glorious is the object of faith, and the more worthy to be believed by a Christian. This deplorable argument for the truth of Christianity I met with in a book lately published by an admirable man, Dr. Joseph Smith, provost of Queen's College, Oxon. In his third section of *A Clear and Comprehensive View of the Being, Nature, and Attributes of God, from* p. 61, to p. 78, the reader may see this *plea* for *darkness, confusion* and *implicit faith.*

that he was sent to destroy sin and the kingdom of Satan ; and to bring the human race to a perfect obedience to the will of the Supreme Being.

" All this, Madam, was as plain to me as the sun in summer's bright day ; and therefore, instead of laying aside my under-standing, and believing things without any rational ground or evidence at all ; instead of going into orders, to draw revealed conclusions from revealed propositions, and by a deep logic, make scripture consequences, that have no meaning in the words, for the faith of the people ; I was so free and ingenuous as to let my father know, that of all things in the world I never would be a parson, since the character obliged me to swear and subscribe to articles I could not find in my Bible ; nor would I, as a layman, ever read or join in the service of reading the tritheistic liturgy and offices he used in his family. I was determined, though I lost his favour and large fortune by the resolution, to live and die a Christian deist ; confessing before men the personal unity and perfections of the true God, and the personal mediatorial office of Jesus Christ. As St. Paul maintained the personal unity and absolute supremacy of the true God, and in his description of the Deity, did not tell the Athenians, that he was a Triune Being, to be considered under the notion of three persons, of three understandings and will, in a co-ordinate triplicity of all divine attributes and perfections ; but one individual personal Agent— one great Spirit, or mind, self-existent, and omnipotent in wisdom and action—one supreme Almighty Creator and Governor of the world, the God and Father of Jesus Christ ; I shall therefore, in obedience to the apostle, and to the other inspired writers, believe in and worship the same God, the one God, the only true God, as our Lord says in Matthew and Mark ; through the alone media-tion and intercession of Jesus Christ, our Redeemer and only be-gotten Son of God ; depending upon the effectual aid and assist-ance of the blessed Spirit, in hope of a glorious immortality. This is, this shall be my religion, whatever I may feel from an antichristian tyranny, on account of the confession. Though an outrage of uncharitable zeal should strip me of every worldly comfort, and reduce me to a want of bread. If I should become a spectacle to men and angels by the faith, yet I will believe as Jesus Christ and his apostles have ordered the world to believe. No unintelligible cant, or scholastic jargon for me. The Holy Ghost has in scripture expressed it sufficiently and unexception-ably clear, that there is One Supreme Independent First-Cause of all things, a Spirit, that is, One Spirit, One God ; I am God, and there is none like Me : I am God and there is none else, beside Me ; with Me ; none but Me ; Thus does the Holy Ghost declare ; and what signify the despicable, heretical declarations of the doctors, in respect of this ?

" Then, as a test of Christianity, the same blessed Spirit adds, that Jesus is the true Messiah, was sent from God to reveal his will for the salvation of man, and is the only Mediator betwixt God and man. Thus has the Holy Ghost regulated our faith and practice, and I think it incumbent on me to mind what he says, and flee the invented pieties of our theologers. I did so, and disobliged my father. I lost his favour entirely. He would take no farther notice of me, and I became as you see a wanderer."

This discourse, delivered with my fire and action, amazed Miss HARCOURT so greatly, that for some time after I had done, she could not speak, but continued looking with great earnestness at me. At last however she said, " I am glad, Sir, it has been my fate to meet with you, and must, when there is more time, converse with you on this subject. My father and I have had some doubts as to the truth of the Athanasian creed ; but he told me, he did not choose to examine the thing, as it had the sanction of ages, and was believed by the greatest divines in all nations. If it be wrong, let the churchmen answer for it. But this does not satisfy me ; and since I have seen one that has forsaken all rather than live a disciple of Athanasius, after a thorough examination of the system ; and that you have now said some things against it that shew the folly of believing it, and make it a faith the most preposterous and unreasonable, I am determined to enquire into the merit of it, and see if Christians ought to acknowledge the supreme dominion and authority of God the Father ; that the Father is absolutely God, the great God in the absolute supreme sense by nature ; and the Son, only a God by communication of divinity from the Father, that is, by having received from the Father, the supreme cause, his being, attributes, and power over the whole creation : or, if they ought to ascribe supreme authority, and original independent absolute dominion to God the Father, God the Son, and God the Holy Ghost ; three distinct supreme Gods, and yet but one supreme God, as the church informs us in her famous creed, and thereby makes us swallow a contradiction, as I have often thought, and a doctrine against which a great number of texts can be produced. This I will examine. My reason shall be no longer silent in so important a case. If a Trinity in unity of equal minds or Gods is not to be proved by the inspired writings, the doctors preaching it, and by creed requiring it, will be no justifiable plea or excuse for me, I am sensible, in the great rising day. I had better, in such case, leave all as you have bravely done, were my father so orthodox and furious a bigot as to force me to be a religionist against my conscience. What I have to beg of you, Sir," Miss HARCOURT continued, " is that you will to-morrow, oblige me with your thoughts on the texts I have marked, as produced by orthodox divines for their mysterious religion*. If you make me sensible that those texts do not prove the doctrine they are brought for, and of consequence, that the doctrine of the Trinity as by them taught, is the work of uninspired writers, I shall renounce it to be sure. I will no longer mistake contradictions for mysteries. The schemes and inventions of men shall not pass with me for the revelations of God."

Here Mr. HARCOURT came up to us, and desired to know, if it was a fair question, what we two had been talking so earnestly. on ; for it seemed at a distance to be something more than ordinary. " I will tell you, Sir," his daughter replied, and immediately began to relate the whole conference, and her resolution.   " Your resolution," the father said, " is excellent. You have not only my consent, but I recommend it to you as the noblest work you can employ any time on. For my part, Sir," Mr. HARCOURT continued, turning himself to me, " I never liked this part of our protestant religion, and have often wished our public prayers had seen more conformable to the simplicity of the gospel ; that we had been contented with what our Master and the Holy Spirit delivered, and not made human compositions the standard of salvation : but since the church in her wisdom has thought it should be otherwise, I have submitted to her authority, and been silent on the doctrines she claims a right to determine ; though some of them to me appear doubtful, and others repugnant to scripture : beside, my studies have been in other fields than that of controversy : mathematics and antiquities have employed my time, and I have neither taste nor capacity for that criticism which is necessary for the examination of such points : greatly however do I honour those who have the ability and patience to go through the work, as I must own it is of the utmost importance, and that the orthodox faith is a sad thing, if the truth be, after all our Athanasian believing, that Christ is no more than God's instrument, as St. Peter and St. Paul name him ; a successful teacher of wisdom, righteousness, sanctification, and redemption : and that God is to be owned and praised, as the true, chief and original cause of all spiritual blessings, according to the counsel of his own will, his own good pleasure, purpose, &c., without partner or second person to intreat and satisfy for us. If this be the case, may the Lord have mercy on our poor orthodox souls : and as it may be so, I honour you for enquiring into the matter, and especially for your good Spirit in preferring the things that are eternal, when what you thought truth could not be held with things temporal. I have," Mr. HARCOURT continued, " a very

* The texts produced by Miss HARCOURT, the next day, in a sheet of paper, she gave me and in my written explication of them in answer, I satisfied her, that the letter of scripture was not full in favor of contradiction, and that where it had any appearance of being so, reason allowed the purest modesty to use some freedom in interpreting, and take the texts in a lower meaning, such a liberty as protestants take with the words ' this is my body,' when they reject the doctrine of transubstantiation. By this means I made a convert of her. This lady became a strict Christian-Deist.

great esteem for you on this account, and if I can be of service to you, I will." He imagined I might want money, and if I did, he would lend me a hundred guineas, without interest, payable on my note of hand, when I could. He immediately took out of his pocket-book a bank note for that sum, and pressed me to accept it. He likewise invited me to stay at his house, while he continued in the country, which would be for a month longer. He assured me also, that I might make it my residence after he left it, if I pleased ; there would be two servants to attend me, and there was excellent mutton, and other things for my table. Nor is this all, you shall have the key of my study."

These offers astonished me, and I said, " most generous Sir, I return you the thanks of a grateful heart, and will ever remember your goodness to me with that sense such uncommon kindness deserves, though I cannot enjoy the benefits you would make me happy with. As to money I do not want any yet, and when I do it will be time enough for me to borrow, if I should find any one, like you, so benevolently disposed as to lend me cash without security and interest : and as to staying at your house, that offer I cannot accept, as I am engaged to a near and rich friend, who will be to me a subaltern providence, if he can be found, and secure me from the evils my attachment to truth has exposed me to. One week however I will stay with you, since you are so good as to invite me in this kind manner."

Here then I stayed a week, and passed it in a most happy way. Mr. HARCOURT was fond of me, and did every thing in his power to render the place agreeable. His lovely daughter was not only as civil as it was possible to be, but did me the honour to commence a friendship with me, which lasted from that time till death destroyed the golden thread that linked it.

Reader, this young lady, HARRIET EUSEBIA HARCOURT, was the foundress of a religious house of protestant recluses, who are still a society in that part of Richmondshire where I first saw her and her father. They are under no vow, but while they please to continue members, live as they do in nunneries, and in piety, and in all the parts of the Christian temper, endeavour a resemblance of their divine Lord and Master ; with this distinction however, that to the plan of the regards due from man by the divine Law to God, to his fellow-creatures, and to himself, they add music and painting for their diversion, and unbend their minds in these delightful arts, for a few hours every day. This makés them excel in these particulars. They are great masters in all kinds of music, and do wonders with the pencil.

EUSEBIA was but just turned of twenty when I first saw her, in the year 1725, and then her musical performances were admirable ; her pictures had the ordonnance, colouring, and expression of a great master. She was born with a picturesque genius, and a capacity to give measure and movement to compositions of harmony. Her music at the time I am speaking of had a most surprising power ; and in painting, long before this time, she astonished. When she was a child, nine years old, and had no master, she would sketch with a black lead pencil on a sheet of paper the pictures of various kinds that came in her way, and make such imitations as deserved the attention of judges. This made her father get her an eminent master, and she had not been long under his direction, when she was able to infuse a soul into her figures, and motion into her compositions. She not only drew landscapes, and low subjects with a success great as Teniers, but evinced by her paintings, that she brought into the world with her an aptitude for works of a superior class. Her pictures shew that she was not the last among the painters of history. They are as valuable for the merit of the execution as for the merit of the subjects.

Her histories of the *Revelations of St. John*, which she finished a little before her death, from the first vision to the last, demonstrated a genius very wonderful, and that her hand was perfected at the same time with her imagination. If this series of pictures is not in every respect equal to Giotto's on the same subject, which I have seen in the cloister of St. Clare at Naples ; they are at least treated with greater truth, and shew that the imagination of the painter had a hand and eye at its disposal to display the finest ideas. The great artist is obvious in them.

The first picture of this Series is a representation of the inside of the glorious temple, that was made the grand scene of all the things St. John saw in the Spirit ; the golden-lamp-sconce, called the seven candlesticks, which afforded the sanctuary all its light and the august personage, who appears in refulgent brightness in the vision, in the midst of the seven golden candlesticks. The majestic and godlike form which the apostle beheld is wonderfully painted. He is represented with more than human majesty. Like Raphael in his picture of the Eternal Father, in one of the Vatican chapels, she does not inspire us merely with veneration, she strikes us even with an awful terror : elle n'inspire pas une simple vénération, elle imprime une terreur respectueuse. In his right hand, this grand person holds the main shaft that supports the six branches of the six lighted lamps, and the seventh lamp at the top of the main trunk, which gleam like a rod of seven stars, as it is written, "having in his hand seven stars," and in this attitude with his face to the apostle, he appears in the midst of the seven golden candlesticks, the emblems of the churches walking, or attending to trim them, the churches ; with a sharp two-edged sword, that is, the powerful word of God, as Aaron walked to trim the real lamps with the golden snuffers. St. John is seen on the floor. He is looking in great surprise at the whole appearance, and as with amazement he beholds the divine Person in the vision, he seems struck with dread, and going to faint away ; as he says in the *Apocalypse*, " When I saw him, I fell at his feet as dead." The next picture in this series is a continuation of, or another representation of the inside of the temple, the golden lamp-sconce of seven golden candlesticks, and the august personage in reful- gent brightness, and splendors transcendently glorious ; but with this difference, that in this piece, the divine personage does not hold the main shaft of the branches of lights in his right-hand, or stand in the midst of the candlesticks ; but, notwithstanding his sublime dignity, is painted with a godlike compassion in his face and manner, and with the greatest tenderness raises and supports the apostle. You see him, as described by St. John ; " he laid his right-hand upon me," the hand which before held the seven stars, or lighted golden lamps, that exhibited an appearance not unlike a constellation of stars; "saying unto me, fear not. I am the first and the last. I am he that liveth, even though I was dead, and behold I am alive for evermore, Amen. And I have the keys of hell and of death." One almost hears these words from the lips of the august form, so wonderfully is the figure painted, so happily has the pencil counterfeited nature, and the apostle appears to revive in transports, as he knows from the words that it is his Lord and Master is speaking to him. It is a fine picture.

The third painting in this series is the subsequent vision in the 4th and 5th chapters of the *Revelation of John the Divine*. In a part of the heavens that are opened, the throne of God is repre- sented by a crystal seat of glory, and from it proceed flashings of a bright flame like lightning and thunder, to represent the awful majesty of the One, and One Only, True God, the Supreme Lord of all things : seven lamps of fire are burning before this throne, as emblems of the seven spirits, or principal servants of God, to shew with what purity, constancy, and zeal, the spirits of the just made perfect serve God in the heavenly church ; and next them appears a crystal sea of great brightness and beauty ; much more glorious than the brazen sea in the temple, which held the water for the use of the priests. This sea alludes to that purity that is required in all persons who have the honour and happiness of a near approach to God, as he manifests himself on the throne of inaccessible light, or, in the moral *shechinah* in this lower world.*

---

* As the first notion of God's glory, in the scripture, is a physical notion, and signifies the manifestation of God, by fire, light, clouds, brightness, and other meteorous symbols, such as the marching pillars of fire and cloud that went before the Israelites, and the *shechinah* in the Holy of Holies, which the Jews called the visible presence ; so is there a glory of God in a moral signification. There is a *shechinah* in a physical sense by fire, light, and refracted colours : and there is a moral *shechinah*, or glory, when men live in obedience to all the divine laws, and walk as children of light. This shews the special presence of God in the righteous, as much as the cloud of glory did manifest him in the temple. The power and wisdom and

The next figures are the four living creatures, or cherubim of Ezekiel, which our English translation very badly renders four beasts ; and they are placed in the middle of each side of the throne, in the whole circle round about, full of eyes, not only before but behind, so as to have a direct and full view every way, without-side them ; on seats, are the four and twenty elders placed, in white and shining garments, with crowns of gold upon their heads. The person who sits on the throne appears in great majesty and glory, and round about his throne the most beautiful rainbow is seen ; to express the glory of God, and his faithfulness to his covenant and promise : the four living creatures next the throne, who represent the angels attendant on the *shechinah*, and have the appearance of a lion, a calf, a man, and an eagle full of eyes, and with six wings, to express the great understanding and power of the angels, their activity, constancy, and good will ; they are drawn in the act of adoring and praising the eternal living God ; and are answered by the four and twenty elders, the representatives of the people, the churches. So inimitably are all these things painted, that the faces of the cherubim and the four and twenty elders seem to move in worship and thanksgiving : one acquainted with the divine songs, cannot help fancying that he hears the four living creatures, saying, " Holy, holy, holy, Lord God Almighty, which was, and is, and is to come ; who for ever wast, and for ever wilt be, the one true God, the everlasting Lord;" and that the elders, that is, the Christian people, reply, "Thou art worthy, O Lord, to receive glory, and honour, and power : for Thou hast created all things, and for Thy pleasure they are and were created."

The apostle St. John, appears in great admiration, on account of the things before him, but seems more particularly affected by a book sealed with seven seals, which the person who sits on the throne holds in his right-hand ; an angel who is painted in the act of proclaiming with a loud voice, " Who is worthy to open the book, and to loose the seals thereof;" and a lamb with seven horns and eyes, standing just before the throne, within the circles of the cherubim and elders : this Lamb, represented as a sacrifice, and with seven horns and eyes, to shew the power, wisdom, and goodness of our Lord in the work of redemption, and the accomplishment of all God's designs of wisdom and grace, engages the attention and wonder of the apostle ; and as this Lamb of God receives the book from the person on the throne, a rising joy appears through the astonishment of St. John, and seems to be

goodness of God are displayed in the holy lives of men. Like the heavens they declare his glory, and are the visible epistle of Christ to the world, written not with ink, but with the spirit of the Living God. " Know ye not that ye are the temple of God, and that his Spirit dwelleth in you ? "

encreasing, as he hears the living creatures and the elders sing a
new song, or hymn of a new composition, which expresses the
peculiar honour of the Son of God, and our peculiar engagements
to him, in these words " Thou art worthy to take the book, and
to open the seals thereof : for thou wast slain, and hast redeemed
us unto God by thy blood, out of every kindred, and tongue, and
people, and nation.   Worthy is the Lamb that was slain to receive
power and riches, and wisdom and strength, and honour, and glory
and blessing.   Blessing, and honour, and glory, and power, be
unto him, that sitteth upon the throne, and unto the Lamb for
ever and ever."   And as the angels conclude this solemn act of
worship by saying " Amen ; " and the people by worshipping him
that liveth for ever and ever, the true God, who liveth and reigneth
from everlasting to everlasting ; and having raised up his Son
Jesus, sent him to bless you in turning every one of you from his
iniquities ; the apostle seems in pleasure to join them, and shews
a sensibility and action that is very wonderful.   It is a charming
picture.   The divine artist has treated the whole subject with
the most elaborate and beautiful expression, and with a delightful
richness of local colours.   This painting gives the beholder a full
and fine idea of the vision.

But it was not only in painting, and in music, that Miss HAR-
COURT excelled : she had when I first saw her, made great progress
in her studies, and discovered in her conversation extraordinary
abilities.   She talked wisely and learnedly on many subjects,
and in so charming a manner, that she entered into the possession
of the heart, and the admiration of all that heard her : nor was it
only in pure Italian, Spanish, and other languages that she could
express her notions ; but, in the correctest Latin she often spoke
to me, and for an hour would discourse in the Roman tongue,
with as great ease as if she had been talking English.   She spoke
it without any manner of difficulty, which was more than I could
do.   I was slow, and paused sometimes ; but that young lady
went on with that volubility of tongue the women are born with.
The language being Latin was no check to her natural fluency
of speech.

To all this let me add, and with truth I can add it, that EUSEBIA,
from the time I was first acquainted with her to her death, walked
in the fear of the Lord, and of consequence in the comforts of the
Holy Ghost.   Religion from her infancy was her stated and
ordinary business, and her sole concern to know and to do her
duty to God and men.   The *Proverbs* of Solomon and the pattern
of Christ, were her study when a very young girl, and from both
she acquired a conduct so prudent and evangelical, that she
seemed at the greatest heights of grace and goodness which a
mortal can reach, and appeared as one that had made a prodigious
proficiency in divine knowledge, and in every virtue ; yet there

was nothing gloomy, or even formal in her behaviour : she was good-humour itself : frank and free ; quite easy, and for ever cheerful.

Miss HARCOURT, at the time I am speaking of, that is, in the one and twentieth year of her age, had all the qualities that constitute a beauty ; she was tall and graceful, and in every action, and her whole behaviour, to the last degree charming ; her eyes were vastly fine, large and long, even with her face, black as night, and had a sparkling brightness as great as could appear from the refraction of diamonds : her hair was as the polished jet, deep and glossy ; and yet, her complexion fresh as the glories of the spring, and her lips like a beautiful flower.

This lady was nine years abroad with her father, who died of the plague at Constantinople in 1733, and in the course of her travels, did me the honour to write me many fine letters, in which she obliged me with her remarks on the things and people they saw in many countries. We held a correspondence together, for a considerable part of the time, and in return for her valuable favours, I sent her the best account I could give of the matters that came in my way. These letters may perhaps appear some day.

In 1734 Mrs. HARCOURT returned to England, and brought over with her some ladies, who became constituents of her claustral house. They formed the most rational and happy society that ever united, and during the life of the foundress, resided sometime in one of the Western Islands, but for the most part in Richmondshire. Since her death, which happened in 1745, they have lived entirely in the North of England, separated from all the world by the most dreadful mountains. They were but twelve in number for several years, but, in the sixth year of the Institute, Mrs. HARCOURT encreased it to twenty-four members, by taking in twelve elèves or disciples. The twelve seniors govern a year about in their turns, unless it be the request of the house, that the superior for the year past should continue in the office another year. This, and their easy circumstances, secure their peace, and as they are ever wise to that which is good, and simple concerning evil, they lead most happy lives : nor can it be otherwise with mortals who cultivate the grace of humility, the want of which lies at the bottom of all contentions, and by a Christian prudence, make it their main work to facilitate the practice of piety, and to promote the pleasure and the lustre of it. Glorious women ! to letters, arts, and piety, they devote those hours which others waste in vanities the most senseless and despicable ; and pursuant to the advice, and according to the rule drawn up by their illustrious foundress, live as beings that have souls designed for eternity. They act continually upon a future prospect, and give all the diligence in making constant advances toward the perfect day. Mrs. HARCOURT shewed them, what an uninspired mortal could do by the means of grace ; that it was possible for assisted human nature, feeble as flesh and blood is, to resist temptations the most violent, and by the supreme motives of our religion, acquit ourselves like Christians. If there be a devil to assault, a corrupt heart to oppose, and many difficulties to be encountered, yet her conduct was a demonstration, that those who are heirs of the heavenly country, may choose and prosecute their best interests, and improve the divine life to a high degree. " Let us," she used to say, " make salvation not only a concern on the bye, but the governing aim through the present life, and we shall not only live like the primitive Christians, but die for our holy faith, with more resolution than the worthies of Greece and Rome, though death should appear in all his array of terrors. Neither adversity nor prosperity could then tempt us to drop a grain of incense before any idol, or commit any action that dishonoured the gospel. Let what will happen, in all events, we should secure the future happiness of our souls, and thereby provide for the everlasting glory and felicity of our bodies too in the morning of the resurrection. Of Mrs. HARCOURT, a further account will be found in the *Memoirs of Several Ladies of Great Britain*, 1755, 8vo. p. 324.

The twenty-fifth day of June I took my leave of Miss HARCOURT and her father, and the rest of the good company, and on horses I borrowed, we returned to the philosophers at Ulubræ. It was nineteen miles round of most terrible road ; a great part of it being deep and swampy bottom, with holes up to the horses shoulders in some places ; and for several miles, we were obliged to ride on the sides of very deep and craggy mountains, in a path so very narrow, that we risked life, and passed in terror : a wrong step would have been destruction beyond recovery. It was likewise no small perplexity to find, that I was going back again, the course being south and south-west ; and that there was no other way of journeying from Mr. HARCOURT's to Ulubræ, but through the pass I first travelled from Westmoreland ; unless I rode from Mr. HARCOURT's into Cumberland, and then round through Bishoprick to the valley the gentlemen lived in. On then I went at all hazards, and in a tedious manner was forced to creep the way, but to make some amends, the prospects from the hills were fine, and things very curious occurred. Groups of crests of mountains appeared here and there, like large cities with towers and old Gothic edifices, and from caverns in their sides torrents of water streamed out, and tumbled in various courses to the most delightful vales below. In some of the vast hills there were openings quite through, so as to see the sun, at the end of three or four thousand yards ; and in many of them were sloping caverns, very wonderful to behold.

I found in one of them, near the top of a very high mountain, a descent like steps of stairs, that was in breadth and height like the aisle of a church, for three hundred yards, and then ended at a kind of door, or small arched opening, that was high enough for a tall man to walk into a grand room which it led to. This chamber was a square of seventeen yards, and had an arched roof about twenty high. The stone of it was a green marble, not earthy and ópaque, but pure and crystalline, which made it appear very beautiful, as the walls were as smooth as if the best polish had made them so. There was another opening or door at the other side of this chamber, and from it likewise went a descent like steps, but the downward passage here was much steeper than the other I had come to, and the opening not more than one third as wide and high ; narrowing gradually to the bottom of the sloping road, till it ended in a round hole, a yard and a quarter every way. I could see the day at the opening below, though it seemed at a great distance from me, and as it was not dangerous to descend, I determined to go down.

The descent was four hundred and seventy-nine yards in a straight line, and opened in a view of meadows, scattered trees, and streams, that were enchantingly fine. There appeared to be about four and twenty acres of fine land, quite surrounded with the most frightful precipices in the world, and in the centre of it a neat and pretty little country. house, on an easy rising ground. I could discover with my long glass a young and handsome woman sitting at the door, engaged in needle-work of some kind ; and on the margin of a brook hard by, another charmer stood, angling for fish of some sort : a garden appeared near the mansion that was well improved ; and in the fields were sheep and goats, horses and cows ; cocks and hens, ducks and geese, were walking about the ground ; and I could perceive a college of bees. The whole formed a charming scene.

Pleased with the view, and impatient to know who the two charmers were, I quite forgot the poor situation in which I left TIM, holding the horses at the mouth of the cavern, on the dangerous side of so high a hill, and proceeded immediately to the house, as soon as I had recovered myself from a fall. My foot slip'd in the passage, about six yards from the day, and I came rolling out of the mountain in a violent and surprising manner. It was just mid-day when I came up to the ladies, and as they did not see me till they chanced to turn round, they were so amazed at my appearing, they changed colour, and one of them shrieked aloud ; but this fright was soon over, on my assuring them that I was their most humble servant, and had against my will tumbled out of the hole that was at the bottom of that vast mountain before them. This I explained, and protested that I had not thought of paying them a visit, when curiosity led me into an opening near the top of the bill, as I was travelling on ; but that when I did get through so wonderful a passage, and saw what was still more strange, when I arrived in the vale, to wit, two ladies, in so wild and silent a place, I judged it my duty to pay my respects, and ask if you had any commands that I could execute in the world ? This was polite, they said, and gave me thanks ; but told me, they had no other favour to ask than that I would dine with them, and inform them how it happened that I was obliged to travel over these scarce passable mountains, where there was no society nor support to be had. Beside if in riding here you should receive a'mischief, there was not a possibility of getting any relief. There must be something very extraordinary surely, that could cause you to journey over such frightful hills, and through the deep bottoms at the foot of them

"Ladies," I replied, " necessity and curiosity united are the spring that move me over these mountains, and enable me to bear the hardships I meet with in these ways. Forced from home by the cruelties of a step-mother, and forsaken by my father on her account, I am wandering about the precipices of Richmond-shire in search of a gentleman, my friend ; to whose hospitable house and generous breast I should be welcome, if I could find out where he lives in some part of this remote and desolate region : and as my curiosity is more than ordinary, and I love to contem-plate the works of nature, which are very grand and astonishing in this part of the world, I have gone many a mile out of my way while I have been looking for several days past for my friend, and have ventured into places where very few I believe would go. It was this taste for natural knowledge that travelled me down the inside of the mountain I am just come out of. If I had not had it, I should never have known there was so delightful a little country here as what I now see : nor should I have had the honour and happiness of being known to you."

" But tell me, Sir," one of these beauties said, " how have you lived for several days among these rocks and desert places, as there are no inns in this country, nor a house, except this, here, that we know ? are you the favourite of the fairies and genies, or does the wise man of the hills, bring you every night in a cloud to his home ? "

" It looks something like it, Madam," I answered, " and the thing to be sure must appear very strange, but it is like other strange things, when the nature of them is known, they appear easy and plain. This country I find consists, for the most part, of ranges and groups of mountains horrible to behold, and of bogs, deep swampy narrow bottoms, and waters that fall and run in-numerable ways, but this is not always the case, like the charming plain I am now on, there are many flowery and delicious extensive pieces of ground, enclosed by vast surrounding hills ; the finest

intervals betwixt the mountains : the sweetest interchange between hill and valley, I believe in all the world, is to be found in
Richmondshire, and in several of those delightful vales I discovered inhabitants as in this place, but the houses are so separate
by fells scarcely passable, and torrents of water, that those who
live in the centre of one group of mountains, know nothing of
many agreeable inhabitants that may dwell on the other side of
the hills in an adjacent vale.   If there had been a fine spot at the
bottom of the precipice I found the opening in, and people living
there, as might have been the case, you ladies who live here, could
have no notion of them, as you knew nothing of a passage from
the foot to the summit of yonder mountain, within sight of the
vast hill, and if you did, would never venture to visit that way ;
and as there is not a pass in this chain of hills, to ride or walk
through, to the other side of them : but the way out of this valley
we are now in, as I judge from the trembling of the mountains all
round us, must be an opening into some part of Cumberland.   For
this reason Stanemore hills may have several families among them,
though you have never heard of them, and I will now give you an
account of some, who behaved in the most kind and generous
manner to me.   Here I began to relate some particulars concerning my friend PRICE and his excellent wife ; the admirable Mrs.
BURCOT and Mrs. FLETCHER ; the philosophers who lived at
Ulubræ, to whom I was returning ; and the generous Mr. HAR-
COURT, and his excellent daughter, whom I left in the morning ;
and at whose house I arrived by travelling up the dark bowels of a
tremendous mountain ; as, on the contrary, I arrived at theirs by
a descent through yonder frightful hill, till I came rolling out from
within, in a very surprising and comical way; a way that would
have made you laugh, ladies ; or, in a fright, cry out, if you had
happened to be walking near the hole or opening in the bottom of
that hill, when, by a slip of my foot, in descending, a few yards
from the day, I tumbled over and over, not only down what remained of the dark steep within, but the high sloping bank that
reaches from the outside of the opening to the first flat part of the
vale.   There is nothing wonderful then in my living in this lone
country for so many days.   The only strange thing is, considering
the waters and swamps, that I was not drowned ; or, on account
of the precipices and descents I have been engaged on, that I did
not break my neck, or my bones; but so long we are to live as
Providence hath appointed for the accomplishment of the grand
divine scheme.   Till the part allotted us is acted, we are secure.
When it is done, we must go, and leave the stage for other players
to come on.''
The ladies seemed greatly entertained with my histories, and
especially with my tumbling out of the mountain into their vale.
They laughed very heartily ; but told me, if they had happened

to be sitting near the hole, in the bottom of that tremendous rocky mountain, as they sometimes did, and often wondered where the opening went to, and that I had come rolling down upon them, they would have been frightened out of their senses, for they must have thought it a very strange appearance ; without hearing the history of it, they must think it a prodigious occurrence, or exception, from the constant affairs of nature.

" This might be, ladies," I answered, " but from seeing me before your eyes you must own, that many things may be fact, which at first may seem to exceed the common limits of truth. Impossible or supernatural some people conclude many cases to be that have not the least difficulty in them, but happen to be made of occurrences and places they have not seen, nor heard the like of before. Things thought prodigious or incredible by ignorance and weakness, will appear to right knowledge and a due judgment very natural and accountable to the thoughts."

Here a footman came up to us, to let his mistress know that dinner was on the table, and we immediately went in to an excellent one. The ladies were very civil to me, and exerted a good humour to shew me, I suppose, that my arrival was not disagreeable to them, though I tumbled upon their habitation, like the genie of the caverns, from the hollows of the mountains. They talked in an easy, rational manner, and asked me many questions that shewed they were no strangers to books and men and things : but at last it came to pass, that the eldest of those ladies, who acted as mistress of the house and seemed to be about one or two and twenty, desired to know the name of the gentleman I was looking for among these hills, and called my friend. " My reason, Sir, for asking is, that you answer so exactly in face and person to a description of a gentleman I heard not very long ago, that I imagine it may be in my power to direct you right."

" Madam," I replied, " the gentleman I am in search of is CHARLES TURNER, who was my school-fellow, and my senior by a year in the university, which he left two years before I did, and went from Dublin to the North of England, to inherit a paternal estate on the decease of his father. There was an uncommon friendship between this excellent young man and me, and he made me promise him, in a solemn manner, to call upon him as soon as it was in my power ; assuring me at the same time, that if by any changes and chances in this lower hemisphere, I was ever brought into any perplexities, and he alive, I should be welcome to him and what he had, and share in his happiness in this world, while I pleased. This is the man I want, a man, for his years, one of the wisest and best of the race. His honest heart had no design in words. He ever spoke what he means, and therefore, I am sure he is my friend."

To this the lady answered, " Sir, since CHARLES TURNER is the man you want, your enquiry is at an end, for you are now at his house ; and I, who am his sister, bid you welcome to Skelsmore-Vale in his name.   He has been for a year and a half last past in Italy, and a little before he went, gave me such a description of you as enabled me to guess who you were after I had looked a while at you, and he added to his description a request to me, that if you should happen to call here, while I happened to be in the country, that I would receive you, as if you were himself ; and when I removed, if I could not, or did not choose to stay longer in the country that I would make you an offer of the house, and give you up all the keys of it, to make use of it and his servants, and the best things the place affords, till his return ; which is to be, he says, in less than a year.   Now, Sir, in regard to my brother and his friend, I not only offer you what he desired I should, but I will stay a month here longer than I intended ;   for this lady, my cousin, MARTHA JACQUELOT, and I, had determined to go to Scarborough next week, and from thence to London : nor is this all, as I know I shall the more oblige my brother the civiller I am to you, I will, when the Scarborough season is over, if you choose to spend the winter here, come back to Skelsmore-Vale, and stay till Mr. TURNER returns.''

This discourse astonished me to the last degree, to hear that I was at my friend TURNER'S house, he abroad, and to be so for another year ;   the possession of his seat offered me ; and his charming sister so very civil and good, as to assure me she would return from the Spa, and stay with me till her brother came home : were things so unexpected and extraordinary, that I was for some time silent, and at a loss what to say.   I paused for some minutes, with my eyes fastened on this beauty, and then said '' Miss TURNER, the account you have given of your brother, and the information that I am now at his house, his friendly offers to me by you, and your prodigious civility, in resolving to return from Scarborough, to stay with me here till your brother arrives, are things so strange, so uncommon, and exceedingly generous and kind, that I am quite amazed at what I hear, and want words to express my obligations, and the grateful sense I have of such favours.   Accept my thanks, and be assured, that while I live, I shall properly remember the civility and benevolence of this day ; and be ever ready if occasion offered, and the fates should put it in my power, to make a due return.   Your offer, Madam, in particular, is so high an honour done me, and shews a spirit so humane, as I told you I was an unfortunate one, that I shall ever think of it, with pleasure, and mention it as a rare instance of female worth ; but as to accepting these most kind offers I cannot do it.   Since Mr. TURNER is from home, I will go and visit another friend I have in this country, to whom I shall be welcome, I believe, till your brother returns.   To live by myself here at my friend's expence, would not be right, nor agreeable to me : and as to confining you, Madam, in staying with me, I would not do it for the world." " Sir," Miss TURNER replied, " in respect of my staying here, it will be no confinement to me, I assure you. My heart is not set upon going to London. It was only want of company made Miss JACQUELOT and me think of it, and if you will stay with us, we will not even go to Scarborough this season." This was goodness indeed, but against staying longer than two or three days, I had many good reasons that made it necessary for me to depart : beside the unreasonableness of my being an expense to Mr. TURNER in his absence, or confining his sister to the country ; there was Orton-Lodge, where I had left O'FIN, my lad, at work, to which I could not avoid going again : and there was Miss MELMOTH, on whom I had promised to wait, and did intend to ask her if she would give me her hand, as I liked her and her circumstances, and fancied she would live with me in any retreat I pleased to name ; which was a thing that would be most pleasing to my mind. It is true, if CHARLES TURNER had come home, while I stayed at his house, it was possible I might have got his sister, who was a very great fortune : but this was an uncertainty however, and in his absence, I could not in honour make my addresses to her : if it should be against his mind, it would be acting a false part, while I was eating his bread. Miss TURNER to be sure had fifty thousand pounds at her own disposal, and so far as I could judge of her mind, during the three days that I stayed with her at Skelsmore-Vale, I had some reason to imagine her heart might be gained : but for a man worth nothing to do this, in her brother's house without his leave, was a part I could not act, though by missing her I had been brought to beg my bread. Three days then only I could be prevailed on to stay, and the time indeed was happily spent.

Miss TURNER was good-humoured, sensible, and discreet, as one could wish a woman to be, talked pleasantly upon common subjects, and was well acquainted with the three noblest branches of polite learning, antiquity, history, and geography. It was a fine entertainment to hear her. She likewise understood music, and sung, and played well on the small harpsicord ; but her moral character shed the brightest lustre on her soul. Her thoughts and words were ever employed in promoting God's glory, her neighbour's benefit, and her own true welfare ; and her hand very often, in giving to the poor. One third of her fine income she devoted to the miserable, and was in every respect so charitable, that she never indulged the least intemperance in speaking. She detested that calumny and reproach which assassinates a credit, as much as she abhorred the shedding a man's blood. The goodness of her heart was great indeed : the integrity of her life was glorious. She was perfection, so far as the thing is consistent with the nature and state of man here, as it was possible for a mortal to be exempt from blame in life, and blemish of soul. An absolute exemption from faults cannot be the condition of any one in this world : But, to the ladies I now speak, you may, like Miss TURNER, be eminently good, if you will do your best to be perfect, in such a kind and degree as human frailty doth admit.

Miss JACQUELOT was by the head lower than Miss TURNER, and her hair the very reverse of my friend's sister, that is, black as the raven ; but she had a most charming little person, and a mind adorned with the finest qualifications. Reason never lost the command in her, nor ceased to have an influence upon whatever she did. It secured her mind from being ever discomposed, and disengaged her life from the inconveniencies which a disregard to reason exposes us to. By a management it dictated, she enjoyed perpetual innocence and peace. She never uttered a word 'that intrenched upon piety, infringed charity, or disturbed the happiness of any one, nor at any time shewed the least sign of a vein and light spirit : yet she had a sportfulness of wit and fancy that was delightful, when she could handsomely and innocently use it, and loved to exert the sallies of wit in a lepid way, when they had no tendency to defile or discompose her mind, to wrong or harm the bearer, or her neighbour, or to violate any of the grand duties incumbent on us ; piety, charity, justice, and sobriety. Every thing that reason made unfit to be expressed, in relation to these virtues, she always carefully avoided ; but otherwise, such things excepted, would enliven and instruct by good sense in jocular expression, in a way the most charming and pleasing. She was very wise, agreeable and happy. She was very good and worthy.

This young lady was a great master on the fiddle, and very knowing in *connoisance*. She painted well, and talked in an astonishing manner, for a woman, and for her years, of pictures, sculpture, and medals. She was indeed a fine creature in soul and body.

With these ladies I spent three days in Skelsmore-Vale ; and the time we talked, walked, played, and laughed away. Sometimes we rambled about the hills, and low adown the dales. Sometimes we sat to serious ombre ; and often went to music by the falling-streams. Miss TURNER sung, Miss JACQUELOT played the fiddle, and on my German flute I breathed the softest airs. We were a happy three, and parted with regret on every side. Fain would they have had me stay, and Scarborough and London should be thought of no more ; but the reason of things was against it, and the 28th day of June I took my leave. Through the mountain I had descended, I went up again to TIM and my horses ; who were stabled in the mouth of the cavern above, and had got provender from the vale below.

The sun was rising as we mounted the horses, and struck me so

powerfully with the surpassing splendour and majesty of its appearance, so cheered me by the gladsome influences, and intimate
refreshment of its all-enlivening beams, that I was contriving an
apology as I rode on, for the first adorers of the solar orb, and
imagined they intended nothing more than the worship of the
transcendent majesty of the invisible Creator, under the symbol
of his most excellent and nearly resembling creature ; and this
according to some imperfect tradition, that man, as a compound
Being, had, in the beginning, a visible glorious presence of Jehovah
Elohim, a visible exhibition of a more distinguished presence by
an inexpressible brightness or glory : this is some excuse for the
first worshippers of the solar orb : and when the thing consecrated
to the imagery and representation of its Maker, became the rival
of his honours, and from being a help to devotion, was advanced
into the supreme object of it ; yet considering the prodigious glory
of this moving orb, and that all animated nature depends upon its
auspicious presence, we cannot wonder that the Egyptian rura-
lists, without a creed, and without a philosophy, should be tempted
to some warmer emotion than a merely speculative admiration,
and inclined to something of immediate devotion. That universal
chorus of joy that is manifested at the illustrious solemnities of
opening sunshine, might tempt the weak to join in a seemingly-
religious acclamation. At least I am sure there is much more to
be said for this species of idolatry, than for the papists worshipping
dead men, stocks, bones, and clouts. They have not only revelation expressly against them—" Thou shalt worship the Lord
thy God, and him only shalt thou serve." *Matt.* ch. iv. v. 10.—
" Neither shalt thou set up any image or pillar." *Deut.* ch. xvi.
v. 22. But downright reason demonstrates that the things are
useless to the preservers, and offensive to God ; whereas on the
contrary, when the eye beholds that glorious and important luminary of heaven, and considers the benefits dispensed to mankind
by the means of its most beautiful and invigorating beams, it
might strike not only an unpractised thinker, and cause the vulgar
who are not able of themselves to raise their thoughts above their
senses, and frame a notion of an invisible Deity, to acknowledge
the blessings they received, by a devotion to this fancied visible
exhibition of divinity. But even some of the wise ones who were
a degree above the absurdity of popular thinking, might be led to
address themselves to the golden sun, in splendour likest heaven,
They might ascribe the origin of their own existance, and the
world's, to this seemingly adequate cause, and genial power of the
system ; when they beheld him returning again in the east, as I
now see him, after the gloom and sadness of the night ; again the
restorer of light and comfort, and the renewer of the world ; regent of the day, and all the horizon round, invested with bright
rays ; that all inferior nature, the earth's own form, and the sup-

ports of its animated inhabitants, seem to depend on his dispensing authority, and to be the effects of his prolific virtue, and secret operation : they might suppose, in the corruption of tradition, or when the revealed truth and direction was lost, and reason not as now in its maturity of age and observation, that some kind of glory should be given to the subordinate divinity, as they fancied, of this heavenly body, and that some homage was due to the fountain of so much warmth and beneficence.   This, I imagine, may account for the earliest kind of idolatry ; the worship paid to the sun.   The effects of his presence are so great, and his splendour so overpowering and astonishing, that veneration and gratitude united, might seduce those ignorant mortals to deify so glorious an object.   When they had lost the guard of traditionary revelation,* and wanted those helps to judgment which are derived

---

* When the tribes went off from Noah in Peleg's days, in the æra of the deluge 240, that is, so many years after the flood, we must in reason suppose, that they had from the venerable patriarch, a final and farewell relation of the creation, and the state of innocency, and the fall ; the institution of worship ; and the hope of acceptance, and the promised seed.   We may believe they had, at going off, a distinct repetition of all the capital articles of their faith. They received a clear review of the facts and revelations which Adam and Noah had the knowledge of, and in a compend of every doctrine and duty, speculative and practical, especially the doctrine of the being of a God, his unity and perfections, had a sufficient fund of useful knowledge to set up with, in the new world.   This is natural behaviour in all good parents, and we may conclude, that the pious patriarch acted in this manner, when he sent his relations away.   But this oral tradition was liable to a gradual declension, and sunk at last into a state of evanescence.   Doctrines deduced from facts long since past, and known by tradition only, become precarious.   The tradition is rendered obscure and dubious.   It might remain nearly perfect, while Peleg, Reu, Serug, Nahor, and Terah lived, as they had their informations from Noah, and were thoroughly advised to make God the object of their supreme love and fear, and trust and worship ; and to practise all virtue and righteousness towards each other, as the great instruments and means of a general happiness.   With an earnest tenderness, these things were recommended to them.   But as the people who came after them never saw Noah, and their information depended on relators, who had it from relators, a dimness prevailed upon the ancient facts, and distance and other objects overshadowed them.   A deprivation of tradition might likewise arise from relators forgetting material circumstances, and from a misapprehension of ancient facts.   There might likewise be many that designedly corrupted these facts, and out of a dislike to truth, and a distaste to virtue, did their best to weaken the principles of religion.   Ingenious bad men there were among mankind then as well as in our time, and as there was no written system and history to go by, they might give the ancient story a turn more favourable to sinners.   By this means contradiction and obscurity came on, endless fables were introduced, and truth was disguised, corrupted and lost.

In respect however of an infinite mind, the author of the universe, it must be confessed that those men could not have lost a right notion of him, if they had been faithful to themselves ; for the works of nature still remained in all their wond'rous beauty, and useful order, and furnished daily evidence, that neither chance, nor undesigning necessity, could produce the beautiful and harmonious, the regular and convenient, the amiable and good, which their eyes beheld whatever way they turned.   Not only the heavens, the air, the earth, the sea, demonstrated the wisdom and goodness of God ; but every beast ,every fowl, every fish they could take, every plant and tree, shewed an exact proportion of parts, and discovered design in the whole of its constitution.   Their own intelligence ought likewise to have led them to the great original it was formed by, an uncreated mind.   There must be a divine understanding, or there never could be pure intellection in man.   It is impossible to solve the phænomena of moral entities, without the being of God.   If it were possible for atoms, rencont'ring in an infinite void, to produce by collision and undirected impulse, the corporeal systems, and the various beauteous forms which we see ; yet the wild and senseless hypothesis could not be applied by atheism itself to the production of ideas intirely independent of matter, and all its properties and powers.   We must have them from an intelligent cause.   The human mind is so framed, that we may surely infer the cause of the constitution was intelligent.   So that God did not in any age, leave himself without witness, or evidence, of his own being and perfection.   We have full proof of creating, ruling intelligence.   All the works of nature proclaim it, and especially the human soul.

from the experience, observation, and reasoning of past times, the specious idolatry might have been introduced, and something tolerably plausible perhaps was pleaded by the better heads of those times. Exclusive of an imperfect notion of the Deity's appearing by *shechinah*, and that the sun might be the visible exhibition as before observed ; they might, in the next place, conclude from the extraordinary motion of the luminary, that he was an animated being and noble intelligence, placed in the highest post of honour and usefulness, and employed by God as his first minister and servant ; for which reason, they thought it their duty to magnify and venerate the sun, whom the Creator had exalted so high ; as the chief minister of kings are had in honour, which is reflected back on their royal masters. Thus might the novel impiety come on. They might, in the beginning, worship the sun as the *shechinah*, appearing by a glorious light, or in a celestial train attending the presence, which, at so great a distance, must appear in an indistinct, luminous vision ; but more generally as the minister of God ; an animated being, who had a principle of consciousness put into it ; as the human body has, seated in it, a human soul ; and that this glorious creature was enabled to perform the etherial journeys by its own understanding and will, and to make all lower nature happy by his benign and diffusive influence ; could see as far as he is seen, and every way was fitted for the noble work he had to execute. Thus did the sun commence

But through negligence, and false notions of religion brought in by impious men, corrupt customs, and prejudices of education, we find that not only virtue was lost, soon after the dispersion, but even the notion of God. Idolatry and wickedness prevailed for the greatest part of the grand period of tradition, from the dispersion to the imparting the knowledge of letters by Moses. This shews the folly, vanity, and inconsistency of all tradition, and that for the support of virtue, and true religion in the world, a written word is necessary. In the early ages of the postdiluvian world, religious knowledge was decayed, and we can trace the origin and beginning of idolatry very high. Even in Serug's time, who had received a compend of religion from Noah, when he became infirm by years, and was no longer able to inspect the manners of his colony, and go about to take cognizance of their irregularities, we find the innovation had begun. We read in the books, that Terah, the father of Abraham was an idolater, in the 170th year of his age, which was the year that Serug died, and to be sure, that was not the first year of his false religion : and it is not to be supposed, that when he went forth, a worshipper of false gods, from Ur of the Chaldees, with Abraham, his son, and Lot, that the young people were safe from the infection. It prevailed before Abraham was warned to withdraw, and of consequence he was one of the ungodly, that is an idolater. To me it is plain St. Paul says so. They all served other gods. In all probability, that was beginning to be the case when Abraham was born, which was in the year after the flood 352 ; and as he was forty years old when his father marched him from Ur, we may think he was then a settled idolater ; and if it had not been that the divine mercy called him by revelation to true religion, he and the whole world might have remained in their gross innovation, eternal strangers to the original truths. The free grace of the universal Father took him and his posterity into covenant, and used them as a mean to restore true piety and virtue to the world, till such time as he was pleased to shew his astonishing mercy, and inestimable love in Christ Jesus. The Creator and Governor of Gentiles as well as Jews, in his infinite wisdom proceeded in this manner, first selecting one nation to be a beacon upon a hill, a public voucher of the being and providence of God ; and in the fulness of time, blessing the human race with a gospel and Redeemer. Adored be his goodness then for the written word. This only can preserve the doctrine of religion free from corruption. The miserable papists may trust to their traditions, and wander where no covenant is to be found : but the religion of protestants must be the gospel of Christ. The written doctrine of the apostles let us receive. The unwritten word of Rome let us despise, There is no security in tradition. It is unsufficient for the preservation of truth : and for that reason, God gave us the writings of inspired men.

a God. He must, they thought, from every appearance, in his wond'rous, useful course, have the most exalted powers ; be wise and benevolent, great and good. And when the worship of this luminary was once established, it could not be long before the moon was deified, and then the stars became conservators of the universe. From thence idolatry went on, and added to the heavenly bodies the emblematic doctrine, and animal apotheosis. Artificial fire was consecrated, and made the symbol of sidereal splendours. Deity was exhibited to the multitude in the forms of its effects, and innumerable orders of inferior divinities by degrees sprang up. Successive enlargements of the system of natural apotheosis prevailed ; and, at last, the world, which ought only to have been regarded, as the magnificent theatre of divine perfections, was itself blasphemously adored, as the independent proprietor of them.

It is evident from hence that a revealed rule was wanting, or man had need of physics, to suppress the rising transports of a too eager gratitude, and guard against the inclination to worship this rising, lucid being, now so glorious before me ; whose motion is so steady and uniform, swift, regular, and useful, that it seems to manifest itself a wise and intelligent being. Without the lights of philosophers, or the supernatural assistance of religion, it was hard for recent and wondering mortals, to refrain from worshipping that beautiful body, as they saw it proceeded with the greatest harmony, and shed innumerable blessings on them. But pure revealed religion diffuses such a light as manifests the error : and a correct and philosophic reasoning, in this improved age the safe guide, and proper arbitrator of religion, not only refuses to address itself to that God of the ancient popular theology, but proves the worship impious and absurd.

Right, reason, and revelation, demonstrate from the matchless graces and glories of nature, which occur in great variety, and without number, wherever we turn our eyes, that there is a Creator of infinite power, wisdom, and goodness ; who bountifully provides for the uses and occasions of human life, and produces repeated millions of objects that bear the stamp of omnipotence, and remain perpetual monuments of the divine benevolence. Manifold are thy works, O Lord ; in wisdom hast thou made them all !

And especially, when from the earth I lift up mine eyes to the heavens, and behold among the wonders of the firmament that vast and magnificent orb, the sun now rising before me, bright'ning by degrees the horizon, and pouring the whole flood of day upon us ; the wonderful and grand scene strikes powerfully on my mind, and causes an awful impression. With sentiments of the greatest admiration, I consider the illustrious object, and feel the kindly heat of that bright luminary, inspiring me with more than usual gladness. And what power is it that supplies this fountain of light and heat, with his genial and inexhausted treasure, who dispenses it with such munificent, yet wise profusion ? It must be some Almighty Being. It must be the work of the Deity, that is, the powerful, wise, and good parent of mankind, the Maker, Preserver, and Ruler of the world ; for his perfections are stamp'd upon the work. The evidence of reason declares it. Chance or necessity cannot form or guide. An active understanding only, and intending cause, can produce, and direct : and this cause, must be all-ruling wisdom, and unlimited power, in conjunction with the most amiable goodness. This is plain to a thorough and rational examination. A supreme Being, an eternal self-existent mind, who comprehends and presides over all, must impart the benefits of that glorious creature before me, using it as an inanimate, unconscious, instrument of conveying light, heat, and prolific influence to the earth ; which, by infinite power, is rendered as much active in sending the vegete juices through the vessels of all plants, as the sun is in diffusing its rays upon the surface of the globe we inhabit. The sun, and moon, and stars, are but instruments in his hand, for bringing about mechanically whatever good effects he has created them to produce. Our holy religion and philosophic reasoning evince this truth. This glorious sun bears the signatures of its author, and the finger of God is discernible every where. The wisdom and loving-kindness of the Lord are visible, whatever way we turn. His bounty appears by its constant, yet voluntary communication, and is the more to be admired as it is a never-failing principle. This rising luminary that visits our earth, is, in particular, a daily fresh instance of the divine favor ; and did not God's goodness only, prevent its suspension, we should be involved in the utmost horror, nay, inevitable ruin, and when, in the evening it leaves us overspread by the darkness, to visit others with its benign influences ; the change is charming, for night gives man a necessary vacation from the labours of the day. In sleep he takes the sweetest refreshment till this rising sun, by the beneficent direction of its great Author, again appears in grace and splendor, and displays the face of nature in unspeakable beauties. Every where the bounty of the supreme Spirit I see diffused ; through air, through earth, and in the waters. No place is without witnesses of his liberality ; and life is the care of his providence.

Of him then should our songs be, and our talking, of all his wonderful works. We should join in adoring him, and acknowledge him " worthy to receive glory and honour and power, who has created all things, and for his pleasure they are and were created." And it follows, that we should likewise absolutely submit to this sovereign Being, and ever resign ourselves to his direction and disposal. Where can ignorance and impotence find so safe and sure a refuge as in infinite wisdom, and almighty power ?

In this manner were my thoughts employed, as we rode over the brows of many high hills, with the rising sun before me, till we descended to a narrow wet bottom, which trended due west for an hour, and brought us to the foot of another high mountain. This we ascended with the horses as far as it was possible to bring them, and from thence I climbed up to the top, by a steep craggy way, near two hundred yards. This was very difficult and dangerous, but I had an enchanting prospect, when I gained the summit of the hill. A valley near a mile in breadth appeared betwixt the opposite mountains and that on which I stood, and a river was running through it that spread sometimes into little lakes, and sometimes fell headlong from the rocks in sounding cascades. The finest meadows, and little thickets, bordered those waters on every side, and beyond them the vast hills had a fine effect in the view : some were covered with forest ; and some with precipitating streams. I was charmed with this assemblage of the beauties of nature. It is a more delightful landscape than art has been able to form in the fiuest gardens of the world.

The descent was easy to this beautiful vale, and after I had feasted my eyes with the prospect of the place, I went down to see who lived in a house covered with creeping greens, that stood by a sonorous waterfall. Some wise one perhaps, said I, who scorns the character of the libertine, or the sot, and to the pursuits of avarice and ambition leaves the world, to enjoy in this fine retreat the true happiness of man ; by embracing that wisdom which is from above, and aspiring to an equality with saints and angels : happy man ! if such a man be here. Or, it may be, some happy pair possess this charming spot of earth, and in discharging all the duties of the matrimonial relation, enjoy that fulness of satisfaction and felicities, which the divine institution was designed to produce. Happy pair indeed ! if such a pair be here.

But when I came near the mansion, no human creature could I see, nor, for some time, could I find an entrance any way. The gate of the garden, in which the house stood, was fast, and so was every window and door : but as the gardens were in fine order, and full of fruits, vegetables, and flowers, I knew it must be an inhabited place, though its people were from home. With my pole therefore I leaped a deep moat, which surrounded the garden, and for half an hour continued walking about it, pulling some things, and looking at others, in hopes that some one might be seen : no soul however appeared, and I was going to return to my horses, when, by accident, I came to a descent of stairs, that was planted round with a shade of laurel, evergreen, and branching palm. Down I went immediately, and walked through a long

arched passage, in which two lamps were burning, and at the end
of it came to an open door, that admitted me into an entry which
led to a flight of stairs. Should I go any farther, was the question ?
If any one within, I might greatly offend : and if it was the habitation of rogues, I might find myself in a pound. What shall I
do then ? Go on, said curiosity, and bravely finish the adventure.

Softly then I ascended, listening, by the way, if I could hear
any voice, and proceeded upwards, to the first floor. A door was
there open, and on my tiptoes I went to look in, but all I could see
was a room well furnished, and through it I passed to another,
which was likewise full of fine things, and had a door unlocked
that opened into a large library. The books were all bound in
vellum, in an extraordinary manner, the collection valuable, and
most judiciously ordered. Mathematical instruments of all sorts
were on a table, and everything looked as belonging to a scholar
and man of fortune. Great was my amazement, as I saw no
living creature. I knew not what to think of all these things :
nor did my astonishment diminish, when I went from the library
into two very handsome bedchambers, and saw in one of them the
apparel of a woman ; in the other the dress of a man.

Musing on these matters, and looking over the books, I continued near an hour, when I turned round to depart, and saw at
the door of the library I was in, a gentleman, and two young
ladies in riding-dresses, who seemed more than amazed at the
sight of me. The man's face I knew very well, and soon remembered he was one of the company that came over with me from
Ireland in the Skinner and Jenkins, and a person I had thought
a very odd man ; for he never stirred out of his birth all the while
he was on board, nor spoke a syllable to any one, except myself ;
and that only for a couple of hours after we landed ; when he was
pleased to single me out, and requested we might dine together ;
to which I said, " with pleasure, Sir," and he came with MISS MEL-
MOTH and me to our inn. With us he sat for the time I have said,
and talked like a man of sense and virtue. He was but three or
four years older than I was, and yet so very grave, that in respect
of temper, he was fit for the bench. He told me, he lived in too
remote a place, ever to expect to see me in the country ; but he
had a house in London, where he was every winter, if not hindered
by sickness, and to a part of it I should be welcome, if it was agreeable to me to improve our acquaintance. Many other civil things
he said, and shewed a regard for me that I little expected, and
could not but wonder at. All this made me as well known to him
as he was remember'd by me ; but he looked, as it were, scared at
the sight of me, in the place I now appeared in ; where I stood
leaning on my long pole, when he came to the closet door, and
was reading aloud in a book I chanced to take into my hand, the
following lines :

H

Τὰ περὶ τοὺς θεοὺς ποιει μὲν, ἡγοῦ δὲ τοῦτο εἶναι θῦμα κάλλιςον, καὶ
θεραπείαν μεγίςην, ἐὰν ὡς βέλτιςον καὶ δικαιότατον σεαυτὸν παρέχης μᾶλλον
γὰρ ἐλπὶς τοὺς τοιούτους ἢ τοὺς ἱερεῖα πολλὰ καταβάλλοντας πράξειν τι παρὰ
τῶν θεῶν ἀγαθόν.

To which I added a few reflections :

Est ut dicis. Vera prædicas, vir sapiens. Quæ ad Deos spec-
tant, pulcherrimum sacrificium et cultum esse maximum ducito
si tiepsum quam optimum et justissimum præbeas. Παρέχειν ἐαυτὸν
ὡς βέλτιςον καὶ δικαιότατον : Præbere se quam optimum ac
justissimum, pluris apud Deos quam multæ victimæ. Speran-
dum est enim tales potius, quam qui victimas multas prosternunt,
quidpiam boni a Diis immortalibus accepturos. Quam optimum
cor ac justissimum ad aras feramus, et bonum a numine semper
lucrabimus.

True, most excellent sage. Rectitude and Benevolence are the
perfection of rational nature, and when by philosophy we acquire
a temper, disposition and action that are comformable to the truth
of things, and continually display strict justice and universal
charity, we offer the noblest sacrifice to heaven, and are con-
similated with the Deity. By this divine affection, for order and
goodness, we manifest a continual use and employment of ourselves for the glory of the supreme virtue, and may by this means,
expect to obtain the infinite mercy of God ; when slaughtered
Hecatombs are despised ; and the creeds of incomprehensible
mysteries, and the external modes and forms of churchism, may
be considered only as the weakness and blindness of reverend
heads. Thousands of rams and ten thousand rivers of oil ;
speculative faith, rites and ceremonies, are nothing, abstracted
from that temper and affection, which unites us to the Deity, and
to the whole system of rationals. Virtue and charity is religion.

This passage and reflection pronounced very loud, with an enthusiasm that seizes me when I take a classic in my hand, added
greatly to the astonishment of finding me in the closet, and for
some time the gentleman was not able to speak, or come forward ;
but at last, moving towards me, as I did to him, the moment I
saw him, he said, " by what strange chance have I the favor of
seeing you here ? Inform me, I beseech you, in the name of
friendship, what surprising accident has thrown you on this
solitude ; without horse or servant, and how did you get over the
broad moat of water, as the two garden gates were locked ? "

" MR. BERRISFORT," I answered, " You may well wonder at seeing me in this remote and silent part of the world, and especially at
my being in your study, without either horse or attendant in
waiting, that you could find, on coming home ; but the thing was
all natural, in the common course of events, as you shall hear.

" Three weeks after you left me at Whitehaven, I set out from that place for Brugh under Stanemore, and went from thence up the northern mountains, in search of a gentleman I had some business with, who lives but a few miles beyond you, and on my return from his house, as the road lay very high on the side of yonder vast bill, I quitted my horse out of curiosity, to climb up to the top of the mountain, and see what kind of country lay on the other side of this long range of high hills. It was with great difficulty I got up to the pike, and few, perhaps, but myself, would attempt it : I was rewarded however by the fine prospect, and seeing the descent on this side easy, and a house and large gardens before me, I could not refrain from going down to the bottom. I marched on to take a view of the mansion and improvements, and as I saw some very fine things in the gardens, and no sign of any living creature ; the gates shut and every place to appearance fastened, I leaped the moat with this pole, and after I had wandered about the ground, by accident came to the shady inclosure, in which I found the descending stairs from the garden, and seeing the lamps burning in the passage, could not avoid going down, and proceeded till I arrived at this fine library. My admiration was great, you may be sure, and the books too strong a temptation for me not to mind them. With great pleasure I looked into many of them, and at last opened the Greek writer I was reading aloud, when you came to the door of your study. Such were the causes that brought me where you find me."

Mr. BERRISFORT replied, " Sir, I am glad there was anything in the force and operation of casualties, that could bring you to my house, and I assure you upon my word, that you are most heartily welcome. As I lay in my cabin on ship-board I conceived a great regard for you, on account of many things I heard you say, and particularly for your lively arguments with Dr. WHALEY, before the storm began, in defence of the divine Unity, and against that miserable theology which the monks have invented, and continue to support, though it militates with the revealed truths of God, and the reason and fitness of things. I was greatly pleased with your different definitions of churchism and religion, and honoured you not a little for what you said in opposition to unintelligible mystery, and the glare of ceremony ; at the same time, that you contended for the worship of the universal Father, and that sober, righteous and godly life, which springs from the love of truth, virtue, and moral rectitude. Once more then I assure you, Sir, I am most heartily glad to see you, and I shall take it as a great favour if you will pass the summer with me in this wild country place. Every thing shall be made as agreeable as possible, and exclusive of this closet of books, which you shall possess while you stay here, we will hunt, and set, and shoot, and enjoy all the pleasures of the field : but in the mean time, as it is now ten o'clock, we ought to think of breakfast, and he desired his sister,

a most charming creature, to call for it immediately, and I soon
saw several servants bring in every thing that was elegant and
excellent.   He told me I need be under no uneasiness about my
mare and horses, for there was a steep narrow way for them to
come down to his stables, about half a mile from the place I left
them, and he would immediately send one of his servants to
bring them."

This was vastly civil and affectionate, and I told Mr. BERRISFORT,
that I was under great obligations to him for his goodness, which
I should ever have an extreme sense of, but I was obliged to go
on upon business : a few days however I would enjoy the happiness he offered me, and we passed them in a very delightful manner.

Early in the morning, we went out with the hounds, and for
half a dozen hours, had the dogs in full cry before us.   We had
hawks and pointers in the afternoon, and enjoyed abroad all the
sports of the field.   Within, when our labours were over, we had
the most elegant dinners and suppers ; every thing, of meat and
drink, that the best taste could desire : and the conversation was
excellent after the repasts.

Mr. BERRISFORT was a man of letters and breeding : and the
ladies had sense, and were no strangers to the best *English* books.
They understood no other language than their mother tongue,
but the choicest authors of every kind that our country has produced, they had read with great care.   The master of Yeoverin-
Green was a learned, worthy, polite man, free in discourse, if he
knew his company, and liked them, but otherwise quite mute,
and he was instructive in everything he said.   His sister and
cousin were very good ; discreet in their behaviour, temperate in
their discourse, and easy in their manner.   They had no learning ;
they pretended to no criticism ; but talked, without vanity, of
the best things, and what they did say, they expressed in a most
agreeable way.   There was no being dull with such people, in
such a place.   I have seen very few young ladies in my time that
I liked better than those girls.   They both charmed me with
their persons, their faces, their good manners, and their chat ;
but I could not enough admire MISS BERRISFORT for one particular, in which she not only excelled MISS FOX, but all the women
that I have ever seen.   This was in hunting.   In the field, she
seemed the silver-shafted queen.

Mr. BERRISFORT and MISS FOX followed the dogs with caution,
and never attempted anything that could hazard their necks
or their bones : but the charming JULIET BERRISFORT had so
violent a passion for the diversion of the field, that she was seized
with a kind of enthusiasm when she heard the cry of the hounds,
and as if she had been the goddess of the silver bow, or one of her
immortal train, went on without a thought of her having brittle

limbs. She leaped every thing to keep in with the dogs ; five-bar gates ; the most dangerous ditches and pales ; and drove full speed down the steepest hills, if it was possible for a horse to keep his feet on them. She frightened me the first morning I was out with her. She made my heart bounce a thousand times. I expected every now and then that she would break her neck— that neck where lilies grew ! I was reckoned a very desperate rider by all that knew me, and yet, with this young lady, I paused several times at some leaps, when she did not hesitate at all. Over she went, in a moment, without thinking of the perils in her way ; and then, if I broke my neck, I could not but pursue.

> When glory call'd, and beauty led the way,
> What man could think of life, and poorly stay ?

It was not in my complexion to stay, and by that means, I got a terrible fall the second day ; whether by my own fault, or my horse's, I cannot tell : but as no bone was broke, and I had re- ceived no other mischief than a black eye, a bruise in my side, and a torn face, I was soon on my mare again, and by MISS BERRIS- FORT's side. She laughed immoderately at me, while the dogs were at fault, as my bones were safe, and advised me with a humorous tenderness, to ride with her brother and Miss Fox. It was not long however before I had more satisfaction than I desired ; for in half an hour's time, we came to some pales, which the stag went over and I leaped first ; but Miss BERRISFORT's horse though one of the best in the world, unfortunately struck, and cleared them in such a manner, that the lovely JULIET came over his head. She fell very safely in high grass, where I waited for her, for fear of an accident of any kind, and did not receive the least hurt ; but in the violence of the motion, and the way she came down, the curtain was thrown on her breast, and she lay for some moments stun'd upon the ground. In a minute how- ever I snatched her up, and set her on her feet. She came to her- self immediately, and thanked me for my care of her ; but was vexed to the heart at what had happened. She requested I would not mention the thing to her brother or Miss Fox, and hoped I would be so generous as not to speak of it to any one. I assured her, " it was not in my soul to extract mirth from the bad fortune of any one ; and much less is it in my power to ridicule, or laugh at a woman of distinction for an accident like this. You may believe me, when I promise you, upon my word, and swear it by every sacred thing, that I will not so much as hint it to any mortal while you remain in this world." This gave her some relief, and by her foot in my hands I lifted her into her saddle again. Two benefits were derived from this mischance. One was, that for the future, this lady hunted with a little more caution, and did not

take the leaps she was wont to do ; the other, that it gained me
her heart, though I did not know it for many months, and thereby secured for me the greatest happiness, against a day of distress.   From the most trivial things the most important do often
spring, but I proceed.

Vexatious as the fall was to this young lady, it was I however
that had all the pain, by the mischief I received when my horse
threw me.   My eye was in a sad black way, my side troubled
me, and the skin was off half my face ; yet I did not much mind it,
as the diversion was good, and that immediately after the death of
the stag we hastened back to an excellent dinner, and some flasks
of old generous wine ; to which Bob Berrisfort and I sat for
two or three hours.   The ladies had left us to change their dress,
and walk in the gardens, and we fell into very serious chat.

" I am thinking," said Mr. Berrisfort, after a considerable
pause, as we sat smoking a pipe over against each other, " that the
cause you gave Dr. Whaley, on ship-board, for the decay of
Christianity, was the best I have heard.   I remember you told
this divine, that it was not want of faith in the present generation
that made so many renounce Christianity ; for, the world were
no enemies to a republication of the law of nature by the man
Christ Jesus ; but the thing that makes infidels, and supports
infidelity, is the extravagant doctrines which the theologers have
obtruded upon the church, as essential parts of Christianity.
Enthusiasm, absurdity, and error, and the blind and bloody scenes
of cruelty and superstition have been the great stumbling-blocks
to mankind, and given the most sad, severe and lasting stabs,
to the interests and success of the pure and peaceable gospel of
Christ.   This is just.   But exclusive of this, may we not say that
there are so many seeming contradictions, and a multiplicity of
obscure passages in it, that it looks as if it could not be, in its
present condition, a rule of faith, and that Christians differ so
much about the meaning of the texts of their Bible, that reason
knows not what to say to a religion so variously represented.
It is not only the two great camps, papist against protestant, and
protestant against papist, who make the religion as different
as black and white ; that the reformed mission at Malabar tell
the Indians they must not hearken to the jesuits, if they expect
salvation ; and the monks at Coromandel declare, on the contrary, to those Indians, that they will be damned to eternity, if
they are converted to what the Danish ministers call Christianity :
which made the famous bramin Padmanaba say, that it was impossible for him to become a Christian, till the learned Christian
priests had agreed among themselves what Christianity was ;
for he had not erudition and judgment enough to decide in the
intricate controversy ; but, exclusive of this, protestants are so
divided among themselves, even the church of England against

the church of England, dissenters against dissenters, and give such different accounts of the revealed system, that it requires more understanding, and strict serious enquiry, than the generality of people have, or can spare, to be able to determine in what party of the celebrated critics and expositors true religion is to be found : and when the controversy is so dark and various, and the authorised professors can never agree among themselves, what can a man of a plain understanding say to it ? This makes many, I imagine, turn from the scriptures to study nature, and the general laws which are established among the several gradations, ranks and classes of beings, so far as they are connected with intelligent, moral agency. In the natural, agreeable pages of that infinite volume, we see and perceive beauty and order, art, wisdom, and goodness, and are thereby led to the Creator and Governor of the world, the universal cause, preserver, and director of nature. We discover his providence, measures and benevolence, the rules and principles of eternal, immutable wisdom and reason, and by them are compelled to confess a universal, intelligent Efficient ; one infinite, eternal, omnipotent, wise, good Being, from whom all others derive, and on whom all others necessarily depend, and that continually. In short, by studying nature, we discover a God of truth, order and rectitude, and as we find perfect universal truth, and moral rectitude to be the highest perfection in the Deity, our reason informs us, that we ought to show our love of God, by a love of these ; and that a regular, uniform pursuit of them, must be the only true and rational pursuit of human happiness. Here is a plain and good religion. Can we wonder then that many study and follow nature, and disregard those interested commentators, who, like opposite counsel at the bar, multiply and make void the law by different and contradictory pleadings on it ? " Here Bob ended—and lighted his pipe again, while I laid mine down, and went on in the following manner :

" As Christianity was instituted by its great Author and Publisher, for the benefit of mankind, it is to be lamented that the divines should so differ, concerning what genuine revealed religion is, as to cause many to renounce this standing and perpetual rule of faith and manners, but as to contradictions and inconsistencies in the apostle's writings, I have read them over several times, and never could find such things in them. Obscure passages there are a few at first sight ; but a little consideration can explain them by other scriptures, if we do not like some commentators endeavour, by forced constructions, to adapt the sense of them to a system. This is what ruins Christianity. The monks shut out the light of reason, which is to explain scripture by scripture, and in the dark, fancy a metaphysical theology : they speculate a tritheistic mystery, original sin, divine sovereignty, election, reprobation, with many other pieties, and call the things revelation, which are, in reality, an artificial, invented corruption of the gospel. The majority of the doctors insist upon it that their reverend notions are revealed religion, and where they have a power, wattle the people into them ; but men who will use the human understanding their Creator has given them, and employ the reason of men in the choice of their religion, very easily perceive that unnatural representation could never come down from heaven : and that whatever the declaimers on human nature may say in praise of their gospel, it is impossible it should be inspiration, when the propositions rather merit laughter and contempt than the attention of rational creatures. This makes the Indians of any understanding flee Christianity. This causes men of sense, in a free country, to declare against revealed religion. The principal offence must remain, while the majority of the clergy continue to blind the human understanding, and instead of couching the cataract, darken the souls of the people with a suffusion of mystery : to which I may add, and obstinately refuse to make use of unexceptionable, scriptural forms of expression in divine public service, though an alteration might be made without any possible danger or injury to the church, and continue to use in our liturgy unscriptural phrases, and metaphysical notions, the imaginations of weak men. While this is done, the Christian religion must suffer, and of consequence, the divines who contend for mystery, and labour to destroy human reason and the powers thereof : to stifle and extinguish our common notions of things, and preclude all reasoning whatsoever upon the subject of religion ; must have the blood of more souls to answer for, in the approaching day of calamity, than they now seem to imagine, while great preferments blind their understanding, and render them insolent and positive. All this however has nothing to do with the true gospel. If men would read the historical, and the argumentative parts of the sacred writings with honesty, and explain them as right reason and true criticism directs ; if they would study them with that true zeal, which is guided by a good light in the head, and which consists of good and innocent affections in the heart ; and have at the same time a knowledge of the customs which prevailed, and the notions that were commonly received in those distant ages and countries, they would find no inconsistencies and contradictions in the scriptures, even the difficulties would soon disappear. The sacred writings would appear to be what they are, a system of religion that answers to all our wishes and desires ; that requires of us that obedience to which as rational beings we are antecedently bound : and offers us rewards for obeying more than nature could ever claim. In the gospel, we have the religion of nature in perfection, and with it a certainty of mercy and unutterable blessings : but in natural religion, as the reason and understanding of men can collect it, our hopes of pardon and glory have but uncertain foundation. Without revelation, our hopes are liable to be disturbed and shaken by frequent doubts and misgivings of mind : but in revealed religion, that is, the moral law republished by inspired men, the promises of the gospel take in all the wishes of nature, and establish all her hopes. Blessed be God, then for sending his wellbeloved Son into the world. From him we have a law that is holy, and the commandment holy, and just, and good : and by a dutiful submission to this plain and perfect law, in which there is no mystery, no inconsistency, no contradiction, we are delivered from condemnation, by the grace of God through Christ. Here is reason for adoring the divine goodness. The gospel gives a better evidence for the truth and certainty of life and immortality than nature before had given, and thereby displays the love that God has for the children of men."

To this Mr. BERRISFORT said, that " he thought my plea for original Christianity was good, and allowed it was not the gospel that was faulty in mystery and obscurity, contradiction and inconsistency ; but, human ignorance, and human vanity, which have loaded it with absurdities, while they excluded reasoning about it, and warped its fair and heavenly maxims to the interests of systems and temporalities. However," continued Bob, " you will allow I believe, that the sacred writers had not perpetually the aid of an unerring Spirit, and therefore are sometimes inconsistent in their accounts : that as they were sometimes destitute of divine assistance, they were liable to error when guided only by the human spirit, and did act like common men upon several occasions. This seems to be evident from the relations, and the human sentiments of the apostles. The evangelists speak of the same facts differently ; and in citing prophecy, while one adapts a fact to the letter of the prophecy, another accommodates the letter of the prophecy to the letter of the fact : I mean here, the ass and colt in *Matthew*, and the colt only in *John*, and their citing *Zechariah*, ch. ix. v. 9. differently. And as to the other sacred writers, does not the dispute between *Paul* and *Peter*, shew a subjection, sometimes, to ignorance and error ? does not the quarrel between *Barnabas* and *Paul* let us see, that one of them was mistaken, and both of them to be blamed ? Tell me likewise, what you think of *Mark* and *John's* different accounts of the time of the crucifixion, and does not *Matthew* contradict *Mark* in his relation of the resurrection of Jesus ? " To this I replied, " that however some zealots may contend for the perpetual inspiration of the sacred writers, yet he could not think such doctrine necessary to the creed of a Christian : Jesus only is called the truth, and was incapable of error. Christ only in all his actions, was directed by a prophetic spirit. All other men, prophets and apostles, were sometimes left to the guidance of their own spirit ; and therefore all things which they have signified to us by their words or deeds, are not to be considered as divine oracles.   Nec adeo omnia, quæcunque dictis significarunt aut factis, ea pro divinis oraculis habenda.   Nullus, excepto Domino, fuit unquam propheta, qui omnia egerit spiritu prophetico.   So Limborch, Dodwell, and Baxter say, and of the same opinion were Grotius and Erasmus.*   They assert, that the apostles, on

* Erasmus, Grotius, Limborch, Baxter, and Dodwell, were great and excellent men, and their lives and writings highly merit consideration.   Of the former it may justly be said, that he in vain lived and died in the Romish communion, and sustained many reflections from some zealous protestants ; he was not the less ill treated both during his life ,and after his death, by several Romish catholic writers ; for though taking all things together, Erasmus was what they called a Roman catholic ; yet his *Colloquies* shew his hatred of the monks, and it was plain from his writings and behaviour, that he did not see without joy the first steps of Luther.   Bayle says of Erasmus, that he was one of those witnesses for the truth, who were wishing for a reformation in the church, but who did not think it was to be procured by erecting another society to be supported by leagues, and that should pass immediately *a verbis ad verbera*, from words to blows, for speaking of his contemporary Luther, Erasmus says, " had all that he wrote been good, his seditious freedom would still have been disagreeable to me.   I would rather submit to some errors than raise a civil war, and put the whole world in an uproar for the sake of truth.   Jo. Manlius *in Locorum Communium Collectaneis*, printed at Francfort on the Maine, in 1568, in 8vo,. has this passage : " Erasmus Roterodamus moriturus sæpe ingeminavit hanc vocem, Domine, Domine fac finem, fac finem, sed quid voluerit dicere non possum.   Manlius was with Erasmus in his last hour.
   Erasmus was born at Rotterdam, October 28, 1466, and died of a bloody flux at Basil, aged 70.   July 12, 1536.
   The following epitaph is on a marble stone in the cathedral at Basil, where he was buried.

CHRISTO SERVATORI. S.
DES. ERASMO ROTTERODAMO.
VIRO.
OMNIBUS MODIS MAXIMO, CUJUS INCOMPARA-
BILEM IN OMNI DISCIPLINARUM GENERE
ERUDITIONEM PARI CONJUNCTAM PRUDEN-
TIA POSTERI ET ADMIRABUNTUR ET PRÆDI-
CABUNT ; BONIFACIUS AMERBACHIUS, HIER.
FROBENIUS, NIC. EPISCOPIUS, HÆREDES ET
NUNCUPATI SUPREMÆ SUÆ VOLUNTATIS
VINDICES, PATRONO OPTIMO NON MEMORIÆ
QUAM IMMORTALEM SIBI EDITIS LUCUBRA-
TIONIBUS COMPARAVIT, IIS TANTISPER DUM
ORBIS TERRARUM STABIT SUPERFUTURO
AC ERUDITIS UBIQUE GENTIUM COLLOQUU-
TURO, SED CORPORIS MORTALIS QUO
RECONDITUM SIT ERGO HOC
SAXUM POSUERE.
MORTUUS EST IV. B I D. JUL.
JAM SEPTUAGENARIUS, ANN. A CHRISTO NATO
M.D. XXXVI.

   Above this epitaph is the device and seal of Erasmus, to wit, TERMINUS, the god of bounds and the words—
CONCEDO NULLI.
   The inscription to his memory, at Rotterdam, is this :
DESIDERIO ERASMO
MAGNO SCIENTIARUM ATQUE LI-
TERATURAE POLITIORIS VIN-
DICI ET INSTAURATORI
VIRO SUI SÆCULI PRIMARIO
CIVI OMNIUM PRÆSTANTISSIMO
AC NOMINIS IMMORTALITATE'
SCRIPTIS ÆVITERNIS JURE
CONSECUTO.
S. P. Q. ROTTERDAM

ordinary occasions, were ordinary men. All true Christians critics must allow this, and grant that the universal inspiration of the sacred penmen, is a notion founded in the prejudices of pious men and their mistaken sense of scripture. Such infallible

NE QUOD TANTIS APUD SE SUOSQUE
POSTEROS VIRTUTIBUS PRÆMIUM,
DEESSET
STATUAM HANC EX ÆRE PUBLICO
ERIGENDAM CURAVERUNT.

BARBARIÆ TALEM SE DEBELLATUR ERASMUS
MAXIMA LAUS BATAVI NOMINIS ORE TULIT
REDDIDIT EN! FATIS ARS OBLUCTATA SINISTRIS,
DE TANTO SPOLIUM NACTA QUOD URNA VIRO
EST
INGENII COELESTE JUBAR MAJUSQUE CADUCO
TEMPORE QUI REDDAT SOLUS ERASMUS ERIT.

* Froben published an edition in 1540, of all the works of Erasmus at Basle, in nine volumes folio. The first, second, and fourth, contain his *Philosophical, Rhetorical,* and *Grammatical Pieces,* his *Colloquies* and *Praise of Folly* : the third, his *Epistles,* which are very fine, and many of them relate to the affairs of the church : the fifth, his *Books of Piety* : the sixth, his version of the *New Testament,* with notes : the seventh, his *Paraphrases on the New Testament* : the eighth his *Translations of some Greek Fathers* : the ninth, which is the largest, his *Apologies.* His *New Testament, Letters,* and *Colloquies,* are the most valuable of his works. The preface to his *Paraphrase on the Gospel of St. Matthew,* is an admirable thing. An English translation of it, with notes, and a good preliminary discourse addressed to Roman catholics, was printed in 1749. Reader, though the edition of 1540 here mentioned is a good one, yet that of Le Clerc's printed at Leyden, in 1703, in eleven volumes, folio, is infinitely superior, and in better estimation.

Hugo Grotius, the son of Jean de Groot was born at Delft in Holland, the 10th of April, 1583, and died at Rostock in Mecklenbourg, Sept. 8, 1645, aged 62.

[In the former editions of this book, a condensed list of the writings of Grotius followed this note, which was derived from M. de Burigny's excellent Life of that great man, printed in 1752, and translated from the French into English in 1754. With much asperity if not ill-nature, Amory has accused M. de Burgny of being a "bigotted papist," and charges him with having "in a sad and ridiculous manner strained some lines written by Grotius to prove that he died a member of the Church of Rome." The Abbé Raynal, a judicious French writer, observes that ' M. de Burigny, has introduced nothing but facts well supported, or theological discussions delivered, but with the greatest conciseness and accuracy," and that, " the most valuable part of his work, is the just and concise idea which it gives of Grotius's several writings." The commendation given by the Abbé Raynal is wholly and absolutely just ; should the reader, therefore, be desirous of becoming better acquainted with the Life and Writings of Grotius, he will find himself agreeably entertained by perusing the Life written by M. de Burigny, and printed in 1745, in 8vo. The list of the works of Grotius occupies pp. 363-8, and though it has met with the maledictory censure of Amory, will questionless receive its due meed of praise from the reader. ED.]

The great and good Richard Baxter was a nonconformist divine, who suffered much by the severity of that cruel monster of a man, lord chief justice Jefferies, in a prosecution, in Easter Term, 1685, on account of some passages in his *Paraphrase on the New Testament.* He was confined in the King's Bench prison from the beginning of the year 1685, till Nov. 24, 1686 ; when, by the mediation of Lord Powis, he obtained a pardon from King James, and was released out of prison. The passages marked for censure, by Sir Roger L'Estrange ; were his explications of *Matt.* ch. v. v. 19. *Mark,* ch. ix. v. 39 ; xi. 31 ; xii. 38,39, 40. *Luke,* ch. x. v. 2. *John,* ch. xi. v. 57 ; and *Acts,* ch xv. v. 2. Dr. South is said to have likewise put into his enemies, power, some annotations, from *Romans,* ch. xiii. The charge was, that his paraphrase on these places reflected on the prelates of the church of England, and, consequently, that he was guilty of sedition ; but equity at this day can find no such reflection or sedition in the passages so condemned.

Richard Baxter was born November 12, 1615, at Rowton in South Bradford. He was an author fifty-two years, and in that time wrote one hundred and forty-five distinct treatises, whereof four were folios, seventy-three quartos, forty-nine octavos, and nineteen in twelves and twenty-fours ; besides single-sheets, separate sermons, and prefaces to other men's writings. He began with *Aphorisms of Justification,* printed in 1649 ; in his thirty-fourth year ; and ended with the *Certainty of the World of Spirits,* in 1691 ; on the 8th of December, in the same year he died at the advanced age of 76 years, at his house in Charter-house-Yard. The following books of his composing in English, are excellent : *The Saint's Everlasting Rest :*

authority they think the best way to silence all objections, and weakly embrace the hypothesis to advance the honour of religion.

" But our allowing this, and that there are some disagreements and variations in the evangelists, cannot hurt the gospel. St.

Call to the Unconverted: Dying Thoughts: Certainty of the World of Spirits: and his *Paraphrase on the New Tesament.* His Latin pieces are *De Catechisatione Domestica. Aphoris mi de Justificatione et Fœderibus. Apologia. Libellus Rationum pro Religione Christiana contra Gassendum et Habestum. Epistola de Generali Omnium Protestantium Unione adversus Papatum. Dissertatio de Baptismo Infantium. Directiones de Reformatione Ecclesiæ. De Religione Grottana adversus Piercium. De Jure Sacramentorum. Gildas Salvianus, sive Pastor Reformatus. Catechismus Quackerianus. Clavis Catholicorum. De Regimine Ecclesiæ. De Universali Redemptione contra Calvinum et Bezam. De Rep. Sancta. Historia Conciliorum.*

But few I am persuaded in those days of dissipation and pleasure, will sit down to read all or any of what Baxter hath written. It may however, be conscientiously asked, What must become of us when high and low, rich and poor, fly from themselves, and laugh at every thing serious ; run into every extravagance and vanity, and wanton life away in dissipation and diversion ? For shame, rationals, reflect. Consider what ye are. You are beings endued with reason, to the end that you may pursue the true happiness of rational nature, and by a truth and rectitude of life, unite yourselves to the supreme inexhaustible fountain of all intellectual and durable good. You are likewise accountable creatures, standing on the brink of death, resurrection, and judgment ; and when this fleeting scene of vanity is over, moral impotence, or natural weakness, as they are now called, will not be accepted as a plea for the offender against nature and reason, for, let reason be heard, and spend some hours of your every day, in reading good books, and in the closet in prayer, with a resolution to do your best to live as you pray, and that power, which darkens the understanding, enslaves the will, and obstructs the operations of conscience, you may easily remove. You will despise every gratification against truth, and delight in being useful and pious here, that you may secure eternal happiness in some future world. Ponder then, rationals, in time. As you are placed herein a mutable condition capable of bliss and misery ; to be made confirmed blessed spirits above, when the time of probation is over, if you have kept the commandments of God ; or, to live with Lucifer and the apostates for ever in darkness and woe, if you have not fought the good fight, and kept the faith ; therefore, do all that piety and goodness can do in this life. Resolve by the advice of the gospel, and let nothing in nature be able to divert the execution, but a countermand from the same authority. I speak to the rich and gay, who nightly visit the resplendent and delusive scenes of vitiated life, among the higher orders ; as well as to others who frequent the dances given at fairs and sixpenny hops as they are termed ; where people of both sexes, of low and middling condition, assemble together, to their destruction in all respects. Here the ruin of many an honest tradesman's daughter commences ; and from being men of pleasure at these places, idle young fellows come by degrees to the gallows. Their morals are here corrupted, their time is wasted, and money must be got some way or other, to answer the expences. The women there, are for the most part loose characters, and the greatest part of the men, pickpockets and gamblers ; nor do they keep themselves sober ; for the last time I looked into one of their dancing rooms, to see how it was with my kind, one night, as I was walking home, I saw some of the men fuddled, fighting for the women ; and several unhappy girls, so drunk, they could not stand. The whole was a sad scene.

But you, who are great, honourable, and rational—may be called on, I suppose, to stay every wandering or illicit thought, every inconsiderate word, and to bring every intended action before the supreme bar of righteous and impartial reason. You may, perhaps, remember what I beg leave to tell you, that you live under a threefold duty to God, to your neighbours, and to yourselves : and of consequence, that you must flee all those pleasures, and diversions, and alienation of mind, which usually obstruct the love of God, his fear, and honour ; that you must have no immoderate desires, which may tempt you to violate the laws of justice and charity ; and in the regimen of yourselves, that you must observe a strict moderation and temperance, and make your whole life an oblation, and submission to the will of God. This advice I humbly offer to those intelligent, immortal beings, who waste their precious hours in routs and spectacles, and in every species of plays and sports, frolic it all the long day.

Philip de Limborch, a remonstrant divine, and professor of Theology, was born June 19, 1633. He was a learned and excellent man, and hath written the following excellent books : *Système Complet de la Théologie,* which was translated into English, and printed in 8vo. *Collatio Amica de Veritate Religionis Christianæ, cum Erudito Judœo.* At the end of this, is an account of Uriel Acosta, a Portuguese deist, who had been a Jew, and Limborch's *Defence of Christianity* against Acosta's objections. This remarkable life and defence of revealed religion were translated into English in the year 1740. But the *Collatio* has not been published in English by any one : at least I never saw such a thing : and for this reason, I have

Paul might reprove St. Peter, and speak himself sometimes after the manner of men ; yet, we see where they had the divine assistance in their explications, and the power of working miracles to confirm their doctrine ; and there, as rational and thinking men,

begun a translation of it, and intend to finish it with many notes on the arguments of the two disputants ; if death, or sickness, do not hinder. *L'Histoire de ce Terrible Tribunal l'Inquisition* ; that is *The History of the Inquistion* ; was translated into English by Samuel Chandler,* a dissenting minister ; who prefixed, in an introduction, a *History of Persecution*, that cannot be sufficientl praised, or enough admired. The History and introduction were published in 4to, in 1731,yand the introduction was afterwards re-printed in 8vo. and again by Atmore, in 1813, 8vo. *Commentarius in Acta Apostolorum et in Epistolas ad Romanos et Hebræos*, printed in folio. This is one of the most valuable books in Christian learning ; strong and beautiful ; just and rational. Let it stand next your bible in your study, and when you sit down to the *Acts of the Apostles*, and the *Epistles to the Romans and Hebrews*, let Limborch's *Commentary* be open before you, and you will be improved and charmed.

Let me likewise advise you, reader, to open, at the same time, Dr. Sykes *on the Hebrews* ; a glorious performance ; and his most excellent book *on Redemption* : these two have been published very lately. By the way, Dr. Sykes's *Essay upon the Truth of the Christian Religion*, is one of the best, if not the best, of all the good things that have been published for revelation ; and his *Connexion and Discourse on the Miracles*, are admirable.

See likewise his *Essay on Sacrifices*, his *True Foundations of Natural and Revealed Religion*, his *Two Defences of Clarke's Exposition of the Catechism*, his *Phlegon*, his *Two Previous Questions, and Defence of the Two Questions of Dr. Middleton* against *Dr. Chapman, Dr. Church, and Mr. Dodwell*. These, and all his pieces, are delightful, useful learning. They illustrate revelation, and give a just and charming account of the Christian religion.

Limborch wrote some other small things, as Letters, Prefaces, and Essays. Among the former those addressed by him to Locke are excellent ; that on Liberty or Power, was too much even for that distinguished and profound philosopher. But his most celebrated Letter to Locke, in which Limborch gave the history of his arguments, used in bringing back an ingenious lady to Christianity, who had been converted to Judaism, has not been published. It has been seen by several, but is now probably irretrievably lost. 🖛

In 1675, Limborch published the valuable works of his master Etienne de Courcelles, an Arminian divine. Courcelles, born in 1586, succeeded Simon Episcopius, who died April 4, 1643 ; as pastor to the Church of the Remonstrants in Holland, but Courcelles dying May 29, 1659, was followed by Arnold Poelemberg, who was succeeded on his death in 1667, by Limborch ; who in 1693, published the *Sermons* of Episcopius, in a large folio, to which he not only prefixed a preface, but an admirable *Life* of Episcopius, which was published separately, in 8vo. Arnoldus Poelemburg. the writer of the Life of Courcelles, prefixed to his works, in 1675 ; was a learned and pious man. His *Dissertatio Epistolaris contra Hoornbeekium*, and his *Examen Thesium Spanhemii*, are fine things. His preface to the second volume of Episcopius's *Theological Works*, is excellent ; and in a valuable book called *Epistolæ Præstantium Virorum*, you will find many letters by Poelemburg, that are extremely beautiful, in respect of the charms of his style, and his judicious manner of treating his subjects.

---

* This gentleman is still living, [1756,] and greatly to be honoured, on account of several other excellent writings, in defence of true piety, and the gospel of Christ. His *Vindication of the History of the Old Testament* against Dr. Morgan. His *Discourse of the Nature and Use of Miracles* ; and his *Answer* to Anthony Collins' *Grounds and Reasons of the Christian Religion*, his *Re-examination of the Witnesses of the Resurrection*, his *Commentary on Joel*, his two sermons called *The Notes of the Church*, in the second volume of the Salter's Hall, *Sermons against Popery*, his *Sermon on Superstition*, and two funeral sermons ; one on the death of Dr. Hadfield, "For the wages of sin is death, but the gift of God, is eternal life through Jesus Christ our Lord." *Romans*, ch. vi. v. 23. The other on the death of Mr. Smyth. "Who shall change our vile body, that it may be fashioned like unto his glorious body, according to the working whereby he is able to subdue all things to himself." *Phil.* ch. iii. v. 21, are all fine pieces, well written, with a sense and spirit, that renders all Mr. Chandler's performances very valuable ; and therefore, they highly merit the attentive reading of every gentleman. Some other things written by this minister I mentioned in my *Memoirs of Several Ladies of Great Britain*, 1755, 8vo. p. 73, to which the reader is referred.

Reader, on *The Resurrection of Jesus*, first read bishop Sherlock's *Trial of the Witnesses* and Tipping's *Defence of the Trial* : then take up Mr. Chandler's piece ; and when you have seriously read it, see what Dr. Pearce, bishop of Rochester, says on this subject in the first part of his *Four Discourses on the Miracles* ; add to them Grove's *Sermons on the Resurrection*, and I imagine, these fine little pieces will give you satisfaction : if a doubt should still remain, open Mr. West's fine book on the Article, and I think you will be easy as to this point. Reduce the strength of what they all say to a few written arguments, and keep them for use.

we must allow the authority of the sacred books ; the few places that have the marks of weakness, only serve to convince us, that the divine writers of the books made not the least pretension to perpetual inspiration. ' In suo sensu abundat aliquid humanæ fragilitatis dissentio habet ; ' says Jerome. Human frailty and their own sense honestly appear, when there was not an occasion for infallibility and miracle. But whenever the preachers of the *New Testament* were wanted for the extraordinary purposes of divine providence, they were made superior to the infirmities of nature : their understandings were enlarged and enlightened and an inspired knowledge rendered them incapable of error. This in my judgment, is so far from ruining the authority of scripture, that it is the greatest confirmation of its truth. It shews the

---

The best thing of Courcelles is his *Quaternio Dissertationum Theologicarum* in which he treats, as an able, rational divine, of the Trinity, Original Sin, the Knowledge of Jesus Christ and Justification. The next in value to this are his *Institutiones Religionis Christianæ* ; *Diatribe de Jesu Sanguinis : Vindiciæ contra Amyraldum :* and *Avis d'un Personage Desinteressé :* in which he acted the Mediator between the Calvinists aud Arminians ; but without success. It is a vain attempt to unite parties. Every party is a church and infallible in its own conceit. Happy they that are of no party, but devoted to Jesus Christ only, and his plain gospel ; doing their best to be pure and good, even as the Lord Jesus Christ was pure and good, and worshipping God the Father Almighty, in the name of Jesus, as his disciples, without speculating, inventing, or perplexing ourselves with imaginations. This was our Lord's direction. When you pray, say, Our Father, whatever ye ask in my name, without holiness no man shall see the Lord. Here it is, gentlemen of the laity, as the doctors call us, and will have us to be an inferior tribe to them. Adhere to these few, plain things, and you will be for ever happy, though the church damns you by bell, book, and candle-light.

The learned and pious Henry Dodwell, who was some time fellow of Trinity College, Dublin ; and Camden Professor of History in Oxford, till he was ejected for refusing to take the oath to King William ; was born at Dublin, in October 1641. His works are the following : *Prolegomena ad Tractatum Joannis Stearnii de Constantio in Rebus Adversis. Two Letters of Advice on going into Holy Orders, and Theological Studies, with a Tract concerning Sanchoniatho. Considerations of Present Concernment, of how far the Romanists may be trusted by Princes of another Persuasion. An Account of the Fundamental principle of Popery, and an Answer to six queries proposed to a Lady by a Romish Priest. Separation of Churches from Episcopal Government Schismatical, and a Defence of it. Dissertations on St. Cyprian. A Dissertation on a passage of Lactantius. A Treatise of the Priesthood of Laics. Additional Discourses to the Posthumous works of Dr. Pearson,* published by Dodwell. *Dissertations on Irenæus. A Vindication of the Deprived Bishops,* Sancroft, Lloyd, Turner, Ken, Frampton, White ; to whom succeeded Tillotson, Moore, Patrick, Kidder, Fowler, Cumberland ; and a *Defence of the Vindication. Four Camdenian Lectures,* called *Prælectiones Academicæ. The Annals of Velleius Paterculus, &c. An Account of the Lesser Geographers. The Lawfulness of Church Music. An Account of the Greek and Roman Cycle. A Letter against Toland, relative to the Canon of the New Testament. The Annals of Thucydides and Xenophon ;* and an *Apology for the Philosophical Works of Cicero. A Letter on the Soul to Mr. Layton,* and a *Letter to Dr. Tillotson on Schism. Two Dissertations on the Age of Phalaris and Pythagoras. An Admonition to Foreigners concerning Schism. An Epistolary Discourse to prove the Soul a Principle naturally Mortal, but Immortalized by its Union with the Divine Baptismal Spirit : that the Bishops only can give this Immortalizing Spirit : and that Sacerdotal Absolution is Necessary for the Remision of Sins. Three Treatises in Defence of the Epistolary Discourse.*

These are the works of the learned Dodwell. Some are very valuable, many of them good for nothing ; and all of them written with great perplexity ; without any beauty of stile, or any order. Dodwell's learning was very great, but beside the singularity of his notions, which he affected, his learning lay like a lump of puzzled silk in his head, and he could draw few useful threads. Dodwell in the fifty-second year of his age, married a very young girl, the daughter of a gentleman, in whose house he boarded in the country ; having been her preceptor for five years ; from a regard to her fine understanding, and by her had ten children. Two sons and four daughters survived him ; one of the sons is the present [1756] rector of Shottesbrook, well known by the title of ORTHODOX DODWELL, on account of his writings for the fathers against Dr. Middleton ; and to distinguish him from the author of a bad book finely written [by Tindal], called, *Christianity, Founded on Argument.*

Dodwell, the elder, died at Shottesbrook, June 7, 1711 ; aged 70.

honesty of the preachers of the new Testament, in owning they were only occasionally inspired : and when the incredulous see the ingenuous acknowledgment of what is human in the inspired writings, the truth of our religion must be more conspicuous to their eyes : whereas the truths of the Testament are hid from them, by making God the dictator of the whole ; because they think that impossible, and therefore conclude, the Christian religion has no better foundation. In short there is no reason to believe that the apostles were extraordinarily inspired, when they say it not ; and when their discourses have in them no mark of such like inspiration. It is sufficient, says Le Clerc, if we believe that, no prophet of the New Testament has said any thing in the name of God, or by his order, which God has not effectually ordered him to say ; nor has undertaken to foretell any thing, which God had not indeed truly revealed to him : that every matter of fact related in the books is true, and the records, in general, the truest and most holy history that ever was published amongst men, notwithstanding the writers may be mistaken in some slight circumstances : that all the doctrines proposed are really and truly divine doctrines, and there is no sort of reasoning in the dogmatical places of the Holy Scriptures, that can lead us into error, or into the belief of any thing that is false, or contrary to piety ; that Jesus Christ was absolutely infallible, as well as free from all sin, because of the Godhead that was always united to him, and which perpetually inspired him ; insomuch, that all he taught is as certain as if God himself had pronounced ; and in the last place, that God did not often dictate to the apostles the very words which they should use. These five heads are enough to believe. We allow in these things the authority of the Holy Scriptures, and they who affirm more are deceived.*

* Let me recommend to you, reader, two large volumes written in an epistolary form ; the first, is *Sentimens de Quelques Theologiens d'Hollande sur l'Histoire Critique du Vieux Testament, et de Nouveau Testament, par P. R. Simon*, and the second *Defense des Sentimens contre Bolville*. These are fine books :' my reason for mentioning them is, that the eleventh and twelfth letters in the former, are on the Inspiration of the Sacred Writers ; and the tenth and eleventh letters in the *Defence, &c.*, are a continuation of the subject in a very extraordinary manner, i.e. by giving a solid demonstration of the truth of our religion, without interesting it in this controversy, by clearly proving, that the Christian religion is true, though the apostles had not been continually inspired. Le Clerc was the author of these works ; and the letters here spoken of were translated into English, and printed in 1690, in duodecimo. Some account of Le Clerc and his writings, will be found in the *Memoirs of Several Ladies of Great Britain*, pp. 356, 358.

The famous Father Richard Simon, who wrote the *Critical History of the Old Testament*, was born at Dieppe, 13th of May, 1638, became a priest of the Oratory, and was the author of many learned works, which a general reader should be no stranger to. His *Lettres Choisies*, his *Bibliotheque Critique*, and his *Nouvelle Bibliotheque Choisie*, in which there is much curious learning, mixed with no less a portion of prejudice, are still worthy of commendation. Simon was a great man, and bad as the *Histoire Critique* is in respect of design, it is a learned work, and of great use to those, who have heads fit to use it. Simon died at Dieppe, April 7, 1712. Herman Witsius, who defended Simon in his *Miscellanea Sacra*, by abusing Le Clerc, was a Doctor in Divinity and Professor of the faculty at Francker, and beside the *Miscellanea Sacra*, published some other works, entitled, *Œconomia Fœderum, &c.*, *Exercitationes Sacræ in Orationem Dominicum* : and *Ægyptiaca*. If like me, reader, you have nothing else to do but read,

" The case is the same as to differences, want of exactness and small mistakes.   We may justly celebrate the harmony or agreement of the sacred writers with regard to the principal transactions by them mentioned, as a strong proof of the integrity of the evangelists, and of the certainty of the fact.   This evinces the truth of Christianity : but in matters of very small moment, we must allow a want of accuracy, or slips of memory, or different informations.   This cannot hurt the authority of the gospels, as it proves the honesty of the writers by shewing they did not compose by compact : and *I* think, that some of the evangelists having been eye-witnesses of, and actors in the facts of the several gospels ; and others having written for the information of those who had got a perfect information of all things from the very beginning, is an argument solid and rational for the credibility of the evangelical history.   It is sufficient.   I am sure it is better to allow this, than to say the writers of the four gospels were mere organs, when the little omissions and inaccuracies observable in their records, cannot be accounted for, if we suppose that God conveyed the facts and truths through them, as pipes, to the world.   It must needs be a perfect work, which the spirit of God directs.

I advise you to read them as curious things ; there is learning, though not much good in them.   See M. Mark's *Funeral Oration on Witsius.*   Simon's *Eloge* you will find in the *Journal Litter.* tom. 3. p. 225.   And if you have a critical head I recommend to you Father Simon's *Dissertation Critique* against Du Pin's *Nouvelle Bibliotheque des Auteurs Ecclesiastiques ;* it is an arch piece of criticism, though it does not hurt Du Pin's *Bibliotheque.*
The learned and excellent Louis Ellies Du Pin, author of the valuable *Bibliotheque Ecclesiastique,* was born June 17, 1657, and died at Paris, June 16, 1719, aged 62.   He wrote many other excellent works : but the *Bibliotheque Nouvelle des Auteurs Ecclesiastique,* from Jesus Christ to the year 1710, printed in thirty-five volumes in 8vo, was the principal labour of his life.   The best edition in English of this fine work, is that printed by Grierson, at Dublin in folio.
The other works of Du Pin are *Dissertation Preliminaire ou Prolegomenes sur la Bible,* in three volumes, 8vo.   *De Antiqua Ecclesiæ Disciplina, in seven Dissertations.   De la Puissance Ecclesiastique et Temporelle.   La Doctrine Chretienne et Orthodoxe.   Notes on the Pentateuch Les Pseaumes en Latin, et des Notes,* in 8vo.   *Version François des Pseaumes, avec des Notes. A Defence of his Notes on the Psalms.*
He edited in folio, the Works of Optatus Aser, a Numidian bishop, who was living anno 368 ; to this edition, he prefixed an History of the Donatists, and the Sacred Geography of Africa.   He also superintended the edition of Gerson s works in five volumes folio ; to which he joined a work of his own, called *Gersoniana :* containing the Life of Gerson, the History of his Times, and the doctrines and Lives of Contemporary Authors.   *Critique sur l Histoire d Apollonius de Tyanne.   Une Lettre sur l'Ancienne Discipline touchante la Messe.   Un Traite de l'Excommunication.   Une Histoire de l'Eglise en Abregé.   Une Histoire Profane depuis les Tems les Plus Reculex jusqu a Present.   Une Analyse de l'Apocalypse, avec des Dissertations sur Differentes Matieres Curieuses.   Une Histoire du xvii Siecle.   Un Traite de l'Amour de Dieu :* and *Bibliotheque des Historiens Profanes.*   Of this last work, he did not publish more than two volumes, which have been translated into English ; and so far as he went are so well done, that it is to be lamented, that he did not finish his noble design.   As to his edition of Basnage's *Histoire des Juifs,* without mentioning the name of Basnage, and his making many alterations in it contrary to its author's mind, it brought on him a severe castigation from Basnage ; as I mentioned in my account of the writings of that writer, in *Memoirs of Several Ladies of Great Britain,* p. 350 ; where I referred the reader to a fine piece called the *Histoire des Juifs reclaimé.*
Note : next to the *Bibliotheque des Auteurs Ecclesiastiques,* the best books of Du Pin are, his *Seven Dissertations de Antiqua Disciplina Ecclesiæ :* in Latin, in one volume, 4to, and his *Puissance Ecclesiastique et Temporelle:* in one volume, 8vo.   In these volumes, he works the pope in a fine manner, as to supremacy and infallibility.

" As to St. Mark and St. John's accounts, I see no contradiction in the relations. St. John's says, reckoning as the Romans did, as he was then in Asia, and Jerusalem destroyed ; that at the sixth hour, that is, six o'clock in the morning, he brought Jesus out to them again, the last time and strove to mitigate the rage of the Jews, and save the life of Christ : but as this was what he could not do, he washed his hands before them all to let them know he was not the author of the innocent man's death and after that delivered him up to the soldiers, to be crucified, when they had scourged him.

" When all this was done, says St. Mark, reckoning in the Jewish manner ; it was the third hour, that is nine o'clock in the morning, and they crucified him. This perfectly reconciles the two evangelists. There is no sign of a contradiction in the places.

" As to St. Matthew and St. Mark's accounts of the resurrection of Jesus, they are not so free from obscurity, but I can see no inconsistency in them. If St. Matthew says, ' the Lord appeared to Mary Magdalene, and the other Mary,' that might be, without a contradiction, though St. Mark says, ' he appeared first to Mary Magdalene.' The case to me appears to be this. Mary Magdalene, Mary the mother of James, and the other women, went with spices and ointments to embalm the body, Sunday the 28th of April, early in the morning, about six and thirty hours after it had been laid in the sepulchre, and when they arrived at the place found not the body, but two angels, as young men in white apparel, who told them Jesus of Nazareth was risen to life again, as he himself foretold, and therefore they must make haste to his apostles, to acquaint them with the news, and let them know that they would see him in Galilee, according to his prediction. With these joyful tidings the women hastened away to the eleven disciples, and related to them what they had heard and seen. The apostles looked upon this account as a dream or vision ; but however, on Mary Magdalene's assuring Peter and John apart that, she had really been in the tomb, and found it empty ; from whence it was most certain, that either Jesus was risen, or they had removed his body ; these apostles ran both to the sepulchre, and Mary Magdalene went with them. Peter and John then saw that it was as she had affirmed, and after they had viewed the tomb, the clothes, and the napkin, returned from the sepulchre, greatly wondering what was become of their master's body ; but Mary continued at the monument, lamenting very greatly, that she could not see Jesus either alive or dead, and while she thus bemoaned herself, the Lord appeared to her. As St. Mark says ' Jesus appeared first to Mary Magdalene, out of whom he had cast out seven devils ; ' and after she had reverenced her dear Lord and master, he bid her go immediately to his disciples, and tell them she had seen him : ' let them also know that I have

assured thee, I shall quickly leave this world, and ascend to the
God and Father of us all, my Father and your Father, my God
and your God, unto those happy mansions where he manifests
his presence in a most especial manner ; there to receive full power
over all things both in heaven and earth, and to prepare a place
for you ; that where I am, there ye may be also,'   Mary accordingly departed.   She told the apostles that Jesus had appeared
to her; and acquainted them with the joyful message.

" As to the other women, it is evident that they likewise went a
second time to the sepulchre, to look for the body of their master,
and having in vain searched for it, were returning to the apostles
to let them know they had enquired to no purpose, when Jesus
himself met them, saying ' All hail.'   Does not this reconcile
Mark's account with Matthew's ?   I think so.   To me it is so
very plain from what all the sacred relators have declared of the
matter, that I am astonished how Jerome could be so perplexed
with the two accounts, as to say, that Mark's account, which
constitutes the last twelve verses of his gospel ; might be rejected
here as spurious, because it was found only in a few copies of that
gospel, and contradicted the other evangelists.   Non recipimus
Marci testimonium, quod in raris fertur evangeliis, præsertim cum
diversa atque contraria evangelistis ceteris narrare videatur.

" In the next place, if the account I have given was liable to any
objection, and you could shew me that it was not the truth of the
case ; which, at present, I think impossible : If it was evident
from the gospels, that the women were not a second time at the
tomb, but that Jesus appeared to Mary Magdalene and the other
women, the first time they were all there together, yet this may
be, as I apprehend, without Mark's contradicting Matthew.   The
meaning of the words of Mark, ' he appeared first to Mary Magdalene ' might be, that as she and the women were returning from
the monument, to tell the news to the apostles, Jesus appeared to
them, and in particular, addressed himself to Mary Magdalene ;
directing his discourse to her, and speaking familiarly and affec-
tionately to her, to distinguish her as his constant follower in his
life-time, and one on whom he had worked a great miracle of healing.   This, I imagine might very justly be termed " he appeared
first to Mary Magdalene.'   To appear first to any one of a company, as I take it, is to come up to, or stand before some particular
person, in order to speak to such person.   This, in my imagination,
removes the difficulty, and reconciles Mark to Matthew ; but to
this explication I prefer the woman's being a second time at the
sepulchre : that is, Mary Magdalene a second time, when Peter
and John went to the tomb, on what she had earnestly told them
apart : and afterwards, the other Mary, Salome, Joanna, &c. a
second time.   The gospels, in my opinion, make this very plain*''.

* Long since my conversation with Mr. BERRISFORT, I have seen an excellent book, written

"What has been said," rejoined Mr. BERRISFORT, "seems plausible, and ought to satisfy every honest man. It gives me content : but there is one thing still that perplexes me, and that is the various lections of the New Testament. Do they not hurt the book ? "

"No:" I replied, "notwithstanding the cry of infidels, and that some learned men of the church of Rome have endeavoured to shake the credit of the two testaments, and to bring the people to the papal chair, to know the truth, on account of the various readings ; yet, nevertheless, they are rather an advantage and security to the sacred text than a detriment to the written word. They corroborate the authority of the sacred book, and give it additional advantages.

" It is a truth that there are many various readings in Terence, Livy, Virgil, Cæsar, Thucydides, Homer, Plutarch, and others, yet who denies the genuineness and great use of those noble authors of sense and politeness ? who is so hardy as to question whether the works universally ascribed to them be their own and the product of those immortal wits ? On the contrary, men of thought and clear heads, conversant in those studies, will agree that those authors of antiquity of which there are the most various readings, are rendered the most pure and correct. And why should not the various readings of the Bible rather lead men of sound learning and judgment to the true meaning of the divine writers, than endanger their mistaking their genuine language and sense.

" Where there are several readings, it is highly probable one of them is the original ; and it is easier by their help to rectify the mistakes of some copies, for when we have only one manuscript, there may be scope for fancy ; but none for judicious comparison and well-grounded criticism.

" Style and language may be distinguished by a happy genius of natural sagacity, improved by true learning and proper application, as well as statues, pictures and medals. No age can counterfeit Cicero, Terence, St. Mark, St. John, St. Paul, no more than a counterfeit picture, or medal, can be imposed on and deceive the complete masters and judges of those ingenious professions and sciences.

" Secondly, there is nothing in the various lections that affects the essentials of religion, or can imply a considerable depravation of the copies, that alters or weakens one moral contained in the

by the learned minister of Maybole, in which he labours, through several 4to. pages, from p. 213, to reconcile Mark and Matthew, by virtue of a second visit to the monument by Mary Magdalene, when the Lord appeared first to her ; and a second visit to the sepulchre by the other women, when Jesus appeared next to those women ; and in my opinion, he has proved it, beyond a possbility of rational reply. See Macknight's *Harmony*. Le Clerc, in his *Harmony*, does likewise evince the thing clearly to conviction.

divine books. And therefore, though it cannot with reason be supposed, that God Almighty should work perpetual miracles to prevent the mistakes and blunders of every careless or corrupt hand, of those numerous transcribers of those sacred volumes, no more than by a resistless power and restraint to prevent all the errors and villainies committed by free and accountable creatures ; yet the argument receives strength, that notwithstanding the innumerable variations, mistakes and contradictions in small matters, the all-seeing eye of Providence has so watched his own blessed and glorious revelations to mankind, that all the transcripts of that divine volume agree in the essential doctrine and grand design of Christianity. This is a truth that Infidels and Papists cannot disprove.

" I observe in the last place, that exclusive of the care of Providence, there could not possibly happen any detriment to our sacred records by various readings : for though in an innumerable number of copies of the gospel that were made before printing was known, and in the many translations of it into several languages, where the idioms are different, and the phrase may be mistaken, it was almost impossible there should not be various lections, and slips of amanuenses, yet the sacred volumes in the early ages of Christianity, were disposed into innumerable hands, translated into so many languages, kept in so many libraries, churches, and in private families of believers, and so carefully preserved and revered as the authentic deeds and charters of eternal happiness, that they were not capable of being falsified.

" Nor could those inestimable copies, scattered as they were over the then discovered world, and in the noble language so universally known and acceptable, be liable to hazards, by sudden revolutions and public disasters ; because those convulsions and surprizing calamities, could not happen alike in every country at one time.

" Neither could a general corruption of manners, a spirit of profuseness or superstition, nor the wicked example, and strong influence of tyrannical princes, of an apostate clergy, and atheistical ministers of state, prevail over many distant and independent nations, to endeavour to corrupt and destroy their sacred book.

" On the contrary, we are to consider that Christianity was the ecclesiastical law of all Christian nations under the sun. The great law which assured to them their religious rights and properties, their claims and titles to immortality, to the inheritance of the saints in light, an inheritance incorruptible, undefiled, that fadeth not away, reserved for them in the heavens. Which, to every one that deserves the name of man and Christian must be infinitely more dear than titles to lands on this earth. For men are naturally more watchful in a matter so dear to them, and every believer would think himself concerned, no more to let a change of consequence to pass uncorrected, than the children of this world, who are wisest in their generation, would overlook a flaw in deeds of sale, or contract, which would assert their title, and evacuate the main intention of making such indentures.

" The primitive Christians must be supposed to be exceeding watchful and jealous that no corruption or abuses should be put on that sacred book, more dear and valuable to them than all other interests and treasures. When these brave champions of the cross were brought to the tribunals of the heathen persecutors, and were commanded to deliver their Bible to the flames, they most courageously refused it, and gave their bodies to be burnt rather than the divine book.

" In short, it is easier to suppose, a new Bible or a new statute book might be imposed at this time of day upon this nation, without discovery, than to suppose a forged gospel, a New Testament corrupted so far as to be insufficient for the good ends Providence designed by it, could be imposed on the universal Christian world. It is easier to suppose that any forgery might creep into the municipal law of any particular nation, than that all the nations, whither Christianity is spread, should conspire in the corruption of the gospel : which most sacred institution is to all Christians of infinitely greater concern and value than their temporal laws, and all the secular immunities and privileges which they secure to them.

" And without such a wicked concert, or such an astonishing carelessness and negligence in all Christian people and nations supposed, which would be a monstrous supposition. No such forgery, no such alteration of essentials could pass undiscovered in the gospel, which was spread in the hands, hearts, and memories of myriads of rational devout Christians of all ranks, qualities and sex, was constantly read in private families, frefrequently explained in schools, and daily used in public divine offices. It was impossible then in the nature of things that there could be any such alterations or corruptions introduced into the sacred text as would affect its doctrines, morals, or truth of its historical relations, or defeat the blessed end and design of the gospel revelation in any period of time, from the beginning of Christianity to this present age.*

* For further Satisfaction on this Article and to be convinced that the books of the *New Testament*, as we now have them, are the word of God, see, reader, Blackwell on *The Sacred Classics*, and Jones's *Method of Settling the Canonical Authority of the Testament.* By the way, if Jacob Ilive, who stood in the pillory, the 30th of June, 1756, for writing and publishing a thing called *Modest Remarks on* (Dr. Sherlock) *the bishop of London's Sermons in a letter to his lordship*, had read with attention the books I have mentioned, and Dr. Lardner's *Credibility of the Gospel-History*, he would not, I imagine, have composed a pamphlet, that manifests not only an impious licentiousness, but an ignorance at once great and despicable in relation to the subjects he pretended to write on.

" And if from this unanswerable way of reasoning in defence of the genuine purity of the sacred scriptures, we look next upon the Providence of the Great God in this important case, is it not consonant to sound sense, and the notions that rational creatures must have of the supreme and all-perfect Being, firmly to believe that the same goodness and providence, which took care for the writing, would likewise take care for preserving these inestimable books, so free at least from corruption, that they might be sufficient for the gracious ends for which they were written, and be able to make us wise to salvation ? I think so. To me it is evident, that since infinite goodness was pleased to reveal a religion, that teaches men to know Jehovah to be the true God, and to know Jesus Christ, whom he hath sent ; his providence must not only preserve the book on which the doctrine depends, but so secure it from corruption as to render it a plain rule to mankind. While there is a Providence, the Holy Scriptures will remain the sacred and unalterable standard of true religion."

" What you say," replied Mr. BERRISFORT, " seems to me to be true. I have nothing to object. But once more, let me ask you in respect of the ascension, which followed the resurrection of Jesus, is it not very strange, that this is not mentioned by any of the apostles who are said to have been eye-witnesses of the face but *Luke* and *Mark* only are the relators of the thing, who were not apostles, and had all they wrote from the information of the apostles. If the apostles, *Matthew* and *John*, did really see with their eyes the Lord Jesus taken up from them into heaven, might we not expect, that they would write the history of that still more wonderful transaction, as well as they had so exactly related the resurrection of Jesus? for the men who stood gazing up into heaven, after the Lord was carried up in a cloud, as *Luke* says they did, not to mention so very wonderful and interesting an affair in their gospels ; and men who did not see the thing, to relate it as a part of the history they had received from the apostles ; this is what astonishes me. If it was a truth, surely so important a one ought not to be omitted by those who saw it : since *Matthew* and *John* did write histories of Christ, why should they be silent on this grand article, and take no notice of it in their records ? What do you say to this ? "

" I will tell you," I replied ; " in the first place, *nostrum non est providentiæ divinæ rationes reddere*. Placuit spiritu sancto ita dirigere calamos Matthæi et Joannis, ut narratione resurrectionis dominicæ evangelia sua concluderent. Sic refert Limborch. It does not become us to call Providence to account, or assign the ways it ought to act in : infinite wisdom thought fit to appoint, that *Matthew* and *John* should end their gospels with the relation of our Lord's resurrection : the resurrection demonstrated the divine mission of Jesus Christ. To it, as a proof the most valid, and unexceptionable, our Lord referred the Jews, and therefore, to it, as the great fundamental, *Matthew* and *John* appealed : they proved it by declaring that they had conversed with Jesus Christ after he arose from the sepulchre ; and when that was proved, there could be no dispute about any thing else. The divinity of the Christian religion, and the ascension and glory of their Lord, rest on this base. All the blessings likewise of the gospel, regeneration, our resurrection, and life eternal, are ascribed by the apostles, Peter and Paul, to the resurrection of Christ, and for these reasons, to be sure, when John had described his Lord's resurrection, he added, ' and many other signs truly did Jesus in the presence of his disciples, which are not written in this book. But these are written, that ye might believe that Jesus is the Christ, the Son of God, and that believing, ye might have life through his name.' We must allow then, that the account of the ascension by *Luke* and *Mark*, may be authentic, though not mentioned by *Matthew* and *John*.

" In the next place, St. *John* is not totally silent as to the ascension of our Lord. In his sixth chapter, ver. 62, it is written ' What and if ye shall see the Son of Man ascend up where he was before ? ' and in the 7th chapter, ver. 39th. ' But this spake he of the Spirit, which they that believe in him should receive. For the Holy Ghost was not yet given, because that Jesus was not yet glorified.' Here most certainly the apostle speaks of the ascension of his Master, and though he did not write the history of it, yet, not obscurely, says the thing was to be ; which confirms the accounts of St. Luke and St. Mark. And since, in the 14th and 15th chapters of St. John, ver. 16 and 26, the apostle declares, that Jesus foretold he would send to them, his disciples, the Comforter or Holy Spirit from the Father, after his ascension to heaven ; and that the apostles demonstrated by miracles, after the death of their Lord, that they had received this Comforter or divine Spirit, it follows, that the ascension and glorification of Jesus is as much asserted and confirmed by the gospel of St. *John*, as if that apostle, like *Luke*, had wrote the history of it. This is evident to me, and I think, it is not possible to dispute it.

" The sum of the whole is, that the prejudices of the pious, and the arts of the crafty and interested, have defaced the true gospel of Christ, and substituted human notions and conse-quences in the place of divine revelation : but let us strip the sacred records of the false glosses and systems, with which the theorists have covered it, and allow the enemy, that the apostles, sometimes wanting the unerring spirit of their Master, were liable to slight mistakes, and inadvertencies, in the representation of ordinary events : that they did, sometimes, by too great an affection for their Master's doctrine, strain some things, and cite

prophecies that did not relate to Jesus in any sense at all ; *—
let this be done to remove incumbrances, to clear up difficulties,
and to answer objections otherwise unanswerable, and the
writings of the apostles will appear to be a globe of light from
heaven ; to irradiate the human understanding, and conduct the

* Let us now see, says a great man and upright Christian, what use the enemies of Christianity have endeavoured to make of the prophecies, as the evangelists apply them ; and what
answer the truth of the case will oblige us to give to them.
They assert that the foundation of the Christian religion is laid by the evangelists, on the
proof of this point, that the mission and character of Jesus were foretold by the prophets ;
and that the validity of this proof depends entirely on the force of those particular prophecies
which the same evangelists have applied to the illustration of it, in their several gospels.
Upon this hypothesis, the enemy undertakes to shew, that the prophecies, so applied by them
do not at all relate to Jesus, in their proper and literal signification, but only in secondary,
typical, and figurative sense : but then this way of interpreting them is equivocal, precarious
and incapable of yielding any rational satisfaction ; and of consequence Christianity has no
foundation. Such is the use the enemy make of the prophecies applied by the evangelists.
In truth, if we admit that Christianity has no other foundation than what its enemies assign
it, it might not perhaps be difficult for them to make good the rest : for upon that supposition,
many objections are thrown in our way, which it is scarce possible to get rid of.   But while
they fancy themselves to be demolishing foundations, they are battering only such parts of
the edifice as serve for its ornaments rather than its support : and had the enemy gone farther,
and shewn that some of the prophecies cited by Matthew did not relate to Jesus in any sense
at all, they would have done no more than what some of the primitive fathers, as well as
modern critics had done before them, without designing or doing the least hurt to Christianity.
Jesus declared in general that Moses and the prophets had testified of him : but since the
evangelists did not think it necessary to give a precise account, or deduction of the several
prophecies, which were alleged by him in proof of that declaration, it is sufficient to take it
just as we find it, without thinking ourselves obliged to defend all the particular instances
or applications, which were offered afterwards in support of it by fallible men.   Whiston, in
his *Literal Accomplishment of the Scripture Prophecies*, has produced forty-five prophecies
from the *Old Testament*, which are cited in the New, in proof of the Messiahship of Jesus, and
which he declares to have been clearly and directly fulfilled, without the least pretence of any
reply from any author whatsoever.   Now if any number of these, how small soever, are found
to be as clearly accomplished, as he takes them to be, they are sufficient to support the authority of the gospel, though all the rest were thrown aside.
But to say the truth, the grounds of our faith, in these latter ages of the church, do not lie
in the particular interpretations of prophecies, made by men, who might be mistaken, and
who, as Jerome* says more than once, by trusting to their memories, in citing these very
prophecies, were frequently mistaken in the words, and sometimes in the sense of them.   Nor
is the evidence of prophecy so proper in these days, to convert men to the faith of Christ as
to confirm those who have already embraced it : serving chiefly, as St. Paul expresses it, not
to them who believed not, but to them who believe. .
The sum then of this article is, that upon the first promulgation of the gospel, while the
conversion of the Jews was the principal object of our Saviour's ministry, and afterwards of
his apostles, the argument of prophecy was, of all others, the best adapted to persuade, and
conquer the prejudices of that nation.   But in preaching the gospel to the Gentiles, not
acquainted with the Jewish scriptures, nor tinctured with any Jewish prejudices, the testimony
of its miracles, and the purity of its doctrines, were the most affecting proof of its divine
origin.   Yet when by the evidence of these, people had once received the Christian faith,
and acquired a competent knowledge of it, they would then perceive, that the argument of
prophecy was a part also of the evidence, essentially necessary to complete the demonstration
of its truth.

* St. Jerome is one of the four great doctors of the Latin church, who support the magnificent bronze chair of St. Peter, in this saint's church in Rome.   The other three doctors are
St. Augustin, St. Ambrose, and St. Gregory.   Great might be the piety of those doctors, for
any thing I can say to the contrary, but this is certain, from their writings, that they did not
understand Christianity.
St. Jerome, born at Stridon, in Dalmatia, in the year 340 ; was a hot, abusive man, and
quarrelled even with St. Augustin.   In his disputes, he is more like a madman than a saint
and ever in the wrong.   He wrote *comments* on all the prophets, Ecclesiastes, St. Matthew,
and the epistles to the Galatians, Ephesians, Titus, and Philemon ; but they are sad stuff in
respect of some modern performances.   Compare them with the comments of Dr. Clarke
Locke, Dr. Benson, and others of our country, and you will see what a poor creature this

sons of men to the realms of bliss. Their lessons are the dictates of the Spirit of God : their sanctions are of such force, in a certainty of future judgment and retribution, that they incline a rational to have a serious regard to them.

"In a word, the religion of nature is perfect, but men are imperfect, and therefore it pleased God to send our Saviour into the world, to republish the law of reason by his preaching, and in the writings of the apostles, and by him to give many motives to men, to incite them to perform their duty, as set forth in his written laws, and in the more striking example of our Lord, his only-begotten Son. Let us be Christians then, my dear BOB, and adore the divine goodness, for the life eternal prepared for the righteous, as declared in the sacred records, Let us hearken to the apostles, who, knowing the terror of the Lord, persuade men, and so govern and conduct ourselves by the rules of revelation that when the man Christ Jesus, who appeared in the world to redeem us, will return to judge us by the gospel, we may ascend with him to the unbounded regions of eternal day, and in ever-blooming joys, live for ever in the presence of God. I have done. Where you think I am wrong, you will be pleased to say."

My friend replied, that he had no objection to make : he was quite satisfied ; and obliged to me for my advice. Thus ended the conversation between BOB BERRISFORT and JACK BUNCLE.

---

saint was in respect of our English divines and philosophers. He translated the *Old Testament* into Latin from the Hebrew ; without understanding the Hebrew well : and he corrected the antient Latin version of the *New Testament*. This is far from being correct, though the church of Rome has decreed it to be infallible, and appointed it to be used in the church. The best and most useful thing this saint hath written is his *Treatise of Illustrious Men* ; which contain a summary of the lives, and the titles of the books, written by ecclesiastical authors, to his time. The next in worth to this, in my opinion, is his book of letters ; in which are several fine moral sentiments, and much good advice ; though his criticisms on the Bible in this work are weak enough He will have it, that it was *wisdom*, and not a young woman, that David took into bed to him, when he was old and cold ; which is a mere fancy, that plainly contradicts the history of that affair in the Bible. But St. Jerome, in his *Letters*, tells us, he abhorred a woman, as much as Mrs. Astel did a man ; detesting and blackening matrimony and a wife, to extol and exalt that whim of his brain virginity. He owns that he beheld with detestation every pregnant woman though rendered so in the holy matrimonial bed and could not bear looking at her, but as he reflected that she carried a virgin. He was consequently a fit supporter of St Peter's chair. Of the works of St. Jerome, who died in the year 420, aged 80, there is a good edition, in nine volumes, in folio, printed at Paris, in 1623 ; but the later one, edited by Martianay, the Benedictin, is much finer and more valuable.

St. Ambrose is the next supporter and saint. This holy prelate, born at Treves in the year 340, was a great contender for tritheism and the rights of the church, and wrote many worthless pieces for them and persecution. He acted an insolent and senseless part, when the emperor Theodosius, in the affair of Thessalonica, ordered the seditious to be destroyed and died soon after, in April anno 397, "the greatest and most blessed of men," so say Paulinus and Baronus who have both written his life. The best edition of his works is that enriched with many notes by the Benedictins, and printed at Paris in 1691, in two volumes folio.

As to St. Gregory of Neocaesarea, and the four other saints of the name, to wit, the two Nazianzens, Nysse, and Armenia, I shall have occasion to mention them in the next volume of my journal, and therefore shall here only observe, in respect of Neocaesarea, usually called Thaumaturgus, or the *wonder-worker*, that he died in the year 265, according to Buronius, and the saint of Armenia, or into 270, according to Fabricius : and that the best edition of his works that by Gerard Vossus, printed at Mayence in 1604, 4to. His pieces were likewise printed in a collection of things written by some minor saints at Paris, in 1621 in a single volume, in folio.

The third day of July, I left Yeoverin Green, and set out again
for Ulubrae, to get my horses and portmanteau, but proceeded
now on foot ; because, by climbing over a high mountain, which it
was impossible for a horse to ascend, and then walking half a mile
over a shaking-bog, where a beast could not go, I was to save
many miles ; and besides, Mr. BERRISFORT was so obliging as to
send one of his servants back with Mr. HARCOURT'S horses, which
I knew not which way to return.   With my pole in my hand then
I set out, and after I had bade adieu to my friends, who walked
with me a couple of miles to the foot of the hills, I began to mount
the Alp at six in the morning, and at eight arrived on its summit.
Here I had a fine road, due south, for an hour, till I came to a
very steep descent, that led to the shaking-bog, as my paper of
directions informed me.   It was an ugly way down, and the better
to go it, I resolved first to breakfast, and bid TIM see what he had
got in his wallet.   Immediately he produced a roast fowl, a
manchet, and a bottle of cyder, and among some trees, on the
brow of a hill, by the side of a spring, that ran off the way I was
to go, I sat down to the repast.   I gave my lad half the bird,
and the other half I dispatched in a very short time, drank a pint
of cyder, and was on my feet again.   I then began to descend,
and in an hour made a shift to get to the bottom, though the way
was bad ; being very steep, wet, and slippery.   I came to a dirty
lane, about two hundred yards long, and that ended at the
shaking-bog.

This kind of bog I take to be an abyss of standing waters
covered with a thin arch of earth, that is, a water communicating
with the abyss so covered, or weakly vaulted over : and of this
opinion I find the right Reverend Erich Pontoppidan is, in his
Natural History of Norway.   The bishop does not tell his reason
for so thinking ; but mine is, that I have seen in Ireland the arches
of several of those bogs broken, and a deep unfathomable water
at some distance from the arch.   They are very dangerous,
frightful places, and many of them play up and down, like a long
plank, in a very surprising manner.

To go half a mile over such a bog, and the most elastic of them
I had ever tried, was that I did not much like ; though the author
of my paper of directions, an old servant of Mr. BERRISFORT,
affirmed it was quite safe ; and as to TIM, he would not, on any
consideration cross it.,   He was positive we should sink beyond
recovery.   What to do then, was the question ?   I tried for some
time to go round the bog, at the bottom of the enclosing mountains,
but that was soon found impossible, and therefore, it only remained, to go up again to the top of the hill, and try onwards for
some other descent beyond the bog.   We did so, and after walking
two hours south-west, at a good rate, had a view of a deep glen,
to which we descended by an easy slope, and marched through it,

to the west, and north-west for two hours, till it ended at a wood. This we passed without any difficulty, as there were walks cut through it, and came out into a broad valley, that had a river very near us, and a sweet pretty cottage on the margin of the flood. I went up to the house to ask my way, and found at the door three men, the eldest of whom seemed to be about thirty years old. They asked me very civilly to walk in, and seemed to wonder not a little at seeing me and my man, in such a place, with our poles in our hands.

These men were three brothers and Roman catholics. Two of them were gentlemen-farmers, who lived together, and jointly managed the country business. The eldest was a Franciscan friar, who came to visit them. Their good manners, in their plain dress, surprised me ; and their benevolence made me wonder a great deal more. Their maid laid a clean cloth in a minute, and brought some cold roast beef, good bread, and fine ale. They bid me heartily welcome many times, and were so frank and generous, so cheerful and gay ; especially the eldest of the farmers, who sang several good songs over a bowl of punch after dinner, that I could not think of leaving them immediately, if I had known my road, and was easily prevailed on to stay several days. A friendship commenced immediately between the eldest FLEMING and me , and there was not one cold or cross minute in it for the few years that he lived. He loved me as his brother from the first day he saw me, and I had so great a regard for him, that with a sorrow I cannot help, I think of his death to this day. How to account for such sudden passions I know not, and have always appeared to me very strange. FLEMING was a man of a bright and very extraordinary understanding, though no more than a farmer, had a most happy temper, a generosity too great for his fortune, and was for ever cheerful and free ; but these however pleasing, could not be the cause of the sudden and lasting friendship between us, as I have been acquainted with men of fortune who equalled him in these respects, and yet they never struck me more than for the present time. Whatever might be the cause, the fact is certain. No two men ever liked one another more than we did from the first hour of our acquaintance, and as I had the happiness of converting him to the protestant religion,* it is possible, that might cement a friendship, which,

* The arguments I used to make a convert of FLEMING, the reader will find in the appendix of this journal, among other interesting matters, that are too long to be inserted in the story of my life. I shall print them in hopes that they may be of service to some other soul. They were introduced the first day I was at FLEMING's house, by his saying to me, after dinner, "Dear sir, will you give me leave to ask you, by what strange cause it has happened, that you are thus travelling on foot in this unvisited country. It must be an extraordinary affair I am sure. "Sir" I replied, "my case is very uncommon. I do not believe that any thing like it ever was before, and, perhaps, such another affair may never happen again." I little thought then, that I should afterwards meet with two instances of the same kind of thinking and resolution in the female world, to wit, Miss Chawcer and Miss Janson whose histories I

a sameness of disposition had helped to produce.   This is all I can
say as to the reason of this matter.   In respect of the thing, it
was of the greatest service to me.   My new acquired friend
assisted me to the utmost of his power, in the accomplishment
of my designs, in that part of the world I then was.   I had his
head, his hand, and his house at my service, and by them I was
enabled to give a roundness to a system, that was too happy to
last long.

But as to the shaking-bog I was to have passed to go to the
gentlemen at Ulubræ, FLEMING told me, I had had a fortunate
escape in not venturing over it ; for, though it be passable in one
narrow way, about a yard broad, yet a stranger to the bog must
perish in attempting to cross ; as the timber causeway that was
made over the great marsh, time out of mind, is invisible in many
places, and one sinks for ever, the moment he steps off that way
"but I will shew you an easy road," continued my new friend, to the
gentleman's house, to whom I am no stranger, and will make you
acquainted with some passes through the mountains, that will
render it easier riding over this country than you have found it."
He did so, and by his guidance I arrived at Ulubræ, the 7th day
of July ; being the 17th day from the morning I left the philosophers.   The gentlemen were startled at the sight of me, as they
concluded I had perished, and had, as they assured me, mourned
my sad fate : they were impatient to hear the adventure of the
mountain, and by what strange means I was jumbled all the way,
to TOM FLEMING'S ; who lives so far from the hill I went into ; and

have given in my *Memoirs of Several Ladies of Great Britain*, p. 41–64. The critics, I remember,
had some doubts as to the reality of these two cases : but to this I answer, that they may as
well doubt the truth of my own story ; and from thence proceed to deny the reality of my
existence ; because several incidents in my life are strange, and such as they have not heard
of before. It is not, however, in the power of criticism to invalidate what I deliver as facts.
I will tell you my story : and so began to relate the religious dispute between my father and
me, and how it was brought to a head by the devil possessed by a woman, called a mother-in-
law. As the glass went round, I let them know, how a man in the twenty-second year of his
age, forsook all for the true gospel of Christ, and at a time of life, when very few think of religion, resolved to confess himself a Christian deist, to all whom it concerned, if it brought him
to want, and from a morsel of bread to the grave. So far I was heard without interrupting
though I declaimed by the way against the dreadful heresy of three gods : but not thinking
I was in company with catholics, for then I imagined that such subjects of the king of England were only to be found in Ireland, I brought into my oration against false religion, the
diabolism of popery, and gave it several thrusts ; as, indeed, I always do, whenever it comes
in my way ; for, good reader—though I love the catholic men and women, because I am a friend
to man, and nearly related to many Romanists of great fortune ; yet, popery I abhor ; and
look upon it as the greatest woe that ever the devil introduced into this lower world, to ruin
mankind ; but when I began to touch this string, and was raking Rome papal fore and aft,
FLEMING the friar, changed colour several times, which I took notice of, and knew not what
to ascribe to, unless he was very sick ; and at last he told me, by way of game, that I was
an eloquent young gentleman, and had a flow of language ; but my mistakes as to the church
of Rome were very great, and he begged leave, as he was a priest of the holy Roman church,
to set me right [in my notions. This was a great surprise to me. It struck me silent for
some minutes. At last, however, I told the gentlemen, that I asked their pardons for making
so free with their religion, which I should not presume to have done, but that I thought they
had been protestants ; that as to his offer to set me right, he did me great honour, and I would
with pleasure hear him. I would, to be sure, be a convert to the strength of his arguments,
if unanswerable, or offer such reasons for remaining a protestant, as must satisfy a rational
man. He then went on, and my reply followed.

the road from it to his house, scarce passable for a mortal. " Inform us, we beseech you, how these strange things came to pass."

" Gentlemen," said I, " I am extremely obliged to you for your concern for me, and will tell you my story as soon as we have dined, as the servants are now bringing the dishes in," and accordingly, when we had done, I gave them a relation in detail. They were greatly pleased with my history, and much more, to have me returned to them in safety again. If they had not seen me, they said, they could not believe the thing, and they would order the whole account to be entered in the journal of their society, as the most extraordinary case they had ever known : or perhaps, should ever hear related again. Their secretary, as directed, wrote it down in their book of transactions, and it remains in their records to this day. In short, reader, these worthy men were so greatly rejoiced at my being alive, when they thought me for certain among the dead, that they put the bottle round in a festal manner after dinner. We drank and laughed till it was midnight.

The 8th day of July, I took my leave of the gentlemen at Ulubræ, and proceeded to the East-riding of Yorkshire, to look for Miss MELMOTH. FLEMING came with me as far as Eggleston to shew me the passes between the hills, and the best ways over the mountains. Many vast high ones we crossed, and travelled through very wonderful glens. Several scenes were as charming as any I had before seen, and the low ways as bad ; but he knew all the roads and cross turnings perfectly well, and shortened the journey a great many miles. I had told him the business I was going on, and he requested, if I succeeded, that I would bring Miss MELMOTH to his house, that his brother might marry us ; and as to Orton-Lodge, which I had described to him, and told him where to find, for he had no notion of it, nor had ever been among the fells of Westmoreland; as he thought that country unpassable ; he promised me he would go there himself, and bring with him two labouring men to assist my lad, in putting the garden and house in the best condition they were capable of receiving ; that he would bring there seeds, and trees, such as the season allowed, and do every thing in his power, to render the place convenient and pleasing : he would likewise sell me a couple of his cows, a few sheep, and other things, which I should find before me at the lodge, and let me have one of his maids for my servant in the house. This was good indeed. I could not wish for more.

The 9th of July, early in the morning, FLEMING and I parted, and I proceeed as fast as I well could to the appointed station, but when I came up to Mrs. ASGILL's door, on the second day in the evening, July 10, and asked for Miss MELMOTH, an old man, the only person in the house, told me, Mrs. ASGILL had been dead

near a month, and Miss MELMOTH went from thence immediately
after the funeral of her friend ; that she had left a letter with him
for a gentleman that was to call upon her ; but that letter by an
accident was destroyed, and where the lady then was, he could
not so much as guess ; he farther told me, that Miss MELMOTH
had sold the goods of the house, and the stock, bequeathed to her
by her deceased friend, to the gentleman who inherited the late
Mrs. ASGILL's jointure, and she would return no more to the place.
This was news to me. It struck me to the soul. Doleful tidings,
how ye wound. What to do I could not tell, but as I rode to
the next town, determined at last, to try if I could hear of her
at York. To that city I went the next day, asked at the inns,
walked the walls, and went to the assembly-room. [My enquiries
were all in vain. One gentleman only did I see who was acquainted with her, and he knew nothing of her present abode.
From York then I proceeded the next morning to search other
towns, and left no place unexamined where I could think she
might be. Three weeks were spent in this manner, without
hearing a syllable of her, and then I thought it was best to return
to my lodge ; for what signified my five hundred pounds to appear
with in the world. It must be soon gone as I had not the least
notion of any kind of trade; and if I joined any one that was in
business, I might be mistaken in the man, and so cheated and
undone. Then what could I do but carry a brown musket, or go
a hand before the mast ; for, as to being an usher to a school for
bread, were I reduced to want, that was the life of all lives that
I most abhorred. Nothing else then had I for it but my silent
mountain-lodge, which kind Providence had brought me to.
There I resolved to go, and in that charming solitude, peruse alone
the book of nature, till I could hear of some better way of spending
my time.

To this purpose then I went the second of August, 1725, to
Barnard's Castle in Durham, and intended the next morning to
set out for FLEMING's house in Stanemore, to go from thence
to my cottage on the side of a Westmoreland-Fell, but after I had
rode a mile off the road to *Eggleston*, where I purposed to dine,
I called out to my lad to stop. A sudden thought came into my
head, to ride first to Greta-bridge, as I was so near it, to see some
fine Roman monuments, that are in the neighbourhood of that
village. To that place I went then, and passed the day in looking
over all the antiquities and curiosities I could find there. I
returned in the evening to my inn, and while a fowl was roasting
for my supper, stood leaning against the house-door, looking at
several travellers that went by, and some that came to rest where
I did that night. Many figures I beheld, but none I knew. At
last there came riding up to the inn, full speed, a young lady on
a most beautiful beast, and after her, two horses more ; on one

of which was her man servant, and on the other her maid, She
had a black mask on her face, to save her from the dust and sun,
and when she alighted from her horse, she did not take it off, but
went with it on into the house, after she had looked for a moment
or two at me. This I thought very strange. " A charmer to be
sure ? " said I. " With what life and grace did she come to the
ground ! but how cruel the dear little rogue is, to conceal the
wonders of its face." " Landlord," said I, to the master of the
house, who was coming up to me, " can you contrive a way to get
me one view of that masked lady, and I will give you a pint."
" Sir," mine host replied, " that I can do very easily, for this lady
has sent me to let you know she wants to speak with you."
" With me ? Transporting news ! " I flew to her apartment, and
there saw that dear irresistible creature, who had added to the
inferior charms of face and person, that wisdom and goodness of
conduct and conversation, which are the true glory of a woman.
It was Miss MELMOTH. She had heard I had been at Mrs. ASGILL'S
house, and did not get the letter she left for me, which made her
think of riding towards Greta-bridge, on an imagination she might
find me thereabout ; as she remembered to have heard me say,
in one of our conversations, that I intended as soon as I could, to
look at the Roman antiquities in this place ; but she had very little
hopes, she added, of succeeding in her enquiry ; as little as I had of
her riding up to the inn ; and this made the meeting the more
pleasing. It did enhance the pleasure indeed. It turned the
amour into an adventure, and gave it that delicious flavour,
which the moderns read of in the histories of past times, but
rarely experience in these days. The reader that has been engaged
in such a wonderful and tender scene, can only form an idea of
felicity, which words would in vain attempt to express.

As soon as we had supped, I recited my adventures since we
parted, and gave Miss MELMOTH a flowery description of Orton-
Lodge ; then asked if she would bless me with her hand, and sit
down with me in my pretty solitude.

" Sir," replied Miss MELMOTH, " if you required it, I would go
with you to Hudson's-Bay, had I a hundred thousand, instead
of four thousand pounds ; which is my fortune exclusive of some
personal estate, which my friend Mrs. ASGILL by her will bequeathed me : and the whole is at your service, to dispose of as you
please."

" Give me thy hand, then," said I, " thou generous girl. You
make me the happiest of men, and in return I swear by that one,
supreme, tremendous Power I adore, that I will be true and
faithful to thee, till death dissolves the sacred obligation. Twice
do I swear by the great Spirit, in whose dread presence I am, with
your right hand now locked fast in mine across this table, and
call on him as witness to our vows, that neither time, nor chance,

nor aught but death's inevitable hand, shall e'er divide our loves."
" Amen," responded Miss MELMOTH.

Early the next morning, the third of August, we rode to Eggleston, where we breakfasted and proceeded from thence to FLEMING
house up Stanemore hills, where we arrived at nine o'clock
in the evening, and had beds there that night.   My friend
TOM and his brother JEMMY, were gone to a fair ; but the eldest
brother, the Franciscan friar, was at home and entertained us
very well.   We took him with us very early the next day to
Orton-Lodge, which we reached at eight in the evening, and found
the house and garden in good order.   Mr friend FLEMING, had
done everything possible, to make it a convenient and comfortable place.   He had made near the Lodge two little rooms for
servants, and had put a bed in the green-house in the garden for a
friend.   He had likewise sent there a couple of cows, some sheep
and lambs, ducks and geese, cocks and hens, and every necessary
he thought we might want there.   Good TOM FLEMING ! there
never was a better man, or a kinder friend, to his small
power.

We had likewise fish in abundance, in the waters at the foot of
our hills, and goats and kids, and plenty of wild fowl.   Few
things were wanting that reason could desire ; and for us, who
thought that happiness, that is, pleasure and repose did not
precariously depend on what others think, or say, or do ; but
solidly consisted in what we ourselves did feel, and relish, and
enjoy, there could not be a more delightful station discovered on
this globe.

To conclude, the best things that Orton Lodge afforded, were
ordered to the fire, and before they were brought on the table, the
man of God threw the fillet or ribband over our hands, according
to the Romish manner, and pronounced the nuptial benediction
on us.   Husband and wife we sat down to supper.

> Thus did the stars preside with friendly rays,
> And bid me hail at last the happy days,
> When sheltered within this wild retreat,
> Above the scorn, below the rage of fate ;
> Blest in a wife, a friend, and books, alone ;
> To this mad world, and all its plagues unknown ;
> The smooth-paced hours did sweetly pass away,
> And happy nights still clos'd each happy day.

When I consider how happy I have been in the married state,
and in a succession of seven wives, never had one uneasy hour ;
that even a Paradise, without an Eve, would have been a wilderness to me ; that the woods, the groves, the walks, the prospects,
the flowers, the fruits, the day, the night, all would have wanted
a relish, without that dear, delightful companion, a wife ; it amazes
me to hear many sensible people speak with abhorrence of matri-

mony, and insist upon it, that wedlock produces so many troubles, even where the pair have affection, and sorrows so very great, when they have no love for each other, or begin to fail in the kind and obliging offices, that it is contrary to reason to contract, if we have a just regard to peace and satisfaction of mind, and would avoid, as much as possible, the woes and bewailings of this turbid period. If you have acquired the divine habits, marriage may unhinge them. It often forces even the pious into immoralities. True, unhappy are many a wedded pair : years of calamity this engagement has produced to thousands of mortals ; it has made the most pious divines become very cruel, as I could relate ; it has caused the most generous, sensible men to murder the women they adored before they were their wives.

THE HISTORY OF ORLANDO AND BELINDA.

This story has been told before by the Tatler, in his 172d paper ; but as he related it only by hearsay, and was mistaken in several particulars, the account I give of this extraordinary affair may be grateful to the reader.

When I was a little boy in Dublin, between seven and eight, Mr. EUSTACE and his Lady lived next door to my father, in Smithfield, and the two families were intimate. Being a lively prating thing, Mrs. EUSTACE was fond of me, and by tarts and fruit encouraged me to run into her parlour as often as I could. This made me well acquainted in the house ; and as I was a remarker so early in my life, I had an opportunity of making the following observations.

ORLANDO EUSTACE was a tall, thin, strong man, well made, and a very genteel person. His face was pale and marked with the small pox ; his features were good, and yet there was something fierce in his look, even when he was not displeased. He had sense and learning, and, with a large fortune, was a generous man ; but passionate to an amazing degree, for his understanding ; and a trifle would throw him into a rage. He had been humoured in everything from his cradle, on account of his fine estate ; from his infancy to his manhood, had been continually flattered, and in everything obeyed. This made him opinionated and proud, obstinate, and incapable of bearing the least contradiction.

BELINDA COOTE, his lady, with whom he had been passionately in love, was as fine a figure as could be seen among the daughters of men. Her person was charming ; her face was beautiful, and had a sweetness in it that was pleasing to look at. Her vivacity was great, and her understanding extraordinary ; but she had a satirical wit, and a vanity which made her delight in shewing the weakness of other minds, and the clearness of her own conception.

She was too good, however, to have the least malice, in such procedure. It was human weakness, and a desire to make her neighbours wiser. Unfortunately for her, she was married to a man, who, of all men in the world, was the unfittest subject for her quick fancy to act on.

But, notwithstanding this, EUSTACE and BELINDA were, for the most of their time, very fond. As she was formed in a prodigality of nature, to shew mankind a finished composition, and had wit and charms enough to fire the dullest and most insensible heart ; a man of ORLANDO's taste for the sex, could not be without an inflamed heart, when so near the transporting object of desire. She was his delight for almost a year, the dear support of his life. He seemed to value her esteem, her respect, her love ; and endeavoured to merit them by the virtues which fortify love : and therefore, when by his being short, positive, and unreasonable in his dictates, as was too often his wont ; and on her being intemperate in the strong sentiments her imagination produced upon the occasion, which was too frequently the case ; when they seemed to forget the Apostle's advice for a while, "that ye love one another with a pure heart, fervently:" 1 *Peter*, ch. i. v. 22. and had strifes and debates, which showed for the time they lasted, that they were far from being perfect and entire, wanting nothing ; then would her throwing her face into smiles, with some tender expression, prove a reconciling method at once. Till the fatal night, this always had a power to soften pain, to ease and calm the raging man.

But poor at best is the condition of human life here below ; and when to weak and imperfect faculties, we add inconsistencies, and do not act up to the eternal law of reason, and of God ; when love of fame, curiosity, resentment, or any of our particular propensities ; when humour, vanity, or any of our inferior powers, are permitted to act against justice and veracity, and instead of reflecting on the reason of the thing, or the right of the case, that by the influence this has on the mind, we may be constituted virtuous, and attached to truth ; we go down with the current of the passions, and let bent and humour determine us, in opposition to what is decent and fit : if in a state so unfriendly as this is, to the heavenly and divine life, where folly and vice are for ever striving to introduce disorder into our frame, and it is difficult indeed, to preserve, in any degree, an integrity of character, and peace within : if, in such a situation, instead of labouring to destroy all the seeds of envy, pride, ill-will, and impatience, and endeavouring to establish and maintain a due inward economy and harmony, by paying a perpetual regard to truth, that is, to the real circumstances and relation of things in which we stand, to the practice of reason in its just extent, according to the capacities and natures of every being ; we do, on the contrary, disregard the moral faculty, and become a mere system of passions and affections, without any thing at the head of them to govern them ; what then can be expected, but deficiency and deformity, degeneracy and guilty practice ? This was the case of EUSTACE and BELINDA. Passion and own-will were so near and intimate to him, that he seemed to live under a deliberate resolution not to be governed by reason. He would wink at the light he had, struggle to evade conviction, and made his mind a chaos and a hell. BELINDA, at the same time, was too quick, too vain and too often forgot to take into her idea of a good character, a continual subordination of the lower powers of our nature to the faculty of reason. This produced the following scene.

MARIA, sister to BELINDA, returned one evening with a five guinea fan she had bought that afternoon, and was tedious in praising some Indian figures that were painted in it. Mrs. EUSTACE, who had a taste for pictures, said, the colours were fine, but the images ridiculous and despicable ; and her sister must certainly be a little Indian-mad, or her fondness for every thing from that side of the globe could not be so excessive and extravagant as it always appeared to be.

To this MARIA replied with some heat, and EUSTACE very peremptorily insisted upon it, that she was right. With postiveness and passion he magnified the beauties of the figures on the fan, and with violence reflected so severely on the good judgment BELINDA, upon all occasions, pretended to, as he expressed it; that at last, her imagination was fired, and, with too much eagerness she not only ridiculed the opinion of her sister, in respect of such things, but spoke with too much warmth against the despotic tempers of self-sufficient;husbands.

To reverence and obey, she said, was not required by any obligation, when men were unreasonable, and paid no regard to a wife's domestic and personal felicity ; nor would she give up her understanding to his weak determination, since custom cannot confer an authority which nature has denied : It cannot license a husband to be unjust, nor give right to treat her as a slave. If this was to be the case in matrimony, and women were to suffer under conjugal vexations, as she did, by his senseless arguments every day, they had better bear the reproach and solitude of antiquated virginity, and be treated as the refuse of the world, in the character of old maids.

This too lively, though just speech, enraged EUSTACE to the last degree, and from a fury, he sunk in a few minutes into a total sullen silence, and sat for half an hour, while I stayed, cruelly determining, I suppose, her sad doom. BELINDA soon saw she had gone too far, and did all that could be done to recover him from the fit he was in. She smiled, cried, asked pardon ; but 'twas all in vain. Every charm had lost its power, and he seemed no longer man.　When this beauty stood weeping by his chair, and said " My love, forgive me, as it was in raillery only I spoke, and let our pleasures and pains be hereafter honestly shared."　I remember the tears burst from my eyes, and in that condition I went away.　It was frightful to look at EUSTACE, as he shook, started, and wildly stared ; and the distress his Lady appeared in, was enough to make the most stony heart bleed¦; it was a dismal scene.

This happened at nine at night, and at ten ORLANDO withdrew, to bed, without speaking one word, as I was informed.　Soon after he lay down, he pretended to be fast asleep, and his wife rejoicing to find him so, as she believed, in hopes that nature's soft nurse would lull the active instruments of motion, and calm the raging operations of his mind, she resigned herself to slumbers, and thought to abolish for that night every disagreeable sensation of pain, but no sooner did this furious man find that his charming wife, was really asleep, than he plunged a dagger into her breast. The monster repeated the strokes, while she had life to speak to him, in the tenderest manner, and conjured him, in regard to his own happiness, to let her live, and not sink himself into perdition here, and hereafter, by her death.　In vain she prayed ; he gave her a thousand wounds, and I saw her the next morning a bloody mangled corpse, in the great house in Smithfield, which stood at a distance from the street, with a wall before it, and an avenue of high trees up to the door ; and not in the country as the Tatler says.

EUSTACE fled, when he thought she was expiring, though she lived for an hour after, to relate the case to her maid, who heard¦ her groan and came into her room ; and went from Dublin to a little lodge he had in the country, about twenty miles from town.　The magistrates, in a short time, had information where he was ; and one JOHN MANSEL, a constable, a bold and strong man, undertook for a reward, to apprehend him.　To this purpose he set out immediately, with a case of pistols and a hanger, and lurked several days and nights in the fields, before he could find an opportunity of coming at him ; for EUSTACE lived by himself in the house, well secured by strong doors and bars, and only went out now and then to an alehouse, the master of which was his friend.　Near it, at last, about break of day, MANSEL chanced to find him, and, upon his refusing to be made a prisoner, and cocking a pistol to shoot the officer of justice, both their pistols were discharged at once, and they both dropt down dead men.　EUSTACE was shot in the heart, and the constable in the brain.　They were both brought to Dublin on one of the little low-backed cars there used ; and I was one of the boys that followed the car, from the beginning of James-street, the out-side of the city, all through the town.　EUSTACE's head hung dangling near the ground, with his face upwards, and his torn bloody breast bare ; and of all the faces of the dead I have seen, none ever looked like his. There was an anxiety, a rage, a horror, and a despair to be seen in it, that no pencil could express.

Thus fell EUSTACE in the twenty-ninth year of his age, and by his hand his virtuous, beautiful, and ingenious wife ; and what are we to learn from thence ? is it that on such accounts, we ought to dread wedlock and ne'er be concerned with a wife ? No, surely, but to be from thence convinced, that it is necessary in order to a happy marriage, to bring the will to the obedience of reason, and acquire an equanimity in the general tenour of life. Of all things in this world, moral dominion, or the empire over ourselves, is not only the most glorious, as reason is the superior nature of man, but the most valuable, in respect of real human happiness. A conformity to reason, or good sense, and to the inclination of our neighbours, with very little money, may produce great and lasting felicity ; but without this subservience to our own reason, complaisance to company, and softness and benevolence to all around us, the greatest misery does frequently sprout from the largest stock of fortunes.

It was by ungoverned passions, that EUSTACE murdered his wife and died himself ; the most miserable and wretched of all human beings. He might have been the happiest of mortals, if he had conformed to the dictates of reason, and softened his passions, as well for his own ease as in compliance to a creature formed with a mind of a quite different make from his own. There is a sort of sex in souls ; and, exclusive of that love and patience which our religion requires, every couple should remember, that there are things which grow out of their very natures, that are pardonable, when considered as such. Let them not, therefore, be spying out faults, nor find a satisfaction in reproaching ; but let them examine to what consequences their ideas tend, and resolve to cease from cherishing them, when they lead to contention and mischief. Let them both endeavour to amend what is wrong in each other, and act as becomes their character in practising the social duties of married persons, which are so frequently and strongly inculcated by revelation and natural reason ; and then, instead of matrimony being a burthen, and hanging a weight upon our very beings, there will be no appearance of evil in it, but harmony and joy will shed unmixed felicities on them ; they will live in no low degree of beatitude in the suburbs of heaven.

This was my case, wedlock to me became the greatest blessing ; a scene of the most refined friendship, and a condition to which nothing can be added to complete the sum of human felicity. So I found the holy and sublime relation, and in the wilds of West-

moreland enjoyed a happiness as great as human nature is capable
of, on this planet.   Sensible to all the ties of social truth and
honour, my partner and I lived in perfect felicity, on the products
of our solitary farm.   The amiable dispositions of her mind,
cheerfulness, good nature, discretion, and diligence, gave a
perpetual dignity and lustre to the grace and loveliness of her
person ; and as I did all that love and fidelity could do, by practising every rule of caution, prudence and justice, to prevent variance,
soften cares, and preserve affection undiminished, the harmony of
our state was unmixed and divine.   Since the primitive institution
of 'the relation, it never existed in a more delightful manner.
Devoted to each other's heart, we desired no other happiness in
this world, than to pass life away together in the solitude we were
in.   We lived, hoped, and feared but for each other ; and made it
our daily study to be what revealed religion prescribes, and the
concurrent voice of nature requires, in the sacred tie.   Do so likewise, ye mortals, who intend to marry, and ye may, like us, be
happy.   As the instincts and passions were wisely and kindly
given us, to subserve many purposes of our present state, let them
have their proper, subaltern share of action ; but let reason ever
have the sovereignty, the divine law of reason and truth, and be
as it were, sail and wind to the vessel of life.

Two years almost, this fine scene lasted, and during that period,
the business and diversions of our lone retreat appeared so various
and pleasing, that it was not possible to think a hundred years
so spent, in the least degree dull and tedious.   Exclusive of
books and gardening, and the improvement of the farm, we had
during the fine season, a thousand charming amusements on the
mountains, and in the glens and valleys of that sweet silent place.
Whole days we would spend in fishing, and dine in some cool grot
by the water-side, or under an aged tree, or the margin of some
beautiful stream.   We generally used the fly and rod, but had
recourse if in haste to one of the little water-falls, and, by fixing
a net under one of them, would take a dozen or two of very large
trouts, in a few minutes time.

By a little water-fall I mean one of those that are formed by
some small river, which tumbles there in various places, from rock
to rock, about four feet each fall, and makes a most beautiful
view from top to bottom of a fall.   There are many of these falling
waters among the vast mountains of Westmoreland, and I have
seen them likewise in the Highlands of Scotland.

At Glencrow, half way between Dunbarton and Inverary, there
are some very fine ones, and just by them one CAMPBELL keeps
a poor inn.   There we were entertained with water and whiskey,
oatcakes, milk, butter, and trouts he took by the net, at one of
the little falls of a river that descends a prodigious mountain near
his lone house, and forms, like what we have at Orton-Lodge, a

most beautiful scene. Several happy days I passed at this place with a dear creature, who is now a saint in heaven.

At other times we had the diversion of taking as much carp and tench as we pleased, in a large, standing, fenny water, that lies about two miles from the lodge, in a glen, and always found the fish of this water of an enormous size, three feet long, though the general length of fish of this species is eleven inches in our ponds. This vast bigness must be owing to the great age of these fish, which I may suppose, at least, an hundred years ; for it is certain that in garden ponds which have for experiment's sake, been left undisturbed for many years, the carp and tench have been found alive, and grown to a surprising bigness.

A gentleman, my near relation, who lived to a very advanced age, put some fish of these species in a pond, 20th Nov. 1648 ; the day that Colonel *E*wer, at the head of seven other officers, presented to the commons that fatal remonstrance, which in fact took off the head of Charles ; and in the year 1727, seventy-nine years after, on his return to that seat, he found them all alive, and near two feet and a half in length. This demonstrates that fish may live to a very great age. It likewise proves that they continue to grow till they are a hundred years old, and then are the finest eating.

Another of our amusements, during the summer's bright day, was the pointer and gun, for the black cock, the moor cock, and the cock of the wood, which are in great plenty on those vast hills.*
CHARLOTTE was fond of this sport, and would walk with me for hours to see me knock down the game ; till, late in the evening, we would wander over the fells, and then return to our clean, peaceful, little house, to sup as elegantly on our birds, as the great could do, and with a harmony and unmixed joy they are for ever strangers to. After supper, over some little nectared-bowl, we sweetly chatted, till it was bed-time ; or I played on my flute, and CHARLOTTE divinely sung. It was a happy life, all the riches and

---

* The black cock, is as large as our game cocks, and flies very swift and strong. The head and eyes are large, and round the eyes is a beautiful circle of red. The beak is strong, and black as the body ; the legs robust and red. It is very high eating, more so than any native-bird in England except the fen-ortolan ; but in one particular it exceeds the fen birds, for it has two tastes, being brown and whitemeat ; under a lay of brown is one of whitemeat : both delicious, the brown is higher than the black moor cock, and the white much richer than the pheasant.

The moor cock is likewise very rare, but is to be had sometimes in London, as the sportsmen meet with it now and then on the hilly-heaths, not very far from town, particularl on Hindhead-heath, in the way to Portsmouth. It is as large as a good Dorking fowl, and the colour is a deep iron-grey. Its eyes are large and fine as the black cock's ; but, instead of the red circle round them, it has bright and beautiful scarlet eyebrows.

The cock of the wood, as unknown in London as the black cock, is almost as large as a turkey, but flies well. The back is a mixture of black, grey, and a reddish brown ; the belly grey, and the breast a pale brown, with transverse lines of black, and a little white at the tips of the feathers. It has a large round head, of the purest black, and over its fine hazel eyes, there is a naked space, that looks like an eye-brow of bright scarlet. It is delicious eating, but far inferior to the black cock.

honours of the world cannot produce such scenes of bliss as we experienced in a cottage, in the wilds of Westmoreland. Even the winter, which is ever boisterous and extreme cold in that part of the world, was no severity to us. As we had most excellent provisions of every kind in abundance, and plenty of firing from the ancient woods, which covered many of those high hills ; and two men servants, and two maids, to do whatever tended to being and to well-being, to supply our wants, and to complete our happiness. This softened the hard rough scene, and the roaring waters, and the howling winds, appeared pleasing sounds. In short, every season, and all our hours, were quite charming, and full of delight. Good TOM FLEMING, our friend, did likewise enhance our felicity, by coming once or twice a week to see us, and staying sometimes two or three days. In the summer time, we also went now and then to visit him ; and, if one was inclined to melancholy, it was impossible to be dull while he was by. His humour, and his songs, over a bowl of punch, were enough to charm the most splenetic, and make even rancour throw its face into smiles.

1727.—Two years, as I have said, this fine scene lasted ; and during that soft transporting period, I was the happiest man on earth. But in came Death, when we least expected him, snatched my charming partner from me, and melted all my happiness into air—into thin air. A fever, in a few days, snapp'd off the thread of her life, and made me the child of affliction, when I had not a thought of the mourner. Language cannot paint the distress this calamity reduced me to ; nor give an idea of what I suffered, when I saw her eyes swimming in death, and the throes of her departing spirit. Blest as she was, in the exercise of every virtue that adorns a woman how inconsolable must her husband be ! and, to add to my distress, by the same fever fell my friend TOM FLEMING, who came the day before my wife sickened to see us. One of my lads likewise died, and the two servant maids. They all lay dead around me, and I sat like one inanimate by the corpse of CHARLOTTE, till friar FLEMING the brother of TOM, brought coffins and buried them all. Thus did felicity vanish from my sight, and I remained like a traveller in Greenland, who had lost the sun.

"O eloquent, just and mighty death !" says Raleigh. It is thou alone puts wisdom into the human heart, and suddenly makes man to know himself. It is death that makes the conqueror ashamed of his fame, and wish he had rather stolen out of the world, than purchased the report of his actions, by rapine, oppression, and cruelty ; by giving in spoil the innocent and labouring soul to the idle and insolent ; by emptying the cities of the world of their ancient inhabitants, and filling them again with so many and so variable sorts of sorrows. It is death tells the proud and insolent, that they are but abjects, and humbles them at the instant ; makes them cry, complain, and repent ; yea even, to hate their former happiness. It is death takes the account of the rich, and proves him a beggar, a naked beggar, which hath interest in nothing but the gravel which fills his mouth. It is death holds a glass before the eyes of the most beautiful, and makes them see therein their deformity and rottenness ; and they acknowledge it.

Whom none could advise, thou hast persuaded ; what none have dared, thou hast done : and whom all the world hath flattered, thou only hast cast out of the world, and despised. Thou hast drawn together all the far-stretched greatness, all the pride, cruelty, and ambition, of man ; all the powerful charms of beauty ; and covered it all over with these two narrow words, ' Hic jacet.'

Nor is this all, mighty Death ! It is thou that leadest to the resurrection of the dead ; and dissolution of the world ; the judgment day ; and the eternal state of men. It is thou that finishes the trial of men, and seals their characters, for happiness or misery for ever.

Be thou then, Death, our morning and evening meditation : let us learn from thee the vanity of all human things ; and that it is the most amazing folly, to melt away time, and misapply talents, as the generality of reasonable beings do : that we were not made men, thinking, rational beings, capable of the noblest contemplations, to spend all our thoughts and time in sense and pleasure, in dressing, feeding, and sporting ; or in purchases, building and planting ; but to prepare for a dying hour ; that, when at the call of God, we go out of the body, not knowing whither we go, we may, like Abraham, travel by faith, and trust to the conduct of the Lord of all countries. Since we must die, and thy power, O Death, we see, is uncontrollable ; since to the dust we must return, and take our trial at the bar of Almighty God, as intelligent and free agents ; for under moral government, and God is a perfectly wise and righteous governor, the wickedness of the wicked will be upon him, and the righteousness of the righteous will be upon him ; since we must be numbered with the dead, and our circumstances and condition indicate a future judgment, surely we ought to remove our chief concern from this world to the other, and transfer our principal regard to the immortal spirit ; that in the hour of agony, a virtuous mind, purity of conscience, and good actions, may procure us the favour of God, and the guidance of his good spirit to the mansions of the blessed, where now pleasures are for ever springing up, and the happiness of the heavenly inhabitants is perpetually increasing. This is the one thing needful. Death demonstrates, that this world of darkness and error, changes and chances, is not worth fixing our

heart on.   To secure our passage into the regions of perfect and
eternal day, should be the employment of immortal mortals.

Thus did I reflect as I sat among the dead, with my eyes
fastened on the breathless corpse of CHARLOTTE, and I wished, if
it was possible, to have leave to depart, and in the hospitable
grave, lie down from toil and pain, to take my last repose ; for
I knew not what to do, nor where to go.   *I* was not qualified for
the world ; nor had I a friend, or even an acquaintance in it, that
I knew where to find.   But in vain I prayed, it was otherwise
decreed ; I must go on, or continue a solitary in the wild *I* was
in.   The latter it was not possible for me to do ; in the state of
mind *I* was in ; overwhelmed with sorrow, and without a companion of any kind : and therefore, *I* must of necessity go to
some other place.   I sold all the living things I had to friar
FLEMING, and locked up my doors.   My furniture, linen, clothes
books, liquors, and some salt provisions, instruments of various
kinds, and such like things, *I* left in their several places.   There
was no one to take them, or probability that any one would come
there to disturb them ; and perhaps, some time or other, the fates
might bring me back again to the same lone place.   Though it
was then a desolate, silent habitation, a striking memento of the
vanity and precarious existence of all human good things ; yet
it was possible, that hearty friendship, festivity, and social life,
might once more be seen there.   The force and operation of
casualties did wonders every day, and time might give me even a
relish for the solitude in a few years more.   Thus did *I* settle
affairs in that remote place ; and, taking leave of my friend, the
friar, with my lad O'FIN, rode off.

May 5th, 1727.—The sun was rising when we mounted our
horses, and *I* again went out to try my fortune in the world ; not
like the Chevalier La Mancha, in hopes of conquering a kingdom,
or marrying some great Princess ; but to see if *I* could find another
good country girl for a wife, and get a little more money ; as they
were the only two things united, that could secure me from
melancholy, and confer real happiness.   To this purpose, as the
day was extremely fine, and O'FIN had something cold, and a
couple of bottles at the end of his valise, *I* gave my horse the rein
and let him take what way his fancy chose.   For some time he
gently trotted the path he had often gone, and over many a
mountain made his road ; but at last, he brought me to a place *I*
was quite a stranger to, and made a full stop at a deep and rapid
water, which ran by the bottom of a very high hill *I* had not been
before.   Over this river *I* made him go, though it was far from
being safe, and in an hour's ride from that flood, came to a fine
rural scene.

It was pasture-ground, of a large extent, and in many places
covered with groves of trees, of various kinds ; walnuts, chesnuts

and oaks ; the poplar, the plane-tree, the mulberry, and maple. There was likewise the Phœnician cedar, the larix, the large-leaved laurel, and the cytisus of Virgil. In the middle of this place were the ruins of an old seat, over-run with shrubby plants, the Virginia creeper, the box-thorn, the jessamine, the honey-suckle, the periwinkle, the birdweed, the ivy, and the climber ; and near the door was a flowing spring of water, which formed a beautiful stream, and babbled to the river we came from. Charming scene ! so silent, sweet, and pretty, that I was highly pleased with the discovery.

On the margin of the brook, under a mulberry tree, I sat down and dined on some cold tongue and ham, and potted black cock, which O'FIN produced from his wallet ; and having drank a pint of cyder, set out again, to try what land lay right onwards. In an hour, we came to a large and dangerous watery moor, which we crossed over with great difficulty, and then arrived at a range of mountains, through which there was a narrow pass, wet and stony, a long and tedious ride which ended on the border of a fine country ; at four in the afternoon, we arrived on the confines of a plain, of about a hundred acres, which was strewed with various flowers of the earth's natural produce that rendered the glebe delightful to behold, and was surrounded with groves. The place had all the charms that verdure, forest, and vale, can give a country. In the centre of this ground was a handsome square building, and behind it a large and beautiful garden, encompassed by a low, thick holly-hedge. As the door of this house was not locked but opened by a silver spring turner, I went in, and found it was one spacious room, filled on every side with books, bound in an extraordinary manner. Globes, telescopes, and other instruments of various kinds, were placed on stands, and there were two fine writing tables, one at each end of the library, which had paper, ink, and pens. In the middle of the room there was a reading-desk, which had a short inscription, and on it leaned the skeleton of a man. The legend said " THIS SKELETON WAS ONCE CHARLES HENLEY, ESQ."

Amazed I stood, looking on these things, and wondered much at the figure of the bones, tacked together with wires ; once, to be sure, the master of this grand collection of books and manuscripts, and this fine room, so sweetly situated in the centre of distant groves ; had a striking effect on my mind ; and the more so, as it held a scroll of parchment, on which was beautifully written in the court-hand, to appear more remarkable, I suppose, the following lines :

" Fellow-mortal, whoever thou art, whom the fates shall conduct into this chamber, remember, that before many years are passed, thou must be laid in the bed of corruption, in the dark caverns of death, among the lifeless dust, and rotten bones of others, and from the grave proceed to the general resurrection of all. To new life and vigour thou wilt most certainly be raised, to be brought to a great account. Naked and defenceless thou must stand before the awful tribunal of the great God, and from him receive a final sentence, which shall determine and fix thee in an eternal state of happiness or misery.

"What an alarm should this be ! Ponder my fellow-mortal, and remember, God now commandeth men every where to repent, because he hath appointed a day, in which he will judge the world in righteousness, by that man, whom he hath ordained ; whereof he hath given assurance unto all men, in that he hath raised him from the dead. Judge the world ! judgment ! the very sound is solemn. Should it not deaden some part, at least, of your concern for things temporal, and quicken your care and industry for the future life ; ought it not to make us condemn, before the dying hour, our vanity and devotion to bodily things and make us employ the greatest part of our time in the acquisition of wisdom, and an improvement in virtue, that when we appear at the session of righteousness, a sacred knowledge, a heavenly piety, and an angelic goodness, may secure us from eternal punishment, and entitle us to a glorious eternity ? Since a future judgment is most certainly the case, and the consequence eternal damnation or salvation, how contemptible a thing is a long busy life, spent in raking through the mire of trade and business, in pursuit of riches and a large estate ; or in sweating up the steep hill of ambitiou, after fame and ambition ; or in living and dressing as if we were all body, and sent into time for no other purpose, than to adorn like idols, gratify like brutes, and waste life in sensuality and vanity ; how contemptible and unreasonable is this kind of existence for beings who were created to no other end, than to be partakers of a divine life with God, and sing hallelujahs to all eternity ; to separate the creature from error, fiction, impurity, and corruption, and acquire that purity and holiness, which alone can see God. Away then with a worldly heart : away with all those follies, which engage us like fools and madmen ; and let the principal thing be, to follow the steps of our great master, by patience and resignation, by a charity and contempt of the world ; and by keeping a conscience void of offence, amidst the changes and chances of this mortal life ; that at his second coming, to judge the world, we may be found acceptable in his sight.

"What a scene must this second coming be ! I saw, says an apostle, a great white throne, and him that sat on it, from whose face the earth and the heavens fled away, and there was no place found for them ; and I saw the dead small and great stand before God ; and the books were opened, and the dead were judged out of those things which were written i   the books : and the sea gave up her dead, and death and hell delivered up their dead which were in them, and they were judged every man, according to their works. The secret wickedness of men will be brought to light ; and concealed piety and persecuted virtue be acknowledged and honoured. While innocence and piety are set at the right hand of the judge, and the righteous shall shine forth as the sun in the kingdom of their father for ever and ever, shame and confusion must sit upon the faces of the sinner and the ungodly. Damnation will stand before the brethren in iniquity, and when the intolerable sentence is executed, what inexpressible agonies will they fall into ? what amazement and excesses of horror must seize upon them ?

" Ponder then, in time, fellow-mortal, and choose to be good, rather than to be great : prefer your baptismal vows to the pomps and vanities of this world ; and value the secret whispers of a good conscience more than the noise of popular applause.

Since you must appear before the judgment-seat of Christ ; that every one may receive the things done in his body, according to that he hath done, whether it be good or bad, let it be your work from morning till night, to keep Jesus in your hearts ; and long for nothing, desire nothing, hope for nothing, but to have all that is within you changed into the spirit and temper of the holy Jesus. Wherever you go, whatever you do, do all in imitation of his temper and inclination ; and look upon all as nothing, but that which exercises and increases the spirit and life of Christ in your souls. Let this be your Christianity, your Church, and your religion, and the judgment-day will be a charming scene. If in this world, the will of the creature, as an offspring of the divine will, wills and works with the will of God, and labours, without ceasing, to come as near as mortals can to the purity and perfection of the divine nature ; then will the day of the Lord be a day of great joy, and with unutterable pleasure, you shall hear that tremendous voice : Awake, ye dead, and come to judgment. In transports, and full of honour and glory, the wise and righteous will hear the happy sentence, Come ye blessed of my father, inherit the kingdom prepared for you from the foundation of the world."

This, and the skeleton, astonished me not a little ; and my wonder at the whole increased, as I could find no human creature living, nor discover any house or cottage for an inhabitant. This I thought exceeded all the strange things I had seen in this wonderful country. But perhaps, it occurred at last, there might be a mansion in the woods, before me, or somewhere in the groves on either side ; and therefore, leaving the library, after I had spent an hour in it, I walked onwards, and came to a wood which had private walks cut through it, and strewed with sand. They shewed only light enough to distinguish the blaze of day from evening shade, and had seats dispersed, to sit and listen to the chorus of the birds, which added to the pleasures of the soft silent place. For about three hundred yards the walk I was in extended, and then terminated in meadows, which formed an oval of twenty acres surrounded by groves, like the large plain I came from. Exactly in the middle of these fields, part of which were turned into gardens, there stood a very handsome stone house, and not far from the door of it, a fountain played. On either side of the water was a garden-chair, of a very extraordinary make, curious and beautiful ; and each of them stood under an ever-green oak, the broad leaved ilex, a charming shade.

In one of these chairs sat an ancient gentleman, a venerable man, whose hair was white as silver, and his countenance had dignity and goodness. His dress and manner shewed him to be a person of fortune and distinction, and by a servant in waiting it appeared, he was Lord of the seigneurie I was arrived at. He was tall and graceful, and had not the least stoop, though he wanted but a year of an hundred. I could not but admire the fine old gentleman.

On the same chair, next to him, sat a young Lady, who was at this time just turned of twenty and had such diffusive charms as soon new fired my heart, and gave my soul a softness even beyond what it had felt before. She was a little taller than the middle size, and had a face that was perfectly beautiful. Her eyes were extremely fine, full, black and sparkling ; and her conversation was as charming as her person ; both easy, unconstrained, and sprightly. When I came near two such personages, I bowed low to the ground, and asked pardon for intruding into their fine retirement. But the stars had led me, a wanderer, to this delightful solitude, without the least idea of there being such a place in our island, and as their malignant rays had forced me to offend, without intending it, I hoped they would pardon my breaking in upon them.

To this the old Gentleman replied, " You have not offended, Sir, I assure you, but you are welcome to the Groves of Basil. It gives me pleasure to see you here ; for it is very seldom we are favoured with any one's company. It is hard to discover or make out a road to this place, as we are surrounded almost by impassible mountains, and a very dangerous morass, nor can I conceive how you found the way here without a guide, or ventured to travel this country, as there are no towns in this part of the county. There must be something very extraordinary in your case, and as you mentioned your being a wanderer, I should be glad to hear the cause of your journeying in this uninhabited region. But first," said Mr. HENLEY, " as it is now near eight at night, and you must want refreshment, having met with no inn the whole day, we will go in to supper." He then arose, and brought me to an elegant parlour, where a table was soon covered

with the best cold things, and we immediately sat down. *Every*
eatable was excellent, and the wine and other liquors in perfection.
Miss HENLEY sat at the head of the table, her grandfather over-
against her, and placed me at her right hand between them both.
The young lady behaved in a very easy genteel manner ; and the
old gentleman, with freedom, cheerfulness, and good manners.
Till nine this scene lasted, and then Mr. Henley again requested
I would oblige him with an account of my travels in that part
of the world. This, I said, I would do in the best manner I
could, and while he leaned back in his easy chair, and the beautiful STATIA fastened her glorious eyes upon me, I went on in the
following words :

" I am an *English*man, Sir, but have passed the greatest part
of my life in Ireland, and from the western extremity of it I came.
My father is one of the rich men in that kingdom, and was, for
many years, the tenderest and most generous parent that ever
son was blessed with. He spared no cost on my education, and
gave me leave to draw upon him, while I resided in the university
of Dublin five years, for what I pleased. *Ex*travagant as I was in
several articles, he never set any bounds to my demands, nor
asked me what I did with the large sums I had yearly from him.
My happiness was his felicity, and the glory of his life to have
me appear to the greatest advantage, and in the most respected
character, that money can gain a man.

" But at last he married his servant maid, an artful cruel
woman, who obtained by her wit and charms so great an ascendant
over him, that he abandoned me, to raise a young nephew this
step-mother had, to what splendor and power she pleased. He
had everything he could name that money could procure, and
was absolutely master of the house and land. Not a shilling at
this time could I get, nor obtain the least thing I asked for, and
because I refused to become preceptor to this young man, and
had made some alteration in my religion, having renounced that
creed, which was composed nobody knows by whom, and introduced into the church in the darkest ages of popish ignorance ; a
symbol, which strongly participates of the true nature and spirit
of popery, in those severe denunciations of God's wrath, which
it pours so plentifully forth against all those whose heads are not
turned to believe it ; my father was so enraged that he would not
even admit me to his table any longer, but bid me be gone. My
mother-in-law likewise for ever abused me, and her nephew, the
lad, insulted me when I came in his way.

" Being thus compelled to withdraw, I set sail for *E*ngland as
soon as it was in my power, and arrived in Cumberland by the
force of a storm. I proceeded from thence to the mountains
of Stanemore, to look for a gentleman, my friend, who lived among
those hills ; and as I journeyed over them, and missed him, I

chanced to meet with a fine northern girl, and a habitation to my purpose. I married her, and for almost two years past was the happiest of the human race, till the sable curtain fell between us, and the angel of death translated her glorious soul to the fields of paradise. Not able to bear the place of our residence, after I had lost my heart's fond idol, I left the charming spot and mansion, where unmixed felicity had been for some time my portion, and I was travelling on towards London, to see what is ordained there in reserve for me ; when by accident I lost my way, and the fates conducted me to the Groves of Basil. Curiosity led me into the library I found in the plain, without this wood, from whence, in search for some human creatures, I proceeded to the fountain, where I had the pleasure of seeing you, Sir, and this young Lady. This is a summary of my past life ; what is before me heaven only knows. My fortune I trust with the Preserver of men, and the Father of spirits. One thing I am certain of by observation, few as the days of the years of my pilgrimage have been, that the emptiness, and unsatisfying nature of this world's enjoyments, are enough to prevent my having any fondness to stay in this region of darkness and sorrow. I shall never leap over the bars of life, let what will happen ; but the sooner I have leave to depart, I shall think it the better for me."

The old gentleman seemed surprised at my story, and after some moments silence, when I had done, he said, " Your measure, Sir, is hard, and as it was, in part, for declaring against a false religion at your years, you please me so much, that if you will give me leave, I will be your friend, and as a subaltern providence, recompense your loss as to fortune in this world. In what manner you shall know to-morrow, when we breakfast at eight. It is now time to finish our bottle, that we may, according to our custom, betimes retire."

August 4th, 1727.—At the time appointed I met the old gentleman in the parlour, and just as we had done saluting each other, STATIA entered, bright and charming as Aurora. She was in a rich dress, and her bright victorious eyes flashed a celestial fire. She made our tea, and gave me some of her coffee. She asked me a few civil questions, and said two or three good things on the beauties of the morning, and the charms of the country. She left us the moment we had done breakfast, and then the old gentle-man addressed himself to me in the following words :

" I do not forget the promise I made you, but must first relate the history of my family. I do it with the more pleasure, as I find you are of our religion, and I cannot help having a regard for you, on your daring to throw up a fortune for truth ; for bravely daring to renounce those systems, which have an outward ortho-dox roundness given to them by their eloquent defenders, and within are mere corruption and apostacy.

"The skeleton you saw in the library was once my son, CHARLES HEYLEY, a most extraordinary man. He had great abilities, and understood every thing a mortal is capable of knowing, of things human and divine. When he was in his nineteenth year, I took him to France and other countries, to see the world, and on our return to England, married him into a noble family, to a very valuable young woman, of a large fortune, and by her he had the young lady you saw sitting on the chair near the table by me. This son I lost, three years after his marriage, and with him all relish for the world; and being naturally inclined to retirement and a speculative life, never stirred since from this country-house. Here my son devoted himself entirely to study, and amused himself with instructing his beloved STATIA, the young lady you have seen. At his death he consigned her to my care; and as her understanding is very great, and her disposition sweet and charming, I have not only taken great pains in educating her, but have been delighted with my employment. Young as she is, but in the second month of her one and twentieth year, she not only knows more than women of distinction generally do, but would be the admiration of learned men, if her knowledge in languages, mathematics, and philosophy, were known to them: and as her father taught her music and painting, perhaps there is not a young woman of finer accomplishments in the kingdom.

" Her father died towards the end of the year 1723, in the thirty-ninth year of his age, when she was not quite sixteen, and by his will left her ten thousand pounds, and Basil-House and estate; but she is not to inherit it, or marry, until she is two and twenty. This was her father's will. As to the skeleton in the library, it was my son's express order it should be so, and that the figure should not be removed from the place it stands in, while the library remained in that room; but continue a solemn memorial in his family to perpetuate his memory, and be a *memento mori* to the living.

" This is the history of Basil Groves, and the late owner of this seat, and his daughter STATIA. We live a happy, religious life here, and enjoy every blessing that can be desired in this lower hemisphere. But as I am not very far from a hundred years, having passed that ninety-two which Sir William Temple says he never knew any one he was acquainted with arrive at, I must be on the brink of the grave, and expect every day to drop into it. What may become of STATIA, then, gives me some trouble to think, as all her relations, except myself are in the other world. To spend her life here in this solitude, as seems to be her inclination, is not proper; and to go into the world by herself, when I am dead, without knowing any mortal in it, may involve her in troubles and distresses. Hear then, my son, what I propose to you. You are a young man, but serious. You have got some

wisdom in the school of affliction, and you have no aversion to
matrimony, as you have just buried, you say, a glorious woman,
your wife.   If you will stay with us here, till STATIA is two and
twenty, and in that time render yourself agreeable to her, I
promise you, she shall be yours the day she enters the three and
twentieth year of her age, and you shall have with her fortune, all
that I am owner of, which is no small sum.   What do you say
to this proposal ? "

" Sir," I replied, " you do me vast honour, much more I am sure
than my merits can pretend to.   I am infinitely obliged to you,
and must be blind and insensible, if I refused such a woman
as Miss HENLEY, were she far from being the fortune she is.   But
I have not vanity enough to imagine, I can gain her affections ;
especially in my circumstances, and to get her by your authority
or power of disposing of her, is what I cannot think of; I will
stay however, a few months here, since you so generously invite
me, and let Miss HENLEY know, I will be her humble servant, if
she will allow me the honour of bearing that title."   This made
the old gentleman laugh, and he took me by the hand, saying,
" This is right.   Come, let us go and take a walk before dinner."

There I passed the winter, and part of the spring, and lived in a
delightful manner.   The mornings I generally spent in the library,
reading, or writing extracts from some curious MSS. or scarce
books ; and in the afternoons Miss HENLEY and I walked in the
lawns and woods, or sat down to cards.   She was a fine creature
indeed in body and soul, had a beautiful understanding, and
charmed me to a high degree.   Her conversation was rational
and easy, without the least affectation from the books she had
read ; and she would enliven it sometimes by singing, in which
kind of music she was as great a mistress as I have heard.   As
to her heart, I found it was to be gained ; but an accident happened that put a stop to the amour.

1728.—In the beginning of March, the old gentleman, the
excellent Mr. HENLEY, STATIA's grandfather and guardian and
my great friend, died, and by his death a great alteration ensued
in my affair.   I thought to have had Miss HENLEY immediately,
as there was no one to plead her father's will against the marriage,
and intended to send O'FIN for friar FLEMING ; but when STATIA
saw herself her own mistress, without any superior, or controul,
and in possession of large fortunes, money, and an estate, that she
might do as she pleased ; this had an effect on her mind, and made
a change.   She told me, when I addressed myself to her, after
her grandfather was interred, " that what she intended to
do, in obedience to him, had he lived, she thought required very
serious consideration now she was left to herself : that, exclusive
of this, her inclination really was for a single life ; and had it
been otherwise, yet it was not proper, since her guardian was

dead, that I should live with her till the time limited by her father's will for her to marry was come ; but that, as she had too good an opinion of me to imagine her fortune was what chiefly urged my application, and must own she had a regard for me, she would be glad to hear from me sometimes, if I could think her worth remembering, after I had left the Groves of Basil." This she said with great seriousness, and seemed by her manner to forbid my urging any further.

" I assured her, however, that time only could wear out her charming image from my mind, and that I had reason to fear, she would long remain the torment of my heart. She had a right to be sure to dismiss me from her service ; but in respect of her inclination to live a single life, I begged leave to observe, that it was certainly quite wrong, and what she could not answer to the wise and bountiful Father of the Universe, as she was a Christian and by being so, must believe, that baptism was a memorial of the covenant of grace.

The Catholics and the Vision-mongers of the protestant side, the Rev. Wm. Law and others of his row, may magnify the excellence of celibacy as high as they please, and work it into Christian perfection, by sounding words and eloquent pens ; but most surely revelation was directly against them, and required the faithful to produce in a regular way.

" Consider, illustrious STATIA, that when the Most High gave the Abrahamic covenant in these words, I will be a God unto thee, and to thy seed after thee, and in thy seed shall all the families, or nations of the earth, be blessed ; which includes an interest in God, as a God, father and friend, for ever and a share in all the blessings wherewith the Messiah, in the gospel, hath enriched the world ; these inestimable blessings and promises of life and favour, were designed by the divine munificence for rising generations of mankind ; and it was most certainly intended, not only that they should be received with the highest gratitude and duty, but that they should be strongly inculcated upon the thoughts of succeeding generations, by an instituted sign or memorial, to the end of the world.

" Circumcision was the first appointed token or memorial, and at the same time, an instruction in that moral rectitude to which the grace of God obliges : and when the New Testament succeeded the Law, then was the covenant interest of infants, or their right to the covenant of grace, to be confirmed by the token or sign called baptism ; that action being appointed to give the expected rising generation an interest in the love of God, the grace of Christ, and the fellowship of the Holy Spirit, that is, in all covenant blessings. But what becomes of this great charter of heaven, if Christian women, out of an idle notion of perfection, will resolve to lead single lives, and thereby hinder rising generations from sharing in the honours and privileges of the Church of Jesus Christ. Millions of the faithful must thereby be deprived of the token instituted by God to convey to them those covenant blessings, which his love and goodness designed for the rising generations of his people. Have a care then what you do, illustrious STATIA, in this particular. It must be a great crime to hinder the regular propagation of a species, which God hath declared to be under his particular inspection and blessing, and by circumcision and baptism, hath made the special object of divine attention and care. Away then with all thoughts of a virgin life, whatever becomes of me. As God hath appointed matrimony and baptism, let it be your pious endeavour to bear sons and daughters, that may be related to God, their Father ; to Jesus, their Redeemer, and first born in the family ; and to all the excellent, who are to enjoy, through him, the blessings of the glorious world above. Marry, then, illustrious STATIA, marry, and let the blessing of Abraham come upon us gentiles. Oppose not the gospel covenant ; that covenant which was made with that patriarch ; but mind the comfortable promises ; I will circumcise thy heart, and the heart of thy seed. I will pour out my spirit upon thy seed, and my blessing upon thine offspring. The seed of the righteous is blessed. They are the seed of the blessed of the Lord, and their offspring with them. Such is the magna charta of our existence and future happiness : and as infants descending from Abraham, in the line of election, to the end of the world, have as good a right and claim as we to the blessings of this covenant, and immense promise, I will be a God unto thee, and to thy seed after thee, in their generations ; it must be a great crime, to deprive children of this intailed heavenly inheritance, by our resolving to live in a state of virginity. In my opinion, it is a sin greater than murder. What is murder, but forcing one from his post against the will of Providence ; and if the virgin hinders a being or beings from coming on the post, against the will of Providence, must she not be culpable ; and must she not be doubly criminal, if the being or beings she hinders from coming on the stage, or into this first state, were to be a part of the perpetual generations, who have a right to the inheritance, the blessing, and were to be heirs according to the promise made to Abraham ? Ponder, illustrious STATIA, on the important point. Consider what it is to die a maid, when you may, in a regular way, produce heirs to that inestimable blessing of life and favour, which the munificence of the Most High was pleased freely to bestow, and which the great Christian mediator, agent, and negociator, republished, confirmed, and sealed with his blood. Marry then in regard to the gospel, and let it be the fine employment of your life, to open gradually the treasures of revelation to the understandings of the little Christians you produce.

This I am sure your holy religion requires from you : and if from the sacred oracles we turn to the book of nature, is it not in this volume written, that there must be a malignity in the hearts of those mortals, who can remain unconcerned at the destruction and extirpation of the rest of mankind ; and who want even so much good will as is requisite to propagate a creature, in a regular and hallowed way, though they received their own being from the mere benevolence of their divine Master ? What do you say, illustrious STATIA ? Shall it be a succession, as you are an upright Christian ? And may I hope to have the honour of sharing in the mutual satisfaction that must attend the discharge of so momentous a duty ?*

* If succession be the main thing, and to prevent the extirpation of the rest of mankind why may it not be carried on as well without marriage, as in that confined way ? I answer, that as the author and founder of marriage was the Antient of Days, God himself, and at the creation, he appointed the institution : as Christ, who was vested with authority to abrogate any laws, or supersede any custom, in which were found any flaw or obliquity, or had not an intrinsic goodness and rectitude in them, confirmed the ordinance, by reforming the abuses that had crept into it, and restoring it to its original boundary : As he gave a sanction to this amicable covenant, and statuted that men should maintain the dignity of the conjugal state, and by virtue of this primordial and most intimate bond of society, convey down the race of mankind, and maintain its succession to the final dissolution. It is not therefore to be neglected or disregarded. We must not dare to follow our fancies, and in unhallowed mixtures, or an illegal method, have any posterity. As the great God appointed and blessed this institution only, for the continuance of mankind, the race is not to be preserved in another way. We must marry in the Lord, to promote his glory as the apostle says, 1 *Cor.* ch. vii. v. 39. The earth is not to be replenished by licentious junction, or the promiscuous use of women. Dreadful hereafter must be the case of all who slight an institution of God.

I am sensible, the libertine who depreciates and vilifies the dignity of the married state will laugh at this assertion : The fop and debauchee will hiss it, and still do their best to render wedlock the subject of contempt and ridicule. The Roman clergy will likewise decry it, and injuriously treat it as an impediment to devotion, a cramp upon the spiritual serving of God, and call it an instrument of pollution and defilement, in respect of their heavenly celibacy.

But as God thought marriage was suitable to a paradisiacal state, and the scriptures declare it honourable in all : as this is the way appointed by heaven to people the earth ; and the institution is necessary, in the reason and nature of things, considering the circumstances in which mankind is placed ; to prevent confusion, and promote the general happiness ; as the bond of society, and the foundation of all human government ; sure I am, the rake and the mass-priest, must be in a dreadful situation at the sessions of righteousness ; when the one is charged with libertinism and gallantries, with madness and folly, and with all the evils and mischief they have done by illicit gratification, contrary to reason, and in direct opposition to the institutes of God : and when the other, the miserable mass-priests, are called to an account, for vilifying the honour and dignity of the married state, and for striving to seduce mankind into the solitary retirements of celibacy, in violation of the laws of God ; and more especially of the primary law or ordinance of heaven. Wretched priests ; your institutions are breaches in revealed religion, trespasses upon the common rights of nature, and such oppressive yokes as it is not able to bear. Your celibacy has not a grain of piety in it. It is policy and impiety.

Hear me then, ye libertines and mass-priests : I call upon you of the first row, ye rakes of genius, to consider what you are doing, and in time turn from your iniquities : Be no longer profligate and licentious, blind to your true interest and happiness, but become virtuous and honourable lovers, and in regard to the advantages of this solemn institution, called wedlock, as well to the general state of the world, as to individuals, marry in the Lord ; so will you avoid that dreadful sentence. Fornicators and adulterers God will judge, that is, punish, and in this life, you may make things very agreeable, if you please ; though it is in the heavenly world alone, where there shall be all joy and no sorrow. Let there be true beauty and gracefulness in the mind and manners, and these with discretion, and other things in your power will furnish a fund of happiness commensurate with your lives. It is possible, I am sure to make marriage productive of as much happiness as falls to our share in this lower hemisphere as the nature of man can reach to in his present condition. For, as to joy flowing in with a full, constant and equal tide, without interruption and without allay, there is no such thing. Human nature doth not admit of this. " The sum of the matter is this : To the public the **advantages of marriage are certain, whether the parties will or no ; but to the parties engag-**

All the smiles sat on the face of STATIA, while I was haranguing in this devout manner, and her countenance became a constellation of wonders. When I had done, this beauty said, " I thank you, Sir, for the information you have given me. I am a Christian. There is no malignity in my heart. You have altered my way of thinking, and I now declare for a succession. Let Father FLEMING be sent for, and without waiting for my being two and twenty, or minding my father's will, as there is no one to oblige me to it, I will give you my hand." Charming news ! I dispatched my lad for the friar. The priest arrived the next day, and at night we were married. Three days after we set out for Orton-Lodge, at my wife's request, as she longed to see the place. For two years more I resided there ; it being more agreeable to STATIA than the improved Groves of Basil. We lived there in as much happiness as it is possible to have in this lower hemisphere, and much in the same manner as I did with CHARLOTTE my first wife. STATIA had all the good qualities and perfections which rendered CHARLOTTE so clear and valuable to me ; like her she studied to increase the delights of every day, and by art, good humour, and love, rendered the married state such a system of joys as might incline one to wish it could last a thousand years : But it was too sublime and desirable to have a long existence here. STATIA was taken ill of the small-pox, the morning we intended to return to Basil Groves ; she died the seventh day, and I laid her by CHARLOTTE's side. Thus did I again become a mourner. I sat with my eyes shut for three days, but at last, called for my horse to try what air, exercise, and a variety of objects could do.

April 1, 1729.—Very early, as soon as I could see day, I left Orton-Lodge, and went to Basil Groves, to order matters there. From thence I set out for Harrowgate-Spa to amuse myself in that agreeable place ; but I did not go the way I came to Mr. HENLEY's house. To avoid the dangerous morass I had passed, at the hazard of my life, we went over a wilder and more romantic country than I had before seen. We had higher mountains to ascend than I had ever passed before ; and some valleys so very deep to ride through, that they seemed as it were descents to hell. The patriarch Bermudez, in journeying over Abyssinia*, never

---

ing, not so : to them it is a fountain that sendeth forth both sweet and bitter waters. To those who mind their duty and obligations sweet ones; to those who neglect them bitter ones."

In the next place, ye monks, I would persuade you, if I could, to labour no longer in striving to cancel the obligations to marriage by the pretence of religion. The voice of heaven and the whispers of sound and uncorrupted reason are against it. It is will-worship in opposition to revelation. It is such a presumption for a creature against the author of our nature, as must draw down uncommon wrath upon the head of every mass-priest, who does not repent their preaching such wicked doctrine. Indeed I do not know any part of popery that can be called Christianity : but this in particular is so horrible and diabolical, that I can consider the preachers for celibacy in no other light than as so many devils. May you ponder in time on this horrible affair.

* Relation de l'Ambassade, dediée a Don Sebastien, roy de Portugal.

travelled in more frightful glens. And yet, we often came to plains and vales which had all the charms a paradise could have. Such is the nature of this country.

Through these scenes, an amazing mixture of the terrible and the beautiful, we proceeded from five in the morning till one in the afternoon, when we arrived at a vast waterfall, which descended from a precipice near two hundred yards high, into a deep lake, that emptied itself into a shallow fifty yards from the catadure, or fall, and went I suppose to the abyss. The land from this head-long river, for half a mile in length and breadth, till it ended at vast mountains again, was a fine piece of ground, beautifully flowered with various perennials, the acanthus, the aconus, the adonis, or pheasant's eye the purple bistorta, the blue borago, the yellow bupthalmum, the white cacalia, the blue campanula, and the sweet-smelling cassia, the pretty double daisy, the crimson dianthus, the white dictamnus, the red fruximella, and many other wild flowers. They make the green valley look charming ; and as here and there stood two or three ever-green trees, the cypress, the larix, the balm of Gilead, and the Swedish juniper, the whole spot has a fine and delightful effect. On my arrival here, I was at a loss which way to turn.

I could not however be long in suspense how to proceed, as I saw near the water-fall, a pretty thatched mansion, and several inhabitants in it. I found these were a religious society of married people, ten friars and their ten wives, who had agreed to retire to this still retreat, and form a holy house on the plan of the famous Ivon, the disciple of Labadie, so celebrated on account of his connection with Maria Schurman*, and his many fanatical writings.

*Maria Schurman, was born at Cologne, on the 5th of Nov. 1607, and died at Wieuweat in Friesland, on the 5th of May 1678, in the seventy-first year of her age. Jean le Labeurer in his *Histoire du Voyage de la Reyne de Pologne*, printed at Paris in 1648, speaking of her surprising endowments, says, " Elle respondet en Italien a Monsieur d'Orange, qui l'interrogeoit par ordre de la Regne, et elle argumenta tres-subtilement en Latin sur quelques points de theologie. Elle repartit aussi fort ellegamment en mesme langue, au compliment que je lui fis pour Madame la Mareschalle. Elle parla grec avec le Sieur Corrade premier medicin de la Regne. Enfin elle nous eust encore parlé d'autres langues si nous les eussions sçeuès ; car outre la Grecque, la Latine, la Francoise, l'Italienne, l'Espagnole, l'Allemande, et le Flaman, qui lui est naturel, elle a encore beaucoup de connoissance de l'Hebreu, Syriacque 'et Chaldaïque ; et il ne lui manque qu' un peu d'habitude pour les parler." Her writings entitled Opuscula Hebræa, Græca, Latina, were published by Frederic Spanheim, Professor of Divinity, in 1648, in 12mo. There are some admirable Latin letters on moral subjects in this book. Her epistle *de Vitæ Termino* to Berovicius, is a fine thing. See how she concludes : Unam tantum sollicitudinem nobis reliquit Deus, ut, quam nobis imposuit provinciam curemus sedulo ante rerum eventum ; post vero in hoc uno secure acquiescamus, quod ille sic voluit qui nisi optima velle non potest. Audiamus, obsecro, divinam illam Epicteti vocem : semper magis volo quod Deus vult, quam quod ego. Adjungar et adhærebo illi, velut minister et assecla : cum illo appeto, cum illo desidero, et simpliciter atque uno verbo quod Deus vult, volo. Hic unica Halcyonia curarum æstibus ; hic animorum per ancipitia fluctuantium statio tutissima : hic denique terminus in quo mente et calamo acquiesco. This is beautiful.

Her other work is called *Eukleria, or Bona Pars*, in allusion to Mary's chusing the better part. This is hard to be met with. It is one octavo in Latin, and though it be not without some vision, yet it is in the main a beautiful and solid performance. It is in the manner of Law's *Christian Perfection*. and has several sentiments resembling those of Madam Guion in her *Comment on the New Testament*, and Madam Bourignon, in her numerous works. It was

A book called the *Marriage Chretien*, written by this Ivon was
their directory, and from it they formed a protestant La Trappe ;

the famous Labadie, the fanatic, who brought Mrs. Schurman over to the interior life and
silent worship, in the forty-third year of her age, and from that time to her dying-day, she
renounced the world, and never went to public worship. The men of learning and worth
were no longer seen in crouds at her house, engaged with her in the noblest literary conversations ; for the advancement of truth and the sciences ; but in a solitude, purchased by herself, she moped away her remaining life in quietism, and holy reveries, and parting from reason
in religion, sunk into passive unions of nothing with nothing, and became the prey of cunning
and stupid religionists. Her house was always full of them. She would see no other company. The holy Labadie expired in her arms, aged sixty-four, in the year 1674 ; Mrs. Schurman being then sixty-seven. What a deplorable change was here, and owing to no reason
in religion. Adhere to reason I enjoin you, for whoever tells you, you must give it up in religion, is the son of darkness, and the truth is not in him.

Labadie, born Feb. 13, 1610, had been many years a Jesuit, then Jansenist, Carme Soli-
taire, Missionnaire, and Devot, and afterwards by the interest of the marquis de Favas, a protestant, was made minister of Montauban.

Bayle, Bernard, and Basnages, in the *Nouvelles de la Republique des Lettres*, tell a strange
story of this man, while he was minister at Montauban : that he had brought over a beautiful
young lady, Madamoiselle de Calonges, to the interior or spiritual life, and to make her perfect
in what they call ' la spiritualité et l'oraison mentale,' he told her she must be absolutely
alienated from all sensible objects in her meditations, and lost in the depths of reflection,
' dans le reveillement interieure.' To this purpose he gave her a point to meditate on, and
desired she would give it her whole application, as she sighed after Christian perfection. Miss
de Calonges began, and the director left her, under a ' detachement absolu ; ' but returned in
an hour or two to her chamber. He found her like contemplation on a monument ; her eyes
fixed, and her whole body, as if it were a petrefaction. Softly the holy man approached ;
strange pleasures filled his soul, as he gazed upon his heavenly disciple, and believing her
quite perfect, from her attitude, in the interior way, he gently put his pious hand upon her
lovely breast, and began to feel the finest tetons in the world. But as Mademoiselle de
Calonges was a woman of sense and virtue, she could not resign to this part of interior religion,
and started up in a passion, giving the director a pounce, and asking him what he meant by
such behaviour.

The minister replied, " sans étre déconcerté, et avec un air devot ; je vois bien ma fille, que
vous étes encore bien éloignée de la perfection reconnoissez, humblement vôtre foiblesse, et
demandez pardon a Dieu d'avoir été si peu attentive aux mysteres que vous deviez mediter
Si vous y aviez apporté tout l'attention nécessaire,vous ne vous fussiez pas apperçue de ce
qu'on faissoit à votre gorge. Mais vous étiez si peu détachée des sens si peu concentrée avec,
la divinite, que vous n'avez pas été un moment à reconnoitre que je vous touchois. Je voulois
éprouver si votre serveur dans l'oraison vous élevoit au dessu de la matiére et vous unissoit
au souverain etre, la vive source de l'immortalité et de la spiritualité, et je vois avec beaucou p
de douleur, que vos progres sont trés petits : vous n'allez que que terre à terre. Que ce la
vous donnez de la confusion, ma fille, et vous porte à mieux remplir les saints devoirs de la
priére mentale."

This speech, continue the historians, was so far from satisfying the beautiful Miss Calonges,
as she perceived the dreadful consequence of such doctrine, and knew it might be extended
to the most impure transactions, in order to be thoroughly concentered with the divinity,
that it enraged her as much as the action of Labadie, and she would never after have any
more to say to him. " Elle rompit entierement avec luy." Bayle says he will not warrant
the truth of this story, and Bernard tells us he has some doubt about it ; but Henry Basnage
in his *Histoire des Ouvrages des Savans*, assures us he had the account of this affair from the
mouth of Mademoiselle de Calonges : he says he heard her relate it several times, and that she
always spoke of the false and hypocritical devotion of Labadie with horror. But, notwithstanding all this, I have some doubts as to the veracity of Miss Calonges' relation, not that I
think such a behaviour has never been practised by a mystic, for there is a lady now living,
who was debauched by a mass-priest, while he was instructing her how to be perfect in the
interior life and abstraction. He first made a convert of her to popery, and then to raise
her to the tip-top saints, consolidated her soul to an impenetrable centre, and taught her to
pray in silence in the inward sanctuary, without any regard to what was outward ; the more
insensible, the more perfect. This continued for some time, and the confessor told her she
was in a fair way to the highest degree of perfection ; a little more absence from the body,
and she was quite glorious. In short, from touching the tip of her ear, as she sat like one
inanimate, he proceeded to the most illicit liberties. She thought him an angel of a man,
and was undone by the uncommon sanctity he wore, and the strong desire she had to be a
perfect mystic.

But as to Labadie, if he was the man Miss Calonges reported him, is it to be thought Mrs.
Schurman would have made him her nearest friend, and first minister in the management of

with this difference from the Catholic religious men, that the friars of the reformed monastery were to have wives in their con-

her house and religionists, and have travelled with him wherever he went. Beside, Mrs. Bourignon did not make this an objection against joining him and Mrs. Schurman. Among the many books written by Labadie, and by him published, there are some of them moral, and extremely pious : and more than this, Ivon was his principal disciple, and all I think allow he was one of the most pious of mortals, though a thorough visionary. He founded a society at Wiewert, which was another la Trappe. " Espéce d'Abbaye de la Trap dans le parti protestant, tres éloignée de l'esprit de mondanité, reformez dans leurs mœurs et dans leurs dogmes, says Bayle in his *Nouvelles* for November 1685. And the *Marriage Chretien* of Ivon, published immediately after the death of Labadie, is a piece of sanctification too severe I think for mortals. I imagine then, that in contempt of those mystics and visionaries, there may be some things overtold, and some stories received, that would bear mitigation, if all the circumstances relating to them were known. It is bad enough that there are mystics and visionaries in the world : and therefore, if I could, I had rather discover virtue amidst their intellectual immoralities, than have an opportunity of displaying imperfections in any of their hearts. As to Labadie, supposing the worst, and that as Henry Basnage, says, he began to feel the breasts of Miss Calonges, might not the attitude of the charming image, and the privacy of the place, be too much for the poor man, as they say she was a prodigious fine girl, and tempt him to commit an indiscretion he might be very sorry for after ? He was at that time a huge, strong, healthy he-mystic, and perhaps had a bottle of [generous in his stomach.

Madame Bourignon, whom I have mentioned, was separated from her earthly tabernacle the 20th of October, 1680, St. Vet. anno ; having lived sixty-four years, nine months and fourteen days. She died at Franeker, in West Friesland, and had suffered greatly in many persecutions. She had an extraordinary fine understanding, and would have been a valuable and useful creature, if she had not gone in to vision. There are however many admirable things in her works, which she published herself at several times, and to that purpose, had a printing house of her own, in the island of Nord-Strand in Holstein ; which island she purchased from Monsieur Cort, one of the fathers of the oratory. Her works were afterwards printed at Amsterdam, 1686, in nineteen volumes in 8vo. A presiding good sense appears every now and then in her writings, which kept her from sinking into the profundities, unions, and annihilations, of Labadie, whom she despised, though Mrs. Schurman was so fond of him. Labadie wanted her to come and live with him and Mrs. Schurman, and be one of the perfectionists in their retreat. He pressed her to it but she would have no connection with them. She told them their plan and economy were weak, and they had not the operation of the spirit in what they schemed and did. The two best books in this lady's works are, *The Light of the World*, and *Solid Virtue*. They have been translated into English ; but are not now to be found.

Madame Guion, another illustrious visionary died the 9th of June, 1717, at Blois, in the seventieth year of her age. Fenelon, archbishop of Cambray's troubles were all owing to this lady. She debauched his understanding with her splendid visions and notions of perfection and quiet, and to his last moment he had the most singular veneration for her, and thought her to be what our grand visionary, the reverend William Law, calls her in one of his pieces against Dr. Trapp, the ' enlight'ned Guion.' Notwithstanding the prelate made a public recantation, through fear, of his maxims of the saints, yet he was to his extreme unction, a thorough Guionist ; that is, by associating and concentering with the divinity, as Madame directed, he was all light, all eye, all spirit, all joy, all rest, all gladness, all love ; pure love. These are their terms. They rest in quietness, and are absorbed in silent spiritual pleasure, and inexpressible sweetness. Filled with a rapt'rous stillness, they sit the hours away at a royal banquet, and enjoy a divine repose in the sweet fellowship of the bridegroom. They even become sometimes like angels without bodies, so exceeding light and easy do they feel themselves with the body. Wretched delusion. It is all a wild, senseless fancy. It wants the beams of eternal and unalterable reason, and therefore can never be that useful, glorious piety, called Christianity ; can never be that heavenly religion which was promulgated by Jesus ; which consists in offering prayers with our lips, praising and giving thanks to the one true God the Father, at proper seasons ; and in reducing the principles of the gospel to practice ; by a righteousness of mind, and an active universal benevolence.

Madame Guion's works are twenty volumes of *Explications and Reflections on the Old and New Testament, concerning the Interior Life.* Five volumes of *Spirituel Cantiques* and *Emblems on Pure Love.* Two volumes of religious discourses. Four volumes of *Letters.* Her *Life* in three volumes. Three volumes of *Justifications in defence of herself against her persecutors.* And two volumes entitled *Opuscules.*

As to Fenelon, archbishop of Cambray, he was a great and beautiful genius, and his *Telemaque* cannot be enough admired : butythat bright genius he laid at the foot of mystery : His noble reason he would not use in religion, and therefore, in this article, was as poor a creature as any of the people. His maxims of the saints declare the weak visionary ; and

vent ; the better to enable them to obtain Christian perfection
in the religious life.   These regulars, men and women,were a most
industrious people, never idle ; but between their hours of prayer
always at work; the men were employed in a garden of ten acres,
to provide vegetables and fruit, on which they chiefly lived ; or in
cutting down old trees, and fitting them for their fire : and the
women were knitting, spinning, or twisting what they had spun
into thread, which they sold for three shillings a pound : they
were all together in a large, handsome room : they sat quite silent,
kept their eyes on their work, and seemed more attentive to some
inward meditations, than to any thing that appeared, or passed
by them.   They looked as if they were contented and happy.
They were all extremely handsome, and quite clean ; their linen
fine and white, and their gowns a black stuff.   The women dined
at one table, the men at another ; but all sat in the same room.
The whole house was in bed by ten, and up by four in the morning,
winter and summer.   What they said at their table I could not
hear, as they spoke low and little, and were at a distance from me,
in a large apartment : but the conversation of the men, at table,
was very agreeable, rational and improving.   I observed they had
a great many children, and kept four women-servants to attend
them, and do the work of the house.   The whole pleased me very
greatly.   I thought it a happy institution.

As to the marriage of the friars in this cloist'ral house, their
founder, Ivon, in my opinion, was quite right in this notion.
Chaste junction cannot have the least imperfection in it, as it is
the appointment of God, and the inclination to a coit is so strongly
impressed on the machine by the author of it ; and since it is
quite pure and perfect ; since it was wisely intended as the only
best expedient to keep man for ever innocent, it must certainly
be much better for a regular or retreating priest, to have a lawful
female companion with him ; and so the woman who chuses a
convent, and dislikes the fashions of the world, to have her good
and lawful monk every night in her arms ; to love and procreate
legally, when they have performed all the holy offices of the day ;
and then, from love and holy generation, return again to prayer,
and all the heavenly duties of the cloistered life ; than to live
against the institution of nature and providence, a burning,

his submitting them afterwards to the censure of the man of sin, called the sovereign pontiff,
renders his speculating religious character very despicable.   He was a thorough visionary;
and at the same time a thorough papist.   The letter he dictated for Lewis the XIVth's confessor, after he had received extreme unction, shews that no man ever had more at heart that
monstrous, and most audacious corruption of the Christian religion, called popery.   In his
expiring moments he conjures that bloody tyrant, the king of France, to order him a successor
that will, like him do every thing to oppose and suppress the Jansenists ; the only remaining
light within the vast black realms of papacy : Je prendrai la liberté de demander à sa majesté
deux graces, qui ne regardent, ni ma personne ni aucun de miens.   La prèmiere est que le
roi ait la bonté de me donner un successeur pieux, et régulier, bon et ferme contre le Jansen-
sme, lequel est prodigieusement accredité sur cette frontiére."

tortured nun, and a burning, tortured friar ; locked up in walls, they can never pass and under the government of some old, cross, impotent superior. There is some [sense in such a *Marriage Chretien* in a convent. Ivon's convent is well enough. A cloister may do upon his plan, with the dear creature by one's side, after the daily labours of the monk are over. It had been better, if that infallible man, the Pope, had come into this scheme. How confortable has Ivon made it to the human race, who renounce the dress and pageantry, and all the vanities of time. Their days are spent in piety and usefulness ; and at night, after the *completorium*, they lie down together in the most heavenly charity, and according to the first great hail, endeavour to increase and multiply. This is a divine life. I am for a cloister on these terms. It pleased me so much to see these monks march off with their smiling partners, after the last psalm, that I could not help wishing for a charmer there, that I might commence the Married Regular, and add to the stock of children in this holy house. It is really a fine thing to monk it on this plan. It is a divine institution, gentle and generous, useful and pious.

On the contrary, how cruel is the Roman Church, to make perfection consist in celibacy, and cause so many millions of men and women to live at an eternal distance from each other, without the least regard to the given points of contact ! How unfriendly to society ! This is abusing Christianity, and perverting it to most pernicious purposes ; under a pretence of raising piety, by giving more time and leisure for devotion. For it never can be pious either in design or practice, to cancel any moral obligation, or to make void any command of God : and as to prayer, it may go along with every other duty, and be performed in every state. All states have their intermissions ; and if it should be otherwise sometimes, I can then, while discharging any duty, or performing any office, pray as well in my heart, O God be merciful to me a sinner, and bless me with the blessing of thy grace and providence, as if I was prostrate before an altar. What Martha was reproved for, was on account of her being too solicitous about the things of this life. Where this is not the case, business and the world are far from being a hindrance to piety. God is as really glorified in the discharge of relative duties, as in the discharge of those which more immediately relate to himself. He is in truth more actively glorified by our discharging well the relative duties, and we thereby may become more extensively useful in the church and in the world, may be more public blessings, than it is possible to be in a single pious state. In short, this one thing, celibacy, were there nothing else, the making the unmarried state a more holy state than marriage, shews the prodigious nonsense and impiety of the Church of Rome, and is reason enough to flee that communion, if we had no other reasons for protesting against it.   The tenet is so superstitious and dangerous, that it may well be esteemed a doctrine of those devils, who are the seducers and destroyers of mankind; but it is, says Wallace, in his *Dissertation on the Numbers of Manhood*, suitable to the views and designs of a church, which has discovered such an enormous ambition, and made such havock of the human race, in order to raise, establish, and preserve an usurped and tyrannical power.

But as to the Married Regulars I have mentioned ; they were very glad to see me, and entertained me with great civility and goodness.   I lived a week with them, and was not only well fed with vegetables and puddings on their lean days, Wednesdays and Fridays, and with plain meat, and good malt drink, on the other days ; but was greatly delighted with their manner and piety, their sense and knowledge.   I will give my pious readers a sample of their prayers, as I imagine it may be to edification.   These friars officiate in their turns, changing every day ; and the morning and evening prayers of one of them, were in the words following.   I took them off in my shorthand.

A PRAYER FOR MORNING.

" Almighty and everlasting God, the creator and preserver of all things, our law-giver, saviour, and judge, we adore thee, the author of our beings, and the father of our spirits.   We present ourselves, our acknowledgments, and our homage, at the foot of thy throne, and yield thee the thanks of the most grateful hearts for all the instances of thy favour which we have experienced.   We thank thee for ever, O Lord God Almighty, for all thy mercies and blessing vouchsafed us ; for defending us the past night from evil, and for that kind provision which thou hast made for our comfortable subsistence in this world.

" But above all, most glorious *E*ternal, adored be thy goodness, for repeating and reinforcing the laws and the religion of thy creation, by supernatural revelation, and for giving us that reason of mind, which unites us to thee, and makes us implore thy communications of righteousness, to create us again unto good works in Christ Jesus.

" We confess, O Lord, that we have done violence to our principles, and alienated ourselves from the natural use we were fitted for : we have revolted from thee into a state of sin, and by the operation of sense and passion, have been moved to such practices as are exorbitant and irregular : but we are heartily sorry for all our misdoings : to thee in Christ we now make our address, and beseech thee to inform our understandings, and refine our spirits, that we may reform our lives by repentence, redeem our time by righteousness, and live as the glorious gospel of thy Son requires. Let the divine spirit assist and enable us to over-rule, conduct, and employ, the subordinate and inferior powers, in the exercise of

virtue, and the service of our Creator, and as far as the imperfections of our present state will admit, help us so to live by the
measures and laws of heaven, that we may have the humility and
meekness, the mortification and self-denial of the holy Jesus, his
love of thee, his desire of doing thy will, and seeking only thy
honour.   Let us not come covered before thee under a form of
godliness, a cloke of creeds, observances and institutions of
religion ; but with that inward salvation and vital sanctity, which
renounces the spirit, wisdom, and honours of this world, dethrones
self-love and pride, subdues sensuality and covetousness, and
opens a kingdom of heaven within by the spirit of God.   O let
thy Christ be our Saviour in this world, and before we die, make
us fit to live for ever with thee in the regions of purity and perfection.

"Since it is the peculiar privilege of our nature, through
thy mercy and goodness, that we are made for an eternal entertainment in those glorious mansions, where the blessed society of
saints and angels shall keep an everlasting sabbath, and adore and
glorify thee for ever, let thy inspiring spirit raise our apprehensions and desires above all things that are here below, and
alienate our minds from the customs and principles of this mad,
degenerate, and apostate world : mind us of the shortness and
uncertainty of time, of the boundless duration, and the vast
importance of eternity, and so enable us to imitate the example
of the holy Jesus in this world, that we may hereafter ascend,
with the greatest ardour of divine love, to those realms of holiness,
where our hearts will be filled with raptures of gladness and joy,
and we shall remain in the highest glory for ever and ever.

"We live, O Lord, in reconciliation and friendship, in love and
good will, with thy whole creation, with every thing that derives from thee, holds of thee, is owned by thee ; and under the
power of this affection, we pray for all mankind ; that they may
be partakers of all the blessings which we enjoy or want, and that
we may all be happy in the world to come, and glorify thee
together in eternity.   To this end bring all the human race to the
knowledge of thy glorious gospel, and let its influence transform them into the likeness of Christ.

"But especially, we pray for all who suffer for truth and
righteousness sake, and beseech thee to prosper those that love
thee.   Defend, O Lord, the just rights and liberties of mankind,
and rescue thy religion from the corruptions which have been
introduced upon it, by length of time, and by decay of piety.
Infatuate the counsels, and frustrate the endeavours of the priests
of Rome, and against all the designs of those, who are enemies
to the purity of the gcspel, and substitute human inventions in
the place of revealed religion ; prosper the pious labours of those
who teach mankind to worship one eternal and omnipresent

being : in whose understanding, there is the perfection of wisdom ; in whose will, there is the perfection of goodness ; in whose actions, there is the perfection of power ; a God without cause, the great creator, benefactor, and saviour of men :—And that the duty of man is to obey, in thought, word, and deed, the precepts of godliness and righteousness, without regard to pleasure, gain, or honour : to pain, loss, or disgrace ; diligently imitating the life of the holy Jesus, and stedfastly confiding in his mediation.

" In the last place, O Lord God Almighty, we beseech thee to continue us under thy protection, guidance, and blessing this day, as the followers and disciples of thy Christ, through whom we recommend our souls and our bodies into thy hands, and according to the doctrine of his religion, say, Our Father, &c."

In this manner, did these pious Ivonites begin their every day ; and when the sun was set, and they had finished their supper, they worshipped God again in these words.

A PRAYER FOR NIGHT.

" Most blessed, glorious, and holy Lord God Almighty, who art from everlasting to everlasting, God over all, magnified and adored for ever ! we, thy unworthy creatures, humble our souls in thy presence, and confess ourselves miserable sinners. We acknowledge our miscarriages and faults, and condemn ourselves for having done amiss. We deprecate thy just offence and displeasure. We cry thee mercy. We ask thee pardon : and as we are quite sensible of our weakness and inability, and know thou lovest the souls of men, when they turn and repent, we beseech thee to give us true repentance, and endue us with the grace of thy sanctifying spirit, that we may be delivered from the bondage and slavery of iniquity, and have the law of the spirit of life which is in Christ Jesus. Upon thee our God, we call for that help which is never wanting, and beseech thee to give us thy heavenly assistance, that we may recover our reasonable nature, refine our spirits by goodness, and purify ourselves even as the Lord Jesus is pure. O thou Father of Lights, and the God of all comforts, inform our understandings, with truth, and give us one ray of that divine wisdom which sitteth on the right hand of thy throne. O let us be always under thy communication and influence, and enable us, through the recommendation of thy Son, our mediator and redeemer, to lay aside all passion, prejudice, and vice, to receive thy truth in the love of it, and to serve thee with ingenuity of mind, and freedom of spirit : that we may pass through a religious life to a blessed immortality, and come to that eternal rest ; where we shall behold thy face in righteousness, and adore and bless thee to eternity, for our salvation through him who hath redeemed us by his blood.

" We praise and magnify thy goodness, O Lord God Almighty, for our maintenance and preservation, by thy constant providence over us, and we beseech thee to take us into thy special care and protection this night. Defend us from all the powers of darkness, and from evil men and evil things and raise us in health and safety. Do thou, most great and good God, protect us and bless us this night, and when we awake in the morning, let our hearts be with thee, and thy hand with us. And the same mercies we beg for all mankind ; that thy goodness and power may preserve them, and thy direction and influence secure their eternal salvation, through Jesus Christ our Lord, by whom thou hast taught us to call upon thee as our Father, &c."

By the way, I cannot help observing, that these disciples of Ivon are much reformed in respect of what his cloistered followers were in his time. It appears from Ivon's books, that he was as great a visionary and tritheist as his master Labadie, or any of our modern mystics now are. But these Regulars I found among the fells, though on Ivon's plan, are as rational Christians as ever adorned the religion of our Master by a purity of faith. You see by their prayers, that their devotions are quite reasonable and calm. There is no rant, nor words without meaning, no feeling instead of seeing the truth ; nor expectation of covenant mercy on the belief of a point repugnant not only to the reason and nature of things, but to the plain repeated declarations of God in the Christian religion. Their prayer is a calm address to the great Maker, Governor, and Benefactor of the universe ; and honour and obedience to Christ as Mediator, according to the will and appointment of God the Father.

Upon my asking one of these gentlemen, how they came to differ so much from Ivon, their founder, and cease to be the patrons of vision, and an implicit incomprehensible faith ? He told me, they had read all the books on both sides of the question, that had been written of late years, and could not resist the force of the evidence in favour of reason and the divine unity. They saw it go against mechanical impulse, and strong persuasion without grounds, and therefore they dismissed Ivon's notions of believing without ideas, as they became sensible it was the same thing as seeing without light or objects. Without dealing any longer in a mist of words, or shewing themselves orthodox, by empty, insignificant sounds, they resolved that the object of their worship, for the time to come, should be, that one supreme self-existent being, of absolute, infinite perfection, who is the first cause of all things, and whose numerical identity and infinite perfections are demonstrable from certain principles of reason, antecedent to any peculiar revelation ; and confessed that the blessing, with which Jesus Christ was sent by God to bless the world, consists in turning men from their iniquities. They now perceived what the creed-makers, and Ivon, their founder, could not see, to wit, that it is against the sacred texts to ascribe to Each Person of Three the nature and all essential attributes and properties of the One only true God, and yet make the Three the One true God only, when considered conjunctly ; for if Each has all possible perfections and attributes, then each must be the same true God as if and when conjoined ; and of consequence, there must then be Three One true Gods, or One Three true Gods ; Three One Supreme Beings, or One Three Supreme Beings, since to each of the three must be ascribed, as the orthodox say, any thing and every thing, that is most peculiar and appropriated to the divine nature, without any difference. In short by conjobbling matters of faith in this manner, they saw we had three distinct selfs, or intelligent agents, equal in power and all possible perfections, agreeing in one common essence, one sort of species, like a supreme magistracy of distinct persons, acting by a joint exercise of the same power, and so the three are one, not by a numerical but specific identity : three Omnipotents and one Almighty, in a collective sense. This, continued the gentleman on searching the scriptures, we found was far from being the truth of the case. We discovered, upon a fair examination, and laying aside our old prejudices, that there was nothing like this in the New Testament. It appeared to us to be the confused talk of weak heads. In the Bible we got a just idea of one Eternal Cause, God the Father, almighty, all-wise, unchangeable, infinite ; and are there taught how to worship and serve him. The greatest care is there taken to guard against the ill effects of imagination and superstition ; and in the plainest language, we are ordered to pray to this blessed and only potentate, the King of kings, and Lord of lords, who only, or alone hath immortality ; and this in imitation of Jesus, who in the morning very early went out into a solitary place, and there prayed.* Who dismissing his disciples departed into a mountain to pray.† And he continued all night in prayer to GOD. ‡ We are ordered to glorify and bless this only wise God for ever.§ Blessed be the God and Father of our Lord Jesus Christ.‖ To God and our Father be glory for ever.¶ And to love him truly by keeping the commandments.** Cui Jesus sic respondit : primum omnium præceptorum est ; audi Israelita. Dominus Deus vester dominus unus est. Itaque dominum Deum tuum toto corde, toto animo, tota mente, totisque viribus amato. Hoc primum est præceptum. Hear, O Israel, the Lord our God is one Lord. And thou shalt love the Lord thy God with all thy heart, and with all thy soul, and with all thy strength. This is the first commandment.

* *Mark*, ch. i. v. 35. † *Mark*, ch. vi. v. 46. ‡ *Luke*, ch. vi. v. 12. § *Romans* ch. xvi. v. 27. ‖ *2 Cor.* ch. i. v. 3. ¶ *Phil.* ch. iv. v. 20. ** *Mark*, ch xii. v. 29. 30, 31.

·Et voici le second. Vous aimerez vostre prochain comme vous même. And the second is like the first. Hunc simile est alterum, alterum ut teipsum amato. His majus aliud præceptum nullum est. Thou shalt love thy neighbour as thy self. There is none other commandment greater than these.

To say it ; we became fully satisfied, that the supreme God and governor of the world, who exists by a prior necessity, and therefore must be one, a perfect moral agent, and possessed of all moral perfections, is the sole object of religious worship : that Jesus Christ was a temporary minister, with a legatarian power, to publish and declare the spiritual laws of this great God : and that it is incumbent on mankind to yield a perfect obedience to these spiritual laws of this Supreme Being : that is, the duty of all, to make the object proposed by Christ, his God and our God, his Father and our Father, the sole object of faith ; and to expect happiness or salvation, on the term of being turned from all our iniquities. This seemed a matter worthy of the Son of God's appearing in the world. Every thing else must be enthusiasm and usurpation.

Here the Ivonist had done, and I was greatly pleased with his sense and piety. "What a heavenly Christianity should we profess," I said, " if the notions of our modern enthusiasts were as consistent with Christ's great design and profession ! We should then set up the Kingdom of God among men, and be diligent and active in promoting the laws of that kingdom. We should then believe, like Jesus Christ and his apostles, that there is but one God, the Father Almighty. There is no one good, so commonly called, but one, that is God ; or only the one God.* Nullus est bonus nisi unus Deus. *Castalio.* And *Cant. MS. Clem. Alex.* adds, My Father who is in Heaven. This is life eternal, to acknowledge thee, O Father, to be the only true God.† It is one God who will justify.‡ We know that there is none other God but one. For to us there is one GOD the Father.§ There is one GOD and Father of all, who is over all, and through all, and in you all.‖ And we should confess one Mediator,— the man Christ Jesus.¶ We should be consistent, and not throw off those principles upon which Christianity was founded, and alone could be first built. We should invite men into our religion, by representing to them the perfection of that primary law of God, reason or natural religion ; by declaring the plainness and clearness of it to all attentive and well-disposed minds ; and then shew them how worthy it was of the Supreme Governor to give such creatures as he has made us the gospel ; that by the religion of favour, he has, with glory to himself, displayed his paternal

---

* *Mark,* ch. x. v. 18.   † *John,* ch. xvii. throughout.
‡ *Romans,* ch. iii. v. 30.   § 1 *Cor.* ch. viii. v. 4–6.
‖ *Eph.* ch. v. v. 6.   ¶ 2 *Tim.* ch. ii. v. 5.

K

regard for us, by doing much more than what is strictly necessary for our eternal good.   God, on a principle of love, sends his Christ, to advise us and awaken us to a sense of our danger in passing through this world, in case, which he saw would be the thing, we should not constantly attend to the light we might strike out, ourselves with some trouble.   He calls us in an extraordinary manner to forsake vice and idolatry, and practise the whole system of morality.   We might expect, that a good God, would once at least, interpose by such an extraordinary method as revelation, to turn and incline his reasonable creatures, to the study and practice of the religion of nature.   This was acting like the Father of the universe, considering the negligence and corruption of the bulk of mankind.   The reason he gave us, the law of nature, was giving us all that was absolutely necessary.   The gospel was an addition of what is excellently useful.   What, my beloved, might a rational divine say, can be more paternal, and worthy of the Almighty Creator, than to reveal plainly the motive of a judgment to come, in order to secure all obedience to the religion of nature ?   Reason may, to be sure, be sufficient to shew men their duty and to encourage their performance of it with the assurance of obtaining a reward, if they would duly attend to its dictates, and suffer them to have their due effect upon them : it may guide mankind to virtue, and happiness consequent to it, as God must be a rewarder of all those who diligently seek him, and was enough to bring them to the knowledge, and engage them in the practice of true religion and righteousness, if they had not shut their eyes to its light, and wilfully rejected the rule written in their hearts.   But as this was what mankind really did, and now do ; as errors and impieties, owing to an undue use or neglect of reason, became universal ; just as the case of Christians is, by disregarding the New Testament ; and reason, through men's faults, was rendered ineffectual, though still sufficient, which justifies both the wisdom and goodness of God, in leaving man for so many ages to his natural will, and so great a part of the globe to this day with no other light than the law of nature ; and reason, I say, was rendered ineffectual, though still sufficient to teach men to worship God with pious hearts and sincere affections, and to do his will by the practice of moral duties ; to expect his favour for their good deeds, and his condemnation of their evil works ; then was revelation a more powerful means of promoting true religion and godliness.   The gospel is a more effectual light. It is a clearer and more powerful guide ; a brighter motive and stronger obligation to universal obedience than reason can with certainty propose.   And therefore, though there was not a necessity for God to give new rule in vindication of his providence, and in order to render men accountable to him for their actions ; yet the divine goodness was pleased to enforce the principles of reason and morality more powerfully by an express sanction of future rewards and punishments, and by the gospel restore religious worship to the original uncorrupted rational service of the Deity. This displays his paternal regard to his children, with glory to himself. Love was the moving principle of his sending Christ into the world, to reform the corruptions of reason to restore it to its purity, and most effectually to promote the practice of the rules of it. The gospel revelation considered in this manner appears to be the pure effect of the divine goodness. It is a conduct accompanied with the greatest propriety and glory.

If this representation of Christianity was as much the doctrine of the church as it is of the Ivonites I have mentioned, we might then, with hopes of success, call upon the rational infidels to come in. They could hardly refuse the invitation, when we told them, our religion was the eternal law of reason and of God restored, with a few excellently useful additions : that the gospel makes the very religion of nature, a main part of what it requires, and submits all that it reveals to the test of the law of reason : that the splendor of God's original light, the light of nature, and the revelation of Jesus, are the same ; both made to deliver mankind from evils and madness of superstition, and make their religion worthy of God, and worthy of men ; to enable them by the voice of reason in conjunction with the words of the gospel, to worship One God the Maker, the Governor, the Judge of the world ; and to practise all that is good and praise-worthy : that we may be blessed as we turn from iniquity to virtue ; and by entering cordially into the spirit of the meritorious example or exemplary merits of Christ, be determined to be dead to sin, and alive to righteousness : in short, my brethren, in the suffering and death of Jesus, his patient, pious, and meek, his benevolent and compassionate behaviour, under the most shocking insult, indignity, and torture, we have what we could not learn from the religion of nature, a deportment that well deserves both our admiration and imitation. We learn from the perfect example of Jesus, recommended in his gospel, to bear patiently ill usage, and to desire the welfare of our most unreasonable and malicious enemies. This is improving by religion to the best purpose ; and as we resemble the Son of God, the man Christ Jesus, in patience, piety, and benevolence, we become the approved children of the Most High, who is kind and good to the unthankful and to the evil. In this view of the gospel, all is fine, reasonable, and heavenly. The gentile can have nothing to object. We have the religion of nature in its original perfection, in the doctrine of the New Testament, enforced by pains and pleasures everlasting ; and we learn from the death of the Mediator, not only an unprecedented patience, in bearing our sins in his own body on the tree : but the divine compassion and piety with which he bore them.   We have in this the noblest example to follow, whenever called to suffer for well-doing or for righteousness-sake ; and by the imitation, we manifest such a command of temper and spirit, as can only be the result of the greatest piety and virtue.   This added to keeping the commandments must render men the blessed of the Father, and entitle them to the kingdom prepared for the wise, the honest, and the excellent.

But alas, I instead of giving such an account of Christianity, the cry of the doctors is, for the most part, Discard reason, and prostrate your understanding before the adorable mysteries.   Instead of a Supreme Independent First Cause of all things to believe in and worship, they give Three true Gods in number, Three infinite independent Beings, to be called One, as agreeing in one common abstract essence, or species ; as all mankind are one, in one common rational nature, or abstract idea of humanity.   Amazing account !   A triune no infidel or gentile of sense will ever worship.

Instead of fixing salvation or moral rectitude, and our preferring the will of God, as delineated in the words of the gospel, before all other considerations, we are told of an innocent, meritorious, propitiating blood, spilt by wicked hands, and so made an acceptable sacrifice, to a Being who is of purer eyes than to behold iniquity.   This, we are assured, satisfies all the demands of the law.   Here is infinite satisfaction, and most certainly, I add, a cool indifference as to personal rectitude.   When such a faith or credulity becomes the principal pillar of trust and dependance, then mere reliance on such satisfaction to divine justice, may be a stupefying opiate, and make many remiss in the labours of a penitential piety, and that exact rectitude of mind and life, which even reason requires, to render us acceptable to the Deity.   Many an appetite and passion are indulged under this subterfuge ; and with little fervency or zeal for good works, men expect to partake of the heavenly joys, by trusting to the merits of their Saviour, in their last will and testament.   Deplorable case ! Alas I how has Christianity suffered by its doctors I   The infidel laughs at it as thus preached.   It becomes a by-word, and a hissing to them that pass by.

As to the library of my friends, the Ivonites, it was far from being a grand one, but I saw many curious books in it which had not come in my way before.   From them I made several extracts, and to gratify my reader's curiosity a little, I will here favour him with one of them.

The first book I chanced to open in this library, was the second volume of Severin Bini's* edition of the Councils printed at

* Severin Bini, or Binius, as he is commonly called, born in 1543, was a doctor of divinity at Cologne, in the circle of the Lower Rhine in Germany, and canon of that archiepiscopal cathedral.   He published in that city, in the year 1606, an elegant edition of all the *Councils*

Paris, in 1630 ; and over-against a very remarkable passage from Cyril, p. 548, I found several written leaves, bound up in the volume, and these leaves referred to by an asterisk. The passage I call remarkable, is part of a homily pronounced by the Alex-

in four very large volumes, folio, and by this work, made the editions or collections of Uerlin, Peter Crabb, and Lawrence Surius, of no value, but the second edition published by James Binius in the year 1618, in nine volumes smaller folio, is far preferable to the first, and the Paris edition printed in 1638, in ten large volumes, folio, is further enlarged, more correct, and of consequence still better than the second edition of 1618. This is not however the best edition to buy, if you love to read that theological stuff called *Councils.* The Louvre edition of 1644, in thirty-seven volumes, folio, is what you should purchase ; or, that of 1672, printed at Paris, by the Jesuits Labbé and Cossart, in eighteen large volumes in folio. I prefer this last, on account of the additions, correctness, and beauty of the impression. Père Hardouin likewise printed a later edition of the *Councils,* with explications and free remarks, an extraordinary and curious work I have been told ; but I could not even see it in France, as the parliament of Paris had ordered the work to be suppressed, on account of the remarks. Binius died in 1620, æt. 77.

James Merlin, the first editor of the *Councils,* was a doctor of divinity, and chanoine of Notre-dame de Paris. Besides the *Councils,* in two large volumes folio ; he published the works of Durand de St. Pourçain, in 1515 ; the works of Richard de St. Victor, in 1518 ; and the works of Peter de Blois, in 1519. His *Defence of Origen,* in 4to, a good thing ; and *Six Homilies on Gabriel's being sent to the Virgin Mary,* in 8vo ; which homilies are not worth half a farthing, are all that may be considered his. Merlin, born in 1472, died in 1541, æt. 69.

Peter Crabb, the second editor of the councils, born in 1470, was a Franciscan friar, He published two volumes of the *Councils,* in folio, at Cologne, in 1538 ; and a third volume in 1550.—He died in 1553, æt. 83.

Lawrence Surius, the third editor of the *Councils,* born in 1522 ; a monk of the Chartreux, published his edition of them, in four large volumes in folio, in 1560 ; and a few years after printed his *Lives of the Saints,* in six volumes. He wrote likewise a short *History of his own Time :* and *An Apology for the Massacre of St. Bartholomew.* He was the most outrageous, abusive bigot that ever wrote against the Protestants. The great men of his own church despised him, and Cardinal Perron, in particular, calls him *bête* and *l'ignorant.* He died in 1578, æt. 56.

Philip Labbé, the Jesuit, born in 1607 ; the fifth editor, and next after Binius ; lived only to publish 11 volumes of the *Councils,* the eleventh came out the year he died ; the other seven were done by Cossart. Labbé was a man of learning, and besides his collection of *Councils,* wrote several other pieces. The best of them are *Bibliotheca Bibliothecarum ; Concordia Cronologica ; Bellarmini Philologica ;* and the *Life of Galen.* He died in 1667, æt. 60.

Gabriel Cossart, the continuator, who published the other seven volumes in 1672, died at Paris, the 18th of December, 1674, æt. 59.

Richard de St.Victor, whose works were published by Merlin, at Paris, in 1518, was a Scotchman, and prior of the abbey of St. Victor in Paris. He was the author of *Three Critical and Historical Dissertations on the Tabernacle ; Two on the Temple ; Three on the Harmony of the Chronology of the Kings of Judea and Israel ; Commentaries on the Psalms, Canticles, the Epistles of St. Paul, and the Revelation :* as also of some Treatises in Divinity ; and several Disquisitions relating to Spiritual Life. There have been four editions of these pieces, and the best of them is that printed at Rouen in 1650, in two volumes, by Father John de Toulouse, who wrote the life of Father Richard, and added it to his edition. The three other editions are those of Paris, in 1518 ; of Venice, in 1592, and of Cologne, in 1621. Richard de Victor has been highly commended by several celebrated writers, particularly by Henry de Grand, Trithemius, Bellarmine, and Sixte de Sienne. There are many curious and fine things in his writings, it must be allowed ; but in general, he is too subtil, too diffuse, and too full of digressions. His commentaries, for the most part, are weak, and evince that he did not understand St. Paul. He died 10th March, 1173, æt. 91 ; and, for the twelfth century, was an extraordinary man.

But who was St. Victor, to whom the abbey of Chanoines Reguliers in Paris, and the greater abbaye of Chanoines in Marseilles, are dedicated ? He was a Frenchman, who fought under the Emperors Dioclesian and Maximilian with great applause, in the most honourable post, but in the year 302, suffered martyrdom for refusing to sacrifice to the idols. He was executed on the spot where the abbey of St. Victor in Marseilles now stands, and there they have his reliques, ‘ a la reserve du pié,’ that is, except his foot, which lies in the Abbaye St. Victor de Paris. William Grimaud, abbot of St. Victor de Marseille, on his being made Pope, under the title of Urban V. in 1362, took the foot of St. Victor from his abbey, when he left it, and made a present of it to John, Duke of Berry, one of the sons of John I, King of France, who was taken prisoner by Edward the Black Prince, in the battle of Poitiers, Sept. 19, 1356 ; and this duke of Berry gave the inestimable foot to the monks of St. Victor in Paris. There it remains to this day ; and though so small a part of the blessed Victor, sheds immense benefits on the pious Catholics who adore it. Happy Catholics !

andrian Patriarch before the council of Ephesus on St. John's day, in a church dedicated to his name. In rehearsing his discourse

As to Peter de Blois, he was archdeacon of Bath, in the reign of Henry the second, and died in London, in the year 1200, æt. 71. His works comprise one hundred and eighty-three letters on various subjects, twenty sermons, and seventeen tracts of several kinds; they were first printed at Mayence in 1500, then by Merlin at Paris, in 1519, as before mentioned; and afterwards, John Busée the jesuit, gave an edition of them in 1600, which is far preferable to that edited by Merlin. But the most valuable edition is that of Peter de Goussainville, printed at Paris, in 1667, in folio; to this edition is prefixed the life of Peter de Blois, and very learned remarks on his writings, and the subjects he wrote on, are added, by Goussainville. De Blois' works contain many excellent things, and his life is a curious piece. Some of his notions relating to the scriptures are very good, and he writes well against vice. He is a good author for the age he lived in. His letters are well worth reading, especially such of them as relate to his own time. King Henry II. ordered him to make a collection of them for his royal use.

Durand de St. Pourçain, bishop of Meaux, in 1326, died the 13th of September, 1333, in the 89th year of his age. His works are, *Liber de Origine jurisdictionum*, a learned piece; and *Commentaries on the Four Books of Sentences*. The book called the *Sentences*, was written by the famous Peter Lombard, bishop of Paris, who died in the year 1164, æt. 82. In the *Sentences*, one of the propositions argued on is this : Christus secundum quod est homo, non est aliquod. Some call these *Sentences* excellent, which is what I cannot think them; but in Durand's *Commentary* on them, there are several excellent things.

As to the jesuit, Jean Busée, who published the third edition of the works of Peter de Blois; he was the author of many books not worth mentioning, and died at Mayence, 30th of May 1611, aged 64.

The learned Goussainville who printed the last edition of De Blois, with notes, died in the year 1683, extremely poor and miserable. He likewise published the works of Pope Gregory with many valuable remarks and notes. There are four editions of this pope's works; that by Tussiniani, bishop of Venice, by order of Pope Sixtus the Vth; the Paris edition of 1640; Goussainville's edition; and the Benedictine edition; but Goussainville's is, in my opinion, the most valuable.

The *Sermons* in the first and second editions of Peter de Blois' works are not his, but by Peter Comestor. De Blois' sermons are only to be found in Goussainville's edition of this archdeacon's works. Peter Comestor was a regular canon of St. Victor's in Paris, and died in the year 1198, æt. 65. Besides the sermons published by mistake as the work of De Blois, he wrote a large *Scholastic History*, which comprehends the sacred history from Genesis to the end of the Acts. This is reckoned a good thing, and has been abridged by one Hunter, an Englishman.

But as to *Councils*, we have the following account of the eighteen general ones in the Vatican library, and are told, that the several inscriptions affixed to them were made by pope Sixtus V.; the famous Felix Peretti, who was born the 13th of December, 1521, and died the 27th of August, 1590, in the 69th year of his age.

The first Council, which is that of Nice in 325. St. Sylvester being pope, and Constantine the great emperor, Jesus Christ the Son of God is declared consubstantial with his Father; the impiety of Arius is condemned; and the emperor, in obedience to a decree of the council, ordered all the books of the Arians to be burnt.

The second Council, which is that of Constantinople in 381. The holy Damascus being pope and Theodosius the elder emperor, the divinity of the Holy Ghost is defended against the impious Macedonius, and his false doctrine is anathematized.

The third Council, which is that of Ephesus in 431, St. Celestin being pope, and Theodosius the younger emperor; Nestorius, who divided Jesus Christ into two persons, is condemned, and the Holy Virgin is decreed to be the mother of God.

The fourth Council, which is that of Chalcedonia in 451. St. Leo being pope, and Marcian emperor, the unhappy Eutychius is anathematized for maintaining that Jesus Christ had but one nature.

The fifth Council, which is the second of Constantinople in 553. Vigilius being pope, and Justinian emperor, the debates relating to the doctrine of Theodore, bishop of Mopsueste; Ibas, bishop of Edessa, and Theodoret, bishop of Cyr, are suppressed, and the errors of Origen are separated from the holy doctrine.

The sixth Council, which is the third of Constantinople in 680. St. Agatho being pope, and Constantine Pagonatus emperor, the heretics called Monothelites, who admitted but one will in Jesus Christ, are condemned.

The seventh Council, which is the second of Nice in 784. Adrian being pope and Constantine, the son of Irene, being emperor, the impiety of the image-breakers is condemned, and the worship of the holy images is established in the church.

The eighth Council, which is the fourth of Constantinople in 689. Adrian II. being pope, and Basil emperor. Ignatius, patriarch of Constantinople, is re-established in his see, and Photius, the usurper, is with ignominy driven away.

to the Holy Fathers, the Saint cites *Heb.* ch. 1. v. 6, and then addresses himself to the apostle. Ὅταν δὲ πάλιν εἰσαγάγῃ τὸν πρωτότοκον εἰς τὴν οἰκουμένην, λέγει, καὶ προσκυνησάτωσαν αὐτῷ πάντες Ἄγγελοι Θεοῦ. "When he bringeth in the first-begotten into the world, he saith, Let all the angels of God worship him." Μυσταγώγεσον Εὐαγγελιστὰ, εἰπὲ αἱ νῦν, ὦ Μακάριε

The ninth Council, which is the first of Lateran in 1122.

The tenth Council, which is the second of Lateran in 1169. The canons of these two councils are wanting, and they have no inscription in the Vatican.

The eleventh Council, which is the third of Lateran in 1179. Alexander III. being pope and Frederick I. emperor ; the errors of the Vaudois are condemned.

The twelfth Council, which is the fourth of Lateran in 1215. Innocent III. being pope, and Frederick II. emperor ; the false opinions of the abbot Joachim are condemned ; the holy war, for the recovery of Jerusalem, is resolved, and the Croisades are appointed among Christians.

The thirteenth Council, which is the first of Lyons in 1245. Under the pontificate of Innocent IV., the emperor Frederick is declared an enemy to the church, and deprived of the empire ; they deliberate on the recovery of the Holy Land ; St. Lewis, King of France, is declared chief of that expedition. The cardinals are honoured with red hats.

The fourteenth Council, which is the second of Lyons in 1274. Gregory X., being sovereign pontiff, the Greeks are reunited to the church of Rome ; St. Bonaventure does signal service to the church in this council ; friar Jerome brings the king of the Tartars to the council and that prince receives, in the most solemn manner, the blessed water of baptism.

The fifteenth Council, which is that of Vienne in 1311. Under the pontificate of Clement V., the Decretals, called the Clementines from the name of this pope, are received and published ; the procession of the holy sacrament is instituted throughout Christendom ; and professors of the oriental languages are established in the four most famous universities in Europe, for the propagation of the Christian faith in the Levant.

The sixteenth Council, which is that of Florence in 1439. The Greeks, the Armenians, and the Ethiopians, are reunited to the catholic church, under the pontificate of Eugene IV.

The seventeenth Council, which is the fifth of Lateran, began in the year 1517. They declared war against the Turks, who had seized the island of Cyprus, and possessed themselves of Egypt, on the death of the sultan : the emperor Maximilian, and Francis I., king of France, are appointed generals of this war, under the popes Julius II. and Leo X.

The eighteenth Council, which is that of Trent, the last of the œcumenical or general councils ; held from the year 1545 to the year 1563. Paul III. Julius III. and Pius V. reigning at Rome, the Lutherans and other heretics are condemned, and the ancient discipline of the church is re-established in her exact and regular practice.

These, reader, are the eighteen famous General Councils ; and if you will turn to the third volume of a work, called *Notes relating to Men, and Things, and Books,* you will find my observations on them ; my remarks on the popes, the princes, and the fathers, assembled ; their unchristian immoralities, and sad acts against the laws of Christ, in order to establish for ever, that very senseless, and very wicked religion, called Popery ; which is, a composition of sin and error so base and abominable, that we might expect such a thing from the devil ; but it is impossible it could come from heavenly-inspired fathers. In that book you will find many thoughts on the religion delivered to the world by those Councils, and by them established, though it is in reality a disgrace to Christianity ; a dishonour to the religion of nature ; and a faction against the common rights of mankind ; which ought to be the just object of universal contempt and abhorrence ; whether we consider it as a system of idolatry, impiety, and cruelty ; or, as a political scheme, to destroy the liberties, and engross the properties of mankind. Of these things, particularly and largely, in the piece referred to.

Here I have only further to observe, that in the large collections of the *Councils,* it is not only the eighteen œcumenical the collectors have gathered, but so much of all the councils as they could find, their acts, letters, formularies of faith, and canons, from the first council at Jerusalem, in the year 49, to the last council in the eighteenth century ; which was convoked by the archbishop of Ambrun against Jean de Soanem, bishop of Senez. These amount to above 1,600 councils. Note, reader, the condemnation and banishment of old John de Soanem, the most learned and excellent prelate in France, of his time, in the eightieth year of his age, by Firebrand Tartuff, archbishop of Ambrun, and his council, Sept. 21, 1727 ; was on account of the bishop's admirable pastoral instruction against the execrable constitution unigenitus, and the antichristian formulary of pope Alexander VII., and because he recommended the reading of Père Quesnel's very pious and fine *Reflections Morales.*

Pasquier Quesnel, a famous Jansenist, and father of the oratory, was born in 1636, was the author of many books, some of them very good. He was severely persecuted for many years, and died at last in prison, if I mistake not, a sufferer for religion.

Ἰωάννε, &c.—"O blessed John the Evangelist, explain this mystery:" Who is the first-begotten, how came he into the world ? Mysterium hoc aperi, effare etiam nunc, qui voces habes immortales. Resera nobis puteum vitæ. Da, ut nunc quoque de salutis fontibus hauriamus.

This passage of Cyril I have heard several learned Roman Catholic gentlemen call a prayer, and affirm it was a proof of the Father's invocation of saints, in the beginning of the fifth century ; for St. Cyril succeeded his uncle Theophilus in the see of Alexandria, October 16, 412. But to this it may be answered,

First, That Binius, though a zealous pleader for the catholic cause, as the monks of Rome miscall it, was of another opinion, for he takes no notice of this passage in his notes, in calce part 3, *Concil. Ephesiani*, tom. ii. p. 665, &c. and most certainly, he would not have failed to urge it, if he had considered it as a prayer, and believed it did prove the invocation of saints.

Secondly, neither does Bellarmine, in his treatise *de Sanctorum Beatitudine*, Henricus Vicus *de Sanctorum Invocatione*, Gabriel Vasquez *de Adoratione*, or Gregorius de Valentia *de Oratione*, make use of this passage of Cyril, though they do, ex professo, and data opera, diligently quote all the councils and fathers they can, to prove the invocation of saints.

Thirdly, As rhetorical apostrophes, or prosopopæias, are usual in all authors, sacred or civil, this may be one in Cyril, and it seems very plain from the passage, that it was intended for no more. It appears to be a rhetorical figure and not a prayer; such a figure as the Greek fathers were wont very frequently to use in their orations and poems.

Cyril intending, as appears by the sequel, to answer his own question with a passage in St. John's gospel, makes a long rhetorical apostrophe to the apostle, as if he were there present, then adds, Annon dicentem audimus, Ὀυκοῦν ἀκούομεν λέγοντος ? But do we not hear him saying ? Or, as Binius has the reading, Ὀυκοῦν ἀκούομεν λέγοντος. Let us hear what St. John saith, audiamus itaque dicentem, as if they had heard John giving his answer, and then concludes with the first verse of the first chapter of his gospel, Ἐν ἀρχῇ ἦν ὁ Λόγος, &c. In the beginning was the word, &c.

It is therefore very plain, that this passage of Cyril is only a part of his homily or sermon, and that in a rhetorical manner, he quotes a text from a gospel written by John about three hundred and thirty years before, in answer to his own question who the word was ? For Cyril to pray to John to tell them what he had told them long before, were senseless and ridiculous ; but to desire the apostle to do it in a rhetorical apostrophe, was allowable. It amounts to no more than the figurative expression in our liturgy, Hear what comfortable words our Saviour saith. Hear what St. Paul saith.

But if Cyril did in this passage truly pray to St. John, that could be no argument for popish invocation of saints ; for if an hundred fathers in the beginning of the fourth century, had preached up, and practised invocation of saints, yet that could not make it lawful and right, since we are taught by the scriptures to direct our prayers neither to saint nor angel, but to God only, and in the name and mediation of Jesus Christ only. We are not only positively ordered by the apostles to make all our addresses and prayers to God only, and by the mediation and intercession of Jesus Christ, but are told, that God is omniscient, and so able to hear all our prayers : all sufficient and therefore able to supply all our necessities ; and that his mercies in Jesus Christ are infinite. This makes our way sure in this particular.

On the contrary, the papists have no precept to pray to saints nor any promise that they shall be heard ; nor any practice of the primitive church for three hundred years after Christ, to encourage them ; and therefore, such popish invocation is a novel, groundless, and impious error.

We are told by St. Peter, that God had exalted the Lord Jesus Christ to be a Prince and Saviour, that is, an intercessor.* By St. Paul, that Christ is able to save to the uttermost all that come to God by him, seeing he ever liveth to make intercession for them ; † that he is gone to heaven, for this very end, to appear in the presence of God for us ; ‡ that there is no other mediator betwixt God and men but the man Christ Jesus,§ that is, whose prerogative it is to intercede for sinners to the divine Majesty ; being an honour and dignity God hath exalted him unto, after his sufferings, and as a reward thereof : Thus are we informed by the divine oracles, and yet, notwithstanding this, to make prayers and supplications to the Virgin Mary, and a thousand other saints, for aid or help ; and to have by their merit and intercession, the gifts and graces they pray for conferred upon them : this is a doctrine of such dangerous consequence, as it is a depriving of Christ Jesus of that grand dignity and prerogative he is now in heaven exalted to, as much as in men lies, that I should have wondered how it ever came to be embraced by such as profess Christianity ; had not the spirit of God foretold ‖ that some should depart from the faith, giving heed to seducing spirits, that is, seducing men, and doctrines of devils, that is to say, doctrines concerning demons, or souls of famous men departed this life ; which the heathens called demons ; and to whom they gave the worship of prayer or invocation, as intercessors or inferior divini-

* *Acts*, ch. v. v. 31.   † *Hebrews*, ch. vii. v. 25.   ‡ *Ib.* ch. ix. v. 24.   § 1 *Tim.* ch. ii. v. 5.   ‖ *Ib.* ch. iv. v. 4.

ties. This prophecy hinders my wondering at the thing; but
then I must call such modern invocation, gentilism Christianized,
a deplorable corruption.

Ponder then, ye Catholics, in time, and think not to excuse
yourselves by arguing from the command Christians have here
on earth to require each others prayers to God for them: for,
we have no command to supplicate any in heaven but only God.*
We have no reasonable assurance that the saints in heaven do
hear our prayers, and of consequence have not the same reasons
to request the prayers to God for us that we have to request the
prayers of saints on earth: nor is this all: our prayers to each
other in this life are only Christian requests to recommend our
conditions to God: offices only of kindness: no acts of religious
worship.

When St. Paul was on earth, had any one on bended knees, with
hands and eyes lifted up to heaven, in time of public prayer, and
amidst the solemn prayers to God, beseeched him for aid and
help, and for the conference of gifts and graces, he would have
rent his clothes, and said, Why do you these things? and can
we suppose, that now in heaven, the apostle is less careful to
preserve entire God's prerogative.

Besides, there is a great deal of difference betwixt St. Paul's
saying, Brethren, pray for us, or our requesting the prayers of
the faithful here on earth for us, and praying to saints in heaven,
as practised in the Roman church. Our's are only wishes and
requests; their's, solemn prayers on bended knees, made in the
places and proper seasons of divine worship, and joined with the
prayers they make to God. They use the same postures and
expressions of devotions they use to God himself. They pray
to them for help and aid, and make them joint-petitioners with
Christ; relying on their merits as the merits of Christ.

In sum, in the tabernacle of this world, we are to request the
prayers of every good Christian for us; but in the tabernacle
of heaven, we are to call on none but him in whom we believe. As
in the outward court of the Jewish tabernacle, every priest was permitted to officiate, to receive and present the devotions of the people
to the divine majesty; but in the holy place, within the veil, none
but the high-priest was to do any office or service: even so in the
tabernacle of this world, every Christian being a priest to God,
has this honour conferred upon him; but in the holy of holies,
in heaven, none but Christ, our high-priest, is to officiate. He
only is there to appear in the presence of God for us. It is his
prerogative alone to receive our prayers, and present them to the
divine majesty. As none but the high-priest was to offer incense
in the holy of holies, so none in heaven but Christ our high-priest
is to offer our prayers to God his father. He alone is that angel

* *Matt.* ch. vi. v. 8.

to whom much incense was given, that he should offer it with the prayers of all saints, upon the golden altar that was before the throne.* Which alludes to the altar that was before the mercy seat, on which the high-priest only was to offer incense.

But the catholic may say perhaps, that as on earth, men do not presently run to kings to present their requests, but obtain his favours by the mediation of courtiers and favourites ; even so, it is fitting we have recourse to saints, who are favourites in heaven, that we may obtain access to God, and have our suits accepted of him. Thus have I heard some learned men of the church of Rome argue. They should consider, however, in the first place, that if an earthly prince had declared he would have no solicitor but his son, and that all favours and royal graces should come to his subjects through his hands, and by means of his mediation ; such subjects could deserve no favour, if they make their application to other favourites, contrary to their prince's command. In the next place, if the solicitor, the son, was out of the question, and no such one had been declared by the king, yet as we petition earthly princes by such as enjoy their presence, because they cannot give audience to all their subjects, nor do they know the worthy ; but God is omnipresent, his ears always open, and his head bowed down to the prayers of his people ; is no respecter of persons, but gives a like access to the beggar as to the prince, and promises to cast out none that make their application to him ; it follows of consequence, that we ought to address ourselves immediately to God, and ask from him. If an earthly prince should thus invite his subjects to petition him for the supply of their wants, I should account the man no better than a fool or a madman, who would apply himself to any of the king's favourites.

The conclusion is ; O thou that hearest prayer, unto thee shall all flesh come.† Since God, who is infinite in mercy, omnipresent, and omnipotent in wisdom and action, admits every man to the throne of grace, bids him ask in the name of Jesus Christ, and promises, whatever we ask in his Son's name, he will do it. Since the practice of praying to saints is injurious to Christ, and doth manifestly rob him of his royal prerogative, which is to be the one, and only mediator betwixt God and man ; for in this office, he hath no sharers or partners, according to the scripture account ; As God is but one, and there is no other ; so the mediator (by the appointment of God) is but one, and there is, there can be no other.‡ And since, exclusive of these unalterable things, the Roman doctors cannot be certain, that saints in heaven hear the

* *Revel.* ch. viii. v. 3.   † *Psalm* lxv. v. 2.
‡ Quid tam proprium Christi quam advocatum apud deum patrem adstare populorum: *Ambrose in Psal.* 39. Pro quo nullus interpellat sed ipse pro omnibus, hic unus verusque mediator est. *Aug. Cont. Parmen.* lib. ii. c. 8.

requests of suppliants on earth, or know whether our prayers are fit to be accepted of God ; * let us reject that unlawful practice the invocation of saints, and pray for pardon and grace, as the gospel directs, to God the judge of all, through Jesus Christ the mediator of the new covenant.   This do, and thou shalt live.

N.B. Who was the author of these good remarks, these friars could not tell me : as they were in the book when they bought it.   If I mistake not, they are an abstract from a letter of Bishop Barlow to Evelyn, with several additions.   I have not Bishop Barlow's works by me : but I think I have seen something to this purpose, written by this prelate about one hundred years ago.

> " Say why was man so eminently rais'd
> Amid the vast creation : why ordain'd
> Through life and death to dart his piercing eye,
> With thoughts beyond the limits of his frame ;
> But that th' omnipotent might send him forth
> In sight of mortal and immortal powers,
> As on a boundless theatre to run
> The great career of justice ; to exalt
> His gen'rous aim to all diviner deeds ;
> To shake each partial purpose from his breast ;
> And thro' the mists of passion and of sense,
> And thro' the tossing tide of chance and pain,
> To hold his course unfault'ring, while the voice
> Of truth and virtue, up the steep ascent
> Of nature, calls him to his high reward,
> Th' applauding smile of heav'n ?   Else wherefore burns
> In mortal bosoms this unquenched hope,
> That breathes from day to day sublimer things,
> And mocks possession ?   Wherefore darts the mind
> With such resistless ardor to embrace
> Majestic forms; impatient to be free.
> Spurning the gross controul of wilful might ;
> Proud of the strong contention of her toils ;
> Proud to be daring ? "

The eighth of April, 1729, I bade the Ivonites adieu, and by their directions, walked up a very steep and stony mountain, which took me two hours, and then arrived at what I had often seen before in this part of the world, a great lake, the water of

---

* The Roman doctors say, the saints know the transactions that are done here below, by revelation or intuition.   To this I answer, if it is by revelation, that they know our requests and prayers to them, then it must be either from God or from angels ; of which there is not the least assurance or certainty to be any where found : but if we could be sure of it, then, in my opinion, we ought to pray to God or angels to make known our prayers to saints ; which would be strange religion.   If it be by intuition, as the greatest part of the doctors say, and that the saints see the requests in the divine essence, as men see things in a corporeal glass : then, (exclusive of answering that the scriptures say no such thing) the saints must see all things in the divine essence, or only such things as God is pleased to permit them to see : if all things, they would be omniscient : if only the things permitted to be seen, how is it possible for us to know,whether God is pleased to permit them to see therein our prayers, or to know the requests we make to them, unless he had told us so.   Let it be revelation or intuition, it is sad stuff.

which was black as ink to look at as it stood, though very bright in a cup, and must be owing, as I suppose, to its descending to the abyss : by the side of this water, under the shade of oak-trees many hundred years old, we rode for an hour, on even ground, and then came to a descent so very dangerous and dark, through a wood on the mountain's side, that we could hardly creep down it on our feet, nor our horses keep their legs as we led them to the bottom. This declivity was more than a mile, and ended in a narrow lane between a range of precipices that almost met at top. This pass was knee-deep in water, from a spring in the bottom of the mountain we had come down, which ran through it, and so very stony, that it took us three hours to walk the horses to the end of it, though it was not more than two miles : but at last we came to a fine plain, over which we rode for an hour and a half, and arrived at a wood, which seemed very large and stood between two very high and unpassable hills. In this forest was our way, and the road so dark, and obstructed by the branches of trees, that it was dismal and uneasy to go. On however we went for a long time, and about the middle of it came to a circular opening of about four acres, in which four very narrow roads met ; that we had travelled, another before us, and one on each hand. The way straight on we were cautioned by my friends not to go, as it was a terrible ride ; but whether to turn to the right or left, we had forgot. I thought to the right ; but my lad was positive, he remembered the direction was to take the left-hand road. This caused a stop for some time, and as I was a little fatigued, I thought it best while we paused to dine. O'FINN brought immediately some meat, bread, and a bottle of cyder, from his valise, and under a great oak I sat down, while our horses fed on the green. One hour we rested, and then went on again, to the left, as O'FINN advised. For several hours we rode, or rather our horses walked, till we got out of the wood, and then arrived at the bottom of a steep mountain ; one side of which is in the northern extremity of Westmoreland, and the other in the north end of Stanemore-Richmondshire. This vast hill we ascended, and came down the other side of the fell into a plain, which extends south-east for near half a mile to the river Teese, that divides the north end of Stanemore from Bishoprick, or the country of Durham. Yorkshire here ends in an obtuse angle, between two mountains, and the angle, for a quarter of a mile, is filled with that beautiful tall ever-green tree, the broad leaved alaternus, intermixed here and there in a charming manner, with the fir tree, the Norway spruce, and the balm of Gilead. It is as fine a grove as can in any part of the world be seen.

Just at the entrance of it, by the side of a plentiful spring, which runs into the Teese, there stood the prettiest little house I had ever beheld, and over it crept the pretty rock-rose, the cassine, the sea-green coromilla, and other ever-green shrubs. Before the house, was a large garden, seven or eight acres of land, under fruit-trees, and vegetables of every kind; very beautifully laid out, and watered in a charming manner by the stream that murmured a thousand ways from the spring by the house-door. I have not seen a sweeter thing. It appeared so beautiful and useful, so still and delightful a place, so judiciously cultivated, and happily disposed, that I could not help wishing to be acquainted with the owner of such a lodge.

As there was no other fence to this fine spot of ground but a ditch like a ha to keep cattle out, I leaped into the gardens, and roamed about for some time, to look at the curious things. I then went up to the house, in hopes of seeing a human creature either high or low. I knocked at the door, but no one could I find, though the mansion did not look like an uninhabited place. I then sauntered into the grove behind, and in a winding way of three hundred yards, that had been cut through the perennial wood, and was made between banks of springing flowers, beautiful exotics, and various aromatic shrubs, crept on till I arrived at a sleeping parlour, which stood in the middle of a circular acre of ground, and was surrounded and shaded with a beautiful grove; the larix, the Phœnician cedar, and the upright savin. There was a little falling water near the door, that was pleasing to look at, and charmed the ear. Entering this room, I found the walls painted by some masterly hand, in baskets of flowers, and the finest rural scenes. Two handsome couches were on either side the chamber, and between these lits-de-repos was as curious a table for wood and workmanship as could be seen. Pretty stools stood near it, and a one-arm chair. It was a sweet silent place, and in every respect, far beyond the sleeping parlour in the gardens at Stow.*

On one of the couches, as it was then evening, and I knew not what to do, I threw myself down, and very soon fell fast asleep. I lay the whole night without waking, and as soon as I could perceive any day, went to see what was become of O'FINN and the horses. The beasts I found feeding on very good grass in the green; and my lad still snoring under a great tree: but he was soon on his legs, and gave me the following account.

About an hour after my departure from him, he saw a poor man pass over the plain, who had come down the mountain we descended, and was going to cross the Teese in a small skiff of his own, in order to go to his cottage on the other side in Bishoprick: that he lived by fishing and fowling, and sold what he got by land and water to the quality and gentlefolk, twenty miles round him. And on asking who lived in the house before us, on the

* Lord Cobham's, now Earl Temple's seat in Buckinghamshire, fifty-nine miles from London.

skirts of the grove, he said, it belonged to a young lady of great fortune, Miss ANTONIA CRANMER, whose father died in the house I saw, and had been dead about a year ; that she was the greatest beauty in the world, and only nineteen, and for one so young. wise to an astonishing degree ; that she lived mostly at this seat, with her cousin, AGNES VANE, who was almost as handsome as she : that Miss CRANMER had to relish for the word, being used to still life, and seldom stirred from home but to visit an old lady, her aunt, who lived in Cumberland : that she was at present there, about twenty miles off, and would soon return : that she kept four young gentlewomen, who had no fortunes, to attend her and Miss VANE ; two old men servants, a gardener, and a cook ; and two boys ; that whenever she went from her house, she took her whole family with her, and left every place locked up as I saw. O'FINN's account surprised me. It set me athinking if it was possible to get this charming girl. I paused with my finger in my mouth for a few minutes, and then bid him saddle the horses.

As soon as it was possible, I went over the river to the fisberman's house, determining to wait there, till I could see the beautiful ANTONIA, and her fair kinswoman, another AGNES DE CASTRO, to be sure. My curiosity could not pass two such glorious objects without any acquaintance with them.

The poor fisherman gave me a bed very readily for money, as he had one to spare for a traveller, and he provided for me every thing I could desire. He brought bread and ale from a village a few miles distant, and I had plenty of fish and wildfowl for my table. Every afternoon I crossed the water, went to the sleeping parlour, and there waited for the charming ANTONIA. Twenty days I went backwards and forwards, but the beauties in that time did not return. Still however I resolved to wait, and, to amuse myself till they came, went a little way off to see an extraordinary man.

While I resided in this cottage, CHRISTOPHER informed me, that about three miles from his habitation, there lived, in a wild and beautiful glen, a gentleman well worth my knowing, not only on account of his pretty lodge, and lone manner of spending his time, but as he was a very extraordinary man. This was enough to excite my curiosity, and on the first of May, as soon as it was light, I went to look for this solitary. I found him in a vale, romantically situated, indeed, amongst vast rocks, ill-shaped and rude, and surrounded with trees, as venerable as the forest of Fontainbleau. His little house stood on the margin of a fountain, and was encompassed with copses of different trees and greens. The pine, the oak, the ash, the chestnut tree, cypresses, and the acassia, diversified the ground, and the negligent rural air of the whole spot, had charms that could always please. Variety and

agreeableness were everywhere to be seen.   Here was an arbour
of shrubs, with odoriferous flowers ; and there, a copse of trees
was crowned with the enamel of a meadow.   There was a collection
of the most beautiful vegetables in one part ; and in another,
an assembly of ever-greens, to form a perpetual spring.   PAN
had an altar of green turf, under the shade of elms and limes :
and a water-nymph stood by the spring of a murmuring stream.
The whole was a fine imitation of nature ; simple and rural to
a charming degree.

Here lived DORICK WATSON, an English gentleman, who had
been bred a catholic in France, and there married a sister of the
famous Abbé le Blanc.   But on returning to his own country,
being inclined by good sense and curiosity, to see what the
Protestants had to say in defence of their reformation, he read
the best books he could get on the subject, and soon perceived
that Luther, Melancthon, Calvin Zwinglius, Bucer, and other
ministers of Christ, had said more against the Romish religion
than the pretended catholics had been able to give a solid answer
to.   He saw, that barbarity, policy, and sophistry, were the main
props of popery ; and that, in doctrine and practice, it was one
of the greatest visible enemies that Christ has in the world.   He
found that even Bellarmine's notes of his church were so far
from being a clear and necessary proof that the church of Rome
is the body of Christ, or true church, that they proved it to be the
Great Babylon, or that great enemy of God's church, which the
apostles describe.

He saw in the first place, that there has not been, since the
writing of the New Testament, any empire, but that of the church
of Rome, so universal for one thousand two hundred and sixty
years together, as to have all that dwell upon earth, peoples, and
multitudes, and nations, and tongues, to worship it : which is
St. John's description of the new power that prevailed on the
inhabitants of the earth to receive his idolatrous constitutions,
and yield obedience to his tyrannical authority.   And all that
dwell on the earth shall worship him,* except those who are
enrolled in the registers, as heirs of eternal life, according to the
promises of the mediator of acceptance and blessing.   The waters,
which thou sawest, where the whore sitteth, are peoples, and
multitudes, and nations, and tongues.†   Bellarmine's Universality
is then directed against him.

The Cardinal's second note, continued DORICK, is antiquity,
and his third, a perpetual and uninterrupted duration.   But on
examination, I could find no ruling power, except Rome papal,
so ancient, as to have the blood of prophets, and saints, and of
all that were slain upon earth, of that kind for that space of time,
to be found in it.‡   And what rule but papal Rome had ever

* *Revel.* ch. xiii. v. 8.   † *Ibid.* ch. xvii. v. 15.   ‡ *Revel.* ch. xviii. v. 24.

so long a duration upon seven hills, so as to answer the whole length of the time of the Saracen and Turkish empires.

The Cardinal's fourth note is amplitude, and it is most certain, that never had any other church such a multitude and variety of believers, as to have all nations drink of the wine of her fornication and to gain, a blasphemous power over all kindreds, and tongues, and nations.

The fifth note is the succession of its bishops; and the sixth, Agreement with the doctrine of the ancient church. Now it is most true, that none but Rome was ever so eminently conspicuous for so long a time for the succession of its bishops under one supreme patriarch, as to be the living image of all the civil dignities of the empire, where it was under one supreme church-head exercising all the power of the civil head : nor did ever any enemy of God's church act for so long a time like the red dragon in its bloody laws against the followers of the lamb : and yet so far agree with the primitive church in fundamental doctrines as to answer the character of a false prophet with the horns of the lamb, that is, Christ, but speaking like the red dragon to his followers, as the church of Rome has done.*

* Reader, it is well worth your while to turn to the first volume of that admirable work, the *Salter's-Hall Sermons against Popery*, and there see how the Cardinal's notes of his church are considered by that learned and excellent man, Dr. Samuel Chandler. His consideration of the sixth note more immediately concerns me here, and therefore I give you an abstract of it.

The writings of the apostles are allowed even by our adversaries to be the oldest records of Christianity, and therefore to this ancient and infallible rule we ought to appeal, to determine the controversy between us and the papists, that is, to see how far this antiquity favours their doctrine and practices, or is in agreement with ours.

1. The protestants renounce the Pope, and acknowledge one law-giver, the Lord Jesus Christ, for these reasons, That the Pope is not mentioned in the New Testament ; that Christ says, one is your master, even Christ ; and St. Paul says, there is but one Lord, and one Faith : the whole family in heaven and earth is named of the Lord Jesus Christ.

2. Protestants do not pay any worship at all to saints and angels, but as St. Paul directs , consider Jesus Christ as their sole mediator and advocate ; for there is but one God, and one mediator between God and man, the man Jesus Christ. They say, such veneration and prayer to saints and angels is superstition and will-worship, and only worship God with all their hearts and souls, with the most raised affections, and the highest degrees of love and fear, faith and confidence ; for it is written, Thou shalt worship the Lord God, and him only shalt thou serve. And the angel in the Revelation said to John, who fell down at his feet to worship him, See thou do it not, for I am thy fellow-servant.

3. We affirm, that in the sacrament of the Lord's Supper, after consecration, there is nothing existent but bread and wine ; for St. Paul says, ' Whosoever shall eat this bread and drink this cup,' and ' as often as you eat this bread and drink this cup.'

4. We affirm the eucharist is only a memorial of Christ's death . for Christ says, do this in remembrance of me ; and St. Paul assures the Corinthians from Christ himself ; *Cor.* ch. xi. v. 24, that they were to receive the elements with this view only : and in his epistle to the Hebrews he tells us, that by one offering Christ hath for ever perfected those who are sanctified ; and that because there is remission of sins under the new covenant, there is no more offering for sin ; which proves, the eucharist is not a propitiatory sacrifice.

5. We renounce the doctrine of purgatory, and affirm that the future state is no state of probation ; for at death, the dust shall return to the earth as it was, and the spirit shall return to God who gave it. And St. Paul declares, that at the judgment seat of Christ every one shall receive the things done in the body, according to that he hath done, whether it be good or bad.

6. Protestants affirm, that the worship of God ought to be performed in a language which all men understand ; and that they have a right to search the scriptures. For, if I speak, with tongues, says the apostle, in such a language as those I speak to cannot understand , what shall I profit you ? Let all things be done to edifying. And Christ bids us search the

The seventh note of Bellarmine's holy Roman catholic church, is the Union of the members among themselves, and with the head. And sure it is, that no where else but in Rome papal, has there been such union of head and members for that length of time, as to apply the one mind of the ten kings for their agreement together, to give their power, and strength, and their whole kingdoms to the beast.

The eighth note produced by Cardinal Bellarmine is Sanctity. and WATSON saw it fairly proved by the protestant writers, that no church but Rome did ever appear so long together with such a medley of sanctity, in some doctrines, and outward appearances of a strict holiness of life, joined with the most abominable doctrines, and practices, to qualify it for the horns of the lamb, and the speech of the dragon for the idolatrous and cruel commands of the image ; or, for having the form of godliness in the atter times, and yet denying the power thereof.

In short, DORICK not only found, on a careful enquiry, that the system of the church of Rome was error and turpitude, abomination, gain, and cruelty, and her great design the very reverse of the gospel revelation, which came down from heaven to prepare men, by the practice of universal holiness and virtue, for eternal life ; but likewise, that even her Cardinal's notes prove, this church cannot be, in any sense, the true church of Christ ; and Bellarmine was perfectly infatuated to make choice of such things for the marks of his church, as make it the very picture of Babylon the Great. He resolved then to come out of Rome. He determined to forsake a church, which had altered the institutions of Christ, and is therefore guilty of heresy as well as schism.

This change in religion gave DORICK the highest satisfaction,

---

scriptures. And how could the word of Christ dwell richly in us in all wisdom, teaching and admonishing one another in psalms, hymns, and spiritual songs, if we had not the word of Christ, and the scriptures of truth to read and consult for ourselves.

These are the protestant doctrines, and we see they were taught by Christ and by his apostles. We have the sanction of the most venerable antiquity on our side, and this note of the true church of Christ belongeth to us in the highest perfection.

When the papists then scornfully say, Where was your church before Luther and Calvin ? The answer is obvious : the doctrine of our church was in the writings of the inspired apostles, where the church of Rome is never to be found ; the same that was taught by Christ himself, whom they have forsaken, and whose faith they have corrupted. As to our predecessors and professors, they were the persecuted disciples of the crucified Jesus, those martyrs and confessors, whose blood the church of Rome had cruelly spilt. This is the genuine antiquity the protestants have to boast of. Their doctrines are the word of Christ, and their fathers were put to death by papists for the testimony of Jesus.

But the papists on the contrary, exclusive of the example of the devil, who was a murderer from the beginning, and Antiochus Epiphanus, Nero, Domitian, and other monsters of mankind, who went before them in the measures of persecution, cruelty, and blood ; and excepting the idolatrous nations of the earth, and the false prophets and deceivers among the Jews, by whose authority and example they may vindicate their own idolatries, they have no genuine antiquity to plead. Many of their doctrines were unknown to, or abhorred by the primitive Church, and are mere novelties and innovations, that were originally introduced by superstition and then maintained by cruelty and blood.

as he told me, and it was doubled by his being able to convert his beloved ADELAIDE from popery to the church of Christ. But this joy had soon after some mitigation, by losing one of the most agreeable women in the world. Death robbed him of his heart's fond idol, and by that stroke he was so wounded, that he could not heal himself for a long time. He became the real mourner. He kept the reasons of his anguish continually before him, and was more intent upon spending his spirits, than his sorrows. He grew fond of solitude and silence, that he might indulge his passion, and provoke the emotion of that grief that was ready to devour him. In short, he retreated to the silent place I found him in, which was a part of his own estate, and turned hermit. He built the little villa I saw by the water-side, and formed the ground into the natural garden I beheld. Le Blanc mentions it in his letters, as an extraordinary thing, and very justly prefers it to the laboured and expensive Gardens at Chiswick, the work of the late Lord Burlington. Here WATSON laid in every thing he had a mind for, and filled his closet with books. He amused and kept himself healthy by working in his garden, and when he had done abroad, went in to read. His principal study was the contemplation of the best learning, which is the true Christian and from that he went to know what the Greeks and Romans have resolved and taught. In some things I found he was a learned agreeable man, and wondered greatly at his whim in turning hermit. I said a great deal against it, as we sat over a bottle of claret ; told him he might employ his time and talents more usefully in the world by mixing and conversing with his fellow-creatures, and by a mutual participation and conveyance of the common blessings of nature and providence ; and as he was not yet forty, advised him to go over the Teese, and make his addresses to Miss CRANMER or Miss VANE, both of them being most glorious girls, as I was told, and capable of adding greatly to the delights of philosophy. You have not seen two finer creatures, soul and body, than they are, if I have been rightly informed ; and I think, it would be a nobler and more religious act to get one of them with child, in the state of holy wedlock, than to write the best book that was ever printed. For my own part, I had rather marry, and double-rib one of these dear creatures, than die with the character of a father of the deserts. But in vain did I remonstrate to this anchoret. Contemplation was become his Venus, from the hour he lost his ADELAIDE and he had lived so very happy in his lone state for seven years past, that he could not think of hazarding felicity by a change of life. He had all he desired. If at any time, any thing was wanting, CHRISTOPHER the fisherman, who came to see him once or twice a week, very quickly got him whatever he required. This was WATSON's answer to my advice, and seeing it was to no purpose to say any more, I wished my hermit health, and bid him adieu.

Having previously mentioned the famous Abbé Le Blanc, I think I ought to say something of him in this place, by adding a few remarks in relation to this extraordinary man. He was in England in the year 1735, and wrote two volumes of Letters in octavo, which were translated into English, and printed for Brindley in 1747. In this account of England, the French monk pretends to describe the natural and political constitution of our country, and the temper and manners of the nation ; but it is evident from his epistles that he knew nothing at all of any of them.

Voltaire, however, that wonderful compound of a man, half-infidel, half-papist, who seems to have had no regard for Christianity, and yet compliments popery, at the expense of his understanding,* who wrote the history of England with a partiality and malevolence almost as great as Smollett, and pretended to describe the Britannic constitution, though it is plain from what he says, that he had not one true idea of the primary institutions of it, but taking this nation to be just such another kingdom of slaves as his own country, railed at the Revolution, and like all the Jacobite dunces, prated against the placing the Prince of Orange on the throne, and the establishment of the succession in the present protestant heirs ; though it is most certain, that these things were the most natural fruit and effect of our incomparable constitution, and are de jure. In short, that Zolius and plagiary, that carping superficial critic, as a good judge calls him ; who abuses the English nation in his letters, and denies Shakespeare (who furnishes out more elegant, pleasing, and interesting entertainment, in his plays, than all the other dramatic writers, ancient and modern, have been able to do and, without observing any one unity but that of character for ever diverts and instructs, by the variety of his incidents, the propriety of his sentiments, the luxuriancy of his fancy and the purity and strength of his dialogue) almost every dramatic excel-

---

* Voltaire's words are :—And notwithstanding all the troubles and infamy which the church of Rome has had to encounter, she has always preserved a greater decency and gravity in her worship than any of the other churches ; and has given proofs, that when in a state of freedom, and under due regulations, she was formed to give lessons to all others. Is not this facing the world, and contradicting truth with a bold front ? Decency and gravity in the church of Rome ! The licentious whore. And formed to give lessons ! Lessons, Voltaire ! Is not her wisdom, in every article of it, earthly, sensual, devilish ; and her zeal, that bitter, fierce, and cruel thing, which for ever produces confusion and every evil work ? With a just abhorrence, and a manly indignation, we must look upon this mystery of iniquity, and never let that horror decay, which is necessary to guard us against the gross corruptions of the Roman church ; the idolatry of her worship, the absurdity and impiety of her doctrines the tyranny and cruelty of her principles and practices. These are her lessons, Voltaire ; and you ought to ask the world pardon for daring to recommend a church, whose schemes and pieties bid defiance to reason, and are inconsistent with the whole tenor of revelation. This is the more incumbent on you, as you say you are a philosopher, and let us know in more places than one in your writings, that by that word, you mean a man who believes nothing at all of any revelation.

lence ; though in his Mahomet, he pilfers from Macbeth almost every capital scene : Voltaire, I say, speaking of this Abbé Le Blanc, wishes he had travelled through all the world, and wrote on all nations, for it becomes only a wise man to travel and write. Had I always such cordials, I would not complain any more of my ills. I support life, when I suffer. I enjoy it when I read you. This is Voltaire's account of the Abbé. How true and just it is, we shall see in a few observations on what this reverend man says of our religion and clergy.

The substance of what this French monk reports, vol. ii. from 64 to p. 75 in his letter to the President Boubier,* is this :

1. That Cranmer, and the other doctors, who introduced the reformation into England, were downright enthusiasts, and compassed their designs by being seconded by those, who were animated by a spirit of irreligion, and by a greedy desire of seizing the possessions of the monks.

It was the desire of a change established the reformation. The new doctors seduced the people, and the people having mistaken darkness for light, quitted the road of truth, to walk in the ways of error.

2. As to morals, that this boasted reformation produced no change in that respect : for the people are not purer than they were in former times, and the ecclesiastics are despised and hated for the badness of their lives. The bishops sacrifice everything to their ambition ; and the clergy of the second rank have no respect for their office. They spend the whole day in public places in smoking and drinking, and are remarkable for drunkenness, so dishonourable to ecclesiastics. Their talk is the most dissolute, and the vice that degrades these professors, sets a bad example to sober people, and makes them the jest of libertines.

*Reader—Bouhier, president of the French academy, to whom Le Blanc inscribes his fifty-eight letter, died in 1746. He was a scholar. L'Abbé de Olivet, speaks of him in the following manner : " Je me suis prêté à ce nouveau travail, et d'autant plus volontiers, que M. le Président Bouhier a bien voulu le partager avec moi. On sera, sans doute, charmé de voir Cicéron entre les mains d'un traducteur aussi digne de lui, que Cicéron lui-même étoit digne d'avoir pour traducteur un savant du premier ordre." *Tusc. Disp.* tom. i. p. 13. And again : " Le feu M. Président Bouhier, le Varron de notre siecle, et l'homme le plus capable de bien rendre les vraies beautés d'un orginal Grec ou Latin, avoit tellement retouché ses deux Tusculanes, qu'on aura peine à les reconnoître dans cette nouvelle édition." *Tusc. Disp.* tome ii. p. 1.

This is Olivet's account of Bouhier ; and I have heard some gentlemen who knew him say, that he was a very fine genius ; but, they added, a popish bigot to the last degree, and therefore, Le Blanc chose him as the fittest person of his acquaintance, to write an epistle to, that abused the reformation, and the English divines. Great is the prejudice of education ! When so bright a mind as Bouhier's cannot see the deformity of Popery, and the beauty of the reformation ; but, on the contrary, with pleasure reads the despicable defamation in Le Blanc's letter.

N.B. The two Tusculans, so finely translated by Bouhier, are the third, *de Ægritudine Lenienda ;* and the fifth, *Virtutem ad Beate Vivendum seipsa esse Contentam. De la Vertu ; Qu'elle suffit pour Vivre Heureux.* See likewise M. Bouhier's curious and useful remarks on the three books, *De Natura Deorum :* the five *Tusculans : Scipio's Dream :* and on the *Catilinaires,* or three *Orations against Catiline.* These remarks are the third volume of Olivet's fine edition of Cicero.

3. The only remarkable change produced by the reformation was the marriage of priests, and, exclusive of this being against the decisions of the Catholic church, it is contrary to sound policy and experience. The marriage of priests diminishes the respect we should have for them. The misconduct of a woman makes the clergyman fall into contempt. The lewdness of the daughter makes the priest, her father, the object of the most indecent jests ; and for the most part, the daughters of the clergy turn whores after the death of their father ; who, while living, spent more of his income in maintaining himself and children in pleasure and luxury, than in works of charity. He lived profusely, and dies poor.

Besides, if the English clergy were the greatest and most excellent men, yet a great man in the eyes of the world, loses the respect which is due to him, in proportion as he has any thing in common with the rest of mankind. A Madam Newton, and a Madam Fontenelle, would injure the illustrious men whose name they bore. Nor is this all. Those who by their disposition cannot fix that secret inclination, which induces us to love, on one person, are more humane and charitable than others. The unmarried ecclesiastics are more animated with that charitable spirit their function requires, as they have no worldly affections to divert it. People very rarely, as Lord Bacon says, employ themselves in watering plants, when they want water themselves. In short, the English divines are the worst of men, and there is hardly any religion in England. Thus does this French Abbé revile the English reformation and divines. He misrepresents the whole nation, and with a falsehood and outrage peculiar to popery and mass-priests, that is, to devils and the most execrable religion screams against the pure religion of the gospel, and dishonestly blackens some of the finest characters that ever adorned human nature. So very virulent is this reverend French papist against the clergy of England, that he is even positive there is not a divine in the nation knows how to behave like a gentleman.

In answer to the first article of impeachment, I observe, that it is so far from being true, that Cranmer, and other English divines, our reformers, were enthusiasts, and compassed their designs by the assistance of those who were animated by a spirit of irreligion, and by a greedy desire of seizing the possession of the monks, as this mass-priest asserts ; that it is most certain, on the contrary, Cranmer, and the other reformers, were wise and upright Christians, who, from a good understanding of religion, opposed the false pretensions of the church of Rome. They saw that Popery was contrary to the true genius of Christianity ; its spirit insolent and cruel ; and its worship not only a jumble of the most ridiculous fopperies and extravagancies, borrowéd from heathen customs and superstitions ; but the impurest that ever appeared in the world : that the designs of Popish Rome were contrary to all the principles of humanity ; its doctrines abominable and sinful ; and its offices cursed and diabolical ; it was evident, I say, to the conception of these great men, I mean Cranmer, and the other English reformers, that the Romish church was treacherous and inhuman, blood-thirsty and anti-Christian ; that her devotions were horrible and impious ; her ministers false prophets and liars, covered and decked with the livery of Christ, but in everything acting contrary to the salvation wrought by Jesus ; and therefore these wise and excellent reformers renounced popery, and bravely declared for that religion, which promotes the good of all mankind, and inspires men to worship the Father only in spirit and in truth, They threw off the cloak and garments of anti-Christ : they gloriously separated from him, and joined together in purity and simplicity, to please the Lord Jehovah. There was no enthusiasm in the case (as Le Blanc, the mass-priest, has the front to say) but, when the light of the gospel was obscured, and darkness had overspread the earth : when ignorance and superstition universally prevailed, and the immoralities of the Church of Rome were made to pass for Christianity in the world, then did these reformers call the people out of Rome, and preach to them the essential truths of the faith. They called them from an idolatrous religion, and all its train of direful effects ; from that sin of the first rank, which strikes at the being of a God, and ravishes from him the greatest honour that is due to him from his creature, man ; they called them from horrible service of the mass, from their addresses to angels and saints, and their worship of images, to the inward knowledge of one true God, and the worship due to him only ; to the sanctification and honour, which is due to him above all things, and above every name ; to the living hope in God through Christ ; to regeneration, and inward renovation by faith, hope, and charity ; to a holy conversation, and a faithful performance of all the commandments ; to true repentance, perseverance to the end, and life eternal. To these truths (not to be found in the religion of our travelling mass-priest) did the great, the glorious English reformers call mankind. They laboured to establish them in every thing tending to a pure faith, and good life. In this, there is not, there cannot be any enthusiasm.

And as to their being assisted by those who were animated by a spirit of irreligion, and by a greedy desire of seizing the possessions of the monks, it does not appear to be the truth of the case. Supposing there were such irreligious men, the assistance the reformers had from any great men in Henry the Eighth's time, when the abbeys were destroyed, was so very little, that malice only could mention it as an objection to the reformation. Popery, in that monarch's reign, was still the established religion of England, and both sides blame this king's persecutions. If papists were put to death for denying the supremacy of Harry, protestants were no less sufferers, for opposing the adoration of the host, and other religious impieties. And after the short reign of his son, Edward the Sixth what assistance had the reformers under bloody Mary ? Did she not do all that infernal popery could suggest, to destroy Cranmer, his brethren, and their reformation ? And did not they, without any other assistance than what they received from the spirit of God, continue to vindicate the truth as it is in Jesus, and teach the pure doctrines of the gospel, in opposition to the frauds and vile inventions of papal Rome ? Without minding the indignities, the torments, and the cruel death prepared for them, the brave honest men went on with their heavenly work, and, till the flames made them silent, endeavoured to destroy the Romish artifices and immoralities, and to spread the pure religion and undefiled before God and the Father. They were zealous, with the truth of religion on their side, and laboured to convert, out of a pure and friendly regard to the eternal welfare of mankind. They did the work, by the blessing of God, and therefore the malicious Le Blanc, the mass-priest, reviles and blackens them.

What he says of usurpation in respect of church lands, does not deserve any notice. The reforming clergy were not the actors in that scene. It was the king and his council. And as the Pope yet there were others to employ the church lands about, as some of them were in founding new bishoprics. And if in this case, the reformers had been guilty of some wilful errors, that could be no crime of the reformation. The culpable must answer it. For the satisfaction of conscience about the reformation, there can be but three questions fairly proposed. Was there sufficient cause for it ? Was there sufficient authority ? And whether the proceedings of our reformation were justifiable by the rule of scripture, and the ancient church ? Upon these points we ought to join issue, and I am sure the conclusion must be in the affirmative.

As to Le Blanc's second observation in relation to the marriage of priests, which our reformation he says produced, it may be answered, that the doctrine of a priest's marriage being unlawful, was borrowed by the church of Rome from the ancient heretics ; especially from the Manichees, who allowed marriage to their hearers, as the church of Rome doth to laymen ; but forbad it to their elect, as that church doth to her priests. St. Augustin charges the Manichees with this error. Hic non dubito vos esse clamaturos invidiamque facturos, castitatem perfectam vos vehementer commendare atque laudare, non tamen nuptias prohibere, quandoquidem auditores vestri quorum apud vos secundus est gradus ducere atque habere non prohibentur uxores. De Moribus Manichæorum, lib. ii. c. 18.

The first pope we read of that condemned the marriage of priests, was Syricius, the Roman, A.D. 384-398. And upon this account, I wonder Baronius had not a regard to his memory : but it has been the misfortune of his holiness since his death to fall under the displeasure of the Cardinal to that degree, that he has struck him out of his catalogue of his Romish saints.   He does not tell us for what reason.   Perhaps it was because this Pope rather dissuaded priests from marriage than peremptorily forbad it, as appears by his letters.   Syr. epist. 1. et 4. apud Binium.

The next pope, who distinguished himself against the marriage of priests, was the son of Bald-head, count of Burgundy, whose granddaughter was consort to Lewis the sixth, king of France ; I mean the celebrated Guy, archbishop of Vienne, who succeeded Gelasius, A.D. 1119, and had for successor in the year 1124, Lambert of Bononia, commonly called Honorius the second. Calixtus the second, pope and prince of Burgundy, was the first who absolutely forbad priests marriage, and in case they were married, commanded them to be separated.   *Grat. Dist. 27.* c. 8. This was in the beginning of the twelfth century.   And towards the end of it, A.D. 1198, the renowned son of Count Trasimund, I mean Innocent the third, the ever memorable Cardinal Lotharius, pronounced all the marriages of priests null.   And afterwards came on the council of Trent, A.D. 1545—1563, which anathematizes those who say such marriages are valid.   Sess. 24. can. 9.

But one would think, that God sufficiently declared his approbation of such marriages, in that the whole world hath by his appointment been twice peopled by two married priests ; first by Adam, secondly by Noah.   And we are sure, the holy scripture tells us, That marriage is honourable in all ;* and places it among the qualifications of a bishop, That he be the husband of one wife, having faithful children.† This, saith St. Chrysostom, the apostle prescribed to this end, that he might stop the mouths of heretics, who reproached marriage ; declaring thereby that marriage is no unclean thing, but so honourable, that a married man may be exalted to the sacred throne of a bishop.‡ What do you say to this, Le Blanc ?   I fancy you never read this homily of Chrysostom.   And well might this saint think it not unbecoming a bishop to marry, when our Lord thought it not unbecoming an apostle, no not the prince of the apostles, as the Romanists will have him, for it is without doubt, that St. Peter was married ; in that the scripture makes mention of his wife's mother.   *Matt.* viii. 14.   And Clemens of Alexandria tells us, that it was certainly reported that when he saw his wife led to death, he rejoiced ; and having exhorted her and comforted her, he called her by her name, and bid her remember the Lord. *Stromat.* lib. 7. p. 736. lut. 1629.   And that he was not only married, but begat children, the same Clemens in another place

* *Heb.* ch. xiii. v. 4.   † *Titus,* ch. i. v. 6.   ‡ *Chrysost. Hom.* ii. in c. 1. ad tit.

affirms ; *Stromat.* lib. 3. p. 448.   Yea that St. Philip and St. Jude were also married, and had children, Eusebius is witness. *Eccles. Hist.* lib. 3. c. 20–31.   And in like manner we find, that many of the primitive bishops were married.   Charemon, bishop of Nilus, St. Spiridion, St. Gregory Nazianzen, St. Gregory Nyssen, St. Hillary, and many more, were married men.

Nor can it be said, that they took wives while they were laymen, and after they took upon them the sacred ministry, were separated from them ; since the canons, commonly called the apostles, did prohibit either bishop, priest, or deacon, to put away his wife upon pretence of religion. See *Canon* 5.   And if any such shall abstain from marriage, as in itself abominable, command that he be corrected, or deposed, and cast out of the church.   *Canon* 50.

Now supposing these canons, notwithstanding all that Whiston has said, were not made by them whose name they bear, yet they are allowed by all to be of much greater antiquity than the first Nicene council.   And when in that council it was moved that bishops and priests, deacons and sub-deacons, might not cohabit with their wives, which they had taken before ordination, the motion was presently dashed by the famous Paphnutius, who was himself a single person.   *Socrat. Eccles. Hist.* lib. l. c. 11. Yea a long time after this council, we meet with many popes, who were sons of bishops and priests.

Pope Theodorus, Silverius, and Gelasius I were the sons of bishops ; pope Boniface I. Felix II. and Agapetus II. were the sons of priests. *Gratian. Dist.* 56. c. 2. and that we may not think this strange, Gratian himself informs us, that the marriage of priests was in those days lawful in the Latin church.   *Dist.* 56. c. 12.

Nor is this doctrine to be rejected only as contrary to scripture, and to primitive and apostolical practice, but because of the abominable fruits produced in the church of Rome by it.   For when the clergy might not have wives, which God allowed, instead of them they took whores ; and that wickedness so far prevailed, in the church, that the Cardinal of Cambray informs us, *De Reform Eccles*, many clergymen were not ashamed publicly, in the face of the world, to keep concubines. And the gloss upon Gratian says " A priest may not be deposed for simple fornification, because there are few priests to be found without that fault."   This made Pius II. say, that though priests were by the western church forbid to marry for good reason yet there was stronger reason to restore marriage to them again. *Hist. Council. Trent.* lib. vii. p. 680.   And many in that council were so sensible of this, that they alleged the great scandal given by incontinent priests, and that there was want of continent persons fit to exercise the ministry. *Paoli.* p. 679, &c.

The Emperor and the Duke of Bavaria did therefore require, that the marriage of priests might be granted. *Paoli*, p. 660, &c. And many bishops desired that married persons might be promoted to holy orders ; but this request was not granted, because, as the fathers observed, if the clergy once come to be married, they will no longer depend on the Pope, but on their prince.

To conclude this article, and I shall do it in the words of a great man, a prelate of the church of England ; To make war against the very Being of their species, they, the Romish priests, devote themselves to a single life, in blasphemous opposition to that first great command and blessing, increase and multiply.

As to Le Blanc's third observation, relating to the immoralities and bad behaviour of the English clergy ; I answer, if there are several bad men among so large a body as the protestant divines are, which is not strange, as it is the common case of all societies, yet the majority of them, orthodox and other dox, are as worthy men as can be found among the human race. I am very sure my acquaintance among them has been much larger than Le Blanc's could possibly be ; and I can affirm from my own know-ledge, that there are very many of this order of men, not only as fine gentlemen as I have ever conversed with ; but, a clergy holy in heart, superior to pride, to anger, to foolish desires : who walk as Christ also walked, and by their example and doc-trine, labour to make the people what the gospel requires they should be ; that is, pious and useful, pure and honest, meek and charitable ; to walk by faith, and not by sight ; and so pass through things temporal, that they may be sure of obtaining the things eternal. This I can say of many English divines of my acquaintance : and I may add, that this testimony from me who am not over-fond of the clergy, as the main of the Chris-tianity of too many of them lies in their opinion ; decked with a few outward observances, says Wesley very truly, in his letter to Bishop Warburton, and only upon occasion, endeavour now to do them justice, is certainly of more weight in their favour, than the calumny and abuse of a furious bigot and mass-priest, can be to make the world have as bad an opinion of them, as popery, and its wretched emissaries, would have the public entertain. Consider this then when you read Le Blanc's letters.

On the other hand, I have had a very large and intimate ac-quaintance with mass-priests in my time, in many parts of the world ; and, a few excellent once excepted. I can affirm, that more wicked and more worthless men than these Romish monks, I have never seen. If adultery, fornication, drunkenness, and swearing, are crimes, then the greatest criminals I could name in these respects, are Roman-catholic priests. Let this assertion of mine be set over against the character the Abbé Le Blanc

gives the English protestant ministers. Consider all I have
said, when you read this mass-priest's fifty-eighth letter, and
then judge of our reformation and clergy.* But it is time to
return to the cottage of Christopher the fisherman, and see
what happened to Antonia and Agnes.

When I came back to the poor man's cottage, he told me the
ladies were come home, and as he had given Miss CRANMER some
account of me, as a traveller who had journeyed into that remote
corner of the world, in search of antiquities and curiosities, he
did not think this lady would be averse to seeing me and hearing
me too, if I contrived any plausible pretence to throw myself
in her way.

Immediately then I crossed the water, went up to the house,
and as I saw her and the fair AGNES, her cousin, walking in the
garden, near the ha, leaped it over immediately, broad as it was,
and with my hat in my hand, made her a low bow, began an
apology for presuming to introduce myself to her presence in
such a manner, and concluded with my being in love with her
charming character, before I had the honour and happiness
of seeing her. What a condition then must I be in, when
a heaven-born maid, like her, appeared ! Strange pleasures
filled my soul, unloosed my tongue, and my first talk could not
be any thing but love. I said much on the subject, not worth
repeating to the reader ; and the issue of the matter was, that I
became so well acquainted with this innocent beauty, that, on
taking my leave, I had an invitation to breakfast with her the
next morning. I was there by eight, and really and truly quite
charmed with her. She was pretty as it was possible for flesh
and blood to be, had a beautiful understanding ; and as she
had very little notion of men, having seen very few, except
the two old servants who lived with her, she had not a notion

* Note, reader, in the fourth volume of a work, called *Notes relating to Men, and Things,
and Books*, you will find some more of my remarks on the Abbé Le Blanc's epistles. You
will see, among other observations on this monk, a vindication of Archbishop Tillotson.
The Abbé rails at one of this prelate's fine sermons, with great malice and impudence, and
has the vanity to think his miserable declamation an answer. This wretched and despicable
Romish apostate has the impudence and impiety to defend the worship of his God of dough,
and would, if it were in his power, persuade the readers of his letters, to adore the tiny cake
he prostrates himself before. For this the reader will find the mass-priest well chastised
in the work I have referred to ; and see the doctrine of the Lord's Supper set in a true light.
You will find there a curious history of the mass, from the time the popish doctors first drew
it out of the bottomless pit ; and see it made quite evident, that in this abominable article
of their faith, as well as in every other part of their execrable religion, they make void the law
of God, and sink the human race into the vilest slavery and idolatry. Beware, then, Christians,
of popery. Still bravely dare to protest against her infernal schemes and inventions, and draw
your religion from the book of God, that holy volume of inestimable treasure. It is our light
in darkness, our comfort under affliction, our direction to heaven, and let us die in defence
of it, if ever there should be occasion, rather than suffer the blood-thirsty papists, the red-
handed idolaters, to snatch it out of our hands. They will give us for it the despicable
legends of fictitious saints and false miracles ; a history of diseases cured instantly by
relics ; accounts of speaking images—stories of travelling chapels—wonders done by a
Madonna ; and the devil knows what he has crowded into their wretched heads. Down with
popery then, the religion of hell, and may that happy state be erected, when truth and love
shall embrace and reign. Come, Lord Jesus, come quickly.

of any danger that could come from conversing freely with a man she knew nothing of, and who might be an enemy in disguise.

After breakfast, I offered to go, but she asked me to stay and dine ; and to sum up the matter, I did dine, sup, and breakfast with her every day, for a month, till my good priest, FRIAR FLEMING, arrived, on a letter I had sent him, and we were married before the end of six weeks. We loved to excess, and did enhance human happiness to a high degree. She was good as an angel, and for two years we lived in unspeakable felicity. For the greatest part of that time, we were at Orton-Lodge, as she liked the wild place. There she likewise died of the small-pox, in the first month of the third year, and left me the most disconsolate of men. Four days I sat with my eyes shut, on account of this loss, and then left the Lodge once more, to live if I could, since my religion ordered me so to do, and see what I was next to meet with in the world. As grief sat powerfully on my spirits, and if not dislodged, would have drank them all up very soon, I resolved to hasten to Harrogate, and in the festivities of that place forget my departed partner as soon as I could. I laid my Antonia by my Charlotte and my Statia, and then rode off. What happened at the Wells, and all the observations I made there, and thereabout, the reader will find shortly narrated.

As I mention nothing of any children by so many wives, some readers may perhaps wonder at this, and therefore, to give a general answer, once for all, I think it sufficient to observe, that I had a great many, to carry on the succession ; but as they never were concerned in any extraordinary affairs, nor ever did any remarkable things, that I heard of ; only rise and breakfast, read and saunter, drink and eat, it would not be fair, in my opinion, to make any one pay for their history.*

In the year 1731 I arrived at Harrogate, in the West-riding of Yorkshire, in order to amuse my mind with the diversions and company of the place. It is a small straggling village on a heath two miles from Knaresborough, which is thirteen miles from York, and one hundred and seventy-five from London. The sulphur wells are three, on the north side of the town, about five hundred yards east of the bog. They rise out of a little dry hill. The second is a yard from the first, and the third is five yards and a half from the second. The water rises into stone-basins, which are each inclosed in a small neat building

---

* The author of *John Buncle, junior*, printed in 1776, a second volume of which appeared n 1778, endeavours to exculpate himself and brethren from this concise but severe satire which the author has passed upon his children, by observing that being already stamped with the character of a fool, and consequently no character to lose, he with more boldness published those letters, as the only chance left him, by which he might gain the good opinion of the reader, and as a means of wiping off the reproach their dear father had entailed upon them. *Anecdotes of John Buncle, junior*, vol. i. p. 72.

of stone and lime a yard square on the insides, and two yards high, covered over with thick flagstones laid in a shelving direction.

The soil out of which these springs rise is first, corn-mould, then a marle lime-stone, and a stratum of plaster : the lime-stone is so abraded by the salt in the water, that when dried, it swims: and where the water stagnates between the basins and the brook, the earth is ink black, and has a dry white scum, which smells like sulphur, and burns with a blue flame. The water does likewise throw up much candied sea salts, that is, salts to which sulphur adheres, and the pigeons resort from all parts to pick them up. In moist or rainy weather, these waters send forth a strong smell at a distance, and before rain, they bubble up with an impetuous force ; yet neither rain nor drought increases or decreases the springs.

From the large quantities of fine flower of brimstone which these waters throw off, it is plain, that sulphur is the principal thing in them ; but experiment likewise proves, that besides sulphur, the stinking well has vitriol, nitre, copper, and salt. These lie in solutis principiis in earth from which the water comes, and may be separated by operation ; some, I know, deny there is any copper in these waters ; but they do not consider that the glittering glebes of a gold colour found here, can be nothing else than glebes gilt with copper.

As to the diseases wherein this strong sulphur water is proper, it is good for everything, except a consumption. For this I recommend the Scarborough purging chalybeate above all waters. But if, reader, you have obstructions in your liver and other viscera, and are tormented with vicious humours in your intestines ; if your bowels are full of worms, the ascarides, or the broad round worm, or the worms called the dog and the wolf, from their likeness to these animals ; or if, from a venereal cause, the malady of many a priest and layman, you have an ulcer in the anus, or in the neck of your bladder, go to Harrogate, drink the stinking-water, live temperate, and you will be cured. For the scurvy, that universal disease, it is better than all other medicines. It is excellent in the jaundice, though of many years standing. It cures the asthma, the scotomia, and palsy, and in many other deplorable cases gives wonderful relief. Whatever ails you, consumption excepted, fly to Harrogate, and the water will do you good, if your hour be not come : and if you are well, the waters will promote long life, and make you the more able to dance with the ladies.

Four pints of water are enough for a patient, to be taken from half an hour to two hours after sunrising, upon an empty stomach. You should take some preparatory medicine ; and walk drinking the waters to warm the body a little, and make the passage the easier. Some people I have known drink their dose in bed, and it does well enough : but exercise and the thin open air do better, and contribute not a little to the patient's recovery ; and there is no finer fresher air in England than at this place.

In short, these wells are the strongest sulphur water in Great Britain, and, from the superior strength of the impregnating sulphur, it does not lose but retain the sulphureous smell, even when exposed to a scalding, and almost a violent heat ; and, in distilling it, when three pints had been taken off from a gallon of it, the last was as strong as the first, and stunk intolerably.

Make haste then to Harrogate, if you are sick, and have money, and in all probability you will find the waters efficacious, unless thy distemper be a consumption, or in its nature incurable, which is the case of many, as death is the common fate of mankind.

But when you are there, let me advise you to exercise as much as you can bear, without fatiguing yourself ; and in the next place, to be regular in meats and drinks, and as temperate as possible. Without these things, you will lose the benefit of the waters. No good can be expected, if men will indulge during a course of drinking the spa, and be not only excessive in quantity, but indiscreet as to the quality, of meats and liquors.

I have known some worn-out hard drinkers come to the Wells for relief, and at the same time increase by intemperance what they had contracted by the same measure. I have likewise seen some in a diabetes drink white wine ; in a cachexy, ale ; in the stone and gravel, claret. I have known a man in a dropsy, eat nothing but cooling, insipid, mucilaginous foods, and drink malt-drink plentifully ; a man in a jaundice, eat nothing but flesh meat and claret ; in a scurvy prefer the pungent, saline diet ; in obstinate obstructions, and a chronic hyppo, feed on thickening, hardening, and drying meats ; and in a hectic, vomiting, and spitting of blood, chuse only such things as increase the blood's momentum and velocity. I have known some gentlemen, who sat up late, never exercised, could not eat a dinner, and therefore would indulge in a flesh supper. All these, and many other irregularities, have I known expect surprising effects from the waters, and when they received no benefits say, there were no sanative principles in them. Unreasonable, unhappy men ! Be temperate and regular, use exercise, and keep the passions within bounds, and you may expect very astonishing cures ; provided your bodies are not become irreparable, and no longer tenantable ; your juices not to the last degree glutinous and acrimonious, and the corrosiveness of your blood not bringing on mortifications ; nor inflammations, filling, dilating, and breaking your vessels into suppuration and putrefactions. Then, live how you will, the waters can be of no use. You must pay the debt of nature by an incurable disease. Neither mineral waters, nor physic, can create and enliven new bodies, or make and adapt particular members to the old. But if you are only hurt a little, and the disease is curable, the waters will certainly be efficacious, and recover you, if you use moderate exercise, riding especially, diversion, a strict regularity, and great temperance.

O temperance ! Divine temperance : Thou art the support of the other virtues, the preserver and restorer of health, and the protracter of life ! Thou art the maintainer of the dignity and liberty of rational beings, from the wretched inhuman slavery of sensuality, taste, custom, and example ; and the brightener of the understanding and memory ! Thou art the sweetener of life and all its comforts, the companion of reason, and guard of the passions ! Thou art the bountiful rewarder of thy admirers and followers, thine enemies praise thee, and thy friends with rapturous pleasure raise up a panegyric in thy praise.

O hunger, hunger, immortal hunger ! Thou art the blessing of the poor, the regale of the temperate rich, and the delicious gust of the plainest morsel. Cursed is the man that has turned thee out of doors, and at whose table thou art a stranger ! Yea thrice cursed is he, who always thirsts, and hungers no more !

As to the company at these wells, I found it very good, and was pleased with the manner of living there. In the day-time we drank the waters, walked or rode about, and lived in separate parties ; lodging in one or other of the three inns that are on the edge of the common ; but at night, the company meet at one of the public-houses, the inns having the benefit of the meeting in their turn, and supped together between eight and nine o'clock on the best substantial things, such as hot shoulders of mutton, rump steaks, hot pigeon pies, veal-cutlets, and the like. For this supper, ladies and gentlemen pay eight-pence each, and after sitting an hour, and drinking what wine, punch, and ale, every one chuses, all who please get up to country-dances, which generally last till one in the morning ; those that dance, and those who do not, drinking as they will. The ladies pay nothing for what liquor is brought in, either at supper or after, and it costs the gentlemen five or six shillings a man. At one the ladies withdraw, some to their houses in the neighbourhood, and some to their beds in the inns. The men who are temperate, do then likewise go to rest.

In short, of all the wells I know, Harrogate is in my opinion the most charming. The waters are incomparable, no air can be better ; and with the greatest civility, cheerfulness, and good humour, there is a certain rural plainness and freedom mixed, which are vastly pleasing. The lady of pleasure, the well-drest tailor, and the gamester, are not to be found there. Gentlemen of the country, and women of birth and fortune, their wives, sisters, and daughters, are for the most part the company. There were at least fourscore ladies in the country-dances every night while I was there, and among them many fine women.

Among the company I found at this agreeable place, were six Irish gentlemen, who had been my contemporaries in Trinity-College, Dublin, and were right glad to see me, as we had been Sociorums,* at the conniving-house at Ringsend, for many a summer's evening, and their regard for me was great. They thought I had been long numbered with the dead, as they could not get any account of me for so many years ; and when they saw me, on their entering the public room, sitting by a beauty, in deep discourse, " God-zounds," said one of them, " there he is, making love, to the finest woman in the world." These gentlemen were MR. GOLLOGHER, MR. GALLASPY, MR. DUNKLEY, MR. MAKINS, MR. MONAGHAN, and MR. O'KEEFE, who was descended from the Irish kings, and first cousin to the great O'Keefe, who was buried not long ago in Westminster Abbey. They were all men of large fortunes, and, MAKINS excepted, were as handsome fine fellows as could be picked out in all the world. MAKINS was a very low, thin man, not four feet high, and had but one eye, with which he squinted most shockingly. He wore his own hair, which was short and bad, and only drest by his combing it himself in the morning, without oil or powder. But as he was matchless on the fiddle, sung well, and chatted agreeably, he was a favourite with the ladies. They preferred ugly MAKINS, as he was called, to many very handsome men. I will here give the public the character of these Irish gentlemen, for the honour of Ireland, and as they were curiosities of the human kind.

O'KEEFE was as distinguished a character as I have ever known. He had read and thought, travelled and conversed, was a man of sense, and a scholar. He had a greatness of soul, which shewed a pre-eminence of dignity, and by conduct and behaviour, the faithful interpreters of the heart, always attested the noblest and most generous sentiments. He had an extreme abhorrence of meanness, treachery, revenge, envy, littleness of mind, and shewed in all his actions the qualities that adorn a man. His learning was of the genteel and most useful kind, a sort of agreeable knowledge, which he acquired rather from a sound taste and good judgment than from the books he had read. He had a right estimation of things, and had gathered up almost every thing amusing or instructive. This rendered him a master in the art of pleasing, and as he had added to these improvements

* A phrase used by Swift.

the fashionable ornaments of life, languages and bodily exercises, he was the delight of all that knew him.

MAKINS was possessed of all the excellent qualities and perfections that are within the reach of human abilities. He had received from nature the happiest talents, and he had singularly improved them by a successful application to the most useful and most ornamental studies. Music, as before observed, he excelled in. His intellectual faculties were fine, and, to his honour I can affirm, that he mostly employed them, as he did his great estate, to the good of mankind, the advancement of morality, and the spread of pure theism, the worship of God our Saviour, who raised and sent Christ to be a Redeemer. This gentleman was a zealous Unitarian, and, though but five and twenty, when we met at Harrogate, he was a religious man ; but his religion was without any melancholy, nor had it any thing of that severity of temper, which diffuses too often into the hearts of the religious a morose contempt of the world, and an antipathy to the pleasures of it. He avoided the assemblies of fools, knaves, and blockheads, but was fond of good company, and condemned that doctrine which taught men to retire from human society to seek God in the horrors of solitude. He thought the Almighty may be best found among men, where his goodness is most active, and his providence most employed.

GALLASPY was the tallest and strongest man I have ever seen, well made, and very handsome. He had wit and abilities, sung well, and talked with great sweetness and fluency, but was so extremely wicked, that it were better for him he had been a natural fool. By his vast strength and activity, his riches and eloquence, few things could withstand him. He was the most profane swearer I have known, fought everything, whored everything, and drank seven in a hand ; that is, seven glasses so placed between the fingers of his right hand, that in drinking, the liquor fell into the next glasses, and thereby he drank out of the first glass seven glasses at once. This was a common thing, I find from a book in my possession, in the reign of Charles the Second, in the madness that followed the restoration of that profligate and worthless prince. But this gentleman was the only man I ever saw who could or would attempt to do it, and he made but one gulp of whatever he drank ; he did not swallow a fluid like other people, but if it was a quart, poured it in as from pitcher to pitcher. When he smoked tobacco, he always blew two pipes at once, one at each corner of his mouth, and threw the smoke of both out of his nostrils. He had killed two men in duels before I left Ireland, and would have been hanged, but that it was his good fortune to be tried before a judge, the late Sir John St. Leger, who never let any man suffer for killing another in this manner. He debauched all the women he could, and many whom he could not corrupt, he ravished. I went with him once in the stage-coach to Kilkenny, and seeing two pretty ladies pass by in their own chariot, he swore in his horrible way, having drank very hard after dinner, that he would immediately stop them, and ravish them ; nor was it without great difficulty that I hindered him from attempting the thing, by assuring him I would be their protector, and he must pass through my heart before he could proceed to offer them the least rudeness. In sum, I never saw his equal in impiety, especially when inflamed with liquor, as he was every day of his life, though it was not in the power of wine to make him drunk, weak, or senseless. He set no bounds or restrictions to mirth and revels. He only slept every third night, and that often in his clothes in a chair, where he would sweat so prodigiously as to be wet quite through, as if come from a pond, or that a pail of water had been thrown on him. While all the world was at rest, he was either drinking or dancing, scouring the bawdy-houses, or riding as hard as he could drive his horse on some iniquitous project. And yet he never was sick, nor did he ever receive any hurt or mischief. In health, joy, and plenty, he passed life away, and died about a year ago at his house in the county of Galway, without a pang, or any kind of pain. This was JACK GALLASPY. There are, however, some things to be said in his favour; and as he had more regard for me than any of his acquaintance, I should be ungrateful if I did not do him all the justice in my power.

He was in the first place far from being quarrelsome, and if he fought a gentleman at the small-sword, or boxed with a porter or coachman, it was because he had in some degree been ill used, or fancied that the laws of honour required him to call an equal to an account, for a transaction. His temper was naturally amicable.

In the next place, he was the most generous of mankind. His purse of gold was ever at his friend's service, was kind and good to his tenants, and to the poor a very great benefactor. He would give more money away to the sick and distressed in one year, than I believe many rich and pious people do in seven. He had the blessings of thousands, for his charities, and, perhaps this procured him the protection of Heaven.

As to swearing, he thought it was only criminal, when it was false, or men lied in their affirmations ; and for whoring, he hoped there would be mercy, since men will be men while there are women. Ravishing he did not pretend to justify, as the laws of his country were against it ; but he could not think the woman was a sufferer by it, as she enjoyed without sinning the highest felicity. He intended her happiness ; and her saying No, kept her an innocent.

How far all this can excuse JACK GALLASPY, I pretended not to determine : but as I thought it proper to give the world the picture of so extraordinary a man, it was incumbent on me, as his friend, to say all I could, with truth, in his vindication.

DUNKLEY had an extensive capacity, an exquisite taste, and fine genius. Besides an erudition which denominates what we call a man of learning, he happily possessed a social knowledge which rendered him agreeable to everybody. He was one of the men that are capable of touching every note. To all the variety of topics for conversation, the diversity of occurrences and incidents, the several distinctions of persons, he could adapt himself. He would laugh like Democritus, and weep like Heraclitus. He had the short, pert trip of the affected ; the haughty, tragic stalk of the solemn ; and the free, genteel gait of the fine gentleman. He was qualified to please all tastes, and capable of acting every part. He was grave, gay, a philosopher and a trifler. He had a time for all things, relative to society, and his own true happiness, but none for anything repugnant to honour and conscience. He was a surprising and admirable man.

MONAGHAN had genius and knowledge, had read many books, but knew more of mankind. He laughed at those men who lose among their books the elegancy of mind so necessary in civil society. He had no relish but for nice studies and fine literature, and despised the too serious and abstruse sciences. This was reckoned a fault in him by several judges, but with me it is a quere, if he was much to blame. Politeness is certainly preferable to dry knowledge and thorny inquiries. This gentleman's was such as rendered him for ever agreeable and engaging. He was continually an improving friend, and a gay companion. In the qualities of his soul, he was generous without prodigality, humane without weakness, just without severity, and fond without folly. He was an honest and charming fellow. MONAGHAN and DUNKLEY married ladies they fell in love with at Harrogate Wells. DUNKLEY had the fair ALCMENA, Miss Cox of Northumberland ; and MONAGHAN, ANTIOPE with haughty charms, Miss Pearson of Cumberland. They lived very happy many years, and their children I hear are settled in Ireland.

GOLLOGHER was a man of learning and extraordinary abilities. He had read very hard for several years, and during that time, had collected and extracted from the best books more than any man I ever was acquainted with. He had four vast volumes of common-place, royal paper, bound in rough calf, and half filled them with what is most curious and beautiful in works of literature, most refined in eloquent discourses, most poignant in books of criticism, most instructive in history, most touching and affecting in news, catastrophes, and stories ; and with aphorisms, sayings, and epigrams. A prodigious memory made all this his own, and a great judgment enabled him to reduce everything to the most exact point of truth and accuracy. A rare man ! Till he was five and twenty, he continued this studious life, and but seldom went into the mixed and fashionable circles of the world. Then, all at once, he sold every book he had, and determined to read no more. He spent his every day in the best company of every kind ; and as he had the happy talent of manner, and possessed that great power which strikes and awakens fancy, by giving every subject the new dress and decoration it requires ; could make the most common thing no longer trivial, when in his hand, and render a good thing most exquisitely pleasing. As he told a story beyond most men, and had, in short, a universal means towards a universal success, it was but natural that he should be everywhere liked and wished for. He charmed wherever he came. The specific I have mentioned made every one fond of him. With the ladies especially he was a great favourite, and more fortunate in his amours than any man I knew. Had he wanted the fine talents he was blest with, his being an extremely handsome man, and a master on the fiddle, could not but recommend him to the sex. He might, if he had pleased, have married any one of the most illustrious and richest women in the kingdom. But he had an aversion to matrimony, and could not bear the thought of a wife. Love and a bottle were his taste. He was however the most honourable of men in his amours, and never abandoned any woman to distress, as too many men of fortune do, when they have gratified desire. All the distressed were ever sharers in GOLLOGHER'S fine estate, and especially the girls he had taken to his breast. He provided happily for them all, and left nineteen daughters he had by several women a thousand pounds each. This was acting with a temper worthy of a man ; and to the memory of the benevolent TOM GOLLOGHER I devote this memorandum.

Having said above, that too many men of fortune abandon the girls they have ruined, I will here relate a very remarkable story, in hopes it may make an impression on some rake of fortune, if such a man should ever take this book in his hand.

Travelling once in the summer-time, in the county of Kildare in Ireland, I came into a land of flowers, and blossoms, hills, woods, and shades ; where I saw upon an eminence à house, surrounded with the most agreeable images of rural beauties, and which appeared to be placed on purpose in that decorated spot for retirement and contemplation. It is in such silent recesses of life, that we can best enjoy the noble and felicitous ideas, which more immediately concern the attention of man, and in the cool hours of reflection, secreted from the fancies and follies, the business, the faction, and the pleasures of an engaged world, thoroughly consider the wisdom and harmony of the works of nature, the important purposes of providence, and the various reasons we have to adore that ever-glorious Being, who formed us for rational happiness here, and after we have passed a few years on this sphere, in a life of virtue and charity, to translate us to the realms of endless bliss. Happy they who have a taste for these silent retreats, and when they please, can withdraw for a time from the world.

The owner of this sweet place was CHARLES HUNT, a gentleman of a small estate and good sense, whom I knew many years before fortune led me to his house. His wife was then dead, and he had but one child left, his daughter ELIZABETH. The beauties of this young lady were very extraordinary. She had the finest eyes in the world, she looked, she smiled, and she talked with such diffusive charms, as were sufficient to fire the heart of the most morose woman-hater that ever lived, and give his soul a softness it never felt before. Her father took all possible pains to educate her mind, and had the success to render her understanding a wonder, when she was but twenty years old. She sung likewise beyond most women, danced to perfection, and had every accomplishment of soul and body that a man of the best taste could wish for in a wife or a mistress. She was all beauty, life, and softness.

Mr. HUNT thought to have had great happiness in this daughter, though it was not in his power to give her more than five hundred pounds for a fortune, and she would have been married to a country-gentleman in his neighbourhood of a good estate, had not death carried off both her father and lover in a few days, just as the match was agreed ou. This was a sad misfortune, and produced a long train of sorrows. For two years however after the decease of her father, she lived very happily with an old lady, her near relation, and was universally admired and respected. I saw her many times during that term, at the old lady's villa within a few miles of Dublin, and took great delight in her company. If I had not been then engaged to another, I would most certainly have married her.

In this way I left ELIZA, in Ireland, and for several years could not hear what was become of her. No one could give me any information : but, about a twelvemonth ago, as I was walking in Fleet Street, I saw a woman who cleaned shoes, and seemed to be an object of great distress. She was in rags and dirt beyond all I had ever seen of the profession, and was truly skin and bone. Her face was almost a skull, and the only remaining expression to be seen was despair and anguish. The object engaged my attention, not only on account of the uncommon misery that was visible ; but, as her eyes, though sunk, were still extraordinary, and there were some remains of beauty to be traced. I thought I had somewhere seen that face in better condition. This kept me looking at her, unnoticed, for near a quarter of an hour ; and as I found she turned her head from me, when she saw me, with a kind of consciousness, as if she knew me, I then asked her name, and if she had any where seen me before ? The tears immediately ran plentifully from her eyes, and when she could speak, she said, I am ELIZABETH HUNT. What, Mr. HUNT'S daughter of Rafarlin ? I replied with amazement, and a concern that brought the tears into my eyes. I called a coach immediately, and took her to the house of a good woman, who lodges and attends sick people, ordered her clean clothes, and gave the woman a charge to take the greatest care of her, and let her want for nothing proper, till I called next day.

When I saw her again, she was clean and whole, and seemed to have recovered a little, though very little, of what she once was ; for a more miserable spectacle my eyes have not often seen. She told me, that soon after I went to *England*, Mr. R. a gentleman of my acquaintance of great fortune, got acquainted with her, courted her, and swore in the most solemn manner, by the supreme power, and the everlasting gospel, that he would be her husband, and marry her as soon as a rich dying uncle had breathed his last, if she would consent, in the mean while, to their living in secret as man and wife ; for his uncle hated matrimony, and would not leave him his vast fortune, if he heard he had a wife ; and he was sure, if he was married by any of the Church, some whisperer would find it out, and bring it to his ear. But notwithstanding this plausible story, and that he acted the part of the fondest and tenderest man that ever lived, yet, for several months, she would not comply with his proposal. She refused to see him any more, and for several weeks he did not come in her sight.

The fatal night however at last arrived, and from the Lord Mayor's ball, he prevailed on her, by repeated vows of sincerity and truth, to come with him to his lodgings. She was undone, with child, and at the end of two months, she never saw him more. When her relations saw her big belly, they turned her out of doors ; her friends and acquaintances would not look at her, and she was so despised, and ashamed to be seen, that she went to *England* with her little one. It fortunately died on the road to London, and as her five hundred pounds were going fast by the time she had been a year in the capital, she accepted an offer made her by a great man to go into keeping. Three years she lived with him in splendour, and when he died, she was with several in high life, till she got a cancer in her breast ; and after it was cut off, an incurable abscess appeared. This struck her out of society, and as she grew worse and worse every day, the little money she had, and her clothes, were all gone in four years' time, in the relief she wanted and in support. She came the fifth year to a garret and rags, and at last, to clean shoes, or perish for want. She then uncovered the upper part of her body, which was half eaten away, so as to see into the trunk, and rendered her, in the emaciated condition she was in, an object shocking to behold. She lived in torment, and had no kind of ease or peace but in reflecting, that her misery and distress might procure her the mercy of Heaven hereafter, and in conjunction with her true repentance bring her to rest, when she had passed through the grave and gate of death.

Such was the case of that Venus of her sex, Miss HUNT. When I first saw her, it was rapture to be in her company ; her person matchless, and her conversation as charming as her person ; both easy, unconstrained, and beautiful to perfection. But when I last saw her, she was grim as the skeleton, horrid, loathsome, and sinking fast into the grave by the laws of corruption. What a change was there ! She lived but three months from the time I put her into a lodging, and died as happy a penitent as she had lived an unhappy woman. I gave her a decent private funeral ; a hearse, and one mourning-coach, in which I alone attended her remains to the earth ; the great charnel-house, where all the human race must be deposited. Here ends the story of Miss HUNT.

And now a word or two to the man who ruined her. BOB R. is still living, the master of thousands, and has thought no more of the wretched ELIZA, than if her ruin and misery were a trifle. He fancies his riches and power will screen him from the hand of justice, and afford him lasting satisfaction ; but, cruel man, after this short day, the present life, the night of death shall come, and your unrelenting soul must then appear before a judge, infinitely knowing and righteous ; who is not to be imposed upon, and cannot be biassed. The sighs and moans of ELIZA will then be remembered, confound and abash you for your falsehood and inhumanity to this unhappy woman. In your last agony, her spirit will haunt you, and at the sessions of righteousness appear against you, execrable R. R.

But to return to Harrogate. While I was there, it was my fortune to dance with a lady, who had the head of Aristotle, the heart of a primitive Christian, and the form of Venus de Medicis. This was Miss SPENCE of Westmoreland. I was not many hours in her company, before I became most passionately in love with her. I did all I could to win her heart, and at last asked her the question. But before I inform my readers what the consequence of this was, I must take some notice of what I expect from the Critical Reviewers. These gentlemen will attempt to raise the laugh. Our moralist, they will say, has buried three wives running, and they are hardly cold in their graves, before he is dancing like a buck at the Wells, and plighting vows to a fourth girl, the beautiful Miss SPENCE. An honest fellow, this Suarez, as Pascal says of that Jesuit, in his *Provincial Letters.*

To this I reply, that I think it unreasonable and impious to grieve immoderately for the dead. A decent and proper tribute of tears and sorrow, humanity requires ; but when that duty has been paid, we must remember, that to lament a dead woman is not to lament a wife. A wife must be a living woman. The wife we lose by death is no more than a sad and empty object, formed by the imagination, and to be still devoted to her, is to be in love with an idea. It is a mere chimerical passion, as the deceased has no more to do with this world, than if she had existed before the flood. As we cannot restore what nature has destroyed, it is foolish to be faithful to affliction. Nor is this all, if the woman we marry has the seven qualifications which every man would wish to find in a wife, beauty, discretion, sweetness of temper, a sprightly wit, fertility, wealth, and noble extraction, yet death's snatching so amiable a wife from our arms can be no reason for accusing fate of cruelty, that is, providence of injustice ; nor can it authorise us to sink into insensibility, and neglect the duty and business of life. This wife was born to die, and we receive her under the condition of mortality. She is lent but for a term, the limits of which we are not made acquainted with ; and when this term is expired, there can be no injustice in taking her back : nor are we to indulge the transports of grief to distraction, but should look out for another with the seven qualifications, as it is not good for man to be alone, and as he is by the Abrahamic covenant bound to carry on the succession in a regular way, if it be in his power. Nor is this all, if the woman adorned with every natural and acquired excellence is translated from this gloomy planet to some better world, to be a sharer of the divine favour, in that peaceful and happy state which God hath prepared for the virtuous and faithful, must it not be senseless for me to indulge melancholy and continue a mourner on her account, while she is breathing the balmy air of paradise, enjoying pure and radiant vision, and beyond description happy ?

In the next place, as I had forfeited my father's favour and estate, for the sake of christian-deism, and had nothing but my own honest industry to secure me daily bread, it was necessary for me to lay hold of every opportunity to improve my fortune, and of consequence do my best to gain the heart of the first rich young woman who came in my way, after I had buried a wife. It was not fit for me to sit snivelling for months, because my wife died before me, which was, at least, as probable, as that she should be the survivor ; but instead of solemn affliction, and the inconsolable part, for an event I foresaw, it was incumbent on me, after a little decent mourning, to consecrate myself to virtue and good fortune united in the form of a woman. Whenever she appeared, it was my business to get her if I could. This made me sometimes a dancer at the Wells, in the days of my youth.

As to Miss SPENCE, she was not cruel, but told me at last, after I had tired her with my addresses and petitions, that she would consider my case, and give me an answer, when I called at her house in Westmoreland, to which she was then going ; at present, however, to tell me the truth, she had very little inclination to change her condition, she was as happy as she could wish to be, and she had observed that many ladies of her acquaintance had been made unhappy by becoming wives. The husband generally proves a very different man from the courtier, and it is luck indeed, if a young woman, by marrying is not undone. During the mollia tempora fandi, as the poet calls it, the man may charm, when, like the god of eloquence, he pleads, and every word is soft as flakes of falling snow ; but when the man is pleased to take off the mask, and play the domestic hero ; Gods ! What miseries have I seen in families ensue ! If this were my case, I should run stark mad.

Miss SPENCE'S mentioning the memorable line from Virgil, surprised me not a little, as she never gave the least hint before, though we had conversed then a fortnight, of her having any notion of the Latin tongue, and I looked at her with a raised admiration, before I replied in the following manner. " What you say, Miss SPENCE, is true. But this is far from being the case of all gentlemen. If there be something stronger than virtue in too many of them, something that masters and subdues it ; a passion, or passions, rebellious and lawless, which makes them neglect some high relations, and take the throne from God and reason ; gaming, drinking, keeping ; yet there are very many exceptions, I am sure. I know several, who have an equal affection to goodness, and were my acquaintance in the world larger than it is, I believe I could name a large number, who would not prefer indulgence to virtue, or resign her for any consideration. There are men, madam, and young men, who allow a partial regard to rectitude is inconsistent and absurd, and are sensible, it is not certain, that there is absolutely nothing at all in the evidences of religion : that if there was but even a chance for obtaining blessings of inestimable worth, yet a chance for eternal bliss is worth securing, by acting as the spotless holiness of the Deity requires from us, and the reason and fitness of things makes necessary, in respect of every kind of relation and neighbour. This is the case of many men. They are not so generally bad as you seem to think.

" On the other hand, I would ask, if there are no unhappy marriages by the faults of women ? Are all the married ladies consistently and thoroughly good, that is, effectually so ? Do they all yield themselves entirely and universally to the government of conscience, subdue everything to it, and conquer every adverse passion and inclination ? Has reason always the sovereignty, and nothing wrong to be seen ? Are truth, piety, and goodness, the settled prevailing regard in the hearts and lives of all the married ladies you know ? Have you heard of no unhappy marriages by the passions and vices of women, as well as by the faults of men ? I am afraid there are too many wives as subject to ill habits as the men can be. It is possible to name not a few ladies who find their virtuous exercises, the duties of piety, and the various offices of love and goodness, as distasteful and irksome to them as they can be to a libertine or a cruel man. I could tell some sad stories to this purpose ; but all I shall say more is, that there are faults on both sides, and that it is not the ladies only run a hazard of being ruined by marrying. I am sure, there are as many men of fortune miserable by the manners and conduct of their wives, as you can name ladies who are sufferers by the temper and practice of their husbands. This is the truth of the case, and the business is, in order to avoid the miseries we both have seen among married people, to resolve to act well and wisely." " This is the thing to be sure," replied Miss SPENCE. " This will prevent faults on either side. Such a course as virtue and piety require must have a continued tendency to render life a scene of the greatest happiness ; and it may gain infinitely hereafter. Call upon me then at Cleator as soon as you can," she concluded, with her face in smiles, " and we will talk over this affair again." Thus we chatted as we dined together in private, and early the next morning Miss SPENCE left the Wells.

Miss SPENCE being gone from Harrogate, and finding myself very ill from having drank too hard the preceding night, I mounted my horse, and rode to Oldfield-Spa, a few miles off, as I had heard an extraordinary account of its usefulness after a debauch. There is not so much as a little ale-house there to rest at, and for six days I lodged at the cottage of a poor labouring man, to which my informer directed me. I lived on such plain fare as he had for himself. Bread and roots, and milk and water, were my chief support ; and for the time, I was as happy as I could wish.

O Nature ! Nature ! would man be satisfied with thee, and follow thy wise dictates, he would constantly enjoy that true plea-

sure, which advances his real happiness, and very rarely be tormented with those evils, which obstruct and destroy it ; but, alas !
instead of listening to the voice of reason, keeping the mind free
of passions, and living as temperance and discretion direct, the
man of pleasure will have all the gratifications of sense to as high
a pitch, as an imagination and fortune devoted to them can raise
them, and diseases and calamities are the consequence.   Fears,
anxieties and disappointments are often the attendants, and too
frequently the ruin of health and estate, of reputation and honour,
and the lasting wound of remorse in reflection, follow.   This is
generally the case of the voluptuary.   Dreadful Case ! He runs
the course of pleasure first, and then the course of produced evils
succeeds.   He passes from pleasure to a state of pain, and the pleasure past gives a double sense of that pain.   We ought then surely,
as reasonable beings, to confine our pleasure within the bounds of
just and right.

As to the place called Oldfield-Spa, it is seven miles from Harrogate, and four from Rippon, lies on a rising ground, between two
high hills, near an old abbey, about five yards from a running
stream, and in a most romantic, delightful situation, which resembles Matlock in Derbyshire, so very much, that one might
almost take it for the same place, if conveyed there in a long deep
sleep.   The same kind of charms and various beauties are everywhere to be seen ; rocks and mountains, groves and valleys, tender
shrubs and purling currents, at once surprise and please the wandering eye.

As to the mineral water at Oldfield-Spa, it is an impetuous
spring, that throws out a vast quantity of water, and is always of
the same height, neither affected by rain or drought.   It is bright
and sparkling, and when poured into a glass, rises up in rows like
strings of little beads.   It has an uncommon taste, quite different
from all other mineral waters that ever came in my way ; but it
is not disagreeable.   What impregnates it I know not.   Dr.
Rutty I suppose never heard of this water, for it is not in his valuable quarto lately published ; and Dr. Short, in his excellent
History of Mineral Waters, printed in two quarto volumes in 1734,
says little more than that there is a medicinal spring there.   What
I found upon trial is, that two quarts of it, swallowed as fast as I
could drink it in a morning, vomits to great advantage ; and that
four quarts of it, drank by degrees, at intervals, works off by siege
or stool, and urine, in a very beneficial, manner.   I was appre-
hensive of a high fever from my night's hard drinking at
Harrogate, which I could not avoid ; and the Oldfield-water,
operating as related, carried off the bad symptoms, and restored
me to sanity in two days' time.   This is all I can say of this fine
water.   It is very little in respect of what it deserves to have said
of it.

By the way, it is to me a matter of great admiration, that so many rich and noble persons not only endure the fatigues and hazards of sailing and travelling to remote countries, but waste their money, to drink spa-waters abroad, when they can have as good of every kind in England, by riding a few miles to the most delightful places in the world, in summer time. Our own country has healing waters equal to the best in France, Italy, and Westphalia. Harrogate-water, in particular, has all the virtues of the famous baths of Aponus, within a mile of Padua in Italy, and is in every respect exactly alike. See the analysis of Aponus-water by Fallopius and Baccius, and the analysis of the English sulphur-spa by Dr. Rutty. It is injustice then to our country to visit foreign nations upon this account.

The mineral waters called Moffat-waters, which are as good as any in the known world, are found at the distance of a long mile northward from Moffat, a village in Annandale, thirty-five miles south-west of Edinburgh. The springs are situated on the declivity of a hill, and on the brow of a precipice, with high mountains at a distance, and almost on every side of them. The hill is the second from Hartfield, adjoining the highest hill in Scotland.

A vein of spar runs for several miles on this range of hills, and forms the bottom and lower sides of the wells. It is of a greyish colour, having polished and shining surfaces of regular figures, interspersed with glittering particles of a golden colour, which are very copious and large.

There are two medicinal springs or wells, which are separated from one another by a small rock; the higher well lies with its mouth south east. It is of an irregular square figure, and about a foot and a half deep. The lower well is surrounded with naked rocks, forming a small arch of a circle. Its depth is four feet and a half, and by a moderate computation, the two springs yield forty loads of water in twenty-four hours, each load containing sixty-four or sixty-eight Scotch pints; a Scotch pint is two English quarts. The higher shallow well is used for bathing, as it is not capable of being kept so clean as the lower well, on account of the shallowness and the looseness of its parts.

These waters are strongly sulphureous, and resemble the scourings of a foul gun, or rotten eggs, or a weak solution of sal polychrestum, or hepar sulphuris. The colour of the water is somewhat milky or bluish. The soil on every side of the wells is thin, and the hills rocky, only just below the wells there is a small moss caused by the falling of water from the hill above it.

Great is the medicinal virtue of these waters, in relieving inwardly, cholics, pains in the stomach, griping of the guts; bilious, nephritic, nervous and hysteric cholics; the gravel, by carrying off the quantities of sand, though it does not dissolve the slimy gravel, clearing the urinary passages in a wonderful manner;

curing ischuries, and ulcerated kidneys ; the gout, the palsy, obstructions of the menses, old gleets, and barrenness ; it is a sovereign remedy in rheumatic and scorbutic pains, even when the limbs are monstrously swelled, useless, and covered with scales.   Outwardly, ulcers, tumors, itch, St. Anthony's fire, and king's evil.

The waters are used by bathing and drinking : to drink in the morning three chopins, i. e. six pints or a Scotch quart, four English quarts, at most, between the hours of six and eleven.   After dinner to drink gradually.

Medicines commonly used during the drinking of the waters are, an emetic or two at first, and a few cathartic doses.   The doses sal Glauberi and polychrestum : syrup of buckthorn, and sulphur, is used along with the water.

But the cathartic prescription most in use, which was given by an eminent physician, for a general recipe, to be taken by all who should at any time use the water, is pills that are a composition of gambozia, resin of jalap, aloes, and scammony ; these to all intents are a strong hydragogue.

The large vein of spar three feet thick, runs in one direction for six miles to the wells, crosses obliquely the rivulet at the bottom of the precipice, and ascends the hill on the opposite side.   Small veins of the same spar which appears on the precipices, are on the side of the rivulet, and six small gushes of water of the mineral kind proceed from them.   The rocks and stones about the tops of the wells, and in other parts of the hill, and precipices differ not from common stones, no more than the water of the small springs in the neighbourhood with the common water.

The virtue of this water was discovered by Miss Whiteford, daughter of bishop Whiteford, in 1632.   She had been abroad, and all over England, drinking mineral waters for the recovery of her health, but found little benefit, till by accident she tasted these waters in her neighbourhood, and fiuding they resembled those she had used elsewhere, made a trial of them, and was cured of all her disorders.

Upon this she recommended the use of them to others, and employed workmen to clear the ground about the springs, their overflowing having made a small morass, that the poor and the rich might come, and make use of a medicine, which nature had so bounteously offered to them.

The 19th of May, 1731, at that hour when the break of day offers the most magnificent sight to the eyes of men, though few who have eyes will deign to view it ; I mounted my horse, and intended to breakfast at Knaresborough, in order to my being at Harrogate by dinner time, with my friends again ; but the land I went over was so enchantingly romantic, and the morning so extremely beautiful, that I had a mind to see more of the country, and let my horse trot on where he pleased.   For a couple of hours, he went slowly over the hills as his inclination directed him, and I was delightfully entertained with the various fine scenes.

The rising sun, which I had directly before me, struck me very strongly, in the fine situation I was in for observing it, with the power and wisdom of the author of nature, and gave me such a charming degree of evidence for the Deity, that I could not but offer up, in silence, on the altar of my heart, praise and adoration to that sovereign and universal mind, image of his benignity, and in its circle, which it traces unweariedly round ; not only to illustrate successively the opposite sides of this globe, thereby enlivening the animal, and supporting the vegetable world, ripening and preparing matter for all the purposes of life and vegetation ; but, to enlighten and cheer surrounding worlds, by a perpetual diffusion of bounties, to dispel darkness and sorrow, and like the presence of the Deity, infuse secret ravishment and delight into the heart. This cannot be the production of chance. It must be the work of an infinitely wise and good Being. The nature, situation, and motion of the sun, brings the Deity even within the reach of the methods of sense assisted by reason, and shows such constant operations of his power and goodness, that it is impossible to consider the present disposition of the system, without being full of a sense of love and gratitude to the Almighty Creator—the parent of Being and of Beauty ! By this returning minister of his beneficence, all things are recalled into life, from corruption and decay ; and by its, and all the other heavenly motions, the whole frame of nature is still kept in repair. His name alone then is excellent, and his glory above the earth and heaven. It becomes the whole system of rationals to say, Hallelujah.

> Come CHEERFULNESS, triumphant Fair,
> Shine through the painful cloud of care.
> O sweet of language, mild of mien,
> Fair virtue's friend, and pleasure's queen !
> Fond guardian of domestic life,
> Best banisher of home-bred strife ;
> Nor sullen lip, nor taunting eye
> Deform the scene where thou art by :
> No sick'ning husband damns the hour,
> That bound his joys to female power ;
> No pining mother weeps the cares,
> That parents waste on hopeless heirs :
> Th' officious daughters pleas'd attend ;
> The brother rises to the friend :
> By thee our board with flowers is crown'd,
> By thee with songs our walks resound ;
> By thee the sprightly mornings shine,
> And evening hours in peace decline.

While I was thinking in this manner of the sun, and the author of it, I came into a silent unfrequented glade, that was finely adorned with streams and trees. Nature there seemed to be lulled into a kind of pleasing repose, and conspired as it were to soften a speculative genius into solid and awful contemplations. The woods, the meadows, and the water, formed the most delightful scenes, and the charms of distant prospects multiplied as I travelled on ; but at last I came to a seat which had all the beauties that proportion, regularity, and convenience can give. This delightful mansion was situated in the midst of meadows, and surrounded with gardens, trees, and various shades. A fountain played to a great height before the door, and fell into a circular reservoir of water, that had foreign wild-fowl swimming on its surface. The whole was very fine.

Here I walked for some time, and after roaming about, went up to the house, to admire its beauties. I found the windows open, and could see several ladies in one of the apartments. How to gain admittance was the question, and I began to contrive many ways ; but while I was busied in this kind of speculation, a genteel footman came up to me, and let me know, his lady sent him to inform me I might walk in and look at the house, if I pleased. So in I went, and passed through several grand rooms, all finely furnished, and filled with paintings of great price. In one of those chambers the servant left me, and told me, he would wait upon me again in a little time. This surprised me, and my astonishment was doubled, when I had remained alone for almost an hour. No footman returned, nor could I hear the sound of any feet. But I was charmingly entertained all the while. In the apartment I was left in, were two figures, dressed like a shepherd and shepherdess, which amazed me very much. They sat on a rich couch, in a gay alcove, and both played on the German flute. They moved their heads, their arms, their eyes, their fingers, and seemed to look with a consciousness at each other, while they breathed, at my entering the room, that fine piece of music, the masquerade minuet ; and afterwards, several excellent pieces. I thought at first, they were living creatures ; but on examination, finding they were only wood, my admiration increased, and became exceeding great, when I saw, by shutting their mouths, and stopping their fingers, that the music did not proceed from an organ within the figures. It was an extraordinary piece of clockwork, invented and made by one JOHN NIXON, a poor man.

At length however, a door was opened, and a lady entered, she was vastly pretty, and richly drest beyond what I had ever seen, and had diamonds enough for a queen. I was amazed at the sight of her, and wondered still more, when, after being honoured with a low courtesy, on my bowing to her, she asked me in Irish, how I did, and how long I had been in England. My surprise was so great I could not speak, and upon this, she said, in the same language, I see, sir, you have no remembrance of me. You cannot recollect the least idea of me. You have quite forgot young

IMOINDA, of the county of Galway in Ireland ; who was your partner in country dances, when you passed the Christmas of the year 1715, at her father's house. What Miss Wolf of Balineskay ? O my IMOINDA ! I exclaimed, and snatching her in my arms, I almost stifled her with kisses. I was so glad to see her again, and in the situation she appeared in, that I could not help expressing my joys in that tumultuous manner, and hoped she would excuse her Valentine, as I then remembered I had had that honour when we were both very young.

This lady, who was good humour itself in flesh and blood, was so far from being angry at this strange flight of mine, that she only laughed excessively at the oddness of the thing ; but some ladies who came into the apartment with her seemed frightened, and at a loss what to think, till she cleared up the affair to them, by letting them know who I was, and how near her father and mine lived to each other in the country of Ireland. She was indeed extremely glad to see me, and from her heart bid me welcome to Clankford. Our meeting was a vast surprise to both of us. She thought I had been in the *Elysian* fields, as she had heard nothing of me for several years, and I little imagined, I should ever find her in England, in the rich condition she was in. She asked me by what destiny I was brought to Yorkshire ; and in return for my short story, gave me an account of herself at large. Till the bell rung for dinner, we sat talking together, and then went down to as elegant a repast as I had ever seen. There were twelve at table, six young ladies, all very handsome, and six gentlemen. Good humour presided, and in a rational, delightful cheerfulness, we passed some hours away. After coffee, we went to cards, and from them to country dances, as two of the footmen played well on the fiddle. The charming IMOINDA was my partner, and as they all did the dances extremely well, we were as happy a little set as ever footed it to country measure. Two weeks I passed in this fine felicity. Then we all separated, and went different ways. What became of Miss WOLF after this, the extraordinary events of her life, and the stories of the five ladies with her, I shall relate in the second volume of my *Memoirs of several Ladies of Great Britain*. Four of them were Mrs. CHESLIN, Mrs. FANSHAW, Mrs. CHADLEY, and Mrs. BISSEL ; the fifth was Miss FARMOR ; all mentioned in the Preface to the first volume of my *Memoirs* aforesaid.

A fortnight, as said, I stayed with Miss WOLF, that was ; but, at the time I am speaking of, the relict of Sir LOGHLIN FITZGIBBONS, an old Irish knight, who was immensely rich, and married her when he was creeping upon all-fours, with snow on his head, and frost in his bones, that he might lie by a naked beauty, and gaze at that awful spot he had no power to enjoy. I did intend, on leaving this lady, to be at Knaresborough at night ; but the fates, for a while, took me another way. At the inn where I dined I became acquainted with a gentleman much of my own age, who was an ingenious, agreeable man. This was OLIVER WINCUP, Esq.; who had lately married Miss HORNER of Northumberland, a fine young creature, and a great fortune. This gentleman, by his good humour, and several good songs, pleased me so much, that I drank more than I intended, and was easily prevailed on to go with him, in the evening, to Woodcester, the name of his seat ; which was but ten miles from the house we had dined at. We came in just as they were going to tea. There was a great deal of company, at least a dozen ladies, besides half a score gentlemen, and all of them as gay and engaging as the best-bred young mortals could be.

The villa here was very odd, but a charming pretty thing. The house consisted of, I think, ten several ground rooms, detached from one another, and separated by trees and banks of flowers. They were entirely of wood, but finely put together, and all disposed with the greatest symmetry and beauty. They were very handsome on the outside, and the inside was furnished and adorned with the finest things the owner could get for money. Easy hills, little valleys, and pretty groves, surrounded the sweet retreat, and the valleys were watered with clear streams. The whole had a fine appearance. The varied scenes for ever pleased.

At this delightful place I stayed ten days, and was very happy indeed. We drank, we laughed, we danced, we sung, and chatted and when that was done, 'twas night. But country-dances were the chief diversion ; and I had a partner, who was not only a wonder in face and person, being divinely pretty ; but did wonders in every motion. This was Miss VEYSSIERE of Cumberland : the dear creature : Reader, when I was a young fellow, there were few could equal me in dancing. The famous PADDY MURPHY, an Irish member of the house of commons, commonly called the *Little Beau,* well known at Lucas's coffee-house in Dublin, in 1734 ; and LANGHAM, the miller, who danced every night at the renowned Stretch's puppet-show, before the curtain was drawn up, danced one night, that I was at the castle, before the late Duke of Dorset and his Duchess, at their graces' request ; and were both deservedly admired for their performance in the hornpipe, yet they were nothing to me in this particular ; Miss VEYSSIERE however out-did me far ; her steps were infinite, and she did them with that amazing agility, that she seemed like a dancing angel in the air. We footed it together eight nights, and all the company said, we were born for each other. She charmed me exceedingly, and I should have asked her the question, to try her temper, if WINCUP had not told me, her father intended to sacrifice her to a man old enough to be her grandfather, for the sake of a great jointure ; and in a week or two she was to dance the "reel of Bogee" with an old monk. Poor Miss VEYSSIERE ! said I, What connection can there be between the hoary churl and you :—

> While side by side the blushing maid
> Shrinks from his visage, half afraid ?

I do not wish you may feather him, but may you bury him very quickly, and be happy.

Another of our diversions at Woodcester, was a little company of singers and dancers WINCUP had hired, to perform in a sylvan theatre he had constructed in his gardens. These people did the mime, the dance, the song, extremely well. There was among them one Miss HINXWORTH, a charming young creature, who excelling in everything, singing especially, had no equal I believe in the world. She was a gentleman's daughter, and had been carried off by one O'REGAN, an Irishman, and dancing-master, and who was the head of this company. He was the most active fellow upon earth, and the best harlequin I have ever seen. Every evening we had something or other extraordinary from these performers. He gave us two pieces which so nearly resembled to two favourite entertainments called *Harlequin Sorcerer*, and *The Genii*, though in several particulars better ; that I cannot help thinking Rich owed his *Harlequin Sorcerer* to O'Regan ; and that *The Genii* of Drury-Lane was the invention of this Irishman.

You know, reader, that in the first scene of *Harlequin Sorcerer* there is a group of witches at their orgies in a wilderness by moonlight, and that harlequin comes riding in the air between two witches, upon a long pole : Here O'Regan did what was never attempted at Covent-Garden house, and what no other man in the world I believe did ever do. As the witches danced round and round, hand in hand, as swift as they could move, O'Regan leaped upon the shoulder of one of them, and for near a quarter of an hour, jumped the contrary way as fast as they went, round all their shoulders. This was a fine piece of activity. I think it much more wonderful, than to keep at the top of the outwheel of a water-mill, by jumping there, as it goes with the greatest rapidity round. This MUN. HAWLEY, of Loch-Gur in the county of Tipperary, could do. He was a charming fellow in body and mind, and fell unfortunately in the twenty-second year of his age. In a plain field, by a trip of his horse, he came down, and fractured his skull. He did not think he was hurt, but at night as soon as he began to eat, it came up. A surgeon was sent for, to look at his head. It was cracked in several places, and he died the next day. He and I were near friends.

The first of June, 1731, at five in the morning, I took my leave of honest WINCUP, as cheerful and worthy a fellow as ever lived, and set out for Knaresborough ; but lost my way, went quite wrong, and in three.hours' time, came to a little blind ale-house, the sign of the *Cat and Bagpipe,* in a lonely silent place. The master of this small inn was one TOM CLANCY, brother to the well-known MARTIN CLANCY in Dublin. He came to England to try his fortune, as he told me, and married an old woman, who kept this public-house, the sign of the *Cat,* to which TOM added the *Bag-pipe.* As he had been a waiter at his brother's house, he remembered to have seen me often there, and was rejoiced at my arrival at the *Cat and Bagpipe.* He got me a good supper of trouts, fine ale, and a squib of punch, and after he had done talking of all the gallant fellows that used to resort to his brother MARTIN'S, Captain MACCAN of the county of Kerry, and many more, the heroes of Trinity-college, Dublin, he let me go to sleep.

The next morning, betimes, I was up, and walked into a wood adjoining to Clancy's house. I sauntered on for about an hour easily enough, but at last came to a part of the forest that was almost impenetrable. Curiosity excited me to struggle onwards, if possible, that I might see what country was before me, or if any house was to be found in this gloomy place ; this cost me a couple of hours, much toil, and many scratches ; but at length, I arrived at the edge of a barren moor, and beyond it, about a quarter of a mile off, saw another wood. Proud to be daring, on I went, and soon came to the wood in view, which I found cut into walks, and arrived at a circular space surrounded with a forest, that was above a hundred yards every way. In the centre of this was a house, enclosed within a very broad deep mote, full of water, and the banks on the inside, all round, were so thick planted with trees, that there was no seeing any thing of the mansion but the roof and the chimnies. Over the water was one narrow draw-bridge, lifted up, and a strong door on the garden side of the mote. Round I walked several times, but no soul could I see : not the least noise could I hear ; nor was there a cottage anywhere in view. I wondered much at the whole, and if I had had my lad O'FIN with me, and my pole, I would most certainly have attempted to leap the foss, broad as it was, and if it was possible, have known who were the occupants of this strange place. But as nothing could be done, nor any information be had, I returned again to the *Cat and Bagpipe.*

It was ten by the time I got back, and at breakfast I told CLANCY, my landlord, where I had been, and asked him if he knew who lived in that wonderful place. " His name," he replied, " is Cock, an old lawyer and limb of the devil, and the most hideous man to behold, upon the face of the earth. Everything that is bad and shocking is in his compound ; he is to outward appearance a monster, and within, the miser, the oppressor, and the villain. He is despised and abhorred, but so immensely rich, that he can do anything, and no one is able to contend with him. I

could relate," said TOM, " a thousand instances of his injustice
and cruelty ; but one alone is sufficient to render his memory for
ever cursed. Two gentlemen of fortune, who had employed him
several years in their affairs, and had a good opinion of him, on
account of a canted uprightness and seeming piety, left him sole
guardian of a daughter each of them had, and the management of
fifty thousand pounds a-piece, the fortune of these girls, with power
to do as he pleased, without being subject to any controul, till
they are of age. These ladies, as fine creatures as ever the eye of
man beheld, he has had now a year in confinement in that prison
you saw in the wood ; and while he lives, will keep them there to
be sure, on account of the hundred thousand pounds, or till he
shall be able to dispose of them, to his own advantage some way
or other. He intends them, it is said, for two ugly nephews he
has, who are now at school, about fourteen years old, and for this
purpose, or some other as bad, never suffers them to stir out of
the garden surrounded by the mote, nor lets any human creatures
visit them. Greatly as they are to be pitied, they bear his severe
usage wonderfully well. Miss MARTHA TILSTON, the eldest, is in
her twentieth year ; and the other, Miss ALITHEA LLANSOY, in her
her nineteenth. They are girls of great sense, and would, if any
kind of opportunity offered, make a brave attempt to escape, but
that seems impossible. They are not only so strictly confined,
and he for ever at home with them, except he rides a few miles ;
but they are attended continually in the garden, when they walk,
by a servant who is well paid, and devoted to the old man her
master. This makes them think their state is fixed for life, and
to get rid of melancholy, they read, and practise music. They
both play on the fiddle, and do it extremely fine."

Here CLANCY had done, and I was much more surprised at his
relation than at the place of their residence which I had seen. I
became very thoughtful, and continued for some time with my
eyes fixed on the table, while I revolved the case of these unfortunate young ladies. " But is all this true, or only report ? " said
I. " How did you get such particular information ? " " I will
tell you," answered TOM, " Old COCK is my landlord, and business
often brings me to his house in the wood, to pay my rent, or ask
for something I want. Besides, I sometimes take a fat pig there,
and other things to sell. My daughter, likewise, has sometimes
a piece of work in hand for the ladies, and she and I take a walk
with it there by a better and shorter way than you went. You
cannot think how glad they are to see us, and then acquaint us
with all their perplexities and distress."

On hearing this, a sudden thought of being serviceable to these
ladies came into my head, and I was about to ask a question in
relation to it, when two horsemen rode up to the door, and one
of them called " House ! " " This " says my landlord, " is Old

Cock and his man ; " and immediately went out to him, to know his will.   He told him, he came for the ride-sake himself, to see if any letters were left for him by that day's post at his house, and would dine with him if he had anything to eat.   " I have " said Tom, " as fine a fowl, bacon and greens, as ever was served up to any table, and only one gentleman, a stranger and traveller, to sit down to it."   Cock upon this came into the room I was sitting in, and after looking very earnestly at me, said " Your servant, sir." I told him I was his " most humble," and right glad to meet with a gentleman for society in that lone place.   I immediately began a story of a cock and a bull, and made the old fellow grin now and then.   I informed him among other things, that I was travelling to Westmoreland, to look after some estates I had there, but must hurry back to London very soon, for my wife was within a few weeks of her time.   " You are a married man then, sir," he re- plied.   " Yes, indeed, and so supremely blest with the charms and perfections, the fondness and obedience of a wife, that I would not be unmarried for all the world : few men living so happy as I am in the nuptial state."   Here dinner was brought in, and to save the old gentleman trouble, I would cut up the fowl.   I helped him plentifully to a slice of the breast, and the tips of the wings, and picked out for him the tenderest greens.   I was as com- plaisant as it was possible, and drank his health many times. The bottle after dinner I put about pretty quick, and told my old gentleman, if affairs ever brought him up to London, I should be glad to see him at my house, in Golden-Square, the very next door to Sir John Heir's ; or, if I could be of any service to him there, he would oblige me very much by letting me know in what way. In short, I so buttered him with words, and filled him with fowl and wine, that he seemed well pleased, especially when he found there was nothing to pay, as I informed him it was my own dinner I had bespoke, and dined with double pleasure in having the satis- faction of his most agreeable company.   I further said, he was a fine politician, and talked extremely well of the government and the times ; that I had received more true knowledge from his just notions, than from all I had read of men and things, or from con- versing with any one.   The glass during this time was not long still, but in such toasts as I found were grateful to his Jacobite heart, drank brimmers as fast as opportunity served ; and he pledged me and cottoned in a very diverting way.   He grew very fond of me at last, and hoped I would spare so much time, as to come and dine with him the next day.   This honour I assured him I would do myself, and punctually be with him at his hour. He then rode off, brim full, and I walked out to consider of this affair.   But before I proceed any farther in my story, I must give a description of this man.

Cock, the old lawyer and guardian, was a low man, about four feet eight inches, very broad, and near seventy years old. He was humped behind to an enormous degree, and his belly as a vast flasket of garbage projected monstrously before. He had the most hanging look I have ever seen. His brows were prodigious, and frowning in a shocking manner ; his eyes very little, and above an inch within his head ; his nose hooked like a buzzard, wide nostrils like a horse, and his mouth sparrow. In this case, was a mind quite cunning, in the worst sense of the word, acute, artful, designing and base. There was not a spark of honour or generosity in his soul.

How to circumvent this able one, and deliver the two beauties from his oppressive power, was the question : it seemed almost impossible ; but I resolved to do my best. This I told CLANCY, and requested, as I was to dine with COCK the next day, that he would be there in the morning, on some pretence or other, and let the ladies know, I offered them my service, without any other view than to do them good ; and if they accepted it, to inform me by a note, slipt into my hand when they saw me, that if they could direct me what to do, I would execute it at any hazard, or let them hint the least particular that might have any tendency to their freedom in some time to come, though it were three months off, and I would wait for the moment, and study to improve the scheme. This my landlord very carefully acquainted them with, at the time I mentioned ; and by two o'clock I was at COCK's house, to see these beauties, and know what they thought of the service offered them. The old man received me much civiler than I thought he would do when he was sober, and had, what my land-lord told me was a very rare thing in his house, to wit, a good dinner that day. Just as it was brought in the ladies entered, two charming creatures indeed, and made me very low courtesies, while their eyes declared the sense they had of the good I intended them. COCK said, " These are my nieces, sir," and as I had saluted them, we sat down to table. The eldest carved, and helped me to the best the board afforded, and young as they were, they both showed by their manner, and the little they said, that they were women of sense and breeding. They retired, a few minutes after dinner, and the youngest contrived, in going off, to give me a billet, in an invisible manner. I then turned to COCK entirely, heard him abuse the government in nonsense and falsehoods, as all Jacobites do ; and after we had drank and talked for better than an hour, took my leave of him very willingly, to read the following note.

" SIR,

" As you can have nothing in view but our happiness, in your most generous offer of assistance, we have not words to express our grateful sense of the intended favour. What is to be done

upon the occasion, as yet we cannot imagine, as we are so confined and watched, and the doors of the house locked and barred
in such a manner every night that a cat could not get out at any
part of it.—You shall hear from us however soon, if possible,
to some purpose ; and in the mean time we are,
          " SIR,
              " Your ever obliged servants,
                                              " M. T.
                                              " A. L."

What to do then I could not tell ; but as I rode back I consulted with my lad O'FIN, who was a very extraordinary young
man, and asked him what observations he had made on the
servants and place.   He said, he had tried the depth of the
water in the mote all round, and found it fordable at one angle,
waist high, and the rock he trod on about two feet broad.   He
had stripped, and walked it over to be sure of the thing.   As to
the people, he fancied there was one young man, a labourer by
the year under the gardener, who would, for a reasonable reward
for losing his place, be aiding in the escape of the ladies ; for he
talked with pity of them, and with great severity of his master :
that if I pleased, he would sound this man, and let me know
more in relation to him : that if he would be concerned, he could
very easily carry the ladies on his back across the water, as he
was a tall man, and then we might take them behind us to what
place we pleased ; or, if it was not safe trusting this man, for fear
of his telling his master, in hopes of more money on that side,
then, he would himself engage to bring the ladies and their clothes
over, on his own back, with wetting only their legs, if they could
be at the water-side some hour in the night.   This was not bad
to be sure, but I was afraid to trust the man ; for, if he should
inform old COCK of the thing, they would be confined to their
chambers, and made close prisoners for the time to come.   It
was better therefore to rely entirely upon O'FIN, if they could
get into the garden in the night.
In answer then to another letter I had from the ladies by my
landlord's daughter the next morning, in which they lamented
the appearing impossibility of an escape, I let them know immediately the state of the water, and desired to be informed what
they thought of the gardener's man ; or, if he would not do,
could they at any particular hour, get to that angle of the mote
I named, to be brought over on my man's back, and then immediately ride off behind us on pillions, which should be prepared.
Their answer was, that they dared not trust any of their guardian's men, but thought my own servant would do, and the
scheme reasonable and seemingly safe, if they could get out.
They gave me a million of thanks for my amazing care of them,

and called the immortal powers to witness the high sense they had of their unutterable obligation to me.

Waiting then for them, I staid at the little inn three days longer, and at last received a billet to let me know, that at twelve o'clock that night, which was the sixth of June, they could, by an accident that had happened, be at the appointed place, and ready to go wherever I pleased. To a minute my man and I were there, and in a few moments, O'FIN brought them and their clothes over safe. In an instant after they were behind us, and we rode off as fast as we could. Six hours we travelled without stopping, and in that time, had gone about thirty miles. We breakfasted very gaily at our inn, and when the horses had rested a couple of hours, we set out again, and rode till three in the afternoon, when we baited at a lone house in a valley, called Straveret Vale, which had every rural charm that can be found in the fiuest part of Juan Fernandes. A young couple, vastly civil kept here a small clean public house, the sign of the *Pilgrim*, on the very margin of a pretty river, and the plain things they had were as good as we could desire. Their bread, their drink, their fowl, their eggs, their butter, cheese, vegetables, and bacon, were excellent, and as they had good beds, I thought we could not do better than lie by for two or three days in this charming place, till it was determined, where the ladies should fix. We were at least sixty miles from old COCK's house, and in an obscurity that would conceal us from any pursuers ; for we had kept the' cross roads and by-ways, and were on the confines of Westmoreland. Here then we agreed to rest for a little time. In reality, it was just as I pleased. The ladies were all acknowledgment for what I did to deliver them, and all submission to my direction. They had each of them thirty guineas in their purses, as they showed me, but what to do after that was gone, or where to go while it lasted, to be in safety, they could not tell.

The affair perplexed me very much, and I turned it a thousand ways, without being able to settle it as I would. I had two young heiresses on my hands, who wanted more than a year of being at age, and I must support them, and place them in some spot of decency, security, and peace, since I had gone thus far, or I had injured them greatly, instead of serving them, in bringing them from their guardian's house. This took up all my thoughts for three days. I concealed however my uneasiness from them, and endeavoured to make the house and place quite pleasing to them. I kept up a cheerfulness and gaiety, and we sat down with joy and pleasure to breakfast, dinner, and supper. Within doors, we played at cards, we sung, and I entertained them with my german-flute. Abroad, we walked, fished; and sometimes I rowed them up the river in a boat which the man of the house had. The whole scheme was really delightful, and as the girls had great quickness and vivacity, and were far from being ignorant, considering their few years, I could have wished it was possible to stay there much longer : but it was no place for them, and I was obliged to call at Claytor, in a little time. I could not forget my promise to the lovely Miss SPENCE. My honour was engaged, and there was no time to lose. It is true, if I had not been engaged, I might immediately have married either the beautiful Miss TILSTON, or the more beautiful Miss LLANDSOY, then become my wards ; but as they were minors, if such a wife died under age, I could be no gainer, and might have children to maintain without any fortune. All these things sat powerfully on my spirits, and I was obliged at last to make the following declaration to the ladies, which I did the third day after dinner.

" Miss TILSTON, Miss LLANDSOY, I am sensible you have too high an opinion of what I have done to serve you, and think there is more merit in it than there really is ; for a man of any generosity and ability would, I imagine, do all that was possible to deliver two young ladies of your charms and perfections, from the slavery and misery your guardian kept you in : I am likewise sure you believe I would do everything in my power, to secure your happiness, and give you the possession of every blessing of time. I honour, I admire, I regard you both, to a high degree ; and if I were some powerful genie, I would crown your lives with stable felicity and glory. But nature, ladies, has irrevocably fixed limits, beyond which we cannot pass, and my sphere of action is far from being large. My fortune is not very great, and thereby prevents my being so useful a friend to you as I would willingly be. However, though it is not in my power to do according to my inclination, in regard to your case, and with security place you in some station fit for your rank and worth, yet I can bring you to a spot of tranquillity, and in still life enable you to live without perplexity or care of any kind. You shall have peace and little, and may perhaps hereafter say, you have enjoyed more real happiness, for the time you had occasion to reside there, than you could find in the tumult, pomp, and grandeur of the world."

Here I gave the ladies an account of Orton-Lodge, in the northern extremity of Westmoreland, where I had lived a considerable time, told them the condition it was in, the goods, the books, the liquors, and other necessaries and conveniencies that were there, and if, in that charming romantic spot, where no mortal could come to hurt them, they could bear to live for a while, I would settle them there, and get a man to work in the garden, and a couple of maids. I would likewise procure for them two cows, a few lambs, some poultry, and corn, and seeds

for the ground : in short, that they should have every thing
requisite in such a place ; I would return to them as soon as
possible ; I would write to them often, directing my letters to the
nearest town, to be called for by their man. " What do you
say, ladies, to this proposal ? In London it is not possible for
you to be : at a farm-house you might have no satisfaction :
and any where that was known and frequented, you may be
liable to discovery, as COCK, your guardian, will inquire every
where ; and if he hears of you, you will be carried home most
certainly to his dismal habitation, and be used ten times worse
than before. What do you think then of this scheme ? "

" Sir," they both replied, " you are to us a subaltern power,
by Heaven sent to deliver us from misery, and secure our happiness in this world. We have not words to express the gratitude
of our souls for this further instance of your goodness in the
offer you make us, nor can it ever be in our power to make
you the return it deserves. You will be pleased to accept our
grateful thanks, and all we have to add at present, our
prayers for your preservation and health. Conduct us, we
beseech you, immediately to that sweet spot of peace you have
described."

This being agreed on, the next thing to be done was to get
two horses for the ladies, for mine were not able to carry double
any farther, if there had been a turnpike road before us ; then
up the mountains we were to go, where no double horse could
travel ; and when they were at the Lodge, they would want
horses to ride sometimes, or to remove, if the necessity of their
case should happen to require it : to my landlord therefore I
applied upon the occasion, and he very quickly got me not only
two pretty beasts, but a young labouring man, and two country
girls to wait upon the ladies. I then sent to the next town for a
couple of side-saddles, gave the servants directions to go to the
Rev. Mr. FLEMING'S house, to wait there till they heard from
me, and then we set out for Orton-Lodge. Two days we spent
in travelling there, feeding on cold provisions we had with us,
and lying a night on the fern of the mountains. The second
evening we arrived at the Lodge. There I found every thing
safe, and the place as I had left it. I opened my various store-
houses, to the surprise of the young ladies, and brought them
many good things ; biscuits, potted char, potted black-cocks,
sweetmeats, and liquors of various kinds ; O'FIN likewise got us
a dish of trouts for supper, and the two beauties and I sat down
with cheerfulness to our table. Vastly amazed they were at all
they saw. Every thing was so good, and the wild charms of the
place so pleasing, that they could not but express the transports
they were in at their present situation. The whole they said,
was charming as enchantment, and in language there was not a

force sufficient to express their grateful sentiments upon the occasion. This gave me much pleasure, and till the end of June, I lived a very happy life with these fine young creatures. They did all that was possible to show their esteem and gratitude. Exclusive of their amazing fine faces, and persons, they were ingenious, gay, and engaging, and made every minute of time delightful. If I had not been engaged to Miss SPENCE, I should certainly have sat down in peace with these two young ladies, and with them connected, have looked upon Orton-Lodge as the Garden of Eden. They were both most charming women. Miss LLANDSOY was a perfect divinity !

On the first of July, just as the day was breaking, I mounted my horse, and again left Orton-Lodge. The morning being extremely fine, and every thing appearing in the loveliness of Nature, I rode on softly for three or four hours, and was so delighted with the beauty and infinite variety of enchanting objects my eyes were feasted with, that heedlessly instead of coming to the turning that was my road, I got into a bending valley, which ended at a range of rocky mountains. For half an hour I travelled by the bottom of these frightful hills, and came at length to a pass through them, but so narrow, that the beasts had not above an inch or two to spare on each side. It was dark as the blackest night in this opening, and a stream came from it, by the waters falling in several places from the top of the high inclosing precipices. It was the most shocking foot-way I had ever seen, and therefore requested O'FIN, as the bottom was hard, to try where the pass ended and let me know what kind of country and inhabitants were beyond it ? " That I will," said O'FIN, and immediately entered the cleft or crevice between the mountains. A couple of hours I allowed my adventurer to explore this dark way, but if in that time he could make nothing of it, then his orders were to return : but there was no sign of him at the end of six hours, and I began to fear he had got into some pound. After him then I went, about one o'clock, and for near half a mile, the narrow way was directly forward, a rough bottom, and ankle deep in water ; but it ended in a fine flowery green of about twenty acres, surrounded with steep rocky hills which it was impossible to ascend. In walking up to the precipice before me, I found many caverns, which extended on either hand, and onwards, into a vast variety of caves ; some of them having high arched openings for entrance, and others only holes to creep in at ; but all of them spacious within, and high enough for the tallest man to walk in.

In these dismal chambers I apprehended my fellow had lost himself, and therefore went into them as far as I could venture, without losing sight of day, and cried out FIN ! FIN ! but could hear no sound in return. This was a great trouble to me, and I knew not what to do. Back however I must go to my horses, and after I had spent two hours in searching, shouting, and expecting my lad's return, by some means or other, I was just going to walk towards the crevice, or dark narrow pass I had come through to this place, when casting my eyes once more towards the caverns in the mountains, I saw my boy come out, leaping and singing for joy. He told me, he never expected to see daylight more : for after he had foolishly gone too far into the caves, till he was quite in the dark, in hopes of finding a passage through the mountain to some open country, he was obliged to wander from chamber to chamber, he knew not where, for many hours, without one ray of light, and with very little expectation of deliverance ; that he did nothing but cry and roar, and was hardly able to stand on his legs any longer, when by a chance turn into a cave, he saw some light again, and then soon found his way out. Poor fellow ! he was in a sad condition, and his escape was very wonderful.

After this, we made what haste we could to our horses, which we had left feeding in the vale ; and O'FIN brought me some cold provisions from his wallet for my dinner. I dined with great pleasure, on account of the recovery of my lad, and when we had both recruited and rested sufficiently, on we went again. We found the valley winded about the mountains for three miles, and then ended at the highest hill I had ever seen, but which it was possible to ascend. With great difficulty we and our horses got to the top of it, and down on the other side. Six mountains of the same height, whose tops were above the clouds, we had to cross, and then arrived at a bottom, which formed a most delightful scene.

The Vale of Keswick, and Lake of Derwentwater, in Cumberland, are thought by those who have been there, to be the fiuest point of view in *England*, and extremely beautiful they are, far more so than the Rev. Dr. Dalton has been able to make them appear in his Descriptive Poem, addressed to two ladies, the late excellent Lord Lonsdale's charming daughters, on their return from viewing the coal-mines, near Whitehaven ; or than the Doctor's brother, Mr. Dalton, has painted them in his fine drawings ; and yet they are inferior in charms to the vale, the lake, the brooks, the shaded sides of the surrounding mountains, and the tuneful falls of water, to which we came in Westmoreland. In all the world, I believe, there is not a more glorious rural scene to be seen, in the fine time of the year.

In this charming vale, I found one pretty little house, which had gardens very beautifully laid out, and usefully filled with the finest dwarf fruit trees and ever-greens, vegetables, herbs, and shrubs.   The mansion, and the improved spot of ground, were at the end of the beautiful lake, so as to have the whole delightful piece of water before the door.   The projecting shaded fells seemed to nod or hang over the habitation, and on either hand, a few yards from the front of the house, cascades much higher than that of dread Lodore, in Cumberland, fell into the lake.   There is not any thing so beautiful and striking as the whole in any part of the globe that I have seen : and I have been in higher latitudes, north and south, than most men living.   I have conversed with nations who live many degrees beyond the poor frozen Laplander ; and have travelled among the barbarians who scorch beneath the burning zone.

Who lived in this delightful valley, was, in the next place, my inquiry, after I had admired for an hour the amazing beauties of the place.   I walked up to the house, and in one of the parlour windows, that had a view up the loch, I saw a young beauty sitting with a music-book in her hand, and heard her sing in a masterly manner.   She could not see me, but I had a full view of her fine face, and as I remembered to have seen her somewhere, I stood gazing at her with wonder and delight, endeavouring to recollect where I had been in her company, when another young one came into the room, whom I had reason to remember very well, on account of an accident, and then I knew they were the two young ladies I had seen at Mr. Harcourt's, and admired very greatly for the charms of their persons, and the beauties of their minds.   Upon this I walked up to the window, and after a little astonishment at seeing me, they behaved with the greatest civility, and seemed to be highly pleased with the accidental meeting.   While we were talking, their mamma came into the apartment, and on their letting her know who I was, and where they had been acquainted with me, the old lady was pleased to ask me to stay at her house that night, and to assure me she was glad to see me, as she had often heard her daughters speak of me.   Three days I passed with great pleasure in this place and then with much regret took my leave.

The fifth of July I left Mrs. THURLOE's, and by the assistance of a guide, had a fine ride to the house of Friar FLEMING, in Richmondshire, where I arrived by noon.   I dined with this good Franciscan, and should have lain there that night, but that I could not help being melancholy, on missing my dear friend TOM, the monk's brother, who died of a fever, as before related.   From him then I parted in the evening, and rode to a Carthusian monastry, which consisted of seven monks, men of some estate, who had agreed to live together in this remote place, and pass their lives in piety, study, and gardening.   I had a letter from FLEMING to one of these gentlemen, the superior, letting him know I was his near friend, and desiring he would receive me as himself ; that, although a protestant, I was of no party, but in charity with all mankind. This letter procured me all the kindness and honours these gentlemen could show me. They behaved with great civility and tenderness, and gave me the best they had, good fish, good bread, good wine, excellent fruit, and fine vegetables ; for as to flesh, they never eat any, by their rule.

They were all learned and devout men, very grave and silent for the most part, except when visited, but without anything stiff or morose in their manner. They had a large collection of books, and seemed to understand them well. What time they had to spare from the hours of divine service, and working in their gardens, according to the rule of St. BRUNO, which they follow, they give to study, and had many volumes of their own writing ; but mostly old manuscripts which they had transcribed, in Greek, Latin, and French. Making such copies was their principal work in the closet.

I stayed two days with these gentlemen, and had a good deal of useful conversation with them, on various subjects. On looking into the writings of the Rabbies, which I saw in their library, I told one of these Chartreux, that it was a wonder to me, that any one read such extravagant fabulous relations and despicable fictions as these books contained, and should be glad to know, what good could be extracted from them.

The Friar replied, that notwithstanding their being fictitious and extravagant to a high degree, yet great use might be made of the works of the Rabbies, and especially of the *Talmud of Babylon.* * We obtain from thence a knowledge of the cus-

---

* Reader, that you may the better understand the conversation I had with this learned Carthusian, I must inform you what the *Talmud*, and other writings of the Rabbies are.

The Talmud, a celebrated piece of Jewish literature, full of Rabinical domination and enthusiasm. The Rabbins pretend, that this book contains the Oral laws, and other secrets, which God communicated to Moses. It consists of two parts, each of which is divided into several books. In the first part, which they call *Mishna*, is the text. In the other, is a sort of comment on the text, and this is stiled the *Gemara*.

This oral law, or tradition of the Jews, was collected after the destruction of the Temple, A.D. 150, by Rabbi Judah, and is by them preferred before the scripture. They suppose it was orally delivered by Moses to Israel, and unlawful to be written ; but when Jerusalem was destroyed, they were constrained to write it, least it should be lost ; but yet it is so written, as that none but themselves might understand it.—This *Mishna* and *Gemara* complete the two *Talmuds ;* that of Jerusalem, A.D. 230 ; and that of Babylon, five hundred years after Christ. Many parts of these *Talmuds* are translated by several learned men, who have endeavoured to render them intelligible : but in order to understand them fully, you must read the *Jad Chaska*, or *Mishna Torah* of Moses Maimonides, who was physician to the king of Egypt about six hundred years ago. This Rabbi hath comprized the substance of the *Mishna* and *Gemara* of the *Talmud*, in his books, and enabled us to understand all the *Mishna* with ease and pleasure. See likewise the *Clavis Talmudica*, Cock's *Excerpta*, and the works of the excellent Ludovicus de Campeigne du Veil, who had been a Jew, but after becoming a Roman Catholic, went over to the Church of England, in which he continued for several years in the character of a great divine : but at last turned Baptist, and died a member of that Christian Church ; which lost him all his friends and interest. He died the beginning of this century, with the reputation of an upright Christian and a most learned man. There is no tolerable account given of him in any of the Biographical Dictionaries. What they

toms and opinions of the Jews, which afford some benefit. In
the next place, they serve to the confirmation of the history of
Jesus Christ ; for it appears by the Babylonish *Talmud,* that
there was one Jesus, who had disciples, lived in such and such
a place, and did and said divers things ; and in the Bible many
texts relating to the Messias are confirmed and explained by
these books of the Rabbies, though not by them intended. This
I have since found to be the truth of the case. I have read the
works of the Rabbins since, and find it to be as the Carthusian
said. For example—

It is said in *Genesis* ch. iii. v. 15. " I will put enmity between ·
thy seed and her seed. It shall bruise thy head, and thou shalt
bruise his heel." Now the *Targum of Onkelos* gives the sense
thus : The man shall be mindful of, or remember, what thou
(Satan) hast done to him in times past, and thou shalt observe,
watch or haunt him till the end of days ; that is, the serpent or
devil should pursue and have dominion over the world till the
last days, and then the prince of this world should be cast out,
and the works of the devil destroyed. Beacharith Heyamin,
the end of days, or last days, is, by a general rule, given by the
most learned Rabbins, meant of the Messias. So Kimchi on
Isaiah, ch. ii. v. 2.—and Abarbriel and R. Moses Nachm on
Genesis, xlix. v. 1. inform us.

It is likewise very remarkable, that the *Targum of Jerusalem,*
and that of Jonathan Ben Uziel, apply this place to the coming
of the Messias. They give the words the following sense. I
will put enmity between thy seed and her seed ; when the sons
of the woman keep my law, they shall bruise thy head, and when
they break my law, thou shalt bruise their heel ; but the wound
given to the seed of the woman, shall be healed, but thine shall
be incurable ; they shall be healed in the last days, in the days
of the Messias. Such is the opinion of the most learned Jews :
and from thence it follows, that the Christians have not put
their sense upon the text I have cited to serve their own turn ;
the Rabbins, we see, give the very same meaning to the place.

Again in *Numbers,* ch. xxiv. v. 17, we have the famous prophecy of Balaam : " There shall come a star out of Jacob, and
a sceptre shall rise out of Israel," and in *Isaiah,* ch. xi.v. 1. it is written. " And there shall come forth a rod out of the stem of
Jesse, and a branch shall grow out of his roots, and the spirit
of the Lord shall rest upon him." And in *Jeremiah,* ch. xxiii.
vv. 5, 6. " Behold the days shall come, saith the Lord, that I will
raise unto David a righteous branch,—and this is his name where-

say is short and next to nothing. And the Popish accounts are not only short, but false, and
sheer calumny. I took much pains some years ago, to collect among the Baptists, and from
others who knew this great man, everything I could get relating to him and his works, and
formed what I had got into a life of him, which I did intend to insert in this place : but by
some accident or other, it is gone. I cannot find it anywhere.

by he shall be called, The Lord our Righteousness." That the Christians apply these texts to the Messias, I need not inform the reader : but it must be grateful to observe, that the paraphrases of Onkelos, Jonathan, and Jerusalem, all of them expressly attribute the prophecy of Balaam to the Messias. And Rabbi Moses Hadarsan and Maimon, say, he is here called a Star, which signifies what *Malachi* expresses by the Sun of Righteousness, *Mal.* ch. iv. v. 2 ; and *Zachariah* by the East, " I will bring forth my servant the East." *Zach.* ch. iii. v. 8. as it is translated in the Vulgat, Septuagint, Arabic, and Syriac, is here, say these Rabbins, called a Star, because he should come and destroy idolatry, among the heathen nations, by becoming a light to the Gentiles, and the glory of Israel.

As to the other two texts, the Jews do likewise attribute them to the Messias. Rabbi Joseph Albo, speaking of the words, " The Lord our Righteousness," in particular, says expressly, that this is one name given to the Messias. Albo, *Sep. ikker.* lib. 2. c. 28. Thus do the Jews concur with us in the application of texts to the Messias. But what is become of this Messias, they cannot tell. They are amazed, perplexed, and confounded at him. They dispute on the article, and have the wildest fancies in relation to it. Whereas the Christians give a clear and consistent account of the Messias, and by every argument that can be desired by a rational, prove the truth of Christianity.

Again : in *Isaiah* ch. ix. v. 6 we have these words ; " Unto us a child is born, unto us a son is given, and the government shall be upon his shoulders : and his name shall be called Wonderful, Counsellor, the Mighty God, the Everlasting Father, the Prince of Peace." Or as the Alexandrian Manuscript hath it, " He shall call his name the Angel, Wonderful, Counsellor, Mighty, the Governor, the Prince of Peace, the Father of the age to come." This is thought by all Christians to be a plain declaration of the Messias ; for to apply it to any mere mortal, as to Hezekiah, or Isaiah's son, cannot be done without the greatest absurdity, and therefore Ben Maimon, *Epist. ad Afric,* fairly yields that these words belong to the Messias, and so doth Jonathan Ben Uziel in his Chaldee paraphrase. The *Talmud* itself allows it. *Tract. Sanhedrim,* that it relates to a person not come in the time of the prophets, but to the man, whose name is the " Branch, which was to come forth out of the stem of Jesse, and to grow out of his roots. My servant the Branch. Behold the man whose name is the Branch." *Zach.* ch. iii. v. 8. and ch. xii. and *Isaiah* ch. iv. v. 1. " Even the person that shall be sent ; " Shilo, that remarkable person God had promised to his people. So says the *Talmud.*

But further ; as to the birth of the Messias, in respect of the

M

manner and the place, it is thus set down by the prophet *Micah*, v. 2, " And thou Bethlehem Ephrata, though thou be little among the thousands of Judah, yet out of thee shall come forth unto me, that is to be ruler in Israel ; whose goings forth have been of old, even from everlasting." And in *Isaiah*, ch. vii. v. 14, are these words, " Behold a virgin shall conceive and bring forth a son, and call his name Immanuel." In these two texts, the Christians say, the place of the birth of the Messias, and the manner of it, are as plainly described as words can do ; and if they cannot, without absurdity, be explained as relating to any other person, then it must be perverting the meaning of the records to oppose this explication : but this the Jews are far from doing. The place is acknowledged in the *Talmud*, in the Chaldee paraphrase of Jonathan, and all their most famous masters declare with one voice, that Bethlehem indisputably belongs to the Messias. " Exte Bethlehem coram me prodibit Messias, ut sit dominium exercens in Israel, cujus nomen dictum est ab æternitate, a Diebus seculi." *Talmud. lib. Sanhedrim, et Midrasch.* The hillinic Rabbi Selemoh, *Paraph. Jonath. in Loc. Rabbi David Kimchi.* And as to the manner, though it be true that some Jews say, the Hebrew word Gnalma signifies a young woman as well as a virgin ; yet Kimchi, Jarchi, and Sele-moh, three of their greatest Rabbins, confess that here is some-thing wonderful presaged in the birth and generation of this person, and that he was not to be born as other men and women are born. What can we desire more, in the case, from an enemy ? And in truth, the behold, or wonder, with which the text begins, would be nothing, if it was only that a young woman should have a child : and as to the Hebrew word Gnalmah, if it ever does signify a young woman, which I very much doubt, yet the translation of the Seventy, who well understood the original surely, they render the word by parthenos, παρϑένος in Greek, which always signifies a virgin in the strict propriety of the phrase. And in the Punic language, which is much the same as the Hebrew, the word Alma signifies a virgin, " virgo intacta," and never means a young woman.

. Such are the advantages we may gain by reading the books of the Rabbins ; and to me it is pleasing to see these great Hebrew masters granting so much to us for our Messias, while they hate our holy religion beyond every thing. Even the gay among the Jews, if I have been truly informed by one who danced a night with them, have, in contempt and abhorrence of our faith, a country-dance called " The Little Jesus."

The eighth of July, I left the little Chartreuse, and went from thence to Knaresborough, where I arrived that night, and re-sided three days. It is a fine old town, and borough by prescript ion, in the West-riding of Yorkshire, and wapentake of Claro.

The vast hills of Craven look beautifully wild in its neighbour-hood, and the rapid river Nid, which issues from the bottom of those mountains, almost encompasses the town. It is a hundred and seventy five measured miles from London, and the best way to it is from Ferrybridge to Wetherby, by the left-hand road, where there is an excellent inn, and from that to Knaresborough.

When this very ancient town passed from the posterity of Surlo de Burgh, the founder of it, we know not, but we find that Henry III granted the honour, castle, and manor, to the *E*arl of Kent, Margaret his wife, and their issue and heirs, and that on failure of issue and right heirs, it returned again to the crown ; for *E*dward II, among other lands, gave this lordship of Knaresborough to his favourite Pierse de Gaveston, *E*arl of Cornwall, and his heirs. Gaveston was taken not long after by the Barons, in Scarborough castle, after a short siege, and was beheaded on Gaversly-heath, near Warwick, by order of the *E*arl of Warwick, June 20, 1312. On the fall of the insolent Gaveston, who had been banished by *E*dward I but recalled, ere that monarch's funeral rites were performed, by the weak and inefficient *E*dward II, whose interest becoming blended with that of his favourite, rendered the public displeasure against Gaveston the want of duty to the prince, and which eventually in his death involved the ruin of his Sovereign ; Knaresborough again reverted to the Crown, and so continued till the forty-fourth of *E*dward III, when this king made a grant of the honour, castle, and manor of the town, and the cell of St. Roberts, to John of Gaunt, the king's fourth son, who was *E*arl of Richmond, and created Duke of Lancaster, on his having married one of the coheiresses of Henry, Duke of Lancaster. Other great estates were likewise given at the same time to this fourth son of *E*dward, that he might maintain his grandeur : and ever since, this town has belonged to the dutchy of Lancaster. It is an appendage to the crown.

Not far from this town are two wells, as strong of sulphur as Harrogate-water, and as valuable, though no one takes any notice of them. One lies in the way to Harrogate, in a low ground by a brook-side. The other is Bitton-spa, in a park by Mr. Staughton's house.

As to the famous dropping-well or petrifying water, it lies on the west side of the town and river, about twenty-six yards from the bank of the Nid, and it rises fifteen yards below the top of a mountain of marle stone, and in four falls, of about two yards each fall, comes to an easy ascent, where it spreads upon the top of an isthmus of a petrified rock, generated out of the water, which falls down round it. This isthmus or rock is ten yards high, and hangs over its base or bottom about five yards. It is near sixteen yards long and thirteen broad, and as it started from the bank about fifty years ago, leaves a chasm between them, that is about three yards wide. In this chasm, you will find petrified twigs of trees, shrubs, and grass-roots, hanging in most beautiful pillars, all interwoven, and forming many charming figures ; and on the common side are whole banks like stalactites, hard and inseparable from the rock, where the water trickles down. These petrefactions, the falling water, and the little isthmus or island being beautifully clothed with ash, osier, elm, sambucus, servicana major, geraniums, wood-mercury, hart's-tongue, sage, lady's mantle, cowslips, wild angelica, &c., form altogether a delightful scene. The first spring of this water is out of a small hole on the little mountain, in the middle of a thick-set of shrubs. It sends out twenty gallons in a minute of the sweetest water in the world, and twenty-four grains in a pint heavier than common water.

Most people are of opinion, that petrifying water is dangerous drink, and may produce abundance of mischief, in causing the stone and gravel in the body : the original particles or principles of the stony substance called spar, which are in abundance suspended in this kind of water, must get into the flood-gates of the kidneys and ureters, as they opine, and create great misery in a little time.

But this fear of petrefactions in living animal bodies is grounded upon neither reason nor experience ; for the spar in these waters forms no petrefactions whilst in a brisk motion, or in a temperate season, or on vegetables while they preserve their vegetating life. While there is warmth and circulation of juices, there can be no incrustation or petrefaction from the suspended stony particles. Besides, if the minims of spar are not within the spheres of sensible attraction, whilst in motion ; much less are they so when mingled with the fluids of the human body : you may therefore very safely drink these limpid petrifying waters at all times, as a common fluid, if they come in your way, as the best, and most grateful or pleasant water in the world, on account of the infinitesimals, or original leasts, of spar that are in them, in vast quantities, but infinitely small particles : and if you are sick, in many cases they are the best of medicines. Human invention has nothing equal to them for fluxes of any part of the body, or colliquations from an acid salt. So far are they from being in the least dangerous, that in all unnatural discharges, by spitting, stool, or urine ; by excessive menstrual or hæmorrhoidal fluxes, in the fluor albus, diabetes, profuse sweatings ; in the diarrhœa, dysentry, or lienteria where the springs are not quite worn out ; in ulcers of the viscera, hectic fevers, atrophy, and colliquations or night sweats, there is not any thing in physic more profitable or pleasant, to recover a patient. Let your dose, in such cases, be three half-pints of

Knaresborough dropping-well in the forenoon ; and before you begin to drink this water, remember to take two doses of rhubarb, to cleanse off the excrements of the first viscera. You must not drink ale, drams, or punch, during a course of these waters : and take but very little red port. You must likewise have a strict regard to diet. Let it be milk, eggs, jellies, barley-broth, chickens, kid, lamb, and the like. You must avoid all salt, sharp, stimulating things, day-sleep, and night-air ; but agreeable conversation, and diversions that require very little exercise, conduce to the success of this kind of water, in the distempers I have mentioned. If such diseases are curable, you may expect a restoration of health.

But, in the dropsy, jaundice, diminished or irregular menses ; in hyppo, melancholy, stuffings of the lungs, obstructions of the viscera, stoppages of the lacteals and misentery, glandular swellings, king's-evil, or any case, where thinning, relaxing, opening, deterging, attenuation or stimulation are wanting, such water is death.

Note, reader, there is another excellent petrifying-water at Newton-Dale in Yorkshire, N. R. thirteen miles from Scarborough. Another near Castle-Howard, the fine seat of the Earl of Carlisle, ten miles from York. Another, near Skipton in that rough, romantic, wild and silent country, called Craven, in the West-riding of Yorkshire. And one, called Bandwell, at Stonefield in Lincolnshire, west of Horncastle, which is a hundred and twenty-two miles from London. These springs, and many that are not to be come at among the vast fells of Westmoreland, and the high mountains of Stanemore, have all the virtues of Knaresborough dropping-well ; though Knaresborough-water is the only one resorted to by company : and as to this spring, I can affirm from my own knowledge, that it is as excellent, and truly medicinal, as the famous petrifying-water at Clermont. There is no manner of need for Britons going to the mountain Gregoire in Basse-Auvergne.

A POSTILLA, *

Containing an Account of Wardrew Sulphur-water ; the Life of Claudius Hobart ; and A Dissertation on Reason and Revelation.

In my account of sulphur-waters, I forgot to mention one

---

* A Postilla, reader, is a barbarous word made up of the words post illa, and was brought into use in the twelfth century, when the marginal explicators of the Bible left the margins and under their text writ short and literal notes, before which they put the word postilla instead of the words post illa, meaning the particular words in the text, from whence, by a letter, they referred to the little note below : but in the thirteenth century, the barbarou word tookyso much, that all the commentators following, appropriated the name to their most copious commentaries, contrary to the first practice in the use of the word, and for three centuries after the biblical learning was all postilla, till at length the word disappeared, according to the wonted inconstancy and agitation of all human things, and gave place to a new and fifth invention, called tractatus, or homily. This is the history of a POSTILLA.

very extraordinary spring of this kind, and therefore, make a postilla of it here, that the reader may find in one section all I have to say on mineral waters. And as I found by the side of this water, a man as extraordinary as the spring, I shall add his life to my account of the water, and a couple of little pieces written by him.

In Northumberland, on the borders of Cumberland, there is a place called Wardrew, to the north-west of Thirlwall-castle, which stands on that part of the Picts-Wall, where it crosses the Tippel, and is known by the name of Murus Perforatus in Saxon Thirlwall, on account of the gaps made in the wall at this place for the Scots' passage. Here, as I wandered about this wild, untravelled country, in search of Roman antiquities, I arrived at a sulphur-spring, which I found to be the strongest and most excellent of the kind in all the world. It rises out of a vast cliff, called Arden-Rock, over the bank of the river Arde or Irthing, six feet above the surface of the water, and comes out of a chink in the cliff by a small spout. The discharge is fifty gallons in a minute from a mixture of limestone and iron-stone ; and the water is so very fœtid, that it is difficult to swallow it. The way to it is not easy, for there is no other passage than along a very narrow ledge, about nine inches broad, which has been cut off the rock over the deep river, and if you slip, as you may easily do, having nothing to hold by, down you go into a water that looks very black and shocking, by the shade of the hanging precipice, and some aged trees which protect from the vast cliff.

This dangerous situation, and its remoteness, will prevent its being ever much visited, admirable as the spaw is ; yet the country-people thereabout make nothing of the ledge, and drink plentifully of the water, to their sure relief, in many dangerous distempers. It is to them a blessed spring.

The land all round here was one of the finest rural scenes I have seen, and made a pensive traveller wish for some small public-house there, to pass a few delightful days. Its lawns and groves, its waters, vales, and hills, are charming, and form the sweetest, softest region of silence and ease. Whichever way I turned, the various beauties of nature appeared, and nightingales from the thicket inchantingly warbled their loves. The fountains were bordered with violets and moss, and near them were clumps of pine and beech, bound with sweet-briar, and the tendrils of woodbine. It is a delightful spot : a paradise of blooming joys, in the fine season of the year.

One inhabitant only I found in this fine solitude, who lived on the margin of the river, in a small neat cottage, that was almost hid with trees. This was CLAUDIUS HOBART, a man of letters, and a gentleman, who had been unfortunate in the world and retired to these elysian fields, to devote the remainder of his time to religion, and enjoy the calm felicities of contemplative life. He was obliged by law to resign his estate to a claimant, and death had robbed him of a matchless mistress, of great fortune, to whom he was to have been married. The men who had called themselves his friends, and as Timon says in Lucian, honoured him, worshipped him, and seemed to depend on his nod, ἐμοῦ νέυματος ανηρ τημῦνοι, no longer knew him ; jam ne agnoscor quidem ab illis, nec aspici ne dignantur me, perinde ut eversum hominis jam olim defuncti cippum, ac temporis longitudine collapsum pretereunt quasi ne norint quidem ; μηδέ ἀναγνόντες : so true, continued HOBART, are the beautiful lines of Petronius ;

> Nomen amicitiæ si quatenus expedit, hæret,
> Calculus in tabula mobile ducit opus.
> Quum fortuna manet, vultum servatis amici :
> Cum cecidit, turpi vertitis ora fugâ.

And so Ovid says was his case,

> Eandem cum Timone nostro sortem
> Expertus naso, qui sic de seipso :
> En ego non paucis quondam munitus amicis :
> Dum flavit velis aura secunda meis :
> Ut fera terribili tumuerunt æquora vento,
> In mediis lacera puppe relinquor aquis.

So HOBART found it, and as his health was declining from various causes, and he had nothing in view before him but misery ; he retired to Wardrew, while he had some money, built the little house I saw on a piece of ground he purchased, and provided such necessaries and comforts as he imagined might be wanting : he had a few good books, the Bible, some history, and mathematics, to make him wiser and better, and abroad he diverted himself mostly in his garden, and with fishing : for fifteen years past he had not been in any town, nor in any one's house, but conversed often with several of the country people, who came to drink the mineral-water : what he had fresh occasion for, one or other of them brought him, according to his written directions, and the money he gave them, and once or twice a week he was sure of seeing somebody : as the people knew he was not rich, and lived a harmless life, they were far from being his enemies, and would do any thing in their power to serve the hermit, as they called him : but he seldom gave them any trouble. His food was biscuit, honey, roots, fish, and oil ; and his drink, water, with a little rum sometimes. He was never sick, nor melancholy ; but by a life of temperance and action, and a religion of trust and resignation, enjoyed perpetual health and peace, and run his latent course in the pleasing expectation of a remove, when his days were past, to the bright mansions of the blest.

Such was the account HOBART gave me of himself, which made me admire him much, as he was but fifty then ; and to convince me his temper had nothing Timonean or unsocial in it from his solitary life, he requested I would dine with him. He entertained me with an excellent pickled trout and biscuit, fine fruit, and a pot of extraordinary honey : with as much cream of tartar as lay on a sixpence, infused in warm water, he made half a pint of rum into good punch, and he talked over it like a man of sense, breeding, and good humour. We parted when the bowl was out, and at my going away, he made me a present of the following in manuscript, and told me I might print it, if I could think it would be of any use to mankind. It was called

THE RULE OF REASON, WITH A FEW THOUGHTS ON REVELATION.

The throne of God rests upon reason, and his prerogative is supported by it. It is the sole rule of the Deity, the Mind which presides in the universe and therefore is venerable, sacred, and divine. Every ray of reason participates of the majesty of that Being to whom it belongs, and whose attribute it is ; and being thereby awful, and invested with a supreme and absolute authority, it is rebellion to refuse subjection to right reason and a violation of the great and fundamental law of heaven and earth.

To this best, and fittest, and noblest rule, the rule of truth, we ought to submit, and in obedience to the sacred voice of reason, resist the importunities of sense and the usurpations of appetite. Since the will of that Being, who is infinitely pure and perfect, rational and righteous, is obliged and governed by his unerring understanding ; our wills should be guided and directed by our reason. In imitation of the wisest and best of Beings, we must perpetually adhere to truth, and ever act righteously for righteousness' sake. By acting in conformity to moral truths, which are really and strictly divine, we act in conformity to ourselves, and it is not possible to conceive any thing so glorious, or godlike. We are thereby taught the duties of piety, our duties toward our fellows, and that self-culture which is subservient to piety and humanity.

Reason informs us there is a superior Mind, endued with knowledge and great power, presiding over human affairs ; some original, independent Being, complete in all possible perfection, of boundless power, wisdom and goodness, the Contriver, Creator, and Governor of this world, and the inexhaustible source of all good. A vast collection of evidence demonstrates this.

Design, intention, art, and power, as great as our imagination can conceive, everywhere occur. As far as we can make observations, original intelligence and power appear to reside in a Spirit distinct from all divisible, changeable, or moveable substance ; and if we can reason at all it must be clear that an original omnipotent Mind is a good Deity, and espouses the cause of virtue, and of the universal happiness ; will gloriously compensate the worthy in a future·state, and then make the vicious and oppressive have cause to repent of their contradicting his will. It follows then most certainly, that with this great source of our being, and of all perfection, every rational mind ought to correspond, and with internal and external worship adore the divine power and goodness. His divine perfections, creation and providence, must excite all possible esteem, love, and admiration, if we think at all ; must beget trust and resignation ; and raise the highest sensations of gratitude. All our happiness and excellency is from his bounty, and therefore not unto us, but to his name be the praise. And can there be a joy on earth so stable and transporting as that which rises from living with an habitual sense of the Divine Presence, a just persuasion of being approved, beloved, and protected by him who is infinitely perfect and omnipotent ?

By reason we likewise find, that the excesses of the passions produce misery. and iniquity makes a man completely wretched and˜despicable : but integrity and moral worth secure us peace and merit, and lead to true happiness and glory. Unless reason and inquiry are banished, vice and oppression must have terrible struggles against the principles of humanity and conscience. Reflection must raise the most torturing suspicions, and all stable satisfaction must be lost : but by cultivating the high powers of our reason, and acquiring moral excellence, so far as human nature is able : by justice and the benevolent affections, virtue and charity, we are connected with and affixed to the Deity, and with the inward enjoyment of all the felicities suitable to our transitory condition. Happy state surely ! There are no horrors here to haunt us. There is no dreadful thing to poison all parts of life and all enjoyments.

Let us hearken then to the original law of reason, and follow God and nature as the sure guide to happiness. Let the offices of piety and beneficence be the principal employment of our time ; and the chief work of our every day, to secure an happy immortality, by equity, benignity, and devotion. By continual attention and internal discipline, reason can do great things, and enable us so to improve the supreme and most godlike powers of our constitution, and so discharge the duties imposed upon us by our Creator, that when we return into that silence we were in before we existed, and our places shall know us no more, we

may pass from the unstable condition of terrestrial affairs to that
eternal state in the heavens, where everlasting pleasures and
enjoyments are prepared for those who have lived in the delightful exercise of the powers of reason, and performed all social
and kind offices to others, out of a sense of duty to God.   Thus
does truth oblige us.   It is the basis of morality, as morality is
the basis of religion.

This, I think, is a just account of moral truth and rectitude,
and shows that it is essentially glorious in itself, and the sacred
rule to which all things must bend, and all agents submit.   But
then a question may be asked, What need have we of revelation,
since reason can so fully instruct us, and its bonds alone are
sufficient to hold us ;—and in particular, what becomes of the
principal part of revelation called redemption ?

The system of moral truth and revelation, it may be answered,
are united, and at perfect amity with each other.   Morality
and the gospel stand on the same foundation, and differ only in
this, that revealed religion, in respect of the corrupt and degenerate state of mankind, has brought fresh light, and additional assistance, to direct, support, and fix men in their duty.
We have histories which relate an early deviation from moral
truth, and inform us that this disease of our rational nature
spreads like a contagion.   The case became worse, and more
deplorable, in succeeding ages ; and as evil examples and prejudices added new force to the prevailing passions, and reason
and liberty of will, for want of due exercise, grew weaker, and
less able to regain their lost dominion, corruption was rendered
universal.   Then did the true God, the Father of the Universe,
and the most provident and beneficent of Beings, interpose by
a revelation of his will, and by advice and authority, do all that
was possible, to prevent the self-destructive effects of the culpable ignorance and folly of his offspring.   He gave the world
a transcript of the law of nature by an extraordinary messenger,
the Man Christ Jesus, who had power given him to work miracles,
to rouse mankind from their fatal stupidity, to set their thoughts
on work, and to conciliate their attention to the heavenly declaration.   In this republication of the original law, he gave
them doctrines and commandments perfectly consonant to the
purest reason, and to them annexed sanctions that do really
bind and oblige men, as they not only guard and strengthen
religion, but affect our natural sensibility and selfishness.   Religion appears to great disadvantage, when divines preach it
into a bond of indemnity, and a mere contract of interest ; but
exclusive of this, it must be allowed, that the sanctions of the
gospel have a weight, awfulness, and solemnity, that prove to
a great degree effectual.   Safety and advantage are reasons for
well-doing.

In short, the evidence of the obligation of the duties of natural religion is as plain and strong from reason, as any revelation can make it ; but yet the means of rendering these duties effectual in practice, are not so clear and powerful from mere reason, as from revelation. The proof of obligation is equally strong in reason and inspiration, but the obligation itself is rendered stronger by the gospel, by superadded means or motives. The primary obligation of natural religion arises from the nature and reason of things, as being objects of our rational moral faculties, agreeably to which we cannot but be obliged to act ; and this obligation is strengthened by the tendency of natural religion to the final happiness of every rational agent : but the clear knowledge, and express promises which we have in the gospel, of the nature and greatness of this final happiness, being added to the obligation from, and the tendency of reason or natural religion to the final happiness of human nature, the obligation of it is thereby still more strengthened. In this lies the benefit of Christianity. It is the old, uncorrupt religion of nature and reason, intirely free from superstition and immorality ; delivered and taught in the most rational and easy way, and enforced by the most gracious and powerful motives.

But if this be the case, it may be asked, Where are our holy mysteries—and what do you think of our Redemption ? If natural reason and conscience can do so much, and to the gospel we are obliged only for a little more light and influence, then Trinity in Unity, and the Sacrifice of the Cross are nothing. What are your sentiments on these subjects ?

As to the Trinity, it is a word invented by the doctors, and so far as I can find, was never once thought of by Jesus Christ and his apostles ; unless it was to guard against the spread of tritheism by taking the greatest care to inculcate the supreme divinity of God the Father : but let it be a trinity, since the church will have it so, and by it I understand one Uncreated, and one Created, and a certain divine virtue of quality. These I find in the Bible, God, Jesus the Word, and a Divine Assistance or Holy Wind, not Holy Ghost, as we have translated it : called a Wind, because God, from whom every good and perfect gift cometh, gave the most extraordinary instance of it under the emblem of a Wind ; and holy, because it was supernatural. This is the scripture doctrine, in relation to the Deity, the Messias, and the Energy of God ; of which the Wind was promised as a pledge, and was given as an emblem, when the day of Pentecost was come ; and if these three they will call a Trinity, I shall not dispute about the word. But to say Jesus Christ is God, though the apostles tell us, that God raised from the dead the Man Jesus Christ, whom they killed ; that he had exalted him at his right hand, and had made him both Lord and Christ ; and to affirm that this Ghost, as they render the word Wind ; is a person distinct and different from the person of God the Father, and equally supreme ; this I cannot agree to. If the scripture is true, all this appears to me to be false. It is a mere invention of the Monks.

As to Redemption, it may be in perfect consistence and agreement with truth and rectitude, if the accomplishment of it be considered as premial, and as resulting from a personal reward : but to regard the accomplishment as penal, and as resulting from a vicarious punishment, is a notion that cannot be reconciled to the principle of rectitude. Vicarious punishment or suffering appears an impossibility : but as Jesus, by adding the most extensive benevolence to perfect innocence, and by becoming obedient to death, even the death of the cross, was most meritorious, and was entitled to the highest honour, and most distinguished reward, his reward might be our deliverance from the bonds of sin and death, and the restoration of immortality. This reward was worthy of the giver, and tended to the advancement and spread of virtue. It was likewise most acceptable to the receiver. It no way interfered with right and truth. It was in all respects most proper and suitable. These are my sentiments of Redemption. This appears to me to be the truth on the most attentive and impartial examination I have been capable of making.

To this, perhaps, some people may reply, that though these notions are, for the most part, just, and in the case of redemption, in particular, as innocence and punishment are inconsistent and incompatible ideas, that it was not possible Christ's oblation of himsel could be more than a figurative sacrifice, in respect of translation of guilt, commutation of persons, and vicarious infliction ; though a real sacrifice in the sense of intending by the oblation to procure the favour of God, and the indemnity of sinners : yet, as the author appears to be a Socinian, his account is liable to objections. For, though the Socinians acknowledge the truth and necessity of the revelation of the gospel, yet, in the opinion of some great divines, they interpret it in such a manner, as no unprejudiced person, who has read the scriptures, with any attention, nor any sensible heathen, who should read them, can possibly believe. They make our Redeemer a man, and by this doctrine reflect the greatest dishonour on Christianity, and its Divine Author.

This is a hard charge. The Socinians are by these divines described as people who read the scriptures with prejudice, and without attention ; men more senseless than the Heathens, and as wicked too : for, in the highest degree, they dishonour Christ Jesus and his religion. Astonishing assertion ! It puts me in mind of an imputation of the celebrated Waterland in his second charge ; " What atheism chiefly aims at, is, to sit loose from present restraints and future reckonings ; and these two purposes may be competently served by deism, which is a more refined kind of atheism." . Groundless and ridiculous calumny ! True and proper deism is a sincere belief of the existence of a God, and of an impartial distribution of rewards and punishments in another world, and a practice that naturally results from, and is consonant to such belief ; and if atheism aims to sit loose from restraints and reckonings, then of consequence, deism is the grand barrier to the purposes of atheism. The true Deist is so far from breaking through restraints, that he makes it the great business of his life to discharge the obligations he is under, because he believes in God, and perceives the equity and reasonableness of duties, restraints, and future reckonings. The assertion therefore demonstrates the prejudice of Dr. Waterland, in relation to the Deists.

And the case is the same in respect of the charge against the Socinians. It is the divines that are prejudiced against them, and not the Socinians in studying the New Testament. It is the grand purpose of our lives to worship God, and form our religious notions according to the instructions of divine wisdom. We examine the sacred writings, with the utmost desire, and most ardent prayer, that we may be rightly informed in the truest sense of the holy authors of those divine books : and it appears to our plain understandings, after the most honest labour, and wishes to Heaven for a clear conception of holy things, that the Father is the supreme God, that is, the first and chief Being, and Agent ; the first and chief Governor ; the Fountain of Being, Agency, and Authority ; that the Christian Messiah, the Man Christ Jesus, was sent into the world to bear witness to the truth, and preach the gospel of the kingdom of God, that kingdom of God which is within you, saith the Lord, *Luke*, ch. xvii. v. 21, not a kingdom of Monks, a sacerdotal empire of power, propositions, and ceremonies. He came to call sinners to repentance and amendment of life, to teach them the law of love, and assure mankind of grace and mercy and everlasting glory, if they kept the commandments, and were obedient to the laws of Heaven ; laws of righteousness, peace, giving no offence, and unanimity in the worship of the God and Father of our Lord Jesus Christ : but that, if they did not repent, and cease to be hurtful and injurious ; if they did not open their eyes and turn from darkness to light, from the power of Satan unto God, and put on such an agreeable and useful temper and behaviour, as would render them a blessing in the creation, they would be numbered among the cursed, and perish everlastingly, for want of real goodness and a general sincerity of heart. This the Socinians think is what Christ proposed and recommended, as the only and the sure way to God's favour, through the worthiness of the Lamb that was slain. We say this is pure religion. It is true, original

Christianity, and if the glorious design of our Lord is answered by his miracles and preaching, by his death, his resurrection, his ascension, and by the grace of the holy, blessed, and sanctifying Spirit, it could reflect no dishonour on Christianity, and its divine author, if our Redeemer was a mere man. If by the assistance of God Almighty, a mere man performed the whole work of our redemption, all we had to do was to be thankful for the mighty blessing. The love of God in this way had been equally inestimable. The worth of Jesus would be still invaluable.

But it is not the opinion of the Socinians that Christ was a mere man. It is plain from his assertion, that the Rev. Dr. Heathcote, in his *Remarks on Free and Candid Disquisitions*, knows nothing of them : the account they give of Jesus Christ is very different. They say, he was a most glorious agent united to a human body, and so far from being a mere man, that he was superior to angels. He was the next in character to the necessarily existing Being. He is the brightness of the Father's glory, and the express image of his person : he has an excellency transcendent, and to the life represents what is infinitely great and perfect.

If they do not allow that he made the worlds, or had an eternal generation ; if they say, he had no existence till he was formed by the power of God in the womb, and assert this eminency is proper to the Man Christ Jesus ; yet they are far from affirming he was therefore a mere man : no ; they believe he was decreed to be as great and glorious as possible, and that God made the world for him ; that he was made the image of the invisible person of the Father ; an image the most express and exact ; as great as God himself could make it ; and of consequence, so transcendent in all perfections, that what he says and does is the same thing as if God had spoken and acted. This is not making him a mere man. No : they say he is the first of all, and the head of all creatures, whom the infinite love of God produced, to promote greatness, glory, and happiness among the creatures, by the superlative greatness and glory of Jesus ; and that angels, and the spirits of the just made perfect, might have the pleasure of beholding and enjoying the presence of this most glorious Image, that is, of seeing their invisible Creator in his Image, Jesus Christ. He is not a mere man ; but the brightness of the glory of God, the express Image of his person, and raised so much higher than the angels, as he has inherited from God a more excellent name than they, to wit, the name of Son, and is the appointed heir of all things.

So that this Socinianism reflects no dishonour on Christianity and its Divine Author. It conduces as much to the glory of God, and the benefit of man, as any Christianity can do. There is something vastly beautiful and satisfactory in the notion of Christ's being the most glorious Image of the invisible Father, whenever his existence began. The many transcendent excellencies of the Messias, in whom all fulness dwells, are exercised upon men to their happiness, and to his glory ; and we learn from thence, that greatness and glory are the result of the exercise of virtue to the relief and happiness of others. The Redeemer of the world is, in this account, the next in dignity and power to the Great God ; and the perfections of the Father do most eminently shine forth in him. We are hereby made meet to be partakers of the inheritance of the saints in light, and delivered from the power of darkness. We give thanks unto the Father, who hath translated us into the kingdom of the Son of his love.

It is certain then that the divines have misrepresented the people, who are injuriously called Socinians, as the religion they profess is Scripture-Christianity. I say injuriously, because, in the first place, the word Socinian is intended as a term of great reproach to Christians, who deserve better usage for the goodness of their manners, and the purity of their faith : and in the next place, that Socinus was so far from being the author of our religion, that he was not even the first restorer of it. He did not go to Poland to teach the people there his religious notions, but because there was a Unitarian congregation there, with whom he might join in the worship of the Father, through Jesus the Mediator, as his conscience would not suffer him to assemble with those who worship a Being compounded of three divine persons.

But it is time to have done, and I shall conclude in the words of a good author in old French.* The extract must be a curious thing to the reader, as the valuable book I take it from is not to be bought.

" Nostre confession de foy até depuis la premiere predication de l'evangile puisque nous luy donnons la sainte ecriture pour fondement, mais il arrive de nous ce qu'il arrive des tous ceux qui se sont detachés de l'eglise Romaine aux quels le papistes donnent malgré eux pour autheurs de leur religion Luther, Calvin, et autres docteures qui n'ont eté que les restorateurs, des dogmes et de verites qui s'etoyent presque perdues sous le gouvernement tyrannique de l'eglise Romaine pendant lequel l'ecriture sainte etoit devenue un livre inconnu a la pluspart de chretiens la lecture en ayant été defendue communement. Mais par un decret de la providence de Diue le periode de la revolution etant venu chacun a commencé a deterer la verité la mieux qu'il a pu, et comme dans chaque revolution il y a des chefs et des gens illustres, ainsi dans le retablissement des dogmes etouffès si longtems par le papisme Luther, Calvin, Arminius, et Socin, ont été des hommes illustres et dont on a donné le nom aux religions. Vous scaurez donc s'il vous plaist que Socin bien loin d'avoir été autheur de nostre religion n'en a pas été meme la premier restaurateur : car

* Or rather in bad French, as the writer was no Frenchman.

il n'etoit venu en Pologne que parce qu'il avoit appris qu'il s'y etoit deja formée une assemblée de gens qui avoyent des opinions semblables aux siennes : Je vous diray de plus, que la seule chose que le fait un heros dans nostre religion c'est qu'il en a ecrit des livres, mais il ny a presque personne qui les lise, car comme Socin etoit un bon jurisconsulte il est extremement long et ennuyeux ; et outre que nous ne voulous point avoir d'autre livre de religion que le nouveau Testament et point d'autres docteurs que les apostres. C'est pourquoy, c'est bien malgré nous qu'on nous appelle Sociniens ou Arriens : cc sont des noms dont la malignité de nos ennemys nous couvre pour nous rendre odieux. Nous appellons entre nous du simple nom de Chretiens. Mais puisque dans cette desunion de la chretienté, on nous dit qu'il ne suffit pas de porter cc nom universel, mais qu'il encore necessairement se distinguer par quelque appellation particuliere, nous consentons donc de porter le nom de chretiens unitaires pour nous distinguer de chretiens trinitaires. Ce nom de chretiens unitaires nous convient fort bien comme a ceux qui ne voulant en aucune façon encherye sur la doctrine de Jesus Christ, n'y y subtiliser plus qu'il ne faut, attachent leur croyance et leur confession positivement a cette instruction de Jesus Christ qui se trouve dans le 17 chap. de l'evangile de St. Jean, quand il dit Mon pere l'heure est venue, glorifiez vostre fils afin que vostre fils vous glorifie, comme vous luy avez donné puissance sur tous les hommes a fin qu'il donne la vie eternelle a tous ceux que vous luy avez donné ; or la vie eternelle consiste a vous connoistre, vous qui estes le seul Dieu veritable, et Jesus Christ que vous avez envoyé. La meme leçon nous donne l'apostre St. Paul dans le 8 chap. aux Cor. disant, qu'il n'y a pour nous qu'un seul Dieu qui est la pere duquel sont toutes choses et nous pour luy, et il n'y a qu'un seul seigneur qul est Jesus Christ, par lequel sont toutes choses et nous par luy. C'est donc a cause de cette confession que nous nous appellons chretiens unitaires par ce que nous croyons qu'il n'y a qu'un seul Dieu, pere et Dieu de nostre seigneur Jesus Christ, celuy que Jesus Christ nous a appris d'adorer, et lequel il a aussy adore luy meme, l'appellent non seulment nostre Dieu mais son Dieu aussy selon qu'il a dit, je m'en vay a mon pere et vostre pere, a mon Dieu et a vostre Dieu.

"Ainsy vous voyez que nous nous tenons aux verités divines. Nous avons la religieuse veneration pour la sainte ecriture. Avec tout cela nous sommes serviteurs tres humble des messieurs les trinitaires,—penes quos mundanæ fabulæ actio est, et il ne tient pas a nous que nous ne courrions de tout nostre cœur a leurs autels, s'ils vouloyent nous faire la grace de souffrir nostre simplicité en Jesus Christ, et de ne pas vouloir nous obliger a la confession de supplemens a la sainte ecriture."*

* *La Verité et la Religion en Visite, Alamagne*, 1695.

The great and excellent Faustus Socinus was born at Sienna, in the year 1539, and died at Luclavie, the third of March, 1604, aged sixty-five. His book in defence of the authority of the sacred scriptures is a matchless performance ; and if he had never written any thing else, is alone sufficient to render his memory glorious, and precious to all true Christians. Get this book, if you can. It is the finest defence of your Bible that was ever published. Steinfurti, 1611. edit. Vorst. And yet, such is the malignity of orthodoxy, that a late great prelate, Dr. Smalbroke, Bishop of Litchfield and Coventry, who died in 1749 ; in his *Second Charge to the Clergy of St. David's*, p. 34 ; could not help blackening the author when he mentioned the work : his words are these, " And if Grotius was more especially assisted by the valuable performance of a writer, otherwise justly of ill fame, I mean, Faustus Socinus' little book *De Auctoritate S. Scripturæ*, this assistance," &c. Here the admirable Socinus, a man of as much piety and as good morals, as hath lived since the apostles' time, who truly and godly served the Almighty and everlasting God, through our Lord and Saviour Jesus Christ, is painted by this eminent hand " a man of ill fame ; " and for no other reason but because his heavenly religion made him oppose the orthodox heresy of three Gods, as taught in the creed of Athanasius ; and piously labour, by the purity of his doctrine and example, to keep the world from corruption.

Let us then be careful to confess the holy unitarian faith. Let us take the advice of Socinus, and be original Christians. Let there not be in our religion a God compounded of three supreme spirits, equal in power and all possible perfections. Let us worship the Invisible Father, the first and chief Almighty Being, who is one supreme universal Spirit, of peerless Majesty ; and, as the inspired apostles direct, let us worship him through his most glorious Image, the Man Christ Jesus ; our Redeemer and Mediator, our King and our Judge.

N.B. Though the reverend Dr. Heathcote hath been very unfriendly in his account of the Christians he calls Socinians, in his observations before mentioned, yet you are not from thence to conclude that he belongs to the Orthodox Party. He is far from it, and therefore I recommend to your perusal not only his *Cursory Animadversions upon Free and Candid Disquisitions*, and his finer *Boyle-Lecture Sermons on the Being of God*, but also his *Cursory Animadversions upon the Controversy, concerning the Miraculous Powers*, and his *Remarks on Chapman's Credibility of the Fathers' Miracles*. They are three excellent pamphlets. The first is against the scholastic Trinity. And the others on the side of Dr. Middleton, against the miracles of the Fathers.

Note, Reader, Dr. Heathcote's two pamphlets on the side of Dr. Middleton, and the Rev. Mr. Toll's admirable pieces in vindication of the Doctor against the miracles of the Fathers, will give you a just and full idea of the late controversy. Mr. Tolls pieces are called, *A Defence of Dr. Middleton's Free Enquiry ; Remarks upon Mr. Church's Vindication ;* and his *Sermon and Appendix against Dr. Church's Appeal.*

If you would see all that can be said in relation to this matter, get likewise Dr. Syke's *Two Previous Questions :* ard *The Two Previous Questions impartially Considered* ; by the same author. *Remarks on two Pamphlets against Dr. Middleton's Introductory Discourse ; Two Letters to the Rev. Mr. Jackson, in Answer to his Remarks on Middleton's Free Inquiry ;* and *A View of the Controversy, concerning the Miraculous Powers, supposed to have subsisted in the Christian Church through several successive Centuries.*   These pamphlets will bind into two large octavo volumes, and make a valuable collection of critical religious learning.

Note, Reader, of that admirable work, called *Bibliotheca Fratrum Polonorum*, by Socinus, Crellius, Sclichtingius, and Wolzogenius, six volumes, printed in *Irenopoli*, 1656, folio.   The first and second volumes are the writings of Socinus ; the third and fourth by Crellius ; the fifth by Sclichtingius ; and the sixth by Wolzogenius : they are all well worth your reading, as they contain the most valuable and excellent learning ; and especially Socinus and Crellius.   In another place, where you will find me alone in a solitude ; I shall give some curious extracts from the works of these great, injured men, and a summary of their lives.

But to return to my narrative ; from Knaresborough, I went to Harrogate again, and there found the following letter, of an old date, left for me,

" SIR,

" As you told me, you intended to go to London soon, and business obliges me to ride up to the capital a few weeks hence, I should take it as a great favour, if you would make Westmoreland your way, and through Lancashire to the Chester road, that I may have your protection and guidance in this long journey.

"I am, Sir,
"Your humble servant,
"MARIA SPENCE.

" Cleator, six miles to the south-
    west of Wharton-Hall."

This letter surprised me.   Yes, dear creature, I said, I will make Westmoreland my way to London.   At four in the morning I mounted my horse, and rode to Cleator.   I arrived there at six in the evening, and had travelled that day seventy-five miles ; to wit, from Harrogate to Boroughbridge, eight ; from thence to Catarric, twenty-two ; to Gretabridge, fifteen ; to Bows, six ; to Brugh in Westmoreland, twelve ; to Kirkby Steven, near

Wharton-Hall, six ; to Cleator, six ; in all, seventy-five miles. I dined at Catarric on a hot pigeon-pye just drawn, and ale of one ear, that is, admirable, as Rabelais means by the phrase, " We had wine of one ear," alluding to the one shake of the head to the right shoulder, when a thing is excellent ; and I gave the horses another feed of corn at Bows, at the George, kept by RAILTON, the Quaker ; an excellent inn, and the master of it an instructive and entertaining orator.* I mention these things for your benefit, reader, that you may know where to stop to advantage, if you should ever ride over the same ground I went that day.

* While I waited at the inn, till the horses had eaten their corn, the landlord brought me a paper dropt, by a lady he knew not, some days before at his house. He added, it was a curiosity, and worth my serious consideration.

A MORNING AND EVENING PRAYER.

" Almighty and ever-living God, have mercy on me. Forgive me all my sins, and make my heart one, to fear thy glorious fearful name, Jehovah. Guide me with thy counsel, I beseech thee, and be the strength of my life and my portion for ever.

" O Lord Jehovah, defend me from the power and malice, the assaults and attempts, of all my adversaries, and keep me in health and safety, in peace and innocence. These things I ask in the name of Jesus Christ, thy Son, our Lord ; and in his words I call upon thee as , Our Father, who art in heaven," &c.

This prayer pleased me very much. In the most beautiful manner, as well as in a few words it expresses all we need ask from Heaven ; and if Miss Dudgeon of Richmondshire was the composer of it, as I have been assured since, upon enquiry, I here place it to her honour, as a monument of her piety and sense ; and in hopes the illustrious of her sex will use so short and excellent a form of devotion in their closets morning and night.

There is an expression in this prayer, which for some time I could not well comprehend the meaning of it ; that is, Make my heart one : but on considering it, I found it supported by the greatest authorities.

Among the sayings of Pythagoras, one is, be simply thyself. Reduce thy conduct to one single aim, by bringing every passion into subjection, and acquiring that general habit of self-denial, which comprehends temperance, moderation, patience, government, and is the main principle of wisdom. Be simply thyself, and so curb desire, and restrain the inclinations and controul the affections, that you may be always able to move the passions as reason shall direct. Let not every foremost fancy, or every forward appearance, have the least mastery over you ; but view them on every side by the clear light of reason, and be no further influenced by the imaginations of pleasure, and apprehensions of evil, than as the obvious relations and nature of things allow. Let the result of a perception which every rational mind may have of the essential difference between good and evil, be the cause or ground of obligation. This will add greatly to quiet, and be productive of much real felicity. It will render every present condition supportable, brighten every prospect, and always incline us more to hope than to fear. This is the doctrine of Pythagoras.

I likewise find that David expresses the same thought in the 86th Psalm, ver. 11, which is rendered in the Bible translation, " Unite my heart to fear thy name ; " in the Common-Prayer Book, " O knit my heart unto thee, that I may fear thy name : " but the Hebrew is, " Make my heart one," to fear thy name ; meaning, Let the fear of thee be the one ruling disposition of my soul, in opposition to the double-minded man, which the Hebrew elegantly expresses by a " heart and a heart ; " one that draws to the riches, pleasures, and honours of this world ; and another to the practice of all virtue.

As to the other part of the prayer, which has the words—glorious—fearful—Jehovah ; whereas in the 86th *Psalm* it is only said, " To fear thy name ; " the author certainly took them from *Deuteronomy*, ch. xxviii. ver. 58. The design of the dreadful threatenings in this chapter set before the people, is there thus expressed, " That thou mayest fear this glorious and fearful name, Jehovah thy God ; " or as in our translation, " the Lord thy God "—And therefore I think these words are very finely used in this prayer.

" It is amazing to me," says the Rev. Mr. Peters, rector of St. Mabyn, " that throughout the Bible, the translators have every where changed the word Jehovah for the word Lord, when God himself gave the word Jehovah as his name to be uttered ; and as in this word the whole mystery of the Jewish and Christian dispensation seem to have been wrapped up.

" Say to the people, Ami Jehovah. I am Jehovah. Ye shall know that I Jehovah am your God, which bringeth you out from under the burdens of the Egyptians." *Exod.* ch. vi. vv. 6, 7. *Deut.* ch. vi. ver. 4. " Hear, O Israel, Jehovah our God is one Jehovah."

When I came to Miss SPENCER's door, I sent in my name by a servant, and immediately MARIA came out herself to welcome me to Cleator.   She told me she was glad to see me, and extremely obliged to me, for riding so many miles out of my way, to travel

Then as to this word's comprehending the two dispensations, a good writer observes that though God was known to his true worshippers by many other names, as God Almighty, the High God, the Everlasting God, &c. yet Jehovah was his one peculiar name; a name which he had appointed to himself, in preference to all others, and by which he declared by Moses he would be distinguished for the time to come.

And as of all the names of God, this seems to be the most expressive of his essence, as it can only be derived from the root which signifies to be, and denotes the one eternal self-existent Being, from whom all other things derive their being, and on whom they must depend ;— As the word does likewise signify "makes to be what was promised or foretold," and by such meaning declares, as often as the word is repeated, that Jehovah our God is not only self-existent, and the Creator of the world, but Him in whom all divine prophecies and predictions centre ; it follows, in my opinion, that we should utter this awful name in our addresses to God, and not, like the Jews, through a superstition omit it, and use another instead of it." This passage is to be found in an excellent Preface to the octavo edition of his admirable *Dissertation on the Book of Job*, in reply to that part of the *Divine Legation of Moses demon-strated*, in which the author, my Lord of Gloucester, sets himself to prove, that this book is a work of imagination, or dramatic composition, no older than Ezra the priest, whom he supposes to be the writer of it, in the year before Christ 467, or the year 455, in the twentieth year of the reign of Artaxerxes, king of Persia, when Daniel's seventy weeks begin ; that is, the period of 490 years, that were to be fulfilled before the passion of our Saviour.   And further, according to the author of the *Legation*, that this "allegorical drama or poem," was written to quiet the minds of the Jewish people under the difficulties of their captivity, and to assure them, as represented by the person of Job, of those great temporal blessings which three prophets had predicted.

Now in the Preface to the book aforementioned, in answer to all this and fully and beauti-fully answered it is, you will find the passage relating to the word Jehovah, and more than I have quoted from it.

As to Pythagoras the Samian, mentioned in this note, on account of his saying, " Be simply thyself ; " he was famous in the 6oth olympiad, as Jamblicus informs us ; that is, his Elikia, or Reign of Fame, began in the first year of this olympiad, which was the year before Christ 540 ; for 60 × 4 gives 240—777 leaves 537 + 3, the plus years of the olympiad ; i.e. 2, 3, 4 = 540. . And he died in the 4th year of the 70th olmypiad, that is, the year before Christ 497 : for 70 × 4 = 280—777 remains 497 : there are no plus years to be added here, as it happened in the 4th or last year of the olympiad.   This philosopher was contemporary with, and a near friend to, the renowned Phalaris, who was murdered in the year before Christ 556, when the Belshazzar of Daniel ascended the throne of Babylon.   And as Pythagoras lived to the age of 90, according to Diogenes, he must have been born in the beginning of the reign of Nebuchadnezzar : the year this conqueror took Jerusalem, and its king Zedekiah, which was Olymp. 47. 3. and of consequence before Christ 590 : for 47 × 4 = 188—777, remain, 589 + 1 = 590.   This was 54 years before Thespis invented tragedy,* and 11 years before the birth of Æschylus, the reformer of tragedy.   Cyrus was then in the tenth year of his age.

It is likewise evident from hence, that Pythagoras must have lived through the reigns of Cyrus, Cambyses, and the greatest part of the reign of Darius Histaspes, who slew Smerdis the Magi, and is called in scripture Ahasuerus, the king of Persia, who married Esther, and ordered Haman the Amalekite to be hanged on the gallows he had erected for Mordecai the Jew, in the year before Christ 510.

Note, David was before Pythagoras 519 years.

Reader, As to the word Elikia, which I have used to express the reign or time of flourishing of Pythagoras, I have an observation or two to make in relation to it, which I think worth your attending to.

Clemens Alexandrinus says, *Stromata*, p. 40, ʻΑπὸ Μούσεος επι τὴν Σολομόντος ἐλικιαν ἔτη τὰ πάντα ἐχακόσια δέκα: that is, The years from Moses to Solomon's Elikia are 610 ; to wit, Moses's life! -   -   -   -   -   -   -   -   -   -   -   -   - 120

From his death to David's accession   -   -   -   -   - 450
David's reign   -   -   -   -   -   -   -   -   - 40

                                                                610

From this passage it is plain, that the Elikia of Solomon is not meant of his nativity, but of the beginning of his reign, when he was 33 years of age.

It is then very surprising that Dodwell should insist upon it, that Elikia always signifies nativity.   It is the more wonderful, as Dodwell quotes this passage from Clement ; and as it is impossible to make out 610, without coming to the 33rd of Solomon, as I have reckoned it.

---

* Olymp. 61. 1. Selden's *Comment on the Arundel Marble*.

up with her to London ; but as she had never been farther from home than Harrogate, and was afraid of going such a journey by herself, she had written to me, in hopes curiosity and my great complaisance to the ladies, might induce me to take Cleator in my way to town, though so much about ; but as so many weeks had passed since she came away from the Wells, and she heard nothing of me, she had laid aside all expectation of my coming, though this made the visit the more pleasing.

In answer to this, I replied, that if I had got her letter sooner, I would have been with her long before : but that was not possible, as I had been at a little lodge and farm of mine in the northern extremity of Westmoreland, to settle things there, and returned to Harrogate but yesterday, when I had the honour of receiving your letter, and upon reading it, set out at daybreak this morning to kiss your hand, and execute any commands.

Here an excellent hot supper was brought in, and after it, Miss SPENCE said, she was surprised to hear I was an inhabitant of Westmoreland, as she had never heard of me in the north, nor seen me at Harrogate before the other day.

I told her I was a stranger in the country, and by a wonderful accident, as I travelled a few years ago out of curiosity, and in search of a friend, up Stanemore-hills, I became possessed of a lodge I had on the northern edge of Westmoreland, where I lived

Nay, in another place of the *Stromata*, Clement says, Isaiah, Hosea, and Micah lived after the Elikia of Lycurgus ; where he can only mean the time when that lawgiver flourished ; for, from the destruction of Troy to the Akmé'of Lycurgus, was 290 years : and from Solomon, in whose time Troy was taken, to the time of the prophets, was 360 years.

Thus does learning accommodate things. Dodwell wanted to fit a passage in Antilochus to his own calculation and so 312 years from the Elikia of Pythagoras, that is, says Dodwell, from the nativity of the philosopher, he meant taking the word in that sense, to the death of Epicurus, brings us exactly to the time. Who can forbear smiling ? A favourite notion to many learned men a sacred thing. Dodwell settles his passage in Antilochus to his mind, by perverting the word Elikia.

This, to be sure, in prophane things, can do no great harm : but when the practice is brought into things sacred, it is a detriment to mankind. Some divines, for example, to support a notion as unreasonable as it is dear to them, tell us that the word Isos signifies strict equality, not like : and that when St. Paul says ἴσα Θεῷ, we must construe it, Jesus Christ was strictly equal to the most High God. This is sad construction, when Homer, Euripides, Æschylus, make the word Isos to import no more than like. Isanemos, swift as the wind ; Isatheos phos, like a God ; Isanerios, like a dream.

And when a divine is positive that os and kathos, as, and even as, words occurring in the New Testament, signify a strict equality, and not some sort of likeness ; this is miserable perversion, and hurts the Christian religion very greatly ; as they endeavour, by such a given sense, to prove that the man Christ Jesus is to be honoured with the same divine honours we offer to God the Father Almighty, by the command and example of Jesus, who was sent from God, and was a worshipper of God ; who lived obedient to the laws of God, preached those laws and died for them in the cause of God ; who was raised from the dead by God, and now sits on God's right hand ; intercedes with God, and in his Gospel owns his Father to be his and our only true God. This is sad accommodation. Though the words never signify more than a degree of likeness in the Greek classics, yet our headstrong orthodox monks will have them to mean strict equality ; and Alexander the Great and Alexander the Coppersmith are the same Being. Amazing ! Gentlemen ; here is but One Ball, and out of itself you shall see this one ball send forth two other balls, big as it, and yet not lose one atom of its weight and grandeur. Hocus pocus, Reverendissimi spectatores, the One is Three.

And now, Gentlemen, be pleased to observe the miracle reversed. Pilluli pilluli, congregate, Presto presto, unite : observate, Signori Dottissimi, the Three are One. Such is the hocus pocus the monks have made of their Trinity.

a considerable time, and once imagined I should never leave it, as it is the most romantic and the most beautiful solitude in the world.

While I was giving this short relation, Miss SPENCE seemed greatly amazed, and her uncle, an old clergyman, who had looked with great attention at me, hoped it would be no offence to ask how old I was.

" None at all, Sir," I replied. " I want some months of twenty-six ; and though I dance and rattle at the Wells, and am now going up to London, where all is tumult and noise, yet my passion for still life is so great, that I prefer the most silent retreat to the pleasures and splendours of the greatest town. If it was in my power to live as I please, I would pass my days unheard of and unknown, at Orton-Lodge, so my little silent farm is called, near the southern confines of Cumberland, with some bright partner of my soul. I am sure I should think it a complete paradise to live in that distant solitude with a woman of Miss SPENCE's form and mind."

" But tell me, I request," said MARIA, " how did you get to the confines of Westmoreland over Stanemore hills, and what was that accident that put you in possession of Orton-Lodge ? It must be a curious account, I am sure."

" This," I replied, " you shall hear to-morrow morning after breakfast ; there is not time for it now. All I can say at present is, that it was love kept me among the mountains for some years, and if the heaven-born maid, vastly like you, Miss SPENCE, she was, had not, by the order of heaven, been removed to the regions of immortality and day, I should not have left the solitude, nor would you ever have seen me at Harrogate : but destiny is the dirigent : mutable is the condition of mortals, and we are blind to futurity and the approaches of fate. This led me over the vast mountains of Stanemore, enabled me to cross the amazing fells of Westmoreland, and brought me to that spot, where I had the honour and happiness of becoming acquainted with Miss SPENCE." Thus did we chat till eleven, and retired to our chambers.

But the old gentleman, the doctor, when he came with me into my apartment, told me we must have one bottle more, for it was his nightcap, without which he could not sleep : he then bid the servant make haste with it, and when that was out, we had another. He was a sensible agreeable man, and pleased me very much, as he appeared a zealous friend to the illustrious house of Hanover ; whereas almost all the clergymen I had been in company with since I came to England, were violent Jacobites.

I remember, among other things, I asked this Divine, over our wine, If popery is ever so corrupt, could men be debarred of their rights for an attachment to it ? Are not clowns hereditary ? And is not treason in our country stamped with so peculiar an infamy, as involving the delinquent's innocent children in the forfeitures, or penal consequences that await it, on purpose to check the rebellion of Britons by such an accumulated punishment of evil doers ?

To this the doctor replied, that the exclusion of a popish prince must be lawful, if we ought to secure our property and religion, and, as in duty bound, oppose his trampling upon the laws, and his own solemn declarations. If the people have privileges and interests, they may defend them, and as justifiably oppose notorious domestic oppressions, as foreign invasions. The head of the community, has no more a license to destroy the most momentous interests of it, than any of the inferior members, or than any foreign invader. If a king has no passion to indulge, incompatible with the welfare of his people, then, as protection and obedience are reciprocal, and cannot subsist, the one without the other, it must be a crime in the people not to honour, and obey, and assist the royal authority. It is not only the interest but the duty of the subject to obey the prince, who is true to the important trust reposed in him, and has the welfare of the people at heart. But such a king cannot be a papist. The Romish prince will not only stretch a limited prerogative into lawless power, and grasp at absolute monarchy ; but will break through the most sacred ties, and subvert the rights he was sworn to guard, to re-establish popery in this kingdom. Could James II have kept the seat of government, and baffled all opposition, we may conclude from what he did, from his trampling upon the laws, and his own solemn declarations ; from his new court of inquisition, the high commission court ; to subvert the constitution of the church of England, and to lay waste all its fences against popery ; from that furious act of his power, which fell on Magdalen-college, and his two cruel acts of parliament in Ireland, the repeal of the act of settlement, by which the protestant gentlemen were deprived of their estates ; and the act of attainder, by which they were to be hanged, for going to beg their bread in another country, after they had been robbed of all in their own by their king, who had sworn to protect them ; from hence, I say, it is plain, that if James could have sat firm upon the throne, his misguided conscience would have induced him to the most inhuman acts of violence. He would have proceeded to the barbarities, and rekindled the flames of Mary. Had he continued to reign over these kingdoms, it is most certain, that instruction and persuasion only would not have been the thing, but where instruction and persuasion failed, imprisonments, tortures, death, would have been used, to compel us to believe all the gross absurdities of Rome, their impieties to God,

and contradictions to common sense. We must throw away
our reason and our bibles, the noblest gifts of heaven, and neither
think nor speak, but as we are bid by men no wiser than ourselves ;
or, we must expire under torments as great as the devil and the
monks could devise. It was therefore necessary, for the preservation of our church and state, to exclude James and his popish
heirs. The common welfare required this salutary precaution.
The collected interest of the community is the primary end of
every law.

All this, I said, seems quite right. To be sure, during that
short twilight of power, which dawned upon popery in England
in the years 1689 and 1690, its rage was imprudent. It did
discover its fury and resentment. In one of the Irish acts you
have mentioned, more than two thousand people were attainted,
and some of them the most noble and venerable characters in
Ireland. Yet had success attended the arms of James, this
would have been but the beginning of sorrows. And probably
a son of Christian Rome would have proscribed more in these
two islands, than in heathen Rome, out of the whole vast Roman
empire, were given up to destruction for their virtue, by the
cruel triumvirate, Augustus, Antony, and Lepidus. And of
consequence, since dear experience convinced, it was equally
absurd and vain, to imagine that a popish head would govern a
protestant church by any councils, but those of popish priests, as
it was to imagine that a popish king would govern a protestant state by any councils, but those of popish counsellors ;
it must therefore be owned, that the Lords, and others, assembled
at Nottingham, were just in declaring, "that King James's
administrations were usurpations on the constitution ; and that
they owned it rebellion to resist a king that governed by law ;
but to resist a tyrant, who made his will his law, was nothing but
a necessary defence." This, to be sure, is just. But still, if
crowns are hereditary, and one severe punishment of treason
was intended to check all rebellion, were we not a little too hasty
in the affair of the Revolution ? And might we not have expected something better from the good sense and good nature
of James, if we had waited a while, till he could see the folly of
his proceedings ?

To this the Doctor replied, that as to James's good sense, it
never appeared he had any : and in respect of his many real
good qualities, they were extinguished by his bigotry, and could
never be of service to a protestant spirit, the spirit of freemen :
it was therefore incumbent on them, who knew and loved the
invaluable blessings they enjoyed, to act as they did ; that is,
as the wisdom of our constitution requires in such cases.

As to the crown being hereditary, and the severe punishment
of treasons ; in respect of the first particular, there is no natural
or divine law declares crowns hereditary. If a certain rule of

succession has been established in most kingdoms, the single point of view in it was public good, or a prevention of those intestine commotions, which might attend an election : But as every rule is dispensible, and must give way when it defeats the end for which it was appointed ; should the customary succession in a kingdom prove at any time productive of much greater evils than those it was intended to obviate, it may questionless be superseded occasionally. This point is evident from reason. Though the crown in our own country is generally hereditary, yet that right is to be set aside, if the security of our civil and religious liberty requires it. If the pretence of James was a right to dominion, in opposition not only to the sense of the legislature, but to that of the nation, then the popish prince was justly excluded, for denying the public good to be the supreme law. Had the right he claimed been established, then our religion, our liberties, and the safety of our fortunes, had been no longer our own. In case of such establishment, the glory of our constitution was no more. The sum of the matter is, the royal family of the Stuarts being Roman Catholics, makes their case similar to an extinction of it.

And as to the accumulated punishment of treason in Great Britain, that can only be designed as a powerful check to rebellion, against a king whose darling view is the welfare of the people. No infamy, forfeitures, or death, can be too severe for the man who rebels against a prince that governs for the good of the people, and endeavours to transmit our state safe to posterity. To plot against such a sovereign is a great crime indeed. To conspire against a prince, whose life is of the utmost consequence to the community, is an enormity that ought to be stamped with a peculiar infamy, and punished in the severest manner. But it can be no treason to act against a papist, who violates every maxim of our constitution, and by every maxim of popery labours to destroy our religion and liberties. Every man may repel unlawful attempts upon his person and property, and is armed by God with authority for self-defence.

To this it was replied, that I thought the Doctor quite right, and for my own part was determined to oppose a popish prince, whenever he comes on with his unalienable and indefeasible claim, to introduce his absurd and cruel religion, to deprive us of our rational Christianity, and to make us slaves, instead of free-born subjects. No popish James, to write our themes, but (filling a bumper) may this nation be ever happy in a king whose right is founded upon law, and who has made it the rule of his government. May Britons ever remember the merciless rage of popery, and the envious malice of France ; each ready to lay waste the whole fabric of our excellent constitution, and cry aloud, with all the embittered sons of Edom, Down with it, down

with it, even to the ground.   Here the clock struck one, and we
parted.

Early the next morning I was up, according to my wont, and
walked out, to look at the place.   Cleator is one of the finest
spots that can be seen, in a wild romantic country.   The natural
views are wonderful, and afford the eye vast pleasure.   The charming prospects of different kinds, from the edges of the mountains,
are very fine.   The winding hills, pretty plains, vast precipices,
hanging woods, deep dales, the easy falls of water in some places,
and in others cataracts tumbling over rocks, form all together
the most beautiful and delightful scenes.   All the decorations
of art are but foils and shadows to such natural charms.

In the midst of these scenes, and in a theatrical space of about
two hundred acres, which the hand of nature cut, or hollowed
out, on the side of a mountain, stands Cleator-Lodge, a neat and
pretty mansion.   Near it were groves of various trees, and the
water of a strong spring murmured from the front down to a
lake at the bottom of the hill.

This was Miss SPENCE's country-house.   Here the wise and
excellent MARIA passed the best part of her time, and never went
to any public place but Harrogate once a year.   In reading,
riding, fishing, and some visits to and from three or four neighbours now and then, her hours were happily and usefully employed.   History and Mathematics she took great delight in,
and had a very surprising knowledge in the last.   She was
another of those ladies I met with in my travels, who understood
that method of calculation, beyond wh'ch nothing further is to
be hoped or expected ; I mean the arithmetic of fluxions.

Very few men among the learned can consider magnitudes
as generated by motion, or determine their proportions one to
another from the celerities of the motion by which they are
generated.   I question if the Critical Reviewers can do it ; I am
sure they cannot, though they have made so licentiously free
with me.   They may, however, pretend to know something of
the matter, and so did Berkeley, the late Bishop of Cloyne in
Ireland ; yet that prelate, in reality, understood no more of the
method than a porter does, though he presumed to write against
it, and the divine Newton, the inventor of it.   But MARIA SPENCE,
in the twenty-fourth year of her age, was at this time a master
in the fluxionary way.   She had not only a clear and adequate
notion of fluxions, but was able to penetrate into the depths of
this science, and had made sublime discoveries in this incomparable method of reasoning.   She astonished me.   I thought Mrs.
BURCOTT and Mrs. FLETCHER, mentioned in my first volume,
were very extraordinary women, on account of their knowledge
in algebra, and the fine answers they gave to the most difficult
problems in universal arithmetic ; but this sort of reasoning

is far inferior to the fluxionary method of calculation ; as the
latter opens and discovers to us the secrets and recesses of nature,
which have always before been locked up in obscurity and darkness. By fluxions, such difficulties are resolved, as raise the
wonder and surprise of all mankind, and which would in vain
be attempted by any other method whatsoever. What then
must we think of a young woman well skilled in such work ;
not only able to find the fluxions of flowing or determinate
quantities, that is, the velocities with which they arise or begin
to be generated in the first moments of formation, called the
velocities of the incremental parts and the velocities in the last
ratios, as vanishing or ceasing to be ; but from given fluxions
to find the fluents ; and be ready in drawing tangents to curves ;
in the solution of problems de maximis et minimis, that is, the
greatest or least possible quantity attainable in any case ; in the
invention of points of inflection and retrogression ; in finding the
evoluta of a given curve ; in finding the caustic curves, by reflection and refraction, &c., &c., this was amazing beyond anything
I had seen ; or have ever seen since, except Mrs. BENLOW, of
Richmondshire, with whom I became acquainted in 1739.*
With astonishment I beheld her. I was but a young beginner,
or learner, in respect of her, though I had applied so close to
fluxions after I had learned algebra, that my head was often
ready to split with pain ; nor had I the capacity, at that time,
to comprehend thoroughly the process of several operations she
performed with beauty, simplicity, and charming elegance.
Admirable MARIA ! No one have I ever seen that was her
superior in this science : one equal only have I known, the lady
a little before mentioned. And does not this demonstrate, that
the faculties and imagination of women's minds, properly
cultivated, may equal those of the greatest men ? And since
women have the same improvable minds as the male part of the
species, why should they not be cultivated by the same method ?
Why should reason be left to itself in one of the sexes, and be
disciplined with so much care in the other. Learning and knowledge are perfections in us not as we are men, but as we are rational
creatures, in which order of beings the female world is upon the
same level with the male. We ought to consider in this particular,
not what is the sex, but what is the species they belong to. And
if women of fortune were so considered, and educated accordingly,
I am sure the world would soon be the better for it. 'It would
be so far from making them those ridiculous mortals Moliere
has described under the character of learned ladies ; that it
would render them more agreeable and useful, and enable them
by the acquisition of true sense and knowledge, to be superior

---

* See *Memoirs of several Ladies of Great Britain*, 1755, 8vo.

to gayety and spectacle, dress and dissipation. They would see that the sovereign good can be placed in nothing else but in rectitude of conduct ; as that is agreeable to our nature ; conducive to well-being ; accommodate to all places and times ; durable, self-derived, indeprivable ; and of consequence, that on rational and masculine religion only they can rest the sole of the foot, and the sooner they turn to it, the happier here and hereafter they shall be. Long before the power of sense, like the setting sun, is gradually forsaking them, that power on which the pleasures of the world depend, they would, by their acquired understanding and knowledge, see the folly of pleasure, and that they were born not only to virtue, friendship, honesty, and faith, but to religion, piety, adoration, and a generous surrender of their minds to the supreme cause. They would be glorious creatures then. *Every family would be happy.*

But as to Miss SPENCE, this knowledge, with a faultless person, and a modesty more graceful than her exquisite beauty, were not the things that principally charmed me : nor was it her conversation, than which nothing could be more lively and delightful : nor her fine fortune. It was her manners. She was a Christian Deist, and considered Benevolence and Integrity as the essentials of her religion. She imitated the piety and devotion of Jesus Christ, and worshipped his God and our God, his Father and our Father, as St. John expressly stiles the God of Christians, ch. xx. v. 17. She was extremely charitable to others, and considered conscious virtue as the greatest ornament and most valuable treasure of human nature. *Excellent* MARIA !

With this young lady, and her two servants, her footman and her woman, I went up to London. We set out from Cleator the 31st day of July, and without meeting with any mischief in all that long way, came safe to London. We were nine days on the road ; and as the weather was fine, and our horses excellent, we had a charming journey. My companion was so agreeable, that had it been two thousand miles from Cleator to London, instead of two hundred and seventy-two, I should still have thought it too short. Her conversation was so various and fine, that no way could seem tiresome and tedious to him that travelled with her. Her notions and remarks were ever lively and instructive. It was vast pleasure to hear her, even on the driest and most abstruse subjects, on account of the admiration her discourse raised, and the fine knowledge it communicated, to one who understood her. I will give an instance.

In riding over the mountains the first day, we missed the road in the evening, and instead of getting to a very good inn, where we intended to rest, we were forced to stop at a poor little public house, and right glad to get in there as the evening was tempestuous and wet, dark and cold. Here we got some bacon and fresh eggs for supper, and the ale was good, which amused us well enough till nine o'clock. We then proposed to play at cribbage for an hour, and called for a pack of cards ; but they had none in the house, and we were obliged to divert ourselves with conversation, till it was time to retire. Miss SPENCE began in the following manner.

" Was Newton, Sir, or Leibnitz, the author of that method of calculation, which lends its aid and assistance to all the other mathematical sciences, and that in their greatest wants and distresses ? I have heard a foreigner affirm, that the German was the inventor of fluxions."

" That cannot be," I replied. " In 1696, Dr. Barrow received from Newton a demonstration of the rule of the quadrature of curves, which the Doctor communicated to Collins; and as this is the foundation of fluxions, and the differential calculus, it is evident Newton had invented the method before that time.

" In the beginning of 1673, Leibnitz was in England, again in October, 1676 ; and the interval of this time he spent in France, during which he kept a correspondence with Oldenburgh, and by his means with Collins ; and sometimes also with Newton, from the last of whom he received a letter, dated June 18, 1676, wherein is taught the method of reducing quantities into infinite series, that is, of exhibiting the increments of flowing quantities. This method was utterly unknown to Leibnitz, before he received the abovesaid letter of Newton's, as he himself acknowledges in a letter to Oldenburgh, dated August 27, 1676 ; for before that time, he says in his letter, he was obliged to transform an irrational quantity into a rational fraction, and thence by division, after the method of Mercator, to reduce the fraction into a series.

" It is likewise certain, that Leibnitz did not then understand these series, because, in the same letter, he desires Newton would explain to him the manner how he got these series. And again in a second letter from Newton to Leibnitz, dated October 24, 1676, he gives yet clearer hints of his method, and illustrates it by examples, and lays down a rule, by which, from the ordinates of certain curves, their areas may be obtained in finite terms, when it is possible.

" By these lights, and assisted by such examples, the acute Leibnitz might have learned the Newtonian method, and indeed it is plain he did so ; for in 1684, he first published, in the *Leipsic Acts*, his *Elements of the Differential Calculus*, without pretending to have had the method before the year 1677, in which he received the two letters from Newton : and yet, when Sir Isaac published his books of the number of curves of the first kind, and of the quadrature of figures, the editors of the *Acts* said Leibnitz was the first inventor of the differential calculus, and Newton had substituted fluxions for differences, just as Honoratus Faber, in his *Synopsis Geometrica*, had substituted a progression of motion for Cavallerius' method of indivisibles ; that is Leibnitz was the first inventor of the method. Newton had received it from his *Elements of the Differential Calculus*, and had substituted fluxions for differences ; but the way of investigation in each is the same, and both centre in the same conclusions.

"This excited KEILL to reply, and he made it appear very plain from Sir Isaac's letters, published by Dr. Wallis, that Newton was the first inventor of the algorith, or practical rules of fluxions ; and Leibnitz did no more than publish the same, with an alteration of the name, and manner of notation. This however did not silence Leibnitz, nor satisfy the foreigners who admired him. He abused Dr. Keill, and appealed to the Royal Society against him ; that they would be pleased to restrain the Doctor's vain babblings and unjust calumniations, and report their judgment as he thought they ought to do, that is, in his favour. But this was not in the power of the Society, if they did justice ; for it appeared quite clear to a committee of the members, appointed to examine the original letters, and other papers, relating to the matter, which were left by Oldenburgh and Collins, that Sir Isaac Newton was the first inventor of fluxions ; and accordingly they published their opinion. This determines the affair. When this is the case, it is senseless for any foreigner to say Leibnitz was the author of fluxions. To the divine Newton belongs this greatest work of genius, and the noblest thought that ever entered the human mind."

"It must be so," replied MARIA. "As the case is stated, Sir Isaac Newton was most certainly the inventor of the method of fluxions : and supposing Leibnitz had been able to discover and work the differential calculus, without the lights he received from Newton, it would not from thence follow, that he understood the true method of fluxions : for, though a differential has been, and to this day is, by many, called a fluxion, and a fluxion a differential, yet it is an abuse of terms. A fluxion has no relation to a differential, nor a differential to a fluxion. The principles upon which the methods are founded shew them to be very different, notwithstanding the way of investigation in each be the same, and that both centre in the same conclusions : nor can the differential method perform what the fluxionary method can. The excellency of the fluxionary method is far above the differential."

This remark on the two methods surprised me very much, and especially as it was made by a young lady. I had not then a notion of the difference, and had been taught by my master to proceed on the principles of the Differential Calculus. This made me request an explication of the matter, and MARIA went on in the following manner.

"Magnitudes, as made up of an infinite number of very small constituent parts put together, are the work of the Differential Calculus ; but by the fluxionary method, we are taught to consider magnitudes as generated by motion. A described line in this way, is not generated by an apposition of points, or differentials, but by the motion or flux of a point ; and the velocity of the generating point in the first moment of its formation, or generation, is called its fluxion. In forming magnitudes after the differential way, we conceive them as made up of an infinite number of small constituent parts, so disposed as to produce a magnitude of a given form ; that these parts are to each other as the magnitudes of which they are differentials ; and that one infinitely small part, or differential, must be infinitely great, with respect to another other differential, or infinitely small part : but by fluxion, or the law of flowing, we determine the proportion of magnitudes one to another, from the celerities of the motions by which they are generated. This most certainly is the purest abstracted way of reasoning. Our considering the different degrees of magnitude, as arising from an increasing series of mutations of velocity, is much more simple, and less perplexed than the other way ; and the operations founded on fluxions, must be much more clear, accurate, and convincing, than those that are founded on the Differential Calculus. There is a great difference in operations, when quantities are rejected, because they really vanish ; and when they are rejected, because they are infinitely small : the latter method, which is the differential, must leave the mind in ambiguity and confusion, and cannot in many cases come up to the truth. It is a very great error then to call differentials, fluxions, and quite wrong to begin with the differential method, in order to learn the law or manner of flowing."

With amazement I heard this discourse, and requested to know by what master, and what method, she obtained these notions ; for they were far beyond everything on the subject that I had ever met with. What she said concerning the nature and idea of fluxions, I thought just and beautiful, and I believe it was in her power, to show the bases on which they are erected.

"My master, sir," said MARIA, "was a poor traveller, a Scotchman, one MARTIN MURDOCH, who came by accident to my father's house, to ask relief, when I was about fifteen years old. He told us, he was the son of one of the ministers of Scotland, and came from the remotest part of the Highlands : that his father taught him mathematics, and left him, at his death, a little stock on a small farm ; but misfortunes and accidents

obliged him in a short time to break up house, and he was going
to London, to try if he could get anything there, by teaching
arithmetic of every kind. My father, who was a hospitable
man, invited him to stay with us a few days, and the parson
of our parish soon found, that he had not only a very extraordinary understanding, but was particularly excellent at figures,
and the other branches of the mathematics. My father upon
this agreed with him to be my preceptor for five years, and
during four years and nine months of that time, he took the
greatest pains to make me as perfect as he could in arithmetic,
trigonometry, geometry, algebra, and fluxions. As I delighted
in the study above all things, I was a great proficient for so few
years, and had MURDOCH been longer with me, I should have
been well acquainted with the whole glorious structure : but
towards the end of the fifth year, this poor Archimedes was
unfortunately drowned, in crossing one of our rivers, in the
winter time, and went in that uncomfortable way, in the thirty-
sixth year of his age, to the enjoyment of that felicity and glory,
which God has prepared for a virtuous life and honest heart.
Why such men, as the poor and admirable MURDOCH, have
often such hard measure in this world, is not in my power to
account for, nor do I believe any one can ; but what I tell you
is one of those surprising things, and I lamented not a little the
loss of such a master. Still however I continued to study by
many written rules he had given me, and to this day, mathematics are the greatest pleasure of my life.

   " As to our method, my master, in the first place, made me
perfectly understand arithmetic, and then geometry, and algebra
in all their parts and improvements, the methods of series,
doctrine of proportions, nature of logarithms, mechanics, and
laws of motion : from thence we proceeded to the pure doctrine
of fluxions, and at last looked into the Differential Calculus.
In this true way my excellent master led me, and in the same
difficult path every one must go, who intends to learn Fluxions.
It would be but lost labour for any person to attempt them,
who was unacquainted with these Precognita.

   " When we turned to fluxions, the first thing my master did,
was to instruct me in the arithmetic of exponents, the nature
of powers, and the manner of their generation. We went next
to the doctrine of infinite series ; and then, to the manner of
generating mathematical quantities. This generation of quantities was my first step into fluxions, and my master so amply
explained the nature of them, in this operation, that I was able
to form a just idea of a first fluxion, though thought by many
to be incomprehensible. We proceeded from thence to the
notation and algorithm of first fluxions ; to the finding second,
third, &c., fluxions ; the finding fluxions of exponential quan-

tities ; and the fluents from given fluxions ; to their uses in drawing tangents to curves ; in finding the areas of spaces ; the valves of surfaces ; and the contents of solids ; their percussion, oscillation, and centres of gravity. All these things my master so happily explained to my understanding, that I was able to work with ease, and found no more difficulty in conceiving an adequate notion of a nascent or evanescent quantity, than in forming a true idea of a mathematical point. In short, by the time I had studied fluxions two years, I not only understood their fundamental principles and operations, and could investigate, and give the solution of the most general and useful problems in the mathematics ; but likewise, solve several problems that occur in the phænomena of nature."

Here MARIA stopped, and as soon as astonishment would permit me to speak, I proposed to her several difficult questions, I had heard, but was not then able to answer. I requested her, in the first place, to inform me, how the time of a body's descending through any arch of a cycloid was found : and if ten hundred weight avoirdupoise, hanging on a bar of steel perfectly elastic, and supported at both ends, will just break the bar, what must be the weight of a globe, falling perpendicular 185 feet on the middle of the bar, to have the same effect ?—My next questions were, how long, and how far, ought a given globe to descend by its comparative weight in a medium of a given density, but without resistance, to acquire the greatest velocity it is capable of in descending with the same weight, and in the same medium, with resistance ?—And how are we to find the value of a solid formed by the rotation of this curvilinear space, A C D about the axis A D, the general equation, expressing the nature of the curve,

$$being \ y = \frac{\overline{a - x \times x}^{\frac{m}{n}}}{\frac{m}{a^{n}}}$$?—How is the centre of gravity to be found

of the space enclosed by an hyperbola, and its asymptete ? And how are we to find the centre oscillation of a sphere revolving about the line P A M, a tangent, to the generating circle F A H, in the point A, as an axis ?—These questions MARIA answered with a celerity and elegance that again amazed me, and convinced me that, notwithstanding the Right Rev. metaphysical disputant, Dr. Berkeley, late Bishop of Cloyne in Ireland, could not understand the doctrine of fluxions, and therefore did all he could to disgrace them, and the few mathematicians who have studied magnitudes as generated by motion ; yet, the doctrine, as delivered by the divine Newton, may be clearly

N

conceived, and distinctly comprehended ; that the principles upon which it is founded, are true, and the demonstrations of its rules conclusive.   No opposition can hurt it.

When I observed, that some learned men will not allow that a velocity which continues for no time at all, can possibly describe any space at all : its effect, they say, is absolutely nothing, and instead of satisfying reason with truth and precision, the human faculties are quite confounded, lost, and bewildered in fluxions.   A velocity or fluxion is at best we do not know what ; whether something or nothing : and how can the mind lay hold on, or form any accurate abstract idea of such a subtile, fleeting thing ?

"Disputants," answered MARIA, "may perplex with deep speculations, and confound with mysterious disquisitions, but the method of fluxions has no dependance on such things. The operation is not what any single abstract velocity can generate or describe of itself, but what a continual and successively variable velocity can produce in the whole.   And certainly, a variable cause may produce a variable effect, as well as a permanent cause a permanent and constant effect.   The difference can only be, that the continual variation of the effect must be proportional to the continual variation of the cause. The method of fluxions therefore is true, whether we can or cannot conceive the nature and manner of several things relating to them, though we had no ideas of perpetually arising increments, and magnitudes in nascent or evanescent states. The knowledge of such things is not essential to fluxions.   All they propose is, to determine the velocity or flowing wherewith a generated quantity increases, and to sum up all that has been generated or described by the continually variable fluxion. On these two bases fluxions stand."

This was clear and just, and showed that the nature and idea of fluxions is agreeable to the nature and constitution of things.   They can have no dependance upon any metaphysical speculations, such speculations as that anti-mathematician, my Lord of Cloyne, brought in, to cavil and dispute against principles he understood nothing of, and maliciously run the account of them into the dark ; but are the genuine offspring of nature and truth.   An instance or two may illustrate the matter.

1. A heavy body descends perpendicularly $16\frac{7}{12}$ feet in a second, and at the end of this time, has acquired a velocity of $32\frac{1}{6}$ feet in a second, which is accurately known.   At any given distance then from the place the body fell, take the point A in the right line, and the velocity of the falling body in the point may be truly computed : but the velocity in any point above A, at ever so small a distance, will be less than in A ;

and the velocity at any point below A, at the least possible distance, will be greater than in A. It is therefore plain, that in the point A, the body has a certain determined velocity, which belongs to no other point in the whole line. Now this velocity is the fluxion of that right line in the point A ; and with it the body would proceed, if gravity acted no longer on the body's arrival at A.

2. Take a glass tube open at both ends whose concavity is of different diameters in different places, and immerse it in a stream, till the water fills the tube, and flows through it. Then, in different parts of the tube, the velocity of the water will be as the squares of the diameters, and of consequence different. Suppose then, in any marked place, a plane to pass through the tube perpendicular to the axis, or to the motion of the water, and of consequence, the water will pass through this section with a certain determinate velocity. But if another section be drawn ever so near the former, the water, by reason of the different diameters, will flow through this with a velocity different from what it did at the former, and therefore to one section of the tube, or single point only, the determinate velocity belongs. It is the fluxion of the space which the fluid describes at that section ; and with that uniform velocity the fluid would continue to move, if the diameter was the same to the end of the tube.

3. If a hollow cylinder be filled with water to flow freely out through a hole at the bottom, the velocity of the effluent will be as the height of the water, and since the surface of the incumbent fluid descends without stop, the velocity of the stream will decrease, till the effluent be all out. There can then be no two moments of time, succeeding each other ever so nearly, wherein the velocity of the water is the same ; and of consequence, the velocity, at any given point, belongs only to that particular indivisible moment of time. Now this is accurately the fluxion of the fluid then flowing ; and if, at that instant, more water was poured into the cylinder, to make the surface keep its place, the effluent would retain its velocity, and still be the fluxion of the fluid. Such are the operations of nature, and they visibly confirm the nature of Fluxion. It is from hence quite clear, that the fluxion of a generated quantity, cannot retain any one determined value for the least space of time whatever, but the moment it arrives at that value, the same moment it loses it again. The fluxion of such quantity can only pass gradually and successively through the indefinite degrees contained between the two extreme values, which are the limits thereof, during the generation of the fluent, in case the fluxion be variable. But then, though a determinate degree of fluxion does not continue at all, yet, at every determinate

indivisible moment of time, every fluent has some determinate degree of fluxion ; that is, every generated quantity has everywhere a certain rate of increasing, a fluxion whose abstract value is determinate in itself, though the fluxion has no determined value for the least space of time whatever. To find its value then, that is, the ratio one fluxion has to another, is a problem strictly geometrical ; notwithstanding the Right Rev. anti-mathematician has declared the contrary, in his hatred to mathematicians, and his ignorance of the true principles of mathematics.

If my Lord of Cloyne had been qualified to examine and consider the case of fluxions, and could have laid aside that unaccountable obstinacy, and invincible prejudice, which made him resolve to yield to no reason on the subject ; not to regard even the great Maclaurin's answer to his *Analyst*, he would have discovered, that it was very possible to find the abstract value of a generated quantity, or the contemporary increment of any compound quantity. By the binomial theorem, the ratio of the fluxion of a simple quantity to the fluxion of that compound quantity, may be had in general, in the lowest terms, and as near the truth as we please, whilst we suppose some very small increment actually described. And whereas the ratio of these fluxions is required for some one indivisible point of the fluid, in the very beginning of the increment, and before it is generated, we make, in the particular case, the values of the simple increments nothing, which before was expressed in general : then all the terms wherein they are found vanish, and what is left accurately shews the relation of the fluxions for the point where the increment is supposed to commence. As the abstract value of the fluxion belongs only to one point of the fluent, the moments are made to vanish, after we have seen by their continual diminution, whither the ratio tends, and what it continually verges to ; and this becomes as visible as the very character it is written in.

But Bishop Berkeley was unacquainted with mathematical principles, and out of his aversion to these sciences, and zeal for orthodoxy, cavilled and disputed with all his might, and endeavoured to bring the matter to a state unintelligible to himself, and everybody else. Here MARIA had done, and for near a quarter of an hour after, I sat silently looking at her, in the greatest astonishment.

But as to our travels, the 10th of August we got safe to London, and the consequence of the journey was, that the last day of the same month, I had the honour and happiness of being married to this young lady.

Wise is the man, who prepares both for his own death and

the death of his friends; who makes use of the foresight of troubles, so as to abate the uneasiness of them, and puts in practice the resolution of the 'philosopher Cleanthes.* "I am thinking with myself every day, says one of the philosophers, how many things are dear to me; and after I have considered them as temporary and perishable, I prepare myself, from that very minute, to bear the loss of them without weakness." I thought of this the morning I married the beautiful and ingenious Miss SPENCE, and determined if I lost her, to make the great affliction produce the peaceable fruits of righteousness. The man must feel, in such a case: the Christian will submit. Before the end of six months, she died, and I mourned the loss with a degree of sorrow due to so much excellence, endearment and delight. My complaint was bitter, in proportion to the desires of nature. But as nature says, "Let this cup pass:" Grace says, "Let thy will be done." If the flower of all my comfort was gone, the glory departed! yet thy glory is, O man, to do the will of God, and bear the burthen he lays upon thee! Let nature, grace, and time, do their part, to close the wound, and let not ignorance impeach the wisdom of the Most High. The cup which my Father hath given me: shall I not drink? I will. I will not quarrel with Providence. In short, I resigned, and not long after I had buried this admirable woman, who died at her seat in Westmoreland, I went into the world again, to relieve my mind, and try my fortune once more. What happened there, I will report, when I have related the extraordinary case of my wife Miss SPENCE, and the four physicians I had to attend her. It is a very curious thing.

This young lady was seized with that fatal distemper, called a malignant fever: Something foreign to nature got into her blood, by a cold, and other accidents, it may be, and the luctus or strife to get clear thereof became very great. The effervescence or perturbation was very soon so violent as to shew, that it not only endangered, but would quickly subvert the

---

' * Cleanthes was a native of Assus in Lysia, in Asia-Minor, and so very poor, when he came to Athens to study, that, for his support, he wrought at nights in drawing water for the gardens, and in grinding behind the mill. He attended the lectures of Zeno, succeeded him in his school, and grew into very high esteem with the Athenians. He lived to ninety-nine, but the year he died we know not. His master Zeno died 342 years before Christ, and had conversed with Socrates and Plato.

The antient academics were Plato, the disciple of Socrates; Speucippus, Zenocrates, Polemo, Crates, and Crantor; and from Crates, the fifth academic, sprung the old stoics, to wit, Crates, Zeno, Cleanthes, Chrysippus, and Diogenes the Babylonian; not he that was surly and proud. Cicero in his works often mentions this Babylonian, the stoic. We find in the Roman history, that he was living in the year of Rome 599, that is, 155 years before Christ; but when he died we know not. These gentlemen of the two old schools were to be sure great philosophers, excellent men; but then, to be strictly impartial, we must own, that all they knew in relation to the will of God, and a kingdom to come, was but poor moral learning, in respect to what is written in the *New Testament* for our Instruction, if we will lay aside our fancies and systems, and let reason explain revelation. The Christian religion is really more for the glory of God, and the good of mankind, than 'reason, without inspiration, has been able to teach. Christianity, without the additions and supplements of monks, s not only above all just exception, but preferable to any other scheme.

animal fabric, unless the blood was speedily dispersed, and nature got the victory by an exclusion of the noxious shut-in particles. The thirst, the dry tongue, the coming causus, were terrible, and gave me too much reason to apprehend this charming woman would sink under the conflict. To save her, if possible, I sent immediately for a great physician, Dr. Sharp, a man who talked with great fluency of medicine and diseases.

This gentleman told me, the Alkaline was the root of fevers, as well as of other distempers, and therefore, to take off the effervescence of the blood in the ebullitions of it, to incide the viscous humour, to drain the tartarous salts from the kidnies, to allay the preternatural ferment, and to brace up the relaxed tones, he ordered orange and vinegar in whey, and prescribed spirit of sulphur, and vitriol, the cream, chrystals, and vitriolate tartar in other vehicles. If anything can relieve, it must be plenty of acid. In acidis posita est omni curatio. But these things gave no relief to the sufferer.

I sent then in all haste for Dr. Hough, a man of great reputation, and he differed so much in opinion from Sharp, that he called an acid the chief enemy. It keeps up the luctus or struggle, and if not expelled very quickly, will certainly prove fatal. Our sheet anchor then must be the testacea, in vehicles of mineral water, and accordingly he ordered the absorbent powers to conflict with this acidity, the principal cause of all diseases. Pearl and coral, crab's eyes, and crab's claws, he prescribed in diverse forms ; but they were of no use to the sick woman. She became worse every hour.

Dr. Pym was next called in, a great practitioner, and learned man. His notion of a fever was quite different from the opinions of Sharp and Hough. He maintained that a fever was a poisonous ferment or venom, which seized on the animal spirits : it breaks and smites them ; and unless by alexipharmics the spirits can be enabled to gain a victory in a day or two, this ferment will bring on what the Greeks call a synochus, that is, a continual fever. In that state, the venom holds fast the animal spirits, will not let them expand, or disengage themselves, and then they grow enraged, and tumultuating, are hurried into a state of explosion, and blow up the fabric. Hence the inflammatory fever, according to the diverse indoles of the venom ; and when the contagious miasms arrive at their highest degree, the malignant fever ariseth. The spirits are then knocked down, and the marks of the enemies' weapons, the spots, &c. appear. This, continued the Doctor, is the case of your lady, and therefore the thing to be done is, to make the malignant tack about to the mild and produce an extinction of the ferment, and relief of the symptoms. This I endeavour to do by alexipharmics and vesicatories, and by subduing the poison by the bark and the warmer antidotes. Thus did my Doctor marshal his animal spirits, fight them against the enemy venom, to great disadvantage. If his talk was not romance, it was plain his spirits were routed, and venom was getting the day. His alexipharmics and warm antidotes were good for nothing. The malady increased.

This being the case, I sent again in haste for a fourth doctor, a man of greater learning than the other three, and therefore in opinion, opposite, and against their management of the fever. This great man was Dr. Frost. He was a mechanician, and affirmed that, the solid parts of the human body are subjected to the rules of geometry, and the fluids to the hydrostatics ; and therefore, to keep the machine in right order, that is, in a state of health, an æquilibrium must be maintained, or restored, if destroyed. The balance must not turn to one side or the other. To restore sanity in acute cases, and in chronic too, our business is to prevent the vessels being elevated or deprest beyond the standard of nature : when either happens, the division of the blood is increased, the motion is augmented, and so beget a fever. There cannot be an inordinate elevation of the oily or fiery parts of the blood, till the vessels vibrate above the standard of nature.

In a slight fever, the blood increases but little above the balance ; but if more than one day, turns to a synochus, which is but the same fever augmented beyond the balance of nature. This turns to a putrid synochus, and this to a causus. This is the case of your lady. From an elevated contraction, the Doctor continued, to my amazement, her blood obtains a greater force and motion ; hence greater division, hence an increase of quantity and fluidity : and thus from greater division, motion and quantity increased, arises that heat and thirst, with the other concomitant symptoms of her fever ; for the blood dividing faster than it can be detached through the perspiratory emunctories of the skin, is the immediate cause of the heart's preternatural beating : and this preternatural division of the blood arises from the additional quantity of obstructed perspirable matter, added to the natural quantity of the blood.

Things being so, the Doctor went on ; and the fever rising by the blood's dividing faster than can be detached by the several emunctories ; and this from an elevation of the solids above the balance, we must then strive to take off the tension of the solids, and subtract the cause. This makes me begin in a manner quite contrary to the other physicians, and I doubt not but I shall soon get the better of the fury and orgasm, make an alteration in the black scabrous tongue, and by according with the modus of nature, throw forth the matter of the disease, I will enable nature to extricate herself. I hope to disentangle her from the weight.

Thus did this very learned man enlarge ; and while he talked of doing wonders, the dry and parched skin, the black and brushy tongue, the crusty fur upon the teeth, and all the signals of an incendium within, declared her dissolution very near. As the serum diminished fast, and the intestine motion of the crassamentum increased, nature was brought to her last struggles. All the dismal harbingers of a general wreck appeared, to give the bystanders notice of approaching death. She died the ninth day, by the ignorance of four learned Physicians. Had these Gentlemen considered the fever no otherwise than as a disease arising from some unusual ferment, stirred up among the humours of the blood, disturbing both those natural motions and functions of the body, hindering perspiration, and thereby giving quick and large accession to such parts of the aliment or liquors taken down, as are disposed to ferment ; and there is always a strong disposition that way ; for the blood has a three-fold motion, fluidity, common to all liquors, protrusive, from the impulse of the heart and arteries, and fermentative, that is, a motion throughout of all its parts, which quality is owing to the dissimilar parts of the blood ; for being a compound of various particles, there must be a colluctation when they occur, and of consequence, a continual fermentation. As this is just and moderate, it is for the good of the animal, and purifies the blood : if it is too much, it tends to a fever ; if it still increases, it produces the burning causus. Hard is the struggle then, and if nature cannot dispume, even helped by art, the patient has no hazard for life. Hence it is, that we are so subject to fevers, and that it carries away more people than all the rest of the diseases. Out of every forty-two that have it, twenty-five generally die. It was so in the time of Hippocrates, 430 years before Christ. And so Dr. Sydenham and Dr. Friend found it, in their practice. But had my four Doctors considered the fever as I have plainly stated it, without vainly pretending to be so wise as to know the essential causes of it ; and in the beginning of it, before the terrible appearances, the vigil, delirium, subsultus, the dry black tongue, the furred teeth, and the pale, unconcocted urine, had caused a depletion by large bleeding, had opened the pores by a mild sudorific, had then given a vomit, Rad. Ipecacuanha in small sack-whey or chicken-water, and let the sufferer indulge in that thin diluting liquor, an emulsion of the seeds and almonds in barley water, and if the patient required it, a draught of table-beer with a toast, between whiles ; had this been done very soon, there might be relief as quickly ; or if the fever still run high, to bleed again, and wash down some proper alexipharmic powder with a proper cordial julap, it is possible nature would have been able to accomplish the work, and health had been again restored.

I use the word proper alexipharmic, and proper cordial julap, because the Theriaca and Mithridatium of the shops, which are commonly, almost always ordered as an alexipharmic bole, are rather poisons than useful in a fever ; and because the tincture and syrup of saffron, the treacle-water, or any other distilled compound, are not fit cordials in the case ; but it should be the conserva lujulæ in an emulsion ex sem. fr. cum amygd. in aq. hordei. This is the true alexipharmic, and the only cordial, to be given in a fever. But it was the destructive alexipharmics and cordials of the shops they forced down Maria's throat, and this, with the other bad prescriptions and management, killed one of the finest and most excellent women that ever lived.

And now to give the world a better idea of this admirable woman than any description of mine can exhibit, I shall here place a few religious little Pieces, which she wrote while Miss SPENCE, and which I found among her papers.

MORAL THOUGHTS.
Written by Miss Spence.
MORALITY.

Abstract, mathematical, or physical truth, may be above the reach of the bulk and community of mankind. They have neither the leisure, nor the necessary helps and advantages to acquire the natural knowledge of arts and sciences. The many calls and importunities of the animal kind, take up the greatest part of their time, thoughts, and labour, so that the more abstract speculations, and experimental disquisitions of philosophy, are placed by Providence quite out of their reach and beyond their sphere of action.

On the contrary, moral truth, right and wrong, good and evil, the doing as we would be done by, and acting towards all men as they really are and stand related in society ; these things are as evident to the understanding, as light and colours are to the eye, and may be called the intellectual, moral sense. Here needs no deep learning, or trouble and expence of education, but the same truths are as evident, and as much seen and felt by the learned and unlearned, the gentleman and the plough-man, the savage or wild Indian, as by the best instructed philo-sopher. The divine perfections shine through all nature, and the goodness and bounty of the Creator to all his creatures, impress the obligation of imitating this wisest and best of Beings upon every man's heart and conscience.

But notwithstanding the maxims of morality are thus solidly established, and adapted to all capacities ; and though every man has a happiness to seek, and a main end to secure, which must be infinitely preferable to any concerns of life, yet here it is we find, that mankind in general have been most lost and bewildered, as if Providence had placed their own happiness, and the way to it, more out of their power than anything else. How this should happen, might seem unaccountable at first sight, and yet it can be no great mystery to any man tolerably acquainted with the world and human nature. It is no difficult matter to discover the reasons hereof, and it is withal highly useful to give them their due consideration.

1. The principal cause I take to be the prevailing strength and bias of private, corrupt, animal affection, and desires. Reason is silenced and borne down by brutal appetite and passion. They resolve to gratify their sensual appetites and desires, and will therefore never taste or try the superior pleasures and enjoyments of reason and virtue. But such men as these having declared open war against their own reason and conscience, and being resolved at all risks to maintain the combat, must be self-condemned, and cannot plead ignorance, or error of judgment in the case.

2. Another fundamental cause of moral error, is the prejudice and prepossession of a wrong education. False principles and absurd notions of God and religion, wrought early into the tender, unexperienced mind, and there radicated and confirmed from time to time, from youth to riper age, by parents, teachers, our most intimate friends and acquaintance, and such as we have the best opinion of, and confide most in ; such causes make such strong impressions, that the grossest errors, thus riveted and fixed, are with the greatest difficulty ever conquered or cleared off. In this case, men turn out well-grounded believers, and are well-armed against conviction. Circumcision or baptism fixes their religion in their infancy, and their church is as natural to them as their country. Free enquiry is with them an apostasy from the orthodox party, and as the great and sure trial of their faith and fortitude, they will hear no reasonings about the holy religion they have taken upon trust.

3. Then the few, who have applied themselves to the study of morality, have done it for the most part in a manner confused ; and superficial enough : and often so, as even to build upon principles either entirely false, or obscure and uncertain ; either foreign to its proper business, or mixt up with gross errors, and absurdities. From whence it comes to pass, that in all languages, the terms of morality, both in common discourse, and in the writings of the learned, are such as have the most obscure, confused, indetermined, and unfixed ideas, of any other terms whatever ; men for the most part despising the things which are plain and ordinary, to run after such as are extraordinary and mysterious ; and that they either will not know, or reject even truth itself, unless she brings some charm

with her, to raise their curiosity, and gratify their passion for what is marvellous and uncommon.

In sum, the prejudices of the understanding, the illusions of the heart, and the tyranny established in the world, with relation to opinions, form a grand obstacle to the serious study of morality ; and to the attainment of a more exact knowledge of our duty. Nor is it to be expected that any will very much apply themselves to make discoveries in these matters, whilst the desire of esteem, riches, or power, makes men espouse the well-endowed opinions in fashion, and then seek arguments either to make good their beauty, or varnish over and cover their deformity. Whilst the parties of men, cram their tenets down all men's throats, whom they can get into their power, without permitting them to examine their truth and falsehood ; and will not let truth have fair play in the world, nor men the liberty to search after it ; what improvements can be expected of this kind ? What greater light can be hoped for in the moral sciences ? The subject part of mankind in most places might, instead thereof, with *Egyptian* bondage, expect *Egyptian* darkness, were not the candle of the Lord set up by himself in men's minds, which it is impossible for the breath of man wholly to extinguish ; how much soever the infallible guides of one church, and the orthodox rulers of another, may scheme and labour to subject conscience to human jurisdiction, and bring the inward principle and motive of action within the cognizance of their political theocracy, or theocratic policy.

After all this, is it to be wondered at, that such, whose occupations and distractions of life, or want of genius and outward helps, do not allow them to engage in long and profound meditations, are found to have generally understandings so short and narrow, and ideas so false or confused, in matters of morality ?

And since this is the case of the greatest part of mankind, it has no doubt been always God's will, that they, who had the greatest light, and whom his providence had furnished with the greatest helps, should communicate their knowledge to such as were not able of themselves to acquire it so easily, or in so great a degree.

RELIGION.

What is religion ? The true, eternal, immutable religion of God and nature, consists, as I opine, in the filial love and fear of God, and the brotherly love of mankind ; in the practice of all those moral duties of truth and righteousness, which result from it, under a fiducial trust in, and dependance on God, and the constant sense of his power and presence in all our actions, as the rewarder of good and punisher of bad men. This is the religion founded in nature and reason, and which must be at all times and everywhere the same. As this religion was in a great measure lost, and neglected, amidst the general ignorance, superstition, and idolatry of the world, it was the great business and design of revelation to restore it, and set moral truth and reason in its original light, by bringing mankind to the right use of their reason and understanding in such matters.

After Epicurus and Zeno, there were no new succeeding schemes of morality, but each man betook himself to that sect, where he found what most suited his own sentiments.

In the reign of Augustus, Potamo of Alexandria introduced a manner of philosophising, which was called the Eclectic, because it consisted in collecting from all the tenets of preceding philosophers, such as appeared most reasonable ; out of which they formed each man his own system of philosophy. It appears from Cicero's works that he was an Eclectic.

And why should it not be good in religion, as well as in philosophy ? I own I am an Eclectic in divinis. And the sum of my religion is, without regard to modes or parties, so to live to the glory of the Father, without attachment to the creature, for the sanctification and happiness of mankind ; that when this fleeting scene of sin and sorrow shall vanish, and pass away from sight, the angels of God may give my soul a safe transition to that heavenly happiness, which no thought can lay hold on, and which no art can describe.

The practice of reason and truth is the rule of action to God himself, and the foundation of all true religion. It is the first and highest obligation of all rational beings, and our divine Lord came down from heaven to earth to teach it to mankind. Christ preached a plain doctrine to men, fitted to reform their hearts and lives, intended to make them perfect in self-denial, humility, love, goodness, and innocence ; and to enable them, with hearts raised above the world, to worship the Father in spirit and in truth.

But this glorious religion the Romish priests have perverted into a system of mysteries, and staring contradictions, the better to support the worst and most deplorable purposes of temporal wealth, power, pride, malice, and cruelty. In direct opposition to reason and common sense, we must commence generous believers in an ecclesiastical Christianity, and confess the symbol of their holy Athanasius, though it be no more, or better, than the effects of a luxuriant fancy, without likeness and correspondency, in the real nature and reason of things ; 17, 4, and 19 are 41, says convocation to his believers, and your religion, my brethren, is all a tremendous mystery : You must adore as such, what the Infidels renounce as a contradiction.

Thus shamefully do these priests sink the credibility of our gospel, and impose upon the silly people, a ball of wax for the religion of Jesus ; making them believe contrary to knowledge, and prefer a system that is a lye against the light of nature, and the gospel.

But the chief end, duty, happiness, and highest perfection that man can arrive at, consists, and is found, in a perfect exercise of human reason.

We read in *Chronicles*, that Hezekiah began his good reign with the revival of religion, which had long suffered by the neglect and profanation, or through the neglect and omission of his predecessors. To this purpose he opened the doors of the house of the Lord, and issued a decree, that all Israel should come to keep the passover, which they had not done of a long time. But as the legal cleansing and purifying, could not be performed by great numbers that did eat the passover, by the appointed time, on account of many things, and particularly the force of long interval and disuse ; therefore this irregularity employed the devotion of the good king, as the canon of the passover, under the strictest prohibition, and the severest penalty, forbid any one to eat, that did not come with outward and legal purity. No unclean person shall eat of it : and he prayed for the people, saying, The good Lord pardon every one that prepareth his heart to seek God, the Lord God of their fathers, though he be not cleansed according to the purification of the sanctuary ; and the Lord hearkened unto Hezekiah, says the next verse, and healed the people, that is, took off the penalties of the canon, and gave them the benefit ·of the rite. From hence it follows, that, however defective we may be in outward rites and ceremonies of a church, yet inward truth and purity will be accepted in default of outward things. Inward disposition is the substance of religion, and may compound for the want of outward matters ; but outward service can never be accepted instead of inward purification.

And it farther follows, if the outward solemnities of religion cannot be obtained upon lawful terms, which is the case of many, in respect of Popery and Athanasian worship ; then will the good Lord pardon and be propitious to those who prepare their heart to seek him, though they be not cleansed according to the solemn institution, and ritual puriffcation.

This text is in the vulgar Latin, Dominus bonus propitiabitur cunctis qui in toto corde requirunt Dominum, Deum patrum suorum, et non ʼimputabit eis quod minus sanctificati sunt. The good Lord will be propitious to all those, who in their whole heart seek the Lord God of their Fathers, and will not impute to them their being less sanctified than they ought.

* Histories in all ages are full of the encroachments of the

* Note. This article relating to the encroachments of the clergy, was not found among Miss Spence's papers, but is inserted here as in a proper place.

clergy, yet they all omit one of the most successful stratagems to ingross money. We are indebted to our statute-book for informing us of one of the most notorious pieces of priestcraft that ever was practised. Would one believe, that there is a country, and in Europe too, where the clergy gained such an ascendant over the minds of the people, as tamely to suffer the moveable estate of every man who died intestate, to be swallowed up by them ; yet so prevalent was superstition in our country, that it produced a law preferring the Bishop to the next of kin ; and in its extension excluding the children, the wife, and the relations of the deceased, nay the creditor ; and giving all to the Bishop per aversionem. Such was the shameful rapacity of the clergy here for ages. Such a monstrous practice was established upon this foundation, that the moveable effects of every deceased person, his own appointment failing, ought to be laid out for promoting the good of his soul ; and so the Ordinary took possession, without deigning to account with any mortal. This began temp. Hen. I. when the Ordinary, for the good of the soul of the deceased, obtained a directing power, and was in the nature of an overseer, and somewhat more. In the time of King John, [the Ordinary drew blood, as Bacon well expresses it * ; for though the possession was as formerly, yet the dividend must be in the view of the church, and by which means, the dividers were but mere instruments, and the right was vanished into the clouds. But temp. Hen. III. it was settled, the Ordinary had not only gotten the game, but gorged it. Both right and possession were now become the clergy's, the Ordinary was to distribute it according to pious uses, and no use seemed so pious as to appoint to himself and his brethren.

The first statute that limited the power of the Ordinary was 13 Edw. I. c. 19. By this the Ordinary was obliged to satisfy the intestate's debts so far as the goods extended. And 31 Edw. III. cap. 2, the actual possession was taken from the Ordinary, by obliging him to give a deputation to the next and most lawful friends of the intestate, for administrating his goods. But this statute proved but a weak check to the avarice of the clergy. Means were fallen upon to elude it, by preferring such of the intestate's relations, who were willing to offer the best terms : this corrupt practice was suffered in the days of Hen. VIII., when the clergy losing ground, the statute 21 Hen. VIII. was enacted, bearing " That in case any person die intestate, or the executors refuse to prove the testament, the Ordinary shall grant administration to the widow, or to the next of kin, or to both, taking surety for true administration."

This statute, as it points out the particular persons who are in-

* *Discourse of Laws*, pp. 1, 66, and *New Abridgment of the Law*, p. 398.

titled to letters of administration, without leaving any choice to the Ordinary, was certainly intended to cut him out of all hope of making gain of the effects of persons dying intestate. But the church does not easily quit its hold. Means were fallen upon to elude this law also. Though the possession given by this statute was wrested out of the hands of the Ordinary, yet his pretentions subsisted intire, of calling the administrator to account, and obliging him or her to distribute the effects to pious uses. This was an admirable engine in the hands of a churchman for squeezing money. An administrator who gave any considerable share to the Bishop, to be laid out by him, without doubt, in pious uses, would not find much difficulty in making his accompt. This rank abuse moved the judges solemnly to resolve, that the Ordinary, after administration granted by him, cannot compel the administrator to make distribution.* And at last, the right of the next of kin was fully established by statute 22 and 23 Car. II. cap. 10. This cut out the Ordinary entirely.

If I thought the Athanasian creed was a part of the religion of Jesus, I should be induced to entertain a hard thought of Christianity. I should think it enjoined a slavish submission to the dictates of designing men : and instead of a reasonable service, required us to renounce our understandings, to apostatize from humanity, and degenerate into brutes, by giving up our reason, which alone distinguishes us from them. Most unjust charge upon our holy religion ! A religion, which enlarges our rational faculties, filling the mind with an astonishing idea of an eternal duration, and thereby giving us a contempt of the mean, transient pleasures of this life, and which we and the brutes enjoy in common : a religion that requires only the highest degree of reverence towards the MOST HIGH, the most refined purity of heart and mind, and the most noble and diffusive charity towards all mankind. In short, that establishes righteousness upon earth, and intire obedience to the will of God ; that so having put the oil into our lamp, according to the gospel parable, it may not only measure the course of time, but light us beyond it, to the coming of the bridegroom, and the morning of eternity.

But this will not do for the Doctors, they must have established Credenda for judgments of all sizes, they must have a formulary of dogmatic theology, an Athanasian Jumble, to support the Holy Church ; though their creed burlesques mathematical certainty, and renders their ecclesiastical Christianity inferior to the antient pagan religion. A trinity is the ecclesiastical God ; but whether three distinct conscious beings of co-ordinate power, equal independency, and unorigination, and so three proper Deities ; or, only three symbols of natural powers. In this the Doctors are not agreed ; but the majority are for the three proper Deities : this

* *New Abridgment of the Law*, p. 398.

heresy of three Gods we must subscribe to, or the priests will number us with the infidels, and do us all the mischief they can. Hence it comes to pass, that humanity, sweetness of temper, and moderation, are banished from society'; religion, like a cloak, is made use of to authorise hatred, violence, and injustice ; and the Christian religion, as the priests have forged it, and shew it off, that is, upon its present footing, as an establishment, is pernicious to mankind, and ought to go, that the people may be restored again to Christ's religion, and be led to attend to the command of God ; which is to believe in the name of his Son Jesus Christ, and to love one another.

FAITH.

" Faith is the substance of things hoped for, the evidence of things not seen ; " *Hebrews*, ch. xi. v. 1, that is, faith is such a firm persuasion as gives, as it were, a substance or present existence to the good things which we hope for, and which are not yet in being, and as engages us to depend upon the truth of unseen things, as really, as upon ocular demonstration.

" He endured, as seeing him who is invisible ; " ver. 27, that is, Moses, as really believed the being and attributes of the invisible God, as if he had seen him with his eyes ; and fully depended upon his conduct and assistance.

The better thing provided for Christians.

" And these all having obtained a good report through faith, received not the promise, God having provided some better thing for us, that they without us should not be made perfect ; *Hebrews*, ch. xi. v. 39, 40, that is, Though the upright under the law have a good character in Scripture, and of consequence were accepted of God upon the account of their faith in the divine power and goodness, yet they received not the promised reward of another life, immediately on their leaving this world : God provided this better thing for us Christians, that we should be made happy immediately, as soon as we leave this world, that so they might not be made happy in heaven, till Christianity commenced, and Christians should be there received to happiness with them.

Note 1. It is plain from what the Apostle says before, that the thing promised is the better and more enduring substance in heaven.

2. The better thing provided for Christians, cannot be the resurrection from the dead, and the being, after that, received into the heavenly Jerusalem ; since herein we shall have nothing better than the good people who lived under the law : therefore better things can only mean our enjoyment of God immediately upon our leaving this world.

It is strange then that Bishop Fell and Whitby say, the better thing means the Messias, or the heavenly country to be fully possessed at the end of the world.

Of the same opinion is Pyle. He says, our pious ancestors under the law, though in a state of rest and happiness, after death, yet received not the full and complete enjoyment of celestial glory, that being deferred till the last and great dispensation of the Messiah be past, that so they and sincere Christians, may be all rewarded and crowned together, with the happiness both of body and soul, at the final day of judgment : but if so, tell me, Mr. Pyle, where is the better thing provided for us Christians ?

3. Besides, if the Apostle may be his own interpreter, the word perfect means the intermediate state of good souls in paradise and not the complete state after the resurrection. In the next chapter, he speaks of the spirits of the just made perfect, by which he means undoubtedly the separate souls now in glory.

In a word, the design of the Apostle was to prove that, since God has provided some better thing for us, we appear to be more in his favour ; and therefore the argument from their being justified to our being justified by faith, is stronger, that is, such a faith as has an operative influence, by rendering our lives a comment upon the blessed nature of God.

And that this was the meaning of the Apostle in the something better provided for us Christians, appears yet plainer from the consequence drawn by the inspired writer, to wit, that we ought with the greater patience and courage to endure persecution, since God has provided something better for us than for them. If the antient believers held out, who expected but a state of sleep, till the time of the general resurrection : much more should we patiently suffer affliction, and even death itself, for the sake of truth, and of the gospel, when we know, that God has promised us something better ; to wit, that we shall be conducted to paradise immediately after death, and be there spirits of just men made perfect, and be with Christ, which is far better than either to sleep after death, or to live longer in this world.

Let us lay aside then every weight, and the sin which doth so easily beset us, and let us run with patience the race that is set before us. Let us put away every thing from us, that would hinder us from improving in virtue and goodness ; looking to and imitating Jesus, the leader and captain of the faithful, and an example of spotless virtue and perfect obedience. The love of the world is enmity with God, and to place our affections here, is to vilify that better provision which he has made for us. We are but strangers and pilgrims here. The human state is but a passage, not a place of abode. It is a station of exercise and discipline, and was not designed for the place of enjoyment. That happy country is before us.

AVOIDINGS.

Avoid all indirect arts in the pursuit of a fortune. All unlawful methods of self-preservation.   And every gratification that militates with reason and benevolence.

The Offices of a Christian.

These are heavenly-mindedness, and contempt of the world, and chusing rather to die than commit a moral evil.   Such things, however, are not much esteemed by the generality of Christians : Most people laugh at them, and look upon them as indiscretions ; therefore there is but little true Christianity in the world.   It has never been my luck to meet with many people that had these three necessary qualifications.   And as for the people, exclusive of their going to church to make a character, or to ogle one another, or out of superstition to perform so much opus operatum, a job of lip service, which they idly fancy to be religion, they, I mean the great and the small, might as well be Heathens as Christians, for any real Christian purpose they answer, in a strict adherence to the three offices aforementioned.   The name of Christian sounds over Europe, and large parts of Asia, Africa, and America : but if a Christian is what St. Paul defines it, to wit, a man that is heavenly-minded, that contemns the world, and would die rather than commit a moral evil, then is the number of Christians very small indeed.

The meaning of John, ch. vi. v. 44.   " No man can come to me, except the Father draw him."

That is, no one can be a Christian, unless his regard for the Deity and natural religion inclines him to receive a more improved scheme of religion.

But Dr. Young, in one of his sermons, explains this text in the following manner.   No one can live up to the religion of Jesus, and reach Christian perfection, unless the Father enlightens and enables him, by the operative influence of his holy spirit.   We can do nothing, in respect of what ought to be done, to be more than nominal Christians, without the inward principle of sanctification. This I think is mere methodism.   The excellent Dr. Lardner expounds the text in the following words : " No man will come to me, and receive my pure, sublime, and spiritual doctrine, unless he have first gained some just apprehensions concerning the general principles of religion.   And if a man have some good notions of God, and his perfections, and his will as already revealed, he will come unto me.   If any man is well disposed, if he has a love of truth, and a desire to advance in virtue, and religious knowledge ; he will readily hearken to me, and believe in me." *Sermons*, vol. i. p. 303.

Of Baptism, in the name of the Father, Son, and Holy Spirit.

What is the meaning of baptizing them into the **name** of the Father, and of the Son, and of the Holy Ghost ?

It signifies receiving men by baptism to the profession and privileges of that religion, which was taught by the Father, Son, and Spirit, that is, which the Father taught by the Son, in his lifetime, and by the Spirit, after his ascension.

Or, to be baptized, is solemnly to profess our resolution to adhere to that holy doctrine, which is the mind and will of God the Father, published to the world by his Son, whom he sent from heaven for that purpose, and confirmed by the power of the Holy Ghost.

Note, An able writer, *St. Hillary de Trinitate*, lib. 2. *ad calcem* on Matt. ch. xxviii. v. 19, says that baptising in the name of the Father, and of the Son, and of the Holy Spirit, signifies, In confession of the author of all things, and of the only begotten, and of the gift.

Of Christian Idolatry.

What a surprising incident is idolatry in the church of Christ ! that after the religion of Jesus had accomplished its glorious design, and subverted idolatry and superstition throughout the world, it should itself be wounded almost to death, by the enemy it had subdued l This is the case all over the realms of popery. And can they be said to have any true religion among them, where the theology of Athanasius prevails ?

Churchism and Creeds.

I have no very good opinion of creeds. Jesus Christ came with a legatarian power from God, the Supreme Being, to declare his will to mankind ; and the great work to be done, so far as I can find in the gospel, is, the perfecting our minds in all that is truly excellent ; by labouring to excel in all the virtues of the gospel, by loving the whole race of mankind with an universal charity, and striving to add to the satisfaction and happiness of all about us, and with whom we have any connection.

Having lost MARIA, I went up to London, and on my way to the metropolis, dined at a pleasant village, not far from Nottingham, where I saw two gentlemen well worth mentioning. They were sitting in a room the waiter shewed me into, and had each of them a porringer of mutton broth. One of them seemed a little consumptive creature, about four feet six inches high, uncommonly thin, or rather exsiccated to a cuticle. His broth and bread however he supped up with some relish. He seemed to be past threescore. His name was RIBBLE.

The other was a young man, once very handsome, tall and strong, but so consumed and weak, that he could hardly speak or stir. His name was RICHMOND. He attempted to get down his broth, but not above a spoonful or two could he swallow. He appeared to me to be a dying man.

While I beheld things with astonishment, the servant brought

in dinner, a pound of rump steaks, and a quart of green peas ; two
cuts of bread, a tankard of strong beer, and pint of port wine :
with a fine appetite, I soon dispatched my mess, and over my wine,
to help digestion, began to sing the following :

> Tell me, I charge you, O ye sylvan swains,
> Who range the mazy grove, or flow'ry plains,
> Beside what fountain, in what breezy bower,
> Reclines my charmer in the noon-tide hour ?
>
> Soft, I adjure you, by the skipping fawns,
> By the fleet roes, that bound along the lawns ;
> Soft tread, ye virgin daughters of the grove,
> Nor with your dances wake my sleeping love.
>
> Come, Rosalind, O come, and infant flow'rs
> Shall bloom and smile, and form their charms by yours ;
> By you the lily shall her white compose,
> Your blush shall add new blushes to the rose.
>
> Hark ! from yon bow'rs what airs soft warbled play !
> My soul takes wing to meet th' inchanting lay.
> Silence, ye nightingales ! attend the voice !
> While thus it warbles, all your songs are noise.
>
> See ! from the bower a form majestic moves,
> And smoothly gliding, shines along the groves ;
> Say, comes a goddess from the golden spheres ?
> A goddess comes, or Rosalind appears.

While I was singing, and indeed all the while I was at dinner,
the gentlemen looked with wonder at me, and at last, as soon as I
was silent, old RIBBLE expressed himself in the following words :

" You are the most fortunate of mortals to be sure, Sir. A happy
man indeed. You seem to have health and peace, contentment
and tranquillity, in perfection. You are the more striking, when
such spectacles as my cousin RICHMOND (pointing to the dying
gentleman in the room) and I are in contrast before you. I will
tell you our stories, Sir, in return for your charming song, and
hope what I am going to say may be of service to you, as you are
coming on, and we going off from this world.

" My kinsman there, the dying RICHMOND, in that chair, was
once a Sampson, and the handsomest man of his time, though the
remains of beauty or strength cannot now be traced. By drinking and whoring he brought himself to what you see ; to a state
that eludes all the arts of medicine. He has an aggravated cough,
which produces a filthy pus of an ash-colour, streaked with blood,
and mixed with filaments torn from his lungs and membranes,
and with the utmost difficulty he respires. He has a perpetual
violent pain in his breast, a pricking soreness in his paps when he
coughs, and defects in all his functions. He has that flux of the
belly, which is called a lientery, and the fluids of his body are
wasted in colliquative sweats. A stretching pain racks him if he
lies on either side, by reason of some adhesion of the lungs to the
pleura. His hair is fallen off, and his nails you see are dead-

coloured, and hooked. His countenance, you observe, is Hippo-
cratical, the very image of death : his face a dead pale, his eyes
sunk, his nose sharp, his cheeks hollow, his temples fallen, and his
whole body thin like a skeleton. What a figure now is this once
curled darling of the ladies : it was done, good Sir, by the hand of
Intemperance.

"As to myself," he continued, "I brought a consumption into
the world with me, and by art have supported under it. I was
born with the sharp shoulders you see, which are called pterogoi-
des, or wing-like, and had a contracted thorax, and long chest, a
thin and long neck, a flaccid tone of all parts about the breast,
and a very flabby contexture of the muscles all over my body :
but nevertheless, by a strict temperance all my life, and by following the directions of Dr. Bennet in his *Theatrum Tabidorum*, I
have not only made life tolerable, but so removed the burden of
stagnant phlegm from the thorax, by throwing it down by stool,
and up by expectoration, exhaling it sometimes through the skin,
and at other times digesting it with fasting, that I contrive more
useful hours to myself than the strong and young can enjoy in
their continued scenes of dissipation and riot. In me is seen the
wonderful effect of rule and sobriety. I am now past fifty by
several years, notwithstanding my very weak and miserable constitution, and by attending to nature, and never indulging in gratification or excess, am not only able to live without pain, but to
divert life by experimental philosophy. I came down to this pleasant place, chiefly for the benefit of poor RICHMOND, my kinsman,
whom you see with his eyes shut before you, the very picture of
death ; and also, with a view to do some good to myself, as it is
the finest air in the world. I took a house in the village to live the
more easily, as the lodging-houses are all crowded here, and resolved to amuse the days I have left in cultivating the science of
chemistry ; not in order to finish what nature has begun, do you
see me, as the alchymists talk, and procure to the imperfect metals
the much desired coction ; but, to examine substances, and by
the examination, obtain ideas of the bodies capable of the three
degrees of fermentation, spiritous, acetous, and putrid ; and of
the products of those fermentations, to wit, ardent spirits, acids
analogous to those of vegetables and animals, and volatile alkalis.

"To this purpose, I made for myself a laboratory, and about a
year ago, began to employ my vessels and furnaces in various pro-
cesses. A vast variety of entertaining things have since occurred,
and my life is thereby made agreeable and pleasing ; though to
look at my poor frame, one would think me incapable of any satisfactions. I will give you an instance or two of my amusements,
and do you judge, if they may not afford a mind more than the
tumultuous joys of love and wine, horse-racing, cock-fighting,
hunting, and other violent pleasures can yield.

" You know, good Sir, I suppose, that there are six metals, two perfect, and four imperfect.   Gold and silver, perfect: the others, copper, tin, lead, and iron.   Quicksilver is by some called a seventh metal : but that I think cannot be, as it is not malleable.   Yet it is not to be confounded with the semi-metals, as it differs from the metals no otherwise than by being constantly in fusion ; which is occasioned by its aptness to flow with such a small degree of heat, that be there ever so little warmth on earth, there is still more than enough to keep mercury in fusion.   It must be called then, in my opinion, a metallic body of a particular kind : And the more so, let me add, as art has not yet found out a way of depriving it wholly of its phlogiston.

" I must observe to you, good Sir, in order to be intelligible in what I am saying, that the phlogiston in metals is the matter of fire as a constituent principle in bodies.   It is the element of fire combined with some other substance, which serves it as a basis for constituting a kind of secondary principle ; and it differs from pure fixed fire in these particulars, that it communicates neither heat nor light, it causes no charge, but only renders body apt to fuse by the force of a culinary fire, and it can be conveyed from body to body, with this circumstance, that the body deprived of the phlogiston is greatly altered, as is the body that receives it.

" As to the semi-metals, which I mentioned, you will be pleased to observe, that they are regulus of antimony, bismuth, zinc, and regulus of arsenic.   They are not malleable, and easily part with their phlogiston.   Zinc and bismuth are free from the poisonous quality, but arsenic is the most violent poison ; especially the shining crystalline calx of it, or flowers raised by the fire, and named white arsenic ; regulus of antimony is likewise a poison, not in its nature, but because it always contains a portion of arsenic in its composition.

" Antimony is a pretty white bright colour, and has the splendour, opacity, [and gravity of a metal, but under the hammer crumbles to dust.   A moderate heat makes it flow, and a violent fire dissipates it into smoke and white vapours.   They adhere to cold bodies, and when the farina is collected, we call these vapours flowers of antimony.

" Butter of Antimony, good Sir, that wonderful corrosive, is a compound made by distilling pulverized regulus of antimony, and corrosive sublimate.   The production, on operation, is a white matter, thick and scarce fluid, which is the regulus of antimony united with the acid of sea-salt.   Here the corrosive sublimate is decompounded, the mercury revivified, and the acid combined with it, quits it to join the regulus of antimony, because its affinity with it is greater."   Little RIBBLE, the Chemist, went on, and with difficulty I could refrain from laughing ; not on account of the man's talking nonsense, for his discourse was the very reverse of that ; but by reason of the gripe he had of my arm, the pulls he gave me, if I happened to look another way, and the surprising eagerness with which he spoke ; which shewed, that he was chemically struck to an amazing degree, and following up closely, " But liver of antimony, good Sir," he continued, " is made of equal parts of nitre and antimony. On the mixture's being exposed to the action of fire a violent detonation ensues, and the deflagrating nitre consumes the sulphur of the antimony, and even a part of its phlogiston. A greyish matter remains after the detonation, and this is what we call liver of antimony. It contains a fixed nitre, a vitriolated tartar, and the reguline part of antimony vitrified.

"The principal use the Chemists make of antimony is to separate gold from the other metals. All metals, gold excepted, have a greater affinity with 'sulphur than the reguline 'part of antimony. As to gold, it is incapable of contracting any union with sulphur. If therefore I have a mass compounded of various 'metals, and want to get the gold out, I melt it with antimony, and as soon as it flows, every thing in the mass which is not gold, unites with the sulphur, in or of the antimony, and causes two separations, that of the sulphur of antimony from its reguline part, and that of the gold from the metals with which it was mixed. This produces two new combinations, the metals and the sulphur, in fusion, being lighter, rise to the surface ; and the gold and the reguline part of antimony being heaviest, the combination of them sinks to the bottom. Now the business is to part these two, and to this purpose, I expose the combination to a degree of fire, capable of dissipating into vapours all the semi-metal the mass contains. The reguline being volatile, goes off by the great heat, and my gold remains pure and fixed in my crucible.

" As to the antimonial wine, made by the essence of antimony, that is, by impregnating the most generous white wine, with the minims or leasts of antimony, which the physicians have found out, it is not the part of a chemist to speak of that ; and therefore, I shall only observe to you, that it is the best vomit, the best purge, and the best thing for a sweat, in the world. I will tell you, good Sir, what I heard an eminent Doctor say of it. Affirmo sanctissime, nihil inde melius, nihil tutius, nihil efficacius, deprehendi unquam, quam tritum illum, ac simplicem vini automonialis infusum ex vino albo generoso, aromate aliquo stomachico adjecto. Epotus largiter maximas movit vomitiones, in minuta tantum quantitate, ad guttas puta viginta, aut triginta, adhibitus sudores elicit benignos ; paulo tamen majoræ aleum solvit leniter. Medicamentum, paratu quidem facillimum, at viribus maximum. And therefore, good Sir, when any thing ails you, let me recommend the antimonial wine to you. Thirty drops will sweat you effectually, and about forty or fifty will effect a purge in a happy manner.

" But as to the second semi-metal, bismuth, it has almost the same appearance as regulus of antimony, but of a more dusky cast inclining somewhat to red.   It requires less heat than antimony to flow, and like it, and the other semi-metals, is volatile, by the action of a violent fire, and under the hammer is dust.   In fusion, it mixes well with all metals, and whitens them by union, but destroys their malleability.   In flowing, it loses its phlogiston with its metallic form.   And it has a singular property, which the other semi-metals have not, of attenuating lead so as to make it amalgamatic with mercury, so perfectly as to make it pass with it through shamoy leather.   As soon as the amalgama is made, the bismuth goes off or separates ; but the lead for ever remains united with the mercury.

" It is of a solution of the ore of bismuth, we make that very curious and useful thing called sympathetic ink, which is a liquor of a beautiful colour, like that of the lilach or pipe-tree blossom. The process in preparing this liquor is tedious and difficult by aqua fortis, aqua regis, and fire, and therefore the ink is rarely to be met with.   It is not to be had, unless some gentleman who makes chemistry his employment, gives one a present of a bottle of it ; as I do now to you, in hopes it may some time or other be of singular service to you ; for I have conceived a great regard for you, though I never saw you before, as you seem not only more teachable than any I have met with, but to delight in the information I give you relating to chemical things."

Here I returned my Chemist many thanks, and professed my eternal obligation to him : that I could listen for years to him ; and wished it was possible to become his disciple, that I might see him by experiment facilitate the study of a science, more entertaining, instructive, and extensively useful than any other. " But how, dear sir, am I to use this ink, you are so vastly good as to give me, to make it more useful than any other ink could be ?"

" I will tell you," replied he, " you must write with this lilach-coloured liquor, on good well gummed paper that does not sink ; and the singularity of the ink, consists in its property of disappearing entirely, and becoming invisible, though it be not touched with anything whatever, and this distinguishes it from all others.   The writing must dry in a warm air, and while it is cold no colour can be perceived : but gently warming it before the fire, the writing gradually acquires a greenish blue colour, which is visible as long as the paper continues a little warm, and disappears entirely when it cools.   When other sympathetic inks are made to appear by proper application, they do not disappear again ; but this liquor from the ore of bismuth must have the fire or heat kept to it, to render it legible.   If a man writes to his mistress, suppose, or to a minister of state, with lemon juice, once the writing has been warmed by the fire, and the letters by that means appear, the epistle may be afterwards read at any time and place ; but if the lady's father should by accident get your letter, written in lilach-coloured liquor, it must still remain a secret to him, for if on getting it, and opening the seal, he could see no writing, and therefore imagining it was written with lemon juice, or some other sympathetic ink, he should hold it himself to the fire, or bid his servant hold it to the heat, that the letters might be produced, and made visible, yet the moment bismuth ink is taken away from the fire, and begins to cool, it is as invisible again, as a sheet of white paper. How serviceable this may be on various occasions, may be easily conceived.

" But as to our third semi-metal, called Zinc, this is so like bismuth in appearance, that some have confounded it with Zinc ; though it differs from it essentially in its properties, and will unite with all metalline substances, except bismuth. It is volatile by fire above all things, and makes a sublimate of the metallic substances with which it is fused. Zinc mixed with copper in the quantity of a fourth part, produces brass. If the Zinc is not very pure, the composition proves Tombac, or Prince's metal.

" Regulus of arsenic, the fourth semi-metal, has a colour resembling lead, unites readily with metallic substances, and renders them brittle, unmalleable, and volatile. The calx of it produced by fire, may be made volatile by more fire, and in this differs from the calx of all metalline substances ; for all other calxes are fixed, and cannot be moved. It has likewise a saline character, in which its corrosive quality or poison consists : a quality from which the other metallic substances are free, when they are not combined with a saline matter. These things being noticed, in relation to metals, and semi-metals in general, I will now proceed to relate a few curious cases, in respect of the metals.

" Gold, our first metal, has ten sensible criterions. It is the heaviest and densest of all bodies : the most simple of all bodies : the most fixed of all bodies : the only body that cannot be turned into scoriæ, by antimony and lead ; the most ductile of all bodies : so soft as to be scarcely elastic or sonorous : must be red hot to melt : is dissolvable by sea-salt and its preparations, but remains untouched by any other species of salts ; and of consequence not liable to rust ; as aqua regia and spirit of sea-salt do not float in the air, unless in laboratories, or chemists' shops, where we find them sometimes : it unites spontaneously with pure quick-silver, and never wastes by emitting effluvia, or exhalations. These are the ten sensible properties or characteristics of this metal. It is certainly pure gold, if it has these criterions, and they are of great use in life ; especially to persons who have to do with that subtil tribe, the alchemists.

" As to the weight of gold, it is more than nineteen times heavier than water, bulk for bulk, and this property is inseparable from it ; it being impossible to render gold more or less heavy ; and for this reason, the specific gravity of gold, if it had no other criterion, might demonstrate real gold. To make gold, other metals must be rendered equiponderant to it, and therefore, if an alchemist should offer to obtrude a metal on you for gold, hang an equal weight of pure, and of suspected gold by two threads to a nice balance, and on immerging them in water, if the alchemist's gold be pure, the water will retain both pieces in æquilibrio ; otherwise, the adulterate metal will rise, and the pure descend.

" The reason is, all bodies lose some of their weight in a fluid, and the weight which a body loses in a fluid, is to its whole weight, as the specific gravity of the fluid is to that of the body. The specific gravity of a body is the weight of it, when the bulk is given ; thirty-eight grains of gold weighed in the air, is not the true weight of it : for there it loses the weight of an equal bulk of air : it weighs only thirty-six grains in the water, and there it loses the weight of as much water, as is equal in bulk of itself, that is, two grains, and as the gold weighs thirty-eight grains, it follows, that the weight of water is to that of gold, bulk for bulk, as two to thirty-eight, that is as the weight lost in the fluid is the whole weight.

" And so, if a piece of gold, and a piece of copper, are equiponderant in air, yet in water the gold will outweigh the copper ; because their bulks, though of equal weight, are inversely as their specific gravities, that is, the gold must be as much less than the copper, as the specific gravity of gold is greater than that of copper : and as they must both lose weight in proportion to bulk in water, therefore the gold, the lesser of the two, loses less of its weight than the copper does, and consequently, out-weighs the copper in water. I hope this is clear. The case is the same, in proportion, in pure gold, and gold mixed with other metals. The bulk of the pure gold must be less than that of alloyed gold, and its weight greater in water ; though both equiponderate, a pound suppose, in air."

" It is very plain, sir, and I request you will proceed. You give me valuable information, and oblige me very much." This pleased the Chemist, and the ingenious little RIBBLE went on.

" As to the simplicity of gold, we mean, by simple body, that whose minutest part has all the physical properties of the whole mass. Now dissolve a grain of gold in aqua regia, and from a single drop of the solution, a particle of gold may be separated, and have all the characters of gold, except those of magnitude, though the separated particle of gold shall only be the millionth part of the grain. Or, fuse a single grain of gold with a mass of silver, and mix the whole together, so that the gold shall be equally distributed : then take a particle thereof, and you will have a particle of perfect gold ; for dissolve the least part of the mixture in aqua fortis, and a quantity of gold will precipitate to the bottom. It will bear the same proportion to the grain, that the part dissolved did to the whole mass.

"Having mentioned aqua regia and aqua fortis, I must, to be intelligible, say two or three words in relation to them. Aqua regia is an extract by fire from sea-salt and spirit of nitre. The acid liquor that comes over from them into the receiver, is aqua regis. Aqua fortis, or spirit of nitre, is a nitrous acid separated from its basis, nitre, by the vitriolic acid. Aqua regis only will dissolve gold. Silver is not soluable by aqua regis ; its proper solvent is the acid of nitre or aqua fortis. But if you want to separate a mass of gold and silver, either will do. You may dissolve the gold by aqua regia, and let the silver remain pure ; or, dissolve the silver by aqua fortis, and let the gold remain pure. Only note in this case of a mixed lump of gold and silver the operation by aqua fortis is preferable, for this reason ; that aqua regis in dissolving the gold, takes up likewise a little silver ; but aqua fortis hath not the least effect on gold ; and note further, that if there be equal parts of gold and silver in the mixture, they cannot be parted by aqua fortis. It has not then the least effect on the silver, which is very strange. To make aqua fortis act duly on silver mixed with gold, the silver must be at least in a triple proportion to that of the gold. The reason of the singular effect is, that when the gold exceeds, or the parts of both are equal in quantity, then, as both are intimate, united in the mass, the parts or minims of the gold coat over the parts of the silver, and defend them from the action of the aqua fortis. In this case, aqua regia must be used to dissolve the gold, and leave the silver pure : or, as aqua regia takes up a little of the silver, when it dissolves the gold, melt the metalline mass, and add as much silver as will make it a triple proportion to the gold. Then you may by aqua fortis take up all your silver in the dissolution, and leave all the pure gold.

"But as to the third criterion of gold, its being the most fixed of all bodies, this is evident from the violence of fire having no effect on it. An ounce of it exposed for the space of two months, in the eye of a glass furnace, does not lose half a grain. It may from thence be said to be incorruptible.

"As to gold's resisting antimony, and not turning into scoriæ by its force, it is most certain from hence, that if you take a mass consisting of gold, silver, copper, the other metals, with stones, &c., and fuse it with antimony, the bodies will flow on the surface, and be easily blown off by the bellows : the antimony all evaporates, and leaves the gold alone. This is called the last test of gold, to try the purity of it. If the remaining gold have lost nothing of its weight, it is allowed perfectly pure, and called gold of twenty-four carats ; or if it be found one twenty-fourth lighter, it is said to be twenty-three carats fine.

" But as to the ductility of gold, this is the most extraordinary property of it. The arts of gold-beating and wire-drawing, show us things quite amazing. In leaf-gold, a grain and a quarter of the metal, may be made to cover an area of fifty square inches ; and if the leaf be divided by parallel lines a hundredth part of an inch, a grain of gold will be divided into five hundred thousand minute squares, all discernible by the eye : yet this is not the most can be done by the hammer. A single grain of gold may be stretched into a leaf that will cover a house, and yet the leaf remain so compact, as not to transmit the rays of light, nor ever admit spirit of wine to transude. This however is nothing to the effects of wire-drawing.

" A gold wire is only a silver one gilt, and if you coat a silver cylinder of forty-eight ounces weight, with one ounce of gold, which is sufficient, this cylinder may be drawn out into a wire so very fine, that two yards thereof shall weigh only one grain, and ninety-eight yards only forty-nine grains, so that one grain of gold gilds ninety-eight yards ; and of course the ten thousandth part of a grain, is above one-third part of an inch long. And since the third part of an inch is yet capable of being divided into ten lesser parts visible to the eye, it is evident that the hundred thousandth part of a grain of gold, may be seen without the help of a microscope. And yet so intimately do its parts cohere, that though the gold wherewith the wire is coated, be stretched to such a degree, there is not any appearance of the colour of silver underneath. Nor is this all.

" In supergildings, that is, to make the richest lace, they employ but six ounces of gold, to cover or gild forty-five marks of silver, that is, twenty-two pounds and a half avoirdupoise weight, rounded into the form of a cylinder or roller, which hath fifteen lines in diameter, and twenty-two inches in length ; and here the stratum of gold which envelops the ingot that is to be drawn into wire, hath no more thickness than the fifteenth part of a line, which is extremely thin ; as a line is the twelfth part of an inch.

" But to make the common gold-thread, they do not use more than two ounces of gold, and sometimes not more than one, to gild or cover the ingot I have mentioned, and then the enveloping stratum is not more in thickness, if two ounces be employed, than the forty-fifth part of a line ; and if one ounce be used, but the ninetieth part of a line. Two ounces of gold are generally used, in gilding or covering the ingot I have mentioned, and vastly thinner must the stratum be, when the ingot is drawn till it surpasses the fineness of a hair, and the diameter is nine thousand times smaller than what it had in the mass. By weighing out half a dram of this thread or wire, it is found by measuring the length of the half dram, that the ingot of twenty-two pounds and a half, and twenty-two inches long, is changed into a length of one hundred and sixteen millions three thousand five hundred and twenty feet, that is, ninety-six leagues and one hundred and ninety-six fathoms ; for the half dram of wire or thread measures two hundred and two feet ; by consequence, an ounce of it, three thousand two hundred and thirty-two feet ; a mark of it, or eight ounces, twenty-five thousand eight hundred and fifty-six feet. And yet, astonishing as this length is, for two ounces of gold to be drawn to, the gold which covers the silver never ceases to gild it. The gold still keeps pace with the wire, stretch it to what length the drawers can, through the wire-drawing irons, and holes much smaller one than another. The silver never appears.

"It does not however rest there. Before the thread or wire is wound on silk, and before they spin it, it must be flatted by passing it between steel wheels extremely well polished, and this flatting increases its length to more than a seventh part. One ingot, therefore, of eight marks, or twenty-two and a half pounds, and twenty-two inches long, by this increase of a seventh part, is brought to the length of a hundred and eleven leagues, that is, about three hundred English miles.

"But amazing as this extent is, it is not the utmost bounds to which the ductility of gold may be carried. One ounce only of gold is sometimes used to cover one ingot, and drawn to the length I have mentioned, and by the time it has passed the flatting wheels, the gold that covers the silver laminæ, must have its thickness reduced to less than the millionth part of a line ; that is, a twelve millionth of an inch. This is beyond the reach of our conception. Imagination cannot plumb her line so low."

"But, sir," said I, "may not the gold be divided into small grains separate one from another, but yet near enough to give their colour to the silver ? Though we may not be able to see the thing, yet I think it may be imagined ; the gold on the laminæ doth not form a continued leaf."

"Experience, good sir, demonstrates the contrary, that every point of silver hath its cover of gold. Put a piece of this gilt wire in aqua fortis, the silver will be dissolved, and the gold left a perfect, continuous tube. It is an amazing thing ! and shews the astonishing power of the first cause ! As to the reason of this ductility, and why gold in such a manner adheres to silver, so as never to part from it, if the twenty-two and a half pounds of silver gilded with one ounce of gold could be extended by art for ever, this is past our finding out. It is a secret of nature we cannot form any idea of—

Calignosa nocte premit Deus."

RIBBLE went on. "These are the things most remarkable in relation to gold ; and I have only to add, that as to the manner of getting it, it is found sometimes in glebes or clods, consisting of gold alone ; sometimes in a powdery form, and then called gold-dust, or sand-gold, in the sands and mud of rivers and brooks ; but most commonly in whitish clods, dug out of mines of vast depth, and intermixed with silver and various fossils. This they reduce by fire to a mass of metal, and by aqua regia or aqua fortis, the gold is easily taken out of the ore.

" As to gold's being so yielding and ductile by human art, it is to be observed, that in return it exerts a greater power on the human mind. Passive it is in its ductility, but more active in its influence on man. It is a greater tyrant than a slave. It drives repeated millions of the human race to death and hell. King of metals as it is, bright and glorious to behold, and what procures innumerable blessings to mankind ; yet, without the grace of God, to moderate the passion for it, and to direct the mind in a true use of it, it is more dangerous to beings on a trial in a first state, than even poverty can be in this lower hemisphere. What villainies are daily committed to get it ! What iniquities daily perpetrated by those who have plenty of it ! Lead us not into temptation, should relate as well to too much of it, as to a total want of it ; and it is well prayed, In all time of our wealth, good Lord deliver us.

" In my opinion, neither poverty nor riches, but a middle state, is the thing we should desire. It is in this condition, we can best live soberly, or with a sound mind, and conduct ourselves as those who have an intelligent spirit to preside in body. Too much gold most commonly inverts this order, and produces an apostasy that sets the inferior powers in the throne, and enslaves the mind to the body. It gives the passions the commanding influence, and makes reason receive law from appetite.

" If we look into the world, we find too often, in this case, that wealth is big with innumerable sins. The rich are filled with wine, wherein is excess, and shew an unbridled dissoluteness of manners. Their eyes behold strange women, and their hearts utter perverse things. Instead of regarding the common good, they commit the most extravagant injuries. Of such a hardening nature is too much gold, that it tends to make conscience insensible and stupid, and renders it for ever unapt for impression. Then whoredom and wine, and new wine, take away the heart, and men are made to forget the law of God.

" But having neither poverty nor riches, in the calm middle state, having all reasonable conveniences, we can fairly come by ; a vast variety of creatures for our food, and wine in its season, to make glad the heart ; we may then partake of the bounties of Providence, with a sober freedom, and at the same time, can best lay up for ourselves a good foundation, or security for the time to come, that we may lay hold of eternal life.

" Though it is with a prospect of difficulties, that all must enter upon religion, and with labour and difficulty, maintain our ground, and acquit ourselves like Christians, that is, resist the devil in all his assaults, overcome the world in its ensnaring influence, and mortify the irregular inclinations of nature ; yet in the happy middle state, where there is no poverty nor riches, that is, great wealth, we can make everlasting glory and felicity our governing aim, and bound our ambition and desires by nothing short of the resurrection of the dead. We may live in a full and ready sub-mission of the soul to the authority of God's word. Things eternal may have the ascendant in our practical judgment, and then with pleasure we become followers of them who through faith and patience inherit the promises.

" Good sir, this is all our sowing time, and whatsover a man soweth, that shall he also reap. He that soweth to his flesh, shall of his flesh reap corruption ; but he that soweth to the spirit, shall of the spirit reap everlasting life. And therefore, whether your lot be cast in the middling state, or you were born to thou-sands a year, let wisdom be your rule, and prefer that happiness which has everlasting duration, in the realms of light above, to any present good that can come in competition with it. Do not spend money for that which is not bread—and your labour for that which satisfieth not. Do not employ your pains for that which hath vanity written upon it, by the word of God, by the testimony of the wisest men, and by frequent experience : but let your principal regard be for your immortal soul, when nothing can be given in exchange for the soul. Implore the light and grace of the good spirit, and by the quickening influences of the Father of the universe, and the exertion of your whole strength, let it be the principal labour of your every day, to make advances in the divine life, and be a blessing to society wherever you come. In virtue and charity may you excel.

" You will pardon old RIBBLE, I hope, good sir, and excuse his addressing himself to you in this manner. It is an odd con-clusion, I own, to a discourse on metals and semi-metals ; but it is from an extreme regard I have conceived for you, that I talk as I do, and presume to call upon you, (as you are a young man of fortune, I suppose) to consider seriously of that decree, which is the result of unerring wisdom, and the will of the Rector of the universe, to wit, that we are all under the law of death, and through that gate must pass, perhaps at a day's, an hour's warning, to the resurrection of the dead, to be adjudged to happiness or misery, as time has been employed, and life spent here. This is the decree of the Most High God, and of consequence, it is incumbent on us, to prepare for the awful hereafter, and endeavour by good action, and a virtuous mind, by purity of conscience, and an exalted piety, to come off well in judgment. Happy, thrice happy they that do so.''

Here little RIBBLE the Chemist had done, and I had reason to return him my very hearty thanks for the favour of his whole discourse. I was vastly obliged to him for the knowledge he had given me, in relation to the philosophy of metals, and taking him by the hand, promised him, that I would ever gratefully remember his moral conclusion. This pleased the old gentleman, and at four in the afternoon we parted.

Reflecting on the wonders of the metals, which I had heard old RIBBLE so well discourse of, and being more intent on what had been told me of these things, that I might never forget such useful learning, I trotted on for several hours without minding the road, and arrived as the sun was setting in a deep and melancholy vale, through which a pleasant river ran, that by the murmur of its streams, seemed to be marked out for the rendezvous of the thoughtful, who love the deep recesses, and embowering woods, with the soft thrillings of gliding streams, as much as the sprightly court the gayest scenes. In this sweet spot, I found a pretty country house, and not knowing where I was, rode up to the door, to enquire my way. A gentleman, who seemed to be about forty, immediately appeared, let me know I was at a considerable distance from any town, and as it was near ten, told me I had best rest with him that night, and I was most heartily welcome. This was humane and civil. I accepted the kind invitation, and immediately went in with him. He brought me into a decent room, and gave me a handsome meal. We had a couple of bottles after supper, talked of a thousand things, and then withdrew to wind up the machines. He would not let me stir the next morning, and after dinner we became well acquainted. Six days this gentleman prevailed with me to stay at his house, and then I left him with regret. He was so generous, so civil, and in every thing so agreeable, that I could not avoid admiring him, and regarding him to an extreme degree. His name was MONCTON.

AVERY MONCTON had seen the world, when he was a young man, and by reading much, and thinking a great deal, had acquired an extensive knowledge, and a deep penetration : in him the gentleman and the scholar were visible. He seemed superior to folly, and his philosophy appeared to be an assiduous examination of his ideas, fancies, and opinions, in order to render them true and just. His religion consisted in a cheerful submission to the divine pleasure, with respect to all things independent of us, or absolutely external to us ; and in a continued exertion of benevolence, in doing all the good he could. ·What the theology of sects was, and the notions of divines, he never minded. It was his opinion, that an active charity is the only thing that can liken and approve us to the original benevolent mind : and that it is reasonable to submit to all his dispensations, since the providence of an infinitely perfect Being, must do all for the best in the whole. This was AVERY MONCTON, Esq. In his person he was tall, and very thin.

This gentleman told me the following remarkable story relating to himself, on my asking him, if he had ever been married ? " Yes, sir," he replied. " When I was about five and twenty, a young lady came in my way, who had all the external charms that ever adorned a woman, and I thought, her mind as perfect in goodness of every kind, as minds can be on this earth. I made my addresses to her, and with some difficulty persuaded her to accept of a good jointure, and be a wife ; for she had got it into her head, that Christian perfection consisted in a virgin-life. I loved her to an extreme degree, and fancied myself beyond mortals happy, as her fondness seemed equal to my passion, and she expressed it in a most transporting way. Three months passed on in this delightful manner, and I should have thought an age but minutes, if the scene was to have no change. But every thing must have an end in this poor state. Business called me one morning early into the city, and till it was late at night, I thought not to return ; back however I was compelled to go for some papers, I had forgot, and designing to surprise my wife agreeably, came in by a key I had, at the wash-house door, and unseen went softly up to my chamber, where I expected to find my beloved in a sweet sleep. Gently I touched the lock, and intended as my charmer slumbered, to give this idol of my heart a kiss. But, as I opened the door without being heard, I saw a man by my bedside, and my fond faithful wife, buttoning up his breeches. Amazement seized me, but I was not in a rage. I only said ' Is that Louisa I see ? ' and shut the door. Down stairs I went immediately, and out again the same way I came in. I was done with love for ever, and from that time never saw my wife more. A ship being to sail the next day for Constantinople, I went a passenger in it, and resolved to live abroad some years.

" Six years I resided in Greece, and visited every curious place. Four I spent in Asia Minor, and two in Italy and France. I diverted myself with noting down the extraordinary things I saw, and I purchased several fine antiquities by the way. When done, I came back to my country again, and this little seat I now live at, being to be sold, I bought it immediately, and have resided here ever since. My study, my garden, and my horse, divert me fully and finely every day. I have all I desire in this world, and reign more happily over my few subjects, in this airy, silent, secret spot, than the greatest monarch can do on a throne. My people are only one young man, who is my gardener, my footman, and my groom, and two old women, my maids. These are ever attentive to my will, and by their good behaviour and management, make

O

my lodge as agreeable, and life as pleasing, as can be expected in this system of things.''

MONCTON'S story pleased me much, and I wondered greatly at his happy temper, when he saw his beloved wife buttoning up the breeches of the man. '' But did you ever hear what became of her after ? Faulty as she was, may there not be found an honest charming woman, to render your hours more delightful than study and contrivance can make them, without a soft part-ner through life ? Come into the world with me, sir, and I will engage to find out for you a primitive Christian of a woman, with all the beauties of body that Lucian gives his images.''

'' You are very good, sir,'' replied MONCTON '' in offering to look out for another wife for me, and I thank you very heartily, for your well-meant kindness ; but as I never inquired what be-came of my first wife, from the morning I left her, and know only that she is dead, as her jointure has not been demanded for several years past ; so shall I never be concerned with a second. Per-haps there are some honest women in the world, I hope so ; but I have had enough of marriage. Beside, I think it time now to turn my thoughts a better way. In the forty-fifth year of my age, it cannot be weak, to begin to consider the great change before me, and fix my hopes on a good remove into some better and happier region. If I was unfortunate with a wife when a young man, I have little reason to expect better days with one, as age comes on. I might find myself again most sadly mistaken. But there can be no disappointment in making it the principal work of life, to prepare, in such a retirement as this, for that ap-proaching hour, when we must submit to the power and tyranny of death and corruption. By this means, the greatest happiness may be secured. In everything else, there is uncertainty and vanity. I speak principally in respect of my time of life, who am hastening fast to fifty ; but at every time, it is my opinion, that men, as rationals, and beings who take on themselves the honourable profession of the Christian religion, should not comply with the criminal liberties allowed in the world, and give into the illicit usages and customs of place and company, for fear of ridicule, or to avoid giving offence ; but keep strictly to the will and laws of their higher country, and in all things have a special regard to holiness, truth, and purity.

'' I do not say this by way of preaching, but that you may thereby have a truer idea of the man you chanced to find in a lone house on the vast common. Seven years have I now lived here, and in all that time, have not been once in London : but sometimes I ride to a neighbouring village, and if on the road, or at an inn, I can pick up a sensible agreeable man, I love to dine with him, and drink a pint of wine. Such a man I frequently ride in quest of, and if he be entirely to my mind, which is very rarely the case, I invite him home with me, to pass at my lodge two or three days. Far then am I from being unsocial, though I live in solitude ; I left the world, because I was ill-used in it, and happen to think very differently from the generality of men." Here MONCTON ended his story, and a little after we parted.

I rode on for six hours without meeting with any thing remarkable, but as I baited about three o'clock at a lone inn, the situation of which was so fine in forest and water, that I determined to go no farther that day, there arrived a little after, a young lady, her maid, and two men servants. They were all well-mounted, and the lady's beast in particular, as great a beauty of its kind, as its mistress was among women. I thought I had seen the face before, and had been somewhere or other in her company ; but as it must have been several years ago, her face and person were a little altered, and I could not immediately recollect her ; but FIN, my lad, coming up to me, asked me, if I did not remember Miss TURNER of Skelsmore-vale ? "Miss TURNER," said I, " to be sure, now I think, it is she ; but this lady just arrived here is much fatter, and, if it be possible, something handsomer." "It is her, believe me," quoth FIN, "and you ought to wait upon her instantly." I went. It was Miss TURNER, one of the beauties that adorn a gallery of pictures in the North ; and who is with great truth in the following lines described, in a Poem written on this collection of paintings.

> "But see ! Emilia rises to the sight
> In every virtue, in every beauty bright !
> See those victorious eyes, that heavenly mien !
> Behold her shine like Love's resistless Queen !
> Thou fairest wonder of thy fairest kind !
> By heav'n some image of itself design'd !
> As if in thee it took peculiar care,
> And form'd thee like some fav'rite seraph there.
> But tho' thy beauty strikes the ravish'd sight,
> Thy virtues shine distinguishingly bright !
> And all the graces of thy form combin'd,
> Yield to the charms of thy unblemish'd mind ;
> Where all is spotless, gentle, and serene,
> One calm of life untouch'd by guilt or pain '
> Could I in equal lays thy worth design,
> Or paint exalted merit such as thine !
> To latest ages should thy name survive,
> And in my verse Emilia ever live ;
> Th' admiring world should listen to thy praise,
> And the fair portrait charm succeeding days."

This lady knew me at once, on my entering the room where she was, and we dined together. She told me, her brother, my friend, died in Italy, on his return home ; and Miss JAQUELOT, her cousin and companion, was happily married ; and that being thus left alone, by these two accidents, she was going up to London, to reside in the world.

" Miss TURNER," said I, " as you are now your own mistress, I may with justice tender you my addresses, and tell you, that from the first hour I saw you, I was in love with you, and am so still ; that if you will do me the honour to be my wife, I will make the best of husbands.   I have now some fortune, and if you will allow, that an honest man is the best companion for an honest woman, let us marry in the country, and instead of going up to that noisy tumultuous place London, retire to some still delightful retreat, and there live, content with each other, as happy as it is possible for two young mortals to be in this lower hemisphere. What do you say, Miss TURNER ? "

" You shall have my answer, sir, in a few days ; but as to going up to London, I think I had best see it, since I am come so far. It may give me a new relish for still life, and make the country seem more charming than I thought it before.   On the other hand, it may perhaps make me in love with the town, and put me out of conceit with the country.   In short, on second thoughts, I will not go up to the capital. I will return to Skelsmore-vale.   I think so now ; but how I may think in the morning, at present I do not know.   In the mean time," she continued, " ring, if you please, for a pack of cards, and let us pass the evening in play. The cards were brought in, the game began, and before we had played many hours, I saw this dear charming creature was all my own.   She sat before me, like blushing beauty in the picture in the gallery of Venus, enriched with thought, warm with desire, and with delicate sensations covered over : I could not help wishing for father FLEMING, my friend, to qualify us for the implanted impulse, and sanctify the call.   Early the next morning I sent FIN for him, and he was with me in a few days.   The evening he arrived we were married.   Man and wife we sat down to supper.

Here the morose, the visionary, and the dunce, will again fall upon me, for marrying a fifth wife, so quickly after the decease of the fourth, who had not been three months in her grave ; but my answer is, that a dead woman is no wife, and marriage is ever glorious.   It is the institution of heaven, a blessing to society, and therefore hated by the devil and mass-priests.   Satan by opposing it, promotes fornication and perdition.   The priests by preaching against it, drive the human race into cloisters ; destroy every thing gentle, generous, and social ; and rob the people of their property.   Celibacy is popery and hell in perfection.   It is the doctrine of devils, and a war with the Almighty.   It is against the institutions of nature and providence ; and therefore, for ever execrable be the memory of the mass-priests, who dare to call it perfection.

My dear Reader, if you are unmarried, and healthy, get a wife as soon as possible, some charming girl, or pretty widow, adorned with modesty, robed with meekness, and who has the grace to attract the soul, and heighten every joy continually; take her to thy breast, and bravely, in holy wedlock, propagate. Despise and hiss the mass-priests, and every visionary, who preaches the contrary doctrine. They are foes to heaven and mankind, and ought to be drummed out of society.

For six weeks after our marriage, we resided at the inn, on account of the charms of the ground, and seemed to be in possession of a lasting happiness it is impossible for words to describe. Every thing was so smooth and so round, that we thought prosperity must be our own for many years to come, and were quite secure from the flames of destruction; but calamity laid hold of us, when we had not the least reason to expect it, and from a fulness of peace and felicity, we sunk at once into an abyss of afflictions. Instead of going back to Skelsmore-vale, as we had resolved, my wife would go up to London, and pass a few weeks there, and thereabout, before she retired to the mountains. I was against it, but her will was my law. We set out for the capital, and the first day's journey was delightful: but her fine beast having met with an accident in the night, by a rope in the stable, which got about its foot, cut it deep, and rendered it unable to travel; we took a chariot and four to finish our way, but on driving by the side of a steep hill, the horses took fright, ran it down, overcame the carriage, and my charmer was killed. This was a dismal scene. She lived about an hour, and repeated the following fine lines from Boissard, when she saw me weeping as I kneeled on the ground by her,

> Nil prosunt lacrumæ, nec possunt fata moveri:
> Nec pro me queror; hoc morte mihi est tristius ipsa,
> Mœror Atimeti conjugis ille mihi.*

* These lines from the *Antiquities of Boissard*, are a real inscription on a tomb in Italy, which this antiquary found in his travels, and copied it as a curiosity to the world. Homonœa was a great beauty at the court of the Emperor Honorius, and married to Atimetus, a courtier and favourite, who preferred her to the most illustrious of ladies of that time, on account of her extraordinary charms, and uncommon perfections; but she did not long enjoy the honour and happiness she was married into. Before she was twenty, death snatched her away, in the year of the reign of Honorius, A.D. 401, and the following beautiful epitaph was cut on her monument, and remains to this day; I place it here for the entertainment of my readers, and likewise La Fontaine's elegant translation of it.

HOMONŒA'S EPITAPH.

> Si pensare animas sinerent crudelia fata,
> Et posset redimi morte aliena salus:
> Quantulacunque meæ debentur tempora vitæ
> Pensarem pro te, cara Homonœa, libens.
> At nunc quod possum, fugiam lucemque deosque,
> Ut te matura per stuga morte sequar.
> (Atimetus *the husband, is the speaker of these six lines*.)
> Parce tuam conjux fletu quassare juventam.
> Fataque merendo sollicitare mea.
> Nil prosunt lacrumæ, nec possunt fata moveri.
> Viximus: hic omnes exitus unus habet.

Just as she expired, she took me by the hand, and with the spirit of an old Roman, bid me adieu.

> Parce, ita non unquam similem experiare dolorem.
> Et faveant votis numina cuncta tuis !
> Quodque mihi eripuit mors immatura juventæ,
> Hoc tibi victuro proroget ulterius.

(Homonœa *is supposed to speak these eight lines, to her husband : and then relates her case to the traveller, who is passing by.*)

> Tu qui secura procedis mente parumper
> Siste gradum quæso, verbaque pauca lege.
> Illa ego quæ claris fueram prælata puellis,
> Hoc Homonœa brevi condita sum tumulo,
> Cui formam paphia, et charites, tribuere decorem,
> Quam Pallas cunctis artibus eruduit.
> Nondum bis denos ætas compleverat annos,
> Injecere manus invida fata mihi.
> Nec pro me queror ; hoc morte mihi est tristius ipsa,
> Mœror Atimeti conjugis ille mihi.
> Sit tibi terra levis, mulier dignissima vitâ
> Quæque tuis olim perfruerêre bonis.

(*These two lines may be the words of the Public, or of whoever erected the monument to the memory of* Homonœa.)

Now see how finely La Fontaine has done this inscription into verse.

> Si l'on pouvoit donner ses jours pour ceux d'un autre
> Et que par cet échange on contentat le sort,
> Quels que soint les momens qui me restent encore
> Mon âme, avec plaisir, racheteroit la votre.
> Mais le destin l'ayant autrement arrété,
> Je ne sçaurois qui fuir les dieux et la clarté,
> Pour vous suivre aux enfers d'une mort avancée.
> Quittez, ô chere epoux, cette triste pensée,
> Vous alterez en vain les plus beaux de vos ans :
> Cessez de fatiguer par de cris impuissans,
> La parque et le destin, deïtez inflexibles.
> Mettez fin â des pleurs qui ne le touchent point ;
> Je ne suis plus : tout tent â ce suprême poinct.
> Ainsi nul accident, par des coups si sensibles
> Ne vienne à l'avenir traverser vos plaisirs !
> Ainsi l'Olimpe entier s'accorde a vos desirs !
> Veüille enfin atropos, au cours de vôtre vie
> Ajoûter l'etenduë à la mienne ravire !
> Et toy, passant tranquille, apprens quels sont nos maux,
> Daigne icy t'arréter un moment a les lire,
> Celle qui preferée aux partis les plus hauts,
> Sur le cœur d'Atimete acquir un doux empire ;
> Qui tenoit de Venus la beauté de ses traits,
> De Pallas son sçavoir, des graces ses attraits,
> Gist sous ce peu d'espace en la tombe enserrée,
> Vingt soleils n'avoient pas ma carriere éclairés,
> Le sort jetta sur mois ses envieuses mains :
> C'est Atimete seul qui fait que je m'en plains,
> Ma mort m'afflige moins que sa douleur amere.
> O femme, que la terre à tes os soit legere ?
> Femme digne de vivre ; et bientôt pusses tu
> Recommencer de voir les traits de la lumieres,
> Et recouvrer le bien que ton cœur a perdu.

Or thus in prose.

S'il suffisoit aux destins qu'on donât sa vie pour celle d'un autre, et qu'il fût possible de racheter ainsi ce que l'on ayme, quelque soit le nombre d'années que les parques m'ont accordé, je le donnerois avec plaisir pour vous tirer de tombeau, ma chere Homonée ; mais cela ne se pouvant, ce que je puis faire est de fuïr le jour et la presence de dieux, pour aller bientôt vous suivre le long du Styx.

Can you form any idea, Reader, of the distress I was then in ? It is not possible I think unless you have been exactly in the same situation ; unless you loved like me, and have been as miserably separated from as charming a woman. But it was in vain for me to continue lamenting. She was gone for ever, and lay as the clod of the valley before me. Her body I deposited in the next church-yard, and immediately after, rode as fast as I could to London, to lose thought in dissipation, and resign the better to the decree. For some days I lived at the inn I set up at, but as soon as I could, went into a lodging, and it happened to be at the house of the famous EDMUND CURLL the bookseller ; a man well known in Pope's *Dunciad,* and his *Letters to his Friends,* on account of

O mon chere époux, cessez de vous affliger ; ne corrompez plus le fleurs de vos ans ; ne fatiguez plus ma destinée par de plaintes continuëlles toutes les larmes sont icy vaines ; on ne sauroit émouvoir la parque : me voila morte, chacun arrive à ce terme la. Cessez donc encore un fois : ainsi puissiez-vous ne sentir jamais une semblable douleur ! Ainsi que les dieux soient favorable a vos souhaits ! Et veüille la parque ajoûter a vôtre vie ce
Et toy ayi à la mienne.
ce peu de mots ces tranquillement, arreté icy je te prie un moment ou deux, afin de lire
Moy, cette Homonœ
donna la beauté, les graces ferra Atimete a de filles considerables ; moy a qui Venus arts, me voilà icy renfermée dans mens ; que Pallas enfin avoit instruite dans tous les vingt ans quand le sort jetta ses mains environ de peu d'espace. Je n'avois pas encore que je m'en plains, c'est pour mon mari, de qui la ma personne. Ce n'est pas pour moy ma propre mort.   est difficile à supporter que
Que la terre te soit legere, ô épouse digne de retourner à la vie, que tu a perdu !   ouvrer un jour

The legend on the monument of Homonœa, *translated into English.*

Atimetus.

If it was allowed to lay down one's life for another, and possible by such means, to save what we loved from the grave, whatever length of days was allotted me, I would with pleasure offer up my life, to get Homonœa from the tomb ; but as this cannot be done, what is in my power I will do, fly from the light of heaven, and follow you to the realms of lasting night.

Homonœa.

My dearest Atimetus, cease to torment your unhappy mind, nor let grief thus feed on your youth, and make life bitterness itself. I am gone in the way appointed for all the mortal race : all must be numbered with the dead. And since fate is inexorable, and tears are in vain, weep not for me, once more I conjure you. But may you be ever happy, may Providence preserve you, and add to your life those years which have been taken from mine.

The person who erected the monument to the memory of
Homonœa.

Stop, traveller, for a few minutes, and ponder on these lines.
Here lies Homonœa, whom Atimetus preferred to the greatest and most illustrious women of his time. She had the form of Venus, the charms of the graces ; and an understanding and sensibility, which demonstrated that wisdom had given to an angel's form, a mind more lovely. Before she was twenty, she was dissolved. And as she had practised righteous-ness, by carrying it well to those about her, and to all that were specially related, she parted with them, as she had lived with them, in justice and charity, in modesty and submission, in thankfulness and peace. Filled with divine thoughts, inured to contemplate the perfec-tions of God, and to acknowledge his providence in all events, she died with the humblest resignation to the divine will, and was only troubled that she left her husband a mourner. Excellent Homonœa.
May the earth lie light upon thee, and in the morning of the resurrection, may you awake again to life, and rise to that immortality, and glory, which God, the righteous Judge, will give to true worth and dignity ; as rewards to a life adorned with all virtues and excellencies, the *dikaiomata,* that is, the righteous acts of the Saints.

CURLL's frauds in purchasing and printing stolen copies of Pope's Works. It is in relation to these tricks, that Pope mentions CURLL in his *Dunciad* and *Letters*. A succinct history of him I shall here give : but had I complied with his requests, it would have been a long relation, to the advantage and glory of this extraordinary man : for he came one morning into my closet, with an apron full of papers ; being letters, memorandums, parodies, and notes, written by or concerning himself ; and requested I would, on a good consideration, write his life, to his profit, and honour, and make it a five shilling book. That I said was not then in my power to do ; but I would, one time or another, give the public a true account of him, and make it conclude I hoped to the glory of his character. Here it is.

EDMUND CURLL was in person very tall and thin, an ungainly, awkward, white-faced man. His eyes were a light-grey, large, projecting, goggle, and pur-blind. He was splay-footed, an baker-kneed. _ acquainted

He had a good natural understanding, and talked well on some with more than the title pages of books. Rowe represents him in subjects. He was not an infidel, afterwards Dutchess of Somer- one of her letters to lady quite evident to him, that the scriptures set. He told New Testament contained a real revelation. There of the Old rational, a natural, a traditionary, and a supernatural testimony ; which rendered it quite certain to him. He said, he no more doubted the truth of the Christian religion, than he did the existence of an independent supreme Creator ; but he did not believe the expositions given by the divines. So far CURLL was right enough. His fault was, that with such a belief, he took no pains with his heart. Trusting entirely to the merits of the Saviour, like too many other mistaken Christians, he had no notion of religion as an invisible thing within us, called the kingdom of God : he did not even consider it as a good outside thing, that recommends a man to his fellow-creatures. He was a debauchee to the last degree, and so injurious to society, that by filling his translations with wretched notes, forged letters, and bad pictures, he raised the price of a four shilling book to ten. Thus, in particular, he managed Burnet's *Archæology* : and when I told him he was very culpable in this, and other articles he sold, his answer was, What would I have him do ? He was a bookseller. His translators in pay, lay three in a bed, at the Pewter-Platter Inn in Holborn, and he and they were for ever at work, to deceive the Public. He likewise printed the lewdest things. He lost his ears for *The Nun in her Smock*, and another thing. As to drink, he was too fond of money, to spend any in making himself happy that way ; but at another's expence, he would drink every day till he was quite blind, and as incapable of self-motion as a block.

This was EDMUND CURRL, but he died at last, as great a penitent, as ever expired. I think in 1748, I mention this to his glory.

As CURLL knew the world well, and was acquainted with several extraordinary characters, he was of great use to me at my first coming to town, as I knew nobody, nor any place. He gave me the true characters of many I saw, told me whom I should avoid, and with whom I might be free. He conducted me to the play-houses, and gave me a judicious account of every actor. He understood those things well. No man could talk better on theatrical subjects. He took me likewise to Sadler's Wells, to the night-cellars, and to TOM KING'S, the famous night-house in Covent Garden. As he was very knowing, and well-known at such places, he soon made me as wise as himself in these branches of learning ; and, in short, in the space of a month, I was as well acquainted in London, as if I had been there for years. My kind preceptor spared no pains in lecturing.

But what of all things I thought most wonderful was the company I saw at the Sieur CURLL'S. As he was intimate with all the high whores in town, many of them frequented his shop, to buy his dialogues, and other lively books. Some of these girls he often asked to dine with him, and then I was sure to be a guest. Many very fine women I thereby saw, but none worth mentioning, till CAROLA BENNET arrived, and surprised me exceedingly. Her mind and body were very wonderful, and I imagine a description of her, and her story afterward will not be ungrateful to my readers.

CAROLA BENNET was at this time in the two and twentieth year of her age, a dazzling beauty in the height of life and vigour. Her eyes were black and amazingly fine, her mouth charming, her neck and breast very beautiful, and her stature was just what it ought to be. She had a glow of health, a luscious air, and a bewitching vivacity : her manners were wonderfully winning, and the tone of her voice so sweet and insinuating, that her words and looks went directly to the heart. She had read many books of gaiety, wit, and humour, especially the French ; and talked delightfully on such subjects. She sang to perfection, but her conversation was too free, and she seemed to have no sense of any religion. It was a fine entertainment to be in her company, as I often was, yet I could not help sighing, to see so many perfections on the brink of everlasting destruction. This young lady all of a sudden disappeared, CURLL knew not what was become of her ; but as I rode ten years after through Devonshire, in the finest part of that romantic county, I saw her one morning, as I stopped to water my horse in a brook that ran from a park, sitting on a seat, under a vast beautiful cedar tree, with a book in her hand. I thought I was no stranger to the fine face, and as I was pretty near to her, I called out, and asked, if she was not Miss BENNET ?

She knew me at once, and pointing to a gate that was only latched desired I would come to her. I went and found she was the mistress of the fine seat at a small distance off. She brought me into the house, would not suffer me to stir that day, and told me the story of her life. I think it worth placing here.

CAROLA BENNET was the daughter of JOHN BENNET, Esq. a Yorkshire gentleman, who died when she was in her 19th year, and left her in the care of her aunt, an old lady who was outwardly all saint, and within a devil. This CAROLA knew well, and requested her father to get another guardian for her, or leave her to manage herself ; for Mrs. HUNFLEET, her aunt, was far from being that primitive Christian he took her for, and so great a miser, that exclusive of all her other vices, her avarice alone was enough to ruin her niece. She would sacrifice the whole human race for half a thousand pounds. But all his daughter said was in vain. He believed his sister was godliness itself, in its utmost latitude and extent ; that she lived a continued opposition to our mortal enemies, the world, sin, and the devil ; and that her heart was a mere magazine of universal honesty, probity of manners, and goodness of life and conversation. Integrity and rectitude, and benevolence, as he thought, were the bright criterions of her soul. She will teach you, CAROLA, to fast and pray, and make you like herself, a perfect saint.

It was to no purpose then for the daughter to remonstrate, she could only weep, as her father was positive, and after his death was obliged to go home with Mrs. HUNFLEET. There, as she expected, she had too much of the outward bodily exercise of religion, every thing that can be named within the circle of external worship ; such as public and private services, fastings, macerations, bowings, expanded hands and lifted eyes, which Lord Halifax in his *Advice to a Daughter*, calls " the holy goggle ; " but that all this accompanied the internal acts of the old woman's mind, and went along with her heart and soul, CAROLA had reason to doubt. She saw it was but outward profession, all hypocrisy, that her life belied her creed, and that her practice was a renunciation of the Christian religion. This appeared to be the case very quickly. The aunt sold her to one CANTALUPE for five hundred pounds. Under pretence of taking her to visit a friend, she brought her to a private bagnio, or one of those houses called convents.

In describing a London convent, it is but proper to observe that such houses stand in back courts, narrow lanes, or in the most private places, and seem to be uninhabited, as the front windows are seldom opened, or like some little friary, where a company of visionaries reside ; but within are elegantly furnished, and remarkable for the best wines. The woman who keep the house is the only person to be seen in them, unless it be sometimes, that a high-priced whore, who passes for the gentlewoman's daughter, by accident appears.

In these brothels the Sieur CURLL was well known, and as the wine in them is always excellent, but a shilling a bottle dearer than at the tavern, and one sits without hearing the least noise, or being seen by any one, I have often gone with this ingenious man to such places, on account of the purity of the wine, and the stillness of the house ; as there are no waiters there, nor any well-drest hussies to come in the way. You are as silent as in a cave ; nor does a woman appear, except as before excepted, unless it be by appointment at this kind of meeting-house, as such places may well be called ; for there not seldom does many a married woman meet her gallant. One evening that I was there with CURLL, there came in the wife of a very eminent merchant, a lady of as excellent a character as any in the world ; who was never as much as suspected by any of her acquaintance, but allowed by every body to be a woman of pure morals and unspotted chastity. She came in first with a black mask on her face, from her chair, and was by the woman of the house shewn into a chamber up stairs ; half an hour after, there was another soft tap at the door, and a gentleman was let in, who was shewed up to the chamber the lady was in. As the door of the room CURLL and I were sitting in, happened to be open as this adventurer passed by, I knew the man. He was an Irish gentleman of large fortune, with whom I was well acquainted. He was ever engaged in amours, and was some years after this hanged at Cork, for ravishing SALLY SQUIBB, the quaker. His name then can be no secret, but as to the lady's name, I shall never tell it, as she left several children, who are now living in reputation ; but only observe, that there are, to my knowledge, many women of such strict virtue in the world. If you ask me reader, how I came to know who she was ? I will tell you. As she came down stairs in a mask at ten at night, in the manner she went up, I concluded she was a married woman of distinction, and followed her chair, when it went off. She changed at Temple Bar, and then took a hackney coach, which drove beyond the Royal Exchange ; I followed till it stopped at a grand house, into which she went without a mask, and had a full view of her fine face. I enquired next day who lived in the house I saw her go into, and was told it was Mrs.*****, a merchant of the greatest repute. Often did I see this lady after this, was several times in her company, and if I had not known what I did, should have thought her a woman of as great virtue as ever lived. There was not the least appearance of levity or indecency in her. To all outward appearance, she was chastity and discretion in flesh and blood. But as to CAROLA BENNET.

Soon after her aunt and she arrived at Mrs, Bedewell's, in came CANTALUPE as a visitor, and after tea, they went to cards. Then followed a supper, and when that was over, they gave the innocent Miss BENNET a dose, which deprived her of her senses, put her to bed, and in the morning she found herself ruined in the arms of that villain CANTALUPE. Distraction almost seized her, but he would not let her stir. She called, but no one came near to her relief. He swore a million of oaths, that it was pure love made him buy her of her aunt, as he heard she was going to marry another man, and if she would but share with him in his great fortune, since the thing was done, he would, by every sacred power he vowed, marry her that evening or the next, the first time they went out, and be the most true and tender husband that ever yet appeared in the world. This, and the situation she was in, naked and clasped in his strong arms, without a friend to aid her, within doors or without, made her sensible her resentments were in vain, and that she had better acquiesce, and make the man her husband, if she could, since it was her hard fate, and that in all probability she might conceive from the transactions of the night. This made her have done. She lay as he requested till noon, and hoped he would prove as faithful as he had solemnly swore to her.

But when the night came, an indisposition he feigned, made him unable to stir out that evening, and he requested the idol of his heart, whom he loved more than life, to give him leave to defer it till the next. For six days he put it off in the same manner, during which time, they never stirred out of the bagnio, and the seventh day he left her fast asleep in bed. A billet-doux on the dressing-table informed her, that he was obliged to set out that morning for France, and as he intended to be back in a few months, he hoped she would not think him faithless at once. He left her a hundred pound bank note, which was all he had then to spare, as he had paid to her aunt five hundred pounds a few days before.

Thus fell the beautiful Miss BENNET by the treachery of her ever-cursed aunt, and was made a whore very much against her will. The aunt, in the mean time, had shut up her house, and was gone no one knew where. She took several jewels with her, and a large sum of money, both the property of her niece. She left her but little of her fortune, and reported every where, that CAROLA was gone into keeping with a great man, and had before been debauched by her footman. In short, all that could be done this woman did, to impoverish and defame her niece, and as she had passed upon the world for a praying, virtuous old piece, her reports were thought so true, that all the female acquaintance Miss BENNET had, laughed at the story she told, and shunned her as a foul fiend. She was banished from all modest company. They considered her as the most detestable prostitute, for excusing herself, they said, by blackening the character of so pious and upright a woman as Mrs. HUNFLEET, her aunt, was.

Thus did iniquity ruin and triumph over innocence, in the

mask of religion, and a thousand times, to my own knowledge, it has done the same thing. I have often known wretches pretend to seek the kingdom of God, and his righteousness, in the first place, and by believing all the monks have invented, by constantly attending public worship, and an unnatural kind of sobriety, pass for people that were ready and willing to suffer every thing the cause of God and truth can require from rationals ; yet these holy mortals could make the service of God not only stand with unwilling infirmities, the common case of the best humanity, but consist with wilful and presumptuous sinning, and a malevolence as great as the devil had against our first parents. A minister of the gospel, who passed for an admirable man, did his best to ruin my character for ever with my father. One of the holiest men in the world, cheated me of a thousand pounds, left in his hands for my use, for fear I should spend it myself. And a rich man, commonly called piety and goodness, from the seeming simplicity of his manners, the softness of his temper, and the holy goggle of his eyes in his public devotion, arrested me on a note of hand, one-third of which was interest thrown into the principal, and made me pay interest upon interest, without mercy, or waiting as I intreated, till it was more convenient. Many more such praying, sanctified villains I could mention, in respect of whom EDMUND CURLL was a cherubim, fond as he was of a girl and a flask. CURLL owned he was a sinner, and that he was led by thirst and repletion to indulge ; but the hypocrites with professions of esteem for the pearl of great price, and that they have parted with their Herodias, for the sake of eternal life ; yet wilfully disobey from a passion for substance, and the shrine of bright Mammon in this world has a greater influence on their souls than all the joys of an ever-lasting heaven to come. What they do is a farce. Upon what they have, they rest their all.

But as to Miss BENNET, in this sad condition, she secreted herself for some months from the world, and notwithstanding her constitution and taste, intended to retire among the mountains of Wales, and live upon the little she had left ; but unfortunately for so good a design, the matchless Sir FREDERIC DANCER came in her way, and by money, and the force of love, persuaded her to be his companion while he lived, which was but for a short time. A young nobleman prevailed on her next, by high rewards, to be the delight of his life for a time ; and at his death, she went to the arms of an Irish peer. She had what money she pleased from these great men, and being now very rich, she determined, on the marriage of her last Lord, to go into keeping no more, but to live a gay life among the agreeable and grand. She had lost all her notions of a weeping and gnashing of teeth to come, in the conversation of these atheistical men, and on account of her living

as happily as she could in this world. What religion she had
remaining, was placed in giving money to the sick and poor,
which she did with a liberal hand ; and her charity, in all its
charms, she often shewed to the most deserving men. Those who
had much of this world's goods paid dear, but she had compassion
on the worthy, though they could not drive in a chariot to her
door. This was the case of CAROLA, when I saw her at CURLL'S.

But all of a sudden she disappeared, and no one could tell what
was become of her ; that I, however, learned from herself, when I
chanced to see her under the cedar tree, in the park, as before
related.

A young clergyman, one TENCH, an Irishman, of the county of
Galway, who was very rich, and had a fine seat in Devonshire,
saw her at the opera, and fell in love with her. He soon found
out who she was, waited upon her, and offered to marry her,
if she would reform. At first, she shewed very little inclination
to a virtuous course, and, as her manner was, ridiculed the interest
of another life. The blessedness of heaven she laughed at, and made
a jest of riches, honours, and pleasures to be found on the other side
the grave. This did not however dishearten TENCH. He was a
scholar and a man of sense, and as he loved her most passionately,
and saw she had a fine capacity, he was resolved, if possible, to
reclaim her, by an appeal to her bright understanding.

He observed to her, in the first place, as she informed me, that,
exclusive of future happiness, godliness was profitable in all
things, that is, even in this life, in prosperity and adversity, in
plenty and in want, in peace and in war, in confusion and security,
in health, in honour and disgrace, in life and in death, and in what
condition soever we may be. This he proved to her satisfaction,
and made it plain to her conception, that by it only we can
acquire a right judgment of persons and things, and have a just
and due estimate of ourselves ; that unless held in by reason and
religion, pleasure, though innocent of itself, becomes a thing of
deadly consequence to mortals ; and if we do not use it in due
time, place, circumstance, measure and limits, it necessarily
involves us in difficulties and troubles, pain and infamy ; if we
stifle the grand leading principles, reason and religion, by sin and
vice, and let desire and inclination range beyond bounds, we
must not only plunge into various woes in this world, but as
creatures degenerated below the beast, become the contempt
and abhorrence of the wise and honest. To this sad condition
must be annexed a reflective misery, as we have conscience or
reason, that will examine, now and then, the whole procedure of
life, do all we can to prevent it, and the remorse that must ensue,
on account of our wretched and ridiculous conduct, is too bitter
a thing for a reasonable creature to acquire, for the sake of illicit
gratification only ; and this becomes the more grievous in re-

flection, as pleasures are not forbidden by religion, but allowed
to the most upright, and ordained for the holy service of God to
recruit nature, and enliven the spirits; to propagate the human
species, and preserve the flame of love in the married state. If
there was then no other life but this, it is most certainly our
interest in regard to fame and advantage, to be governed by
reason and religion.

And if we are not to be annihilated with the beast, but are to
answer hereafter for what we have done, whether it be good or
bad, surely the main business of life should be to govern ourselves
by godliness, that is to be Christians in our principles, holy in our
conversation, and upright in our behaviour. If the gospel be true,
as has been proved a thousand and a thousand times, by the
wisest men in the world, to the confusion and silence of infidelity,
and the Son of God came into the world, not to make Judea the
seat of absolute and universal empire, and establish a temporal
dominion in all possible pomp and magnificence, as the Jews most
erroneously and ridiculously fancied, and to this day believe,
but to prepare greater things for us; to relieve us from the power
of sin, and the endless and unspeakable miseries of the life which
is to come; to propose a prize far more worthy of our expectations
than the glories of civil power, and to secure to us the happiness
both of soul and body to all eternity, in the kingdom of God;
then certainly, in regard to ourselves, we ought to attend to his
heavenly lessons, and turn from the unlawful enjoyments of this
life, to the endless and solid happiness of a future state. As this
is the case, we should cherish and improve a faith of invisible
things, by serious and impartial consideration. We should attend
to the evidence which God has given us for the truth of Christianity,
evidence very cogent and sufficient; and then shew our faith by
works suited to the doctrine of Christ; that is, by recommending,
the practice of virtue, and the worship of one God, the Creator
of the Universe.

"Consider then, Miss BENNET," said he, "that you stand on
the brink of death, resurrection, and judgment; and it is time
to begin by serious and humble enquiry to arrive at a faith of
strength, and activity; that by your eminence in all virtue and
holiness, you may make the glorious attempt to be greatest in
the kingdom of heaven. This will be a work worthy of an immortal Soul. Nor will it hinder you from enjoying as much
happiness in this lower hemisphere, as reason can desire. For
godliness is profitable unto all things, having promise of the life
that now is, and of that which is to come."

"Thus," continued Miss BENNET that was, "did this excellent
young clergyman talk to me, and by argument and reasoning
in the gentlest manner, by good sense and good manners, made
me a convert to Christianity and goodness. He snatched me

from the gulph of eternal perdition, and from the realms of darkness, and the society of devils, brought me into the kingdom of
the Messiah.   To make me as happy as it was possible even in
this world, he married me, and landed me in this charming spot
you found me in.   For seven years, we lived in great happiness,
without ever stirring from this fine solitude, and since his death,
I have had no inclination to return to the world ; I have one lady
for my companion, an agreeable sensible woman, a near relation
of Mr. TENCH'S, and with her, and some good books, and three or
four agreeable neighbours, have all the felicity I care for in this
world.   When you saw me at CURRL'S, I had no taste for any thing
but the comedy, the opera, and a tale of La Fontaine ; but you
found me with a volume of Tillotson in my hand, under that
aged and beautiful cedar, near the road ; and in those sermons
I now find more delight, in the solemn shade of one of those fine
trees, than ever I enjoyed in the gayest scenes of the world.
In these sweet silent walks I am really happy.   Riches and honour
are with me, yea durable riches and righteousness.   To the
blessings of time, I can here add the riches of expectation and
comfort, the riches of future glory and happiness.   This makes
me fond of this fine retreat.   In contentment, peace, and comfort
of mind, I now live ; and by hearkening to the commandments,
my peace is a river."
⋄ Here Mrs. TENCH had done, and I was amazed beyond expression.   This charming libertine was quite changed.   It was
formerly her wont, when I have sat an evening with her at CURLL'S,
to make a jest of the Christian scheme, to laugh at the ɩdevil and
his flames ; her life was all pleasure, and her soul all whim, but
when I saw her last, she was serious, and seemed to enjoy as happy
a serenity and composure of mind, as ever mortal was blessed
with.   Even her eyes had acquired a more sober light, and in the
place of a wild and luscious air, a beautiful modesty appeared.
    And now to what shall I ascribe this astonishing alteration ?
Shall I say with our methodists and other visionaries, that it must
be owing to immediate impulse, and proceeded from inward impression of the Spirit ?   No, this will not do.   It was owing
clearly to the word, not in-spoken, but taught by Christ in his
gospel.   When her friend TENCH opened the *New Testament* to
her, her good understanding inclined her to hearken.   She began
to consider, she pondered, and had a regard to the gospel, now
laid before her, by that sensible and excellent young clergyman.
She became a believer.   And as the Apostle says, We can do all
things through Christ who strengthens us ; that is, says Dr. Hunt,
in one of his first sermons, through the directions of Christ, and
through the arguments and motives of the Christian doctrine.
Well said, Hunt.   It must be our own choice, to be sure, to be good
and virtuous.   So far as men are passive, and are acted upon,

they are not agents. Without power to do good or evil, men cannot be moral or accountable beings, and be brought into judgment, or receive according to their works.

Dr. Lardner, in his excellent *Sermon on the Power and Efficacy of Christ's Doctrine*, has a fine observation ; would any say, that the necessity of immediate and particular influences from Christ himself, is implied in this context, where he says that he is a vine, and his disciples branches, and that their bearing fruit depends as much upon influences from him, as the life and vigour of branches do upon the sap derived from the root of the tree? It would be easy to answer, that the argument in the text is a similitude, not literal truth. Neither is Christ literally a vine, nor are his disciples, strictly speaking, branches. Men have a reasonable, intellectual nature, above animals and vegetables. They are not governed by irresistible, and necessary, or mechanical powers. But it is sound doctrine, and right principles, particularly the words of Christ, which are the words of God, that are their life, and may, and will, if attended to, powerfully enable them to promote good works, and to excel and persevere therein."

But it is time to return to my own story. While I lodged at CURLL's two Irish gentlemen came to see me, JEMMY KING an attorney, and that famous master in chancery, who debauched NELLY HAYDEN the beauty, and kept her several years. I knew these men were as great rakes as ever lived, and had no notion of religion ; that they were devoted to pleasure, and chased away every sober thought and apprehension by company, and by empty, vicious, and unmanly pleasures. The voice of the monitor was lost, in the confused noise and tumult of the passions, but I thought they had honour at the bottom, according to the common notion of it. I never imagined they were sharpers, nor knew, that being ruined in Ireland, they came over to live by a gaming table. The Doctor especially, I thought, was above ever becoming that kind of man, as he had a large estate, and the best education ; always kept good company ; and to appearance, was as fine a gentleman as ever was seen in the world. With these two I dined, and after dinner, they brought me, as it were, out of curiosity, to a gaming table, they had by accident discovered, where there was a bank kept by men of the greatest honour, who played quite fair, and by hazarding a few guineas, I might perhaps, as they did, come off with some hundreds.

On entering the room, I saw about twenty well-drest men sitting round a table, on which lay a vast heap of gold. We all began to play, and for two or three hours, I did win some hundreds of pounds ; the Doctor and the other cheat, his friend, seemed to lose a large sum ; but before morning they won all back from me, with much more : and I not only lost what I had then, but the thousands I had gained by my several wives ; and excepting a few pounds, all I was worth in the world. I had sold my wives' estates, and lodged the money in my banker's hands. The villains round this table got it all, and my two Irishmen were not to be seen. They disappeared, and left me madly playing away my all. I heard no more of them, till I was told several years after, that they were in the Isle of Man, among other outlawed, abandoned, wicked men, where they drank night and day, according to the custom of the place, and lived in defiance of God and man. There these two advocates of impiety dwelt for some time, and died as they had lived ; enemies to all good principles, and friends to a general corruption.

As to the well-drest company round the table, they went off one by one, and left me alone to the bitter thought, which led me to reflect on what I was some hours before, by what I then found myself to be. I was almost distracted. What had I to do with play ? I wanted nothing. And now by villains, with a set of dice that would deceive the devil, I am undone. By sharpers and false dice I have sat to be ruined. The reflection numbed my senses for some time : and then I started, became wild, and raved.

This transaction made me very thoughtful, and I sat within for several days, thinking which way to turn. CURLL saw I was perplexed, and on his asking me if I had met with any misfortune, I told him the whole case ; that I had but one hundred pounds left, and requested he would advise me what I had best do. To do justice to every one, CURLL seemed deeply concerned, and after some silence, we sat over a bottle at a Coffee-house, he bid me take notice of an old gentleman, who was not far from us. " That is DUNK the miser, who lives in a wood about twenty miles off. He has one daughter, the finest creature in the universe, and who is to succeed to his great estate, whether he will or not, it being so settled at his marriage ; but he confines her so much in the country, and uses her so cruelly every way, that I believe she would run away with any honest young fellow, who could find means to address her. Know then," continued CURLL, "that I serve Mr. DUNK with paper, pens, ink, wax, pamphlets, and every thing he wants in my way. Once a quarter of a year, I generally go to his country-house with such things, as he is glad to see me sometimes ; or if I cannot go myself, I send them by some other hand. Next week I am to forward some things to him, and if you will take them, I will write a line by you to Miss his daughter, recommend you to her for a husband, as one she may depend on for honour and truth. She knows I am her friend, and who can tell, but she may go off with you. She will have a thousand a year, when the wretch her father dies, if he should leave his personal estate another way."

This thought pleased me much, and at the appointed time, away I went to Mr. DUNK's country-house with a wallet full of things,

and delivered CURLL's letter to Miss. As soon as she had read it, I
began my address, and in the best manner I could, made her an
offer of my service, to deliver her from the tyrant her father. I
gave her an account of a little farm I had on the borders of Cumberland, a purchase I had made, on account of the charms of the
ground, and a small pretty lodge which stood in the middle of it,
by a clump of old trees, near a murmuring stream ; that if she
pleased, I would take her to that sweet, silent spot, and enable her
to live in peace, with contentment and tranquillity of mind ;
though far away from the splendours and honours of the world,
and considering, that a Christian is not to conform to the world, or
to the pomps and vanities of it ; its grand customs and usages ;
its dress and entries ; its stage representations and masquerades,
as they minister to vice, and tend to debauch the manners ; but
are to look upon ourselves as beings of another world, and to form
our minds with these spiritual principles ; it follows then, I think,
that a pleasing country situation for a happy pair must be grateful
enough. There peace and love and modesty may be best preserved ; the truth and gravity of our religion be strictly maintained, and every lawful and innocent enjoyment be for ever the
delights of life. Away from the idle modes of the world, perpetual
love and unmixed joys may be our portion, through the whole of
our existence here ; and the inward principles of the heart be ever
laudable and pure. So will our happiness as mortals be stable,
subject to no mixture or change ; and when called away from this
lower hemisphere, have nothing to fear, as we used this world, as
though we used it not ; as we knew no gratifications and liberties
but what our religion allows us, as our enjoyments will be but the
necessary convenience and accommodation, for passing from this
world to the realms of eternal happiness. Follow me then, Miss
DUNK ; I will convey you to a scene of still life and felicity, great
and lasting as the heart of woman can wish for.

The charming AGNES seemed not a little surprised at what I had
said, and after looking at me very earnestly for a minute or two,
told me, she would give me an answer to Mr. CURLL's letter in less
than half an hour, which was all she could say at present, and with
it I returned to give him an account of the reception I had.
" It will do," said he, after he had read the letter I brought
him from Miss DUNK, but you must be my young man for a week or
two more, and take some more things to the same place. He then
shewed me the letter, and I read the following lines :—

" SIR,
" I am extremely obliged to you for your concern about my
happiness and liberty, and will own to you, that in my dismal
situation, I would take the friend you recommend, for a guide
through the wilderness, if I could think his heart was as sound as
his head. If his intentions were as upright as his words are fluent

and good, I need not be long in pondering on the scheme he proposed.   But can we believe him true as Lucinda says in the play ?

> The sunny hill, the flowr'y vale,
> The garden and the grove,
>   Have echo'd to his ardent tale,
> And vows of endless love.
>
> The conquest gain'd, he left his prize.
> He left her to complain,
>   To talk of joy with weeping eyes,
> And measure time by pain.

To this CURLL replied in a circumstantial manner, and vouched
very largely for me.   I delivered his letter the next morning, when
I went with some acts of parliament to old DUNK and I found the
beauty, his daughter, in a rosy bower ; *Simplex munditiis*, neat and
clean as possible in the most genteel undress ; and her person so
vastly fine, her face so vastly charming ; that I could not but
repeat the lines of Otway :—

> Man when created first wander'd up and down,
> Forlorn and silent as his vassal brutes ;
> But when a heav'n-born maid, like you appear'd,
> Strange pleasures fill'd his soul, unloos'd his tongue,
> And his first talk was love.

I said much upon the occasion, we became well acquainted that
day, as her father had got a disorder that obliged him to keep his
bed, and by the time I had visited her a month longer, under
various pretences of business invented by the ingenious CURLL,
AGNES agreed to go off with me, and commit herself entirely to my
care and protection.   But before I relate this transaction, I think it
proper to give my readers the picture of this lady ; and then an
apology for her flying away with me, with whom she was but a
month acquainted.

AGNES in her person was neither tall nor thin, but almost both,
young and lovely, graceful and commanding ; she inspired a respect, and compelled the beholder to admire, to love and reverence
her.   Her voice was melodious ; her words quite charming ; and
every look and motion to her advantage.   Taste was the character-
istic of her understanding, her sentiments were refined, and a
sensibility appeared in every feature of her face.   She could talk
on various subjects, and comprehended them, which is what few
speakers do ; but with the fiuest discernment she was timid, and
so diffident of her opinion, that she often concealed the finest
thoughts under a seeming simplicity of soul.   This was visible to a
hearer, and the decency of ignorance added a new beauty to her
character.   In short, possessed of excellence, she appeared unconscious of it, and never discovered the least pride or precipitancy
in her conversation.   Her manner was perfectly polite, and mixed

with a gaiety that charmed, because it was as free from restraint as from boldness.

In sum, exclusive of her fine understanding, in her dress, and in her behaviour, she was so extremely pleasing, so vastly agreeable and delightful, that she ever brought to my remembrance, when I beheld her, the Corinna described in the beautiful lines of Tibullus :—

> Illam quicquid agit, quoquo vestigia flectit,
> Componit furtim subsequiturque decor ;
> Seu solvit crines, fusis decet esse capillis ;
> Seu compsit comptis est veneranda comis.
> Urit seu tyria voluit procedere pulla ;
> Urit seu nivea candida veste venit.
> Talis in æterno felix Vertumnus Olympo
> Mille habet ornatus, mille decenter habet.

> When love would set the gods on fire, he flies
> To light his torches at her sparkling eyes.
> Whate'er Corinna does, where'er she goes,
> The graces all her motions still compose.
> How her hair charms us, when it loosely falls,
> Com'd back and ty'd, our veneration calls !
> If she comes out in scarlet, then she turns
> Us all to ashes,—though in white she burns.
> Vertumnus so a thousand dresses wears,
> So in a thousand, ever grace appears.

Such was the beautiful AGNES, who went off with me, and in doing so acted well and wisely, I affirm, on her taking me only for an honest man ; for there is no more obedience due from a daughter to her father, when he becomes an unrelenting oppressor, than there is from a subject to an English king, when the monarch acts contrary to the constitution. Passive obedience is as much nonsense in a private family, as in the government of the prince. The parent, like the king, must be a nursing father, a rational humane sovereign, and so long all service and obedience are due. But if, like the prince, he becomes a tyrant, deprives his daughter of her natural rights and liberties ; will not allow her the blessings of life, but keep her in chains and misery ; self-preservation, and her just claim to the comforts of existence and a rational freedom, give her a right to change her situation, and better her condition. If she can have bread, serenity, and freedom, peace and little, with an honest man, she is just to herself in going off with such a deliverer. Reason and revelation will acquit her.

Thus justly thought Miss DUNK, and therefore with me she fled at midnight. We met within half a mile of her father's house, by the side of an ancient wood, and a running stream, which had a pleasing effect, as it happened to be a bright moonshine. With her foot in my hand, I lifted her into her saddle, and as our horses were excellent, we rode many miles in a few hours. By eight in the morning, we were out of the reach of old DUNK, and at the sign of the Pilgrim, a lone house in Esur-vale, in Hertfordshire, we breakfasted very joyfully. The charming AGNES seemed well pleased with the expedition, and said a thousand things that rendered the journey delightful. Twelve days we travelled in a fulness of delights, happy beyond description, and the thirteenth arrived at a village not far from my little habitation. Here we designed to be married two days after, when we had rested, as there was a church and a parson in the town, and then ride on to Foley-farm in Cumberland, as my small spot was called, and there sit down in peace and happiness.

But the second day, instead of rising to the nuptial ceremony, to crown my life with unutterable bliss, and make me beyond all mankind happy, the lovely AGNES fell ill of a fever. A sense of weight and oppression discovered the inflammation within; and was attended with sharp and pungent pains. The blood could not pass off as it ought in the course of circulation, and the whole mass was in a violent fluctuation and motion. In a word, she died in a few days, and as she had requested, if it came to that, I laid her out, and put her into the coffin myself. I kept her seven days, according to the custom of the old Romans, and then in the dress of sorrow, followed her to the grave. Thus was my plan of happiness broken to pieces. I had given a roundness to a system of felicity, and in the place of it saw death and horror, and disappointment before me.

What to do next I could not tell. One question was, should I return to Orton-lodge, to my two young heiresses ? No, they wanted two years of being at age. Then, shall I stay at Foley-farm where I was, and turn hermit ? No : I had no inclination yet to become a father of the deserts. Will you return to London then, and see if fortune has any thing more in reserve for you ? This I liked best, and after six months' deliberation left my farm in the care of an old woman, and set out in the beginning of January.

It was as fine a winter's morning as I had seen, which encouraged me to venture among the Fells of Westmoreland ; but at noon the weather changed, and an evening very terrible came on. A little after three, it began to blow, rain, and snow very hard, and it was not long before it was very dark. We lost the way quite, and for three hours wandered about in as dismal a night as ever poor travellers had. The storm rattled, the tempest howled ; we could not see our horses' heads, and were almost dead with cold. We had nothing to expect but death, as we knew not which way to turn to any house, and it was impossible to remain alive till the day appeared. It was a dismal scene. But my time was not yet come, and when we had no reason to expect deliverance, the beasts of a sudden stopt, and *Soto* found we were at the gate of a walled yard. There he immediately made all the noise he could, and it was not long before a servant with a lantern came. He related our case within, and had orders to admit us. He brought me into a common parlour, where there was a good fire, and I got dry things. The man brought me half a pint of hot alicant, and in about half an hour I was alive and well again. On enquiring where I was, the footman told me, it was Doctor STANVIL's house ; that his master and lady were above in the dining-room, with some company, and he had directions to light me up, when I had changed my clothes, and had recovered. Upon this I told him I was ready, and followed him.

On the servant's opening a door, I entered a handsome apartment, well lighted with wax, and which had a glorious fire blazing in it. The doctor received me with great politeness, and said many civil things upon fortune's conducting me to his house. The conversation naturally fell upon the horrors of the night, as it still continued to rain, hail and blow, beyond what any of the company had ever heard ; and one of the ladies said, she believed the winter was always far more boisterous and cold among the Fells of Westmoreland, than in any other part of England, for which she gave several good reasons. The solemn mountains ; the beautiful valleys, the falling streams constitute to form this one of the most charming countries in the world in summer-time ; but in winter, it is surely the most dreadful spot on earth.

The voice of the lady who talked in this manner, I thought I was well acquainted with, but by the position of the candles, and the angle of a screen in which she sat, I could not very well see her face. Amazement however began to seize me, and as an elegant supper was soon after brought in, I had an opportunity of seeing that Miss DUNK whom I had buried, was now before my eyes in the character of Dr. STANVIL's wife ; or, at least , it was one so like her, it was not possible for me to distinguish the figures : there was the same bright victorious eyes and chestnut hair ; the complexion like a blush, and a mouth where all the little loves for ever dwelt ; there was the fugitive dimple, the enchanting laugh, the rosy fingers, the fine height, and the mien more striking than Calypso's. O heavens ! said I to myself, on sitting down to supper, what is this I see ! But as she did not seem to be at all affected, or shewed the least sign of her having ever seen me before that time, I remained silent, and only continued to look with admiration at her, unmindful of the many excellent things before me. In a minute or two, however, I recovered myself. I ate my supper, and joined in the festivity of the night. We had music, and several songs. We were easy, free, and happy as well-bred people could be.

At midnight we parted, and finding an easy-chair by the side of my bed, I threw myself into it, and began to reflect on what I had seen ; FIN standing before me with his arms folded, and looking very seriously at me. This lasted for about a quarter of an hour and then the honest fellow spoke in the following manner. " I beg leave, Sir, to imagine you are perplexing yourself about the lady of this house, whom I suppose you take for Miss DUNK, we brought from the other side of *England*, half a year ago, and buried in the next church-yard to Blenkern.   This, if I may be so free, is likewise my opinion.   I would take my oath of it in a court of justice, if there was occasion for that.   However she got out of the grave, and by whatever casualty she came to be Mrs. STANVIL, and mistress of this fine house ; yet I could swear to her being the lady who travelled with us from the west to Cumberland.   But then, it seems very wonderful and strange, that she should forego you, Sir, so soon, or be able to act a part so amazing, as to seem not to have ever seen you before this night.   This has astonished me, as I stood behind your chair at supper, looking full at her ; and I observed she looked at me once or twice.   What to say to all this, I know not ; but I will make all the inquiry I can among the servants, as to the time and manner of her coming here, and let you know to-morrow, what I have been able to collect in relation to her. In the mean time, be advised by me, Sir, though I am but a poor fellow, and think no more about the matter to the loss of your night's rest.   We have had a wonderful deliverance from death by getting into this house, I am sure, and we ought to lie down with thankfulness and joy, without fretting ourselves awake for a woman, or any trifling incident that could befall.   Beside, she is now another man's property, however it came to pass, and it would be inconsistent with your character to think any more of her.   This may be too free, but I hope, Sir, you will excuse it in a servant who has your interest and welfare at heart."   Here the sage O'FIN had done.   He withdrew, and I dosed into sleep.

Betimes the next morning O'FIN was with me, and on my ask-ing what news, he said, he had heard something from all the ser-vants, and more particularly had got the following account from the doctor's own man : that Dr. STANVIL had a small lodge within three miles of the house we were in, and retired there sometimes to be more alone, than he could be in the residence where we were at ; that this lodge was a mere repository of curiosities, in the middle of a garden full of all the herbs and plants that grew in every country of the world, and in one chamber of this house was a great number of skeletons, which the doctor had made himself ; for it was his wont to procure bodies from the surrounding church-yards, by men he kept in pay for the purpose, and cut them up himself at this lodge : that some of these dead were brought to him in ham-pers, and some in their coffins on light railed cars, as the case required : that near six monthe ago, the last time the doctor was at this lodge, there was brought to him by his men the body of a young ·woman in her coffin, in order to a dissection as usual, and the bones being wired ; but as it lay on the back, on the great table he cuts up on, and the point of his knife at the pit of the stomach, to open the breast, he perceived a kind of motion in the subject, heard a sigh soon after, and looking up to the head saw the eyes open and shut again ; that upon this, he laid down his nife, which had but just scratched the body, at the beginning of the linea alba, as my informer called it, and helped himself to put it into a warm bed : that he took all possible pains, by administering every thing he could think useful, to restore life, and was so fortunate as to set one of the finest women in the world on her feet again. As she had no raiment but the shroud which had been on her in the coffin, he provided every thing belonging to dress that a woman of distinction could have occasion for, and in a few days' time, she sparkled before her preserver in the brightness of an Eastern princess. He was quite charmed with the beauties of her person, and could not enough admire her uncommon understanding ; he therefore offered to marry her, to settle largely on her, and as she was a single woman, she could not in gratitude refuse the request of so generous a benefactor. My informer further related, that they have both lived in the greatest happiness ever since ; and the doctor, who is one of the best of men, is continually studying how to add to her felicities, that he offered to take her up to London to pass the winters there, but this she refused, and desired she might remain where she was in the country, as it was really most agreeable to her, and as he preferred it to the town.

This account made the thing quite plain to me. And to judge impartially, considering the whole case, I could neither blame the lovely AGNES for marrying the doctor, nor condemn her for pretending to be a stranger to me. She was fairly dead and buried, and all connexion between us was at an end of course, as there had been no marriage, nor contract of marriage. And as to reviving the affair, and renewing the tenderness which had existed, it could answer no other end than producing unhappiness, as she was then Mrs. STANVIL, in a decent and happy situation. And further, in respect of her marrying the doctor, so soon after her separation from me, it was certainly the wisest thing she could do, as she had been so entirely at his disposal, was without a stitch to cover her, and I in all probability, after burying her, being gone up to London, or in some place, where she could never hear of me more ; I might likewise have been married, if anything advantageous had offered after laying her in the churchyard. And beside, she neither knew the place she fell sick in, nor the country the doctor removed her to, as soon as he could get her clothes to put on. So that, naked and friendless as she was, without any money, and ignorant of what became of me, without a possibility of informing herself, I could not but acquit her. I even admired her conduct, and resolved so far to imitate her, in regard to the general happiness, that nothing should appear in my behaviour, which could incline any one to think I had ever seen her before the night the tempest drove me to her house. I was vexed, I own, to lose her ; but that could be no reason for making a senseless uproar, that could do nothing but mischief.

As composed then as I could be, I went down to breakfast, on a servant's letting me know they waited for me, and found the same company, who had so lately parted to slumber, all quite alive and cheerful, easy and happy as mortals could be. At the request of Dr. STANVIL, who was extremely civil, I staid with them two months and passed the time in a delightful conversation, intermixed with music, cards, and feasting. With sadness I left them all, but especially on account of parting for ever with the late Miss DRINK. It was indeed for the pleasure of looking at her, that I staid so long as I did at Dr. STANVIL's ; and when it came to an eternal separation, I felt on the morning of my departure an inward distress it is impossible to give an idea of to another. It had some resemblance, I imagine, of what the visionaries call dereliction, when they sink from ecstacy to the black void of horror, by the strength of fancy, and the unaccountable operation of the animal spirits.

Here, before I proceed, I think I ought to remove some objections that may be made against my relation of Mrs. STANVIL's coming to life again, and her being brought from the couch of lasting night to a bridal bed. It is not easy to believe, that after I seemed certain she was dead, and kept her the proper number of days before interment ; saw her lie the cold wan subject for a considerable time, and then let down into the grave ; yet from thence she should come forth, and now be the desire of a husband's eyes. This is a hard account sure. But nevertheless, it is a fact. As to my being mistaken, no less a man than Dr. Cheyne thought Colonel Townsend dead ; See his *Nervous Cases.* And that several have lived for many years, after they had been laid in the tomb, is a thing too certain, and well-known, to be denied. In Bayle's *Dictionary,* there is the history of a lady of quality, belonging to the court of Catharine de Medicis, who was brought from the church vault, where she had been forty-eight hours, and afterwards became the mother of several children, on her marriage with the Marquis D'Auvergne. The learned Dr. Connor, in his *History of Poland,* gives us a very wonderful relation of a gentleman's reviving in that country, after he had been seemingly dead for near a fortnight ; and adds a very curious dissertation on the nature of such recoveries. The case of Dun Scotus, who was found out of his coffin, on the steps going down to the vault he was deposited in, and leaning on his elbow, is full to my purpose. And I can affirm from my own knowledge, that a gentleman of my acquaintance, a worthy excellent man, was buried alive, and found not only much bruised and torn, on opening his coffin, but turned on one side. This many still living can attest as well as I. The reason of opening the grave again, was his dying of a high fever in the absence of his lady, who was in a distant county from him ; and on her return, three days after he was buried, would have a sight of him, as she had been extremely fond of him. His face was sadly broke, and his hands hurt in striving to force up the lid of the coffin. The lady was so affected with the dismal sight, that she never held up her head after, and died in a few weeks. I could likewise add another extraordinary case of a man who was hanged, and to all appearance was quite dead, yet three days after his execution recovered as they were going to cut him up. How these things happen, it is not easy to explain or account for ; but they do happen sometimes. And this case of Mrs. STANVIL, may be depended on as a fact.

Opinion's foot is never, never found
Where knowledge dwells, 'tis interdicted ground;
At wisdom's gate opinions must resign
Their charge, those limits their employ confine.
Thus trading barks, skill'd in the wat'ry road,
To distant climes convey their precious load.
Then turn their prow, light bounding o'er the main.
And with new traffic store their keels again.
Thus far is clear. But yet untold remains,
What the good genius to the crowd ordains,
Just on the verge of life.
                    He bids them hold
A spirit with erected courage bold.
Never, he calls, on fortune's faith rely,
Nor grasp her dubious gift as property.
Let not her smile transport, her frown dismay,
Nor praise, nor blame, nor wonder at her sway,
Which reason never guides : 'tis fortune still,
Capricious chance, and arbitrary will.
Bad bankers, vain of treasure not their own.
With foolish rapture hug the trusted loan.
Impatient, when the pow'rful bond demands
Its unremember'd cov'nant from their hands
Unlike to such, without a sigh restore
What fortune lends : anon she'll lavish more.
Repenting of her bounty, snatch away,
Yea, seize your patrimonial fund for prey.
Embrace her proffer'd boon, but instant rise,
Spring upward, and secure a lasting prize,
The gift which wisdom to her sons divides ;
Knowledge, whose beam the doubting judgment guides,
Scatters the sensual fog, and clear to view
Distinguishes false int'rest from the true.
Flee, flee to this, with unabating pace,
Nor parley for a moment at the place,
Where pleasure and her harlots tempt, nor rest,
But at false wisdom's inn, a transient guest :
For short refection, at her table sit,
And take what science may your palate hit :
Then wing your journey forward, till you reach
True wisdom, and imbibe the truth she'll teach.

Such is the advice the friendly genius gives,
He perishes who scorns, who follows lives.
SCOTT'S CEBES.*

With this advice of the genius in my head, which by chance I had read the morning I took my leave of Dr. STANVIL, I set out, as I had resolved, for York, and designed to go from thence to London ; hoping to meet with something good, and purposing, if it was possible, to be no longer the rover, but turn to something useful, and fix. I had lost almost all at the gaming-table, as related, and had not thirty pounds of my last hundred remaining ; this, with a few sheep, cows, and horses at Orton-lodge, and a very small stock at my little farm, on the borders of Cumberland, was all I had left. It made me very serious,and brought some dismal apprehensions in view : but I did not despair. As my heart was honest, I still trusted in the Providence of God and His administration of things in this world. As the infinite power and wisdom of the Creator was evident, from a survey of this magnificent and glorious scene ; as his care and Providence over each particular, in the administration of the great scheme was conspicuous ; can man, the favourite of heaven, have reason to lift up his voice to complain if he calls off his affections from folly, and by natural and supernatural force, by reason and revelation, overbears the prejudices of flesh and blood : if he ponders the hopes and fears of religion, and gives a just allowance to a future interest ? " Hearken to the commandments," saith the Lord, " and your peace shall be as a river."

On then I trotted, brave as the man of wood, we read of in an excellent French writer,† and hoped at the end of every mile to meet with something fortunate ; but nothing extraordinary occurred till the second evening, when I arrived at a little lone public-house, on the side of a great heath, by the entrance of a wood. For an hour before I came to this resting-place, I had rid in a tempest of wind, rain, lightning, and thunder, so very violent, that it brought to my remembrance Hesiod's description of a storm.

---

* As the *Table of Cebes* does best in prose, and Jeremy Collier the Nonjuror's translation of this fine mythological picture is not good, the reader will find another version of *Cebes' Table*, as an appendix at the end of this volume. I made it at the request of a young lady, who did not like Collier's version. The fine picture in his English, looks more like a work in the cant language of L'Estrange, or Tom Brown, than the antient and charming painting of Cebes the Theban philosopher. It is fitter to make the learned men of a beer-house laugh, than to delight and improve people of breeding and understanding.

† In Claude's reply to Arnaud, the French papist, we are told it was the humour of the Prince of Condé, to have a man of wood on horse-back, drest like a field-officer, with a lifted broad sword in his hand ; which figure was fastened in the great saddle, and the horse it was on always kept by the great Condé's side, when he travelled or engaged in the bloody field. Fearless the man of wood appeared in many a well-fought day ; but as they pursued the enemy one afternoon through a forest, in riding hard, a bough knocked off the wooden warrior's head ; yet still he galloped on after flying foes, to the amazement of the enemy, who saw a hero pursuing without a head. Claude applies this image to popery.

Then Jove omnipotent display'd the god,
And all Olympus trembled as he trod:
He grasps ten thousand thunders in his hand,
Bares his red arm, and wields the forky brand;
Then aims the bolts, and bids his light'nings play,
They flash, and rend through heav'n their flaming way:
Redoubling blow on blow, in wrath he moves,
The singed earth groans, and burns with all her groves:
A night of clouds blots out the golden day,
Full in their eyes the writhen lightnings play:
Nor slept the wind; the wind new horror forms,
Clouds dash on clouds before th' outragious storms;
While tearing up the sands, in drifts they rise,
And half the deserts mount th' encumber'd skies:
At once the tempest bellows, light'nings fly,
The thunders roar, and clouds involve the sky.

It was a dreadful evening upon a heath, and so much as a bush was not to be met with for shelter : but at last we came to the thatched habitation of a publican, and I thought it a very comfortable place. We had bread and bacon, and good ale for supper, and in our circumstances, it seemed a delicious meal.

This man informed me, that about a mile from his habitation, in the middle of the wood, there dwelt an old physician, one Dr. FITZGIBBONS, an Irish gentleman, who had one very pretty daughter, a sensible woman, to whom he was able to give a good fortune, if a man to both their liking appeared ; but as no such one had as yet come in their way, my landlord advised me to try the adventure, and he would furnish me with an excuse for going to the doctor's house. This set me a thinking. Dr. FITZGIBBONS, an Irish gentleman, said I, I know the man. I saved his son's life in Ireland, when he was upon the brink of destruction, and the old gentleman was not only then as thankful as it was possible for a man to be, in return for the good I had done him, at the hazard of my own life, but assured me, a thousand times over, that if ever it was in his power to return my kindness, he would be my friend to the utmost of his ability. He must ever remember, with the greatest gratitude, the benefit I had so generously conferred on him and his. All this came full into my mind, and I determined to visit the old gentleman in the morning.

Next day, as I had resolved, I went to pay my respects to Dr. FITZGIBBONS, who remembered me perfectly well, was most heartily glad to see me, and received me in the most affectionate manner. He immediately began to repeat his obligations to me, for the deliverance I had given his son,* and that if it was in his power to

* The case was this,—As I was returning one summer's evening from Tallow-Hills, where I had been to see a young lady mentioned in the beginnng of my first volume, I saw in a deep glen before me two men engaged ; a black of an enormous size, who fought with one of those large broadswords which they call in Ireland, an Andrew Ferraro ; and a little thin man with a drawn rapier. The white man I perceived was no match for the black, and must have perished very soon, as he had received several wounds, if I had not hast'ned up to his relief. I knew him to be my acquaintance, young FITZGIBBONS, my neighbour in the same square

be of service to me in *England*, he would leave nothing undone that was possible for him to do, to befriend me   He told me, that darling son of his, whose life I had saved, was an eminent physician at the court of Russia, where he lived in the greatest opulence and reputation, and as he owed his existence as such to me, his father could never be grateful enough in return.   " Can I any way serve you, Sir ?   Have you been fortunate or unfortunate, since your living in *England* ?   Are you married or unmarried ?   I have a daughter by a second wife, and if you are not yet engaged, will give her to you, with a good fortune, and in two years time, if you will study physic here, under my direction, will enable you to begin to practice, and get money as I have done in this country.   I have so true a sense of that generous act you did to save my son, that I will with pleasure do any thing in my power that can contribute to your happiness."

To this I replied, by thanking the doctor for his friendly offers and letting him know, that since my coming to *England* several years ago, which was occasioned by a difference between my father and me, I had met with several turns of fortune, good and bad, and was at present but in a very middling way, having only a little spot among the mountains of Richmondshire, with a cottage and garden on it, and three or four beasts, which I found by accident without an owner, as I travelled through that uninhabited land ; and a small farm of fifty acres with some stock, on the borders of Cumberland, which I got by a deceased wife.   This, with about thirty guineas in my purse, was my all at present; and I was going up to London, to try if I could meet with any thing fortunate in that place ; but that, since he was pleased to make me such generous offers, I would stop, study physic as he proposed, and accept the great honour he did me in offering me his daughter for a wife.   I told him likewise very fairly and honestly, that I had been rich by three or four marriages since my being in this country; but that I was unfortunately taken in at a gaming-table, by the means of two Irish gentlemen he knew very well, and there lost all; which vexed me the more, as I really do not love play ; that as to my father, I had little to expect from him, though he had a great estate, as our difference was about religion ; which kind of disputes have always the most cruel tendency ; and the wife he had,

---

of the college that I lived in ; and immediately drawing an excellent Spanish tuck I always wore, took the Moor to myself, FITZGIBBONS not being able to stand any longer, and a glorious battle ensued.   As I was a master of the small sword in those days, I had the advantage of the black by my weapon, as the broad sword is but a poor defence against a rapier, and gave him three wounds for every slight one I received : but at last he cut me quite through the left collar-bone and in return, I was in his vast body a moment after.   This dropt the robber, who had been a trumpeter to a regiment of horse ; and FITZGIBBONS and I were brought, by some people passing that way to his father's house at Dolfin's-barn, a village about a mile from the spot where this affair happened.   A surgeon was sent for, and we recovered in a few weeks time ; but my collar-bone was much more troublesome to me, than the wounds FITZGIBBONS had were to him, though he lost much more blood.   This was the ground of the obligation the doctor mentioned, in his conversation with me.

a low cunning woman, did all she could to maintain the variance, and keep up his anger to me, that her nephew might do the better on my ruin. That I had not written to him since my being in England ; nor had I met with any one who could give me any account of the family.

"And what," said Dr. FITZGIBBONS, " is this fine religious dispute, which has made your father fall out with a son he was once so proud of ?" " It was about Trinity in Unity, Sir ; a thing I have often heard your son argue against by lessons he had from you, as he informed me. My father is as orthodox as Gregory Nazienzen, among the ancient fathers, or Trapp and Potter, Webster and Waterland, among the modern doctors ; and when he found out that I was become an unitarian, and renounced his religion of three Gods, the horrible creed of Athanasius, and all the despicable explications of his admired divines, on that subject ; that I insisted ; that notwithstanding all the subtle inventions of learned men, through the whole Christian world, yet God Almighty hath not appointed himself to be worshipped by precept or example in any one instance in his holy word, under the character of Father, Son, and Holy Ghost ; that the worship of three persons and one God is expressly contrary to the solemn determination of Christ and his Apostles ; and in numbers of instances in the New Testament it is declared, that the one God and Father of all is the only supreme object, to whom all religious worship should be directed : that for these reasons I renounced the received doctrine of a co-equal trinity, and believed our great and learned divines, who laboured to prevent people from seeing the truth as it is in Jesus, would be in some tribulation at Christ's tribunal ; where they are to appear stripped of all worldly honours, dignities, and preferments, poor, naked, wretched mortals and to answer for their supplement to the gospel, in an invented heresy of three Gods. When my father heard these things, and saw the religious case of his son, his passion was very great. He forbid me his table, and ordered me to shift for myself. He renounced me, as I had done the triune God."

The doctor wondered not a little at the account I had given him, as my father was reckoned a man of great abilities, and taking me by the hand, said, I had acted most gloriously ; that what lost me my father's affection, was the very thing that ought to have induced him to erect a statue to my honour in his garden—that since I was pleased to accept of his offer, his friendship I might depend on—that if I would, I should begin the next day the study of physic under his direction, and at the end of two years, he would give me his daughter, who was not yet quite twenty.

Just as he had said this, Miss FITZGIBBONS entered the room, and her father introduced me to her. The sight of her astonished me, though I had before seen so many fine women, I could not help

looking with wonder at her.   She appeared one of those finished
creatures, whom we cannot enough admire, and upon acquaintance
with her, became much more glorious.

What a vast variety of beauty do we see in the infinity of nature.
Among the sex, we may find a thousand and a thousand
perfect images and characters ; all equally striking, and yet as
different as the pictures of the greatest masters in Italy.   What
amazing charms and perfections have I beheld in women as I have
journeyed through life.   When I have parted from one ; well I
said, I shall never meet another like this inimitable maid ; and
yet after all, JULIA appeared divinely fair, and happy in every
excellence that can adorn the female mind.   Without that exact
regularity of beauty, and elegant softness of propriety, which
rendered Miss DUNK, whom I have described in these *Memoirs*, a
very divinity, JULIA charmed with a graceful negligence, and
enchanted with a face that glowed with youthful wonders, beauties that art could not adorn but always diminished.   The choice
of dress was no part of JULIA's care, but by the neglect of it she
became irresistible.   In her countenance there ever appeared a
bewitching mixture of sensibility and gaiety, and in her soul, by
converse was discovered that generosity and tenderness were the
first principles of her mind.   To truth and virtue she was inwardly
devoted, and at the bottom of her heart, though hard to discover
it, her main business to serve God, and fit herself for eternity.   In
sum, she was one of the finest originals that ever appeared among
womankind, peculiar in perfections which cannot be described ;
and so inexpressibly charming in an attractive sweetness, a natural
gaiety, and a striking negligence, a fine understanding, and
the most humane heart ; that I found it impossible to know
her without being in love with her : her power to please
was extensive indeed.   In her, one had the loveliest idea of
woman.

To this fine creature I was married at the end of two years from
my first acquaintance with her ; that is, after I had studied
physic so long, under the care and instruction of her excellent
father, who died a few weeks after the wedding, which was in
the beginning of the year 1734, and the 29th of my age.   Dying,
he left me a handsome fortune, his library, and house ; and I
imagined I should have lived many happy years with his admirable
daughter, who obliged me by every endearing means, to be excessively fond of her.   I began to practise upon the old gentleman's
death, and had learned so much in the two years I had studied
under him, from his lecturing and my own hard reading, that I
was able to get some money among the opulent round me ; not
by art and collusion, the case of too many doctors in town and
country, but by practising upon consistent principles. The method
of my reading, by Dr. FITZGIBBON'S directions, was as follows ;

and I set it down here for the benefit of such gentlemen, as chuse to study in the private manner I did.

A method of studying Physic in a private manner : by which means a gentleman, with the purchase of a Diploma, may turn out a Doctor, as well as if he went to Padua, to hear Morganni.

⸰ The first books I got upon my table, were the *Lexicons* of Castellus and Quincy ; one for the explication of ancient terms ; and the other of modern. These, as Dictionaries, lay at hand for use, when wanted.

I then opened the last edition of Herman Conringius's *Introductio in Universam Artem Medicam, singulasque ejus partis ;* I say the last edition of 1726, because that has an excellent preface by Hoffmann. This book, which comes down to the beginning of the seventeenth century, I read with great care ; especially Gonthier Christopher Schelhammer's notes, and additions, which have enriched the work very much. By the way, they were both very great men, and bright ornaments to their profession. They wrote an amazing number of books on medicine. Conringius died December, 1681, aged 75 ; and Schelhammer, in January, 1716, in the 67th year of his age.

The next introductory book to the art, was *Lindenius Renovatus de Scriptis Medicis, quibus præmittitur Manuductio ad Medicinam.* This book was first called *Libro duo de Scripturis, &c.* and written by John Antonides Vander Linden, a famous professor at Leyden, who published it in 1637, in a small octavo. It was again printed in the same form, in 1651 and 1662, at Amsterdam ; but the most valuable edition is that printed at Nuremburg in 1686, edited by George Abraham Merklinus, who made very many and excellent additions to this fourth edition, and called it *Lindenius Renovatus*, as he had augmented it to a thick quarto. Vander Linden died in March, 1664, aged 55 ; and Merklinus in April, 1702, in the 58th year of his age. They have both written many books on physic, but there have been such improvements made by the diligence and success of modern physicians, that it would be only loss of time to read over all their works, or all the authors of the seventeenth century.

The next books I opened, were the learned Daniel Le Clerc's *History of Physic*, which commences with the world, and ends at the time of Galen ; and the great Dr. Friend's *History*, in two vols. octavo, which is a continuation of Le Clerc, down to Linacre, the founder of the College of Physicians, in the reign of Henry VIII. These books shewed me the origin and revolutions of physic, and the ancient writers and their works on this subject. Daniel Le Clerc died in June, 1728, aged 76, and some months.

P

When I had read these things,* I turned next to botany, and read Raii *Methodus Plantarum Emendata*, 1703. Raii *Synopsis Methodica Stirpium*, third edition ; and Tournefort's *Institutiones Rei Herbariæ*. These books, with a few observations of my own, as I walked in the gardens, in the fields, and on the plains, furnished me with sufficient knowledge of this kind for the present. The vast folios on this subject are not for beginners.

Chemistry was the next thing my director bid me look into, and to this purpose I perused Boerhaave's *Elementa Chemiæ*. and Hoffman's *Observationes Physico-Chemiæ*. These afford as much chemistry as a young physician need set out with ; but as books alone give but an imperfect conception, I performed most of the common operations in Beecher's portable furnace.

The *Materia Medica* in the next place had my attention, that is, those animal, vegetable, and fossil substances, which are used to prevent, cure, or palliate diseases. And in order to know the names of all the drugs, their history, the adulterations they are subject to, their virtues, their dose, their manner of using them, and the cautions which they require, to get a sufficient knowledge of this kind, I looked into Geoffrey's *Materia Medica*, and made a collection of the *Materia* at the same time, that I might conceive and remember what I read.

Pharmacy, or the art of preparing and compounding medicines, was the next thing I endeavoured to be a master of. And that I might know how to exalt their virtues, to obviate their ill qualities, and to make them less nauseous, I read to this purpose Quincy's *Pharmaceutical Lectures* and *Dispensatory*, and took care to be well versed in all the *Pharmacopœia's*, those of London, Edinburgh, Paris, Boerhaave, Bate, and Fuller. And I read very carefully Gaubin's *Methodus Præscribendi*. This gave me the materials, and taught me the form of prescribing.

Anatomy I studied next, that is, the art of dividing the several parts of a body, so as to know their size, figure, situation, connexions, and make. I began with Drake and Keil, and then read over Winslow. I had likewise open before me at the same time, at my entrance upon this study, a good set of plates, the tables of Eustachius and Cooper, and turned them carefully over as I read. The doctor then showed me how to dissect, but chiefly by the direction of a book entitled *Culter Anatomicus : on Methode Courte, Facile, et Claire de Dissequer les Corps Humaines*. I was soon able to perform myself. It was the third edition of the above book, by Lyserus, in 1679 ; which has many curious anatomical observations added to it by Gaspar Bartholin, the son of the celebrated Thomas Bartholin, professor at Copenhagen. Michel Lysère was the disciple of the great Thomas

---

* If Mangetus had published his *Bibliotheca Scriptorum Medicorum*, 2 vols. folio, at the time I am speaking of, the Doctor, my friend, would have recommended it to a beginner.

Bartholin, who died in December, 1680, in his 64th year. Michel died early in life, in 1656, a very young man, " regretté à cause de son merite." I had also Nichol's *Compendium*, and Hunter's *Compendium*. By these means, and by reading the authors who have written upon some one part only ; such as Peyerus *de Glandulis Intestinus. Experimenta circa Pancras*. De Graaf *de Organis Generationis*. Gasp. Bartholin *de Diaphragm*. Malpigius *de Pulmonibus, de Venibus, de Liene, et de Cornuum Vegetatione*. Lower *de Corde, de Ventriculo, et de Cerebri Anat*. Willis *de Respiratione*. Glisson *de Hepatæ*. Casserius *de Vocis Auditusque Organis*. Walsalou *de Aure*. Havers *on the Bones*. Munro *on the Bones*. Douglas *on the Muscles*. Morgagni *Adversaria*. Ruyshii *Opera*. Nuck's *Adenographia*. Wharton's *Adenographia*. Ridley's *Anatomy of the Brain*. Santorini *Observationes*. Boueti *Sepulchrum Anatomicum*. Blasii *Anatomia Animalium*. Tyson's *Anatomy of the Oran-Outang*. By these means, I cut up the body of a young woman I had from a neigh-bouring churchyard, and acquired knowledge enough of anatomy.

N.B.—If all the pieces written upon some one part of the body are not to be had single, the reader inclined to the delightful study of physic will find them in the *Bibliotheca Anatomica*, 2 vols. folio.

Here, before I proceed, I will mention a very curious case, which occurred in my dissecting the body I have spoken of. It was as remarkable an example of preternatural structure as ever appeared. In cutting her up, there was found two vaginas, and a right and left uterus. Each uterus had its corresponding vagina, and the uteri and the vaginæ lay parallel to each other ; there was only one ovarium ; but two perfect hymens. The labia stretched so as to take in the anus, terminating beyond it ; and as they were in large ridges, and well armed, the whole had a formidable appearance. If it should be asked, Could a perfect superfœtation take place in such a person ? Most certainly there might be one conception upon the back of another at different times ; therefore, I should not chuse to marry a woman with two vaginas, if it was possible to know it before wedlock.

But to proceed. The next things I read, were the institutes of medicine, that is, such books as treat of the economy and con-trivance of nature in adapting the parts to their several uses. The books purely physiological are Keil's *Tentamia*. Sanctorii *Aphorismi*. Bellini *de Pulsibus et Urina*. Borellus *de Motu Animalium*, both admirable pieces. Friend's *Emmenologia*. Simpson's *System of the Womb*. And Pitcairn's *Tracts*. These are the best things relating to physiology, which may be called the first part of the Institutions of Physic.

The second part of the Institutes is the Art of preserving such a system as the body, in an order fit for the exercise of its functions as long as possible. The third part is pathology, which teaches the different manners in which diseases happen ; and the various causes of these disorders, with their attendants and consequences. The fourth part is the doctrine of signs, by which a judgment is formed of the sound or bad state of the animal. And the fifth is Therapeutica, that is, the means and method of restoring sanity to a distempered body. Treatises on all these matters are what we call institutions of physic, and in relation to the four last mentioned, the best books are Hoffman's *Systema Medicinæ Rationalis*, and Boerhaave's *Institutions*, with his lectures upon them. These books I read with great attention, and found them sufficient.

Being instituted in this manner, I turned next to the practical writers, and read the history of diseases and their cure from observations of nature. This is called *pathologia particularis*, and is the great business of a physician. All that has been said is only preparatory to this study. Here then I first very carefully read the authors who have written a system of all diseases ; and then, such writers as have considered particular cases. The best system writers are Boerhaave's *Aphorisms and Comment.* Hoffman's *Pathologia Particularis ;* being the last part of his *Systema Medicinæ.* Jumher's *Conspectus Medicinæ.* Allen's *Synopsis.* Shaw's *Practice of Physic ;* and Lomnii *Opusculum Aureum.*

The writers on a few and particular distempers are Sydenham *Opera.* Moreton's *Puretologia.* Bellini *de Morbis Capites et Pectoris.* Ramazzini *de Morbis Artificium.* Wepsemus *de Apoplexia.* Hoyes on *Asthma.* Astruc *de Lue Venerea.* Turner's *Synopsis,* and *of the Skin.* Musgrave *de Arthritide.* Highmore *de Passione Hysterica et Hypocondria.* Glisson *de Rachitide.* Clericus *de Lumbrico Lato.* Daventer *Ars Obstetricandi.* Mauriceau *des Femmes Grosses.* Harris *de Morbis Infantium.* Turner's *Letter to a Young Physician.* All these books I read very carefully, and to your reading add the best observations you can any where get, or make yourself. I wrote down in the shortest manner, abstracts of the most curious and useful things, especially the representations of nature ; and refreshed my memory by often looking into my note-book. Every thing taken from nature is valuable. Hypothesis is entertaining rather than useful.

And when I was reading the history of diseases in the authors I have just mentioned, I looked into the ancient Greek and Latin medical writers ; for all their merit lies in this kind of history. Their pharmacy and anatomy is good for nothing. They scarce knew any thing of the human bodies, but from the dissections of other animals, took their descriptions. The great Vesalius in the beginning of the sixteenth century, was the first that taught physicians to study nature in dissecting human bodies ; which was then considered by the church as a kind of sacrilege.* As to chemistry, they had no notion of it. It was not heard of till some hundred years after the latest of them. In botany they had made little progress, in short, as they knew little of botany, and nothing of chemistry ; as their systems of natural philosophy and anatomy were false and unnatural, and it is upon anatomy and natural philosophy that physiology or the use of the parts is founded, we can expect nothing from the ancients upon these heads, but mere imaginations, or notions unsupported by observation or matter of fact. It is their history of diseases that supports their character. Hippocrates, in particular, excels all others on this head ; but this great man was not perfect even in this. Knowledge in nature is the daughter of time and experience. Many notions of the animal economy were then absurd, and if Hippocrates was too wise to act always up to his theory, yet he could not be entirely free from its influence.

The names of the ancient original Greek medical writers are Hippocrates, Dioscorides, Aritæus, Galen, and Alexander. The Latin writers of physic are Celsus, Scribonius Largus, Cælius Aurelianus, Marcellus Empericus, Theodorus Priscianus, and Sextus Placitus. We have besides several collectors, as Oribasius, Aetius, Paulus Æginita, etc. Nicander, the medical poet ; and the fragments of Soranus, Rufus Ephesius, Zonorates, Vindicianus, Diocles Carystius, Cassius, and a few others ; but all these may be looked into afterwards. The original authors are sufficient in the noviciate.

As to the Latin medical writers, Celsus, and Cælius Aurelianus only, are worth reading. Celsus lived in the latter end of the reign of Augustus, and is admirable for the purity of his Latin, and the elegance of his sense. You must have him night and morning in your hands, till you are a master of the terms and expressions peculiar to physic, which occur in him. The style of Cælius is very bad, and his cavils tedious ; but his description of diseases is full and accurate. In this respect he is a very

* When Vesalius began to dissect human bodies, he was considered by the people as an impious cruel man, and before he could practice publicly, was obliged to get a decision in his favour from the Salamanca divines. "C'est ce qui engagè Charles V. de faire une consultation aux theologiens de Salamanque, pour savoir si en conscience on pouvoit dissequer un corps humain, pour en connoître la structure." *Memoirs de Niceron.* They would not let him settle in France, but the republic of Venice gave him a professor's chair at Padua, where he dissected publicly, and taught anatomy seven years. He was but eighteen, when he published his famous book, *La Fabrique du Corps Humain,* which was the admiration of all men of science ; and a little after, he made a present of the first skeleton the world ever saw, to the university of Basle ; where it is still to be seen. This great man, Andrew Vesal, was born the last of April, 1512 ; and in the 58th year of his age, October 15, 1564, he was shipwrecked on the isle of Zante, and in the deserts there was famished to death. His body was found by a goldsmith of his acquaintance, who happened to land there not long after, and by this man buried. Vesal's works were published by Herman Boerhaave, in two volumes, folio, in 1725. Every physician ought to have them.

valuable writer.   He lived in the second century, as did Galen likewise.

As to Hippocrates, who was contemporary with Socrates, he was born in the first years of the 8oth Olympiad, 460 before Christ, René Chartier's edition printed at Paris, 1639, is the most pompous : but Vander Linden's, printed at Leyden in 1668, two vols. 8vo., is the best.   When I read Hippocrates, I also looked into Prosper Alpini's good book *de Presagienda Vita et Morte Ægrotantium*, in which he has with great care collected and methodized all the scattered observations of Hippocrates, relating to the dangerous or salutary appearances in diseases. At the same time, I likewise read this great man's *Medicina Methodica*.   Alpinus, born in November, 1553, died professor of botany at Padua, February, 1617, Æt. 64.   The best commentators on Hippocrates, whose names you will find in Conringius's Introduction, are also worthy of reference.

The best edition of Dioscorides' *Materia Medica*, is that of Frankfort, 1598, folio.   The best edition of Aritæus, who lived before Julius Cæsar's time, as Dioscorides did, A.D. 46, is Boerhaave's, 1731, folio.   The best editions of Galen's works are those of Basle, 1538, in 5 vols. and of Venice, 1625, in 7 vols., folio. Alexander of Tralles flourished in the' sixth century, under Justinian the Great, and left the following works.   *Therapeutica*, Lib. xii.   *De Singularum Corporis Partium Vitiis, Ægritudinibus, et Injuriis*, Lib. v.   *Epist. de Lumbricis.   Tractatus de Puerorum Morbis.   Liber de Febribus.*   The best Greek copy is that of Stephens, Paris, 1548, folio.   In Greek and Latin, Basil, 1658. But in neither of these editions is to be found the *Epistle de Lumbricis.*   You must look for that in the 12th volume of Fabricius's *Bibliotheca Græca*.

In the last place, besides all the authors I have mentioned, I likewise looked into the original observation writers and miscellaneous books relating to physic.   They afford excellent knowledge, where the authors are faithful and judicious.   Such are the *Observationes Medicæ* of Nicolaus Tulpius, a curious book ; and the dedication of it to his son Peter, a student in Physic, good advice.   The second edition of 1652 is the best, being a fourth part larger than the first which came out in 1641. The *Observationes et Curationes Medicinales* of Petrus Forestus, Lib. xxii.   The *Observationes Medicæ* of Joannes Theodorus Schenkius, and the various Journals and Transactions of learned Societies, which are repositories in which the physician fiuds much rare and valuable knowledge.   And as a physician ought to have a little acquaintance with the modern practice of surgery I concluded with Heister's, Turner's, and Sharp's *Surgery*.

By this method of studying physic in the middle of a wood, and employing my time and pains in reading the ancients, and considering their plain and natural account of diseases, I became a Doctor, as well as if I had been a regular collegiate. But it is time to think of my various story. Having married the illustrious JULIA, as related in a preceding page, and by the death of her father soon after the wedding, acquired a handsome settlement, a considerable sum of money, and a valuable collection of books, I thought myself so happily situated in the midst of flourishing mercies, and so well secured from adversity, that it was hardly possible for the flame of destruction to reach me. But when I had not the least reason to imagine calamity was near me, and fondly imagined prosperity was my own, infelicity came stalking on unseen : and from a fulness of peace, plunged us at once into an abyss of woe. It was our wont, when the evenings were fine, to take a boat at the bottom of a meadow, at the end of our garden, and in the middle of a deep river, pass an hour or two in fishing); but at last, by some accident or other, a slip of the foot, or the boat's being got a little too far from the bank's side, JULIA was drowned. This happened in the tenth month of our marriage. The loss of this charming angel in such a manner sat powerfully on my spirits for some time, and the remembrance of her perfections, and the delights I enjoyed while she lived, made me wish I had never seen her. To be so vastly happy as I was, and be deprived of her in a moment, in so shocking a way, was an affliction I was hardly able to bear. It struck me to the heart. I sat with my eyes shut ten days.

But losses and pains I considered were the portion of mortals in this trying state, and from thence we ought to learn to give up our own wills ; and to get rid of all eager wishes, and violent affection, that we may take up our rest wholly in that which pleaseth God. Carrying our submission to Him so far, as to bless His correcting hand, and kiss that rod that cures our passionate eagerness, perverseness, and folly.

We ought likewise to learn from such things, to look upon the sad accidents of life, as not worthy to be compared with what Christ underwent for our sakes, who, though he was a Son, yet He learned obedience by the things that He suffered ; and with Christian resignation live in a quiet expectance of a future happy state, after our patience has had its perfect work. Considering that these light and momentary afflictions are not worthy to be compared with the glory that Christ hath purchased for us ; and if we are faithful to death, hath promised to bestow upon us.

In all these things resigning to the wisdom of God, and not merely to His will and authority, believing His disposal to be wisest and best ; and that His declarations and promises are true, though we cannot in some cases discern the reason of such an end, and such means being connected, nor can imagine how

some promises can be made good. Patience, I said, my soul !
Patience, and what thou knowest not now, thou shalt know in a
little time. Thus I reasoned, as I sat with my eyes shut, and
Juvenal's observation recurred to my recollection—

> Omnibus in terris quæ sunt a Gadibus usque
> Auroran et Gangen, pauci dinoscere possunt
> Vera bona, atque illis multum diversa, remota
> Erroris nebula : quid enim ratione timemus
> Aut cupimus ? Quid tam dextro pede concipis, ut te
> Conatus non pœniteat, votique peracti ?

Having thus given vent to reflection, I called to Soto O'Einn,
my man, to bring the horses out immediately, and I would go
some way or other to see new scenes, and if I could, get another
wife ; as I was born with the disease of repletion, and had made
a resolution not to fornicate, it was incumbent on me to have a
sister and companion, with whom I might lawfully carry on the
succession. As a friend to society, and passively obedient to
the laws of my higher country, a wife for ever, I declared ; for,
if on losing one, we can still be so fortunate as to get another,
who is pretty without pride ; witty without affectation ; to
virtue only and her friends a friend—

> Whose sense is great, and great her skill,
> For reason always guides her will ;
> Civil to all to all she's just,
> And faithful to her friend and trust :
> Whose character, in short, is such,
> That none can love or praise too much.

If such a charmer should again appear, and ten thousand such
there ever are among the sex, silly and base though the
majority may be ; what man could say he had had enough of
wedlock, because he had buried seven such wives ? I am sure
I could not. And if, like the men who were but striplings at
fourscore, in the beginning of this world, I was to live for ages,
and by accidents lost such partners as I have described ; I would
with rapture take hundreds of them to my breast, one after
another, and piously propagate the kind. The most despicable
of all creatures is a w——. An abomination to heaven : and
if God was a mere fanciful fear ; yet such a wretch the prostitute
is, that neither honour nor honesty can ever be expected from
her. But, in defiance to divine and human laws, she lives a foe
to mankind ; to ruin the fortune, disease the body, and for ever
damn the soul of the miserable man, who is dunce enough to
become a Limberham to the execrable wretch. The misfortunes
I have known happen to gentlemen of my acquaintance by street-
w——, chamber-w——, and kept-w—, would make a volume
as large as this I am writing, and leave another world quite out
of the history. I have seen gentlemen of the best fortunes and

education, become worn-out beggars in the streets of London, without anything hardly to cover them, by the means of these execrable harlots ; some have become bullies to brothels ; and many I have beheld going to the gallows by maintaining the falsest and least-engaging of women ; but take a modest sensible woman to your heart, who has the fear of the great God before her eyes, and a regard to the laws of her country, share your fortune generously with her, that she may have her innocent amusements and dress, be for ever good-humoured, be true to her bed, and every felicity you may taste that it is possible to enjoy in this lower hemisphere. Let a wife be our choice, as we are rationals.

With these notions in my head, I mounted my horse ; and determined, in the first place, to pay a visit to my two beauties at Orton-lodge, who were by this time at age, and see what opinions they had acquired, and if they had any commands for me. But when I arrived at my romantic spot, I found the ladies were gone, all places shut up, and no soul there ; the key of the house-door was left for me, and a note fastened to it, to inform me how the affair was.

" SIR,

" Not having had the favour of hearing from you for almost three years, and despairing of that honour and happiness any more, we have left your fine solitude, to look after our fortunes, as we are of age ; and on enquiry have found that old Cock, our cruel guardian, is dead and gone. We are under infinite obligations to you, have an extreme sense of your goodness, and hope, if you are yet in the land of the living, that we shall soon be so happy as to get some account of you, to the end we may return the weighty balance due from,
SIR,
Your most obliged,
and ever humble servants."

From the date of this letter it appeared that they were not a month gone before my arrival ; but to what place they said not, and it was in vain for me to enquire. I found every thing in good order, and all the goods safe ; the garden full of fruits and vegetables, and plenty of various eatables in the house, pickled, potted, and preserved. As it was in the month of June, the solitude looked vastly charming in its vales and forest, its rocks and waters ; and for a month I strove to amuse myself there in fishing, shooting, and improving the ground ; but it was so dull, so sad a scene, when I missed the bright companions I had with me in former days, who used to wander with me in the valleys, up the hills, by the streams, and make the whole a paradise all the day long, that I could not bear it longer than four weeks, and rode from thence to Dr. STANVIL'S seat, to ask him how he did, and look once more at that fine curiosity, Miss DUNK that was, but at the time I am speaking of, his wife. However, before I left my lodge, I made a discovery one day, as I was exploring the wild country, round my little house, that was entertaining enough, and to this day, in remembrance, seems to me so agreeable, that I imagine a relation of this matter may be grateful to my Readers. It contains the story of a lady, who cannot be enough admired, can never be sufficiently praised.

THE HISTORY OF THE BEAUTIFUL LEONORA.

As I rambled one summer's morning, with my gun and my dog, over the vast mountains which surrounded me at Orton-lodge, I came as the sun was rising to a valley about four miles from my house, which I had not seen before, as the way to it, over the Fells, was a dangerous road. It was green and flowery, had clumps of oaks in several spots, and from the hovering top of a precipice at the end of the glen, a river falls engulphed in rifted rocks. It is a fine rural scene.

Here I sat down to rest myself, and was admiring the natural beauties of the place, when I saw three females turn into the vale, and walk towards the water-fall. One of them, who appeared to be the mistress had an extravagance of beauty in her face and a form such as I had not often seen. The others were pretty women drest like quakers and very clean. They came very near the water where I was, but did not see me, as I was behind two rocks which almost joined : and after they had looked awhile at the headlong river, they went back, and entering a narrow-way between two hills disappeared. I was greatly surprised at what I had seen, not imagining I had such a neighbour in Richmond-shire, and resolved to know who this beauty was. The wonders of her face, her figure, and her mien, were striking to the last degree.

Arising then as soon as they were out of sight, I walked on to the turning I saw them enter ; and in half an hour's time came to a plain, through which several brooks wandered, and on the margin of one of them, was a grove and a mansion. It was a sweet habitation, at the entrance of the little wood ; and before the door, on banks of flowers, sat the illustrious owner of this retreat, and her two maids. In such a place, in such a manner, so unexpectedly to find so charming a woman, seemed to me as pleasing an incident as could be met in travelling over the world.

At my coming near this lady she appeared to be astonished, and to wonder much at seeing such an inhabitant in that part of the world : but on pulling off my hat, and telling her I came to visit her as her neighbour ; to pay my humble respects to her, and beg the honour of her acquaintance ; she asked me, from what vale or mountain I came, and how long I had been a resident in that wild part of the world ? This produced a compend of some part of my story, and when I had done, she desired me to walk in. Coffee and hot rolls were soon brought, and we break-fasted cheerfully together. I took my leave soon after, having made her a present of some black cocks and a hare I had shot that morning ; and hoped, if it was possible to find an easy way to my lodge, which I did not yet know, that I should some time or other be honoured with her presence at my little house ; which was worth her seeing, as it was situated in the most delightful part of this romantic silent place, and had many curiosities near it ; that in the mean time, if it was agreeable, I would wait upon her again, before I left Richmondshire, which would be soon : for I only came to see how things were, and was obliged to hasten another way. This beauty replied, that it would give her pleasure to see me when I had a few hours to spare. From this invitation I went three times more within a short-space, we became well acquainted, and after dinner one day, she gave me the following relation.

"My name was LEONORA SARSFIELD before I married an Irishman, one BURKE, whom I met at Avignon in France. He is one of the handsomest men of the age, though his hopes were all his fortune ; but he has proved himself a villain as great as ever disgraced mankind. His breeding and his eloquence, added to his fine figure, induced me to fancy him an angel of a man; and to imagine I had well bestowed a hundred thousand pounds, to make him great, and as happy as the day is long. For three months he played the god, and I fondly thought there was not such another happy woman as myself in all the world, but I was mistaken. BURKE found out by some means or other, that I concealed five thousand pounds of my fortune from his know-ledge ; and that I was in my heart so good a protestant, that it was impossible to bring me over to popery, or ever get me to be an idolater at the mass, before the tiny god of dough : that I could never be brought to look upon the invented superstitions, and horrible corruptions of the church of Rome, as the true relig-ion ; nor be ever persuaded to assist at the Latin service in that communion, as it must be an abomination to Christ and to God, if the gospel may be depended upon as the rule of faith. When BURKE perceived these things, he threw off the disguise, and appeared a monster instead of a man, a bigot of the first order, as he was a furious papist, which I did not know, when we were married ; and as he was by nature as cruel, as he was avaricious by principle, he began to use me in the vilest manner, and by words and deeds, did all he could to make my life a burden to

me. He was for ever abusing me in the vilest language ; cursing
me for a heretic for ever damned ; and by blows compelling me
to inform him where my money was ; he has left me covered with
my own blood very often, and when he found I still held out, and
would not discover to him what remained of my fortune, nor
violate my religion, which I valued much more than my money ;
by renouncing the customs and practice of the reformed church,
and joining in the sinful worship of the mass ; he came to me one
night with a small oak sapling, and beat me in such a manner as
left me almost dead. He then went out of the house, told me he
would return by twelve, and make me comply, or he would break
every bone in my body. This happened at a country-seat of
mine in the shire ; all the servants being obliged to lie every
night in an out-house, that he might have the more power over
me. His excessive avarice was but one cause of this inhuman
behaviour : it was the zeal of this raging bigot for his ever-cursed
popery, that made him act the unrelenting inquisitor.

" I asked you, Sir, before I began my story, if you were a
catholic, and as you assured me you were the very reverse, I
may indulge myself a little in expressing my resentments against
that religion of Satan, which the Popish doctors drew out of the
bottomless pit. It is a religion formed in hell by devils, and from
them brought by those arch-politicians, the mass-priests, to make
the world their slaves, or rack the human race to death, by
torments that would perhaps melt even devils. O bloody and
infernal scheme of worship ! Surely there is some chosen curse,
some hidden thunder in the stores of heaven, red with just wrath
to blast the men, who owe their greatness to their apostasy from
the religion of Christ Jesus : and to the woes and pains they lay
on mankind. By the religion of modern Rome, you see in me
a wife almost tortured to extinction by a holy Roman catholic
husband : nor am I the only married protestant woman, who
has felt the stripes and bruises of a merciless popish companion.
Thousands to be sure have suffered as well as I upon the same
account, though none in so miserable a manner. Even fathers
have lost all bowels for their children, and become the most
violent persecutors, when the blessed religion of popery has been
in dispute. Children, for its sake, have destroyed their parents,
and the world has been turned into a field of blood, to feed and
support those dreadful slaughterers, the mass-priests ; and gratify
the blind and impious religious fancies of their well-taught
religionists, commonly called catholics. What I have suffered
gives me a true sense of popery. It has made me consider its
errors and iniquities with double attention. I tremble at the
thoughts of its prevailing in this land. How direful is popery,
whether we consider it in a religious view, or regard it as a political
contrivance, to gratify the avarice and ambition of the clergy,

it appears the just object of our contempt, as well as of our abhorrence. It not only makes its priests the slaughterers of mankind ; witness the inquisition, the Morisco's, Thorn,* England,
Ireland, France, the Low Countries, Hungary, and other theatres
of barbarity, the most shocking and inhuman ; but it causes
even husbands to become mere devils to wives who are angels
of women in mind and body, and can only be charged with their
being protestants. Could that religion come down from heaven,
which claims a right not only to persecute single persons, but to
devote whole nations to detruction by the blackest treachery,
and most inhuman massacres ; and which teaches such absurdities as transubstantiation, masses, purgatory, penances, indul-
gences, and attrition ; absurdities that dissipate the poor Romans
of those guilty fears, which natural conscience might otherwise
keep alive in men. Such things, without mentioning the adoration of the cross and other images, and the increasing multitude
of imaginary mediators, entirely destroy the credibility of any
system with which they are connected. God cannot be the author
of a scheme which weakens and corrupts the law of nature.

"But as to my tragical relation," continued LEONORA, "being
thus left by BURKE in this sad situation, bleeding, and miserable
with pains, but still in dread of worse usage on his return, I crawled
down stairs, to a small door in a black place, which opened to a
private way out of the house. This was known only to myself, as it
was a passage my father had made, in case of thieves, or any villains, from a little unfrequented cellar, by a narrow ascending arch,
to a thicket in the corner of a shrubby field, at a small distance
from the house. To a labyrinth made in this small grove I made
what haste I could, and had not been long there, before I perceived through the trees my inhuman husband ; and as he came
near me, heard him say, 'she shall tell me where my money is,
for all she has is mine ; and worship our lady and the host, or I
will burn her flesh off her bones, and make her feel as many
torments here, as the heretics are tortured with in everlasting
pain.' The sight of the monster made me tremble to so violent
a degree, that I was scarcely able to proceed to the cottage of a
poor woman, my sure friend, about two miles from the place I
was hid in ; but I did my best to creep through crossways, and
after many difficulties, and suffering much by going over ditches,
I got to my resting-place. The old woman, my nurse, screeched
at the sight of me, as I was sadly torn, and all over gore. Such
a spectacle as I presented has been seldom seen. But by peace
and proper things, I got well again in two months, and removed
to this lone house, which my father had built in this spot for his

* The Morisco's were expelled Spain in the year 1492 ; the inquisition was erected four
years after, and the doings at Thorn, by which the quantity of blood formerly spilt on the
ground by ever-cursed popery was increased, in the year 1724.

occasional retirement. Here I have been for two years past, and am as happy as I desire to be : nay vastly so, as I am now free and delivered from a monster, whose avarice and cruelty made me a spectacle to angels and men : because, Sir, I would not reduce myself to the state of a beggar, to satisfy his insatiable love of money : nor worship his dead woman, and bit of bread; his rabble of saints, images, relics, and that sovereign cheat, the Pope ; because I would not give up all I had, and become an idolator, as far more despicable and sinful than the antient Pagans ; as the Romish ritual and devotions are more stupid and abominable than the Heathen religion ; for disobedience in these respects, pains and penalties without ceasing were my appointment, and I was for some months as miserable as the damned.

"Such, Sir, was my fatal marriage, which I thought would be a stock of such felicities, that time only by many years could reduce to an evanescent state, and deprive me of.   As Venus was at the bridal with her whole retinue ; the ardent amorous boy, the sister-graces in their loose attire ; Aglaia, Thalia, and Euphrosine, bright, blooming, and gay ; and was attended by Youth, that wayward thing without her ; was conducted by Mercury, the god of eloquence, and by Pitho, the goddess of persuasion ; as all seemed pleasurable and enchanting, my young imagination formed golden scenes, and painted a happiness quite glorious and secure.   But how precarious and perishing is what we mortals call felicity !   Love and his mother disappeared very soon, as I have related ; and to them succeeded impetuous passion, intense, raging, and terrible, with all the furies in the train. The masked hero I had married was a Phalaris, a miser, a papist ; a wretch who had no taste for love, no conception of virtue, no sense of charms ; but to gold and popery would sacrifice every thing that is fair and laudable. *Le Diable a quatre* he shined in as a player, and was the Devil himself in flesh and blood. 'Where is the rest of your gold, you b—— ?' with uplifted arm, was the cry thundered in my ears. 'You shall be catholic, d—— you, or I will pinch off the flesh from your bones.'"

Here the beautiful LEONORA had done, and I wondered very greatly at her relation, nor was her action in speaking it, and the spirit with which she talked, less surprising. With admiration I beheld her, and was not a little pleased, that I had found in my neighbourhood so extraordinary a person, and so very fine an original.   This lady had some reason to abhor the word catholic, and might well be angry with popery, though she carried resentment a little too far ; but had the Reader seen her attitude, her energies, and the faces she made, when she mentioned the corruptions of popery, or the word husband, sure I am, it would be thought much more striking than Garrick in Richard, or Shute, in his exhibition of Old Philpot.   I was greatly delighted with her, and as she was very agreeable in every thing, I generally went every second day to visit her during the short time I continued in Richmondshire.

> Bear me, ye friendly powers, to gentler scenes,
> To shady bow'rs, and never-fading greens ;
> To flow'ry meads, the vales, and mazy woods,
> Some sweet soft seat, adorn'd with springs and floods :
> Where with the muses, I may spend my days,
> And steal myself from life by slow decays.
> With age unknown to pain or sorrow blest,
> To the dark grave retiring as to rest ;
> While gently with one sigh this mortal frame,
> Dissolving turns to ashes whence it came ;
> And my free'd soul departs without a groan,
> In transport wings her flight to worlds unknown.

July 2, 1734, I journeyed from Orton-lodge, to Bassora, to pay my respects to Dr. STANVIL and his charming consort, and was received by them both with the greatest goodness and civility ; but as before, this lady did not seem to have had any former acquaintance, one might well think from the part she acted, that she had never seen me, till the accident I have related brought me to her husband's house. I did not however even hint any thing to the contrary, but turning to the Doctor a little after my arrival, began to ask him some questions.

As he had an *Essay on Fevers* in his hand, when I entered the room, I requested to know how he accounted for the effects of Cantharides, in raising and strengthening a low trembling pulse, and driving the natural heat and efflatus of the blood outward, in giving relief in delirious ravings, stupors, and loss of reason, in reducing continual fevers to distinct remissions, and in cleansing and opening the obstructed glands and lymphatics, so as to bring on the critical sweats, let loose the saliva and glandular secretions, and bring down the thick soluble urine ? How does blistering, so happily brought in by the physical bully of this age, Dr. Radcliffe, so wonderfully cool and dilute the blood ? It seems to me somewhat strange.

" It is easily accounted for," replied Dr. STANVIL. " The Spanish fly, an extremely hot and perfectly caustic insect, is stocked with a subtile, active, and extremely pungent salt, which enters the blood upon the application of the blister, and passes with it through the several glandular strainers and secretory ducts. This stimulating force of the fly's salt, occasions the pain felt in making the water with a blister, which may be taken off by a thin emulsion made with the pulp of roasted apples in milk and water, and causes the liberal, foul, and stinking sweats, while the *E*pispastic is on.

" This being evident, it is plain from thence, that the penetrating salts of the fly, that is, the volatile pungent parts of the cantharides, act in the blood by dissolving, attenuating, and rarifying the viscid cohesions of the lymph and serum ; by stimulating the nervous coats of the vessels, throw off their stagnating viscidities, and by cleansing the glands, and forcing out the coagulated serum, restore the circulation and freedom of lymph from the arteries to the veins ; opening, scouring and cleansing at the same time, the expurgatory glands.

In short, as common cathartics purge the guts, and cleanse and throw off their clammy, stagnating, and obstructing contents, by rarifying and dissolving the viscid cohesions of the fluids, and by stimulating the solids ; so do the active salts of the fly penetrate the whole animal machine, become a glandular lymphatic purge, and perform the same thing in all the small straining conveying pipes, that common purgatives effect in the intestines : and as by this means, all the sluices and outlets of the glandular secretions are opened, the cantharides must be cooling, diluting, and refrigerating in their effects to the greatest degree, though so very hot, caustic, and pungent in themselves. So wonderfully has the great Creator provided for his creature, man ; in giving him not only a variety of the most pleasing food, but so fine a medicine, among a thousand others, as the Spanish fly, to save him from the destroying fever, and restore him to health again.   It is not by a discharge of serum, as too many doctors imagine, that a blister relieves, for five times the quantity may be brought off by bleeding, vomiting, or purging ; but the benefit is entirely owing to that heating, attenuating, and pungent salt of this fly, and this fly only, which the divine power and goodness has made a lymphatic purgative, or glandular cathartic for the relief of man, in this fatal and tormenting malady. Vast is our obligation to God for all his providential blessings. Great are the wonders that he doth for the children of men."

Here the Doctor dropt off his chair, just as he had pronounced the word men, and in a moment became a lifeless sordid body. His death was occasioned by the blowing up of his stomach, as I found upon opening his body, at the request of his lady.   When the blood which is confined within the vessels of the human body, is agitated with a due motion, it maintains life ; but if there be a stagnation of it in an artery, it makes an aneurism ; in a vein, a varix ; under the skin, a bruise ; in the nose, it may excite an hæmorrhage ; in the vessels of the brain, an apoplexy ; in the lungs, an hæmoptoe ; in the cavity of the thorax, an empyema ; and when it perfectly stagnates there, immediate death.

An animal, observe me, Reader, must live so long as this fluid circulates through the conical pipes in his body, from the lesser base in the centre, the heart, to the greater in the extreme parts ; and from the capillary evanescent arteries, by the nascent returning veins to the heart again ; but when this fluid ceases to flow through the incurved canals, and the velocities are no longer in the inverse duplicate ratio of the inflated pipes, then it dies. The animal has done for ever with food and sex ; the two great principles which move this world, and produce not only so much honest industry, but so many wars and fightings, such cruel oppressions, and that variety of woes we read of in the tragical history of the world.   Even one of them does wonders.   Cunnus teterrima belli causa.   And when united, the force is irresistible.

But as I was saying, when this fluid ceases to flow, the man has done with lust and hunger.   The pope, the warrior, and the maid, are still.   The machine is at absolute rest, that is, in perfect insensibility ; and the soul of it is removed to the vestibulum or porch of the highest holy place ; in a vehicle, says Wollaston, and Burnet of the Charter-house, as needful to our contact with the material system, as it must exist with a spiritual body, says the Rev. Caleb Fleming, in his *Survey of the Search after Souls*, because of its being present with its Saviour, beholding his glory, who is in human form and figure, which requires some similitude in the vehicle, in order to the more easy and familiar society and enjoyment.   Or, as the learned Master of Peter-house, Dr. Edmund Law, and Dr. Sherlock, bishop of London inform us, it remains insensible for ages, till the consummation of all things ; from the dissolution of the body, is stupid, senseless, and dead asleep till the resurrection.

Such was the case of my friend, Dr. STANVIL ; he dropt down dead at once.   A rarefaction in his stomach, by the heat and fermentation of what he had taken the night before at supper, destroyed him.   That concave viscus, or bowel, which is seated in the abdomen below the diaphragm, I mean the stomach, was inflamed, and as the descending trunk of the aorta passes down between it and the spine, that is, between the stomach and back part of the ribs, the inflation and distention of the bowel compressed and constringed the transverse section of the artery aorta in its descending branch, and by lessening it, impeded the descent of the blood from the heart, and obliged it to ascend in a greater quantity than usual to the head.   By this means, the parts of the head were distended and stretched with blood, which brought on an apoplexy, and the operation upward being violent, the equilibrium was entirely broken, and the vital tide could flow no more.   This I found on opening the body.   I likewise observed that, exclusive of the compressure of the descending trunk of the artery aorta, the muscular coats of the stomach were stretched, inflated, and distended ; and of consequence, the blood-vessels which enter into the constitution of those muscles, were stretched, dilated, and turgid with blood, and therefore the blood could not be driven forward in the course of its circulation with its natural and due velocity, but must prove an

obstacle to the descent of the blood from the heart, and oblige
almost the whole tide to move upwards. This, and the con-
stringing the aorta, at its orifice or transverse section, between
the costæ and the bowel called the stomach, is enough, I assure
you, Reader, to knock up the head of a giant, and put a stop to
all the operations of nature. Thus fell this gentleman in the
thirty-second year of his age.

Whether the learned Dr. Edmund Law,* and the great Dr.
Sherlock † bishop of London, be right, in asserting, the human
soul sleeps like a bat or a swallow, in some cavern for a period,
till the last trumpet awakens Lewis XIV. the hero of Voltaire
and Henault ; to answer for his treachery, falsehood, and cruelty ;
or, whether that excellent divine Mr. Fleming has declared the
truth, in maintaining in his late *Survey*, that the conscious scheme
was the doctrine of Christ and his apostles ; this however is
certain, that my friend STANVIL is either now present with his
Saviour, beholding his glory, in a vehicle resembling the body
of our Lord ; as the dissenter just mentioned teaches ; or if,
according to Archdeacon Law, the author of *Considerations on
the State of the World*, and my Lord of London, in his *Sermons*,
the scriptures take no account of an intermediate state in death,
and we shall not awake or be made alive until the day of judgment ; then will my friend have eternal life at the resurrection ;
he was as worthy a man as ever lived ; an upright Christian
deist, whose life was one unmixed scene of virtue and charity.
He did not believe a tittle of our priestly mysteries, or regard
that religion which skulks behind the enormous columns of consecrated opinions ; but, as Christianity was revealed from heaven,
to bring mankind to the worship of the one supreme God and
governor of the world, and lead them into the paths of humanity,
he rejected the superstition of Monks and their disciples, and
in regard to the voice of reason, and the words of the gospel,
adored only the supreme Being, manifested his love of God by
keeping the commandments, and his love of his neighbour, by
doing all the good in his power. Such a man was Dr. JOHN
STANVIL. If men of fortune would form their manners on such

---

* Notwithstanding all the fine learning of Dr. Law, I think he is mistaken in many of
his notions, and especially in his Notes on Archbishop King's *Origin of Evil* ; as I intend
to shew in my *Notes* aforementioned. His *Tritheism* likewise requires a few animadversions ;
which I shall humbly offer with plainness, fairness, and freedom.
  † Dr. Sherlock, bishop of London, died at Fulham, after a long and lingering illness, Saturday, July 18, 1761, three months after the great and excellent bishop Hoadley, who departed
this life at Chelsea, April 20, 1761. Sherlock and Hoadley never agreed ; and which of
them was right I attempt to shew in my *Notes on Men and Things and Books*. Which will
be published as soon as possible. Why I think Hoadley's *Sermons* far preferable to Sherlock's,
vastly beautiful though some things are in the *Discourses* of the latter ; and that my Lord
of Winchester's *Plain Account of the Supper* is a most rational and fine performance ; as
gold to earth in respect of all that has been written against this book. Why, I say, all
Hoadley's Tracts are matchless and invulnerable, and that he was victor in the Bangorian
controversy, the Reader will find in many considerations on these subjects in the book
called *Notes*, &c. aforementioned.

a model, virtue by degrees would spread through the inferior world, and we should soon be free from superstition.

Having mentioned the sleeping and the conscious schemes, I would here examine these opinions, and shew why I cannot think a dead inconscious silence is to be our case till the consummation of the ages ; as a happiness so remote would weaken I believe the energy and influence of our conceptions and apprehensions, in respect of faith, hope, and expectations. To curb, desire, or suffer severely here, for the sake of truth and virtue, and then cease to be, perhaps for ten thousand years to come, or much longer ; (for there is not any thing in revelation, or an appearance out of it, that can incline a rational man to think he is near the day of judgment or general resurrection ;) this seems to be an obstacle in the progress of the pilgrim. And therefore, why I rather think, we step immediately from the dark experiences of this first state, to a blissful consciousness in the regions of day, and by death are fixed in an eternal connexion with the wise, the virtuous, and the holy ; this, I say, I would in the next place proceed to treat of, by considering what the scriptures reveal in relation to death, and what is most probable in reason ; but that it is necessary to proceed in my story.

When the beautiful Mrs. STANVIL saw her husband was really dead, and had paid that decent tribute of tears to his memory, which was due to a man, who left her in his will all his estates, real and personal, to be by her disposed of as she pleased, she sent for me to her chamber the next morning, and after a long conversation with her, told me, she could now own who she was, and instead of acting any longer by the directions of her head, let me know from her heart, that she had still the same regard for me, as when we travelled away together from her father's house in the West, to the North of England ; and if I would stay at Bassora where I was, but for three months she must be away, she would then return, and her fortune and hand I might command. This I readily consented to, and when the funeral was over she departed. For the time agreed on, I continued in the house, and to a day she was punctual in her return. We were married the week after, and I was even happier than I had ever been before, which must amount to a felicity inconceivably great indeed. Six months we resided at her seat, and then thought it best to pay a visit to my father in Ireland. We arrived at Bagatrogh Castle in the western extremity of that island, in the spring of the year 1735, and were most kindly received.

My father longed to see me, and was very greatly rejoiced at my coming ; but I found him in a dying way, paralytic all over, and scarcely able to speak. To my amazement, he was become as strict a unitarian as myself, and talked with abhorrence of Athanasian religion. This was owing, he said, to my manuscript Remarks which I left with him on Lord Nottingham's *Answer to Whiston's Letter* to his Lordship ; which manuscript of mine he had often read over when I was gone, and thereby was thoroughly convinced, on considering my reasoning, that Christians are expressly commanded, upon pain of God's displeasure, to worship one supreme God, and him only, in the name and through the mediation of Jesus Christ. Upon this religious practice as a fundamental rule he had at last fixed. He saw it was the safe way, and would never depart from it. He told me, the parson of his parish, a right orthodox divine, who had been his chum in the university, and very intimate with him, was greatly troubled at this change in his sentiments, and said many severe things ; but he no more minded the Athanasians now, than he did the idolatrous papists. This gave me great pleasure, and recompensed me for what I had suffered on a religious account. I gave thanks to God that truth through my means had prevailed.

And now my candid Reader, to take my leave of you at this time, I have only to observe, that as this volume is full large, I can only say in a short summary, that soon after my arrival at Bagatrogh Castle, my father's seat on Mall-Bay, on the coast of Galway in Ireland, the old gentleman died, and as in a passion, he had irrevocably settled the greatest part of his large estate on a near relation of mine, and had it not in his power to leave me more than a hundred a year, a little ready money, and a small ship, which lay before his door in the Bay, he descended to the grave in great trouble, with many tears. Like old Isaac over *E*sau, he wept bitterly, and wished in vain, that it was in his power to undo what he had done.

As soon as my father was buried, I returned to *E*ngland with my wife, in the little vessel, now my own, which lay in the Bay, and immediately after landing, and laying up my ship in a safe place, we went to Bassora again, there lived for one year as happy as two mortals could be ; but in the beginning of the year 1736, she died of the small pox, and to divert my mind, it came into my head to go to sea, and make some voyages in my own little ship, which was an excellent one for strength and sailing, though but a sloop of twenty-five tons. I went captain myself, and had an ingenious young gentleman, one JACKMAN, for my mate, who had been in the *E*ast Indies several times, six good hands, and two cabin-boys. *E*very thing necessary, convenient, and fit, books, mathematical instruments, &c. we took on board, and weighed anchor the 5th of July, 1736.

We went on shore at the Canary Islands, the Cape de Verd Islands, and other places. We passed the Sun in 15 degrees North latitude, and from that time standing South, crossed the Line ; the heats intolerable, and the musquitoes and bugs insufferable. We soon lost sight of the Northern star, and had the Crosiers and Magella clouds in view. In three months time we anchored at St. Catharine's on the coast of Brazil. The second of December we saw the Streights la Maine, that run betwixt Terra del Fuego and Staten, and is the boundary between the Atlantic and Pacific oceans ; but instead of venturing into them, and hazarding our lives among the impetuous blasts and waves which sweep round Cape Horn, as Admiral Anson did on the 7th of March, 1741, two months too late, by the fault of the ministry, in his way to the South Seas ; we kept out at sea to the East of Staten-land, and ran to the latitude 64, before we stood to the Westward. The weather was fine, as it was then the height of summer, to wit, in December and January. All the occurrences in this course, the discovery we made in the latitude above-mentioned of an inhabited island, governed by a young Queen, and what appeared and happened there, and in our run from thence to Borneo and Asia, round the globe ; and from China to Europe, on our return home ; with the events we afterwards met with, and the observations I made in other places, the Reader will find in a book called, *The Voyages and Travels of Dr. Lorimer.*

Nine years of my life were spent in travelling and sailing about, and at last I returned to rest and reflect, and in rational amusements pass the remainder of my time away. I retired to a little flowery retreat I had purchased within a few miles of London, that I might easily know what was doing in this hemisphere, while I belong to it ; and in the midst of groves and streams, fields and lawns, have lived as happily ever since, as a mortal can do on this Planet.

Dr. Cheyne by the way, I observe, calls it a ruined Planet, in his wild posthumous book ;* a notion he had from enthusiastic Law,† his master, but from what I have seen on three continents,

---

* It is a question with some, if this book was not written by the Doctor's visionary daughter or by her and the Rev. Athanasian Bigot, her brother. But as I knew the Doctor after he was a little cracked with imaginary religion, and have heard him talk as in this book, I am positive it is his.

† William Law, the father of our Methodists, and the disciple of Jacob Behmen the theosopher, died at King's Cliff near Nottingham, April 13, 1761, seven days before bishop Hoadley, against whom he was a bitter writer in the Bangorian controversy. I knew this famous visionary very well, and shall remark largely on his writings in my *Notes relating to Men and Things and Books.*

Law was the most amazing compound I have ever seen. He was a man of sense, a fine writer, and a fine gentleman ; and yet the wildest enthusiast that ever appeared among men. His temper was charming, sweet, and delightful ; and his manners quite primitive and uncommonly pious : he was all charity and goodness, and so soft and gentle in conversation, that I have thought myself in company with one of the men of the first church at Jerusalem while with him. He had likewise the justest notions of Christian temper and practice, and recommended them in so insinuating a manner, that even a rake would hear him with pleasure. I have not seen any like him among the sons of men in these particulars. It was wrong to put him in the *Dunciad,* and call him one Law, as Pope does. He was really a very extraordinary man ; and to his honour be it remembered, that he had the great concern of human life at heart, took much pains in the pulpit, and from the press, witness his two fine books *On a devout Life :* to make men fear God and keep his commandments. He was a good man indeed.

and in traversing the ocean round the globe, from West to East, and from the Southern latitude 64, to 66 North ; a Planet in reality so divinely made and perfect, that one can never sufficiently adore and praise an infinitely wise God for such a piece of his handy work. A world so wisely contrived, so accurately made, as to demonstrate the Creator's being and attributes, and cause every rational mortal to acknowledge that Jehovah is our God, and fear and obey so great and tremendous a Being the power and glory of our God.

But as I was saying, after my return, I bought a little spot and country-house, where I might rest from my labours, and easily know what is doing in this hemisphere : how gloriously our most gracious and excellent king endeavours to advance the felicity of his people, and promote the honour and dignity of Great Britain : how indefatigable the present ministry is in pursuing such measures, as demonstrate they have the interest of their country at heart ; as evince how well they supply the deficiencies of their predecessors in office ; and how zealously the combined wisdom of the whole legislature acts for the preservation of the Britannic constitution, and the liberties and properties of the people ; that the ends of the late war may be answered, and the peace at last give universal satisfaction.

To hear such news ; and know what France and Spain are doing ; and what the renowned Anti-Sejanus, who deserves the curse and hatred of the whole community as an abetter of arbitrary power, and for attempting to raise the prerogative, is writing ; I purchased a retirement near the capital, a spot surrounded with woods and streams, plants and flowers ; and over which a silence hovers, that gives a relish to still life, and renders it a contrast to the busy, bustling, envious crowds of men.

Here I sat down at last, and have done with hopes and fears for ever.

> " Here grant me, heav'n, to end my peaceful days,
> And pass what's left of life in studious ease ;
> Here court the muses, whilst the sun on high,
> Flames in the vault of heav'n, and fires the sky ;
> Soon as Aurora from her golden bow'rs,
> Exhales the fragrance of the balmy flow'rs,
> Reclin'd in silence on a mossy bed,
> Consult the learned volumes of the dead ;

But what strange books did he write His *Appeal to the Deity*, His *Spirit of Prayer and Love*, His *Earnest and Serious Answer to Trapp*. His notes and Illustrations on Behmen. His Replies to Hoadley ; and what is stranger still, his abuse of bishop Hoadley, in his *Appeal* I have mentioned.

Here, had I room, I would relate a very curious conversation that passed between Dr. Theophilus Bolton, archbishop of Cashell in Ireland, a most excellent, most sensible, and most learned man, and me, on the third night's sale of archbishop King's library in Dublin, in relation to Mr. Law. It happened on his Lordship's buying Jacob Behmen's works for a pound, and then asking me, who stood by him, if I had read them, and could enable him to understand them ? But this I must place in my Notes aforementioned.

Fall'n realms and empires in description view,
Live o'er past times, and build whole worlds anew :
Oft from the bursting tombs, in fancy rise
The sons of Fame, who liv'd in antient days ;
Oft listen till the raptur'd soul takes wings,
While Plato reasons, or while Homer sings.
    Or when the night's dark wings this globe surround,
And the pale moon begins her solemn round ;
When night has drawn her curtains o'er the plain,
And silence reassumes her awful reign ;
Bid my free soul to starry orbs repair,
Those radiant orbs that float in ambient air,
And with a regular confusion stray,
Oblique, direct, along the aërial way :
Fountains of day ! stupendous orbs of light !
Which by their distance lessen to the sight :
And if the glass you use, t' improve your eyes
Millions beyond the former millions rise.
For no end were they made ? Or, but to blaze
Through empty space, and useless spend their rays ?
Or ought we not with reason to reply,
Each lucid point which glows in yonder sky,
Informs a system in the boundless space,
And fills with glory its appointed place :
With beams, unborrow'd, brightens other skies,
And worlds, to thee unknown, with heat and life supplies.
    But chiefly, O my soul, apply to loftier themes,
The opening heav'ns, and angels robed with flames :
Read in the sacred leaves how time began,
And the dust mov'd and quicken'd into man ;
Here through the flow'ry walks of Eden rove,
Court the soft breeze, or range the spicy grove ;
There tread on hallow'd ground where angels trod,
And rev'rend patriarchs talk'd as friends with God ;
Or hear the voice to slumb'ring prophets giv'n,
Or gaze on visions from the throne of heav'n.
    Thus lonely, thoughtful, may I run the race
Of transient life, in no unuseful ease :
Enjoy each hour, nor as it fleets away,
Think life too short, and yet too long the day ;
Of right observant, while my soul attends
Each duty, and makes heav'n and angels friends :
Can welcome death with Faith's expecting eye,
And mind no pangs, since Hope stands smiling by ;
Nor studious how to make a longer stay,
Views heav'nly plains and realms of brighter day ;
Shakes off her load, and wing'd with ardent love,
Spurns at the earth, and springs her flight above,
Soaring through air to realms where angels dwell,
Pities the shrieking fiends, and leaves the lessning hell."

APPENDIX

THE

MYTHOLOGICAL PICTURE OF CEBES

BY THE REV. AND FAMOUS

JEREMY COLLIER

As we were taking a turn in Saturn's temple, we saw a great many consecrated presents, remarkable enough for their curiosity. Amongst the rest, we took particular notice of a picture hung over the door ; the piece we perceived was an emblem and mythology ; but then the representation was so singular and out of custom, that we were perfectly at a loss whence it should come, and what was the meaning of it. Upon a strict view, we found it was neither a city, nor a camp, but a sort of court, with two partitions of the same figure within it, though one of them was larger than the other. The first court had a crowd of people at the gate, and within we saw a great company of women. Just at the entrance of the first gate, there stood an old man, who by his gesture and countenance seemed to be busy in giving advice to the crowd as they came in. And being long at a stand about the design of the fable, a grave man somewhat in years, making up, begins to discourse us in this manner. Gentlemen, says he, I understand you are strangers, and therefore it is no wonder the history of this picture should puzzle you ; for there are not many of our own countrymen that can explain it. For you are to observe, this is none of our town manufacture.* But a long while ago, a certain outlandish man† of great sense and learning, and who by his discourse and behaviour, seemed to be a disciple of Pythagoras and Parmenides ; this gentleman, I say, happened to travel hither, built this structure, and dedicated both the temple and this piece of painting to Saturn. Sir, said I, had you any acquaintance with this gentleman. Yes, says he, I had the benefit of his conversation, and was one of his admirers a long time. For, to my thinking, though he was but young, he talked at a strange significant rate . ‡

N.B. The remainder of Collier's facetious version is omitted for want of room.

---

* The Greek words which Collier renders town-manufacture, are πολιτικον αναθημα.
† And what he calls outlandish, is αξενος.
‡ The Greek is, διελεγετο πολλα και σωουδαια.

TABLE OF CEBES

A DIALOGUE

BETWEEN AN OLD MAN AND A TRAVELLER

While we were walking in the temple of Saturn, in the city of Thebes, and viewing the votive honours of the God, the various offerings which had been presented to that deity, we observed at the entrance of the Fane, a picture tablet that engaged our attention, as it was a thing entirely new, both with regard to the painting and the design. For some time, we stood considering the device and fable, but still found ourselves unable to guess the meaning. The piece did not seem to be either a city or a camp ; but was a kind of a walled court, that had within it two other inclosures, and one of them was larger than the other. The first court opened at a gate, before which a vast crowd of people appeared, impatient to enter ; and within a group of female figures was represented. Stationed at the porch without, was seen a venerable form, who looked like some great teacher, and seemed to warn the rushing multitude. Long we gazed at this work, but were not able to understand the design, till an old man came up to us, and spoke in the following manner.

§ 1. *O.* It is no wonder strangers, that you cannot comprehend this picture : for even our inhabitants are not able to give a solution of the allegoric scene. The piece is not an offering of any of our citizens, but the work of a foreigner, a man of great learning and virtue, and a zealous disciple of the Samian or Elean sages, who arrived here many years ago, and by his conversation instructed us in the best learning, which is morality. It was he built and consecrated this temple to Saturn, and placed here this picture you see before you.

T. And did you know (I said) and converse with this wise man ?

O. Yes, (he replied) I was long acquainted with him, and as he was but young, and talked with great judgment upon the most important subjects, with astonishment I have listened to him, and with pleasure heard him explain the moral of this fable.

T. Expound to us then, (I conjure you) the meaning of the picture, if business does not call you away ; for we long to be instructed in the design of the piece.

O. I am at leisure, (the old man answered) and willingly consent to your request ; but I must inform you first, there is some danger in what you ask. If you hearken with attention, and by consideration understand the precepts, you will become wise, virtuous and blest :* if otherwise, you will be abandoned, blind, and miserable.† The explanation of the picture resembles the enigma of the Sphinx, which she proposed to every passenger that came that way. If they could expound the riddle they were safe ; but if they failed in the attempt, they were destroyed by the monster.‡ Folly is as it were a Sphinx to mankind. She asks you, How is good and ill defined ? If you cannot explain the problem, and happen to misjudge, you perish by degrees, and become the victim of her cruelty. You do not die immediately, as the unhappy did by the Theban monster ; but by the force and operation of folly, you will find yourself dying from day to day, your rational part wounded and decayed, every noble power of the soul confounded, and like those given up to punishment for life, feel the last of those pangs, which guilt prepares for the stupid ; but if by thinking, you can understand and discern the boundaries of good and ill, then Folly like the Sphinx must perish, and your life will be blest with happiness and serenity. Hear me then with all your attention.

These things being previously observed by the old man, and we intreating him to begin, he lifted up a wand he held, and pointing to the picture, said, the first inclosure represents human life, and the multitude at the gate, those who are daily entering into the world. That aged person you see on an eminence, directing with one hand, and holding in the other a roll, which is the code of reason, is the genius of mankind ; benevolent, he seems to bend, and teach the people what they ought to do ; shews them as they enter into life the path they ought to take ; the way which leads to danger, and that which bears to safety and happiness.

T. And which is the way, (I said) and how are they to find it ?

O. That you shall know hereafter : but at present you must take notice of that painted woman seated on a throne very near the gate. She is called Delusion, and by every art, with fawn and soft infection, presents a bowl of ignorance and error to all that enter into life. They take the cup, and in proportion to what

---

* Εσεσθε φ*ζ*ονιμοι και ευδαιμονες.
† αφρονες, και κακοδαιμονες, και ωικροι, και αμαθεις.
‡ This monster, who lived near Thebes, was said to be the daughter of Typhon and Echidna, and had a head and face like a girl, wings like a bird, and in the rest like a dog.

they have drank of the intoxicating mixture, are lead away by the women you see, at a little distance from Imposture, to destruction some, and some to safety ; less erring and less blind those being who have but tasted of Delusion's cup.

These women so variously drest, and so profusely gay, are called the Opinions, Desires, and Pleasures. You observe how they embrace each mortal as he arrives within the gate, promise the greatest blessings, and compel their votaries to wander with them where they please.

T. But who (I asked) is that woman placed on a globe, who appears not only blind, but seems to be wild and distracted ? Incessantly she walks about, and flings her favours capriciously. From some she snatches their effects and possessions, and bestows them upon others.

O. They call her Fortune (replied the old man). Her attitude marks her character. Her gifts are as unstable as her tottering ball ; and all who depend upon her specious promises, are deceived when most they trust her, and find themselves exposed to the greatest misfortunes.

T. There is a great crowd I perceive surrounding her, and if too commonly she meditates mischief, whenever she smiles, what is the meaning of their attendance.

O. These are the inconsiderate, and stand there to catch the toys she blindly scatters among them ; (wealth, fame, titles, an offspring, strength or beauty, the victor's laurel and arbitrary power). Those who rejoice, and are lavish in their praises of this divinity, have received some favours from her, and call her the goddess of good fortune. But those whom you see weeping and wringing their hands, are such whom she has deprived of every good ; they curse her as the goddess of ill-fortune.

T. But (replied I) as to riches, glory, nobility, a numerous posterity, power, and honour, which you called toys, why are they not real advantages ?

O. Of these things (our instructor answered) we shall speak hereafter more fully. At present it is better to continue the explication of the picture.

§ 2. Cast your eyes next then on that higher inclosure, (proceeded the old man) and take notice of the women on the outside thereof. You observe how wantonly they are drest. The first of them is Incontinence, loosely zoned, her bosom bare ; and the other three are, Riot, Covetousness, and Flattery. They watch for the favourites of fortune. You see they caress them, and try to bring them to the pleasures of their soft retreat ; where the bowl sparkles, the song resounds, and joys to joys succeed in every jocund hour. But at length Distress appears, and the favourite of a day discovers, that his happiness was merely imaginary—under a delusion ; but the evils that attend his pleasures real. When

he has wasted all he had received from fortune, he is forced to
enter himself into the service of those mistresses, and by them
compelled to dare the foulest and most desperate deeds ; villain
and knave he becomes ; stabs for a purse ; his country sells for
gold ; and by deceit and sacrilege, by perjury, treachery, and
theft, endeavours for some time to live.   But shiftless at length,
and unable to acquire support by crimes, they are consigned to the
dire gripe of Punishment.

T. What is she, I beg you will inform us ?

O. Look beyond those women, called the Opinions, (continued
the old man) and you will see a low gate, opening into a dark and
narrow cave : you may observe at the entrance of it, three female
figures very swarthy and foul, covered with rags and filthiness ;
and near them, standing naked by their side, a frightful lean
man.*   Close to him is another woman, so meagre and ghastly you
perceive, that it is not possible for any thing to resemble him
more.

T. We see them, and request to be informed who they are ?

O. The first with a whip in her hand, is Punishment, and next
to her sits Sadness, with her head reclining on her knees ; that
woman tearing her hair is Trouble ; the naked lean man is Sorrow,
and the image by his side wild Despair.   You see they are all
going to seize the unhappy man of pleasure, and make him feel
the greatest pain and anguish.   For they carry him to the house
of Misery, and in the pit of Woe he is to pass the remainder of
life, unless Repentance comes to his relief.

T. And what then follows, (I said) if Repentance interposes ?

O. She rescues him from his tormentors, and gives a new view
of things.   He has from her some account of true learning, but
the hint so short, that it may lead him likewise to false learning.
If he be so happy as to understand, and chuse right, he is delivered
from prejudice and error, and passes the rest of his days in tranquillity and peace : but if he be mistaken, instead of wisdom, he
only gains that amusing counterfeit, which turns him from vices
to studious folly.

T. Great (I replied) are the risks we mortals run.   But who
is this false learning ?

§ 3. *O.* At the entrance of the second inclosure,† you may observe a woman neatly drest, and of a good appearance ; decent
the port,—spotless the form.   This is the counterfeit, but the
vulgar call her true learning.   Even the happy few, who succeed
in the pursuit of wisdom, are commonly detained too long by this
deceiving fair one.   Nor is it strange ; for, skilled as she is in all
the learning, and in every art can grace the head, you see what

* This man Collier calls, an ill-looking skeleton of a fellow, with scarce a tatter to his limbs
Cant ! The Greek is, τις δυσειδης λεπτος, και γυμνος.

† The three inclosures in Cebes, allude to the division of human life into the sensual, the
studious, and the virtuous.

crowds of admirers she has ; poets, orators, logicians, musicians, arithmeticians, geometricians, astrologers, and critics.

T. But who, (I asked my instructor) are those women, so busy on every side, and so earnest in their addresses to this company ? They look like Incontinence and her companions, and the opinions whom you shewed us in the first court. Do they also frequent the second inclosure ?

O. Yes, (replied the old man) Incontinence is sometimes seen here. The opinions do likewise enter ; for the early portion these men received from Imposture still operates. Ignorance finds a place here ; and even *Extravagance* and Folly. They remain under the power of these, till having left false learning, they enter upon the path that leads to Wisdom. When they arrive at the enlightened ground of Truth, they get her sovereign remedy,* and are freed from the ill effects of Ignorance and *Error.* This enables them to throw off the wild hypothesis, the learned romance, and to employ the precious hours of life in thinking to the wisest purposes. Had they staid with false learning, they never could have delivered themselves from these evils.

T. Proceed then, I pray you, (said I) and shew us the way that leads to Happiness and Wisdom.

§ 4. *O.* Do you see (proceeded the venerable man,) that rising ground, which appears so desert and uninhabited. You may observe upon it a little gate, that opens in a narrow and unfrequented path ; the avenue a rugged rocky way. You perceive a little onward, a steep and craggy mountain with precipices on either side, which sink to a frightful depth. This is the way to Wisdom.

T. It seems a dreadful way, as painted in this table.

O. Yet higher still observe that rock, towards the mountain's brow, and take notice of the two figures which sit upon its edge, and appear to be as beautiful and comely as the goddess of health. They are sisters ; Temperance the one, Patience the other. With friendship in their looks, and arms protended over the verge of the cliff, you see them lean, to encourage those who pass this way, and rouze the spirits of the fainting sons of Wisdom, who has stationed these two sisters there. They urge the brave men on ; tell them the hardships will lessen by degrees, the passage will become more easy and agreeable as they advance, and offer them their assistance

---

* Collier translates it,—they enter into a course of physic. The Greek is, και πιωςι την καθαρτικην δυαμιν τουτων. And what Collier a little before translates, " She opens a vein, and gives them a glass of her constitution: " when they have taken the stirrup cup ; brimmers: the lasses frisk about : salute with a deal of welcome, and then lug them off, some to ruin, and some to the gallows." All this, and much more night-cellar stuff, the Theban philosopher had not an idea of, as any one may see who can turn to the Greeks. How Collier learned such guard-phrases, and why he used them, seemed for some time very strange to me, till I was informed by one who knew this divine well, that in the days of his youth he kept very low company, and was known at several night-houses. In that period of his life, he translated Cebes. ˉ

to ascend the summit, and reach the top of the rock. That being gained, they shew them the easiness and pleasantness of the rest of the way to wisdom : the charming road invites one's eyes : how smooth and flowery, green and delightful, does it appear !

T. It does indeed.

§ 5. *O.* Look next (the excellent old man continued) at that distant blooming wood, and near it you will see a beautiful meadow, on which there seems to fall a light as from a purer heaven, a kind of double day. In this lightsome field,* you may perceive a gate which opens into another inclosure, which is the abode of the blessed. Here the Virtues dwell with Happiness. In this region of eternal beauty, the righteous rest.

T. It does appear a charming place.

O. Observe then near the portal, a beauteous form of a composed aspect : She seems mature in life, and her robe is quite plain, without affectation or ornaments. Her eyes are piercing ; her mien sedate : she stands not on a globe, like Fortune, but upon a cube of marble, fixed as the rock she is on before the gate. You see on either side of her two lovely nymphs, the very copies of her looks and air. This matron in the middle is true learning, Wisdom herself ; and the two young beauties are Truth and Persuasion. Her standing on a square, is an expressive type of certainty in the way to her ;† and denotes the unalterable and permanent nature of the blessings she bestows on those who come to her. From her they receive courage and serenity ; that confidence and contempt of fear, which exempts the happy possessors from any disturbance, by the accidents and calamities of life.

T. These are valuable gifts. But why without the walls does Wisdom stand ?

O. To present the purifying bowl to those who approach, and restore them to themselves. As a physician by degrees first fiuds out the cause of a violent disorder, and then removes it, in order to restore the man to health ; so Wisdom, as she knows their malady administers her sovereign medicine, and frees them from all their evils. She expels the mischiefs they had received from delusion, their ignorance and error, and delivers them from pride, lust, anger, avarice, and all the other vices they had contracted in the first inclosure. In a word, she restores them to sanity, and then sends them in to Happiness and the Virtues.

T. Who are they ? (I said).

§ 6. *O.* Do you not see within the gate, (my instructor replied) a society of matrons, beautiful and modest, drest, unaffected, and without any thing of the gay excess ? These are Science and her sisters, Fortitude, Justice, and Integrity, Temperance,

* Δειμωροειδής, καὶ φωτὶ πολλῷ καταλαμπόμενος.
† Καθεστηκυῖα τὸ πρόσωπον, *constanti vultu*, or *constans vultum*.

Modesty, Liberality, Continence, Clemency, and Patience. They hail their guests, and the company seem to be in raptures.

T. But when the friends to virtue are admitted into this charming society, where do they lead them to ?

O. See you not (resumed the good old man,) the hill beyond the grove ; that eminence which is the highest point of all the inclosures, and commands a boundless prospect. There, on a glorious throne, you may observe a majestic person in her bloom, well drest, but without art or lavish cost, and her temples adorned with a beautiful tiar : this is Happiness, the regent of that blessed abode, and as the moral heroes approach her, you may perceive her, with the Virtues who stand assistant round her, going to reward the friends of wisdom with such crowns as are bestowed on conquerors.

T. Conquerors ! (I said) In what conflicts have these persons been victorious ?

O. They have, in their way to the realm of Happiness, destroyed the most formidable and dangerous monsters, who would have destroyed them, if they had not been subdued ; these savage beasts at war with man are, ignorance and error ; grief, vexation, avarice, intemperance, and every thing that is evil. These are vanquished and have lost all their power. The moral hero triumphs now, though their slave before.

T. Great achievements indeed ! A glorious conquest. But exclusive of the honour of being crowned by Happiness and the Virtues, is there any salutary power in the crown that adorns the hero's head ?

O. There is, young man. The virtue of it is great. Possessing this, he is happy and blessed. He derives his felicity from no external object, but from himself alone.

T. O happy victory ! And being thus crowned, what does the hero do, where next his steps ?

O. Conducted by the Virtues, he goes back to survey his first abode, and see the crowd he left ; how miserably they pass their time ; waste all their hours in crimes, and in the whirl of passions live. Slaves to ambition, pride, incontinence, vanity, and avarice they appear tormented with endless anxiety. They have forgot the instructions the good genius gave them, at their entrance into life, and suffer thus because they cannot find the way to Wisdom.

T. True : (I said) But I cannot comprehend, why the Virtues should bring the heroes back to the place they came from : why should they return to view a well-known scene ?

O. The reason (answered my instructor) is, because they had not a true idea what they had seen. Surrounded by a confusion of things as they passed on, they could not distinctly perceive what was done. The mists of ignorance and error obscured the prospect as they journeyed on, and by that means, they were subject to mistakes. They could not always distinguish between good and evil. But now that they have attained to true learning, with concern they behold the mad world the virtues shew them again, and being enlightened by wisdom, are perfectly happy in themselves. The misery of the numberless fools they behold now, strikes them very strongly, and gives them a delightful relish for their present happiness.

T. It must be so. And when they have seen these things, where do they then go ?

O. Wherever they please. Safely they may travel where they will : in all times, and in all places they are secure, as their integrity is their defence. Every where they live esteemed and beloved by all. The female monsters I have mentioned, Grief, Trouble Lust, Avarice, or Poverty, have now no power to hurt them ; but as if possessed of some virtuous drug, they can grasp the viper, and defy destruction.

T. What you say is just. But who are all these persons descending the hill ?

O. Those that are crowned (the old man said) are the happy few I have described. You see what joy is in their faces : and those who seem forlorn and desperate, under the command of certain women, are such who by their folly have not found the way to true learning ; or stopping at the rough and narrow ascent you observed, went to look for an easier path, and so quite lost the road. The tormentors who drive them on are, Trouble, Despair, Ignominy, and Ignorance. Wretched you see them return into the first inclosure, to Luxury and Incontinence ; and yet they do not accuse themselves as the authors of their own ruin, which is very strange ; but rail at Wisdom, and revile her ways ; asserting, that the true pleasures of life are only to be found in luxury and riot. Like the brutes, they place the whole satisfaction of man in the gratification of sensual appetite.

T. But who are those other lovely women, who return down the hill so full of gaiety and mirth ?

O. They are the Opinions, who having conducted the virtuous to the region of light, are coming back to invite and carry others thither, by shewing them the felicity and success of those they brought to the mansion of Wisdom.

T. And do the Opinions never enter with those they bring into that happy place, where the virtues and true learning reside ?

O. No : Opinion can never reach to science ; they only deliver their charge into the hands of Wisdom, and then, like ships that give up their lading, in order to sail for a new cargo, they return to bring other *E*leves to reason and felicity.

T. This explanation of the table (I said) is quite satisfactory : but you have not yet informed us, what the good genius bids the multitude do, as they appear on the verge of life ?

O. He charges them to act with courage and be magnanimous and brave in all events ; a thing I recommend to you, young man ; and that you may have a true idea of this, I will tell you what I mean by a bold spirit in passing through this world.

§ 7. *O.* Then lifting up his arm again, and pointing with his wand to a figure in the picture ; that blind woman standing on a globe, as I told you before, is Fortune. The genius forbids us to trust her, or imagine her smiles will be lasting happiness. Reason is never concerned in what she does. It is Fortune still ; without principle she acts, is arbitrary and capricious, and inconsiderately and rashly for ever proceeds. Regard not then her favours, nor mind her frowns : but as she gives and takes away, and often deprives of what we had before, we are neither to esteem or despise her ; but if we should receive from her a gift, take care to employ it immediately to some good purpose, and especially in the acquisition of true science, the most lasting and precious possession. If we act otherwise, in respect of Fortune, we imitate those wretched usurers, who rejoice at the money paid in to them, as if they received it for their own use ; but pay it back with regret, forgetting the condition, that it was to be returned to the proprietor on demand. Regardless of Fortune then, and all her changes in this mortal life, the genius advises to pass bravely on, without hearkening to the solicitations of Incontinence and Luxury in the first inclosure, to reject their temptations, and go on to false learning : with her he would have us make a short stay, to learn what may be of service to us in our journey to wisdom. This is the advice of the genius to those who enter into life.

T. Here the good old man had done, and I thanked him for his explanation of the picture. Only one thing (I said) there was more, which I must request he would tell me the meaning of. What is it we can get by our stay with false learning ?

O. Things (he answered) that may be of use to us. The languages and other parts of education, which Plato recommends, may hinder us from being worse employed, and keep us from illicit gratification. They are not absolutely necessary to true happiness ; but they contribute to make us better. Something good and useful they do afford ; though virtue, which ought to be the principal business in view may be acquired without them. We may become wise without the assistance of the arts, though (as observed before), they are far from being useless : as by a good translation made into our own tongue, we may know what an author means, and yet by taking the pains to become masters of the original language, might gain many advantages, such as entering better into the writer's sense, and discovering some beauties which cannot otherwise be found : so the useful things in the sciences may be very quickly and easily learned, and

Q

though by great labour in becoming accurately acquainted with them, we might fill our heads with speculations, yet this cannot make us the wiser and better men. Without being learned, we may be wise and good.

T. And are the learned then in no better a condition than the people in respect of moral excellence ? (I said). Are the speculations of the scholar, and the arts and fine inventions of the schools, of no use in perfecting the moral character ? This to me seems a little strange.

O. Blind as the crowd is the men of letters, in this particular (my instructor replied) : all his studies and curious knowledge have no relation to his living right. With all the tongues, and all the arts, he may be a libertine, a sot, a miser, or a knave, a traitor to his country, and have no moral character at all. This we see every day.

T. But what is the cause of so strange a thing, I requested to know ? I observe that these men of letters seem to sit down contented in the second inclosure, and do not attempt to go on to the third, where Wisdom resides ; though they see continually before their eyes so many passing on from the first court, where they had lived, for some time in lewdness and excess, to the habitation of true learning.

O. It is their remaining in this second inclosure, that occasions their being inferior in moral things to those who have not had a learned education. Proud and self-sufficient on account of their languages, arts, and sciences, they despise what Wisdom could teach them, and will not give themselves the trouble of ascending with difficulty to the mansion of true learning. They have no taste for the lessons of Wisdom ; while the humble mount to her exalted dwelling, those scholars, as you see, are satisfied with their speculations and vain conceits. Dull and untractable in the improvement of their hearts, and regardless of that exact rectitude of mind and life, which is only worth a rational's toiling for (as he is an *E*leve for eternity), they never think of true wisdom, nor mind her offered light. Their curious ingenious notions, are what they only have a relish for ; the imaginations of those men of letters cannot reach that ineffable peace and contentment, that satisfaction and pleasure, which flow from a virtuous life and an honest heart. This is the case of our learned heads, unless repentance interferes to make them humble, and scatters the vain visions they had from false opinion.

This, concluded the venerable teacher, is the explication of this parable or allegory. May you oft revolve upon these lessons and lend your whole attention to the attainment of true wisdom, that you may not embrace the shadow, the speculations and inventions of the learned, but, by this instruction, acquire the true principles of morality and goodness.

This is not all the Table of Cebes. There follows a disputation in the Socratic method concerning the claim of wealth, and other externals, to the title of good things : but it is dry, and no part of the picture or mythology. For this reason I stop here.

As to the picture of Cebes, it is to be sure a fine thing, and greatly to the honour of the Theban philosopher, who was one of the disciples of Socrates ; and about twenty at the time of the death of his master : Socrates died by the executioner, in the 70 year of his age, before our Lord 402. Cebes was about eighty, at the birth of Epicurus.

But after all that can be said in praise of this excellent remain of antiquity, still the little system of ethics is but a poor performance, in respect of any section of the gospel of Christ. Cebes says nothing of the Deity : nor does he mention the mischiefs of vice, and the benefits of virtue, as a divine constitution.

An Apostle, on the contrary, (to mention only one particular out of a thousand from the Christian books,) calls to the human race in the following manner : " I beseech you, brethren, by the mercies of Almighty God, the Father of the Universe, who hath graciously admitted you to the faith, and revealed the terms of acceptance ; that ye present your bodies now a living sacrifice, holy and acceptable to the Deity, which is the reasonable and spiritual service required of you in the time of the gospel ; and not offer the bodies of beasts any more as the Heathen world were wont to do.

" And, as persons now wholly devoted to the Lord of heaven and earth, be not conformed to the fashions and ways of this world ; but be ye transformed by the renewing of your mind ; that ye may prove what is the good, the acceptable, and perfect will of God. Abhor that which is evil, in all your dealings : cleave to that which is good : let love be without dis-simulation ; and be kindly affectioned one to another ; not advancing, but in honour pre-ferring one another. Be not slothful in business, but fervent in spirit ; as serving the Lord Jehovah in your several stations. Rejoice in hope of a refreshment to come, in the real. ·s of bliss : be patient in tribulation, which God will reward and continue instant in prayer.

" In sum, let us follow the steps of Christ, and in imitation of his divine humility, his devo-tion, his love, be for ever meek and forbearing, gentle and charitable, and live in the spirit of prayer."

What is there in the Table of Cebes like this spiritual and religious virtue, this love to God, this zeal for his honour and service, and an entire dependence upon him in all conditions of life ? The virtues of the heroes of antiquity are noble and excellent qualities ; their courage, and justice, and temperance, and gratitude, and love to their country are fine things : but they seem to have been calculated for the civil life. Those heroes were virtuous without being pious, and appear rather as self-sufficient independent beings, than as servants and votaries of God Almighty. It is these Christian virtues I have mentioned, that adorn and perfect human nature. It is these things that mostly contribute to the happiness of the world, and of every man in it.

N. B. Scott, at the end of his Notes on Cebes, has the following remark. If this philosopher had represented the effects of virtue and vice as a divine constitution, he would have ennobled his instruction, and done greater service to the interests of morality. But those important interests are effectually provided for by revelation. There the precepts of virtue are the law; of God. There we find a clear and complete system of his will. There our obedience is encouraged by hope in his pardoning mercy and powerful assistance, by the life, death, and resurrection of his own son ; and by promises and threatnings which extend the reward of righteousness, and the punishment of wickedness unto a future state of existence.

No. II.

THE TENTH SATIRE * OF JUVENAL.

Survey mankind, muster the herd
From smoothest chin to deepest beard ;
Search ev'ry climate, view each nation,
From lowest to the highest station ;
From Eastern to the Western Indies,
From frozen Poles to th' line that singes ;
Scarce will you find one mortal wight,
Knows good from ill, or wrong from right :
'Cause clouds of lust and passion blind,
And bribe with interests the mind ;
And while they combat in our heart,
Our fondness crowns the conqu'ring part.
What is the thing under the sun,

---

* The design of this fine Satire is to shew, that endowments and blessings of the mind, as wisdom, virtue, justice, and integrity of life are the only things worth praying for.

That we with reason seek or shun?
Or justly by our judgment weigh'd,
Should make us fond of, or afraid?
Whate'er is luckily begun,
Brings sure repentance at long-run.
The distant object looming great,
Possest proves oft an empty cheat;
And he who wins the wish'd-for prize,
A trouble often dearly buys.
Some for their family importune,
And beg their ruin for a fortune.
The courteous gods granting their prayers,
Have intail'd curses on their heirs.
Of wizards some inquire their doom,
Greedy to know events to come,
And by their over caution run
On the same fate they strove to shun:
Some have petition'd to be great,
And eminent in church and state.
This in the war's a famous leader,
T'other at bar a cunning pleader,
The cause on either side insure you,
By dint of noise stun judge and jury:
And if business won't bear water,
Banter and perplex the matter.
But their obstrep'rous eloquence
Has fail'd ev'n in their own defence:
And saving others by haranguing,
Have brought themselves at last to hanging.
Milo presuming on his strength,
Caus'd his own destiny at length.
　　The greedy care of heaping wealth,
Damns many a soul and ruins health,
And in an apoplectic fit,
Sinks them downright into the pit.
How many upstarts crept from low
Condition, vast possessions show?
Whose estate's audit so immense
Exceeds all prodigal expence.
With which compare that spot of earth,
To which these mushrooms owe their birth:
Their manners to dad's cottage show,
As Greenland whales to dolphins do.
　　In Nero's plotting dismal times,
Riches were judg'd sufficient crimes.
First swear them traitors to the state,
Then for their pains share their estate.
Fat forfeitures their toils reward:
Poor rogues may pass without regard.
Some are hook'd in for sense and wit,
And some condemn'd for want of it.
The over-rich Longinus dies,
His bright heaps dazzled envious eyes
Neither could philosophy,
Wisdom, desert, or piety,
Rich Seneca from his pupil save,
'Tis fit he send him to a grave,
And then resume the wealth he gave.
　　The guards the palaces beset,
For noble game they pitch their net:

While from alarms and pangs of fear,
Securely sleeps the cottager.
If you by night shall happen late,
To travel with a charge of plate ;
With watchful eyes and panting heart,
Surpriz'd, each object makes you start :
While rack'd with doubts, opprest with fear,
Each bush does an arm'd thief appear :
A shaken reed will terror strike,
Mistaken for a brandish'd pike.
Before the thief, the empty clown *
Sings unconcern'd and travels on
    With warm petitions most men ply
The gods, their bags may multiply ;
That riches may grow high and rank,
Outswelling others in the bank.
But from plain wood and earthen cups,
No poison'd draught the peasant sups.
Of the gold goblet take thou care,
When sparkling wine's spic'd by thy heir :
Then who can blame that brace of wise men,
That in diff'ring moods despise men :
Th' old merry lad saunters the streets
And laughs, and drolls at all he meets :
For pastime rallies, flouts, and fools 'em,
Shams, banters, mimics, ridicules 'em.
The other sage in maudling wise,
Their errors mourns with weeping eyes.
Dull fools with ease can grin and sneer,
And buffoons flout with saucy jeer.
What source could constant tears supply,
To feed the sluices of each eye ;
Or t'others merry humour make,
His spleen continually to shake ?
Could he in sober honest times
With sharp conceit tax petty crimes :
And every where amongst the rout,
Find follies for his wit to flout ; †
Which proves that Gotham and gross climes,
Produce prodigious wits sometimes.
The joys and fears of the vain crowd,
And whimp'ring tears he'd jeer aloud ;
Wisely secure, fortune deride,
By foppish mortals deified :
Bid her be hang'd, and laugh at fate,
When threat'ned at the highest rate ;

* The Latin of these two lines is—
        Cantabit vacuus coram latrone viator.
Which Dryden translates thus :
        The beggar sings, ev'n when he sees the place
        Beset with thieves, and never mends his pace.
Shadwell, who was Poet Laureate in King William's time, does it thus :
        While the poor man, void of all precious things,
        In company of thieves, jogs on and sings.
Barton Holiday thus :
        Before the thief, who travels empty, sings.
And Stapylton thus :
        The poor wayfaring man, that doth not bring
        A charge along, before the thief will sing.
† Juvenal here means Democritus.

Whilst fools for vain and hurtful things,
Pour out their prayers and offerings,
Fast'ning petitions on the knees,*
Of their regardless deities.
   For place and power, how many men vie,
Procuring mortal hate and envy ;
Heralds long-winded titles sound,
Which the vain owners oft confound.
Down go their statues in disgrace ;
The party hangs up in the place.
In rage they break chariot triumphant,
Because a knave 'fore set his rump on't :
Poor horses suffer for no fault,
Unless by bungling workmen wrought.
The founder's furnace grows red hot,
Sejanus' statue goes to pot :
That head lately ador'd, and reckon'd
In all th' universe the second,
Melted, new forms and shapes assumes,
Of p—pots, frying-pans, and spoons.†
The crowd o'erjoyed that Cæsar's living,
Petition for a new thanksgiving ;
How the base rout insult to see
Sejanus dragg'd to destiny.‡
   Would you on these conditions, Sir,
Be favourite and prime minister,
As was Sejanus ? Stand possest
Of honours, power, and interest ;
Dispose supreme commands at will,
Promote, disgrace, preserve, or kill;
Have foot and horse-guards, the command
Of armies both by sea and land.
Had you not better ask in prayer,
To be some petty country mayor ;
There domineer, and when your pleasure's

* The Latin of these two lines is—
    Propter quæ fas est genua incerare deorum.
Which Dryden does not translate at all.   His lines are—
    He laughs at all the vulgar cares and fears :
    At their vain triumphs, and their vainer tears :
    An equal temper in his mind he found,
    When Fortune flatter'd him, and when she frown'd :
    ' Tis plain from hence that what our vows request,
    Are hurtful things, or useless at the best.

† Dryden's translation of this passage is thus :
    Sejanus, almost first of Roman names,
    The great Sejanus, crackles in the flames :
    Form'd in the forge, the pliant brass is laid
    On anvils. And of head and limbs are made,
    Pans, cans, and piss-pots, a whole kitchen trade.
The Latin is :
    Jam strident ignes, jam follibus atque caminis
    Ardet adoratum populo caput, et crepat ingens
    Sejanus. Deinde ex facie toto orbe secunda
    Fiunt urceoli, pelves, sartago, patellæ.
‡ Sejanus, the vile minister of Tiberius, was executed by order of the Emperor, A.D. 31, and to prevent his suspecting any such thing, and providing against the calamity, which the favourite might easily have done, as he commanded the Prætorians, and had all power given him, his master named him his colleague in the consulship ; which of all things Sejanus most desired, and thought the highest mark of his sovereign's affection. So true it is that we know not what we wish for.

Condemn light weights, break false measures ;
Though meanly clad in safe estate,
Than chuse Sejanus' robes and fate ?
Sejanus then, we must conclude,
Courting his bane, mistook the good,
Crassus and Pompey's fate of old,
The truth of this sure maxim told :
And his who first bow'd Rome's stiff neck,
And made the world obey his beck.*
   The novice in his accidence,
Dares pray his wit and eloquence
May rival Roman Cicero's fame,
And Greek Demosthenes' high name :
Yet to both these their swelling vein
Of wit and fancy prov'd their bane.
No pleading dunce's jobbernowl
Revenge e'er doom'd to grace a pole.
   The trophies which the vanquish'd field
Do to the glorious victors yield,
Triumphant conquerors can bless,
With more than human happiness :
This, Roman, Grecian, and barbarian,
Spurr'd to acts hazardous and daring ;
In sweat and blood spending their days,
For empty fame, and fading bays.
'Tis the immoderate thirst of fame
Much more than virtue does inflame :
Which none for worse or better take,
But for her dower and trappings' sake.
The fond ambition of a few,
Many vast empires overthrew ;
While their achievements with their dust,
They vainly to their tombstones trust.
For sepulchres like bodies lie,
Swallow'd in death's obscurity.†
   Behold how small an urn contains
The mighty Hannibal's remains :
That hero whose vast swelling mind
To Afric could not be confin'd :
Nature's impediments he past,
And came to Italy at last :
There, after towns and battles won,
He cries, comrades, there's nothing done,
Unless our conqu'ring powers
Break down Rome's gates, level her towers,

* Julius Cæsar, who acquired the sovereign sway by art and slaughter, and when a tyrant
fell by his own desires.
† The Latin of this passage, which is truly beautiful, is :
               Et laudis titulique Cupido
   Hæsuri saxis cinerum custodibus : ad quæ
   Discutienda valent sterilis mala robora ficus :
   Quandoquidem data sunt ipsis quoque fata sepulchris.
Which Dryden renders in the following manner :
     This avarice of praise in times to come,
     Those long inscriptions crowded on the tomb,
     Should some wild fig-tree take her native bent,
     And heave below the gaudy monument,
     Would crack the marble titles, and disperse
     The characters of all the lying verse.
     For sepulchres themselves must crumbling fall
     In time's abyss, the common grave of all.

Root up her posts, and break her chains,
And knock out all opposers' brains :
Whilst our troops scour the city thorough,
And fix our standard in Saburra.*
But what catastrophe of fate,
His conduct's baffled, army's broke,
Carthage puts upon the Roman yoke :
Whilst flight and banishment's his fate,
His ruin'd country's scorn and hate.
Go, madman, act thy frantic part,
Climb horrid Alps, with pains and art,
Go, madman, to be with mighty reputation,
The subject of a declamation.†
    One world's too mean, a trifling thing,
For the young Macedonian king ;
He raves like one in banishment,
In narrow craggy island pent :
In one poor globe does sweat and squeeze,
Wedg'd in and crampt in little-ease.
But he who human race once scorn'd,
And said high Jove King Philip horn'd,
While manag'd oracles declare
The spark great Ammon's son and heir ;
At Babylon, for all his huffing,
Finds ample room in narrow coffin.
Man swells with bombast of inventions,
When stript, death shews his true dimensions.
    So do we read wild Xerxes rent
Mount Athos from the continent,
And in a frolic made a shift,
To set it in the sea adrift :
With ships pav'd o'er the Hellespont,
And built a floating bridge upon't :
Drove chariots o'er by this device,
As coaches ran upon the ice.
He led so numberless a rout,
As at one meal drank rivers out.
This tyrant we in story find,
Was us'd to whip and flog the wind ;
Their jailor Eolus in prison,
Ne'er forc'd them with so little reason :
Nor could blue Neptune's godhead save him,
But he with fetters must enslave him.
Yet after all these roaring freaks,
Routed and broke he homeward sneaks :
And ferries o'er in fishing-boat
Through shoals of carcases afloat ;
His hopes all vanish'd, bilked of all
His gaudy dreams : see pride's just fall.
    The frequent subject of our prayers,
Is length of life and many years :
But what incessant plagues and ills,

---

* The greatest street in Rome.
† The Latin is :
                    I demens curre per Alpes.
        Ut pueris placeas, et declamatio fias.
Dryden has given it thus :
        Go, climb the rugged Alps, ambitious fool,
        To please the boys, and be a theme at school.

The gulph of age with mischief fills !
We can pronounce none happy, none,
Till the last sand of life be run.
Marius' long life was th' only reason,
Of exile and Minturnian prison.
Kind fate designing to befriend
Great Pompey, did a fever send,
That should with favourable doom,
Prevent his miseries to come :
But nations for his danger griev'd,
Make public prayers, and he's repriev'd :
Fate then that honour'd head did save,
And to insulting Cæsar gave.
Tis the fond mother's constant prayer,
Her children may be passing fair :
The boon they beg with sighs and groans,
Incessantly on marrow-bones.
Yet bright Lucretia's sullen fate,
Shews fair ones are not fortunate.
Virginia's chance may well confute you,
Good luck don't always wait on beauty.
  Let not your wills then once repine,
Whate'er the gods for you design.
They better know than human wit,
What does our exigence befit.
Their wise all-seeing eyes discern,
And give what best suits our concern.
We blindly harmful things implore,
Which they refusing, love us more.
  Shall men ask nothing then ? Be wise,
And listen well to sound advice.
Pray only that in body sound,
A firm and constant mind be found :
A mind no fear of death can daunt,
Nor exile, prison, pains nor want :
That justly reckons death to be
Kind author of our liberty :
Banishing passion from our breast,
Resting content with what's possest :
That ev'ry honest action loves,
And great Alcides' toil approves,
Above the lusts, feasts, and beds of down,
Which did Sardanapalus drown.
This mortals to themselves may give ;
Virtue's the happy rule to live.
Chance bears no sway where wisdom rules,
An empty name ador'd by fools.
Folly blind Fortune did create,
A goddess, and to heaven translate.*

---

* As I had not room for all the tenth Satire, what is seen here, is rather an abridgment than an entire version.   The whole sense of the author, however, is preserved, though several of his examples and illustrations are left out.
  Dr. Burnet, bishop of Salisbury, thought this Satire so excellent a thing, that in his famous *Pastoral Letter* he recommends it, and the *Satires* of Persius, to the perusal and practice of the divines in his diocese, as the best common places for their sermons ; and what may be taught with more profit to the audience, than all the new speculations of divinity, and controversies concerning faith ; which are more for the profit of the shepherd, than for the edification of the flock.   In the Satires, nothing is proposed but the quiet and tranquillity of the mind. Virtue is lodged at home, as Dryden expresses it, in his fine dedication to the Earl of Dorset, and diffused to the improvement and good of human kind.   Passion, interest, ambition

mystery, fury, and every cruel consequence, are banished from the doctrine of these stoics and only the moral virtues inculcated for the perfection of mankind.

But so unreasonable and infatuated are our shepherds, too many of them I mean, that a rational Christian cannot go to church without being shocked at the absurd and impious work of their pulpits. In town and country, almost every Sunday, those bright theologers are for ever on the glories of trinity in unity, and teaching their poor people that God Almighty came down from heaven to take flesh upon him, and make infinite satisfaction to himself. This is the cream of Christianity, in the account of those teachers. The moral virtues are nothing, compared to a man or a woman's swallowing the divine mystery of an incarnate God Almighty. Over and over have I heard a thousand of them on this holy topic, sweating and drivelling at each corner of their mouths with eagerness to convert the world to their mysteries. The adorable mystery! says one little priest, in my neighbourhood in Westminster. The more incomprehensible and absurd it appears to human reason, the greater honour you do to Heaven in believing it, says another wise man in the country. But tell me, ye excellent divines, tell me in print if you please, if it would not be doing more honour to the law of Heaven, to inform the people, that the true Christian profession is, to pray to God our Father for grace, mercy, and peace, through the Lord Jesus Christ; without ever mentioning the Athanasian scheme, or trinity in unity: which you know no more of than so many pigs do, because it is mere invention, and not to be found in the Bible. And in the next place, to tell your flocks in serious and practical address, that their main business is, as the disciples of the holy Jesus, a good life: to strive against sin continually, and be virtuous and useful to the utmost of our power; to imitate the purity and goodness of their great master the Author of eternal salvation to all them that obey him, and by repentance and holiness of heart, in a patient continuance in well-doing, make it the labour of their every day, to live soberly, righteously, and godly in this present world: you must become partakers of a divine nature, having escaped the corruption that is in the world through lust, and by acquiring the true principles of Christian perfection, render yourselves fit for the heavenly bliss: This, my dearly beloved brethren, is the great design of Christ and his gospel. You must receive Jesus Christ as your Saviour and Mediator, you must be exercised unto godliness, and have the ways of God in your hearts. By a course of obedience and patience, you must follow the captain of our salvation to his glory.

To this purpose, I say, our clergy ought to preach; and if in so saying, they think me wrong, I call upon them to tell me so in print, by argument; that I may either publicly acknowledge a mistaken judgment; or prove, that too many ministers mislead Christian people in the article of faith and practice. By the strict rules of Christian simplicity and integrity, I shall ever act.

THE END.

Butler & Tanner, The Selwood Printing Works, Frome, and London.

WS - #0027 - 200825 - C0 - 229/152/26 - PB - 9781331323938 - Gloss Lamination